《瑷珲海关历史档案辑要》编委会

主　编：石巍巍

副主编：魏　巍

编　辑：杜　晔　张　念　张丽娜　陈　顿

瑷珲海关
历史档案辑要

地方见闻
（第七卷）

黑龙江省档案馆　编译

社会科学文献出版社

SOCIAL SCIENCES ACADEMIC PRESS (CHINA)

目 录

第一部分 地方见闻(1921～1925)

第二部分　地方见闻（1926 ~ 1928）

第三部分　地方见闻（1929～1932）

第一部分

地方见闻

（1921～1925）

1. 包安济致安格联函

（第 1 号半官函）

H.

S/O No. 1.   Aigun/Taheiho 5th October. 1.

Dear Sir,

Allow me to express my sincere thanks for the trust you have put in me, by appointing me in charge of the Aigun Customs : you may rest assured that I will give the best of my ability and activity in fulfilling my task to the exclusive interest of the Customs.

Outstanding Questions : As soon as received news of my appointment I started work on a few questions which in my opinion require an early settlement. I have nearly completed the draft of definitive Customs Regulations, complemented by Harbour Regulations, for the Aigun District. Many delicate points are involved in the framing of these Regulations, especially **because** the waters of the Amur are shared between two Powers, and nothing is easier for a vessel than to try and escape our jurisdiction and sanctions, by crossing to the Russian side of the River It is too early to even think of a Customs Agreement on a basis of reciprocity with the Russian Authorities in Siberia; so we must take many precautions for a proper control of the River traffic, avoiding at the same time the reproach of being oppressive and inimical to trade.

trade. - I wanted to discuss many points verbally with Mr. d'Anjou, but, since his visit to this Port has been abandoned, I will send him the drafts, inviting his advice and suggestions.

The question of the Liangchiat'u Barrier and Duty levies on Native Goods imported overland for consumption in the District has been amply explained in Despatches from Harbin, and I hope a solution will be found soon. - Another point at issue is the encroachment of the Local Tax Office (   ) in the working of the Taheiho Customs. The matter was reported to the Harbin Commissioner who approved my point of view; acting on his instructions, I have requested the Tax Office to remove their Office on the Bund, and generally not to interfere with Customs-controlled cargo, especially on the foreshore and Bund, where it is essential for us to have exclusive jurisdiction. They have referred the case to the Heilungchiang Financial Commissioner, and I foresee opposition to our contention. I suppose you have been kept informed by the Harbin Commissioner, but, when the case is either settled to our satisfaction or has to be referred to you for settlement, I shall report in full.

General. The conditions of this Port have been explained at length, especially in the Report enclosed in Harbin Despatch No. 2273; I will therefore give you only a brief outline of things as they are just now.

Relations

<u>Relations with Officials</u>. With the exception of the Taoyin, Officials are the same as when Mr. d'Anjou visited this Port in November 1920. The new Taoyin, Jung Hou, who is to act jointly as Superintendent of Customs, has not arrived yet. The Magistrate is acting for him, and he is a very amiable person of the old school, although not very energetic; he can be influenced for the best, and, unrequested, has several times promised his entire support in any difficulty I may experience. General Pa is also quite pleasant, although at times he and his men have **tried** to interfere with - or disregard - the Customs; each time, without undue friction, the Customs have had the last word. The General has a good grip over his men. - The Chinese Consul in Blagovestchensk is a lazy individual, but is socially very pleasant. Other Officials count but little. -

I am in very good terms with each of them, high and small Officials; a man in charge here has to rely on his personal influence and relations more than at many other Ports. What redress could be expected against high-handed action by the local Officials, especially the Military ? - the best policy is therefore to impress them with the prestige of the Customs, and to have a social hold on them, which I am trying to do, so far with success. - They are all friendly, I may say cordial, towards the Customs; but I don't forget the Greek wisdom: "memneso apistein", they said, and I **am** on my guard.

With the Bolsheviks our relations are **indifferent** The Customs enjoy a great prestige with the Russians just now, and a few attempts by unruly subordinates at annoying us have been promptly met with threat of difficulties in their occasional holidays/ in Tahciho. The salutary **fear** of reprisals has always had immediate effect. <u>Blagovestchensk</u>. is now in very distressing conditions. You certainly have read the contributions to the Peking and Tientsin **Times** and the North China Herald, signed Orrin Keith. Well, no Orrin Keith ever came here, and I am almost sure, judging from the experiences recounted and the opinions expressed, that the author of the articles is Prof. Norton, an American, special correspondent of the Japan Advertiser. When he was here, he was often told by reliable people, especially by an American Engineer who has daily dealings with the Reds, of all the horrors that go on in Blagovestchensk; the way he invariably "verified" was by asking his interpreter, who had been supplied by the Russian Mission in Peking <u>pour le besoin de la cause</u> ! And that is how they write history, sometimes; they have the nerve to state that all is for the best here, while I <u>know</u> personally of people who are actually on the verge of starvation, while we know that people are tortured and suddenly disappear, thanks to the Secret

Sergiee

Service, when we have **seen** in Tsheiho the launch of the
Frontier Commissioner come over here and kidnap from the
foreshore, in broad daylight, a Russian, ex-Officer in the
Semenoff Army, who has been "suppressed" at once. In that
occasion the Acting Taoyin showed his usual weakness by
simply accepting apologies for himself and the Customs
whose rules had been incidentally violated; he even released one of the ruffians who had been caught here.

The time has now come when there is no more
money in Blagovestchensk, and, I believe, in the whole Far
Eastern Republic. The last resource was in the **mines**;
but Russian bandits make life so unsafe there, that in
most places work has been stopped. To cler the country of
the bandits requires money, so they are in a **cercle
vicieux**. I know that the Chita people have better intentions than the few scalliwagger who misrule here; but, if
no money is forthcoming, I am afraid we will witness here
a repetition of the terrible chaos now existing in Russia
Proper. The trouble is that nobody would lend money without sufficient security for the proper administration of
the funds; and I think the only Power at present in a
position to exercise an effective control is Japan, by
sheer advantage of her geographical situation. The success
or failure of the Dairen Conference will therefore be
the decisive factor in the immediate future of the Far
Eastern

Eastern Republic. - The Bolscevike are now in such
straights that they do no longer discriminate between
friend and foe: I just had news that Mr. Kim, a very
wealthy Korean merchant residing in Tsheiho, while escor-
ting a consignment of well over 200 oxen destined for
Nikolaievsk, had all his cargo seized and was himself
taken prisoner not far from Habarovsk, although he had
all the required permits and passes from Blagovestchensk.
Yet he is well known for his activity amongst the pro-
Bolshevik Koreans in Siberia, and I heard from reliable
sources that he was in direct telegraphic connection with
Moscow.

Trade. We are in a particularly slack period just now, partly due to the Season, partly to the lack of money on
the other side. - So far, trading has been of a desul-
tory nature, and it is a pity that the Chinese Merchants,
bent on easy and sometimes disgraceful gains of the day,
do not think of the morrow, do not take steps, now that
times are so favourable, for the building up of a legitimate and lasting trade, and for the development of
the natural resources of this country. - A few attempts
have been made, but with little competency and too much
self-conceit. The most striking example of such unlucky
enterprises is afforded by the history of Mr. Wu K'uang,
a Mining Engineer in the employ of the Heilungchiang
Provincial

Provincial Government, who, against the advice of the makers and the American Engineer specially appointed to help him, bought in San Francisco a Gold Dredge; had the materials transported to Harbin in part _via_ Vladivostock, in part _via_ Dairen, with the result that it arrived too late for the Dredge to be mounted in 1920; had it completed early, in 1921, and spent a ridiculous amount of money in having it towed up by certain steamers which were too weak for the purpose and broke down twice. The Dredge arrived here too late for profitable work, and anyhow it was seen that Mr. Wu had no definite ideas as to where and on which ground to employ the Dredge; and the working of the engine (burning Kerosene)costs about $ 250 a day, whereas, if, as advised, he had bought a steam engine fed by firewood which is plentiful here, the cost would have been less than $ 100. Mr. Wu has at last been thanked by the Heilungchiang Government, and the Dredge is here, a real white elephant.

Staff. The whole Staff is keen on working. Mr. Baukham, the Senior Out-Door Officer, is very competent and reliable. He is now sick with typhoid, and his place is very well filled by Mr. Murray. The Chinese Staff is satisfactory; but, if I had a Chinese Assistant with more experience and initiative, I could let him attend to many routine matters which take a lot of my time, and I would be in a better position to tackle the more important questions.

Property.

Property. The question of the buildings to be erected for the Aigun Customs has been gone over with Mr. Davison, Assistant Architect, during his visit here. I do not know what conclusions have been arrived at in Harbin, and I hope to get information soon. It is my opinion that, if we want to build next year, all plans and specifications should be ready by next December or in January at the latest; we ought to procure wood and have it seasoned for many months, and we should invite tenders early, and perhaps accept Russian tenders, if accompanied by suitable guarantees. I am of opinion that we spent too much on the Liangchiat'un Building , because we made a hasty contract in the middle of the summer. Otherwise, I think it would be better to wait another year, since we can renew nearly all of our leases at the present rentals until 1925, rather than do things in haste with poor results.

                              Yours sincerely,

Sir Francis A. Aglen, K. B. E.,
        Inspector General of Customs,
                Peking.

第 1 号半官函   1921 年 10 月 5 日于瑷珲关 / 大黑河

尊敬的安格联先生：

感谢信任并任命本人担任瑷珲关署理税务司,日后定当竭尽全力履行职责,维护海关利益。

主要问题：收到调任通知后,本人立即着手处理需要尽早解决之事。现下已基本完成瑷珲关的各项章程与理船章程的草拟工作,然因黑龙江为中俄两国界河,船只若欲摆脱中国海关之管辖约束过江至俄岸亦绝非难事,故草拟章程过程中需要解决的细节问题着实颇多。另外目前考虑与西伯利亚地区俄国当局签订互惠互利的海关协议还为时过早,只能尽量采取预防措施管控黑龙江上的往来运输,同时还需避免对贸易造成压制或损害而引来非议。此间诸多问题,原希望与覃书（R. C. L. d'Anjou）先生当面探讨,但因其视察瑷珲关之计划已经取消,只得嗣后再向其发送章程草案,征询意见与建议。

梁家屯分卡及经陆路进口并销售本埠之土货的征税问题已由哈尔滨关呈文说明,希望可尽快找到解决办法。另外,当地税捐局之行为已对瑷珲关的工作造成侵扰。本人业已就此事向哈尔滨关税务司征询意见,获得支持及指示后,已请当地税捐局将其检查处搬离堤岸,并提出日后不要再干涉海关管辖之货物,尤其不要对应由海关单独管辖的前滩与堤岸上的货物有何行动。当地税捐局已将此事呈报黑龙江省政府财政厅,但恐怕省政府不会同意海关要求。相信哈尔滨关税务司已及时呈报此事,待事情得以圆满解决,或是须提请阁下裁定时,本人再做详细汇报。

瑷珲关概况：本口岸的具体情况此前已有汇报,哈尔滨关致海关总税务司公署第2273 号呈随附报告中更有详细说明,故此谨简要概述当前之情形。

地方官员：自覃书先生 1920 年 11 月视察本口岸以来,除道尹外,其他地方官员均未换任。不过新任道尹兼瑷珲关海关监督荣厚先生尚未到任,一应事务暂由瑷珲县知事[①]代理,他为人虽有些保守,但十分友善,可为海关所用,而且此前已多次主动表示会全力帮助海关解决所遇困难。巴英额将军为人谦和有礼,虽然有时与其部下会试图阻扰或是漠视海关,但最终还是会遵照海关要求办理,而且双方从未有过切实冲突。巴英额将军对部下的管理十分有方。驻布拉戈维申斯克（Blagovestchensk）中国领事为人有些懒散,但交往起来十分友善。其他地方官员不甚重要,故不做一一介绍。

---

① 此时,瑷珲县知事为孙蓉图。

不过地方官员，无论大小，本人皆与之保持友好关系，因为大黑河口岸与其他口岸的情况多有不同，于此担任税务司，不仅需要有一定的个人影响力，还需要有一定的社会关系。毕竟面对地方官员尤其是军方的专横行为，直接抵抗并无益处，唯有以海关之声望赢得敬重，通过社交拉近关系，方为良策，本人一直致力于此，迄今颇有收效。地方官员对海关的态度十分友好，甚至可以说是亲切热情，但本人亦将希腊智者之言"信任他人又不轻信"牢记心间，时刻保持警惕。

海关虽与布尔什维克党的关系一般，但在俄国人心中仍有较高的声望。此前曾有少数不守规矩的俄国人试图扰乱海关秩序，但被警告日后若欲来至大黑河休假必然会受到阻碍后，便停止此等行为。警告可以让不法之人有所忌惮，总是能够立见成效。

布拉戈维申斯克：如今之情形颇为糟糕。《北华捷报》和《京津泰晤士报》均刊登过奥林·基思（Orrin Keith）署名的文章，相信阁下亦已阅读过。但实际上当地从未有过名为奥林·基思之人造访，而且根据文中所述及所评推断，此等文章的作者应为《广智报》的特约记者美国教授诺顿（Norton）先生。诺顿先生在大黑河停留期间，经常通过可靠的民众，尤其是与苏俄红军日日打交道的美国工程师，获悉布拉戈维申斯克所有恐怖行动，得到消息后再通过询问其来自北京俄国使团的翻译予以证实，有时文章便就此得来。不过他们关于当地情形终会转好之言论，确与事实不符。因为据本人所知，有些人正面临饥饿，更有人饱受折磨，甚至无故失踪。此前曾于大黑河目睹苏俄筹边使的汽艇来至华岸，光天化日之下将已被镇压的谢米诺夫（Semenoff）军队的前俄籍军官从前滩掳走。当时代理道尹表现出一贯的软弱，接受了苏俄方对其和海关的道歉，全然不顾海关规定已然受到侵犯这一事实，甚至还释放了一名此前抓捕的暴徒。

如今布拉戈维申斯克地区，甚至整个远东共和国都已无资金来源。原本矿产还可以有一些产出，但因苏俄匪患猖獗，矿区安全难有保障，大多地方已经停工。但要剿灭匪患，还需资金支持，因此当地实已陷入恶性循环。据悉，与本地区少数扰乱秩序的俄国人相比，赤塔（Chita）地区的民众有更大的企图，但如果再无资金来源，恐怕本地区亦会面临俄国本土的混乱局面。而问题是，如果没有充分的资金管理保障，根本无法获得借款。兹认为，现下唯一可以有效管理远东地区的国家就是拥有地理优势的日本。因此大连会议的成败将直接决定远东共和国近期的局势发展。另外，布尔什维克党目前已不再区分敌友。有消息称，定居于大黑河的朝鲜富商金先生护送200余头牛前往尼古拉耶夫斯克（Nikolaievsk）时，在哈巴罗夫斯克（Habarovsk）附近被捕入狱，所运货物皆遭扣押。但实际上，金先生已于布拉戈维申斯克获取了所有必要的准单和通行凭证，而且西伯利亚地区人人皆知其是朝鲜布尔什维克党的活跃分子。据可靠消息,金先生一直直接与莫斯科方面通过电报联系。

贸易:目前贸易萧条,一部分是因为航运季已接近尾声,一部分是因为俄国方面资金匮乏。迄今为止,贸易状态一直不甚稳定,但现下正是建立长久合法贸易机制,开发中国自然资源的良机。令人惋惜的是,中国商人贪图安逸,满足于蝇头小利,不思未来,不谋进取。当然亦有商人试图有所作为,但大多都是无能自负之辈。其中最为突出之例便是受雇于黑龙江省政府的采矿工程师吴旷先生。吴旷先生不顾厂商和特派前去协助其的美国工程师的意见,执意从旧金山购买一艘采金船,并决定将部件分别经符拉迪沃斯托克(Vladivostock)和大连运至哈尔滨,以致运抵时间严重延误,1920年未能组装采金船,直至1921年初方组装完毕;随后又花费大量资金雇用数艘轮船将采金船拖至本地,但因所雇轮船承重不够,运输途中又出现两次故障。采金船最终抵达本地时,可以获利的工程已所剩无几,而且吴旷先生根本不知何处需要雇用采金船,对雇用条件更是一无所知。该艘采金船的发动机需要依靠燃烧煤油来驱动,每日的工作费用高达250余银圆,如果吴旷先生当初听取意见购买本地盛产的蒸汽发动机,仅依靠燃烧木柴便可驱动,那么每日的费用将不会超过100银圆。不过,黑龙江政府最终还是对吴旷先生表示了感谢,但是这艘采金船在本地也只是一件昂贵的摆设罢了。

人事:瑷珲关关员皆对海关工作充满热情。超等外班关员博韩(G. E. Baukham)先生能力出众,忠诚可靠,但因感染风寒已请病假,其职位暂由马瑞(N. J. G. Murray)先生接任。华籍关员之工作亦令人颇为满意,但希望可以再为本关任命一名经验丰富、能动性强的华籍帮办负责日常事务,以便本人拥有更多时间处理更为紧要之事。

关产:副建筑师戴维森(W. R. Davison)先生在大黑河停留期间,已就为瑷珲关修建房屋一事进行调查研究,但不知哈尔滨关是否已有定论,希望可以尽快收到消息。兹认为,如果要于明年开始动工,那么最迟亦应于今年十二月或是明年一月前准备好一应图纸和设计书。因为不仅需要尽早购置木料,放置风干数月,还需尽快发出承包邀请;如果苏俄承包商能够提供充分担保,或许亦可接受。此前修建梁家屯分卡房屋时,便是因于夏季匆匆签订承包合同,以致费用支出过高。鉴于目前本关所有房屋租赁合同皆可续约至1923年,建议一年之后再行修建之事,以免因为过于匆忙而使结果差强人意。

您真挚的

包安济

2. 包安济致安格联函

（第2号半官函）

S/O No. 2.

Aigun/Taheiho 18th October   1.

Dear Sir,   Entered in Card-Index.

We are in a very slack period now, and our collection is pitifully low; but I have always a full day, and I am therefore late in writing.

Banknotes. Recently I was approached by the Bank of China and the Eastern Provincial Bank (also known as the Bank of Manchuria) with a view to the acceptance of the Bank Notes of the last-named Bank in payment of Duty. Following the advice of the Harbin Commissioner, I replied that officially the Customs could only accept silver, and Notes of the two Government Banks; but that, if the Bank of China wants to accept other notes under its own responsibility, we cannot very well object. I think in this way our Revenue is safe in principle; should the Bank of China suffer from eventual depreciation of the Eastern Provincial Bank Notes, we would suffer anyhow, I am afraid. There is no immediate danger, however, and I am informed that the note-issuing Banks have arranged for a daily clearance of their notes. But now the Kwang Hsin Kung-ssu (广信公司), also known as the Bank of Tsitsihar, has notified its intention of issuing its own Banknotes, and if the mania spreads, a depreciation is not unlikely, especially if the Russians succeed in establishing their own Mint, and the Chinese Notes have to be withdrawn

withdrawn from the Siberian Market. The Russians have already a few days ago issued a Prikase by which people are forbidden to accept Chinese Banknotes; of course, for the time being, only Government Offices refuse notes, and demand payment in gold roubles, which are brought back from Taheiho in exchange for notes, while merchants go on dealing in "tayang". Should there arise a danger of depreciation of Banknotes, I shall devise means to protect Revenue, and particularly Service, Moneys, by withdrawing as quick as possible all Moneys from the Bank of China, discounting cheques on the Hongkong and Shanghai Bank whenever money is needed for the Office, at the local exchange rate.

Chinese Post Office. An Inspector from Harbin has made several arrangements for the improvement of the Service. The Heiho Motor Car Company have agreed to carry letter bags in winter to and from Tsitsihar for a small fee; an agency will shortly be opened in Hsiangohiat'un, which will be very handy, although the mounted Courier will have to be maintained for carrying stores, parcels seizure, moneys, and because the Guards use his horses for patrolling the back roads. The C. P. O. will remove their Office soon to a more decent building, if Directorate sanction is obtained, and this will advantage examination of Parcels. In this connection I have been asked whether the Customs are

are prepared to sell to the C. E. O. the south-eastern
half of our Lot known as the Old Customs Compound; this
question was raised when the Asst. Architect Mr. Davison
visited this Port, and I do not know what results have
been arrived at in Harbin; so I replied that your decision had not been received yet. - I strongly advised at
the time not to alienate any portion of our ground, because we have just enough for a complete Building Programme, and because price will most likely go up.-

Blagovestchensk. I have seen another article by the same
"Orrin Keith", in which he pretends having verified by
reference to Churin's Manager the report of the requisition of his goods. Well, the Manager, or any man that
may be taken for a Manager, has never seen Norton, or
"Keith" or anybody that may resemble him, and the requisition is a fact. Conclusion: either Norton has been misti-
fied, or else he is hired by the Reds for Propaganda,
the only art in which these people excel. - The day before yesterday, we met on the Ferry one Commissar, who is
perhaps the only genuine specimen of honest Communist; he
stated that the Government had given him 1,500 (one thou-
sand five hundred) roubles (gold) *to last all through the winter* with which to buy wood
for all the army in Blagovestchensk; besides, he came to
persuade a certain steamer to sail, because the sailors,
once in Taheiho, refused to leave unless some stores were
put on board. We asked him how much was needed for the
stores; he said,"fifty dollars"; and in order to get

them, he was going to dispose of a little platinum in
his possession - The newly mobilised soldiers are being
more or less clothed, and sent away by batches, but are
fed worse than dogs; I was told they should replace the
older soldiers, soon to be demobilised. - I am told by
several informers that when the Ministers were here they
ordered the Government Bank to be "requisitioned" of all
valuables deposited for safe-custody; some 120,000 dollars
have been realised, according to reports. - Some twothou-
sand children from Russia are expected here; another Commissar informed me that 50 had been asked for by a Manager of a Saw Mill ! Poor kids ! And nobody wants them,
I am afraid , except to get something out of them, as in
the present instance. - I think next winter there is going to be a stream of people seeking refuge from Siberia.

Staff. All well, except Mr. Baukham, the Out-door Senior Office
sick with typhoid, complicated by slight appendicitis. He i
better, but, in the Doctor's opinion, should take a long
rest after his recovery; in such case I shall have to
apply in a haste for another Examiner, winter work being
impossible with one Examiner only. -

Taheiho. On the 9th, the first Temple of this town was i-
naugurated. It is dedicated to the God of War, and has
cost some 10,000 dollars. The local gentry have an idea
that

that the Temple will induce people to a little more
Religion and Morality, and that the Bandits evil may
be stamped out thereby. Spes. Ultima Dea ! - Mr. Pai, the
President of the Chamber of Commerce, left for Tsitsihar
where he will meet Mr. Sun (孙), President of the Tsitsihar Chamber of Commerce; both are to proceed to Shanghai, having been delegated to represent the Heilungchiang
Province. Amongst Arguments to be tackled there is the
Income Tax, and the Imshan Conference. Mr. Pai has been a
costant enemy of the Customs, but I had absolutely nothing
to complain; I must recognise in him a hard-worker and
a stubborn head, but his intelligence is below the average
and I cannot figure that he may do any good in Shanghai.

- May I ask what is the "Republic of China Bu-
"reau of Economic Information" ? They have written that
they placed this Office on their Mailing List, and ask me
to return the compliment. Of course I cannot dispose of
Official Publications, and nothing is published locally. On
the other hand their Bulletins are not worth much, and I
don't think they are worth subscribing to. What have other
Port done, that I may follow the precedents ?

With kindest regards

Yours sincerely,

Boers

Sir Francis A. Aglen, K. B. E.,
Inspector General of Customs,
Peking.

第 2 号半官函 1921 年 10 月 18 日于瑷珲关/大黑河

尊敬的安格联先生：

如今贸易萧条,瑷珲关税收少得可怜,但每日公务依然十分繁忙,此亦为本人延迟呈交半官函之原因。

为纸币事：日前,中国银行和东省银行(亦称满洲银行)前来商议接受使用东省银行纸币支付关税一事。本人依照哈尔滨关税务司之建议回复称,按照规定,海关只能接受银圆及两家政府银行发行的纸币,但如果中国银行愿意自担风险接受其他纸币,海关亦无法反对。相信如此安排,原则上应可确保海关税收不受损失,但如果中国银行因东省银行纸币贬值而遭受损失,恐怕海关亦会受到牵连。无论如何,短期之内应不会有何风险。据报,银行每日都会清理当日发行之纸币。不过,现今广信公司(亦称齐齐哈尔银行)业已宣布要开始发行纸币,如果银行纷纷效仿,纸币贬值亦不无可能,尤其一旦俄国建成自己的铸币厂,中国纸币都将被挤出西伯利亚市场。数日前,苏俄当局已发布指令禁止俄国人接受中国纸币,当然暂时只有俄国政府机构拒绝接受中国纸币,要求以金卢布支付款项,商人私下依然使用"大洋"进行交易。如果日后出现纸币贬值危机,本人将重新调整策略,尽快将资金从中国银行取出,以保护税收、海关及经费免受损失,如有办公经费需要,将按照当地汇率兑换汇丰银行支票。

为中国邮政局事：哈尔滨专员已前来做出数项改善安排。黑河汽车公司已同意负责冬季期间本地与齐齐哈尔之间的信件包裹运输,仅收取小额费用；中国邮政局不日将于梁家屯设立办事处,日后运输将更加便利。但海关陆路马差仍须留用,以运送物品、收缴的包裹及钱款等,而且卫兵亦需使用其马匹巡缉小路。中国邮政局计划尽快将公署搬至更为体面的房屋(此举将利便海关检查包裹),现下正在等待政府批准,日前还曾询问海关是否愿意售卖瑷珲关旧海关办公楼大院东南部分。副建筑师戴维森(W. R. Davison)先生在大黑河期间已知晓此事,但不知哈尔滨关现下有何定论,因此只得告知中国邮政局总税务司尚未下达指令。鉴于瑷珲关亦有建房计划,而且大黑河房产价格极有可能上涨,因此强烈建议不要出让海关关产。

为布拉戈维申斯克(Blagovestchensk)事：近日又读到一篇以"奥林·基思(Orrin Keith)"署名的文章,内称征用秋林公司货物之报道已通过公司经理得到证实。但实际上,秋林公司经理,或是其他可能被认作经理之人,均未曾见过"诺顿(Norton)"先生或是"基思(Keith)"先生或是任何相似之人,不过征用之事确为事实。总结来看,要么是诺顿先生自己未能厘清事实，要么就是其已被苏俄红军雇用撰写宣传文章，毕竟这些红军只擅长撰写此类文章。前日在渡船上遇到一名苏俄政治委员，其或许是唯一一位真正诚实的共产党人。其告知已自政府处获得1500（金）卢布拨款用以为所有驻扎于布拉戈维申斯克的军队购置冬季所需木柈，但因大黑河的水手坚称需要装上一批货物后才能出航，故来此劝说。经询问得知此批货物需花费50银圆，为筹集款项，其将售卖自己的一些白金。当地最近招募的士兵已分批派往各处，虽然有衣服可穿，但饮食极差。据悉他们将替代即将退伍的老兵。另有线报称，俄国各部部长到达当地时，下令"征用"政府银行收存保管的所有贵重物品，据报变卖后约得120000银圆。另外，预计将有2000余名俄国儿童逃难至此。据另一名苏俄政治委员透露，一家锯木厂经理已表示需要50名童工！可怜的孩子们！但如果这些孩子没有利用价值，如锯木厂之例，恐怕亦不会有人愿意收留。兹认为，明年冬季将有大批难民从西伯利亚逃难至此。

为人事事：超等外班关员博韩（G. E. Baukham）先生此前因感染风寒已请病假，之后又查出有轻微阑尾炎，虽然目前病情已有所好转，但医生建议恢复后还应休养一段时日。其他关员一切安好，但考虑一名验货员难以应对冬季期间的验货工作，特此申请尽快再为本关任命一名验货员。

为大黑河事：10月9日，大黑河第一座关帝庙举行了落成仪式，修建费用约10000银圆。当地乡绅认为关帝庙能够保佑平安，引人向善，甚至可以驱逐土匪。黑河商会主席白先生[①]已动身前往齐齐哈尔与当地商会主席孙先生会合，之后二人将代表黑龙江省前往上海参加中华全国商会联合会临时大会及庐山会议等事。白先生一直对海关抱有敌意，但本人对其并无可抱怨之处。必须承认，白先生为人勤恳，只是有些顽固，头脑亦不够灵活，恐怕此次上海之行难以有何有益之举。

另外，国家经济情报局（Republic of China Bureau of Economic Information）[②]近日来函称已将瑷珲关列入其邮寄列表，要求回函。不知此为何等机构？不过，本人自然无权处置官方刊物，本地更无刊物出版，而且其简报内容也无太大价值，不建议订阅。不知其他口岸如何处理此事，能否借鉴？

愿诸事顺遂。

您真挚的

包安济

---

① 指黑河商会主席白良栋。

② 此机构1921年成立，由W. H. 唐纳德担任主任，出版《中国经济公报》和《中国经济月刊》，两份刊物均以英文出版。

3. 包安济致安格联函

（第 3 号半官函）

S/O No. 3

Aigun/Taheiho 5th November 1.

Dear Sir,

Nothing very important to report; trade is at a _record_ point of slackness; for 20 days there has been drifting ice on the River, and communications have been practically closed that way. Quite an amount of goods have been sent to Lahasusu or other intermediate points, and have had to go back via Harbin; some, like cargo carried by Steamer Hsi-King, are ice-bound on the Amur. The overland traffic has not yet started, because the roads are very wet between Mergen and Tsitsihar, and no ice is forming owing to the uncertain season.

Superintendent. I was informed by the Acting Taoyin that Jung Hou insists on his resignations, and that he will not come in, all probability. There is a Superintendent's Office here, and I receive despatches in the usual way, but I have received no notification that anybody is acting for Jung Hou, so the position is rather awkward. I have decided on sending Returns, and exchanging correspondence, being unwilling to ignore the "Office", of which

Sir Francis A. Aglen, K. B. E.,
Inspector General of Customs,
Peking.

Entered in Card Index.

which the Acting Taoyin is actually in charge.

Receipt for Fines. I have started fining the Merchants for discrepancies in value, etc., since my arrival here. My predecessors hardly ever punished such offences, while I believe I am bringing the merchants to a clearer sense of their duty. But I have noticed a certain mistrust as to the ultimate destination of the fines paid on the part of the Merchants; the feeling is in a way justified by our giving receipts for payment of duty. I have yesterday issued a receipt for a Fine, in order to dissipate the wrong impression and suspicion, and, although I know that the Practice at other Ports is against the issue of Receipts, I hope you will approve my action, so that I may go on issueing them. -

Local. The Tung Ya Co., of Harbin, has applied for permission to build a steamer here, during the winter; quite a good prospect of future building of ships may be foreseen, wood being so much cheaper here than in Harbin. The Taoyin is investigating on the true nationality of the firm. - People here feel nervous upon the conditions in Siberia; the Militia (   ) about 120 strong in theory, has begun practicing and drilling with a little more zest than in the past. Some people are very much scared of raids on Taheiho by Partisans or Soldiers from Blagovestchensk, which I consider not impossible

sible. – In Blagovestchensk things are going bad; you will
see from the District Occurrences that people with money are kidnapped for ransom, and you will be interested
to know that they are after me too: one of the carriage drivers which we usually employ over there told us
that two men hired him, and, when away from town, asked
for the Blagovestchensk address of two Americans (one of
whom they know by name), an Estonian, and myself; he said
he did not know, whereupon they beat him. I am going
over very seldom, and always in daytime, and never alone
so I am not scared; and I don't want to make anybody
believe that I am afraid; but I will be prudent, anyhow. –

<u>Bunding of Foreshore and Improving of Harbour.</u> I would like
to take up these most important matters with the Authorities and the Chamber of Commerce, but would like to
tell them that some expert will soon come. May I count
on a Harbour Master for the coming navigation season?
I would even like to have him here some time before,
to help deciding several technical points.

<u>Staff.</u> Baukham improving fast; I think he cannot afford (fi-
nancially) a leave of any kind; it is a pity, because
that would do him a lot of good.

_____

with kindest regards

Yours sincerely,

(G. Bäosi)

第 3 号半官函   1921 年 11 月 5 日于瑷珲关 / 大黑河

尊敬的安格联先生：

近日并无要事，唯本地贸易已萧条至极。自黑龙江上出现浮冰以来已有 20 余日，水路交通几乎皆已停运；已经运至拉哈苏苏或其他中转站的大量货物只得经由哈尔滨运回；另有一些货物，如西京（His-King）号轮船所载，已被浮冰困于黑龙江上。而陆路交通，则因墨尔根与齐齐哈尔之间的道路受天气影响尚未结冰，依然泥泞湿滑无法通行。

为海关监督事：代理道尹告知，荣厚先生已经递交辞呈，很有可能不会来此上任。不过本地设有海关监督公署，本人依然可以如常接收函文，只是不清楚何人接替荣厚任海关监督，尚未收到公告，当前情况着实有些尴尬。兹已决定，为避免忽视"海关监督公署"（如今实由代理道尹监管）的存在，仍照常发送报告，收发函文。

为罚金收据事：自到任以来，凡遇有商人申报时谎报货价等行为者，均处以罚款。虽然前几任代理税务司皆未有此举措，但相信此办法可令商人更加明晰自己应尽之义务。唯近来发现商人对罚款之目的颇有疑虑，但考虑商人缴纳关税后海关皆会发给完税收据，而缴纳罚金后却无任何凭据，引起质疑亦在情理之中，遂已于昨日开始签发罚金收据，以消除商人之误解和疑虑。本人知晓其他口岸并无此等惯例，但仍希望可获总税务司批准，以便日后可继续签发罚金收据。

为地方局势事：哈尔滨东亚公司申请于冬季在此地建造一艘轮船。大黑河木料价格较哈尔滨低廉许多，本地造船行业前景看好。道尹已开始调查东亚公司的所属国家。另外，大黑河百姓对西伯利亚地区的局势发展颇为忧虑，甚至担心布拉戈维申斯克（Blagovestchensk）的激进分子或者士兵会突袭大黑河，不过相信应无此可能。大黑河民兵组织约有 120 人，现今每日操练的热情比以往更甚。布拉戈维申斯克的局势持续恶化。如瑷珲关本口要事所载，当地有钱人已有被掳走并被勒索赎金之例，更有趣的是，本人亦在匪徒绑架目标之列。据瑷珲关在当地经常雇用的司机相告，此前曾有两人雇用其驾车，出城后便开始询问两名美国人、一名爱沙尼亚人和本人在布拉戈维申斯克的住址，他们甚至知道其中一名美国人的姓名。司机回复并不知之情后便遭到毒打。本人如今鲜少过至俄岸，即使有亦只是在白天出门，且总有人陪同，因此并不担心绑架之事，亦不希望给人以胆小害怕之印象，但仍会谨慎行事。

为修筑堤岸改善港口事：兹计划与地方官员和商会商议此等重要事宜，但会说明不日将有专业人士到此。不知明年航运季可否为瑷珲关任命一名理船厅？希望其可于航运季前抵达，以便帮助解决技术问题。

为人事事：博韩（G. E. Baukham）先生身体恢复很快，如果可以继续休养一段时日，应会十分有益，但恐怕其已无法承担继续休假的经济损失。

愿诸事顺遂。

您真挚的

包安济

4. 包安济致安格联函

（第6号半官函）

S/O No. 6.

Aigun/Tsheiho, 2nd December 31.

Dear Sir Francis,

I have duly received your S/O letter of 28th November.

Fines for discrepancies in value: I am going very slowly; the average of the fines amount to the duty on value short declared. Not a protest has been made so far, and I think it is well to show that the Customs go their own way and are firm in their stand, rather than trouble for fear of the Merchants. I realize the danger of pushing too far, and I shall avoid trouble; my situation however is easier now than before: the Superintendent, who gets S/10ths of the Seizures, is at the same time the Taoyin.

Blagovestchensk: State of siege still enforced. The frontier is closed to all but Chinese and Officials; they refuse even Americans to pass on their national Passports, but allow them to go to and fro if recommended by the Chinese Customs. The wildest rumours circulate about the White offensive - troops have been despatched towards Habarovsk. Arrests continue "en masse"; they arrest "by proxy" - e.g. the sister of a certain rich widow here, who has been notified that her sister will only be released when she surrender herself to the Russian Authorities; her crime

Entered in Card-Index.

being connected in possessing money and precious stones. The Reds now officially requisition from Chinese and Foreigners alike, especially furs, generally under pretext that people speculate, or that the furs are intended to be smuggled abroad without paying at the Custom House; when they did the same trick to a certain Mr. Gold, a Jew, they clearly explained to him that the Secret Service and the Party must live somehow, and since funds are no coming from Chita, they must resort to confiscation. In many instances the merchants are offered to re-buy their goods at very reduced prices. - I heard from good source that the Chita Government sent a telegram, transmitted by post, to the effect that an official with gold for the payment of the whole fleet had been sent; the telegram (letter) had arrived over ten days ago, but no news of the official, nor of the money. It is possible that Chita never despatched any, and only wired to quiet down the sailors, who are grumbling, and may join the Whites, if an offensive develops from Habarovsk. - Red troops are said to gather round Blagovestchensk, but I think they won't be strong enough to oust the Reds by themselves. - Another tale which circulated widely among refugees is to the effect that at a secret meeting held (some) six days ago in Blagovestchensk, the Reds propose to hand over all the Chinese Prisoners, against the Russian refugees in Tsheiho: that the Chinese Consul General was

in favour of the scheme, but that taoyin opposed a stern
refusal. - I don't believe one word of this story, which
shows the wild frame of mind of the local Russians. -
__Hunghutzes.__ They have been active on the route to Tsitsihar;
a place near Tsitsihar, called __Bordo__, has been occupied by
them for a couple of days. On the 13th, they wounded one
chinese passenger travelling by motor-car, and killed nine
out of a party of 14 Japanese who were going towards
Mergen, and who, apparently, put up a fight. - The Tuchun
has specially appointed Mr. To (托   ), Military
Adviser, in charge of the suppression of the Hunghutze:
with no results, so far.-

__Finance.__ Market tight here, but not the slightest panic; I am
informed by the Taoyin that the Eastern Provincial Bank
in Harbin was in a rather weak position - but the crisis
is practically over now. The Provincial Treasury on the
contrary is rich, having some 20,000,000 dollars to its
credit.

__Staff.__ All well; I paid a surprise inspection to the two
Sub Stations, and found everything in very good order.

                    Yours truly,

Francis A.   K. B. E.,
    Inspector General of Customs,
                Peking.

第 6 号半官函　　　　　　　　　　　　1921 年 12 月 21 日于瑷珲关／大黑河

尊敬的安格联先生：

11 月 28 日半官函收悉。

为对申报时有谎报货价行为之商人处以罚款事：此事正在缓慢推进，罚款平均金额相当于商人短报货价应纳关税之数，迄今为止尚未有抗议之声。兹认为，海关应态度明确，坚定立场，不惧商人之抗议。当然，本人亦知过于严苛会有风险，定会尽量避免徒惹麻烦，不过如今之境况已有所改善，海关监督兼黑河道尹会抽取罚款金额的三成。

为布拉戈维申斯克（Blagovestchensk）事：当地仍然在实行"封锁令"，已经不允许中国民众及官员入境，美国人亦无法凭本国护照获准入境，须有中国海关推荐方可。盛传俄国白军已开始向哈巴罗夫斯克（Habarovsk）行进。布拉戈维申斯克的抓捕行动仍在继续，通常会通过抓捕"人质"来威胁目标人物。据称，当地一名遗孀十分富有，苏俄当局便将其姐妹逮捕并威胁其自首，否则便不放人，而其罪名则是藏有金钱珠宝。如今苏俄红军已开始以投机买卖或者逃避向海关交税走私出口为由向当地中国及其他外国富人征用财物，尤其是皮货。他们借此理由向一名犹太人戈尔德（Gold）先生征用财物时便明确表示，红军队伍和特务组织需要发展下去，而赤塔（Chita）方面的拨款还未到位，他们只能通过没收征用来维持。但很多时候，商人可以低价购回被征用的货物。

据可靠消息，赤塔政府已经通过邮政发出电报告知已派遣官员送来购置舰队的黄金。此电报十日前便已送达，但迄今仍未有官员和黄金的踪影，或许赤塔政府根本没有做出派遣安排，只是为了安抚士兵的情绪，以免哈巴罗夫斯克方面发动进攻时，士兵们会加入白军队伍。据悉已有白军在布拉戈维申斯克周围集结，但估计兵力不足以推翻红军。另外，难民中盛传约六日前布拉戈维申斯克举行了秘密会议，苏俄红军提出愿意移交收押的所有中国犯人，以交换大黑河的俄国难民，中国总领事已表示赞同，但黑河道尹坚决反对。兹认为，此传闻毫无可信之处，皆为当地俄国人的胡乱臆测。

为红胡子事：红胡子主要活动于通往齐齐哈尔的道路沿线，近日已经占领了齐齐哈尔附近的博尔多（今讷河）镇，11 月 13 日又袭击了一名乘车而行的中国人，并与 14 名前往墨尔根的日本人发生争斗，其中有 9 名日本人遇害。黑龙江督军现已特派一名军事顾问负责镇压红胡子，但迄今仍未见有成效。

为财务事：当地财务状况紧张，但并未引起恐慌。自道尹处得知，哈尔滨东省银行之前出现了财务危机，所幸现已解除。不过黑龙江省地方金库充盈，约有 20000000 银圆。

为人事事：关员一切安好；经突击检查，发现两处分卡工作亦井然有序。

您真挚的

包安济

5. 包安济致安格联函

（第 7 号半官函）

the streets after midnight. All is quiet however, -
Money market still tight, and business very poor.

Superintendent. He has come to me to complain that the 3/10
of Fines and Confiscations will be insufficient for the
upkeep of an Office. I told him I could only refer the
matter to you confidentially. In fact, for the last quarter
his share will only be some 110 Hk.Tls.; as he has
to keep at least two Clerks to write the correspondence and send copy of all the C'hu's instructions.
50 or 60 dollars a month won't cover the expenses; and
an increase in the Amount of Fines is not very likely
for the present. Besides, he has to give time and thought
himself to Customs business, and, if I may express my
advice, it is not right to make people work for nothing. However, I told him to wait and see what the
Amount of Fines (3/10ths) will be this quarter, before
the arrange with the C'hu, which he is willing to do.
I simply write this for your information, and that you
may know how things are, should the C'hu enquire in the
matter at the request of the Superintendent.

The Staff are all well.

                    Yours truly,

第 7 号半官函　　　　　　　　　　　1922 年 1 月 7 日于瑷珲关 / 大黑河

尊敬的安格联先生：

自发送第 6 号半官函以来，本地情况并未有何明显转变。

为布拉戈维申斯克（Blagovestchensk）事：布尔什维克政权仍占主导地位，被捕民众不计其数，百姓生命和财产安全无法获得保障。如今似乎可以确定，俄国白军已经占领了哈巴罗夫斯克（Habarovsk），并将战线延伸至城西约 100 英里处。但布尔什维克党日前却宣称已重新占领哈巴罗夫斯克。难民中又在流传，俄国白军距离布拉戈维申斯克仅有一百英里，日本军队也正大批从齐齐哈尔赶来。不过上述传闻应属子虚乌有。据日本军队指挥官汤上（Yugami）先生告知，赤塔（Chita）方面的白军已派出 3000 名士兵（主要为骑兵）奔赴前线；第五军队（前高尔察克军队）亦已出发，很有可能会突袭红军；布拉戈维申斯克亦有士兵被派往前线，但大多皆于收到枪支后逃离部队，以暗中观察动向。汤上先生还指出，布拉戈维申斯克红军中虽有绝大多数人（约 90%）赞成如有必要可不战而降，但仍有少数激进分子扬言如果白军占据上风，便会于交城之前放火烧城，让尼古拉耶夫斯克（Nikolaievsk）惨案再次上演。此事亦不无可能，因为城内大部分守备军皆来自苏俄本土，撤离此地后亦不怕会遭到报复。

不过苏俄红军如何能够筹到战争所需资金，着实令人费解。据悉，用于舰队的黄金已挪作他用，苏俄政治委员已开始使用实物从大黑河购买供给，他们之前发送过来的多为一两年前购置的铁制器具，如今已开始发送木料和皮货，其中多数为征用没收所得。另外，苏俄红军仍在抓捕富人（或者有些钱银之人）索要赎金，采用一切措施获取利益。然而当地民众日益贫困，市场上有些货物存量还有很多，但买主极少，而且很多人都在试图售卖旧衣服、破帽子或低廉的小首饰，或者以此交换食物。

为地方事：中国政府为避免大黑河受到西伯利亚地区政变的影响，已经采取预防措施：齐齐哈尔增援部队已经抵达大黑河，以加强守备力量；警方已下令禁止民众于午夜之后外出。目前事态较为平稳，但货币市场依然紧张，贸易亦颇为萧条。

为海关监督事：海关监督已前来抱怨称，罚款及充公货物变价的三成不足以应对海关监督公署的支出。对此本人表示只能将此事秘密汇报给总税务司。实际上，上一季度海关监督抽取的金额仅有约 110 海关两，但支出方面，至少包括两名负责撰写函文的供事的薪俸，以及发送税务处训令抄件的费用，每月五六十银圆根本无法应对所需开支，而且罚金方面恐怕亦不会再有增加。此外，海关监督还需为海关事务付出时间与精力，兹认为,让人白白辛苦不给酬劳着实不甚稳妥。不过本人已请其暂且等到本季度最终罚金数额出来之后,再向税务处呈报。其已答允。现下汇报此事仅供知悉,以便税务处应海关监督请求询问之时,阁下可有所准备。

另,关员各司其职,一切安好。

您真挚的

包安济

6. 包安济致安格联函

（第8号半官函）

...nse will only be taken in case of extreme necessity.

In this connection, a new Office has been opened on the road in Takaiho, called the 警马司部 , under the supervision of the General in command of the 3rd Mixed Brigade, General Ba (巴).

In Blagoveschensk nothing specially important; many soldiers have returned from the front, with hands or feet frozen, and many wounded; the Normal School for Girls has been converted in a large Hospital; Puncura go about freely; a Chinese official informed me that a truce had been arranged between Reds and Whites; on the other hand, according to the Japanese consul, the Dairen Conference was proceeding satisfactorily quite recently, and a Treaty between the F.E.R. and Japan was a probability of the near future. All these news must be taken cum grano salis, notwithstanding their official origin.

Hunghutse are active once more : they infest the road from Mergen to Tsitsihar, and quite recently they raided a village between Aigun and Hungnan, called Sun Pi La T'un (巡 卅 拉 屯). A Band 30 or 40 strong robbed the place, carrying away 20 horses and 10 men, including the Police Officer and one of his men. Soldiers have been sent in pursuit, but they won't be caught.

Yours truly,

第 8 号半官函   1922 年 1 月 28 日于瑷珲关 / 大黑河

尊敬的安格联先生：

为布拉戈维申斯克（Blagovestchensk）事：自发送上一封半官函以来，当地华籍商人与西伯利亚当局已形成对峙局面，而且形势或许还会有变。当地局势持续恶化，征用之事愈演愈烈，商人饱受政府与强盗的双面胁迫，个人财产充公之理由更是荒谬至极。而此时，当地政府又增加商铺税，大型商铺每年 500 银圆，中型商铺每年 350 银圆，小型商铺每年 150 银圆，且要求预先支付。此项征税无疑是压倒华籍商人的最后一根稻草。

1 月 25 日，当地中国移民在中国领事的主持下召开集会，会议决定，在布尔什维克政府取消新税，保证中国移民人身和财产安全之前停止一切与俄国人的贸易。中国领事还任命 42 名专员组成工会，负责监督抵制行动的彻底实施。大黑河商会亦已收到通知，本地华籍商人似乎也要中断与俄贸易往来。实际上，1 月 26 日和 27 日确无过江运输，而且可能不仅仅是因中国农历新年之故。

不过事态如何发展，仍难预料。华籍商人虽然对苏俄政府的征用及专制行为颇为愤慨，但依然希望从苏俄获取利益，以谋生计，只是不希望交税或因获取高额利润而涉险。他们能够在远东共和国的领土上宣布并实施抵制活动，已经十分说明问题，而且亦可借此看出事态发展的程度。只不过，如果华籍商人坚持不与俄国人贸易，苏俄当局很有可能会采取恶意手段报复。

大黑河当局业已意识到问题的严重性，齐齐哈尔方面已经增派援军，地方司令还曾表示要派兵前往布拉戈维申斯克保护当地中国居民，但此举很有可能会引发战争，相信不到万不得已，军方应不会如此行动。此外，1 月 22 日大黑河已设立警备司令部，受第三混合旅旅长巴将军指挥。

除此之外，布拉戈维申斯克并无要事发生。很多士兵已从前线返回，手脚均有冻伤，很多人还身负重伤，当地女子师范学校已被改建为大型医院，以救治伤兵。据一名中国上校透露，苏俄红军与白军已经休战。另外中国领事告知，大连会议进展顺利，远东共和国和日本很有可能会于近期达成协约。不过以上消息虽有官方来源，但真实性仍有待考证。

为红胡子事：红胡子活动越发频繁，大批出没于齐齐哈尔与墨尔根之间的道路沿线，近日又袭击了瑷珲与龙门之间一处名为逊别拉屯的村庄。这批抢匪有三四十人，十分强悍,掳走了 60 匹马和 10 名村民（其中还包括一名警官及其一名下属）。军方已派兵追缴,但恐怕难以抓获。

您真挚的

包安济

7. 包安济致安格联函

（第 10 号半官函）

SO No. 10.

Aigun/Taeiho 10th March   2.

Dear Sir Francis,

In the last month or so, the situation has improved in Blagovestchensk; the authorities have adopted a slightly more liberal course, there are not so many arrests, security is greater in town, and even there is the beginning of trade in sight. Whether this will last, it is hard to say, but in the meantime the respite is felt with satisfaction by all. — I think two factors are at work; one is the change of mind of the masses, and in particularly the workmen, who now talk Unions - not Communism or Socialism; the other is a better grip on the affairs of this town, acquired by Chita and by Moscow It is evidently now that the Chita (Moscow) policy, to give a favourable impression and to grant certain concessions to foreigners of the principal european nations and the U.S.A., to offsett the Japanese menace. Several mines have recently been leased to British or American prospectors; two parties have already arrived, one with concessions for the Upper Amur, one for the Zeia; a third party is expected soon. — One of the Engineers, American, and much in

Sir Francis A. Aglen, K. B. E.,
   Inspector General of Customs,
      Peking.

Entered in Conf. Index.

in sympathy with the F. E. R., has been quite recently in Chita, and says that they are terribly short of money, that, notwithstanding, they did not grant a concession to an applicant belonging to one of the smaller european Nations, for the reason that his Nation had no political weight; that things are under the absolute control of the Moscow Government, to the point that Ministers report to Moscow two or three times a week. — I am of opinion that the F. E. R. will soon be formally absorbed by Russia, as it has already been in fact. — The war against the "white" has been mainly waged by troops from Russia Proper - well equipped and fed troops, which easily overcame the white Bands of the Merkuloff. — Many more soldiers have arrived from the front with hands and feet frozen - almost all of them from the local troops, which were poorly clothed, especially at the beginning of the campaign. —

LOCAL. Mr. Ma, Manager of the Bank of China, has arrived at last; I will try and settle the question of collection and remittance of Customs Money with him, as soon as the present wave of lunches and dinners is over. — General Ma left for Mukden on the 3rd of this month; he will discuss the Central China question, and measures to be taken vis-à-vis the Russians, although the situation now does not seem to call for special measures.

PROPERTY : PURCHASE OF PRESENT CUSTOM HOUSE: I was very sorry

sorry to have to ask for a decision by telegram; but I
think the deal is a bargain, and everyone shares my opinion. I have approached the Superintendent, and he also
agrees, and will ask the Shui-wu-ch'u to appropriate the
money for this, and for the "New Customs Site". - I just
got the Engineer-in-chief's comments on this deal; how he
does put the value of the Building at 16,000 I hardly
know, when I think that our Liangchiat'un Building cost the
Customs, (materials, labour and supervision,) about $ 15,000. The
Liangchiat'un Home is built much better, of course, but it
covers approximately 2,500 sq.ft and is a single storey
structure, while the present C. H. covers a surface of over
3,100 sq.ft, has a basement and two floors. And the cost
of materials, and wages, have gone up remarkably since building at Liangchiat'un.

LIANGCHIAT'UN. My despatch was only ready yesterday; I
have been negotiating with the superintendent, and, through
him, the Chamber of Commerce, until a week ago, and I had
to collect a quantity of data; I regret I could not
report before. - I have in mind still another solution,
but it is rather risky and involves an understanding with
the Tax Office, which is undesirable in many ways. It
would consist in closing our Barrier, on condition that
the Tax Office opens one, and forces all goods to be
brought to either Taheiho or Aigun, on importation overland
also

also that the Tax Office Barrier at Liangchiat'un stop
(and report to us) all goods exported overland which are
unprovided with Customs Documents. - The plan is almost
impossible; only that, by closing our Barrier, we would save
enough to allow of a better control of the two River
Stations, without extra expenses. As the question is so
complicated, and it is hard to say what solution can be
best adopted, I give this scheme for what it is worth.-
↓ In the discussions about Liangchiat'un the superintendent
has been supporting me very cleverly - more than I expected
from him, a representative of the Provincial Authorities
as Taoyin. - He still grumbles about his meagre 3/10ths
without any Allowance, and hopes that the Central Government will come back on their ruling as to his salary;
he would like, of course, your intervention in the matter,
but I have repeatedly told him that more than let you
know matters, and my personal opinion, I couldn't do. -
STAFF.One of the Clerksis sick with influenza, and the
work in the Office is greatly hampered, as he is the russian linguist; besides, I am afraid that the desease may
spread, and have asked the N. M. P. P. Doctor to see today
if it isn't a case of removing the patient to Hospital.

Yours truly,

第 10 号半官函   1922 年 3 月 10 日于瑷珲关 / 大黑河

尊敬的安格联先生：

　　为布拉戈维申斯克（Blagovestchensk）事：当地局势已有所好转，当局政策略有宽松，抓捕行动大幅减少，城内治安改善良多，贸易亦开始有些起色。虽然能否持续下去，还难以确定，但众人皆对暂时的缓和十分满意。兹认为，当地局势的转变主要有两方面原因：一是民众观念已发生转变，尤其是工人阶级，不过他们现在拥护的是工会，而不是共产主义或者社会主义；一是赤塔（Chita）和莫斯科方面已加强对布拉戈维申斯克各项事务的管控。

　　显然，赤塔（莫斯科）方面的政策是给予欧洲大国和美国商人特权，以获取相应国家的支持，对抗日本的威胁。近日，当地部分矿井已租赁给英美两国探矿公司，如今已有两组探矿队抵达，一组经授权前往阿穆尔河上游，一组经授权前往结雅河，据悉第三组探矿队不日亦将抵达。据一名刚到赤塔并支持远东共和国的美国工程师透露，莫斯科政府虽然财政资金紧缺，但面对欧洲小国的探矿申请，亦未予特许，主要因这些国家的政治影响力甚微。另外如今莫斯科政府对各项事务均有绝对的把控，各部部长每周须汇报两至三次。兹认为，远东共和国不日即将正式并入苏俄，毕竟实质上已是如此。

　　反"白军"战争主要由苏俄本土部队发起，他们装备精良，军粮充足，已经轻而易举地击溃梅尔库洛夫（Merkuloff）带领的白军队伍。但目前已有越来越多的士兵从前线返回布拉戈维申斯克，他们手脚皆有冻伤，而且几乎都来自当地部队，从反"白军"战争开始便身着破旧衣衫。

　　为地方事：中国银行经理马先生[①]终于来到大黑河，待各种宴请款待结束后，本人将与之商议海关征税及汇款相关事宜。巴将军已于本月 3 日动身前往奉天商议中原问题及对俄措施，不过依照当前情况来看，似乎无须制定特别策略。

　　为购买现海关办公楼大院事：很抱歉通过电报向阁下提请指示。但兹认为，此笔交易的确颇为划算，而且已获多方认同。海关监督对此亦表示赞同，还告知会向税务处申请拨款购置现海关办公楼及"新海关关址"。总营造司关于此事之意见业已收悉，但不知其何以对现海关办公楼仅估价 16000 银圆，梁家屯分卡房屋建造时，物料、人工、监督等费用共计支出约 15000 银圆，虽然相比之下房屋质量更佳，但占地面积仅有约 2500 平方英尺，

---

　　①　指中国银行经理马延喜。

而且是单层建筑,而现海关办公楼占地面积超过 3100 平方英尺,除地上两层,地下还有一层。此外,如今建筑材料费用和人工费用也较建造梁家屯分卡房屋时大幅上涨。

为梁家屯分卡事：昨日方完成相关呈文的草拟工作,很抱歉此前未能呈报此事,但主要因一周以前一直在与海关监督商议相关问题,并通过其与商会交涉,另外还需搜集大量资料。不过除呈文所汇报之办法,还有一种解决方案,只是风险较大,而且涉及与税捐局的协作,从多方考虑,均不甚稳妥。此办法为关闭梁家屯分卡,另由税捐局于当地增设检查处监管途经货物,凡经由陆路进口之货物,均设法令之至大黑河或瑷珲口岸报明,凡经由陆路出口之货物,如未持有海关凭证,均不予放行,并报告海关。然此办法几无实现之可能,除非关闭梁家屯分卡后,瑷珲关可以在不增加费用支出的情况下,确保大黑河和瑷珲两处口岸的管控足够严密。鉴于梁家屯分卡问题过于复杂,哪种解决方案更能有效执行亦难以确定,本人只能尽己所能给出建议。

在商议梁家屯分卡问题的过程中,海关监督,虽然亦为代表黑龙江省政府的道尹,但给予海关的支持非常有力,令人出乎意料。只是其一直在抱怨未得到海关监督津贴一事,认为如今所得罚款及充公货物变价的三成太过微薄,希望中央政府能够尽快恢复之前的薪俸规定,还希望总税务司可以出面干涉。但本人已多次回称海关对此亦无能为力。

为人事事：供事中已有一人因患流感而休病假,但因只有其通晓俄文,办公室的工作现已大受影响。另因担心此疾病会蔓延传染,今日已请北满洲防疫事务处的医生来确诊是否可将病患转移至医院救治。

您真挚的

包安济

8. 包安济致安格联函

（第 11 号半官函）

S/O No. 11.

Aigu /Taheiho   5th April   2.

Dear Sir Francis,

I have been very busy lately preparing various despatches, and, notwithstanding the best will and hard work, I could not get everything ready before march 31st; two despatches will only leave to-morrow.

LIANGCHIATUN QUESTION: The Superintendent has acted on my suggestion, and told the Chamber of Commerce that they will have to agree to what is decided by the proper authorities. The results, as I foresaw, are good; I am privately informed that at the last secret meeting of the Merchants, the majority decided that it is well to take what is offered, rather than risk to irritate the official *Oignez vilain, il vous poindra, poignez vilain, il vous oindra .!* But most of the Merchants are not at all so fierce; it is only a few gangleaders.

GENERAL AND HARBOUR REGULATIONS. I have been unable to send a Russian Translation; if they have to be published in a hurry, could it be done to publish them in English

and

Sir Francis A. Aglen, K. B. E.,

  Inspector General of Customs,

     P e k i n g.

Entered in Card-Index.

and Chinese first, publishing the Russian version later, as soon as ready ?

It is my intention, when and if the New Regulations are published, to explain them to the Merchants, who never understand a word of them, even if they are compiled in the most elementary style; my idea is to ask them all, through the Superintendent and the Chamber of Commerce, to come on a certain date, and ask all the queries they may think of, so as to give them an idea of Inward Transit, Outward Transit, Manchurian Special E. C., etc. I am sure the Customs would be less unpopular if the advantage they afford were better known.

PURCHASE OF CUSTOM HOUSE: the purchase is now effected; the Manager of the Bank of China tried a very dirty coup, by offering 24,000 cash, at a time when I could not give a definite answer, a week ago; the deal did not go through because of the precaution I had taken in securing another year's lease at the same rental, also because the Taoyin warned that the house was marked for the Customs. The idea was to raise the rental, and force the Customs to buy, at a much higher value ; I am nearly sorry he did not try, for I would have liked to see his face when we would have either built our own C.H., or found accommodation elsewhere with plenty time to do it. - Now he says with a broad smile that he missed this good bargain to give a chance to the Customs !

BLAGOVESTCHENSK

BLAGOVESTCHENSK. Things are not so bad now; there is more
freedom, more law. But requisitions have been replaced by
War contributions; firms and individuals are requested to
produce within 24 or 48 hours so much, from 50 to 1,000
dollars - to be repaid later when funds arrive (?). It is
said that the Farmers have decided to force the Government
to stop the War and recall their sons under colours,
under threat to stop the sowing of cereals which must
begin in a month or so ; the rumour needs confirmation. -
The relations between Chinese and Russian Authorities generally are hardly amiable; there is a fight going on just
now on passports. The Russians first started taxing 35 cts
all people going away from Blagovestchensk; the Chinese replied by instituting a Hsiao Piao, cost 21 cents, for all
people leaving Taheiho for Blago; the Russian counterattac-
ked by allowing entrance into Blagovestchensk only to
chinese provided with a Permit to reside by the Russian
Authorities; this morning the Taoyin asked if I had objection to enforcing a similar measure on this side, i.e.
to forbid entry to all Russians unprovided with either a
Huchao of the Chinese Consul, or the Police Permit to
reside in Taheiho. Of course, I could have no objections,
although I pointed out that this means killing trade too,
and it would be better to try and arrange matters. But,
as the Heads over there are not easily persuaded, I cannot
blame the Taoyin for taking energetic measures. - Contrary
to

to this hostility between the Emissar and the Taoyin,
my relations with other Russian Officials have never been
better; the Customs, the Control of Navigation, the State
Fleet, and other public concerns have sent me their Regulations, have given all information I have asked of them,
have asked for information which I have given within the
limits of our published Statistics; their Heads have all
recently called on me, and have discussed all sort of
subjects, on which I maintain a non-committal attitude. Mr.
Romodanovsky, controller of the Government Navigation Office
entered in a discussion about the Chinese and Russian
rights on the Amur, and came to my point of view that
China has a right to navigate the whole of the Amur to
the sea, if nothing else, in exchange of the concession to
Russian Steamers to navigate the Sungari. - He would like
to see an arrangement concluded soon about Aids-to-Navigation, and says that the Russians think of levying River
Dues, as they have no funds. I told him that it would
be difficult also for China to levy the necessary amount
of money ; that the question had been taken up three
years ago, and dropped on that account. - I think it may
be time for trying some arrangement on this point - and
the opportunity for me to advise the Taoyin has just
arisen in connection with a
PROVISIONAL ARRANGEMENT FOR THE NAVIGATION OF AMUR AND SUNGARI which
the Emissar has proposed to the Taoyin, and which I heard
he

he was going to submit to Peking. I obtained a copy of
the draft, and immediately went to see the Taoyin, and
pointed out certain details which conflicted with Customs
jurisdiction, e.g. the obligation for Steamers arriving at -
or leaving - the Russian or Chinese shore, to report to the
Russian Navigation Office (   ). The Taoyin not only
lent an attentive ear to my criticism, but asked me to
draft a new Agreement for him; which I did, as an entirely
unofficial matter - both the original draft, and mine, are
appended for your information. - I trust I acted in
the spirit of the instructions of your despatch No.
2248/78,057 to Harbin, which were "to render all possible
"assistance to the Tuchun in effecting these local arrange-
"ments".

LOCAL. Dearth of cereals; the maximum prices have been fixed
by the Magistrate as follows, per pood: Flour, II grade, $ 3.50;
III grade, $3.30; IV, $ 2.80; wheat, $ 1.90. - The Taoyin wants
to prohibit the export of wheat, and has asked to assist;
I have replied that authority must be solicited from the
Shui Wu Ch'u. In fact, export of flour is allowed freely,
and the whole thing is a humbug; Flour Mills are powerful,
and grease the wheels; while Mr. Ch'ê, one of the Sub-
managers of the Bank of China, and concurrently one of
the Taoyin's Secretaries, is interested in certain wheat
deals, and wants no foreign competition.

CARRIAGE ALLOWANCE. I am going to apply officially for a carriage allowance; everyone has got motor-cars or carriages
here.

down to the Chief of Police, the Sub-Managers of the
various Banks, the leading Merchants, and the Commissioner
cuts too poor a figure besides this crowd. Only a little
while ago I had to call on one of the Colonels at his
camp, and when I arrived there the soldiers pretended to
let me step out of the carriage at the entrance of the
camp, because it was a hired carriage; I had to threaten
to go back at once, in order to enter, driving, to the
Colonel's house.- Such incidents are very annoying, and I
must make an effort and get something. There is a Motor
Car for sale; but that means over 1,000 dollars, and I
haven't got them now; I will try and buy a good horse
and a carriage, or else I will rent one. But renting a
decent "equipage" means at least 100 dollars a month. -
I hope I can get an allowance, as the car is entirely
for the purpose of official "face"; personally, I do not
fell the need for one - and will use it only for
"parades".

Your S/O of 13th March. I hope there will be no curtailment
in the collection of this Port; against our losses (even
tual) at Liangchiat'un, we can more than make good by
levying Duty on Amur Traffic, and Coast Trade Duty .- I
am very busy indeed, and have been especially so lately,
one of the Clerks, Wang Te-mao, having been very ill with
pneumonia; he is still in Hospital after 30 days treatment, but
very much better.-

                              Yours truly,

第 11 号半官函   1922 年 4 月 5 日于瑷珲关 / 大黑河

尊敬的安格联先生：

近日一直忙于撰写呈文，尽管已竭尽全力，还是未能于 3 月 31 日之前完成所有准备工作，明日只能发出两份呈文。

为梁家屯分卡事：海关监督已采纳本人建议，告知商会须遵照政府决定办理。结果与预计一样理想。已从私下得知，在商人最近举行的集会上，多数已决定接受政府指令，不愿冒险惹怒官员。虽说恶人欺善怕凶，但商人大多皆非凶恶之辈，只是有一些是帮会头目而已。

为瑷珲关的相关章程与理船章程事：暂时仍无法提供俄文译本。如急需颁布，可否先刊印汉英两版，俄文版本待翻译完毕之后再行颁布？

此外，新章程颁布后，考虑对于章程规定，即使以最浅显易懂的语言撰写，商人也永远无法真正理解，建议通过海关监督及商会于特定日期将商人召集起来，由海关为之解释章程内容，解答所有疑问，说明如进口货子口税、出口货子口税、满洲特别免重征执照等规定。相信如果海关提供的有利条件能够更好地为商人所知，商人对海关的抵抗情绪亦会大大减弱。

为购买现海关办公楼大院事：现已开始办理购买相关事宜。但一周之前，在本人还未能给出确切答复之时，中国银行经理竟然提出要以 24000 银圆现款购买此地，不过最终交易未能成功，主要因本人早已按照当前租金价格续签下一年的租约，而且道尹业已警告其此房屋应为海关所有。中国银行经理原计划于购入后提高房屋租金，迫使海关以更高的价格购买。很遗憾其未能有机会如此操作，否则倒可以看看，如果海关届时自建办公楼，或是到他处租赁房屋，其脸色会有多么难看。如今其竟然还能大笑称，自己错过此次绝佳的交易，将机会留给了海关！

为布拉戈维申斯克（Blagovestchensk）事：当地局势已有所好转，民众更加自由，社会也更有法治，只是"征用"已改为"战争捐款"。当地商行和个人均被要求于 24 小时或 48 小时之内贡献出 50 到 1000 银圆，等到政府资金到位后再退还捐款。据称，当地农民已决定向政府抗议，要求停止战争，让他们的儿子回归家园，否则一个月之后播种期来临时，便不再播种谷物。不过此传闻还有待进一步证实。

中俄两国地方政府关系一直不甚友好，近期还因护照之事发生了冲突。此事的起因是苏俄政府对离开布拉戈维申斯克的民众收取 35 分的税费，中国政府随后对离开大黑河前往布拉戈维申斯克的民众签发过境小票,每张收取 21 分,苏俄政府顺势又提出唯有获得苏俄政府居留准单的中国人方可进入布拉戈维申斯克。今晨,道尹前来询问,如果大黑河亦采取相应措施,仅允许获得中国领事馆签发之护照或者警察开具之大黑河居留准单的俄国人入境,海关有无异议?对此,本人无法提出反对,唯指出如此一来贸易将会受损,最好可以做出相应安排。不过,鉴于苏俄红军十分顽固,不易劝服,道尹采取激进的反制措施,亦无可厚非。

与道尹和苏俄领事的敌对关系相反,本人与其他苏俄官员相处得倒是颇为融洽。苏俄方面,无论是海关、阿穆尔国家水道局、国家舰队还是其他相关政府部门,均会应本人请求提供所需信息,本人亦会按照他们的请求提供海关公布的信息。这些部门的长官近日还曾来此拜访,讨论各项事宜,不过本人皆是含糊作答,并未明确表态。阿穆尔国家水道局局长罗莫达诺夫斯基(Romodanovsky)先生谈及中俄两国船只在黑龙江上的航行权利问题时,表示同意中国船只应有权于黑龙江上航行至入海口,但同时俄国船只亦应获得于松花江上航行的权利。其希望中俄双方可以尽快就航运之事达成协议,并称他们已无经费,正在考虑通过征收江捐来筹款。本人回复称,中国方面亦难以征收到所需钱款,协议之事三年之前便曾提及,但因资金问题只得搁置。兹认为,现下或许正是协商协议相关事宜的好时机,而且日前刚好有机会向道尹建议签订黑龙江与松花江临时航运协议一事。

为黑龙江与松花江临时航运协议事:苏俄领事已向道尹提出相关建议,据悉道尹亦将向北京方面呈报此事。本人拿到协议草案抄件后,立即面见道尹,指出其中与海关管辖权有冲突之处,例如草案中规定轮船抵达或离开俄岸或华岸时,须向俄阿穆尔国家水道局报明。道尹不但耐心听取意见,还请本人为其重新草拟一份协议。如今新协议已草拟完毕,特将原协议及新协议草案抄件随函附上,以供参考。海关总税务司公署致哈尔滨关第 2248/78057 号令曾指示"尽一切可能协助督军完成地方安排",相信本人此举完全符合此项指示精神。

为地方事:本地粮食不足,地方长官已公布粮食的最高价格。二等面粉每普特 3.50 银圆;三等面粉每普特 3.30 银圆;四等面粉每普特 2.80 银圆;小麦每普特 1.90 银圆。道尹希望禁止小麦出口,并请海关协助。本人已回复此事须由税务处批准。实际上,面粉仍可自由出口,整件事情另有隐情。面粉厂颇有势力,可上下疏通,而中国银行的一名支行经理兼道尹公署秘书对小麦生意亦颇有兴趣,不希望有外国商人竞争。

为马车津贴事:本人打算申请马车津贴。此地官员上至守备队长官,下至警察长,乃至各银行经理及重要商人,出行均有汽车或者马车,唯税务司既无汽车亦无马车,着实有损海关颜面。数日前，前去一名上校的营地拜访时，便因所乘马车为租赁，险些被营地门口士兵请下马车，被要求徒步前往上校住所，无奈之余本人只得威胁称，如不放行便立即返回，最终才得以乘车进入。此等事件着实恼人，而且有损海关颜面，本人必须设法解决。目前，此地正有一辆汽车出售，但需 1000 余银圆，现下资金不足，因此计划购买一匹良马和一驾马车，否则便需租赁，但租赁一驾体面的马车每月至少需要 100 银圆，故此希望可获得一笔津贴。毕竟购置车辆完全是为保海关"颜面"，本人自己并无此需，此车购买后亦仅将用于为出行壮大声势。

为总税务司 3 月 13 日半官函事：希望本口岸税收不会有何缩减。梁家屯分卡方面的损失，应该可以通过对黑龙江往来运输征收江捐，对土货征收复出口 / 复进口半税来平衡。但本关公务着实繁忙，近日尤甚，主要因同文供事王德懋先生身患肺炎，十分严重，已在医院医治 30 余日，所幸如今病情已有好转。

您真挚的

包安济

9. 包安济致安格联函

（第 12 号半官函）

S/O No. 12.

Aigun/Tsheiho 14th April. 2.

Dear Sir Francis,

As I expected, the question of Aids-to-Navigation has come up for discussion. You have probably received my telegram of yesterday, which gives a general review of facts. - On 6th instant I called on the General Director of the Government Water Transport (Govt. Fleet) in Blago-veschensk; I had to return his call, and had heard something about their schemes, and wanted to enquire about them. - Without my asking any questions, the Director asked at once my cooperation in securing the Chinese Government's towards the levy of xx River Dues for the upkeep of Aids-to-Navigation. I agreed with him that the matter was urgent, but said that in my opinion the Chinese Government would require their share in the super-vision, as well as in the contributions. When I heard from him that the question was being studied with a view to starting collection of Dues soon after the ope-ning of the Navigation, and that a Conference of Interest (including the C. M. Customs) was to be called shortly,

I

Francis A. Aglen, K. B. E.,
   Inspector General of Customs,
      Peking.

Entered in Call-Index.

I immediately went to see the Taoyin; he knew practical-ly nothing, and was totally unprepared. He is a good man, and intelligent, and open to advise - so he asked me to get more information, and to devise some plan. - In the meantime he wired to the Provincial Authorities, asking for general instructions. - On the 10th I received a visit from the Board of Directors of the Russian Navigation Office; I took the chance for getting definite informations which I gave you in my telegram, about the Tariff they propose; I am inclined to consider it rather too heavy, but the Amur is a long River. - I pointed out that, as far as I could see, the Taoyin and the Chinese Government would join only on condition that the levy of Duty be equal on both sides, and be levied by the respective Customs; that the Dues collected in China be used only for the upkeep of Aids in the frontier Section of the Amur and Oussouri (if necessary); and Argun that the Admini-stration be joint for that section of the River or Rivers, the Chinese Government appointing somebody to supervise the work and the expenditure. To this the Board replied that they saw no objection. - I know that the Chinese Govern-ment, three years ago, was rather unwilling to commit the upkeep to the Russians only; but they have all the boats and the materials, and a competent staff, which, at least for this year, the Chinese could never put together. The

Russians

Russians so far have not mentioned the question of refund by China of part cost of the materials; but I have
suggested the Taoyin to reply, if the question is brought
up, that for a provisional arrangement there is no possibility of China repaying the cost of original expenses in
buying the materials; further, that, if Russia has spent
much money in the Aids-to-Navigation, China has lost considerably through her Steamers not being allowed to navigate the Amur - and the claims could be called quits. -
I think that, Russia contributing all the Materials, it is
better for the time being (the Arrangement ought to be
only valid for 1922) to let the Russians organise everything, saving China's interests by the appointment of two
or three representatives, who should have access to the
Books and to the Works. This idea was expressed by Mr.
Garden, and I think no other solution is possible, especially for this year. - China is not committed to heavy expenses, which she should meet instead, if she assumed the
responsibility of the upkeep of the Aids ; for the present
year the Russians will do enough with the money they
reckon will be collected as River Dues. The Russians this
time struck me as having a proper plan, an understanding
amongst themselves, and serious intention. The Board of
Navigation is composed of people of a good class - when
I saw them in their Offices they plainly stated that,
being of the **intelligentia**, they are eager to save as much
as

as can be saved. I think that the Board is now established more on technical ground than on political reasons, and that most of the Directors would remain even
in case of a change of Government. - After I secured
all the information, and had tentatively indicated the
minimum desiderata of the Chinese Government (without com-
mitting myself or prejudicing anything), I went again to
the Taoyin, and he asked me to be present at a meeting
of the Chamber of Commerce, the Wut'ung Company, and other
interested. - The meeting took place yesterday morning;
the Chamber of Commerce, through the President started
talking about Treaties, navigation on the Sea, etc etc,
without any competence - Young China style -; the Taoyin
set this question aside, however, and, after my remark that
the important point would be to have one idea and one
programme, if the invitation to the Conference was to be
accepted - the Chamber of Commerce advocated Tonnage Dues
instead of River Dues, as fairer to Trade (the idea is
that they would be redistributed on the freights in exact
proportion to the value of the cargo, and the distances)
with possibly an ad valorem Tax on passengers' tickets.-
The representative of the Wutung Co., objected that the
Steamers should pay irrespective of whether they make profits or not; to which I replied that this would be a
sort of insurance on the Steamer, and, like many other
charges, was to be taken into account by the Company
in

in making their plans (from a Customs point of view, a
tax on the basis of Tonnage Dues is much easier to
collect than River Dues, especially in International Waterway; then there is the question of freights and passengers carried between points where there is no C.H. - which
benefit from the Aids, and are difficult to tax. - In my
telegram I asked your instructions on this point in particular.)- I remarked that it was all well, but the Russians would not agree, very probably, to Tonnage Dues,
because they maintain several lines with many steamers
and little cargo; they would pay Tonnage even with empty
bottoms - and they don't like the idea. - At the meeting
it was finally decided that the Ch. of Commerce would discuss the question with the Shipping Cos., so as not to
present two conflicting points of view on the Chinese side. The taoy
in on the other hand agreed with me that it would be
necessary to inform Peking, and ask for instructions, political on his side, technical on my side. So we both did.
It is understood that I will stand absolutely aside as
long as political issues are being discussed; but I will
privately help the Taoyin to the best of my ability;
for anything technical, I will take advantage of the materials collected by the Mr. Garden - and, if the arrangement
is to be concluded, I venture to suggest that a River
Inspector, with a Russian Interpreter, would be the best
upholder of China's rights and interests - with possibly
an

an expert in accounts (with perfect knowledge of Russian)
to check the expenditure. - The Russian hope to be
able to settle everything at the meeting of the 23rd -
but I am afraid they will be disappointed; there are
too many points at issue.

Agreement with Bank of China. I have spoken again to the
Manager, who is an ex-coolie, and always bargains like a
vendor of imitation-curios; he says that the instructions
of the Head Office were to charge 2 % for collection -
a statement which may just as well be a lie - but that
he is going to write again, proposing 1%. That we shoul
pay more than Harbin is evident, because the proportion
of expenses in Shroffs, etc., to the amount collected, is
much higher here than in Harbin. We have three shroffs,
one of which in Aigun; if no duty is going to be collected on Amur traffic, we may perhaps do away with this
one - but the collection would be in the hands of the
Officer-in-charge, without much control. - The Manager of
the Bank asked what about opening of Stations? I said
that that should be arranged extra, because nobody knows
the money that will be collected there, in the event of
opening new Stations. - I believe we cannot consider new
Stations now; if we do open any, I propose that a Shroff
appointed by the Bank be paid by the Customs, until such
times as the amount collected be ascertained, and the
eventual new Station be included in the Agreement; anyhow the Bank could not remit from those stations, as
they

they have no branches along the River.

I will put all this officially after the Manager of the Bank of China has received a definite answer from the Head Office. - I am in a bad position here, because the Bank of China knows very well that I cannot fall back on any other Bank; that the only alternative to their terms, is to collect by Customs Shroffs - with a certain risk, and without facilities for remitting.

Concerning the rate of remittance, I propose to do like the Harbin Commissioner, i. e. to check the rate quoted by the Bank of China with rates quoted by other Banks, which I can obtain through the Post Office; I have just received Mr. d'Anjou's last despatch on the subject, and I have taken his point of view as a guide in trying to get terms from the Bank.

Blagovestchensk. The situation is about the same; there have been a few requisitions again, and bandits have reappeared in town - besides the Officials. The rumour here is that Japan has sent an ultimatum to Russia, exacting the evacuation of the Neutral Zone round Vladivostock; they say that the Little Entente is acting in concert with Japan with a view to crushing the Bolsheviks. I don't believe that either Japan or the Little Entente would gain by helping in restoring normal conditions in Russia....

Yours truly

第 12 号半官函   1922 年 4 月 14 日于瑷珲关 / 大黑河

尊敬的安格联先生：

黑龙江航路标志：正如本人所料，此事现已提上讨论日程。阁下或许已经收悉瑷珲关 4 月 13 日关于概述此事之电报。

4 月 6 日，本人前往布拉戈维申斯克（Blagovestchensk）拜访俄阿穆尔国家水运局（国家舰队）总督办。此行一则是为回访，二则是因此前已听闻俄方之计划，希望再探究竟。然在提问之前，总督办便提出希望海关可协助确保中国政府能够为航政工作征收足够江捐。本人表示此事的确十分紧急，但指出中国政府摊付经费后，应会要求参与监督工作。总督办随后又表示在研究航路标志的同时，已在考虑于航运季开始后即刻开始征收江捐，并计划尽快召开相关会议（中国海关亦在受邀参加之列）。得知此事后，本人立即返回面见道尹，然其对此事竟全然不知，完全没有任何准备。道尹为人和善明智，善于倾听意见，听完此事后便请本人继续打探消息，拟订应对方案。与此同时，其亦向黑龙江省政府发送电报申请指示。

4 月 10 日，俄阿穆尔国家水道局各科长来访，本人借机确认消息（已于 4 月 13 日电报中汇报），询问俄方拟订之税则。兹认为俄方所定江捐税率偏高，不过黑龙江的河道的确很长。对此本人指出，估计唯有在中俄双方使用相同税率并由各自海关负责征税的情况下，道尹和中国政府方会同意合作，而且中方所征江捐仅可用于黑龙江、（如有必要）乌苏里江及额尔古纳河边界河道的航路标志，同时还应由中国政府委派专员监督工程及费用支出。对此各科长并无异议。

兹了解，三年前中国政府曾表示不愿将航路标志全权委托给俄方，但俄方拥有维护工作所需的一切船艇、物料设备及职员，这些都是中方无法提供的，至少今年确实如此。迄今俄方尚未提出让中方摊付物料设备费用之事，但本人已向道尹提议，如被问及此事，便回复称：对于临时协议而言，中方不可能偿付购买物料的初期经费，而且如果俄方已为航路标志投入大量资金，那么中方摊付后无疑会因中国轮船此前未获准于黑龙江上航行而遭受巨大损失。相信如此一来，俄方应不会继续索要。另外，兹认为，既然暂时（临时协议应仅于 1922 年有效）所有物料设备皆由俄方提供，管理事宜最好亦由其主要负责，中方为确保利益，可委派两到三名代表负责审查账簿，监督工程。已故巡江工司贾登（H. G. Garden）先生当初亦持此观点，相信应该再无其他解决方案，今年更是如此。

中国政府不希望投入过多经费，但如果要承担维护航标的责任，就需要承担相应的费用,俄方今年应会根据江捐税收预算来制定工程方案。俄方此番开展航路标志的态度十分认真,而且已有妥善计划,内部业已达成共识,着实令人刮目相看。俄阿穆尔国家水道局职员层次较高,曾于会面时坦言,作为知识阶层,希望可以尽量节约成本。兹认为,这一机构的设立主要基于技术原因,而非政治因素,即使将来苏俄政府更迭,大多科长亦会继续留任。

经过此次会面,本人已获取俄国关于航路标志的全部信息,亦大概明白中国政府的最低要求(但未亲自允诺任何条件,亦未提出任何批判意见)。随后与道尹会面商议时,又受邀出席商会、戊通公司及相关各方举行的会议。会议于昨日上午举行,由商会主席首先发言,讨论条约及航运等事,但水平不高,而且道尹也未予回应。本人随后提出,当务之急是在受邀参加中俄地方会议之前,统一想法,制定一套应对方案。商会倾向于以船钞代替江捐,认为如此于贸易而言更加公平(即按照货价及运输里程征收船钞),乘客船票则可按照票面价格收税。而戊通公司代表抗辩称,如此一来,轮船无论有无收益均需缴税。对此本人回复称,此费用于轮船而言相当于一种保险,航业公司在制定计划时应将之考虑在内。

从海关角度考虑,与征收税捐相比,征收船钞更易执行,尤其是在国际水道上,但问题是,如果货物及乘客往来于未设税关之地,该如何办理,此等航行均受益于航标,但海关却难以对之征税。对此,兹已向阁下发送电报申请指示。

本人随后在会议上指出,征收船钞固然便利,但俄方很有可能会提出反对,因为他们有几段航道上轮船很多,但货物极少,即使轮船空载行驶亦须缴纳船钞,因此应不会支持此办法。会议最终决定由商会和戊通公司协商讨论,以便于中方内部统一观点。另外,道尹同意向北京方面呈报此事,提请指示,并由其负责政治方面的汇报,由本人负责技术方面的汇报,吾等已如是办理。另商定凡涉及政治方面的讨论,本人概不介入,但只要涉及技术问题,私下仍会竭尽全力帮助道尹,已故贾登先生此前所收集的资料亦会作为参考依据。如果最终要签订协议,兹认为,由一名巡江工司及一名俄文翻译出任中方代表最为合适,如有需要还可任命一名财务方面的专业人士(通晓俄文)负责审查支出账目。俄方希望可于4月23日的会议上解决所有相关问题,但恐怕事实会令他们失望,毕竟需要处理的问题还有很多。

为与中国银行签订协议事:与中国银行大黑河支行经理再次会面时,其表示总行已经指示酬劳费应按照所收税数的2%收取(此言或许并不属实),但答允会再次致信总行建议按照1%收取。大黑河支行经理此前是苦力出身,商讨条件时总有贩卖赝品之态。无论如何,由于本地管账员等费用支出比例均高于哈尔滨,最终支付的酬劳费也一定会高一些。现今瑷珲关共有三名管账员,其中一名驻于瑷珲口岸,如果对黑龙江往来运输征税之事最终未能实现,或许可以将之解雇,只是如此一来瑷珲口岸所征税款将由负责关员掌管,恐怕管理力度会有不足。

大黑河支行经理还询问如果增设分卡,应如何办理。本人回复称,届时需另行安排,因为即使增设分卡,开始时亦难以预计日后能够征收税款之数,不过兹认为现下还不必考虑此事。但如果有一日需要增设分卡,建议在税收确定之前,暂由银行委派一名管账员,由海关支付其薪俸,再于协议中列明分卡相关事宜。无论怎样,中国银行在黑龙江沿岸并无支行,无法直接为分卡办理汇款。

待中国银行大黑河支行经理收到总行明确答复后,本人将就此事进行正式汇报。不过中国银行知道当地已无其他银行可供海关选择合作,这于海关而言十分不利。对于其所提条件,唯一可以变动的便是由海关管账负责管理税款,但汇款方面又将面临风险。

至于汇费,建议参照哈尔滨关现行办法,将中国银行所报汇费与其他银行所报汇费(可从邮局处获得)进行比对后再做决定。兹已收到覃书(R. C. L. d'Anjou)先生关于此事的呈文,业已按照呈文中所述与银行方面协商。

为布拉戈维申斯克事:当地局势并未有何改变,只是政府又开始进行"征用",土匪也开始在城中出没。有传闻称,日本已向苏俄政府下达最后通牒,要求他们撤出符拉迪沃斯托克(Vladivostock)附近的中立区,而且小协约国也已开始与日本合力打压布尔什维克党。兹认为,无论是日本,或是小协约国,均不会从帮助俄国恢复秩序这件事上得到任何好处。

您真挚的

包安济

10. 包安济致安格联函

（第 13 号半官函）

o. 13.   Aigun Taheiho 6th May,   2.

Dear Sir Francis,

I have duly received your of 5th April.

The sooner it is realised that the Russian Government has come to stay and cannot be upset from ouside the better for all !

I am not quite sure of this; it is certainly preferable on many points not to interfere with the internal affairs of any nation. Still England had to intervene at last in France, after the French Revolution and Napoleon; Lenin's Creed is not far distant from the "Rights of man". It maybe wise to let the Bolsheviks consolidate their power; it may be, through, following perinde ac cadaver the shortsided outcry of the Manchester Manufacturers. It is for the Statesman to foresee what is going to result, in ten, twenty years hence, of intercourse with Russia. — I can convey my impression that the "Reds" are only apparently disarming, to entice capitalists and build up new strength with which to fight anew their neighbours and the whole of Europe, perhaps. Mr. Yakovlev, then Emissar, now an all-powerful Jew, a rat-faced, shrewd politician, acting behind the scenes through the Popular Committee, one year ago, after a good dinner and several drinks, stated

Francis A. Aglen, K. B. E.,
Inspector General of Customs,
Peking.

Entered in Card-Index.

stated that the creation of the Far Eastern Republic was only an expedient to avoid trouble; that the democratic Government would only be a facade, that the Reds would entice foreigners for milking their money, and for fattening Russia a little; in about 5 years they would resume their programme, using the forces injected into Russia by foreign help. — The fight in five, or may be ten years hence, may prove much more terrible than the abstention from trade now; caveant consules. — There are many ominous signs which will be little heeded; but I have to report my own impression, which is not biassed by personal sympathies or otherwise. Personally I hate, like smoke in the eyes, all the verbose nonsense which goes under the name of Democracy, let alone socialism and communism; but I am on the best of terms with all the Russian Authorities, even the reddest; my mission here is not to muddle with politics. — The cleverest and most level-headed investor in gold mines now, Lieut-Col Laws, C. M. G, shares my views, and says that he takes the risk, and anyhow takes the mining concession because he believes that in three years at the most he will have recovered all his money and made a profit; he would never invest for a long period. —

Aigun controls frontier and river trade, not inland trade; you want to be sure about our right to function at Liangchiat'un at all. At other ports we have control of railways which do not even go as far as the frontier;

In Yunnan our transfrontier trade is taxed by Customs. eff.

in others, like in Yunnan, in order to control the frontier traffic, the Customs Station is far from the Frontier and has sub-stations at various distance of the frontier. Besides, we change duty on Postal Parcels moved overland in China. Why, if it is demonstrated that frontier traffic here is uncontrollable except through Mongoliat'un and other inland Barriers, should our right be contested? Goods are carried by cart here from Harbin; but very likely, if a railway were built, we would control it - it is only a difference of means of transportation.

Blagovestchensk: the situation is again getting worse. The Officials are not so bad, but bandits are again numerous, in the country and in town, especially for Easter, when they caught many people by surprise. In the country there is a Militia, but without wages, so that they avoid fighting the robbers. - Poverty in town is something distressing; notwithstanding the high price of freight by rowing boat ($ 1.00 per person crossing), a greater amount of flour has been exported in the last fortnight than at any time this year through the rogatka. Inland, in Siberia, a Likin has been established; there are three or four stations between Blagovestchensk and Zeia Pristan, I am informed. - The Reds intimated some time ago to the Japanese Mission that the Japanese Flag could no longer be hoisted, because the Mission has no official standing; the Mission consequently retired to Taheiho; of course all came after the end of

of the Dairen Conference. - By the way, I sent a telegram to inform you; do you approve of short telegrams in case of political events, even if they do not directly affect this Office, as in the present instance?

River. On the 15th the ice was so unsafe that the Police stopped traffic across; on the 16th small boats began to ply between ice blocks. On the 20th the ice moved, and in three days the river was clear. The water has been extremely low; only to-day some steamers have been able to float, but the big ice has not come down yet. But in two days the first steamer will start, for Harbin.

Aids-to-Navigation. I have reported developments by despatch; my position is somewhat funny; my advice is sought for by the Taoyin and Officials, and my mediation by the Russians - but officially I have very little to say. I was present at the Conference of 23rd in Blago, and only listened, and gave certain help to the Taoyin. We had a banquet afterwards, lasting over three hours; the speeches were innumerable, and "the two Republics" provided the main theme; I abstained from any speech, having nothing to say.

Financial. The strife in the North (I am without news, but they say there is fight) may endanger the Eastern Provincial Bank, which will not affect us; but also depreciate the Notes of the Bank of China. What can I do? The safest course would be to either remit to Harbin; but this may complicate and confuse the accounts; or

or to exchange all the available money for, gold coins;
but here, again, what trouble in the accounts ! And that
would not solve the problem of collection; there is no
silver in circulation, and notes should be discounted every
day, and gold bought with them. The rate of remittance on
Shanghai is now 15%; fortunately I have little to remit
just now.- The worse will be, that in case of emergency
the telegraph line may be interrupted. I think I would
first see if it possible and convenient to remit telegraphically to Harbin (deposit on the N. & S. Bank); if not,
then I would buy gold.

Local. Much excitement lately, when it was reported that
a rich gold mine had been discovered, two li noth of
the Custom House, in Taheiho ! But the quantity of gold
in the sand does not warrant for the trouble of mining,
and after a week the thing has dropped.

Staff. Mr. Wang Te-mao has returned to duty four days
ago; he has been sick for two months, to great inconvenience to me, because he is the russian linguist; I had to
translate documents and letters without his help, while the
general Office was busy, and the preparation of the quarterly Service Accounts (without specimen, and mostly after
memory) gave a lot of work and trouble.

Yours truly,

第 <u>13</u> 号半官函 　　　　　　　　　　1922 年 5 月 8 日于瑷珲关 / 大黑河

尊敬的安格联先生：

4 月 5 日半官函收悉。

苏俄政府已日趋稳定且不会受到他国干扰之事实如能尽早为外界所意识到,于各方而言均会十分有益。

但事实是否如此,并不确定。从诸多角度考虑,不干涉别国内政自然更为可取,但此前法国大革命和拿破仑战争爆发后,英国最终还是干预了法国内政。列宁(Lenin)伸张的原则与"人权"极为接近,让布尔什维克党独自巩固政权或为明智之举,但也很有可能会起到反作用。如今政客们应当对与苏俄建交十几、二十年后之结果有一定的预计。兹认为,苏俄红军或许只是在假意解除武装,以诱使资本家前去投资建设,同时建立新的武装力量,以便与邻国乃至整个欧洲重新开战。一年前,前苏俄使节雅科夫列夫(Yakovlev)先生曾于晚宴后说道,远东共和国的建立仅是为避免麻烦的权宜之计,民主政府也只是虚有其表,红军将以此吸引外国人投资,促进本国经济发展,五年之后再通过外国势力的帮助重新开战。

若果然如此,那么五年或者十年之后的战争带来的后果将比目前的贸易停滞还要严重。当前已有很多不祥之兆,但可能很少会被注意到。对于此事,本人汇报时从未掺杂任何偏见或个人感情,但从自身来说,着实厌恶所有以民主名义暗地进行的荒唐之举,更不用说什么社会主义和共产主义,不过本人深知自己于此地之任务并不是参与政治斗争,因此与苏俄各方政治势力,包括红军,一直都能保持良好关系。如今金矿业最有头脑的投资人劳斯(Laws)先生亦赞同本人之观点,称其此番冒险接受苏俄政府授予的采矿特权,主要是因相信自己至多三年便可收回所有成本并赢利,但绝不会长期在此投资。

瑷珲关的管辖范围应仅限于边境贸易和过江贸易,内陆贸易并不在管辖之列,需明确海关是否有权于梁家屯行使职能。

在其他口岸,海关管辖权亦有扩展至远离边境的铁路之例。又如在云南等地,税关驻地距离边境较远,但为有效管控边境运输,亦会在边境沿线设立诸多分卡。此外,海关亦对在中国内陆往来运输的邮政包裹征税。如果经证实,对于瑷珲关区的边境运输,唯有通过梁家屯分卡或是其他内陆分卡监管,方能实现有效管控,那么海关在梁家屯的管辖权又有何需要质疑之处呢?如今货物主要由货运马车自哈尔滨运至本埠,如果两地之间通有铁路,海关很有可能会予以管控,但实际上,货运马车和铁路亦只是运输方式不同而已,为何如今不可列入海关管辖之列？

为布拉戈维申斯克（Blagovestchensk）事：当地局势再次恶化，虽然政府官员并无太多过分之举，但土匪再次大批出没于城内及周边乡村，复活节时还出其不意地抓捕了很多人。乡下虽有民兵组织，但因无工饷，并不会与土匪抗争。城内的贫困状况日益严重。划艇运费价格虽然颇高（每人每次 1.00 银圆），但过去两周内出口的面粉量却高于全年其他任何时段。据报，西伯利亚内陆地区已经开始征收厘金，在布拉戈维申斯克和结雅两地之间已设立三、四个厘金税卡。日前，苏俄红军当局已暗示日本军方使团不得再于当地悬挂日本国旗，因为他们不具备官方身份。随后日本军方使团便撤回至大黑河，当然这一切均发生于大连会议结束之后。关于此事，兹已向阁下发送电报。不知日后可否继续通过电报简短汇报当地政治事件，即使与本关并无直接关联？望指示。

为黑龙江事：4 月 15 日，冰面开始消融，为防止发生意外，警察已禁止行人在冰面上往来。4 月 16 日，小型船只已开始穿梭于冰块之间。4 月 20 日，冰面开始移动，三日后浮冰完全消失，只是水位一直极低，直至今日轮船方可航行，但上游的大冰块还未漂流过来。不过两日后，首艘驶往哈尔滨的轮船将起航。

为黑龙江航路标志事：此事相关进展已于呈文中汇报。本人在整件事情中的处境颇为微妙，私下里会应道尹和地方官员之要求提供建议，应俄国官员之要求从中调解，但正式场合确甚少发表言论。4 月 23 日出席布拉戈维申斯克会议时便只是旁听，并从旁协助道尹，在会后长达三个多小时的宴会上亦未讲话，其他官员几乎均有发言，讲话主题主要与"两个共和国"有关。

为财务事：北部发生的冲突（虽未收到确切消息但据称已发生战争）可能会危及东省银行，但不会影响到海关。不过中国银行发行的纸币亦可能会因此而贬值，兹该如何应对？最安全的应对之策应将税款汇至哈尔滨，但如此一来，账目便会出现混乱。另一种办法是将所有现款兑换成金币，但如此操作，账目混乱问题仍难以避免，而且也无法解决征税问题。本地并无银币流通，纸币又日日都在贬值。现在汇款至上海的汇费为 15%，所幸瑷珲关目前需要汇解之款数额极少。更糟糕的是，如有紧急情况，电报线路很有可能会被切断。有鉴于此，兹计划，先确定能否将钱款电汇至哈尔滨（存储于汇丰银行），如此操作是否便利？如不可行，再将现款兑换成金币。

为地方事：日前有报告称，大黑河海关办公楼以北 2 里处探测到一处金矿，且蕴藏量很高，地方各界情绪因此大振。然因开矿难度较高，而沙土下的金矿量恐怕难以保证日后能够收回一应成本，因此开矿计划已在一周后暂行搁置。

　　为人事事：王德懋先生已于四日前返回岗位，但在其生病的两个月期间，因本关其他同文供事均不通晓俄文，函件翻译工作只得由本人独自完成。另因征税汇办处公务繁忙，海关季度报表的编制工作（因无样本大多只得凭记忆填制）亦积压很多，十分麻烦。

您真挚的

包安济

11. 包安济致安格联函

（第14号半官函）

S/O No. 14.

Aigun / Taheiho   22nd May,   2

Dear Sir Francis,

The events in North China have had their repercussion here. I received your telegrams enjoining to remit Revenue frequently; two days before, I had another telegram from Harbin, informing that the Independence was about to be declared, and that the Three Eastern Provinces (i. e. Chang Tso-lin) would pretend to appropriate the Revenue surplus of the Manchurian Ports. - I at once appropriated all the available Revenue to A/c D (in repayment of money advanced for the purchase of the New Customs Building and the Corner Lot) and remitted by telegram to Harbin, to the Hongkong & Shanghai Bank, paying only 6 per mille, while a remittance on Shanghai would have cost at least 11 per cent. The use of the account on a Foreign Bank in Harbin is thus justified at once; and I would ask whether, in the event of serious threats to our Revenue, I could not remit equally to Harbin, either to the Service Account, or by opening a Revenue Account : remittances to Shanghai may not be possible in time of crisis, or may be too expensive. - As to the remittance of moneys belonging to A/c D, which I have just made, I will wait until the remittance rate from Harbin to Shanghai is reasonable, and then make a Remittance from A/c D to your A/c in Shanghai

Entered in Card-Index.

Shanghai. - I calculate that it will take at least two months yet to repay the entire outlay into A/c D, after deducting the moneys to be used for current expenses. When I received your telegram, the position was therefore already clear. But on the 19th, as I went to see the Taoyin-Superintendent about the Kiangshiat'un question, he acquainted me (after considerable roundabout talk) with a telegram received from Chang Tso-lin who claimed the interests on Customs surplus (after payment of the foreign indebtedness) from this Port, saying that Peking is now under compulsion (evidently from Wu Pei-fu) and that moneys should not be remitted to Peking. - I refused at once to enter into discussion, and told the Taoyin that in the matter of remitting Revenue, I can only remit to your account. On my arrival in the Office, I found the Taoyin's despatch and I replied immediately in the negative; at the same time informed the Superintendent, in reply to a verbal query, that there is no surplus whatever, and that for the time being all is absorbed by Service expenses. Next morning I learned that the Bank of China has received a communication from the Taoyin (copy of Chang's telegram) forbidding from making remittances for the Customs without consultation with the Taoyin. I went at once to see the Acting Manager; the Manager, of course, has left here a few days ago, as soon as he scented danger. He was most dignified, and agreed with me that the Bank

keeps

keeps the Moneys to the order of the Commissioner of Customs, and of nobody else; he agreed with me that to act otherwise would be most nuisible to the prestige and independence of the Bank; he replied to the Taoyin as suggested, and told me, anyhows that I might any time transfer moneys from Revenue to Service A/c, which I however would not do, except for legitimate purposes. The same afternoon (20th) the Taoyin came to see me, trying to find out some means of settling the matter; he told me that he had replied to Chang that the Revenue could not be seized, but that he had received another telegram insisting on the order. He asked if I could assure him that no moneys would be remitted to Peking; I replied that moneys are remitted to Shanghai; that, as Superintendent, I may tell him that very likely no remittance would be made for some time, but that I could absolutely not engage myself not to remit, under any circumstances. He left rather disconsolate, because he is conscious of the foolishness of Chang, and annoyed at the perspective of having to relinquish his post in case Chang is ousted (which appears likely); at the same time he is somehow brother-in-law of the said Chang. Poor men! An official report will follow.

AIDS TO NAVIGATION. I insisted on our collecting, because I am afraid, if the collection goes into the hands of the Shui Ch'üan Chü, that they will acquire too much influence at our expenses. Luckily the idea of using the Local Tax Office has not occurred to the Taoyin; he says he has wired the Shui Wu Ch'u for authority to have the Customs collect; but, anyhow, the question will now be put in abeyance, I am afraid, owing to political matters having taken the first rank in the toughts of the local Officials. The General, having excused himself from participating in the war on account of the unsettled state of the border, is bent on an entirely local policy, which will give him a chance of remaining, whoever comes on the top. - The Merchants are very anxious to see the end of the adventure; commerce is dead, except for flour and other cereals exported to Blagovestchensk and Nikolaievsk; money cannot be found even at the most absurd rates of interest.

Coming back to the "Aids", you may rest assured that I will not collect, or engage the Customs, without your explicit authority, in this, as well as in future instances. I feel very much hurt at the way the questions of the Liangchiat'un Barrier and the Local Tax Office have been referred to Peking by the Superintendent, and especially the blunt way of the Shui Wu Ch'u, in deciding about these questions without in the least consulting you, and listening at our reasons. I have expressed my astonishment and displeasure to the Superintendent, in mild terms of course; in future, I will never let my conclusions be known to the Superintendent

Superintendent, but will keep them for myself as far as possible, get all the information I can, and simply report to you, in matters about which I do not know your exact point of view.

SIBERIA. Conditions are short of desperate; there have been shipments over shipments of flour and bran to Blagovestchensk and Nikolaievsk from here the last ten days; the payment is principally made by depositing old iron, silver ware, binding twine, gunny bags, in short anything available, with the Banks or the Mills. Export goes on beautifully, notwithstanding the local scarcity, and the prohibition to export wheat, which is decidedly a shameful protection to Flour Mills and Spirit Factories. - If my informations are correct (and I collect from all sides) hardly only one fourth of the arable land is prepared and will be sown this year; horses (indispensable to agricultural work in this part of the world) have been requisitioned, grains have been requisitioned, and there are none for seeding, except what the farmers buried under the snow, and has been half spoiled; if the season is not exceedingly favourable, a famine will plunge this part of Siberia into a situation as desperate as it is in Russia at present. - Most of the flour, if not all, goes to the front, and still the soldiers are very badly fed and clothed; they would revolt, if they were given arms elsewhere than on the actual battlefield; but the arms always

travel

travel separate from the warriors, in the care of a few Commissars, preferably Jews, who watch the fighting from the rear. - But everyone is so downhearted and the population generally is so apathetic, that the misrule can continue almost indefinitely, especially with the help of foreign charity. On the 1st May, here, the crowd, believing in the permission given to everyone to act as they liked, in commemoration of the Festivity, shouted in many instances "down with communism"; contrary to the program, many arrests were made.

HUNGHUTZE have attacked Mumaho on 13th, over 100 strong; the soldiers made a good stand, according to reports; reinforcements left here on the 14th, and their arrival in Mumaho caused the Russians in Blago. to enquire from the Consul General whether it was true that Su Pei-fu's troops had reached Mumaho !!

The HARBIN-HEIHO RAILWAY, according to the local Paper, is to be built soon; the work to start in June ! Money to be provided by the Province; no foreign help - Sung Hsiao chen to be Tupan.

The Harbin Postal Commissioner, Mr. Ritchie, has just arrived this morning.

Yours truly,

Sir Francis A. Aglen, K. B. E.,
Inspector General of Customs,
Peking.

第 14 号半官函   1922 年 5 月 22 日于瑷珲关 / 大黑河

尊敬的安格联先生：

　　中国北部的战事现已影响到瑷珲关区。总税务司要求经常汇出税款之电令业已收悉。两日前又收到哈尔滨关电报,内称东三省即将宣布独立,张作霖将挪用满洲各口岸的税收盈余。收到电报后,本人立即将税收账户余额转入瑷珲关 D 账户,其中部分款项将用于支付最近购置新海关办公楼及街角商铺的费用,随后又将钱款电汇至汇丰银行哈尔滨分行,未汇至上海分行是因汇至上海的汇费最低为每百元 11 元,而汇至哈尔滨分行仅为每千元 6 元,由此可见于哈尔滨外国银行开立账户确有益处。另请指示,如果瑷珲关税收受到严重威胁,可否直接汇至哈尔滨,比如汇至海关经费账,或者重新开立税收账户,因为如有危机情况,恐怕无法向上海汇款,或者汇费太过高昂。至于瑷珲关 D 账户已经汇至哈尔滨的款项,待自哈尔滨至上海的汇费降至合理范围后,将立即汇至总税务司上海账户。经计算,D 账户的经费支出,除去当前费用,至少还需要两月时间才能全部结清。

　　收悉阁下电报后,税款处理办法已经明了。但 5 月 19 日前去与道尹兼海关监督商议梁家屯分卡问题时,一番闲谈过后,其告知张作霖已发来电报要求瑷珲关(付清外国债务后)上交关余,并称北京现已受到(吴佩孚)压制,关余不得汇至北京。本人当即拒绝继续讨论此事,说明只会将税收汇至海关总税务司账户。待回至海关办公室后,发现道尹函文已经发来,遂立即回函说明无法遵照办理,同时口头回复海关监督瑷珲关暂无关余,所征税款皆已用于海关支出。

　　5 月 20 日上午又得知中国银行业已收到道尹函文(即张作霖电报抄件),内称如无道尹批准不得为海关汇款。本人随后立即前去与中国银行代理经理见面(中国银行经理数日前因为担心会有危险已经离开本地),指出银行如果允许税务司以外之人干涉海关钱款,信誉必将受损。代理经理对此表示赞同,答允将仅按照海关税务司之命令保管税款,并称可以随时将税款转移至海关经费账,不过如无正当原因,本人自不会如此操作。代理经理之后便向道尹回函表明中国银行无法遵照其指令行事。

　　当日下午,道尹前来商议解决办法,称其已向张作霖说明无法上交关余,但之后又再次收到电令要求继续如此行事,遂请本人说明是否可以保证不会向北京汇款。本人回复称,如今所有关余均汇至上海,另鉴于其为海关监督,可以告知其近期之内很有可能不会汇款,但任何情况下都不可能承诺绝不汇款。谈话结束后道尹悻悻而回,一方面因其已经意识到张作霖的做法并不明智,同时考虑到张作霖失势后(很有可能),自己会被革职,而恼怒不已，另一方面又因自己是张作霖的连襟，于道义而言不能袖手旁观。可怜的道尹！关于此事，随后将呈文正式报告。

为黑龙江航路标志事：兹认为，征税之事必须由海关负责，因为一旦税捐局获得征税权利，定会继续扩大影响力，海关亦会因此而付出代价。所幸道尹并未提出启用地方税捐局，而且表示已经向税务处发送电报申请批准由海关征税。不过恐怕此事会暂行搁置，因为目前政治事务方为地方官员首要关心之事。将军以边境问题尚未解决为由已获准不必奔赴前线，如今正致力于施行地方政策，以便日后无论由何人执政，其皆有机会于此留任。商人也在焦急地等待结果，贸易已经基本停滞，只有面粉和部分谷物出口至布拉戈维申斯克和尼古拉耶夫斯克（Nikolaievsk），但无论利率如何变化，仍无人存款。

至于为"航标"征税一事，阁下尽管放心，如未收到明确指示，本人断不会开始征收，更不会使海关卷入其中。但海关监督向北京方面汇报梁家屯分卡及地方税捐局问题的方式，着实令人气恼，而且税务处在下达决定之前竟未向阁下询问意见，了解原委。对此，兹已向海关监督委婉地表达了不满与讶异，另已决定日后绝不会再向其透露自己的决定，凡未收到阁下明确意见之事，均会尽可能保密，待收集所有信息后再直接汇报。

为西伯利亚事：当地局势简直令人绝望。过去十日，一批又一批的面粉和豆类自大黑河运至布拉戈维申斯克和尼古拉耶夫斯克，但俄国人只能以旧铁器、银器、绳索及麻布袋等一切可用之物与银行及面粉厂交易。尽管大黑河也缺少粮食，小麦出口禁令（显然是为保护面粉厂和酒厂）业已颁布，但出口并未受阻，依然顺利进行。

若本人所收消息（多方搜集而来）无误，西伯利亚今年可以耕种的耕地连四分之一都不到，而且当地农业劳作必不可少的马匹已被征用，谷物亦被征用，仅剩下农民埋在雪地中的种子（一半都已腐坏）可以播种。如果今年再遇上天灾，西伯利亚将遭遇严重饥荒，陷入与当前俄国本土一样令人绝望的境地。

据悉，面粉主要（或者全部）运往前线，但士兵依旧缺衣少粮。如果不是在战场上，他们拿到武器后很有可能会造反，不过武器并不由士兵们随身携带，而是由在后方观察的政治委员（多为犹太人）看管。如今人心涣散，百姓对战事更是漠不关心，恐怕这种错误的统治方式还将无限期地继续下去，尤其还有外国势力的帮助。

5月1日，当地人们以为可以按照自己的方式庆祝劳动节，遂走上街头高喊"打倒共产主义"，结果与他们的预计相反，很多人都被抓捕起来。

为红胡子事：5月13日，呼玛河遭遇100多名红胡子袭击。据报，当地士兵已经奋力抵抗，大黑河援军业已于5月14日动身，援军抵达后，布拉戈维申斯克的民众还向中国总领事询问是不是吴佩孚的军队抵达了呼玛河!

为哈尔滨至大黑河铁路事：据地方报道,哈尔滨至大黑河的铁路即将开始修建,预计6月动工,修建费用由黑龙江省政府提供,无外国援助,由孙烈晨(Sung Hsiao chen)出任工程督办。

哈尔滨邮政司里奇(Ritchie)先生已于今早抵达大黑河。

您真挚的

包安济

12. 包安济致安格联函

（第 15 号半官函）

S/O No. 15.

Aigun/Taheiho 19th June,   2.

Dear Sir Francis,

I am terribly late in writing, but I have had my full share of work. The Aids-to-Navigation business has supplied an _extra_, which was not necessary to keep me busy. I am anxiously awaiting the arrival of the new Clerk, who is due shortly, because, the General Office being busier, I derive almost no help from the Assistant now.

I am in receipt of your S/O of 12th and 13th May, and 5th June.

Aids-to-Navigation. It is fortunate that my status is now better defined. The trouble is, the Taoyin knows nothing about this matter, and is too lazy to try and learn He leaves practically all to one of his Assistants. Mr. Ch'ê, who is also a Sub-Manager of the Bank of China, and has no other qualification than the knowledge of Russian. He mixes up all the issues, and makes even fanciful translations, which I have to correct. Thus it happened that, while I had suggested a better text, the Agreement has been signed on a Chinese text of which I would be ashamed, because I could not interfere in the last stage of the

Sir Francis A. Aglen, K. B. E.,
        Inspector General of Customs,
            P e k i n g.   Entered in China-Index.

negotiations, which were on the contrary concluded without my knowledge. But now this won't happen again; and I have already discussed additional articles in matters of detail; I had to correct all the drafts, in Chinese and Russian, (the two were far apart) submitted by the Taoyin, add several articles, and revise the text altogether. Saturday I went over with Mr. Ch'ê, and presented _my_ text; I am glad to say that the Russians accepted all the points, and withdrew their own draft. I am awaiting now to see what becomes of the draft in the hands of Mr. Ch'ê - but he will not have an easy time now. In the add. articles I have introduced (subreptitiously) the eventual right of Chinese vessels to navigate the Amur from Habarovsk to the sea. - This question however can only be settled in a definite manner if the Chinese Government will negotiate openly - not through _local_ agreements - ; when we discuss the thing locally, the Navigation Office replies that they have power only as refers to economical issues within their jurisdiction. - An Agreement like the one drafted by the Boards concerned and transmitted in your S/O of 24th May, is highly desirable, is clear and just - but it should be concluded between the Peking Government and the Chita Government - or their acknowledged Agents, even in Taheiho - not by the local Authorities as such. Luckily nothing is prejudiced by the Agreement signed on 27th may - and the draft sent, will be be ever present to my mind, especially now that my position has so much improved. - I hope I can have the River Inspector soon; Ignatieff would be preferable, but if his pretentions are too high, another competent man will do well, and will soon be trained, especially if he is willing to learn Russian. I do not know Ignatieff personally, and have to go by hearsay; they say that he is quite capable and decent, but ambitious; that is why I am afraid he may use the Customs as a step to re-enter the Russian Inspectorate of the River, when conditions improve. - I am very glad to see that my action meets with your approval; I have my own mind, and I am generally not in doubt what course to follow; but I must bring my methods in line with your views - and my activity must be subordinate to your general plans - it is therefore of the highest value for me to see that I am not following a wrong direction.

As to the negotiations re Aids-to-Navigation on the Amur, I am astonished that the Wai-Chiao Pu is not aware of them, for the Taoyin has assured that he had telegraphic approval of the fundamental principles of the Agreement, from the Pu.

Your S/O of 5th June : Our control at Liangchiat'un. Except in special cases we do not control cart traffic, or junk traffic. This can well be considered a special case - on a land frontier of such extention !

Control

Control of Amur Traffic. It is all right not to levy Coast Trade Duty, for various reasons. But what about Duty on Amur Traffic ? Could not the Ch'u make it yet a necessary counterpart of our concessions on the Liang-chiat'un Barrier ?

Motor Launch. I am thinking of substituting, in part, cruises by Motor launch to control at Barriers on the two sides of the Harbour (control of overland goods); the launch would also be of great help to the River Inspector - when I have to go over to Blagovestchensk now, I lose more time in waiting for the Ferry, or for some
                    I use
other boat, than ∧ in actual business.

Political situation. Nothing new here; only that, according to information from the Telegraph Office, the Taoyin and Defence Commissioner receive their orders from Peking, no longer from Mukden. - Martial Law has, however, been declared from 25th May; this, in order to give a pretext to the General, and not go to war, in which all merchants support him heartily. All sort of rumours have been circulating - but I knew their origin, and was not alarmed

Blagovestchensk. Not much change; lack of money, and of everything; the Ministers, Nikiforoff and Petzoff, have come down recently, and have put a little order in some of the Administrations. The Emissar has again changed ! The political elections are being prepared; arrests en masse of leaders of Anti-Communist Parties, and Newspapers publishers

democratic

democratic papers closed. Two regiments recalled from Habarovsk; bulletins sent to foreigners (I have seen one).- The
Military
Control have found a new way of "squeezing"; at the
regatta, they ask for subscriptions to Benefit Performances,
to Concerts, to the Popular University, to a Raffle; you are
free, of course, to refuse - but be careful how they handle
you when you cross the frontier ! Money is so scarce that
people I know, being in straits, pawned gold objects(over
60 dollars worth of pure gold in them), and got 20
roubles (gold) loan - they have to pay four gold roubles
Taheiho. a month interest ! In Taheiho, pawnshops now charge 10 %
per month, two months interest prepaid. If one were a
shark, money could be made by heaps in the most filthy
way. The Bank of Communications, here, refuses to renew
loans - the merchants are practically boycotting her Notes,
and even started a rumour to the effect that the Customs
refused them - which of course, is false. I suppose the
Bank wants to charge interest at the new rate. It is
said that probably by the Autumn festival, some 60 shops
will go bankrupt; they are running at a loss now. There
is practically no export trade, except Flour (enormous a-
mounts) and timber.-

Various. Mr. Ritchie, Harbin Postal Commissioner, has
visited this place from 22nd to 24th May; he proposes to
make this a 1st Class Post Office; we hope for an amelior-
ation of communications and the service generally. Mr. Ritchie would still like to buy part of our land, but
this

this question I will report separately (officially) It
may be advisable to sell, in my opinion a) if the cost
of the land is sufficiently high; b) if we can buy with
less money another place, better suitable for residence.

The Telegraphic Cable between Helampo and Blago. has
been repaired by a Danish Engineer; telegrams can now be
sent to Europe from here, through Russia. The Pin-Hei
Ry. was reported in the Paper as having been granted to
a Dutchman (formerly of the Cheefoo Breakwater) by the
Chiao T'ung Pu - concession for 20 years - to be built
in 3 years.

The Conclusion of the Agreement for Aids-to-Navigation was solemnised by a banquet, at which much was spoken. At the end, under the influence of liquor, two of
the Military (Soldiers of the Revolution, as they styled
themselves) made most violent and aggressive speeches,
which, diplomatically, nobody translated into Chinese. Trahit
sua quemque voluptas ! I must say I am not reassured at
all by the bad omen that are accumulating. I think it
is a hard task to try and tame this rabble; it is
something like improving the Cholera, or like cultivating
the bacillus of typhoid fever for domestic purposes.
Yours truly,

第 15 号半官函　　　　　　　　　　　1922 年 6 月 19 日于瑷珲关／大黑河

尊敬的安格联先生：

　　此次呈交时间延误许久，主要因需要处理之事过多，包括日益增多的航路标志。征税汇办处现下十分繁忙，帮办无法脱身帮助本人，希望新任同文供事可以尽早到来。

　　5 月 12 日、13 日和 6 月 5 日半官函收悉。

　　为黑龙江航路标志事：虽然本人在此事上的身份已经明确，但问题是，道尹对航路标志一无所知，且不愿尝试了解，现已全权交由其秘书车先生^①（亦为中国银行代行长）处理。但车先生除了通晓俄文，并无其他可以胜任此项工作的能力，不仅会将所有事务混为一谈，就连翻译文本都会错漏百出，需要本人做出纠正。然因无法参与中俄双方最后的协商，签订协议时本人并不知晓，协议汉文文本更是令人耻于接受，而且实际上，在此之前本人早已推荐过一份更好的文本。不过如今已经不会再有此等情况出现，本人已就相关细节问题拟订附加条款，但在此之前不得不对道尹提供的协议汉文及俄文草案（两份文本出入较大）进行修正，同时还需添加一些新条款，最后再整体修订。

　　周六已将修订文本交与车先生。令人欣慰的是，苏俄代表已经接受修订协议中的所有条款，并将自己拟订的协议撤回，但不知车先生会如何处理自己此前的协议草案，相信其现下之处境亦不会太轻松。本人已于附加条款中列入中国船只应有权于黑龙江自哈巴罗夫斯克（Habarovsk）至入海口河段航行一条。但此问题若想明确解决，还须由中国政府出面协商谈判，地方无法议定。此前于地方商议此事时，俄阿穆尔国家水道局表示他们只能在管辖职责内协商经济层面的问题。总税务司 5 月 24 日半官函所附各部代表草拟的航行条例虽然非常可取，条款亦明确公正，但应由北京政府和赤塔（Chita）政府签订，或者由经授权的机构签订，而非当前状态下的地方政府。所幸双方于 5 月 27 日签署的协议并未造成任何损失，而且之后协议草案的拟订亦会征询本人意见。

　　此外，希望巡江工司的人选可以尽快选定。如果是易保罗（P. I. Ignatieff）先生，当然最好，但如果其过于自恃，亦可选用其他有能力之人，只要愿意学习俄文，相信很快便可胜任。不过，本人并不认识易保罗先生，只是听闻其才干出众，为人正直，但很有野心，亦正因如此，方会担心其会将在中国海关任职一事当作跳板，待时机成熟后再重返俄国担任巡江官员。

---

　　① 黑河支行代行长"车席珍"

获悉此前所采取之行动已获阁下支持，甚为欢喜。本人虽自有主意，在应对办法上通常亦不会有何疑虑，但必须保证一应办法均符合阁下之意，均与海关总税务司公署总体方向保持一致，因此于本人而言，确保路线正确才最为有益。

但得知外交部对于地方就黑龙江航路标志进行协商一事竟毫不知情，着实讶异，因为道尹曾表示外交部已通过电报对协议的基本原则予以批准。

为总税务司6月5日半官函事：关于海关于梁家屯的管辖权，如无特别情况马车运输或者民船运输均不在海关管辖之列，海关于梁家屯监管陆路运输是为确保有效管控边境，应可视为特别情况。

为管控黑龙江往来运输事：对于黑龙江上的往来运输，鉴于种种原因，不征收土货复进口／复出口半税亦属合理，但不知是否可以征收正税？海关既已放弃梁家屯分卡，税务处是否可以批准此项征税以作抵偿？

为摩托艇事：现正在考虑购置一艘摩托艇，主要用于巡航，以替代对港口上下游两处分卡（监管陆路运输的货物）的管控，待巡江工司到任后亦将对其工作有极大助益，如今本人前往布拉戈维申斯克（Blagovestchensk）时，等待渡船或者其他船只的时间比正常处理事务的时间还要长。

为政治局势事：本地局势并无新进展，唯从电报局得知，如今道尹及镇守使接收的命令均来自北京，而非奉天。5月25日，地方宣布实施戒严令，以便将军有理由留在此地，不必奔赴战场，所有商人对其均十分拥戴。现下流传各种传闻，但本人了解其来源，因此并未紧张。

为布拉戈维申斯克事：当地局势并未有何变化，钱财和所有物资仍十分紧缺。近日两名部长尼基弗洛夫（Nikiforoff）和彼得罗夫（Petroff）下到当地，管理秩序已有所恢复。但特使再次更换，政治选举已在筹备当中，选举公报业已分发给外国人（本人亦阅读过）。反共政党的领导人和报纸出版人大批被捕。宣传民主的报纸已被查封。两个团已从哈巴罗夫斯克撤回。此外，当地军方又开始实行新的"压榨"办法，他们于出入港口检查处要求往来民众为义演、音乐会、人民大学及抽彩活动等捐助费用，当然也可以拒绝，但要当心过境时可能会遭到不公对待。当地货币稀缺，据本人所知，有些深陷困境的人们已开始典当黄金制品（其中有价值60银圆的纯金制品），以换取20金卢布的贷款，但每月的利息高达4金卢布！

为大黑河事：当地当铺每月的利息为10%，并要求典当者预先支付两个月的利息。如有坑蒙拐骗之辈，定可借此机会大发横财。交通银行大黑河支行不再允许续借贷款，商人实际上已在抵制交通银行发行的纸币,并制造谣言称是海关拒收交通银行纸币,但事实当然并非如此。估计交通银行此举是为了调整利息。据称,中秋节后将有60余家店铺倒闭,这些店铺现在已处于亏损状态。如今除了面粉(出口量极大)和木料,再无出口贸易。

为其他各事:哈尔滨邮政司里奇(Ritchie)先生于5月22日至24日到访大黑河,提议将本地邮政局设为一级,以期整体改善邮政通信服务,同时表示希望购置部分海关关产。关于此事,将单独呈文汇报。兹认为,如果对方出价足够高,而且海关可以较低价格在别处购置适宜居住之所,便可考虑出售之事。

大黑河与布拉戈维申斯克之间的电报线路已由一名丹麦工程师修理完毕,现在大黑河可经苏俄向欧洲发送电报。此前报纸所报道的哈尔滨至大黑河铁路修建工程,已由交通部承包给荷兰人,承包期为20年,3年内动工。

中俄双方签订黑龙江航行地方临时协议后举行宴会庆祝,宴会上双方均有致辞。宴会接近尾声时,两名醉酒的俄国军方人士(自称为革命军)发表了充满暴力和挑衅的言论,但出于外交礼仪,现场未有人将此等言论翻译成汉文。虽说人各有志,但这些不祥之兆愈来愈多,着实令人难安。想要驯服这些桀骜不驯的士兵,相信必定十分艰难,就如同治愈霍乱,或是培养伤寒杆菌一样艰难。

您真挚的

包安济

13. 包安济致安格联函

（第 17 号半官函）

S/O No. 17.

Aigun / Taheiho, 1st Aug. 22

Dear Sir Francis,

Nothing very striking since writing last. But we are waging a daily struggle against encroachments from the Police, the Local Tax Office, even the Ferry Office now, which has brought action against a Junk which carried flour across to Blagovestchensk, duly cleared by us. They contend that they have the monopoly of ferrying things across; of course, they do not take such a free hand against the <u>russian</u> vessels carrying freight across; but here they dare. I am asking for the payment of a fine, and if the case is not satisfactorily settled locally, I will report to you officially.

<u>Aids to Navigation.</u> I am informed that Lahasusu started collection; they do not collect much, however. A despatch will tell you some fine mess made in the translation of the Agreement by the usual individual (Mr. Ch'e) who acts as Interpreter and Adviser for Foreign matters to the Taoyin. He is the most conceited fool in town, and there is nothing to do with him, just because he is conceited.

Francis A. Aglen, K. B. E.,
Inspector General of Customs,
P e k i n g.

Entered in Card-Index.

I am very much annoyed at the thought that, perhaps, I may take part, officially or unofficially, to the forth-coming Conference on Navigation on the Amur, etc, if business has to be transacted through that fool. I hope the delegates will, bring with them a really competent inter-preter. - I am unofficially informed that the Conference should be held here, the Taoyin being the representative of the WaiChiao Pu, while the Chiao T'ung Pu would send two delegates, who should at the same time enquire into the doings of the Wut'ung S. S. Co., which has been losing terribly last year, and into the question of the Harbin-Haiho Railway (which it is now rumoured would be granted to an American concern). If they are to look into so many and diverse things, I am afraid they will be competent in none ; the Taoyin is too lazy, and does not know much, anyhow, so that I may have to do all, (including re-dressing mistakes) and be my own translator. I have started <u>studying</u> russian, but I cannot possibly be very proficient two months hence !

Concerning the River Inspector, I would be much obliged if one could be appointed <u>soon</u>; he could gain so much experience <u>now</u>, so useful for the future. I have sent the Senior Out-Door Officer on a tour of inspection of the Aids down River; but his absence is felt in the Office; still, I preferred to go to a certain inconvenience, rather than be in the dark of all that is being done. - The

first

first accounts rendered by the Water Transport on work
and expenditure has been very unsatisfactory - and I have
sent it back, with request to give a proper detailed
statement. - We will always have to fight for proper
supervision - that is one of the reasons why I would
still advocate the taking in hand of conservancy work
on half of the River (possibly the section from here to
Habarovsk or Kasakevich), where we have already two points
d'appui : Lahasusu and Aigun), the other being that we may
undertake it at about the same cost as the russians, by
employing chinese labour (but I want the River Inspector to
confirm my estimates) - besides the question of obtaining
a better hold of the River; the technical establishments
can facilitate Customs work proper, give interesting informa
tion on Trade, be the nucleus for development of our
action. -

Blagovestchensk is still suffering from lack of food
and supplies; there is no work, only gains for a few
commission Agents, and for the Chinese who carry articles
of food across; the Government Bodies are offering all
sort of guarantees to the Chinese (including steamers) for
flour; but the Chinese only accept cash, as they have
been caught several times. - Politically, nothing new. The
American Consul, Mr. Thomas, who was here on a visit, went
away to Habarovsk four days ago, with a Military attache,
who had been visiting certain mines (gold).

Local.

Local. The Russians are trying to open a Consulate or
Representation in Taheiho; Mr. Tujilin, former Consul (up to
the closing of the Consulate) has come back, and will be,
if not Consul, because he is not a Communist, the technical
adviser to the Consul. - More trouble ahead, probably !
A short while ago the first foreign Club of Taheiho was
opened, and I was elected President; I accepted on condition that no politics be allowed therein. - After the
opening, the "Amurskaya Pravda", Bolshevist paper of Blago.,
published a rabid article about the "reactionary Club", which
had opened on most inflammatory speeches against the present Russian Regime, which was anti-jews, etc.- Now, I had
been the only one to speak, just two words to welcome the
guests and wish well to the Club - and the Chinese Authorities had been invited to be present, and had come. So
I went to the Emissar, and complained; he asked me to send
a rectification, which I did - but in the meantime the Direc
tor of the Water Transport had seen the Newspaper Editor -
who sent a representative to see me; I was absent, and Mr.
Baukham saw him. Next day a fine article appeared on the
"Pravda", all flowers for the C.M.C, but full of inexactitudes
I will not rectify this time, as they are harmless. Small
as this incident was, it took me good time, too valuable
here to be spent on trifles. -

The Magistrate is changed; a fire occurred in his Yamen,
and the Taoyin ascribes it to negligence; the substitute,
who

who has not arrived yet, is said to be very smart and
honest ! Wait and see. The present Magistrate, Mr. Sung, has
handed over on the 31st July to a Secretary of the Taoyin.
Several more changes are announced or have taken place; the
representative of the Yen Wu Shu, the Manager of the Mutung,
the Director of the Local Tax Office. — It is even
rumoured that the Taoyin is shortly going; but I have no
ground for believing this. — Soldiers (chinese) fired at
the S.S. Su-chow, which they wanted to board for Taheiho,
while the steamer did not want to stop; nobody was hurt,
happily.

Staff all well, with the exception of one excellent
Chinese Tidewaiter — who is not seriously ill, but whose
absence is felt.

Yours truly,

第 17 号半官函   1922 年 8 月 1 日于瑷珲关 / 大黑河

尊敬的安格联先生：

自发送上一封半官函以来，本地并无要事发生，唯警方和地方税捐局时常侵犯海关管辖权。如今轮渡公司亦开始有此趋势，日前竟对一艘已于海关办理结关并载运面粉前往布拉戈维申斯克（Blagovestchensk）的民船进行拦截，还扬言渡运货物过江乃其独有之权利，不过对于载运货物过江的俄国船只，他们并不敢如此插手，只敢针对华籍船只。对于此事，兹已向轮渡公司索要罚金，如果最终无法在地方妥善解决，将呈文正式汇报。

为航路标志事：据悉，拉哈苏苏分关已开始征收江捐，只是所收数额不多。另外，道尹公署外交顾问兼翻译车先生对地方协议的翻译错漏百出，具体情况将发送呈文汇报。车先生是镇上最为狂妄自大之人，本人平时与之毫无往来，但一想到在接下来的黑龙江航务相关会议中很有可能需要与之交涉，便十分恼怒。希望届时中方代表可以选用一名真正有能力的翻译出席会议。现已从私下得知，会议将于大黑河召开，道尹将代表外交部出席，交通部亦会派出两名代表，估计会调查戊通航业公司去年严重亏损一事及哈尔滨至黑河铁路的修建事宜（有传闻称此项工程已承包给一家美国公司）。但如果他们想要审查之事如此繁杂，恐怕最终难有成果。鉴于道尹为人懒惰，又不了解航务之事，届时本人很有可能需要承担所有工作，包括更正错误的翻译，因此现已开始学习俄文，但距离会议召开仅有两个月的时间，可能不会有显著成效！

此外，如果可以尽快为瑷珲关任命一名巡江工司，本人将不胜感激，因为目前正是为日后工作积累经验的好时机。另已派遣超等外班关员前往黑龙江巡查航标的修建情况，虽然日常公务方面因此已有些不便，但亦好过对航标工事的进展一无所知。苏俄阿穆尔国家水运局提交的首批航标工事及支出相关账目令人很不满意，现已退回并要求提供详细报表。在航路标志的监督问题上，中方总是要通过抗争方能得到正当权利，因此本人仍然认为，中方应当自行承担黑龙江一半航道的维护管理工作。可以是自大黑河至哈巴罗夫斯克（Habarovsk）或嘎杂克维池（Kasakevich）河段，因为在这一河段，海关已有拉哈苏苏和瑷珲两处关卡，维护工作可以雇用华籍劳工来做，这样一来，费用方面应该与俄方当前支出相差无几，但此预算还需由巡江工司核定。若如此，中方不仅可以更好地管控黑龙江航道，海关工作亦会更加便利，最为重要的贸易信息也可及时获得。

为布拉戈维申斯克事：当地仍然紧缺粮食和物资，亦无工作机会，唯有一些佣金代理商和运送粮食过江的中国商人可以获得一些收益。当地政府机构向中国商人（包括轮船主)提出以各种抵押品交换面粉,但中国商人只接受现金,因为此前已因接受抵押品而被扣押过数次。政治方面,并无新情况。之前造访当地的美国领事托马斯(Thomas)先生已于四日前前往哈巴罗夫斯克,随行的还有一名军方官员,此人一直在探访(金)矿地。

为地方事:苏俄方面计划重新于大黑河设立领事馆或者代表处。前领事(任职至领事馆关闭之前)图吉林(Tujilin)先生已经返回大黑河,但因其不是共产主义人士,很有可能不会再次担任领事,不过即便如此,估计亦会担任领事的专门顾问。不久前,大黑河首家洋人俱乐部成立,本人被推选为主席,但接受这一职位时已经申明不得涉及政治问题。不料,随后布拉戈维申斯克布尔什维克党的报纸《阿穆尔真理报(Amurskaya Pravda)》刊登了一篇题为"反动俱乐部"的文章,该报纸曾以极具煽动性的言论大肆批判苏俄当前政府。俱乐部成立当日,中国官员亦受邀出席,本人也只是对来宾发表了简短的欢迎致辞,同时表示希望俱乐部可以顺利发展。看到报道后,本人便前去拜访苏俄特使说明此事,之后又按照其要求发送了一份更正说明。与此同时,苏俄阿穆尔国家水运局督办也面见了《阿穆尔真理报》的编辑,该编辑随后便派遣一名代表来此了解情况,但本人当时不在海关,博韩(G. E. Baukham)先生接见了他。次日,《阿穆尔真理报》便发表了一篇赞扬中国海关的文章,只是内容并不属实。但鉴于该报道对海关无害,因此不会再次要求更正。此事虽小,但颇为耗时,本人的时间不应浪费在此等琐事上。

日前,瑷珲县公署失火,县知事因此被免职,道尹认为此次失火是疏忽所致。据称继任县知事为人正直,且十分机敏,但至今还未到任。离任县长孙先生已于7月31日将职务移交给道尹秘书。除此之外,地方官员还有一些变动,包括盐务署代表、戊通公司经理及地方税捐局局长的更换等。还有传闻称,道尹不日亦将离职,但相信并不属实。此外,有几名华籍士兵向"苏州(Su-chow)"号轮船开火,起因是他们意图乘坐此船前往大黑河,但轮船并未停靠,所幸并无人员伤亡。

为人事事:关员一切安好,唯有一名华籍钤子手已因病请假,不过病情并不严重,但也给海关带来些许不便。

您真挚的

包安济

14. 包安济致安格联函

（第18号半官函）

S/O No. 18.

Aigun/Taheiho 24th august   2

Dear Sir Francis,

I have received Mr. de Luca's letter of 28th July, enclosing copy of communication from the Chief Secretary, Directorate General of Posts, to the Chief Secretary, Inspectorate General of Posts, concerning the Customs examination of Postal Parcels at Taheiho. The question is merely one of Staff: we have only two Examiners, of which the one acts as Senior Officer, and has his time largely taken up in fulfilling what may be termed Tide-surveyor's duties, in preparing valuation Lists, etc, and cannot therefore be available for duty at the G.P.O; while the other has to attend to steamer cargo in summer, overland cargo in winter, besides examination of outgoing parcels in the General Office, and special examination in godowns, when the Senior Officer has to attend to the examination at the Custom House. The Examiners are therefore more than occupied: they are crowded with work at times, exactly the times when traffic in postal parcels is heavier. - Of the Tidewaiters of Senior rank, with sufficient knowledge of Examination work, one,

Mr.

Sir Francis A. Aglen, K. B. E.,

Inspector General of Customs,

P e k i n g.   Entered in Card-Index.

Mr. Grundul, helped by an excellent Chinese Tidewaiter (Mr. Tsang Lan-hsien) is permanently detached at the Ferry Office in summer, at the Winter Road Office in winter, while another yet is in Aigun (Mr. Irahenko). Until recently I had no more; but now Mr. Emiliano having replaced Mr. Matser(Senior Tidewaiter) he not only does his share as the senior of Tidewaiters, but occasionally helps in examination, and is most useful in checking cargo duty-paid from Harbin, and is fairly advanced in knowledge of goods and values. Right now he is replacing(to a certain extent, and greatly helped by the Senior Officer) Examiner Murray, laid up with liver trouble. - I think I may now do something for the Post Office, i.e. propose to detach Mr. Emiliano for duty there three times a week, say, from 9 to 10.30 a.m., or from 2 to 3.30 p.m.; the Officer should be given a special room)which is available in the building now occupied - and to be shortly purchased - by the G.P.O), with a Desk and all facilities. - The short hours are necessary, because there may be a rush of work in the Custom House or Bund, while the Officer would be sitting in the G.P.O., idle, waiting for some late customer; but, of course, should "application" presented up to 10.30 (or 3.30) be outstanding, the Officer will go on working on them till 12, or till finished.

Incidentally, these arrangements would be very opportune in improving the handling of export Parcels; which so far,

by

by an established practice, and because no other arrangements could be made, are examined in the General Office
(or Examiners' Office at Head Office), handed back to applicant, who takes them to the C.P.O., and there re-inspected
(not always - and summarily anyhow) by our Examiner before
mail bags are despatched; substitution of goods and shipment of opium chiefly, are quite easy now. - I would
therefore propose that, on accordance with practice at other
Ports, parcels be handled solely at the C.P.O (Inward as
well as Outward Parcels), duty paid there (the amount to
be handed to the G.O. daily), and the parcels stamped by
our Officer with a copy of the Office seal. Complete original waybills should be handed by the C.P.O., so we
could see that no parcel escapes payment of duties.

However, I should be sure that the present strength and
standard of staff is maintained, especially in the event
of transfers: besides two capable Examiners (or Assistant
Examiners) there should always be three Foreign Tidewaiters
of senior rank with fairly good knowledge of Examination,
and one at least of the Chinese Tidewaiters should be
of the type of Mr. Tsang : exceptionally reliable and
experienced.

Your S/O of 26th July: Trip up River by Commissioner:
provided work can be carried on, he should go, and learn
as much about the river as possible :

1

I am trying to have all outstanding questions settled
and, if possible, will leave for Humaho and Moho (i.e.
practically the confluence of the Shilka and Argun) about
the 10th of September; the trip takes only ten days, and I
intend obtaining permission from the Russian to have the
Chinese Steamer stop also on the Russian side, so I can
inspect some of the Aids-to-Navigation too. The cost to the
service will be trifling, since no tickets are to be paid
by Officers on Inspection of Aids-to-Navigation. As to leaving the Office alone, I think I can manage it: the Chinese
Assistant is quite capable of running the G.O.; the
Senior Out-door Officer knows his business well, and I have
already asked the Superintendent to see that no questions
are brought up during my short absence; if anything should
happen, I can be reached by wire at Humaho, Moho, and at
some of the Russian places I intend to visit. It will
have to be a hurried trip, but I am collecting materials
in advance, which I will check on the spot.

Patrol system and Motor Launch for Taheiho: the rumour
that we may buy the launch and open the Barriers has
already had a wholesome effect on contraband; it has
dropped considerably, according to all reports. - The gig is
working, and effecting considerable saving of time in
boarding vessels, which now have to stop in front of the
Custom House without exception.

Property .

<u>Property.</u> Extraordinary slackness in the Magistrate Yamen
has made it impossible to, effect the registration of any
of the Title Deeds so far unregistered (previous to the
seperation); I am afraid several months will be necessary
to put all Property Records on a proper footing. As to
the Property "New Custom House Side", purchased in 1921 with
Service Money, which has recently been refunded from Revenue
(*originally*) I asked the Magistrate to register it under your name
(糸总税务司) as directed by Circular No. 3240; but now,
that an appropriation from Revenue has been made for this
lot, how should it be registered ? 海关, I presume ?

Blagovestchensk: life continues dull there: the crop is
fairly good, and export of flour will soon stop from here.
Just now there seems to be a nervous feeling among the
Reds in power; they have the Bund patrolled at night, one
armed launch is also patrolling the River frontage, and
searchlights have played on the sky for two nights. They
say a "White" insurrection is feared; but I am slow in
believing it; they did absolutely nothing, when the "white"
armies were marching towards Blago. from Habarovsk, and the
"fleet" was tied up by the ice; how could they dare it
now ? - Still, surprises are possible; and I do not know
whether to wish one, or to deprecate it. - If things have
not cleared up, I shall not go on my trip, anyhow. - On
the 10th the New Bank of the Far Eastern Republic opened
in Blagovestchensk; many speeches, the one of the Manager
insisting

insisting on the fact that the capital as well as the
deposits would be absolutely free from confiscation or
requisition ! The capital should consist of three million
gold roubles; I hear that only 1,800,000 has been subscri-
bed, 55% belonging to the Government. - There is no business there anyhow, and the Bank may perhaps live on
loans, like a pawnshop.

<u>Local.</u> The Chinese Post Office has been changed from
the 16th into a First Class Post Office; they are about
                                    but smaller, and
to buy a building, similar to ours, without basement,
without outhouses, and with a smaller yard; the price is
somewhere about $ 18,000. - The Heilungchiang Assembly, as
you probably have learned, elected as Civil Governor a certain
Liang Shang-ta, native of Heilungchiang, against Chang Tso-lin's
candidate; Tuchu Wu seems to be flirting with Peking; developments may be expected if that is the actual case. -
I hear that Chang presented to the Consular Body at Harbin a
proposal to open Sansing as a Port; it was, apparently, all a
speculation; but that may open a prospect for opening Taheiho.
- The Italian Consul General in Hankow, detached for duty
(temporarily) at Harbin, Mr. G. Ros, has visited Taheiho and
Blagovestchensk, from 12th to 17th. - Staff well, except Examiner Murray, laid in bed with inflammation of the liver, consequent upon a gastritis contracted in Harbin; he is improving. -
I have put up a very fine russian horse with a carriage which,
however fine, is also in russian style, and looks something like
"a matchbox behind an elephant". It shows all right !
                                Yours truly,

第 18 号半官函　　　　　　　　　　　　　　**1922 年 8 月 24 日于瑷珲关 / 大黑河**

尊敬的安格联先生：

卢立基（L. de Luca）先生 7 月 28 日函已收悉，内附其与总务科税务司和总邮政司就大黑河海关查验邮政包裹一事的往来函抄件。实际上，此事仅仅是人事上的问题。瑷珲关目前只有两名二等验货，其中一名还是超等外班关员，大部分时间都在履行头等总巡的职责，同时还要负责编制估值表等事，因此无暇兼顾中国邮政局之工作。另外一名需于夏季负责查验船载货物，冬季负责查验陆路货物，同时还需于征税汇办处负责查验出口包裹，当超等外班关员于海关办公楼验货时，还要前往关栈验货。两名二等验货已是繁忙不堪，邮政包裹运输量增加时，更是分身乏术。

超等钤子手中虽有熟悉验货工作的关员，但其中葛伦德（J. D.Grundul）先生在优秀的华籍钤子手臧郎轩先生的协助下，于夏冬两季分别负责横江码头检查处和冬令过江检查处的验货工作，尹贞固（A. A. Irshenko）先生则负责瑷珲口岸的验货工作。除此之外，再无可以负责验货的关员。直到近日，埃米利尔诺（A.Emiliano）先生为接替超等钤子手马蒂尔（N. C. Mateer）先生来至本口岸后，情况方有所缓解。因为其不仅可以负责超等钤子手之职务，偶尔还可以帮忙验货，尤其擅长查验哈尔滨关运来的完税货物，而且熟悉货物及估值方面的知识，如今在超等外班关员的帮助下已经开始负责因肝病休假的二等验货马瑞（N. J. G.Murray）先生的部分工作。

依目前情况来看，或许可以派遣埃米利尔诺先生前去负责邮政局的查验工作，每周可以去三次，工作时段可以为上午 9 时至 10 时 30 分，或者下午 2 时至 3 时 30 分。关员应当有专门的办公室（在中国邮政局即将购买的办公楼内安排一间即可），配备办公桌和办公设备。缩短关员在邮政局的工作时间，主要考虑海关办公室和堤岸上的验货工作可能会很多，而邮政局可能有时并没有验货工作，关员只能在那里闲坐等待，浪费时间，不过如果到上午 10 时 30 分（或者下午 3 时 30 分），仍有很多待处理的"报单"，关员可工作至 12 时，或者直到完成所有查验工作为止。

若能如此安排，出口包裹的处理办法亦可借机调整。按照惯例（亦无其他办法），出口包裹一直在征税汇办处（或者验查课）接受查验，通过后再由报关人送至中国邮政局接受海关验货员的复验（偶尔且为大致查验），之后再寄出。按照此办法，替换货物或者偷运鸦片等行为便颇为容易。有鉴于此，兹建议，按照其他口岸的现行办法，仅于中国邮政局处理（进口及出口）包裹，并收税（税款按日送交海关征税汇办处），海关关员验货后须于包裹上加盖关封,中国邮政局随后应送交所有运搬凭单原件,以便海关确认无包裹漏交关税。

但在此之前,必须确保瑷珲关保持现有人力,即使人事上有调动,亦不宜改变当前的人员配置。即除两名有能力的二等验货(或者三等验货)外,还须有三名熟悉验货工作的洋籍超等钤子手,至少一名如臧朗轩先生一样可靠且经验丰富的华籍钤子手。

为总税务司 7 月 28 日半官函事:只要不影响海关事务税务司可前往黑龙江上游巡查望竭尽所能获取所需信息。

现正在尽力解决所有待处理之事,如果情况允许,将于 9 月 10 日左右动身前往呼玛河和漠河(即石勒喀河与额尔古纳河交汇处附近)。此次行程往返仅需十日,本人还计划向苏俄当局申请允许所乘华籍轮船停靠俄岸,以便检查航标的情况。费用方面,海关需承担之数应会很少,因为巡查航标的官员不必支付船票费。至于海关事务,相信亦不会有何问题,华籍帮办可以妥善处理征税汇办处的日常事务,超等外班关员亦能处理好自己的分内之事,海关监督业已答允帮忙照看,确保在本人离开期间关内不会出现问题。如有意外情况,关员还可向呼玛河、漠河及此次巡查将会到访的俄镇发送电报与本人联络。此次巡查时日较短,但本人已事先收集相关资料,届时可实地核验。

为大黑河口岸巡缉办法和摩托艇事:一直有传闻称,瑷珲关或将购置摩托艇并增设分卡,走私事件因此已受到影响。据多方报告,走私情况已大幅减少。如今船只进港后均停靠在海关办公楼前方,关员借助小船登船检查,可以节约大量时间。

为关产事:由于瑷珲县公署办事效率极低,地契登记之事迄今仍未完成,恐怕还需数月时间才能落实所有关产的登记事宜。另外,对于"新海关办公楼关址"的地契登记一事,本人仍有些疑问。此前因考虑 1921 年购置此关产时使用的是海关经费,故已按照海关总税务司公署第 3240 号通令指示请县知事将之登记于总税务司名下,但此笔款项近日已由税收偿付,不知还应如何登记?是否应登记在"海关"名下?

为布拉戈维申斯克(Blagovestchensk)事:当地百姓生活依旧艰辛,不过庄稼长势甚好,估计不久之后便不会再有面粉自大黑河出口至当地。近来,红军当局似乎颇为紧张,夜间还派兵于堤岸上巡逻,此外还有一艘武装汽艇于前滩巡缉,最近两晚还使用探照灯巡视。据称,他们是担心遭遇"白军"突袭,但对此本人并不相信,因为当初"白军"队伍从哈巴罗夫斯克(Habarovsk)向布拉戈维申斯克行进时,红军的"舰队"被冰困于江中,他们都未曾有任何行动,如今又怎会惧怕?不过世事难料,"白军"是否会突袭,目前无法断言。无论如何,在事态明朗之前,本人无法前往黑龙江上游巡查。8 月 10 日,远东共和国新银行于布拉戈维申斯克开办,当日有很多官员发表讲话,银行经理坚称银行资产和存款绝不会被政府充公或者征用！银行资产应有 300 万金卢布，但据悉仅有 180 万金卢布被认购，其中 55% 属于政府所有。不过，当地仍无贸易，银行或许只能依靠贷款维持经营，如典当行一般。

为地方事：自 8 月 16 日起，大黑河中国邮政局已被列为一级邮政局，现正计划购置一处办公楼。此建筑与海关办公楼相似，但面积小一些，而且无地下室和附属建筑，庭院亦相对较小，价格约 18000 银圆。此外，阁下或许已经听闻，黑龙江省议会已推举一位名叫梁声德（Liang Shang-ta）的黑龙江当地人出任省长，并未推选张作霖选定之人。吴督军①似乎对北京方面十分殷勤，若果真如此，局势可能会有转变。据悉，张作霖已向驻于哈尔滨的领事机构提议将三姓设为口岸，显然此消息仅为推测，但若为事实，或许大黑河亦有望开放。驻汉口意大利总领事罗斯（G.Ros）先生暂被派遣至哈尔滨处理事务，并于 8 月 12 日至 17 日到访大黑河和布拉戈维申斯克。

为人事事：关员一切安好，唯二等验货马瑞先生因于哈尔滨感染胃炎后又患上肝炎，现卧病在床，不过已经有所好转。

本人已购入一匹俄国良驹和一驾俄式马车，质量较好，只是行动时如同"大象拖着火柴盒"，但总体状况尚好。

您真挚的

包安济

---

① 英文为 Tuchu Wu，鉴于文中其他华人之姓名皆为姓在前名在后，因此 Tuchu 不应为姓名，而为官职；另查 1921 年吴俊升被任命为黑龙江督军兼署省长，此后七年一直统治黑龙江，故推测 Tuchu 或为拼写错误（文中经常出现此类错误），实应为 Tuchun，即督军吴俊升。

15. 包安济致安格联函

（第 19 号半官函）

S/O No. 19.

S/O No. 19.

Aigun/Tuheiho 30th August 2

Dear Sir Francis,

Since writing six days ago, the situation has become more serious on the Russian side, and I have collected further interesting information. - There is undoubtedly an insurrectional movement extensively planned; the farmers will revolt after the harvest; from a traveller just returned from a trip on the Zeia (as far as Dombuky) I learn that the discontent amongst the farmers and gold-washers is just as rife there as along the Amur; they say that anything they possess is taken away by the Government. I know that, again, after a period of free breathing due to an inflow of gold from Chita (Moscow) for the war against Vladivostock, the Government is broke : employés have been mostly paid only till May, sailors on board merchant vessels are only few, and sometime receive 30 or 40 cents a month - the surplus they make as they can, by smuggling chiefly - the Government Offices are selling out all they can, in order to raise funds. Recently consignments of old shells and bombs (broken up as scrap iron) have been shipped

ir Francis A. Aglen, K. B. E.,

Inspector General of Customs,

Peking.

Entered in Card-Index.

to Harbin; Govt. automobiles and motor-bycicles, are freely offered for sale; arms are sold and smuggled to China, to bandits mostly. - The outlook is this : if the present Government remains, it will have to start confiscating the crops from the farmers; the farmers know it, and they are ready for an insurrection. - I have approached one of the "white" leaders here, by asking him abruptly when he was going to lead his own men into Blagovestchensk. He could not deny, and confirmed that the movement is to start very shortly, i.e. after the harvest (about the middle of September) ; that it is connected with the re-organisation in Vladivostock, under General Diderichs (while Gondatti, a great hope of the Whites, and a really capable man, prudently declined to join); that the money, of course, will come chiefly from Japan - that it is even the idea of some of the Whites to settle things with Japan by giving up the northern portion of Sagalien and Niko-laievsk to Japan. My unwilling informant is of the opinion that the movement will be successfull, that, if the new Government can stand the test of a few months, they can revive Trade, reopen the Mines, in a word restore confidence, and resume functions like a regular Government. - I am not judging, only reporting. - In my opinion, the success is not sure, although there are signs that the Reds are scared - Commissars have left Blagovestchensk for Harbin in number, lately, with all their belongings and families, and the sale

sale on a large scale of Government property, the patrolling of the River by Gunboats, the searchlights at night,
all tend to confirm the impression that the Reds feel
uncomfortable. - But they are a decided lot, and, if they
give way, they will *probably* only do so in the last moment, not
without doing damage, and with the idea of coming back.-
If the "Whites" succeed, I do not know where they will
get enough money from, to last, without extortions and requisitions, until collecting of taxes on a more or less
normal trade and industry will allow them to live like a
decent Government .. unless they obtain large loans from
Japan in exchange for concessions as hinted above.- If the
they start requisitioning they will soon be as impopular
as the Communists, especially with the farmers. Besides, I
believe that the White terror will be as bad as the
Red terror; that they will be unwise enough to seek
revenge, not only on the leaders (which is justice) but on
the poor people, without distinction. By the way, feelings
are very high against the Jews (ils ne l'ont pas chire)
and a massacre is not improbable. -

My informer also gave me to understand that, should
the advance from Vladivostok be slow, they are thinking
to stop the running of vessels, russian and chinese alike,
between here and Harbin, so that Red leaders may not
run away and escape punishment. I gave to understand as
clearly that I would take the matter very much to heart,
and

protest in the most vigorous way against any stoppage
of goods passed by this Customs for Harbin. - In fact, I
do not see why they couldn't do like the Reds, i.c.
visit Boats at the mouth of the Sungad, without stopping
navigation. -

If these informations are exact (and they are most
reliable) I will not be able to leave for my trip up
river, which should have started on the 7 or 8th september.
However, the harvest may not be over before the 20th
september, in which case I can go and be back in time.-
Partisans are already active not far from Blago., and they
were heard of at Jalinda (opposite Lien Yin). -

The effect of these activities on local trade is
good; much foodstuff (beans, peas, oil) has been sent over
to Blago. to private merchants; it is clear to me that
partisans are behind the merchants, else there would be
no market for the goods. - Several local shops earmarked
for bankrupcy have taken a new lease of life; some, I am
afraid, are making money by purchasing arms from the Reds
and reselling them to the partisans. It is an ill wind....

Yours truly,

P. S. The propaganda against the present
Govt. is made in the name (if without
the consent) of Empress Dowager Maia Feodorovna, who
is considered as the rightful "ointed" pretender. The choice is good,
as it appeals to the religious feeling of the people, connected with
the idea of legitimacy. There is a great religious revival here, right
under the eyes of the Poles and the Cosmopolitonrans, and it must be
taken into serious consideration as a political factor.

第 19 号半官函   1922 年 8 月 30 日于瑷珲关／大黑河

尊敬的安格联先生：

自上次呈交半官函至今的六天以来，俄岸的局势愈发紧张，特于此汇报最新情况。

毫无疑问的是，俄岸大多地区都有爆发叛乱之势，农民很有可能会于秋收后起义。据一名刚从结雅河远至多姆比基（Dombuky）返回的平民透露，结雅河沿岸的农民和淘金工人与黑龙江沿岸的工农一样对当局十分不满，称自己的所有财产均已被政府占用。当地政府能够维持一段和平时期，主要是因为赤塔（Chita）（莫斯科）方面此前为支持其与符拉迪沃斯托克（Vladivostock）的战争拨发了一批金子，但如今已再次亏空。各部门职员的薪俸自 5 月以后便未再发放，商船上的水手亦只能获得食物供给，有时每月还可以通过走私货物等办法获取三、四十分的额外收入，政府官员已开始贩卖一切可卖之物，以筹得资金。近日还有大批废旧炮弹（已被炸碎成废铁片）运至哈尔滨，政府的汽车和摩托车也在自由出售，军火被贩卖或走私至中国，买家大多为土匪。依目前情况来看，当前政府若想继续维持下去，就不得不征用农民的粮食，而农民也已意识到这一点，正在筹划暴动。

本人此前与一名暂居于大黑河的俄国"白军"领导人谈话时，直接询问其准备何时带兵攻入布拉戈维申斯克（Blagovestchensk）。其坦承不日（即九月中旬秋收之后）即将动身，并称此行与迪德里茨（Diderichs）将军在符拉迪沃斯托克的重组行动有关，但真正有能力的贡达基（Gondatti）先生，亦是"白军"最大的希望，却谨慎地拒绝参与此次行动，还表示经费方面将主要由日本提供。据称，"白军"中甚至有人希望通过割让库页岛北部和尼古拉耶夫斯克（Nikolaisevsk）来获得日本的支持。此"白军"领导人相信他们的行动会取得胜利，认为只要新政府能够维持数月，便可恢复贸易，重开矿井，总之便是可以重新获得民众的信任，发挥政府的正常职能。

以上仅是在汇报实际情况，绝无评判之意。不过，兹认为，"白军"的行动未必一定会成功，因为虽有种种迹象表明苏俄"红军"已经有所忌惮，比如近日已有大批政治委员携家眷和财物离开布拉戈维申斯克前往哈尔滨，政府财产也在大批出售，江上一直有炮艇往来巡缉，夜间还有探照灯巡视，这一切似乎都在表明"红军"当局已经察觉事态有变，但他们大多意志坚定，估计只有到最后时刻才会决定放弃，而且不会就这样逃离，一定会进行破坏，还会抱有卷土重来的信念。此外，即使"白军"取得胜利并组建政府，在贸易和工业得以恢复，所收税款足以支持政府正常运作之前，如果不强夺征用，实不知他们还能如何筹得资金，除非如上所述，通过割地等妥协办法从日本获取大量贷款。然而，一旦开始征用，

"白军"政府就会与"红军"政府一样受到百姓（特别是农民）的唾弃。兹认为，"白军"将施行与"红军"一样糟糕的恐怖统治，甚至会发起报复行动，不仅会报复"红军"领导人（无可厚非），还会无差别地报复贫苦百姓。另外，"白军"的反犹太人情绪十分强烈，恐怕会有一场屠杀。

此"白军"领导人的言语间还透露，如果符拉迪沃斯托克的"白军"队伍行进缓慢，他们会考虑阻止中俄两国船只往来于大黑河与哈尔滨两地之间，以防"红军"领导人出国避难，逃脱制裁。本人当即表示非常不希望出现此等情况，坚决反对阻碍由海关放行之货物运往哈尔滨的行为。其实他们完全可以效仿"红军"于松花江与黑龙江交汇处登船检查，根本无须阻止航运。

如果上述消息皆属实（其中大部分内容十分可靠），本人原定于9月7日或8日开始的黑龙江上游巡查之旅恐怕无法如期进行，不过秋收可能会于9月20日之后结束，若是如此，本人仍可及时往返。"白军"拥护者现已开始于布拉戈维申斯克附近活动，此前已出现在加林达（Jalinda）（连崟对岸）。

苏俄方面的活动对本地贸易产生了积极影响。大量的粮食（大豆、豌豆、食用油）从大黑河出口至布拉戈维申斯克，买家虽为私营商人，但实际买主应为"白军"拥护者，否则这些粮食在当地根本没有市场。本地有几家商铺此前已面临破产，如今重焕生机，其中有些商人可能是通过从"红军"手中购买武器再转卖给"白军"拥护者来获取利润。由此可见，任何坏事都会利于某些人。

您真挚的

包安济

另："白军"此次是以皇太后玛利亚·费奥多罗夫娜（Maria Feodorovna）的名义（但或许并未获得准许）对"红军"政府发起讨伐行动，认为其才是最合法的统治者。"白军"此举将唤起民众心中的宗教感，让他们对"红军"当局的合法性产生怀疑。如今当地已开始有宗教复兴之势，而且就在契卡（全俄肃反委员会）的监视之下，这于政治局势而言十分重要。

地方见闻

16. 包安济致安格联函

（第 20 号半官函）

-0 No. 20

Aigun/Tsheits 9th september 2

Dear Sir Francis,

I am only leaving to-day, because yesterday a gale
of unprecedented violence swept the Harbour, and made it
impossible to load the Steamer. - I have been reliably
informed that the farmers over in Siberia are waiting to
see what happens in Vladivostock, and only when events
there take a more definite shape will they start (or
otherwise). That gives me about one month breathing time,
and I put it to use in going up inspecting the River,
so much the more as that Mr. Ignatieff will not be here
before the end of September, too late to take the trip
himself. I am taking with me a Chinese Clerk, for investigating matters at all small ports where we only stop
a few hours; and two Russia Engineers from the other
side. - I have received your letter of 25th August from
Peitaho; your approval of my action is a great encouragement to me - until a few months ago I have been more
or less feeling my way, and I am glad to give you
satisfaction, and to be out of the dark and surer of
my way. The appointment of Mr. Ignatieff will be a great
                                                    boon

ir Francis A. Aglen, K. B. E.,
    Inspector General of Customs,
        Peking.   Entered in Card-Index.

boon, and I will certainly use his work to the utmost. -
I think that his appointment for three years, and on contract gives the Commissioner a better hold on the man, a
he will do his best to be recommended for re-appointmen
- and, if not entirely satisfactory, he can easily be
discarded, and an "understudy" found to him; but I believe
he is anxious to prove himself useful. - As to taking
one section over ourselves, may I insist on a few point
It will be difficult to snatch this concession from the
Russian, but we should get it if we want to be
on a footing of equality with Russia; if we are not
prepared to take the section over next year, this will
be one reason in favour of the Russians for not giving
way; a fait accompli is better than ten Agreements; if
the Russians can maintain the Aids with the money now
available, we can too, although on the poor standard of
the russian upkeep at present. I would like to make every
effort to secure the passing over of one section to us;
personally, I would prefer to rest, and let the job to
somebody else later. - As to estimates, we will certainly
collect 20,000 dollars this, a bad, year, for five months;
we can rely on a minimum of ₤ 30,000, besides which we
should collect a clearance tax on every steamer, like at
Harbin; expenses, as presented by the Water Transports, for
the whole of the Amur from the Shilka to Habarovsk, they
amount to something like 36 or 37,000 gold roubles, i.e.
                                                    might

might almost be paid out of _our_ collection, exclusive of
duties collected on the Russian side, for the whole River.
- I will submit closer estimates and detailed report
of the _personnel_, etc, as soon as returned from my trip.-

Situation in Blagovestchensk slightly better owing to
the good crop, which however, so far, does not help Offici
cials out of their financial troubles. They are waiting a
German diplomatic Mission, which has left Stretensk, and
which I am sorry to miss; the head is, if I remember
rightly, is named Amyss (?).

Remittances. The Taoyin is still opposing the remittance of Revenue Moneys; I tried with the Bank, and the
were scared of Chang Tso-lin. I do not want to make an
official break with the Taoyin-Superintendent, which would
be most unpolitical here; so I have made a most irregular thing : I have switched money to my account, and I
am remitting from it through Mr. d'Anjou. - I am afraid of
leaving so much money in the Bank here, and I resort to
the only method; the money I kept so far, being uncertain
whether duty on flour exported abroad would be sanctioned,
and whether to have to refund heavy sums as drawbacks,
which I hope will not be the case. - If the Taoyin
insists, however, on my remitting, I will start collecting myself, not through the Bank, remitting as I can. - In the
mean time I have suspended the despatch of the Monthly
Return of Collection and Expenditure to the Superintendent-
Taoyin,

-Taoyin, seeing that that Official uses the information
therein contained against the Customs, thus betraying his
trust as Superintendent. I will simply delay until things
get settled, without hurting that official directly. Does
my action meet with your approval ? - If not, I will simply have to keep the money in the Bank of China unre-
mitted, and trust to fortune that it be not confiscated
one day. - The Taoyin, by the way, is going to Harbin
(and Mukden) shortly; apparently he goes to solicit a
better post; but his move may be taken in connection with
the alleged hostilities between Chang and Tuchun Ti Cheng-
sheng ; the Taoyin being a brother-in-law of Chang he may
run for safety. -

Arms moved within the Province. There are many instances of arms moved over Liangchiehtun, for villages, for
garrisons, etc. They should have the Lu Chun Pu's sanction
(Circ 2508)
sanction, and pass under Tuchun Huohao; three times have I
passed consignments, under guarantee from the Superintendent
and the Garrison Commander that proper permission would be
obtained; the Tuchun Huohao has some, but no sanction from
the Ministry of War. In view of the conditions here, and
the independence of this Province from Peking, could I go
back to the ruling of Circ. No. 1941 ? I am in an awkward
position; if I am too strict, I risk having everything passed without permission right under my nose.

Yours truly,

第 20 号半官函　　　　　　　　　　　1922 年 9 月 9 日于瑷珲关 / 大黑河

尊敬的安格联先生：

昨日暴风席卷港口，无法登船，本人只得于今日出发。据可靠消息，西伯利亚地区的农民正在等待符拉迪沃斯托克（Vladivostock）方面的行动，在局势明朗之前不会发起暴动。如此一来，一个月之内应不会有何动乱，本人正好利用这段时间前往黑龙江上游巡查，但易保罗（P. I. Ignatieff）先生应该无法于 9 月末之前抵达，亦无法参与此次巡查。此次巡查随行的还有一名华籍同文供事，主要负责协助调查沿途短暂停留的小口岸的情况，另有两名苏俄方面派来的俄籍工程师。

阁下 8 月 25 日自北戴河发来之函业已收悉，得知此前所采取之行动已获得支持，备受鼓舞。数月来，本人一直摸索行事，如今能够得到认可，着实欢喜，日后办事亦可更加笃定。易保罗先生的任命于瑷珲关而言着实有益，本人定会竭力让其发挥自己的优势，签署三年雇用合同，不仅可以让税务司对其有更好的管控，亦会令其更加努力地工作，以换取与海关续约的机会，而且如果其工作表现差强人意，合同到期后便可不再继续雇用，另择合适人选接替其职位，不过相信其定会尽力为海关服务，以体现自己的价值。

关于由中方独立管理黑龙江一段航道一事，兹认为，要让苏俄方面妥协，确实有些难度，但中国如果想与俄国保持平等，就必须争夺独立管理的权利。如果明年中方不打算接管黑龙江一段航道的航标维护工作，苏俄方面便会有理由不再让步，毕竟既成事实要比十份协议更为有用，如果苏俄方面能够使用现有经费完成航标的维护工作，那么中方也同样可以，不过工程质量会低于俄方当前的维护标准。本人愿意竭尽全力为中国争取独立管理黑龙江一段航道的权利，但从个人角度出发，并不愿参与此事，希望日后可由他人办理。预算方面，今年贸易状况虽然不佳，但应当可以于五个月内征得 3 万银圆的税收，除此之外，还可以效仿哈尔滨关对每艘轮船征收结关税。俄阿穆尔国家水道局为黑龙江自石勒喀河至哈巴罗夫斯克（Habarovsk）河段所制定的费用预算为 36000—37000 金卢布，也就是说，不算苏俄方面征收的关税，单凭瑷珲关所征之税款，便基本可以承担黑龙江整条航道的费用支出。待巡查结束返回瑷珲关后，再呈交更为精确的预算及人员方面的详细报告。

为布拉戈维申斯克（Blagovestchensk）事：当地农作物长势良好，局势已经因此而有所缓解，但政府官员并未就此摆脱财政困境，现正在等待德国外交使团的到来。据悉，使团已离开斯列坚斯克（Stretensk）。遗憾的是，待他们到来时，本人可能会错过会面的机会，如果未记错，使团领导人的名字应是阿米斯（Amyss）。

为汇款事：道尹仍然反对将税款汇出，与银行方面商议后亦未有任何结果，因为他们也惧怕张作霖。鉴于如果因此事与道尹兼海关监督正式决裂，从政治角度考虑，将会十分不利于海关在本地发展，因此本人已做出一个有反常规的安排，先将税款转入自己的账户，再通过罩书（R. C. L. d'Anjou）先生的账户汇出。出此下策，主要是因为担心将大笔税款留在这儿的银行会有风险，另考虑对出口面粉征税一事能否获得批准，是否需要退税，还难以确定，因此特保留一部分税款，以备需要时使用，不过希望不会如此。

如果道尹坚持不允许本关将税款汇至总税务司，本人将自行征收关税，不再通过银行，同时尽量寻找其他办法汇款。另外，现已停止向道尹兼海关监督发送瑷珲关税收及支出月报，以防其以政府官员之身份利用报告信息对付海关，违背其身为海关监督的原则。不过待汇款问题解决后，还将继续按照规定发送月报，不会对其造成直接伤害。不知上述安排能否获得批准？如若不能，本人则只能将税款存入中国银行大黑河支行，且不再汇出，希望日后不会被充公。此外，道尹不日即将前往哈尔滨（和奉天），此行显然是为谋得更好的职位，不过也可能和张作霖与督军吴俊升[①]变成敌对关系的传闻有关，道尹是张作霖的连襟，很有可能是为保命而逃跑。

为黑龙江省内军火运输事：近来，经梁家屯分卡向乡村、守备部队等地运送军火之事已有多例。根据海关总税务司公署第 2508 号通令指示，此等军火须有陆军部的批准和督军签发的护照，本人已放行三批军火，当时海关监督和守备司令均担保之后会按照规定申请批准，现已收到督军签发的护照，但还未收到军务部的批准。鉴于黑龙江省已脱离北京当局宣布独立，而本地情况又较为特殊，特此询问是否可遵照海关总税务司公署第 1941 号通令之规定办理？本人如今之处境颇为尴尬，若过于严苛，很有可能会造成所有货物都会在未经批准的情况下从海关眼皮底下运输之局面。

您真挚的

包安济

---

① 英文为 Tuchun Wu Cheng-sheng，经查 1922 年黑龙江督军应为吴俊升，此处原文应是拼写有误（经常出现）。

17. 包安济致安格联函

（第 21 号半官函）

/O No. 21.

Aigun/Taheiho, 2nd October 2

Dear Sir Francis,

I have returned over a week ago from my trip up river, and I haven't found time to write yet. The trip has been satisfactory, and I have collected much information, and formed a good idea, about both sides; I am going to write a Report which I will submit as soon as possible, I am therefore not going into details now; the conclusions I formed are mainly two : with regard to our control, it would be inexpedient to establish sub-stations until trade has recovered, and developed, unless we decide on collecting Amur River Dues, in which case Humaho would afford a good station for taxing all the rafts from up-river; - with regard to Aids-to-Navigation, the work done by the Russians is nothing very difficult or intricated - the nature of the river is not so bad as on the Sungari, - the scarce trade would not justify any conservancy work on a large scale (such as on the Whangpoo), therefore there is no necessity of highly-trained Staff, and the Russians never had Engineers to compare with those of other

Sir Francis A. Aglen, K. B. E.,

Inspector General of Customs,

Peking.

Entered in Card Index.

other Conservancy Boards - there is, in fact, no technical difficulty in taking over the Aids from the Russian. As to Finances, I believe that we should get more than this year, since we cannot pay indefinitely the same salaries that the Russians pay (when they pay); but the local merchants may consent to an increase in the Tariff, if they know that the money will go only to the Aids - and it will, of course. On the other hand the Taoyin, who would be very keen on taking part of the Aids over for China, says he can promise the active support of all the Chinese Authorities along the River. - To me the chief financial difficulty would not so much arise out of running expenses, as from the necessity of new equipment, which we do not possess. - I will make a more detailed report by despatch so far our collection has amounted to $ 21,683.79, which means, for a full average season, a minimum of $ 30,000. We should have, in my opinion, at least $ 50,000 to be sure in our positions, and to do some improvements to the navigation - Political situation in Siberia. There have been risings here and there, and even now the reports say that not far from Alexeief the "whites" are giving a very bad time to the Red soldiers; when I was passing Kumare there was fighting going on, and there was fight in Ushakovo also when I stopped at Humaho; the reds were ousted for a time but they came back in number and the "whites" withdrew. Many soldiers from Soviet Russia were dispatched from Chita to Habarovsk, and we met several barges loaded with them

them, on our way up; some 5,000 are reported as transport-
ted by River, and 5,000 by railway.- What can the "whites"
do in Vladivostock ? No reliable news I have yet received.
The discontent is certainly at its height amongst farmers;
and I doubt whether any Government in Russia can stand
long against the farmers, once they have become active, as
the case appears to be.- The German mission was in Blagovestchensk, but it is reported to be a purely commercial
mission; they came over here, during my absence, visiting the
town.

   Pin-Hei Railway. According to the local Daily, the
hope has been dropped of constructing this line in the
near future, and the Provicial Assembly has decided to
entrust the construction of a section from Hulan (呼蘭)
to Hai Lun (海倫) to the British firm Reiss & Co. Cost
about $ 6,000,000, to be advanced by the contractors without
interest, and to be repaid in instalments. The said Daily
has given so many accounts of the construction of this Railway, that I do not vouch for the accuracy of this report.
- Local. The Taoyin-Superintendent left on the 12th for
Harbin and Mukden, leaving one of his Secretaries in charge.
The General accompanied him to Aigun, whence he returned
on 13th.- Martial law was abolished in Tsheiho from 16th
september; still the General refuses to send his troops
to Mukden, alleging that his duty is to keep watch at the
frontier; the rumour has circulated several times that Chang
Tso-lin wants to replace him with a young Officers with
a

a good education from the Higher Military Colleges. I hope
he will not succeed, as General Pa is very kind, has much
influence locally, but does not meddle in local gossip, and
has his troops rather well in hand.- On the 12th an
Office of the "Unofficial Representative of the Ministry of
Foreign Affairs of the F.M.R." was opened in Tsheiho; his
position is somewhat similar to that of the Chinese Consul
General in Blagovestchensk; visits have been exchanged, but
I am waiting to see the attitude of the Representative
before coming to any de facto recognition of his authority
- It has been reported that russians are not allowed to
enter Blagovestchensk on a pass of the Chinese Police, as
before, but that they must have a visé by the Representative;
this does not directly concern the Customs, however.- A fire broke
out on the 27th and destroyed, amongst others, a pawnbroker's
shop.- The weather has been rather bad; snow fell on
20th sept, a most unusual event at that time of the year.
I felt the cold intensely on my trip, as I staid outside
practically all day, mapping and "absorbing" the features of
the country visited; for three days there was ice everywhere
on board, and for the rest I had rain almost every day.
I came back quite tired, but in excellent health.- Mr.Murray
Examiner, who fell sick on his return from three months'
leave, is still in bed, suffering from liver and stomach
disease -; he is slightly better, but it will be a long
time before he can attend to duty again.
                    Yours truly,

第 21 号半官函   1922 年 10 月 2 日于瑷珲关／大黑河

尊敬的安格联先生：

本人从黑龙江上游返回已有一周时间,但因事务繁忙未能及时汇报。此次巡查十分圆满,本人不仅收集了大量信息,还想到了一个于中俄双方皆为有利的办法,关于此事,将会尽快呈文报告,故在此不做详细叙述。

经过此行,主要得出两个结论：首先是关于海关的管控。兹认为,在贸易恢复并发展之前,暂无增设分关之必要,但如果海关决定对黑龙江往来运输征收江捐,则可于呼玛河设立分关,以便对黑龙江上游往来木筏征税。其次是关于航标。经查,苏俄方面开展的航标工事并非艰难复杂之工作,黑龙江航道的自然条件亦不像松花江航道那般苛刻,而且现下贸易正处于萧条时期,根本不必开展大范围的维护工程（如黄浦江）,亦无须雇用训练有素的职员,俄方也从未选用特别出众的工程师。实际上,就技术层面而言,从俄方接管航路标志,并无困难。至于财务方面,兹认为,接管后需要增加税收,而且中方不可能一直按照俄方的现行标准为雇员发放薪俸,不过本地商人如果知道所有税款都将用于航标的维护工作,相信亦会同意提高税率。另一方面,道尹也十分希望由中国接管部分航路标志,并表示会动员黑龙江沿岸的地方政府全力配合。兹认为,主要的财务问题,不是航标维护工作的费用支出,而是购置必要设备的初期经费。关于此事,本人将呈文详细汇报。

迄今为止,瑷珲关已征收税款 21683.79 银圆,也就是说,待航运季结束后,至少可征收 30000 银圆。不过为确保航标维护工事的顺利进行,同时改善黑龙江上的航行条件,估计至少需要 50000 银圆。

为西伯利亚地区政治局势事：近来,西伯利亚地区到处都在爆发起义,现下还有报告称,阿列克谢夫（Alexeief）附近的"白军"正在向红军士兵发动猛烈进攻；我们巡查期间经过库马拉（Kumara）时,当地也是战乱不断,之后在呼玛河停留时发现乌沙科夫（Ushakovo）也发生了战争。此间,红军曾被击败,但很快又以更多的人数卷土重来,将"白军"击退。苏俄士兵中有很多都是从赤塔（Chita）派往哈巴罗夫斯克（Habarovsk）,我们在前往黑龙江上游的途中还曾遇到过几艘装载士兵的驳船,据报告称,红军方面经水路和铁路运至战场的士兵人数,约各有五千名。至于符拉迪沃斯托克（Vladivostock）"白军"的情况,暂时还未收到可靠消息。如今,当地农民的不满情绪已达到顶点,一旦开始积极反抗,无论是哪个政府执政,恐怕都无法与之长期抗衡。德国使团已经抵达布拉戈维申斯克（Blagovestchensk）,在本人巡查期间,还曾到访大黑河,但据报他们仅仅是贸易方面的使团。

　　为哈尔滨至黑河铁路事：据本地日报报道，于近期修建此条铁路之希望已经落空。黑龙江省议会业已决定将呼兰至海伦一段铁路的修建工程承包给英国公司茂和洋行，工程费用约需 6000000 银圆，将由承包商预付，不收取利息，且允许分期偿还。此日报使用大篇幅报道铁路修建之事，但不知是否属实。

　　为地方事：道尹兼海关监督已于 9 月 12 日离开大黑河前往哈尔滨和奉天，并委派其秘书主理各项事务。巴英额将军将其护送至瑷珲，随即于 9 月 15 日返回大黑河。自 9 月 16 日起大黑河已撤销戒严令，巴将军仍以监视边境为由拒绝将其部队派至奉天。有传闻称，张作霖意图选调一名在高等军事学校受到过良好教育的年轻军官顶替巴将军的位置，希望不会成真，因为巴将军平易近人，在地方的声望颇高，但从不插手地方事务，而且对属下管教有方。

　　9 月 12 日，"远东共和国外交部非官方代表"办事处于大黑河设立，该代表之职位与中国驻布拉戈维申斯克总领事类似，待知晓其立场后，本人再决定是否应承认其权威性。据汇报称，俄国人已无法如从前一般仅凭中国警察签发的通行证便可进入布拉戈维申斯克，必须持有该代表签发的签证才可以，不过此事与海关并无任何关系。

　　9 月 27 日，本地发生一场大火，被烧毁的店铺中还有一家典当行。天气方面，已开始转冷，9 月 20 日还迎来一场降雪，比历史同期早了许多。本人前往黑龙江上游巡查期间，便已感受到天气的寒冷，当时几乎整日都在室外绘制地图，收集所到地区的信息，甚至有三日甲板上都结有冰霜，其他时间几乎日日均有降雨。本人返回时虽然十分疲惫，但身体状况尚佳。

　　为人事事：二等验货马瑞（N. J. G. Murray）先生休假三个月后因患上肝病和胃病一直卧床休养，如今虽已有所好转，但仍需调养一段时日方可返回海关任职。

　　　　　　　　　　　　　　　　　　　　　　　　您真挚的

　　　　　　　　　　　　　　　　　　　　　　　　包安济

18. 包安济致安格联函

（第 22 号半官函）

S/O No. 22.

Aigun/Taheiho 15th October 2.

Dear Sir Francis,

I have received your despatch about the settlement of the Liangchiat'un question, and I am taking steps to carry out your orders. — Still I am not quite convinced that my proposals were either illegal or imprudent, and you will allow me to present semi-officially a few more remarks on the subject, not, of course, by way of personal defence, but for what I consider to be the best interest of the Customs here.

1. There is a question about our rights. These originate from two sources : Foreign Treaties and Chinese laws and Regulations. Which one are we offending ?

a) Not Treaties with Foreign Powers: the foreign merchant can send to- or receive from - the interior his merchandise, either under Special Documents (O.T.P, I.T.P., Manchurian S.E.C) which are to be presented to - and will be honoured by - Barriers met en route, whether likin or Customs Barriers; or by paying at all likin Stations, i.e. by entirely subjecting himself to Chinese fiscal control.

b) The source of fiscal rights in China is - at least

Sir Francis A. Aglen, K. B. E.,
Inspector General of Customs,
Peking.
Entered in Card-Index.

least for us - the Shui Wu Ch'u; if not the source, the proper organ for recognition and delimitation of rights. If we had to open a Barrier on the River, we would be covered by a decision of the Shui Wu Ch'u; which has sanctioned the present arrangement in full. — Besides, it is our main right and duty to tax foreign trade and to guard the frontier; the means of guarding the frontier may vary and, in my opinion, a State can arrange whatever means are deemed most suitable for the purpose, as long as they do not conflict with existing Treaties, with the Code, and do not impose too heavy a burden on the people; one of the means (and most effective) may be to force trade along certain specified routes, giving the Customs, under special conditions, the control and police of these routes. — The simplest way of carrying out this arrangement is to ask the merchants to guarantee the arrival at certain destinations of their merchandise, and in our case the Merchants have no serious objections. Then why, if it was legal to establish a 100 li zone, with a Barrier at Liangchiat'un (entailing collection of duties) and to exact a guarantee from the Inns, or a deposit for the arrival of goods at destination, by force of an agreement with Russia — why is it illegal to make similar, if much milder arrangements - controlling, not taxing, with merchants' own guarantee, simpler and cheaper than guarantee by the Inns — by authority of the Shui Wu Ch'u ? — Still I may be wrong in point of strict right; but, then,

II. There

II. <u>There is a question of opportunity</u>. The local Authorities and merchants are more or less antagonist to the Customs, and ready to snatch any privilege they can at our expense; we are daily fighting the encroachments of the Local Tax Office, the Police, the Military, in fact everyone who is given the opportunity. Nor can the Central Government protect us; in fact it does not ensure the smooth running of our righful activities. — Under these circumstances a policy of extreme retrenchment within the strict limits of our rights, will find no response in the local Officials; and while any decision against us will be readily enforced by them, the Government will be unable to enforce those in our favour. We are thrown on our forces; and I think it is unadvisable to weaken our position; we will embolden the local authorities, encourage them to question every step we take, even perhaps our right of being in Taheiho, which is not an open Port. When the Government will be strong enough to enforce its decision against anybody, then we can give up our <u>surplus</u> of rights, in exchange for a perfect freedom within our limits; to give way now in the hope that our example be followed seems to me, in the present conditions, a sure loss

III. <u>There is a question of Revenue</u>; and you know that, if we do not see that goods imported overland come to Aigun or Taheiho, our Revenue in winter may be considered as lost. — If you so decide, I shall set my mind working

working for a plan to definitely abolish the Barrier and do away with the merchants' guarantees; a solution may come out, but, at present, I am afraid it would entail either enormous expenses, or big losses to the Revenue. You have excluded the collaboration of the Soldiers — and of course there would be inconveniences to have them work for the Customs; besides, I am afraid their help would not amount to much anyhow.

<u>Fine on foreign goods passing Liangchiat'un inward, and failing to report to Aigun or Taheiho</u>: this is the natural consequence of recognising the principle that those foreign goods are dutiable. — If they fail to report how can we only levy duty ? We ought to know the exact amount of duty leviable; and this would mean

a) that we should have a very competent Officer at the Barrier, capable of appraising foreign goods, and deciding of the value of the documents that may cover them;

b) a very careful examination of all foreign goods <u>en route</u>.(at the Barrier).

Naturally enough, merchants prefer an occasional heavy fine on the dishonest merchant who does not report his goods at destination as guaranteed, than the worry of a close scrutiny at Liangchiat'un, so that the duty payable be ascertained there with exactitude. —

It is at present the practice to examine goods at Liangchiat'un very summarily (and it has been for years), inspecting the packings, the invoices, and opening, if necessary only

only a few packages. - This is goods enough for the
Native goods which pass the Barrier (living animals, spirit,
samshu, bean oil), which, besides, are now free of duty, and
going to be
will be charged duty if not presented at destination, only
for the suspicion that they have crossed the frontier. But,
not so for Foreign goods; and in levying a fine we continue existing practice, which applies to foreign and native
goods as well. -

BARRIERS East and West of Taheiho. This District is
certainly more law-abiding than Harbin: much less robberies
on the Amur than on the Sungari, much less outlawry
round Taheiho and Aigun than Harbin. Still there are two
Barriers in Harbin, at about the same distance from Fuchia-
tien as the proposed ones from Taheiho. - There is no
danger of attack by outlaws on the Barriers, especially
under protection of the soldiers; soldiers are always
obtainable at the Lower Barrier, where there is a Military
are at the mercy of
Post ; but, for the Upper Barrier, we depend upon a change
of Garrison Commander - the present one has agreed, another
one may object to displace his soldiers for the Customs.
As for Soldiers on patrols, their position may be, if
anything, less easy when operating from a more remote
base (Taheiho); besides which/ their work will be less
efficient, their movements more liable to detection and
their presence easier to avoid by smugglers.

I am now taking the following steps:

1. The

1. The regulations are notified as approved by the
Shui Wu-ch'u.

2. If you so direct, I will, however, enforce as little
as possible fines for failure to bring foreign goods to
the Aigun or Taheiho Custom Houses.

3. I am buying 12 horses, 10 for Head Office , 2 for
Liangchiat'un.

besides
4. I am engaging 4 guards, to be used with the 6 boat
men now at Taheiho.

5. I would rather not ask the Superintendent for one
soldier to accompany each of our patrols; it means very
little, if any, advantage, as the man would not be so well
in hand - and possibly delays, and the leaking out of
information of on our movements.

6. I will see that, especially at the beginning, the
Patrols are led by a good and steady and self-possessed
Foreign Officer, when possible the Senior Officer; also that,
at first, their task be limited to bringing information, on
which I shall decide what action to take for checking contraband.

But, if my arguments seem strong enough to you,
I shall, with your permission, ask officially for :

a) the establishment, as soon as possible, of the two
Barriers, with accommodation for soldiers in the upper one;

b) the provision of two more guards (mounted) for Liangchiat'un, in order to intensify our patrol system on the
back roads.

I

I have seen the representatives of the Chamber of Commerce; they have proposed the 1st November as the date for starting the new procedure, and are perfectly satisfied. If we do not take the advantages accruing from the arrangement sanctioned by the Ch'u, I am afraid we will appear "plus royalistes que le Roi". -

Blagovestchensk: Nothing of importane since writing last. I have it confirmed that the crop has been good where the farmers had seeds, which is only in a few places; the potato crop has been plentiful, luckily. Near Alexsieff, about 1/10th of the land has been cultivated (wheat). - A certain merchant has obtained sanction from the Authorities to the opening of a distillery; half of the profits should go to the Government; if the price is too high, smuggling will not cease from this side, and the chinese spirit merchants so far feel no anxiety as to the possible competition. - A large quantity of firewood from the Chinese side has been already imported in Blago. without paying duty, for the distillery; I cannot do anything, so far, as the crossing takes place up river, not far from Upper Blagovestchensk. - The political situation is not clear; fighting goes on between troops and bands of rebels - but nothing definite is in view.

Mr. Murray is still sick; another month before he can return to duty.

Yours truly,

第 22 号半官函　　　　　　　　　1922 年 10 月 13 日于瑷珲关/大黑河

尊敬的安格联先生：

关于梁家屯分卡问题解决办法的令文已经收悉,现已开始遵照办理。然本人并未发现此前之提议有何不合规矩之处,特于此以半官方的形式补充说明几点内容,相信阁下亦不会反对。以下所述绝无自我辩护之意,仅是出于对海关利益的考虑。

1. 关于海关权利：海关权利受制于两方面,外国条约和中国法律规章,那么梁家屯分卡的管理办法有违哪项规定呢?

（1）并未违背与外国签署的条约。外国商人运送商品往来内地时,既可以选择向沿途关卡（厘金税卡或是海关关卡）出示特别凭证（出口过境单、进口过境单或者满洲特别免重征执照）,亦可以选择向沿途所有厘金税卡缴税,即完全受中国财政办法的管理。

（2）税务处是中国海关财政权利的源头,即便不是权利授予方,亦是权利承认或界定的官方机构。如果海关需要沿江设立分卡,就必须由税务处下达决定,而梁家屯分卡的管理办法早已获得批准。此外,对外贸易征税和保护边境是海关的权利与责任,兹认为,保护边境的办法可以因地制宜,为有效实现这一目的,政府可以根据实际情况做出最为合理的安排,只要不与现行条约或法典有何冲突,只要不会给百姓造成过重的负担即可。最为有效的办法或许便是迫使贸易运输按照特定的路线往来,并于特殊情形下,赋予海关管控之权和警力支持。实现这一安排最简单的办法就是让商人确保会将货物运至指定地点,实际上,商人也从未对梁家屯分卡的安排有过严重反对。

既然当初按照与俄国签署之协议开设 100 里免税区,于梁家屯设立海关分卡（需要征税）,要求商人提供当地旅馆出具的担保书或者为确保货物运至目的地缴存押款等安排均合理合法,那么为何如今想要施行类似且更为和缓的办法,就不合乎规矩了呢? 也就是海关仅于梁家屯分卡管控货物,不再征税,也不再需要旅馆出具担保书,只需商人自行出具一份即可,手续更简单,费用也更低,当然还需由税务处批准。不过,或许本人仍有理解误之处。

2. 关于机会：地方当局及商人对海关或多或少都抱有敌意,总是伺机夺取特权,使海关利益受损。如今地方税捐局、警察、军方,甚至任何有机会的个人,每日都在侵犯海关的权益,中央政府亦无法保护海关利益,甚至无法确保海关行使合法职能。在此等情况下,即使将海关已经十分有限的权利紧缩到极致,地方官员仍不会感到满足,对于不利于海关的决议,他们都将毫不迟疑地遵照办理,而面对利于海关的决定,中央政府总是难以推行。

海关只能依靠自己的力量，自行削弱权利绝非明智之举，若如此，则无异于是在助长地方当局的气焰，是在鼓励他们对海关的每一项举措都提出质疑，甚至对海关于大黑河的权利提出质疑，毕竟大黑河还未完全开放。如果有一日，中央政府强大到可以让所有人都服从其命令，海关可以放弃额外的权利，只要能够自由行使应有之权即可，但现下便退让，兹认为，定会损失惨重。

3. 关于税收：如阁下所知，如果不能确保经由陆路进口的货物至瑷珲或者大黑河口岸报关，瑷珲关冬季税收将遭受巨大损失。但如果阁下坚持此决定，本人将集中精力为裁撤梁家屯分卡，废除商人担保制度制订方案。当然可能会有解决办法，不过依目前情况来看，恐怕会面临巨额开支或者使税收严重受损。至于与士兵的合作办法，阁下已将之不纳入考虑范围，而且让他们为海关工作，着实有些不便，甚至可能也不会起到很大作用。

为经由梁家屯分卡进口但未至瑷珲或大黑河口岸报关之洋货处以罚款事：此项处理办法乃以洋货应征税这一原则为基础，对于洋货未能按照规定报关者，如果于查实后仅对之征税，又如何足够？不过在此之前，海关应当知悉应征关税的确切数额，如此则须：

（1）于梁家屯分卡安排一名能力出众的关员，负责对洋货估价，确定货物所持凭证能够抵销的金额数；

（2）于梁家屯分卡对途经洋货——仔细查验。

实际上，与对梁家屯分卡仔细查验的担忧相比，正当商人更希望海关能够偶尔对那些未按照担保规定前往目的地报关的商人处以高额罚金，而梁家屯分卡经过仔细查验便可准确估出应征关税之金额。

按照当前惯例，梁家屯分卡仅对货物进行粗略查验（已持续多年），只检查外包装和货单，如需拆箱验货，也只是打开一部分。此办法对于途经分卡的土货（牲畜、烈酒、白酒、豆油）已经足够，而且如今土货还将免税，海关仅会对未至目的地报明的土货征税，因为他们有过境运输之嫌疑，但对于途经的洋货则远远不够，因此才会在现行办法（适用于洋货及土货）的基础上施以罚款。

为于大黑河口岸上游及下游设立分卡事：虽然与哈尔滨关区相比，瑷珲关区的治安更好，大黑河和瑷珲口岸周围的违法事件更少，黑龙江上的强盗也比松花江上要少，但仍建议于大黑河上下游设立分卡，两处分卡与大黑河之间的距离和哈尔滨关两处分卡与傅家甸的距离基本相同。拟建分卡不会有受到不法分子袭击的危险，尤其是在士兵的保护下，下游分卡所在地设有军事哨所，士兵随时都可以提供支援，而上游分卡能否获得支援，全凭守备司令的决定,虽然现任司令已经同意协助,但新任司令可能不会同意为海关派遣士兵。至于巡缉士兵,如果从大黑河派遣,可能会有诸多不便,工作效率也会受到影响,行动也更容易被走私者察觉甚至躲避。

有鉴于此,兹提议:

1. 根据税务处的批准发布章程;

2. 如果总税务司批准,本关将对未能至瑷珲或大黑河口岸报关的洋货收取小额罚金;

3. 购入 12 匹马,10 匹留于大黑河口岸,2 匹送至梁家屯分卡;

4. 雇用 4 名卫兵,作为大黑河口岸现有 6 名水手的补充力量;

5. 不向海关监督申请派遣士兵跟随海关卫兵巡缉,因为士兵不会完全听从海关差遣,还有可能会延误,甚至泄露海关巡缉行动,于海关而言无甚益处;

6. 初期由一名品行良好,性格沉稳的洋籍关员带领巡缉队,如果情况允许,可由超等外班关员带队,巡缉队的初期任务主要是搜集信息,以供本人参考并决定日后查验违禁品的办法。

如果阁下认为上述安排尚属合理,本人将在获得准许后呈文正式申请:

(1)尽快设立两处分卡,并于上游分卡为士兵提供住宿;

(2)再为梁家屯分卡提供两名(陆路)卫兵,以加强对小路的巡缉。

本人已与商会代表会面,他们提议于 11 月 1 日开始实行新办法,并表示十分满意。兹认为,对于税务处已经批准的办法,海关如不能加以利用,恐怕会显得"过于保守"。

为布拉戈维申斯克(Blagovestchensk)事:自发送上一封半官函以来,当地并无要事发生。可以确定的是,当地谷物收成较好,但农民播种的面积有限,所幸马铃薯产量较大,阿列克谢夫(Alexeief)附近约有十分之一的土地都种植了小麦。据称,一名商人已经获得当局批准开办酿酒厂,但半数利润都将上交政府,如果酿酒厂生产的酒类价格过高,估计还会有人从大黑河走私烈酒,迄今为止,中国酒商还未因这一潜在竞争对手而感到焦虑。目前因为此酿酒厂,布拉戈维申斯克已从黑龙江华岸进口大量木桦,且未缴纳关税,然因木桦皆于布拉戈维申斯克上游附近运输过江,本人对此亦是束手无策。当地政治局势尚不明朗,政府军队与叛军仍在对抗,但具体会如何发展,还难以确定。

为人事事:马瑞(N. J. G. Murray)先生仍病中,还需休养一个月,方可返回海关工作。

您真挚的

包安济

19. 包安济致安格联函

（第 24 号半官函）

S/O No. 24.

Aigun/Taheiho 20th November, 2.

Dear Sir Francis,

I have duly received your S/o of 16th October :

I. G. Cannot approve action of Commissioner if he has remitted moneys through private account:

I plead guilty: the Banks declined to remit for the Customs, whether Revenue or Service Moneys. I was going to leave for Moho, and I thought it unsafe to leave in the Bank of China (thus terrorised by the Taoyin) a sum too large for this Port. I therefore resorted to remittance in my own name, giving probably too free an interpretation to the words of your S/O of 5th June, 1922: "Do whatever is necessary to ensure safety first". The money has safely arrived in Shanghai, long ago; but I will not resort to this means again.

Your despatch No. 84/91,667 : Commissioner is going out of his "fan wei" in suggesting a fine on Ferry Co., for tueing vessels duly cleared by the Customs.

My action was prompted by the belief that a) it was necessary to punish the Ferry Co. for their impertinence in terrorising

Sir Francis A. Aglen, K. B. E.,
Inspector General of Customs,
Peking.

Entered in Sk Index.

terrorising applicants who were perfectly within their rights; b) the alleged Monopoly being entirely illegal according to Treaties and Regulations, the damage was mainly supported by the Customs and their prestige; if Permits issued by the Customs according to Laws are to be thus challenged by a private firm, and applicants are persecuted for the fact of having complied with Customs regulations, where is our credit ? c) that we should do our/utmost to ensure a smooth and practical application of the rights deriving by the observation of our Regulations, and the payment of duties to the Customs.— As I did not want to stop the clearance of the Ferry (out of consideration for the public), I asked the Taoyin-superintendent to help in collecting a fine. — My conviction was strengthened by what happened on 12th August: the Ferry Co. then had the SS. "Vera", duly cleared for Blago with a cargo of flour, stopped by an order of the Magistrate. On the owner reporting the case, I raised a storm and had the steamer released the same day; the negotiation, being in such a hurry, were carried on verbally, but I intended to report the case in full officially, once it had been settled. Things, however, were dragging along, and I sent in the meantime copy of my despatch to the Supt.— I must add, incidentally, that the owner of the Vera asked me in writing to get him a compensation for damages from the Ferry Co., and that I declined, and referred him to the Magistrate. —

This

This case leads me to ask whether we are to allow the present arrangements to go on. - The Ferry Co., since several years, pays an annual sum (said to be 6,000) to the local Authorities for a privilege which it is not in their power to grant. The only privilege (going and coming without a regular clearance - with manifest - and entry at the General Office) is granted by the Customs, who receive nothing for it; in addition, we keep two tidewaiters and other Out-door staff especially occupied with the Ferry and again we receive no compensation. I would therefore propose to approach the Taoyin with a view to getting a compensation for the Customs, in the shape of a monthly fee of at least Hk.Tls. 150. - It will be a hard nut to crack, for it will probably mean a diminution in the fee paid for nothing to the local Authorities (Taoyin & Police - and I wish therefore to have your approval before mentioning the matter to the Taoyin-Superintendent.

I would also like to ask for your instructions on a few more points :

Taoyin's Tax-Collecting Office erected on foreshore. This case has been reported in Aigun Return of Non-Urgent Chinese Correspondence for October, Case 4. The house alluded to is for use of the Taoyin's underlings in collecting a fee for passes on Chinese going to Blagovestchensk: Apart from the fact that it is an evident squeeze, because passes are sold undiscriminately, and even in blank, to any buyer,

it

it is a distinct slur on us to thus build, on the fore shore, and just in front of our Property "New Customs House Site" without as much as asking permission. I will now wait for an answer; if the Taoyin owns to the property, and asks for permission, I think of giving it (a posteriori) provisionally, until the Customs need the place; if he does not reply, I would like to protest (for the sake of record); and I am afraid that, under present conditions, I cannot go much further.

River Police. This is a branch of the local Police (in Aigun there is no distinction), paid from the same funds as the whole of the Police (gambling and prostitutes taxes chiefly), composed of 3 Officers and 25 men. They are on duty within Harbour limits, and accompany our Officers in the search of steamers, on arrival and departure, when they also re-check passports. At times they interfere with Junks, search them before our Officers, and otherwise encroach on our jurisdiction; they have tried to levy taxes on Junks and steamers at Aigun, when I have protested that such taxes, in Ports where there is a Customs house, must only be levied by us, even if on behalf of the local Authorities, after sanction from you. - The River Police is either a duplicate, or a nuisance. Things however have been going on like this for several years, and I have confined myself to protesting against any abuse or encroachment. - In future, however, it is my opinion that we should do away with this Police; the worst

point

point is, that we have no funds for this; otherwise the
best solution would be to have a small Police force
under our orders; and the money could be found, in more
normal times; perhaps from a small tax on vessels. So we
would be in sole control of foreshore, Bund, and vessels.

Military Control. Besides the Police, a military Officer accompanies our Officers when steamers are entered
and cleared; he looks for suspicious characters, and re-
checks passports together with the Police. This is also an
old practice, which may be justified in time of troubles, and
martial law, but is objectionable in ordinary times: the
Military should watch passengers before they step on
board or after landing.

I am referring these various points, because I want
to keep you informed. I would however not attempt to
redress them all, unless you could assure me of a strong
backing from Peking. This for the present is hardly possible, and
in the same way as I put this matter on record here, I
intend putting it on record in correspondence with those
concerned, without too much hurting feelings, which would be worse
than useless now.

Mr. Kastler arrived, after being robbed by Hunghutze on
the way, but unhurt. The coffin of the late Mr. Murray is
already on the way, and I hope to get the widow and Mr.
Kastler away by tomorrow. - I have made a report of the
robbery to the Taoyin, but it will be of no avail. -
Mr.

Mr. Kastler, by the way, came without even a cheque book;
so that I had to advance money privately, not without
difficulty. - Mr. Rende, the Examiner from Harbin, has also
arrived safely, without bad accidents. -

The Patrols have started making useful work, but I
only bought a few horses, because the prices went up by
50% as soon as it was known that we were buyers. I am
trying to get some through the C.M.O. - We will however be
able to do little in the case of importation of arms
with the connivance of the Military; I heard that the
Garrison Commander is implicated in a plot, which failed;
but that shows what can be expected. Pity we cannot interest the soldiers on our side, by giving them seizure
Rewards !

Against the Hunghutze, the Chamber of Commerce tries
to act; the Volunteers Militia (保卫团) has been increased to 120 (mounted, and well disciplined); the funds
will be provided by a Tax on Spirit (15 cts. a vedro) and
Cigarettes (5%), and other luxuries; the expenditure for
the winter is foreseen in $ 20,000. - The Militia will
only do something for the vicinity of Tsheiho-Aigun.

Blagoveschensk: there is little to report, for the
River has been impassable for quite a while. On 7th, as
reported by telegram, the Red Flag was hoisted; guns were
fired from midnight to midnight; some prisoners were released. Only five days ago traffic was resumed, and yesterday
I went over. At the Rogatka, no sign of change: new
Staff,

Staff, but respectful for the ∧ Customs as usual. In town,
no changes in the various Offices, except that the Revolu-
tionary Comittee has assumed de jure the highest authority
which they had de facto before. – Taxes are being levied, and
an inventory is made of all property, not excluding furniture, on which taxes are leviable, graduated according to
riches, from 6% on. It is expected that paper currency
will be introduced; and that will be a cold douche on
trade, which otherwise has resumed rather briskly, as usual
after an interruption of traffic.

Mr. Ch's, former interpreter and Adviser to the Taoyin,
has left for Peking, as a M.P., in substitution for the
former representative of Heilungkiang, deceased; it is a
good point for me, as he was the most dreadful stick-in-
the-mud of the Taoyin's Office, which is saying much. The
first automobiles left for Tsitsihar on 12th; and arrived
safely. – The River closed on the 14th; on 15th foot traffic began, and on 18th carriages crossed.

The staff is well.

Yours truly,

P.S. About the fine on the Ferry Co.: I propose to let the matter drop,
according to your view of the case. But, should by chance
the Superintendent remit the amount to me, shall I refuse it?
I will not do so without your instructions.

第 24 号半官函   1922 年 11 月 20 日于瑷珲关 / 大黑河

尊敬的安格联先生：

10 月 16 日半官函收悉。

总税务司不同意通过私人账户汇款。

对此深表惭愧，当时银行拒绝为海关汇款，无论是通过税收账户或是海关经费账户，而本人正要动身前往漠河，担心将大笔钱款留在中国银行（会受到道尹威胁）会不安全，另考虑总税务司曾于 1922 年 6 月 5 日半官函中指示"采取一切必要手段确保税款安全！"，遂将钱款汇入本人名下的账户，如今看来，可能是过度解读了指示内容。此笔钱款早已安全汇至上海，嗣后不会再使用此种方式汇款。

海关总税务司公署致瑷珲关第 84/91667 号令：总税务司认为瑷珲关税务司因轮渡公司拦截已于海关办理结关的船只而建议罚款之行为已超出其职权"范围"。

本人有此建议是因为：

（1）轮渡公司对行使正当权利的商人做出无理行为，应当受到惩罚；

（2）轮渡公司的垄断行为完全违背了条约及章程规定，有损海关及条约章程的公信力，如果海关依法签发的准单被私营公司漠视，同时其他商人又因遵守海关章程而受到迫害，那么海关的声望又何在？

（3）海关应当竭力确保商人能够切实自由地行使因遵照海关章程办事而拥有的权利，确保他们能够将税款缴纳给海关。

但出于对公众利益的考虑，本人不愿阻止渡船结关，遂请道尹兼海关监督帮助收取罚金。8 月 12 日，轮渡公司奉瑷珲县知事之命拦截了已于海关办理结关并载运面粉前往布拉戈维申斯克的"维拉（Vera）"号轮船，船主前来汇报后，本人十分恼怒，但因事出紧急，只能与轮渡公司口头协商，轮船最终于当日放行。原本计划待事情彻底解决后再正式详细汇报，无奈事情一拖再拖，不过本人已将呈文抄件发送给海关监督。另外，值得一提的是，"维拉"号轮船船主来函希望可以帮助其向轮渡公司索要赔偿，本人已经回绝，并让其向瑷珲县知事申诉。

经过此事，本人一直在想，海关是否还应继续容忍下去。数年来，轮渡公司每年都会向地方当局缴纳一笔费用（据称 6000 银圆），以换取随意通行的特权，不用按照规定结关，不用出示舱口单，也不用到海关征税汇办处办理手续。然而，地方当局根本无权批准此项特权，唯有海关可以，但海关却从未收到过任何补偿。另外，海关还专门派遣两名铃子手和另外一名外班关员驻守渡船检查处,但同样未收到任何补偿。有鉴于此,建议向道尹申请为海关发放补偿金,比如每月至少150海关两。不过此非易事,毕竟如此一来,地方当局(道尹及警察)不劳而获的收入便会减少,因此希望在向道尹兼海关监督说明此事之前,获得阁下的批准。

另请对以下各项予以指示。

为道尹于前滩设立收税处事:此事已于瑷珲关10月非紧急中文往来函清折(事由4)中汇报。道尹下属于此收税处对前往布拉戈维申斯克(Blagovestchensk)的中国人收取过境小票的费用。实际上,他们的这种行为无异于是在压榨,因为过境小票会无差别地售卖给所有人,有时甚至只是一张白纸。而且收税处就搭建在"新海关办公楼关址"的前方,在修建之前甚至都未曾向海关申请批准,这于海关而言,简直就是赤裸裸的羞辱。如今本人正在等待一个说法,如果道尹承认收税处为其所有并向海关申请使用所占地块,本人便考虑在海关需要使用此地块之前,暂时允许其使用(鉴于房屋已经修建完毕),但如果其不做回应,本人将提出抗议(理由如上所述),恐怕目前亦只能如此。

为江上警察厅事:此为地方警察厅的分支机构(在瑷珲关区实际上并无差别),收入来源亦与其他警察相同(主要来自赌捐和花捐),共有3名警官和25名手下。他们在港口界限以内执勤,陪同海关关员一起于船只入港及离港时登船检查,同时复查护照,有时还会阻扰民船,在海关关员抵达之前先行登船搜查,或者直接侵犯海关管辖权。此外还试图于瑷珲口岸对民船和轮船征税,对此,本人已提出抗议,说明凡设立海关之口岸,如已获得海关总税务司批准,此等税项均只能由海关征收,即使代表的是地方政府。不过,这种情况已经持续多年,本人只能对他们滥用职权或者侵犯海关管辖权的行为提出抗议。兹认为,将来应当裁撤江上警察厅,但问题是海关又无雇用警察的经费,否则最好的办法就是让一小队警察听命于海关,而此笔资金可以通过正常手段获得,比如对船只征收少量税费,如此一来,瑷珲关便可以独立管理前滩、堤岸及船只。

为军方管控事:除江上警察,还有一名军方官员陪同海关关员于船只入港及离港时登船检查,此军官主要负责排查可疑人员,并与江上警察一同复查护照。此亦为旧例,然而,如果发生暴乱,地方施行戒严令,军方有此等行为或许合理,但在普通情形下不免令人生厌,军方应当于乘客登船之前或者下船之后再展开排查。

以上所述仅为向阁下汇报说明,在确保北京方面能够给予足够支持之前,不会对他们做出任何指正行为,而且目前海关恐怕无法采取任何措施。除了于此汇报以便记录,本人还计划向相关各方致函略做说明,言辞上尽量不影响彼此之间的关系,以免弄巧成拙。

为卡斯特勒(Kastler)先生事:汽车公司的卡斯特勒先生已经抵达大黑河,但在来时的路上遭遇红胡子（土匪）抢劫，所幸并未受伤。马瑞（N. J. G. Murray）先生的棺木已在运输途中，希望明日可以安排其遗孀和卡斯特勒先生离开。土匪抢劫一事已汇报给道尹，但恐怕亦不会有任何作用。另外，卡斯特勒先生并未携带支票簿，本人只得私人垫付钱款，很是麻烦。自哈尔滨关调来的二等验货聊德尔（J. R. Rendle）先生已经安全抵达，途中还算顺利。

为巡缉事：巡缉工作已初现成效，但此前购买马匹时，卖家知道是海关求购后，立即将价格调涨了50%，因此仅购入了数匹，现正试图通过中国邮政局再购买几匹。军火进口方面，因为有军方庇护，海关的管控十分有限，据悉，守备司令卷入了一场阴谋之中，不过最终阴谋未能得逞，但通过此事可以预见未来的局势发展。遗憾的是，海关不能给士兵发放缉私奖金，以让他们站在海关一边！

为红胡子事：商会正试图与之对抗。保卫团人数现已增加至120人（皆为骑兵且训练有素），经费主要通过对酒（每俄桶15分）、烟草（价值的5%）及其他奢侈品收税筹得，预计今年冬季的费用支出将达30000银圆。保卫团将仅于大黑河及瑷珲附近活动。

为布拉戈维申斯克事：黑龙江上无法往来通行已有一段时日，当地情形如何亦无法获悉。如此前电报所述，当地已于11月7日开始悬挂红旗，但每晚都有枪火之声，有些囚犯已经获得释放。五日前，黑龙江上的交通重新开通，本人昨日过江后，发现布拉戈维申斯克出入港口检查处并未有何变化，职员虽然都已换新，但对中国海关的关员仍如从前一般尊敬。城内各政府部门亦未改变，唯革命军事委员会已正式成为法律上的最高军事权力机关。当地政府已开始收税，并对百姓的所有财产进行盘查登记，包括家具。据富人称，收税最低标准为财产价值的6%。政府可能会开始引入纸币，若如此，贸易定会受到影响，否则还可如以往一样在过江运输重新开通后迅速恢复。

道尹公署前任翻译兼外交顾问车席珍先生已经离开大黑河前往北京，接替已故去的黑龙江省代表担任议员，这于本人而言是件好事，因为其保守顽固，是道尹公署最令人讨厌的官员。11月12日，大黑河至齐齐哈尔开始通车，首批出发的车辆已经安全抵达。11月14日黑龙江封江，15日开始有商人在冰面上往来，18日开始有马车通行。

关员一切安好。

您真挚的

包安济

另，为对轮渡公司罚款事：现打算按照阁下之意见就此作罢。但如果海关监督将罚款汇来，是否应该拒绝？此事将依照阁下指示办理，本人不会擅自接受。

20. 包安济致安格联函

（第 25 号半官函）

S/O No. 25.

Aigun/Taheiho 28th Dec. 2.

Dear Sir Francis,

I am very late in writing, but I have, and am
very busy. Everything is delayed, if not by the Chinese,
then by the Russian authorities: patience is the greatest
of virtues here. — I regret that the wishes of the
whole Staff will reach you too late; I hope I shall
be excused. — Even my report on the trip to Moho is
far from completed, one of the reasons being that the
light here (electric) is so poor, that one cannot absolutely work after dark, except by candle light, which is
very trying.

Events are taking rather an unpleasant turn in
Blagovestchansk. The economic situation is not too bad,
but there is a new scheme of taxation which will take
the breath away from any one possessing anything. On the
other hand, rumours about an early introduction of paper
money are growing, and I am afraid that the official
denial will count for nothing against the temptation for
the Government to raise money by this simple devise. A
decree has been issued some 15 days ago, by which the
property

Francis A. Aglen, K. B. E.,
Inspector General of Customs,
Peking.

Entered in Conf-Index.

property of all the Churches is confiscated to the
profit of the "people"; the Churches are left to the
use of the believers, if at least 20 of them (for each
Church) promise to provide funds for all the expenses; otherwise
the Church building itself becomes the property of the
people. Besides, all valuables belonging to the churches
have been confiscated. — Again, arrests have been made by
the hundreds: all the Social-Revolutionary are being sent
to Chita, and thence ... to Arkangel, perhaps; anyhow they do
not come back. Even Jews belonging to this Party are
being arrested and sentenced, because the Party made a
very large and successful propaganda lately; even a writer
belonging to that Party (Valerian Petroff), such a harmless
fellow that he was left undisturbed by the "Whites" when
they captured Blagovestofansk, is now in jail, and will
leave in two days for Chita. Of course, I don't feel
like pitying them too much, because, after all, they are
the fathers of communism, and they now reap the fruits
of what they planted; but it goes to show what a change
for the worse the political situation has undergone since
the arrival of the Moscow people. — The situation is
also a little uneasy with regard to the threatened occupa-
tion of the C.E. Railway by the Reds; if they carry their
threat out, and resistance is offered, then there will be
fighting on this side too, the lure of looting Taheiho
being very tempting to the half-starved and embittered
Russians.

Russians; the chinese authorities are rather anxious, and
they are making arrangements for the defense of he frontier - but, if a clash occurred, the Chinese Army would
melt away: the arrogant coolies which compose it are most
cowardly against a real enemy; their leaders are worse
than useless. - However, I am inclined to consider the
russian attitude rather in the nature of a bluff - in
order to get more concessions from China, in the Treaty
to be concluded some time in the near future.

I am also learning that labour troubles are increasing in Blagoveatchensk: labourers claim indemnities when
discharged according to contracts, and are accorded them
by the Commissioner for Labour. There is in accordance a
feeling of great uncertainty, and I know of one instance
when an enterprising owner of a flour mill gave up the
opening of a second Mill for this reason. - The farmers
however are much better off than people in the towns, and
as they are the bulk of the population, there is still
hope, if the people in power do not go for them after
having squeezed out the town folks. I am getting the
tariff of the new taxes, and will give you an idea in
due course: iron beds, for instance, are considered luxuries
and taxed accordingly ! - An increase in robberies and
hold-ups in Blagoveatchensk is also noticeable.

In Tsheibo the most important event has been the
visit to this place of General Chen, a representative of
Chang Tso-lin, and one of his advisers on military matters.
He

He is a foreign-educated man, has been 9 years in Austria
speaks German very fluently, English fairly well; is young
and seems rather energetic - quite a change from the Military one sees here. He has inspected the local Garrison
has visited Blagoveatchensk, and has departed after a few
days: we have had quite a long conversation on local
affairs, with regard to Russia, and I gave him my best
advice, although he did not represent the Central Government. - There was a stoppage of frontier traffic on the
1st December, by order of the Taoyin, as a reprisal
against maltreatment by the Russian Authorities on the
Chinese carriage drivers which are stationed on the
Russian side; the matter was luckily straightened out
the same morning, and normal traffic was resumed at once.
- The 3rd Mixed Brigade (under the Heibo Chen Shou Shih)
has been changed to the 11th Manchurian Brigade ; a matter
of names. - Mr. Lagutin, the General Director of the
Russian Water Transport and Navigation Office, left here
yesterday for Chita via Tsitsihar; he will report also
on the question of Aids: my despatch on this question
(which has been concluded for the 1922 year quite recently) will be ready soon, I hope. The Taoyin, now that his
Adviser has gone, believes that it is better to leave X
everything to the Customs; I hope he will show the same
dispositions when discussing matters for next year, as it
actually means a saving of labour and time.

I

I have received your S/O of 5th December; with regard to the Remittance of Service Moneys through private account. I wish to state once more that the Banks actually refused to remit Service Moneys; it was wrong, but the only action for me would have been to withdraw all the Official Accounts from the Bank of China; this would have been inadvisable for a good many reasons, and I simply lodged a protest with the Bank.

Drawback of Export Duty collected on Flour: this Office is quite busy issueing drawbacks. It seems a pity that we should lose so much rightful revenue. If we were right in collecting, the proper course, in my opinion, was to direct the Harbin Office to collect back duties from 15th April 1 Instead, the Shui Wu-ch'u encourages the local merchants in their insolence by granting refund of on flour lawful duty: we collected Hk.Tls. 23,189.189, out of which I believe we will have to refund some Hk.Tls. 13,000.

The Chunshan Meteorological Observatory of Nantung, Kiangsu (江蘇南通軍山氣象臺) asks for certain meteorological data, to be periodically supplied by this Customs: is this Office to comply with the request ?

Commissioner's house: the lease of this House will expire in the autumn of 1923, and, this being the only suitable house in town, I would like to renew the lease, to have a few repairs done to it by the landlord, and, if possibly, to obtain a further reduction in the rent (although

(although this will prove more difficult). It would be necessary for me to know whether there is a likelihood of building the Commissioner's house (own Customs') in 1924; if not, I propose to renew the lease for two years (to Autumn 1925) with option for another year.

Yours truly,

第 25 号半官函　　　　　　　　　　　　1922 年 12 月 28 日于瑷珲关 / 大黑河

尊敬的安格联先生：

　　近期事务繁忙，延误了撰写半官函的时间，实际上所有事务都因中国地方当局或者俄国地方当局而延误，在此地工作需有极大的耐心。遗憾的是，瑷珲关全体关员对总税务司的新年祝福将无法及时送达，还望谅解。到目前为止，本人前往漠河巡查的报告还未完成，主要因本地电力供应较差，天黑后便只能借助微弱的烛光工作，颇为艰难。

　　为布拉戈维申斯克（Blagovestchensk）事：当地情况不甚乐观，虽然经济形势还不算太糟，但政府实行新的征税办法后，民众的负担将会十分沉重。另一方面，关于当地政府不日即将引入纸币的传闻愈演愈烈，通过这样简单的调整来筹得资金，于政府而言的确颇有诱惑力，恐怕即使他们出面公开否认，亦不会影响这一结果。十五日前，当地政府颁布法令，要求所有教堂将财产全部充公，交给"人民"，但如果某一教堂有 20 名以上的信徒愿意负责各项开支，该教堂便可以留给信徒使用，否则将成为人民的财产。除此之外，教堂内的贵重物品一律充公。

　　迄今又有数百人被捕，所有社会革命党都被押往赤塔（Chita），随后可能会被送至阿尔汉格尔斯克（Arkangel），但无论如何都不会再返回当地。即使是加入社会革命党的犹太人，也已被逮捕判刑。当局采取此等措施，是因为社会革命党近期大肆宣传，而且还颇有成效。其中有一名作家彼得罗夫（Valerian Petroff）虽然是社会革命党，但实际上并无任何危险性，而且在"白军"占领布拉戈维申斯克期间也从未受到过任何打扰，如今却被捕入狱，两日后将被押往赤塔。当然本人并不同情这些囚犯，毕竟他们都是共产主义的始作俑者，现在也算是自食其果，不过他们的遭遇同时也表明，莫斯科当局派遣的人到达布拉戈维申斯克后，当地的政治局势已经开始恶化。

　　此外，苏俄红军扬言要占领中东铁路，如果他们最终付诸行动，而中方予以回绝，恐怕本地也将发生战争，更何况苏俄红军如今饥饿难耐，如何能够抵挡抢掠大黑河的诱惑？中国当局对此事也颇为担心，已开始于边境布防。但如果战争真的打响，只怕中国军队会迅速溃败，因为队伍里都是些傲慢自大的苦力，面对真正的敌人时，必定会怯战不前，而且他们的领导人更是发挥不了任何作用。不过，兹认为，苏俄方面很有可能只是在虚张声势，主要目的是让中国在即将签订的条约中做出更多的让步。

　　据悉，布拉戈维申斯克的劳工问题日益严重。劳工被解雇后要求劳工处根据劳务合同为之发放遣散费作为补偿，但恐怕机会不大。听闻此前便有一名磨坊主因为劳工问题放弃了开办第二家磨坊的念头。不过,农民的生活比城镇中的百姓要好得多,农村人口众多,只要当地政府压榨完城中百姓后不再去找他们的麻烦,估计还有发展的希望。至于当地的新税税率,已在了解当中,嗣后将适时汇报,当地政府已将铁制床列入奢侈品一类予以征税!布拉戈维申斯克的强盗土匪数量也大幅增加。

为地方事:近日来,大黑河地区最重要的事情莫过于张作霖的代表兼军事顾问陈将军的到访。陈将军接受过西方教育,曾在奥地利生活过9年,德文十分流利,英文也很好,而且年纪尚轻,精力充沛,与地方军官的形象十分不同。陈将军在此停留了数日,不但视察了地方守备部队,还访问了布拉戈维申斯克。本人也借此机会就地方事务及苏俄相关事宜与其进行了长谈,并提出了最好的建议,只不过陈将军代表的并不是中央政府。

12月1日,道尹下令暂时关闭边境交通,起因是中国运货马车司机停靠俄岸时受到了苏俄当局的不公对待,所幸此次事件于当日上午便顺利解决,边境交通也随即恢复正常。黑河镇守使下辖的第三混成旅现已改编成满洲第十一旅,但也只是名称上的改变而已。

苏俄阿穆尔国家水运局和水道局局长拉古丁(A. N. Lagutin)先生昨日离开大黑河,将经齐齐哈尔前往赤塔,届时其将向上级汇报航政相关事务。本人也将尽快呈文汇报此事(即对1922年航路标志的总结)。道尹认为,其外交顾问既已调离大黑河,航路标志最好由海关全权处理,希望明年再讨论此问题时,其依然能够保有这一观点,若如此,必定可以节省大量人力和时间。

总税务司12月5日半官函已收悉。

为通过私人账户汇解海关经费事:希望借此机会再次说明,当时银行方面确实拒绝汇出海关经费;本人的做法确有不妥,但当时能够做的也只有从中国银行取出全部钱款,虽然从多方考虑,此举均不可取,但本人也只是希望向银行方面提出抗议。

为对面粉已征出口税退税事:瑷珲关正忙于签发退税存票。失去这么一大笔合法税收着实可惜。兹认为,如果海关对面粉征税合理合法,便应让哈尔滨关自4月15日起将退回的税款重新征收回来!税务处授予地方商人退税特权的举动实际上更加助长了他们蛮横无理的气焰。瑷珲关对面粉征收的税款共计23189189海关两,需要退还的税款约有15000海关两。

为江苏南通军山气象台事:江苏南通军山气象台希望瑷珲关可以定期提供气象数据,不知能否答允?

为税务司住所事:瑷珲关税务司住所的租赁合同将于1923年秋季期满,鉴于此乃大黑河唯一适合此用的房屋,希望可以续租,届时将请房主重新修缮房屋,如果可能,还希望可以让其减少房屋租金(虽然很难做到)。另请告知,1924 年有无修建瑷珲关税务司宅邸的可能,如果没有,建议续约两年(即至 1925 年秋季),同时保留第三年续租的权利。

您真挚的

包安济

21. 包安济致安格联函

（第26号半官函）

S/O No. 26

Aigun/Taheiho 29th January 3.

Dear Sir Francis,

I have received your letter of 10th instant, asking me to supply Mr. Palmer with information about Russian Refugees : this I have already done several days ago at the request (by telegram) of the Harbin Commissioner. Luckily there are no refugees here to speak of; the recent event have not increased their number, and the old ones (stationed here since 1920) have settled down, and do some sort of work. Most of them are Cossacks, who get help from their relatives from the other side; many are poor, none of them starving ; in view of the sore needs of refugees in Harbin, along the Railway, around Kirin, etc, there is no immediate need to start relief work here. —

<u>Blagoveschensk</u>. Things continue in a disagreable way : even the economical situation does not seem very good, and there is a fear that stocks of eatables (chiefly potatoes) may not last until the next crop. I could not ascertain with precision the amount of taxes which are being levied now (some of them even for back years): I have the Prikase, according to which they shoud, not exceed

1 %

Francis A. Aglen, K. B. E.,

    Inspector General of Customs,

      P e k i n g.

               Entered in Index.

1% in the cases of greatest wealth (the taxation being proportional to wealth); but in fact I know of many cases in which the percentage is much higher, and it is to be noted that taxes are collected not only on revenue but also on unproductive property, even beds, chairs, etc, when the value of each exceeds 10 roubles. There are also many special surtaxes; and in one instance, a Kinematograph Show has been asked to contribute $ 7,500 (gold), and another, $ 5,000 a year. — The "cleaning" of all Social-Democrats is progressing thoroughly; and now all Officers not exactly "red" are being replaced: those who served formerly under Koltchak and other "reactionaries", are said to be concentrated in special camps; the others, simply apolitical, are sent to Moscow, Petrograd, etc. — Train loads have already left. — A Mission from Moscow for the reorganisation of Transports has arrived, and stayed here (Blago. and Taheiho) four days; the Chief, a most influential (and intelligent) Bolshevik, named Marchand, said to be of French origin, but, in my opinion, a Jew, spent all his time drinking in Taheiho, and never inspected anything I tried in vain to talk business to him. His technical Adviser, an Ingeneer of the Water Transports, (Ing Petropavlovsk) in few days, tried to suggest certain urgent reforms, but, when told by the present Chief Accountant of the Transports that much money was needed for the reforms to be carried out, he left everything go, and came himself to Taheiho, where

            however

however he kept sober. —The Commission has started a weekly train from Vladivostock to Chita, which should go as quick as before the collapse of Russia. But I do not know whether this is a dream or a reality, and anyhow, the train will not be run during the warm season, because the rails are not safe, except when the frost strengthens the road in its grip of ice; otherwise, all the sleepers, practically, should be changed (an enormous task), without which no orders can allow the fast running of a train on this line. — The Commission had an intention of going up to Peking; probably, if they go, Mr. Lagutin, the local head of the Water Transports, will go too; he is the most decent fellow in the gang, and the only one in Blagovestchensk. (Techn. Adviser to the Moscow Commission)

With Mr. Lagutin and Ing. Petropavlosk I have spoken of the future working of the <u>Aids-to-Navigation on the Amur</u>: they agree that something should be done, but they are tied by the instructions from Moscow not to do anything locally, and let the question be dealt with in Peking. They tell me that they also are thinking of effecting repairs by means of steam-launches, instead of having Staff permanently at various points of the River: this confirms my opinion that the method of repairs by parties working on launches is the best (as stated in despatch No. 91). — Im have also been informed by them and by

by the unofficial Representative of Russia in Tahsihe, that Chinese vessels will not be allowed to touch the Russia shore next year, unless a Treaty is concluded. This will probably lead to reprisals from the Chinese, and seems likely to bring trouble, and losses to the merchants. — I have not seen the Taoyin yet, since his return, which happened yesterday (29th). — On the russian side there is now a remarkable series of trials in connection with murders and robberies happened from 1920 to 1922 : apparently there one Judge who tries to be honest and stern, and it is on this account that the most ghastly stories of crimes, wholesale robberies perpetrated by the former members of the Political Secret Police, intermingled with murders *are coming to light* and, alas, all, or nearly all, the Jews of Tahsihe are strongly implicated, mostly as accomplices, receivers of the stolen goods; in some cases, as instigators, and murderers. They are all, however, let free on bail, of from 50 to 100 dollars ! I believe that the efforts of the one would-be honest Judge will be nullified; for it would be most extraordinary that the <u>regime</u> in force condemn its best supports. In fact, on Christmas night (Russian) at a great dance, the first given since the Revolution at the Blagovestchensk Club, a very fine affair at which several of our Tidewaiters were present, the Secretary of the "Party" shot a young fellow through the head, in the middle of the ballroom, for what is said to be a very slight provocation.

provocation. The murderer was arrested the following morning, but after a few hours was released....

The Chinese Consul-General in Blagovestchensk is
transferred to Peking; I do not yet know the name of the
successor.

Local. Great panic and speculation over Russian action
with regard to the C.E.Railway. On the   the Taoyin,
on receipt of a wire from Tsitsihar asking for a competent representative to go at once to consult about urgent
business, left himself suddenly at night, and only returned on 29th. I do not know exactly what he went for; but
almost certainly it was about russo-chinese politics. The
General in command (Chen Shou Shih) of whom I asked for
information, took all his time and wits in explaining that
the russians should not provoke China, since he keeps his
territory in quite good order, and does nothing provocati-
ve towards them. - The fact is, they are all scared, and
martial law has once more been proclaimed on 25th, with
censorship at the Telegraph Office and Post Office (which
however is not applied to Customs correspondence); but if
things really came to a head, there would be such a
flight of officials, as to leave none here; the merchants
would be left to themselves entirely. - Rumours have been
circulated to the effect that 1,500 chinese soldiers of
the Red Army have arrived in Blago. of which fact I have
no confirmation; on the other hand, reinforcements are coming
from Tsitsihar, said to amount to two "ying". - To this
                                                    must

must be added the activity of the Hunghutze, to give an
idea of the state of panic prevailing. Bandits attacked
merchants (smugglers) near Machang, some 40 li above Taheiho, and stole
5 horses; when they ran to the russian shore, the russian Customs chased them, and shot one of them. But a larger raid
was made against Wanhochen and Taipingkou, down river; it
was said that a band over 1000 strong attacked and
looted the two towns, and an expedition was set on foot
to march against the robbers, which were also said to be
a band formed on the russian side (the fact is quite
possible, but the russian representative energetically denies it). However, before the "expedition" was half-way, one
veteran officer with 30 soldiers made a night attack
against the robbers, who were not over 200 all told, and
dispersed them. - Again, the local Military Officials are
playing a game of bluff, because the latest inspection
from Moukden has been very unfavourable to them on the
point of efficiency, and they want to force the Chamber
of Commerce to protest against their removal, as it was
done when the Fengtien warlord called the local General
to war against Wu Pei-fu. - I forgot to mention that the
Head in Blagovestchensk of the Chinese Residents' Association (華僑會) has been arrested as a spy for the
Whites (which are absent from these parts now), and has
not been released after more than one month; hence more
excitement.

Smuggling. A great deal of smuggling is made over
                                                    the

the Liangchiat'un Barrier: the Military and the Taoyin-Superintendent   the example. They invariably refuse to stop when passing the Barrier, notwithstanding my repeated requests and protests, and they always carry in the motor-cars opium, and, more seldom, arms. As they are always escorted by soldiers, I cannot do anything to stop them, for fear of a conflict; but I know, for instance, that in the Taoyin's car, which left a few days ago, there were about eighty pounds of opium. — Arms they generally send through the Humaho-Hsinglungkow-Mergen route because they do not want to give me proof of their smuggling, and arms are so bulky they cannot very well be carried in motor cars. — But a great deal of opium tryies to go in private motor cars as well; and I have suspicion that some of our Officers may be implicated in this dirty business: I suspect especially two : Morozoff and Pistruiloff. There has been a case when a motor car, which was to be examined here by Mr. Pistruiloff, has been (under my instructions) searched by Mr. Ayaymonnt (a more reliable, if not very bright, man), and opium has been found in a basket, in such open way, that it seems impossible it was placed there without previous understanding with the Customs Officer. Besides, Mr. Pistruiloff fell at once sick with "influenza", and recovered only after four days. But an accomplice there should be at Liangchiat'un, and there too, I have noted that Mr. Morozoff (in charge) failed to report, at times, Motor cars which passed without having cleared at Taheiho; he also seems to have more money

money in his account than warranted by his salary. I have no certain proof against these two men, but I keep them under strict watch, and maybe I will be able to obtain some kind of proof from the merchants, who are said to be talking about this affair. Anyhow I have at once removed all the Staff from Liangchiat'un, substituting men of indisputable rectitude. But I do not know very well what to do with the two men under suspicion. I hope I can clear the matter soon. — The chief point is, that up to the present I have had nothing against these two men, good searchers, rather quiet, although not more efficient than they may be expected in their rank. — Against Officials of course I cannot do anything, but it is a real scandal to see the Superintendent run opium, and put obstacles in my way: in fact I proposed to him to put an actual "Barrier" (wooden fence) at Liangchiat'un, so as to oblige all cars to stop, but he was very much against this proposal, and pour cause ! Without his support, on the other hand, I feel I cannot risk a conflict with the Military. —

The whole In-Door Staff has worked like niggers, even long hours by candle light (the electric light is entirely useless, and, unless new machinery is purchased, we will have to get our own plant), and Messrs. So Yam Su and Yang Dien Fong have done particularly good work at the Returns, which are practically all ready. —

Yours truly,

第 26 号半官函

尊敬的安格联先生：

1 月 10 日半官函收悉，函中要求向帕尔默（W. Morgan Palmer）先生提供本地俄国难民的情况。数日前哈尔滨关税务司亦发来电报要求提供信息，已经照办。幸运的是，瑷珲关区俄国难民的情况并不严重，人数方面也并未因苏联近来的种种事件而有所增加，仍是自 1920 年逃难至此的那些人。他们现已在本地定居，从事各种工作，其中大多数为哥萨克人，主要由对岸的亲戚接济，虽然很多难民依然穷困，但并没有人挨饿。与哈尔滨、铁路沿线及吉林周边等地急需救助的难民相比，瑷珲关区的难民暂无救助之需。

为布拉戈维申斯克（Blagovestchensk）事：当地形势发展依然不甚乐观，经济方面也开始出现危机，食物储量（主要是马铃薯）可能将不足以支撑到今年秋收。至于当地政府现行的征收税率，目前还无法获取准确信息，如果根据以往惯例推断，对富人征收的税率应当不超过 1%（税率根据财富比例而定）。但据了解，实际上多数情况下都会远超这一标准。另外值得注意的是，当地政府不仅对收入征税，还对毫无产出的资产征税，甚至是床、椅子等，只要物品价值超过 10 卢布，便会列入征税之列。此外还有多种特别附加税，例如有一家电影院被要求每年缴纳 7500 元，另一家则被要求缴纳 5000 元。

苏联当局对社会民主党的"清洗"十分彻底，官员中，只要不是完全的"红军"支持者，便均已被撤换。据称，高尔察克曾经的部下和其他"反动派"的下属均被关押在一个特殊的营地当中，其他与政治无关的官员都被押往莫斯科和彼得格勒（Petrograd）等地。

莫斯科方面派来整顿交通的使团已于四日前抵达，负责人马尚德（Marchand）是一名极具影响力（也非常聪明）的布尔什维克党人，据称还有法国血统，但本人认为其应是犹太人。在停留期间，其从未进行过任何视察，整日都在大黑河酗酒，就连本人极力与之商议正事都只是枉费口舌。使团的专门顾问彼得罗巴甫洛夫斯克（Petropavlosk）先生是水运局的工程师，抵达后曾提出一个紧急改革方案，但从水运局现任会计主任处得知实施改革将会需要大量经费后，便不再插手，只身来到大黑河，不过并未酗酒。

莫斯科使团已经安排火车每周往返于符拉迪沃斯托克（Vladivostock）和赤塔（Chita）之间，速度可达到沙俄时期的标准。但不知是否真的会实现，不过无论如何火车都不会在气候温暖时通行，因为铁路只有在出现霜冻后才会更加牢固稳定，其他时间都不太安全，或者将所有轨枕换新（工程量巨大），否则政府不会同意让火车如此高速运行。莫斯科使团还计划前往北京，届时水运局分局督办拉古丁（A. N. Lagutin）先生也将一同前往，其是使团中最正派的官员，也是布拉戈维申斯克唯一的代表。

此外，本人已就日后的黑龙江航路标志与拉古丁先生及莫斯科使团专门顾问彼得罗巴甫洛夫斯克工程师进行商议。他们均赞同应当有所行动，但表示莫斯科方面已指示不得擅自于地方决定任何事宜，此问题须于北京处理。另外还告知，他们正在考虑使用汽艇开展航标维护工作，不再安排职员长期驻守于航道沿线各处。由此可以看出，本人关于由维修队乘坐汽艇对航标进行维护的办法确为最佳方案（参阅瑷珲关致海关总税务司署第91 号呈文）。他们及驻大黑河苏联非官方代表还透露，明年如果无法缔结条约，苏联方面将不会允许中国船只靠近俄岸。若如此，中国政府可能会采取报复措施，届时恐怕会出现麻烦，商人亦会因此遭受损失。道尹已于昨日（1 月29 日）返回，但本人还未与其见面。

苏联地方当局正在审理1920 年至1922 年期间发生的谋杀及抢劫案件，其中有一名法官显然是要力求公正严明，因此那些最为可怕的罪行，那些前政府政治部秘密警探曾经犯下的抢劫罪和谋杀罪都已逐步公之于众，而大黑河的犹太人几乎全部涉案，他们大多是同谋，或者帮助劫犯销赃，但也有些是主谋，甚至参与谋杀。但他们只要能够提交保释金（50 银圆至100 银圆不等），便可获得释放。恐怕那位力求公正严明的法官此次将会徒劳收场，毕竟执政政权不会谴责为其效力之人。

俄历圣诞节前夕，布拉戈维申斯克俱乐部举办了一场盛大的舞会，这是自当地革命爆发以来的首场舞会，瑷珲关铃子手中也有几人出席。然而当晚舞会的组织干事却在舞厅中央朝一名年轻人的头部开枪，而事件的起因据称仅仅是双方当时发生了一点小摩擦。行凶者于次日清晨被捕，但几个小时后便被释放。

中国驻布拉戈维申斯克总领事已被调回北京，暂时还不知继任者为何人。

为地方事：苏联红军将对中东铁路采取行动的传闻已在本地引起极大恐慌，一时间流言四起。日前齐齐哈尔方面发来电报要求道尹派遣一名有能力的代表立即前去商议紧急事务，道尹接到命令后便于当日夜间亲自前往，直到29 日才返回。虽不知道尹此行究竟所为何事，但相信定与中俄两国政治关系有关。本人向镇守使打探消息时，其一直解释称自己将边境管理得井然有序，从未做过任何激怒苏联红军的举动，他们不应挑衅中国。实际上，大黑河地方官员均已有所忌惮，自1 月25 日起又开始施行戒严令，并于电报局和邮政局展开搜查，不过海关信函不在搜查之列。但如果最终发生战事，恐怕地方官员都将逃走，只留下商人独守此地，自生自灭。另有传言称，中国已有1500 名红军士兵抵达布拉戈维申斯克，但是否属实，还难以确定，据称齐齐哈尔方面也有两个"营"的增援部队正在赶来。

此外，红胡子（土匪）活动猖獗，由此更能感受到本地的恐慌气氛。日前，大黑河上游约 40 里处的马厂附近有商人和走私者遭到土匪袭击，共有 5 匹马被偷走，这些土匪逃至俄岸后遭到苏联海关的追击，其中还有一人中枪，黑龙江下游地区的温和镇和太平沟遭遇的袭击更为严重，据称袭击并劫掠这两个小镇的一伙土匪共有 1000 余人，而且个个身强体壮，有消息称这些土匪都是在俄岸集结的，虽然的确有此可能，但苏联代表已极力否认。事件发生后，当局已派遣远征队前去剿匪，行进途中，一名经验丰富的军官带领 30 名士兵夜袭土匪（不足 200 人），并成功将之驱散。地方军官再次开始大肆吹嘘本地的危急情况，主要因为奉天方面近期的巡查对他们十分不利，他们希望借此让商人抗议撤离地方军队，当初奉天军阀要求本地守备司令至前线与吴佩孚的军队对战时，他们便采取了这一策略。

此外，布拉戈维申斯克华侨会负责人已被当地政府以白军（如今远东地区已无白军踪影）间谍的罪名逮捕，现已被关押一月有余，本地氛围因此更加紧张。

为走私事：梁家屯分卡走私情况十分严重，军方和道尹兼海关监督亦参与其中。他们每次经过梁家屯分卡时，都拒绝停车接受海关检查，无论本人如何要求，如何抗议，都无任何作用，他们总是会在汽车里私藏鸦片，有时甚至会私藏军火，但碍于有士兵护送，为避免引起冲突，本人也无法强制停车检查。据了解，道尹数日前离开时，车里便藏有八十磅鸦片。至于军火，他们通常会通过呼玛河—兴隆沟—墨尔根路线运送，一是不希望给海关留下走私证据，二是因为军火占用空间大，不便于使用汽车偷运。此外还有大量鸦片试图通过私人汽车偷运。

现怀疑瑷珲关关员中亦有涉案者，嫌疑最大的是莫罗作福（D. A. Morozoff）和皮士垂（B. E. Pistruiloff）。日前，伊思孟（V. A. Eysymonnt）先生（为人最为可靠虽然可能不太精明）在一辆汽车上搜查出鸦片，当时鸦片就置于一个篮子中，如果没有事先与海关关员串通好，如此放置根本不可能不被发现，而这辆汽车本应由皮士垂先生检查，但其当时并未在现场，而且事发之后突患流感，四日后方恢复。但此事若欲成功，梁家屯分卡必定还有一名关员涉案。本人已注意到，梁家屯分卡的负责关员莫罗作福先生多次故意隐瞒有车辆未在大黑河办理结关便通过分卡之事，经查其账户中的钱款数额远超于其薪俸应得之数。

虽然目前还无切实证据，但本人已将此两名关员严密监视起来。据称，商人都在议论此事，或许可以从他们身上获取一些证据。事件发生后，本人已立即撤回梁家屯分卡的所有关员，替换成绝对正直可靠之人。只是对于这两名有嫌疑的关员，还不知该如何处理，希望可以尽快查清此事。而且关键在于，截至目前，这两名关员从未有过任何差错，他们擅长搜查，行事稳重，只是工作效率有所欠缺。

对于中国地方官员，本人的确无计可施，但就这样眼睁睁地看着海关监督走私鸦片，阻挡海关检查，也确实说不过去。实际上，本人此前已向海关监督提议于梁家屯分卡安置一个木制栅栏作为真正的"屏障"阻挡所有车辆通行，迫使他们停车接受检查，但其极力反对，原因不言而喻！既然无法获得道尹兼海关监督的支持，本人也无法贸然与军方交涉，以免发生冲突。

为人事事：瑷珲关内班关员工作十分勤勉，甚至在夜间还要借助蜡烛工作，如今电灯已无法使用，如果不购买新的设备，便须自建发电厂。苏荫召先生和杨殿芳先生在统计报表的编制工作方面表现非常出色，现已基本完成。

您真挚的
包安济

22. 包安济致安格联函

（第 27 号半官函）

/O No. 27.

Aigun/Taheiho 20th February 3.

Dear Sir Francis,

I have only received your S/O letter of 24th January. I am inclined to believe that the Reds' attitude in the matter of the C. E. R. has changed for the better lately. Fear of Japan, or other reasons, I do not know; I have an idea that Obolsky, the Secretary of the Administration, is for something in the change : he is a brother-in-law of the Manager in Harbin of the Centrosoyus, a moderate but very influential Communist, who went to Moscow recently perhaps in connection with the affairs of the Railway, of which Obolsky expects to become Director when Ostroumoff retires. This is really gossip, but important issues are often decided on such merits. - Should however the Russians decide on action for the recovery of the C.E.R. (it is impossible to foretell : the "Reds" have nothing to lose, and much to gain - and their power is based on the Red Army, which is to be kept busy, if its enthusiasm is to be maintained), I am not sure that they will confine themselves to the Railway. Their hate of the Chinese is great, and they would probably welcome their chance of wrecking Taheiho, against which place, and whose merchants vehement articles are being

Sir Francis A. Aglen, K. B. E.,

Inspector General of Customs,

P e k i n g.

Entered in dark Index.

being edited periodically by the only Blagovestchensk paper, the official Amurskaya Pravda, with such expressions as these :"we must shake the dust of Taheiho" "the Taheiho vampires" etc.- The chinese Administration, inefficient and unreliable, harsh at times, weak at others, and the merciless advantage taken by chinese merchants of the situation are in part responsible for these bad feelings. - I have seen the Taoyin about the situation created by the intimated russian policy of refusing to come to any local agreement on Navigation and aids on the Amur, and of forbidding chinese steamers from trading at Russian Ports; but he is hopeless - does not know what to do, and would rather get my advise. - I believe that a line of conduct should be given by the Peking Ministries; but it seems hardly likely. I have spoken with the Russian Representative in Taheiho about the possible deadlock resulting from the recent decisions of the Moscow Government : he is afraid that, in response to the Russian move, the Chinese Authorities may close the Sungari to Russian boats, but says that the Sungari has now little importance for Russian shipping ; on the other hand he thinks that the Russians may close the Amur (both sides) to Chinese steamers, although he is personally persuaded that the Amur is a River belonging in common to China and Russia, and that such step would be wrong. - He is very doubtful about a Sino-Russian conference in the near future, and says that Russia wants first an agreement with Japan, probably in order to have free hands with China afterwards

afterwards.

In Blagovestchensk, on the 15th, suddenly, a new Import
Tariff has been put into force; it is much higher than
before, and the general basis seems to be 33 % of the
value, although I have had no time to study it. The
Russian Commissioner wired to Chita asking that the Tariff
be suspended for some time, until he may prepare a report
showing the damages that it will inflict on Trade; but
he has been ordered to enforce it as it is. — Such
measures reset on the general situation very much: there is
a sort of panic in town, everyone trying to buy as much
as he can; the Chinese New Year coincident with the
introduction of the Tariff makes it impossible to measure the extent of damage to the Foreign Trade; but it
must be large — and contraband will be encourage further.
The suggestion of my despatch No. 95 — opening of Barriers
for checking cargo at Dalao Hei Ho and opposite Upper
Blagovestchensk — seems to me more urgent than ever, now.
As a result of the visit of the Commission from the Ministry of Communications, the Amur Railway had been handed
over, in part to the Zabaikal R., in part to the Oussouri R.; over 60% of the employees have been discharged. The
Railway is busy transporting towards Russia all sort of
materials (much of it useless, I am assured) taken in
Vladivostock. — The general score has brought a decline in
the price of furs, of which merchants in Blagovestchensk
are trying to dispose in a hurry, for fear of requisitions
On

On the 12th February a big explosion occurred in the
middle of the town, causing several deaths and wounding
many people. It was a factory (so to speak) for conver-
ting shell powder into common shot-gun powder. Chinese worked in it, but it was actually directed by one of the
Cooperatives, and therefore tolerated in the middle of
the town. — The new Consul-General appointed to Blagovestchensk is coming from the Wai Chiao Pu, his name being
Cheng Yen-hsi (鄭延禧).

Smuggling of Opium. Recently an automobile passed
Liangchist'un, and opium was found concealed in the Car.
The chauffeur, when the Chinese watcher was searching, the
hiding-place, told him to go and ask the Foreign Officer
to whom he said he would give the "usual" reward if
he would let the 10 lbs. go. — Naturally enough the Office
seized the opium: he is honest, and I know it (it is
Mr. Rymymontt); the chauffeur they let go, and I cannot
blame them, because all the passengers would otherwise have
been stranded in Liangchist'un. But he cannot go very far,
having only a temporary pass to Tsitsihar, and, if he does
not come back at once, I will have him arrested in Tsitsihar. I went to get all possible information out of him
and see who is at fault, first, because the opium had
been put in the car by somebody else, certainly with the
complicity of the owner (a Russian); second, because more
shipments have certainly been passed in the cars and I may
get serious proofs from this chauffeur. In the meantime I

am getting more details from Mr. Szymontt and his subordinates at Liangchiat'un, and I may go, if I have time, in two or three days to visit that station. — I have practically no doubt that Mr. Morosoff and Mr. Pistruiloff have had dirty dealings with opium smugglers; but I do not want to condemn them without solid proofs. These may be forthcoming from other sides as well; one smuggler, whose property has been confiscated some time ago, comes now and lets me know that he will produce what proofs he can of the connivance of my officers, provided I do not implicate him. — I expect something definite in a few days. — The man named above has mentioned the names of Messrs. Pistruiloff and Morosoff, the officers I deem guilty, of his own accord. —

Yours truly

J. Bohr

第 27 号半官函　　　　　　　　　　　　**1923 年 2 月 20 日于瑷珲关 / 大黑河**

尊敬的安格联先生：

　　1 月 24 日第 21 号半官函收悉。兹认为，苏联红军对中东铁路一事的态度近日已经有所缓和，或许是出于对日本当局的忌惮，或许另有原因，但具体为何，暂时还无法确定。另外中东铁路管理局秘书奥博尔斯基（Obolsky）先生似乎希望能够借此转变有所作为。其不仅与苏联消费合作社中央联社哈尔滨地区的经理有亲属关系，还是一名政治立场温和但极具影响力的共产主义者，近日已前去莫斯科，或许正是为中东铁路一事，而且中东铁路管理局现任局长沃斯特罗乌莫夫（Ostroumoff）先生退休后，很有可能会由其接任局长一职。虽然只是传闻，但也不无可能。

　　然而，如果苏联当局决定让中东铁路恢复运行（目前还无法断定。但恢复运行后，"红军"当局不会有任何损失，反而会受益良多，更何况红色政权的基础是红军，如果要让红军保持热情，就须让他们一直保持忙碌状态），不知他们是否会仅将注意力集中在铁路相关事宜上。因为苏联红军十分痛恨中国人，甚至很有可能会借此机会摧毁大黑河。如今布拉戈维申斯克（Blagovestchensk）唯一的报纸《阿穆尔真理报》已经开始定期刊登反对大黑河及大黑河商人的文章，言辞颇为激烈，甚至会有"要让大黑河化为灰烬""大黑河吸血鬼"等言论。而中国地方政府，效率低下又不可靠，时而严厉，时而软弱，政府管理的弊端又恰恰被中国商人所利用，这也是引起苏联方面敌对情绪的原因之一。

　　鉴于苏联方面拒绝与中国地方政府签订黑龙江航路标志相关协议，又禁止中国船只于其口岸开展贸易，本人遂与道尹商议对策，但其毫无主见，反倒希望采取本人的建议。兹认为，关于此事，应由北京当局下达基本决策，但似乎又不太可能。与驻大黑河苏联代表谈及莫斯科政府近期的决策可能会导致局面僵持一事时，其担心中国政府为反击苏联的举措，可能会禁止苏联船只驶入松花江，不过又表示如今松花江于苏联船运而言已不甚重要，但认为苏联当局很有可能会禁止中国轮船于黑龙江（华俄两侧）上航行，虽然其自己也相信黑龙江为中苏两国共有，苏联方面不应单方禁止。另外，其认为中苏双方可能无法于近期召开会议，因为苏联方面计划先与日本当局达成协议，以便日后可与中国自由交涉。

　　为布拉戈维申斯克事：2 月 15 日，当地突然开始实行新的进口税则，税率远高于此前所定，基本为货物价值的 33%，不过目前并无时间查明核实。苏联海关税务司此前已向赤塔（Chita）方面发送电报申请暂时停止实行新税则，以便其有时间统计出新税则对贸易所造成的损失；但收到的命令仍然是继续遵照执行。然而此举已对当地整体局势造成了颇为严重的影响，城镇内一片恐慌，百姓争相囤积货物。不过，由于中国农历新年与新税则实施的时间有所重合，无法估算出本埠对外贸易的损失，但相信一定非常大，而且之后的走私事件定会增多。兹认为，依目前情况来看，瑷珲关致海关总税务司公署第 95 号呈中关于在小黑河及布拉戈维申斯克上游对岸增设分卡之建议应当尽快实施。

莫斯科交通部使团来访后，阿穆尔铁路一部分移交给后贝加尔斯克铁路①，一部分移交给乌苏里铁路，原有职员中有 60% 已被解雇。该条铁路现正忙于从符拉迪沃斯托克（Vladivostock）向苏联本土运输各种货物（相信大多皆无甚用处）。

由于当地的恐慌局势，皮货价格已开始下跌，布拉戈维申斯克的皮货商人都急于尽快处理掉手中的货物，以避免被政府征用。2 月 12 日，城镇中心发生一场大爆炸，造成数人死亡，多人受伤。据称，发生爆炸的是一家用炮弹粉末制造枪支火药的工厂，厂内亦有中国工人。该工厂实际上是受一家合作社企业管理，因此才会获准设立于城镇中心。新任中国驻布拉戈维申斯克总领事来自外交部，名为郑延禧。

为走私鸦片事：近日，一辆汽车经过梁家屯分卡时，被查出车内藏有鸦片。华籍巡役搜查到鸦片藏匿之处时，该车司机要求面见洋籍关员，并对洋籍关员表示如果可以让其将这 10 磅鸦片带走，便按照"惯例"支付酬金。洋籍关员自然是将鸦片收缴，此关员〔伊思孟（V. A. Eysymontt）先生〕品行正直，本人十分了解。不过司机最终还是被放行，毕竟如果继续扣留，车上的乘客都将滞留在梁家屯，关员有此举亦情有可原。相信司机应该不会逃得太远，因为其手中仅有前往齐齐哈尔的临时通行证，即使其不返回本地，亦可让齐齐哈尔方面将其逮捕。希望可以通过该司机了解更多的信息，查明都有何人牵涉其中，因为一定有人与车主（俄籍人）事先串通好将鸦片藏于车中，而且此前定有更多的走私物品由私人汽车运输过卡，或许可以从该名司机身上得到切实证据。与此同时，伊思孟先生及其梁家屯分卡的下属亦将提供更多细节线索，如果时间允许，本人将于两三日内前去分卡查访。

实际上，本人几乎可以确定莫罗作福（D. A. Morozoff）先生和皮士垂（B. E. Pistruiloff）先生与鸦片走私者有过违反海关规定的交易，只是不希望在无确凿证据的情况下将他们定罪。至于证据，除了上述来源，还有人可以提供。有一名俄籍走私商人因自己的货物日

---

① 英文为 Zabaikal R.，经查 Zabaikal 为后贝加尔斯克的俄文英译。

前被没收，现来到海关表示可以提供其与瑷珲关关员串通走私的证据，但前提条件是不要将其卷入其中。相信事情不久便会水落石出。该名走私商人已经主动说出本人认为有罪的两名关员的名字，即莫罗作福和皮士垂。

您真挚的

包安济

23. 包安济致安格联函

（第 29 号半官函）

O No. 29.

Aigun/Taheiho 30th march, 23.

Dear Sir Francis,

Conversations have been resumed with the Russian Authorities for the conclusion of another tempoary Agreement on <u>Aids to Navigation</u>. On 24th the General Director of the Amur Water Transports (and Navigation Office) returned from a long trip of inspection, during which he visited Habarovsk Vladivostock, the whole railway line, and Harbin. On 26th I went to see him, and he at once agreed that something had better be done. The same day I went to the Taoyin, and discussed matters with him, when he agreed with me on all points, except on the change of Tariff, with regard to which he asked me to be careful not to tax Steamers too heavily (Clearance Fees) since Chinese steamers are already in financial straits such as to foreshadow the closing of the Wut'ung concern. - I have private information which point to the same conclusion: the Wut'ung Co. have not paid their Captains and Pilots for last year, and now they wanted to force on them a contract by which they would work next summer at half the salaries of last year, receiving arrears of pay in small instalements; the Captains and Pilots refuse to accept these conditions; and the Wut'ung Co. tried to get other Staff from Blagovestchensk ; however

Sir Francis A.Aglen, K. B. E,m
Inspector General of Customs,
    P e k i n g.
                                    Entered in Card-Index.

Blagovestchensk; however, the Wut'ung Co,'s Russian Staff belong to the Blagovestchensk Masters' and Pilots' Association, which has forbidden any of its Members from unfairly competing against their colleagues alrady in the services of the Wut'ung Co. - and the Co. is consequently in a fix, apart from the disastrous management which has squandered the moneys in a way too common in China. - But, to go back to the proposed Agreement, I informed the Taoyin that the Russians had approached me on the subject of Navigation on the Sungari, which I altogether declined to discuss, saying that this was for the Taoyin (Commissioner of Foreign Affairs) to brooch M; I then re-presented to the Taoyin the draft which you sent in your S/O of 24th May, 1922. With his usual carelessness, he seemed to have forgotten all about it (I had shown it to him when I received it), and it would appear that the Boards did not send him a copy (?). However, he eagerly seized the suggestion, and I believe he approached the Russian Authorities when they went to see him on 29th (yesterday); for this morning the Taoyin's representatives came to discuss the draft agreement I had prepared and submitted the day before, and manifested the Taoyin's intention of including practically all the clauses unchanged of that draft into the new Agrment. To this, of course, I have no objection, although I would prefer two Agreements, one on Navigation, one on upkeep of the Aids, to be signed at one time preferably; but this part of the Agreement he must discuss by himself, and I politely refused his proposal to entrust the discussion
                                                              of

of the whole question (Navigation and Aids) to me, saying
that I am not prepared on the former argument, and that I
cannot encroach in a field which is absolutely his own.
The redaction of the Agreement has been changed from my
original draft, beause the Taoyin was afraid that, the form
differing from tha Agreement of last year, the Provincial
would be more difficult to persuade; At the start, this
morning, the Taoyin's representative stated that the Provincial Authorities had instructed to renew last year's
Agreement; but I replied that , if the Taoyin did not
want to improve on an Agreement which had to be altered
in fact even last year, it was useless to discuss; that in
that case I would ask for your authority to collect dues
but could not accept an appointment in the Joint Commission.
After which all the modifications I suggested were very nice
ly entered in the draft, which, however, in deference to
"form", still contains a lot of useless (and harmless) clau
ses and words. The Taoyin should let me have the definite
draft as soon as possible, when I shall complete the
Russian translation for the part concerning the Aids, and
submit it to the Russians. However, it has already become
very difficult to cross the River, owing to the surface of
the ice melting, and there being in places as much as three
fet of water, and I do not know whether discussions can
be continued. and concluded as early as desirable. The
Russians, in their preliminary draft, aimed at securing all
our collection, against a very loose supervision on their
work and expenditure, but I turned down this pretense, and
it

it is very likely that they will come to our terms,
because they need money: the whole staff of the Amur
Navigation Office has not ben paid for three months (Janu
ary, February, March).

Conditions in Blagovestchensk : The high Tariff, which
Marchand, the new Director General of the Water Transports,
has branded as "idiotic" in a discussion with me, continues
in force; with the help of the practial monopoly of the
Government Trading Co. (not one permit has ben issued to
others so far), it is he cause of a most serious increase
in the cost of living in Blagovestchensk, notwithstanding the
activity of contrabandists. All business is stopped, and
even on this side there is little doing; the Gostorg (Govt
Trading Co.) has bought supplies, chiefly piece goods, pell-
mell from a local russian merchant, who is bragging that he
has shifted on to them all the stuff that he could not
sell to anybody - and I am informed that this is true and
that the Agent of the Gostorg had no idea of what his
company wanted. I also know of a representative of the
Professional Union (a Red organisation), which, just previous
to the closing of the forntier purchased goods for the Union
from a chinese dealer, and obtained an extra (higher) receipt
for the Union, and an extra one (much lower) for the Russian
Customs. No wonder things are bad over there. - In other ways
however, things are better: order is more respected, communications by Railway are actually more convenient (although
the bridges at Habarovsk and at other points have not been
repaired, and the road is in need of most urgent repairs)
the

the telegraph is working regularly, not only to Russia, but
to all countries in Europe, and is most convenient, costing
only 28 kopeks per word (e.g. to Italy or England). But
the tightness of money is extreme: to start with, all gold
has disappeared from circulation, and only the silver roubles
are left; these are accepted at a discount varying from 5 to
10 % (even by Government Offices, Customs, etc); then the rate of interest charged by the Far Eastern Bank on secured loa
loans is 24% (per annum); and, as the Director of the Naviga
tion Office told me, it is absolutely impossible to remit
even 100 dollars to places like Chernayeva or Jalinda, beause
the Post Office at that place could never scrap together that
sum. - The Officials of the Water Transports are hoping on
the lifting of the ban against imports, and on a modification
of the Tariff: they are making preparation for intasive
navigation during the next season, and they will badly
squash Russian chinese enterprise. They are also talking about supply
of manufactures from Russia proper, via Stretensk; but Marchand has ben more frank with me, and says it is all dream
- Spetial Tax for the maintenance of the Local Militia.
Not long ago the Magistrate and the President of the
Chamber of Commerce came to me and asked the Customs cooperation to the levy of a local tax for the upkeep of
the volunteer Militia, the tax to be about ½ % of the
value of all goods, native and foreign, coming and going.
The Customs's cooperation may take the shape of direct
collection, or of information to the Chamber as to the
amount of goods traded by each firm, so as to avoid
                                               leakage.

leakage. I informed the visitors that the Customs are not
as a rule allowed to collect local taxes, but that, if they
submitted some proposals to the Central Governmen through
the Superintendent, and to you through the Customs, something may perhaps be done; as to giving information of a
confidential nature, I said this could not be done. At the
same time I pointed out all the difficulties in the way of
such tax to be collected through the Customs : I said that
goods under Manchurian E. C, could not be taxed, and they
said they would tax only such goods on which the Customs
collect duty on arrival; I also pointed out that no such
tax could be levied on goods imported or exported by nationals
of Treaty Powers, who, by Treaty, are entitled to trading on
payment of Customs duties only (including Transit Dues when
travelling in the interior). I strongly advised them not to
take decisions without referring the question to the
superior authorities, and to go on in the meantime with
means at their disposition. I have heard nothing more of this
argument, and I am afraid that it may be presented in a
petition to the Shui Wu-Ch'u, or in, some other devious way,
which may obtain results similar to the case of the Liangchiat'un Barrier, or, the case of the Local Tax Office,
which does not yet come to an agreement on the removal of
their Office on the foreshore, notwithstanding the instructions
of the Shui Wu Ch'u to that effect; neither is the Taoyin-
Superintendent doing anything to help the Customs, as usual.

Opening of Hsiao Hei-ho as a Port. Hsiao Hei Ho
                                                is

is a very small village, a few li below Taheiho, opposite
the centre of Blagovestchensk City: it is now active for
the contraband which is carried on on a large scale with
the Russian side, but it has very poor landing accomodation
Steamers could not approach without most expensive works;
besides, the village proper is bordering a channel of the
River which is generally dry: on the outer side of an Island
there may be created a poor anchorage for vessels. It is
this place that the authorities are now planning to declare
an Open Port; there has been already a Weiyüan appointed,
but the area has not been defined. If this place were opened in conjunction with Taheiho, the question may be taken
seriously, but, as it is, it looks like a speculation on
the part of Chang Tso-lin and the local Authorities. Merchants
are in fact taking a keen interest in land at, or near ,
Hsiao Hei Ho, and several russians are thinking of buying
land and establishing a small colony.- As far as I can understand, the move is purely local (provincial). If, notwithstanding the absurdity of the matter, the place is declared an
open Port, we will have a chance of opening a Barrier without
difficulty, and we shall be able to control contraband much
better than at present.

Accusations against Pistruiloff : a smaller incident is
worth reporting. Pistruiloff went to the Senior Out-Door Officer one week ago, and stated that Zeligman would come and
withdraw all the charges, being ready to go to prison, in
order not to have Pistruiloff damaged by his false accusations. He did not explain how he knew this fact, but he
was

was positive. The same morning Zeligman came over from
Blagovestchnsk and, as it happened, went straight into the
Senior Officer's room, without Pistruiloff being able to
get hold of him; questioned, he denied any intention of
recanting, saying he was not mad, and that all his charges
are good and true. - Two days ago Zeligman again came
to see the Senior Officer, and told him that a certain
Popkoff (a local scoundrel, well acquainted with Pistruiloff)
approached him (Zeligman) with a proposal of recanting, against
$ 500 from Pistruiloff. - Zeligman says he turned the
offer down as ridiculous. - I become more and more convinced of Pistruiloff's guilt.

The Staff is well.

Yours truly,

(G.Boezi)

第 29 号半官函   1923 年 3 月 30 日于瑷珲关/大黑河

尊敬的安格联先生:

中俄地方政府已重新开始就航路标志临时协议的签订事宜进行协商谈判。

俄阿穆尔水运局(及水道局)总督办此前一直在外巡查,走访哈巴罗夫斯克(Habarovsk)、符拉迪沃斯托克(Vladivostock),铁路全线及哈尔滨等地,已于 3 月 24 日返回。本人遂于 3 月 26 日前去拜访,总督办当即赞同最好有所行动,同日面见道尹时,道尹对本人所提各项建议亦表示赞同,唯不同意更改税率,指出中国轮船现下经营困难,戊通公司已有倒闭之风险,因此不希望海关对轮船征税(结关费)过高。

据私下消息,戊通公司还未向其船主及水手支付去年的薪俸,如今又要迫使他们签订合同,同意今年夏季工作期间仅收取去年薪俸之半数,而且还须接受公司后期分期付款。船主和水手已经回绝。戊通公司的管理问题颇为严重,与中国大多公司一样过于铺张浪费。此前迫于无奈还曾试图从布拉戈维申斯克(Blagovestchensk)招收人员,但公司的俄籍职员均隶属于布拉戈维申斯克船长与水手协会(Masters' and Pilots' Association),根据协会规定,所有成员均不得与早已就职于戊通公司的成员进行不公平竞争,因此已陷入困境。

关于航路标志协议一事,日前苏方代表来至海关商议其轮船于松花江上航行之事,本人当即拒绝讨论,并说明此事应与道尹(兼瑷珲交涉司)商议。随后面见道尹时,已据实相告,并再次将总税务司 1922 年 5 月 24 日半官函所附协议草案呈予其阅览。无奈道尹一向疏忽大意,似乎已经毫无印象(本人早已于收到后便交与其查阅),而且显然税务处也未曾向其发送抄件。

不过,道尹现急于征询意见,而且相信昨日(29 日)已与来访的苏联代表会面,因为道尹公署代表今日上午特来至海关商议本人前日交与道尹的协议草案,并说明道尹希望将草案中的所有条款原封不动地列入新协议之中。对此,本人当然不会有反对意见,只是认为,航运及航路标志应当各签一份协议,而且最好可以同时签订。但这一切还须由道尹独自决定。道尹希望本人可参与所有事宜的协商,包括航运和航标问题,对此,本人已经婉拒并说明自己对航运问题并不了解,而且此事应由道尹单独决定,本人不可僭越。

道尹担心如果新旧协议的形式有异,将会更难以向黑龙江省政府申请批准,故已对本人起草的协议做出改动。起初,道尹公署代表于今日上午来访时便表示黑龙江省政府指令续签去年的协议,但本人指出,去年的协议确有需要改进之处,如果道尹不愿修改,那么商讨也无甚意义,并表明若如此,本人将仅向总税务司申请批准征收江捐,不会接受联合委员会的任命。之后，新协议草案便完全按照本人建议之改动拟订，但如今为了遵循"形式"上的一致，仍然包含大量无用（又无益）的条款和措辞。道尹应会尽快发来新协议的终稿，以便本人将其中与航标有关的部分译成俄文，交与苏方。

然而，黑龙江江面已开始融化，如今过江颇为艰难，部分地区水深三英尺。中俄双方能否继续商议，尽早签订协议，还难以确定。

苏方于最初的协议草案中意欲让中方投入全部税收，但对苏方工作和支出的监督规定却十分宽松。本人已将此提议驳回。不过，苏方目前缺少资金，极有可能会接受中方的各项条款，俄阿穆尔水道局的职员已有三个月（1月至3月）未领到薪水。

为布拉戈维申斯克局势事：当地依然在实行高税率。新任俄水运局总督办马尚德（Marchand）先生在与本人的一次会谈中，曾表示这样的税率"着实愚蠢"。苏联贸易公司（政府贸易机构）已经基本垄断当地市场（迄今为止还未有准单签发给其他个人或机构），布拉戈维申斯克的生活成本因此大幅增加，尽管走私活动仍在继续。当地所有商业活动都已停止，华岸亦鲜有贸易往来，苏联贸易公司已从本地一名俄籍商人手中买入物资，主要是布匹，该名商人吹嘘自己已将无法卖给他人的货物全部卖给了该公司。据了解，该名俄籍商人所言非虚，而且苏联贸易公司的代理人对于应购置哪类货物也是全然不知。此外，据悉职业联社（Professional Union）（红色组织）的代表在边境关闭前从一名华籍商人手中购置了一批货物，并额外索要了两张收据，一张价格较高用于向联社报销，另一张价格较低用于向苏联海关报税。如此看来，当地局势日益恶化，也就不足为奇了。

当地其他方面倒是有所好转，民众更加遵守秩序，铁路交通更加方便（只是哈巴罗夫斯克（Habarovsk）及其他地区的桥尚未修缮完毕，道路也亟待修缮），电报局也正常运转，可以向苏联其他地区，甚至欧洲其他国家发送电报，每个单词（如意大利或者英国）仅需28戈比，十分方便。当地货币极其紧缺，金卢布已不再流通，只剩下银卢布，但银卢布在使用过程中会被扣掉5%到10%（政府机构及海关等部门亦是如此）。远东银行对贷款征收的利息高达24%（每年），据俄水道局督办透露，如今已无法向切尔纳耶瓦（Chernayeva）及加林达（Jalinda）此等地区汇款，因为当地邮局连100银圆都无法凑齐。

俄阿穆尔水运局的官员希望当局可以取消进口禁令，修改税率，以促进下一航运季的航运工作，他们已开始为此做准备，届时很有可能会狠狠压榨中国公司，他们还在考虑从苏联本土通过斯列坚斯克（Stretensk）运输机制货物，但马尚德先生已坦承这一切都是妄想。

为维持保卫团的运营代收地方税捐事：不久前，瑷珲县知事和商会主席前来请瑷珲关代收地方税捐,以维持地方保卫团的运营,税率为货物价值的 0.5%,征收对象为进出口洋土各货,瑷珲关可以直接收税,也可以依据商会提供的各商行货物交易信息收税,以免漏征。本人回复,按照规定,海关无权征收地方税捐,但如果他们可以通过海关监督向中央政府提此建议,通过瑷珲关向总税务司提出申请,或许有实现之可能,并说明鉴于商会提供的信息可能涉及机密,因此不赞成如此操作,还指出由海关代收地方税捐将有诸多困难。例如,凡货物持有满洲特别免重征执照者,均不在海关征税之列。对此,他们称仅对抵达时应向海关缴纳关税之货物收税即可,本人指出,若如此,有约各国公民进出口之货物亦不在收税之列,因为按照条约规定,此类货物仅须向海关缴纳关税(包括运入内地时应纳的子口半税),不必缴纳地方税捐。本人已强烈建议他们在向上级汇报之前不要贸然做出决定,不要一意孤行。之后便再未听闻与此相关的消息,恐怕他们已呈报税务处,或者使用了更加卑劣的手段以达到目的,梁家屯分卡及地方税捐局之事就是前车之鉴。尽管税务处已下达指令,但地方税捐局还是未同意拆除其设立于前滩上的检查处,道尹兼海关监督也如往常一样未对海关提供帮助。

为将小黑河设为通商口岸事:小黑河是一座极小的村庄,位于大黑河下游数里处,与布拉戈维申斯克城市中心相对,如今与俄岸有大量走私往来,但因无码头,轮船难以停靠,如要修建,费用将会十分高昂,此外,村庄内陆濒临的河道即将干涸,或许可于村庄外部修建一处简易的船只泊地。

目前,地方当局计划将之设为通商口岸,业已任命一名委员,但具体区域还未确定。如果小黑河与大黑河一同成为通商口岸,此事或许还值得重视,但似乎这只是张作霖及地方当局的计划。实际上,商人对小黑河及其附近的土地倒是颇感兴趣,有几名俄籍商人甚至考虑在此地买入土地,以建立一个小型"殖民地"。兹认为,此次开埠纯属是地方(黑龙江省政府)上的行动。尽管听起来确实有些荒唐,但如果小黑河最终真的成为通商口岸,海关于此设立分卡将会更加容易,对走私活动的管控也将更加有效。

为对皮士垂(B. E. Pistruiloff)的指控事:另有一件小事需要汇报。一周前,皮士垂先生向超等外班关员汇报称,泽里格曼(Zeligman)先生已准备好入狱服刑,很快会前来撤回对其的所有指控,因为不希望其因被诬告而受到伤害。皮士垂先生并未说明从何处获得这一信息,但态度却非常肯定。当日上午,泽里格曼先生果然从布拉戈维申斯克来到海关,但到达后便径直走到超等外班关员办公室,皮士垂先生没有机会将其拦截,被询问后,泽里格曼先生否认有反悔之意,表示自己并不愚蠢,此前的所有指控均属实。两日前,泽里格曼再次找到超等外班关员,汇报称有一位名叫波波科夫(Popkoff)的先生(当地的无赖,与皮士垂先生私交甚笃）此前找到他,表示只要撤回对皮士垂先生的指控,便可获得500 银圆,但被其拒绝。本人已更加确信皮士垂先生确实有罪。

　　关员一切安好。

您真挚的

包安济

24. 包安济致包罗函

（第 30 号半官函）

S/O No. 30

Aigun/Taheiho 28th apr 23

Dear Mr. Bowra,

The negotiations with the Russians about a new Agreement
on Aids to Navigation have been progressing rather slowly, the fault this time laying principally with the Taoyin, and
his Adviser on Foreign Affairs, who is a ridiculous extract
of Young China of the most pretentious and ignorant type.
As reported, I presented to the Taoyin the draft Rules for
Navigation on the Amur prepared by the different Boards, and
transmitted to this Office in your S/O of 24th May, 1922.
I intended these rules to be a guide to the Taoyin in case
the Russians brooched with him the question of Navigation on
the Sungari, etc, which they had hinted at in conversations
with me. The Russians, however, were apprised in the meantime
of the fact that a Conference in Peking was being prepared,
and they did not bring up for discussion the general subject of
Navigation on the Frontier Rivers, the Sungari, and the Amur to
the sea; but the Taoyin, having grasped the idea, did not
want to let go of it, and accordingly has insisted that the
Draft Rules be entered in toto in the Agreement on "Aids".
He even added an article saying that steamer could in no
case be confiscated, even for debts or for other reasons
involving a lawsuit. This I had a hard time in persuading
him to withdraw, as contrary to all accepted laws and principl
a steamer being a property like another, having even special
obligations, as, e.g. in the case of salaries to the Crew,

Entered in Gen. Index.   which

which are a first lien on ships, according to Russian (and
European generally) law. - The technical part of the Agreement I discussed with the representatives of the Russian
Navigation Office and Water Transports, and, after a sitting
of about 9 hours, the whole matter was practically settled.
- I hope I can send one of these days the final proposed text for your approval. - But it was quite different for
the general Articles concerning shipping, which the Russian
Delegates said they were unable to discuss. The Taoyin's
first decision was that the Agreement had to be signed
in toto, or nothing. I had a bothersome time in persuading
him that the Agreement is more beneficial to China, even
restricted to the upkeep of the Aids only, than to Russia:
that, if China shares in the upkeep for a few years, she will
be able to claim rights of joint property of the Aids;
that China's abstention may furnish Russia a pretext for rever-
ting to her old policy of excluding Chinese ships from
the Amur: that, if China does not collect the River Dues,
Russia will, on all international trade at least. In the
meantime I obtained from the Russians that they apply for Telegraphic instructions from Moscow, which they did: but the
result was that Moscow directed to let all matters not of
a purely technical matters for discussion at the Conference
which is being prepared. The Taoyin was, lately, presudded of
the soundness of my arguments, and said he would wire to
the Boards concerned asking whether they would allow of the
signature of a technical Agreement only. If the reply is
in the affirmative, as I hope, it will be easy to compile
the

the definitive text of the Technical Agreement between the
Customs and theRussian Authority. In order to avoid the
rediscussion of the Agreement at the beginning of each
Season, I have succeeded in introducing a clause by which,
if the Agreement is not denounced by the end of December,
it will be automatically in force for next year.

Blagovestchensk : No change in the general conditions :lif
very dear, and little activity. I am informedthat seeds , espe
cially in the case of wheat, are very scarce : in places not
onetenth of the normal amount is available,and it is said
that farmers are eating them. On 5th instant the Techni
cal school was totally destroyed by fire. - Traffic across
the River has been difficult the whole month: a few contrabandists have sunk, in their many attemptsat crossing outside
Harbour Limits.

Tax in support of the Pao Wei Tuan. This has been enforced
by theChamber of Commerce for the last month, without the
required help fromthe Customs:I am told the results are rather
meagre : less than 500 dollars for the whole period.

News of Mr, Hedgeland I have received yesterday, from
Shanghai: thank you very much for the instructions given to
him to travel by the quickest route' However, especially if
he knows no russian, he won't be ableto travel by the Railway,
which is quite in good order between Habarovsk and Vladivostock, but not quite advisable between Habarovsk and Blagove-
stehhansk, according to latest reliable reports.

Yours truly,

第 30 号半官函   1923 年 4 月 28 日于瑷珲关／大黑河

尊敬的包罗先生：

　　与苏方协商新航路标志协议的进展极其缓慢，主要原因在于道尹及其外交顾问。其外交顾问为人狂妄自恃，无知愚蠢，可笑至极。

　　如此前所报，本人已将总税务司 1922 年 5 月 22 日半官函所附之由各部草拟的黑龙江航行条例草案抄件交与道尹翻阅，原希望如果苏方代表在协商中提出其轮船于松花江上航行一事，道尹可据此条例所列与之应对。因为苏方代表此前与本人会面时曾谈及此事，但如今他们得知中苏两国政府正在筹备于北京召开会议，便未于地方协商会议中提出界河、松花江及黑龙江至入海口一段的航行问题。然而，道尹因已了解此事，不愿就此放弃，坚持要将黑龙江航行条例草案之内容全部载入"航路标志"协议中，甚至还要附加一条，规定无论出于何种原因，均不得扣留或没收轮船，既使因债务或其他原因遭到起诉，亦不例外。但此规定有违所有公认的法律及原则，因为轮船与其他财产一样，需要履行专门的义务，例如按照苏联（以及欧洲大部分国家）的法律，船员薪俸的支付优先享有扣押轮船之权利。为此，本人已劝服道尹将此项条款撤回，不过过程着实艰难。

　　协议中的技术部分，主要由本人与俄阿穆尔水运局及水道局的代表商议，经过大约 9 个小时的会谈后，所有技术问题已基本解决。希望可以尽快将协议终稿呈交阁下审批。

　　但对于协议中的航运部分，苏方代表表示无权讨论，而道尹最初则坚持仅签署完整协议（即包括航运及航标两部分内容）。本人遂劝谏道尹，协议实际上更利于中国，即使仅签署航标维护协议，亦是如此，因为中国与苏联合维护边界河道航路标志数年后，便有权将航路标志认领为联合财产，但如果中国放弃此次合作，苏方就将有理由再次禁止中国船只于黑龙江上航行，而且如果中国不征收江捐，苏方将对所有国际贸易征收江捐。

　　另一方面，苏方代表告知他们已向莫斯科方面发去电报请求指示，但得到的回复是所有非技术性问题均须留待即将于北京召开的会议上解决。近日，道尹终于认同本人所述的确合理，并表示会向各部发送电报请示能否仅于地方签署单纯的技术协议。希望可以得到肯定答复，届时便可由中国海关与苏方确定最终的技术协议文本。为避免每年航运季之前都需重新讨论协议内容，本人已成功加入一项条款，规定如果双方未于 12 月底前废止协议，协议将于次年自动继续生效。

　　为布拉戈维申斯克（Blagovestchensk）事：当地总体局势并未有何变化，只是生活成本颇高，贸易往来又很少。据悉，当地农作物种子稀缺，尤其是小麦，部分地区的农民可以买到的种子仅有往年的十分之一。据称，是因粮食短缺，农民只能依靠吃种子为生。本月6日，当地一所技术学校发生火灾，房屋损毁严重。这一个月来，过江运输一直十分艰难，有几艘走私船试图于港口界限外过江，但屡屡失败，最终沉船。

为维持保卫团的运营征收地方税捐事：上个月商会开始强制收税，但并未寻求瑷珲关帮助，据悉，收税结果并不乐观，截至目前所收税额还不足 500 银圆。

昨日已收悉贺智兰（R. F. C. Hedgeland）先生自上海来此的消息，感谢阁下指示其由最快的路线来至瑷珲关。不过，贺智兰先生不懂俄文，恐怕无法乘坐火车。据最新可靠报告，哈巴罗夫斯克（Habarovsk）至符拉迪沃斯托克（Vladivostock）一段的铁路沿线治安较好，但至布拉戈维申斯克一段并不安全。

您真挚的

包安济

25. 包安济致包罗函

（第 31 号半官函）

No. 31.

Aigun/Taheiho 8th May, 23.

Dear Mr. Bowra,

I have reported officially on the negotiations on theAgreement for upkeep of Aids to Navigations. I hope that this will be concluded before my departure, but things have been dragging along in a regrettable way, and we are bound to lose much good Collection, anyhow. - I have ascertained in the meantime that the prohibition to chinese steamers calling at Russian Ports, which was communicted, officially, to the Taoyin some two months ago, only applies to purely Russian Ports, like Habarovsk, not Blagovestchensk, which is on frontier waters: it is a retaliation against the prohibition to navigate the Sungari, enforced against Russian steamers flying the Red flag. - The Russian Water Transpots is planning an extensive exploitation of the Amur this year : they will have the transport of the goods seized at Egersheld, from Habarovsk to Stretensk : in addition, they are negotiating with the Wut'ung Co., which would, if the agreement is reached, transport beans and cereals from Sansing (and Fukochin) to Lahasusu, whence the Russian steamers would transport it to Habarovsk, to proceed by rail to Vladivostock. This arrangement would deprive the C.E.Ry of

M, A, V. Bowra, Esquire,
    Officiating Inspector General of Customs,
        P e k i n g,   Entered in Card-Index.

of much valuable cargo, and give much work, both ways, to the Ussouri Railway. - The Wut'ung Co. however has not concluded yet: they ask for 5 cents a pood, while freights are extremely low this year, at least for a beginning. I hear that the Water Transports did not receive the money they were expecting from Moscow, and they will havedifficulties in running their Boats. - In the meantime the Officers and crews of private steamers, all belonging to a Labour Union (which is not tolerated for the crews and Captains of Government Boats) have presented demands for increase in wages, for an eight hours' day, and for the presence of apprentices, paid, but doing no work, on each steamer, according to the complement of crew. The owners say they won't be able to compete with Government vessels, and will have to dismantle their steamers : the crews threaten a strike - so that there seems to be a little ray of hope for the chinese steamers after all. Possibly the discontent is stirred also by the Government Fleet (Water Transports), who had to give up their plan of a syndicate between Government Steamers and private Vessels. - It appear that the Water Transports, on their side, are reducing the wages by something like 50 %. - There is practically no freight for Taheiho: grains are ready for exportation at Chikota, which place should be watched with a view to establishing a Barrier. For Nikolaievsk there are several thousand poods off Potatoes, and still more poods flour.

Opening

135

Opening of the River. The ice only started moving on
April
29th, but it was three days before it cleared away from
Taheiho. Then exceptionally heavy ice drifts began, in quick
succession, and at the time of writing the ice is still
flowing. Very late season, on the whole. But there is an
abnormal volume of water. It appears as if Mr. Hedgeland,
who, according to a telegram, left Harbin on the 5th, will not
be able to arrive before the 15th. The Wut'ung Co. informed
that on the 4th, already, two of her steamers from Harbin
had reached Lahasusu and were waiting for the Amur to be
free of ice !

Mines. The reported discovery of mines on the Fapila
River, some 180 li from Taheiho, seems to prove very
remunerative. Approximately 2,500 miners are already on the
spot, and labour is very scarce now in Taheiho. Another
concession is reported for a gold mine in the Lope
(漠北) District.

Native In-Door Staff. I have been approached by the
Assistant and Clerks who would like to petition you on the
subject of their stay in this Port. They would like to be
put on the same footing as Clerks and Assistants who serve
in Yunnan (Mengtze, Szemao, Tengyueh), who are allowed to
apply for transfer after three years' stay. While, however,
their colleagues serving in the Ports of Yunnan and, I
think, Lungchow, are also given one promotion on appointment
and one on retransfer, the Native In-door Staff in Taheiho
only limit their demand to the length of stay. They
state,

state, in support of their demand, that Taheiho is a less
agreable residence than places in Yunnan, on account of the
extreme cold weather, of the very high cost of life,
of the difficulty in transports, of the expenses entailed
by procuring furs and heavy garments, on account of the
difficulty of bringing families up here, with the dangers
of attack by pirates and the uncongenial environmment ;
on account of the total lack of educational facilities, not
only in the District, but at any place within a reasonable
distance. Formerly, there were special allowances: but now
that these have been abolished, there is no advantage and
many disadvantages to a long stay in this Port. All these
arguments are without reply, and I am of opinion that
the right of applying for transfer after three years'
stay is not too great a privilege in exchange for the
hardship endured while here by all Native In-Door Staff,
except the natives of Manchuria. I must add that very few
people, outside the Customs, dare bring their families here: that
even ordinary unskilled labourers gather enough money after
three years to pay a visit of several months to their home
in Shantung or elsewhere, during the dead season.

The Staff has asked my advice on the best way of
approaching you: I have told them that it would be best
if I first asked your opinion semi-officially. And I should
therefore be obliged if you would let me know whether you have
any objections to an official petition to you from the
concerned.

Yours truly,

第 31 号半官函   1923 年 5 月 8 日于瑷珲关/大黑河

尊敬的包罗先生：

已呈文正式汇报中苏联合维护航路标志协议的协商事宜,希望协议可于本人调任之前签订。遗憾的是,此事一直拖延未决,瑷珲关亦将因此损失大量税收。

可以确定的是,苏联当局禁止中国船只在其港口停靠之规定(已于约两月前正式告知道尹)仅适用于纯粹的苏联港口,如哈巴罗夫斯克(Habarovsk),而界河上的港口,如布拉戈维申斯克(Blagovestchensk)并不受此禁令限制。苏联此举是为应对中国政府禁止其船只悬挂红旗于松花江上航行之规定的报复行为。

俄阿穆尔水运局希望今年能够充分利用黑龙江运输货物,不仅计划将在埃格谢尔德(Egersheld)扣押的货物自哈巴罗夫斯克运至斯列坚斯克(Stretensk),还计划与戊通公司合作运输大豆及谷物。目前双方还在协商阶段,若达成协议,将由戊通公司负责从三姓(及富克锦)运输大豆及谷物至拉哈苏苏,再由苏联轮船运至哈巴罗夫斯克,最后经铁路运至符拉迪沃斯托克(Vladivostock)。若如此,中东铁路将失去大量宝贵的货物运输,而乌苏里铁路的双向运输工作都将大大增加。不过,双方还未达成共识,戊通公司要求的运费为每普特 5 分,但预计今年货运量会非常少,至少初期会是这样。

据悉,俄阿穆尔水运局未能如预期从莫斯科获得拨款,今年的船只运营工作将会十分艰难。另一方面,私营轮船的职员和船员已要求涨薪,而且每日仅工作八小时,船员还提出,每艘轮船上如果有学徒,即使没有工作,亦须支付薪水;私营轮船的职员和船员均隶属于工会,但政府船只的船长和船员并不允许加入。私营船主均称无法与政府船只竞争,日后或将被迫停止运营,卖掉轮船。船员已开始威胁将发动罢工;如此看来,中国船只似乎有望迎来新的商机。苏联国家舰队(水运局)已被迫放弃组建政府轮船和私营船只联合会的计划,船员的不满或许亦与此有关。看来水运局将减少 50% 的薪水支出。

如今几乎已无货物运往大黑河,谷物已准备于奇克特直接出口,应视察此地是否适合设立海关分卡。现有数千普特马铃薯运往尼古拉耶夫斯克(Nikolaievsk),面粉的货运量更大。

为黑龙江开江事:4 月 29 日,冰面开始移动,三日后冰块才开始自大黑河向下游漂流,随后大块浮冰开始不断从上游漂流而下,至今还未停止。今年开江的时间整体较晚,但是水量较大。贺智兰(R. F. C. Hedgeland)先生似乎无法于 5 月 15 日之前抵达瑷珲关,据电报称其已于 5 月 5 日离开哈尔滨。据戊通公司报,其有两艘自哈尔滨出发的轮船已于 5 月 4 日抵达拉哈苏苏,现正在等待黑龙江上的冰块完全消融后再继续航行。

为矿产事：此前有报告称，距大黑河 180 里的法别拉河附近发现矿产，如今来看蕴藏量颇丰，现已开采约 2500 个矿井，大黑河地区的劳工已十分紧缺。此外，萝北地区也汇报发现金矿。

为华籍内班关员事：华籍帮办和同文供事希望就他们于本口岸的任职时间向阁下请愿。他们希望与云南省各口岸（即蒙自关、思茅关和腾越关）的华籍帮办和同文供事一样可于任职满三年后申请调职。而且，云南省各口岸及龙州关的华籍帮办和同文供事还可得享一次调职晋升及一次重新调任的机会，而大黑河口岸的华籍内班关员仅对在此地的任职时长有所要求。为此，他们还指出与云南相比，大黑河的居住环境要糟糕很多。这里冬季极度寒冷，生活成本极高，交通条件极差，冬季还要为购买皮毛和厚重衣物增加支出，而且由于匪患猖獗，环境不适宜，教育资源不足（不仅仅是瑷珲关区，附近所有地区皆是如此），关员无法携带家眷到此任职。此前海关还为他们发放特殊津贴，但如今已经取消，长期在瑷珲关任职已是毫无优势可言。

兹认为，华籍内班关员（满洲籍华籍关员除外）在本地的艰苦环境下工作三年后提出调职申请并不过分，得享此权利亦称不上是获得优待。必须指出，除瑷珲关的关员，没有人愿意把家人带到此地生活；即使是没有任何技能的劳工在此地工作三年，积攒了足够的钱款后，都会在工作淡季返回山东省（或其他省份）老家休息数月。

华籍帮办和同文供事询问应如何向阁下请愿，已告知最好先由本人以半官方的形式向代理总税务司征询意见。故此请示，是否同意关员发送正式请愿书。

您真挚的

包安济

26. 包安济致包罗函

（第 32 号半官函）

.32.

Aigun/Taheiho 31st May, 23.

Dear Mr. Bowra,

Mr. Hedgeland has arrived on the 18th, and I am going to hand over to him this evening. I am afraid I will be another fortnight befor I can leave this place but then I hope to be able to travel at full speed, so as to reach Peking before the end of June.

I am sorry I cannot leave a clean desk to my succcessor : the Agreement on Aids is not concluded yet, and that is the main affair in suspense. But now the Taoyin has once more changed his mind, and he has asked the superior Authorities (so he says) to have an Agreement signed on the lines of last year's. - It is a pity that there should be so much delay, but I believe an Agreement will be signed in the end.

Things, unhappily, are going from bad to worse in Siberia, or at least in the Amur Province. Quite recently, 75 houses, the best in Blagovestchensk were "municipalised" (the name changes, the trick is always the same), after the owner had been made to repair them and pay taxes, in certain instances for 2 years.- Great excitement in Blagovestchensk over the British Memorandum :

demonstrations

oon .A. V. Bowra, Esquire,
la   Of . Inspector General of Customs,
                    Peking.   Entered in Card-Index

demonstrations have been held, in which the bourgeoisie has been bitterly denounced, and Moscow has been encouraged to hold out to the last man, to make war on England, etc : The demonstrations have generally ended in subscriptions for the Ruhr, etc etc. On the 18th , and on the night of the 23rd alarms were raised by the steamers in harbour whistling and bellowing for nearly one hour, the troops going out and surrounding the city; it has been a sort of trial of strength. It is difficult to say why the Reds are nervous, but nervous they are, beyond doubt. There are "partisans" in the Oussouri, but they are the same that harassed the Whites, and are now dissatisfied because they were not paid by the Reds: only a few white officers have left Manchuria for the Oussouri, according to information: the source of nervousness in Blagovestchensk must be found elsewhere, perhaps in the question of the British Memorandum, although why it should affect this far-away district, I cannot understand. One night, the Ferry has been kept all night under pressure, with full complement on board. Finally, now the Russians will no longer recognise the passes issued by the Taoyin for crossing the Frontier, and insist on visa by their representative in Taheiho; lately, no Russian has been allowed to leave Blagovestchensk.

Russian steamers have had to undergo very complicated formalities regarding their crews, not only in Blagovestchensk, but in Habarovsk: consequently no
                                    russian

russian vessels have come to the Chinese side until
to-day, and they lost their time at anchor on the
russian side, since the navigation opened on the 12th.

To the havoc produced by the Red Admnistration,
nature has added floods, which have swept most of the
towns along the Zeya and Selemja: the waters have
covered not only towns, but fields, the crop being lost,
of course; they have carried away the firewood and
timber already prepared for traffic on the River Banks,
they have destroyed houses and houses. A famine is very
much to be dreaded, and it is perhaps to the general
discontent that the nervous feeling of the Bolsheviks is
due : signs would point, once more, to a turn in the
tides, through it is difficult to say who is pulling
the wires, this time : perhaps the attitude of the foreign
Powers, less supine recently, encourages malcontents to
fight the Red Government.

Trade is almost nil: steamers have no cargo : only
a few passengers move along the River. The Russian frontier is closed tight, and contraband has not the same
facilities as in the Winter. A change must come soon,
one way or the other: either the Reds are overthrown,
or they settle down once more and resume trading.

In the meantime, life on the Russian side has become
intolerable.

Yours truly,

J. Foch.

第 32 号半官函   1923 年 5 月 31 日于瑷珲关 / 大黑河

尊敬的包罗先生：

贺智兰（R. F. C. Hedgeland）先生已于 5 月 18 日抵达大黑河，本人将于今晚与其交接工作，但恐怕还需要两周时间才能离开此地。希望届时可以最快的速度前往北京，以便于 6 月底之前抵达。

遗憾的是未能于离开瑷珲关之前完成所有工作；航路标志协议还未签订，此为现阶段最无法确定之事。如今道尹再次改变主意，声称已向省政府申请续签去年的航路标志协议。此事拖延许久，着实令人遗憾，但相信最终还是会成功签署。

为布拉戈维申斯克（Blagovestchensk）事：西伯利亚地区，或者至少是阿穆尔省的局势日益恶化。近日，布拉戈维申斯克最好的 75 间房屋被划归"市有"（只是换了名头，实际上还是"征用"）。在此之前，当地政府还要求房主对房屋进行修缮，缴纳税款，有些房屋甚至缴纳了两年的税款。当地民众对英国通牒 [①] 的反映十分强烈，已游行示威，严厉谴责资产阶级，鼓励莫斯科政府坚持一致对外，向英国宣战等，示威活动最终以为鲁尔（Ruhr）区捐款等事而结束。

5 月 18 日及 23 日晚，布拉戈维申斯克港口内的轮船纷纷鸣笛发出警报，持续将近一个小时，同时军队出动将城镇包围，此次行动为军事演习。虽不知红军当局为何紧张，但事实的确如此。乌苏里江流域倒是有一些"游击队"，不过他们此前也曾与白军对抗，只是因从未得到红军发放工饷，开始有不满情绪。但据悉，目前仅有数名白军官员离开了满洲前往乌苏里江流域。有鉴于此，红军当局的紧张必有其他原因，或许与英国通牒有关，只是此事何以会影响远东地区，着实令人费解。此外，有一日，渡船被滞留整晚，船上还装满了食物补给。

如今，苏方已不再承认道尹签发的过境小票，凡过境者，必须持有驻大黑河苏联代表签发的签证，最近，俄籍人已经不允许离开布拉戈维申斯克。

苏联轮船须为船员办理的手续非常复杂，布拉戈维申斯克，乃至哈巴罗夫斯克（Habarovsk）皆是如此。因此，虽然 5 月 12 日航运便已开通，但苏联船只因办理手续一直滞留俄岸，直至今日方有船只过江来至华岸。

[①] 英文为 British Memorandum，经查 1923 年 5 月苏俄处决了一名以宗教活动为掩护的英国间谍，并扣留了擅自闯入苏俄领海的英国渔船，英国就以此为借口于 5 月 8 日由外交大臣寇松向俄国发出最后通牒。根据时间推断，此处所述应为此事，故译为英国通牒。

除红军当局的迫害，当地还遭遇洪水侵袭，结雅河和谢列姆贾（Selemja）河沿岸的城镇多数受灾，村庄、农田皆被淹没，农作物损失惨重，堆放在江岸上准备运输的木桴和木料亦被冲走，房屋农舍连连被摧毁。如此看来，当地今年极有可能发生灾荒，布尔什维克党的紧张或许与民众普遍的不满情绪有关，种种迹象表明局势可能再次发生转变，只是不知此次转变的导火索会是何事，也许是外国政权对红军当局的态度。近来，外国政权对布尔什维克党的态度日趋强硬，对红军政府颇为不满的民众或许会因此起义暴动。

　　为贸易基本停滞事：黑龙江上虽有轮船往来，但并无货物可运，只有少量乘客。苏联边境已严密封锁，走私货物亦不再像冬季那般便利。相信局势很快会迎来转变，也许是红军政权被推翻，也许是红军政权再次迎来稳定并恢复贸易。

　　但在此期间，苏联百姓的生活极其艰难。

您真挚的

包安济

27. 贺智兰致安格联函

（第46号半官函）

S/O No. 46.   Aigun   27th. December 4

Dear Sir Francis,

The Taoyin's request for the Technical Adviser's attendance at the forthcoming Conference on Amur Aids to Navigation. (Aigun Nos. 193 and 198: I.G. No. 205).   The conclusion drawn by you after reading my despatch is that I adopted an unnecessarily unsympathetic attitude towards the Taoyin's request and that in view of the conditions obtaining I should have telegraphed to you for instructions.   I regret that I did not do so and that any uneasiness should have been created by my action as reported.   Between this office and the Tao Yin Kung Shu there has been no antagonism; on the contrary, there exists harmony and cooperation and the Taoyin's whole attitude negatives the suggestion that I have ever made myself in any way objectionable to him.

The proposal to establish a Joint Commission to control the frontier and inland waters of this district.   This proposal seems to have originated with

The Inspector General of Customs,
         Peking.

with Mr. Ch'ê Hsi-chên, Adviser on Foreign Affairs to the Taoyin and Manager of the local branch of the Bank of China.   It also appears to have found favour with some of the Bolshevist authorities at Blagovestchensk and if this is so the movement, so far as the Soviet people are concerned, may be said to have a political basis that is inherently plausible and is presumably one stage in the accomplishment of a deliberate plan for extending the influence of the Bolshevists by involving the Soviet in China's domestic affairs. I may add that Mr. Chebisheff, Director of the Amur Navigation Office, does not approve of the scheme.   He thinks that the prospect of so complicated an organisation being run with success is remote, and that from no point of view would it be an easy or particularly attractive policy for his own side.   He agrees with Mr. Ignatieff that Mr. Ch'ê shows a disposition to swallow a great change of system whole without sufficient question or examination.   Mr. Sedoroff, President of the Russian Water Transport Company, a political agent and Mr. Chebisheff's immediate chief, appears
                                          to

to agree with Mr. Ch'e that the scheme is feasible
and it may be that they are working together.
Mr. Ch'e is a very ambitious, but disappointed
man. Some of his friends who studied with him
at Petrograd are now holding lucrative appointments
in connection with the Chinese Eastern Railway and
Mr. Ch'e feels that he ought to be given something
good. Mr. Ch'e has now been appointed a
delegate to the Conference and, unless he changes
his mind in the meanwhile, he will be likely to
take advantage of his position as such to argue
that China's interests would best be served by
submitting to this complicated and debatable administrative change. I have accordingly thought
it prudent to inform the Taoyin verbally of the
Technical Adviser's conclusion on this point which
is to the effect that the establishment of a
Board as suggested would not be to China's advantage; that Joint Control on the lines proposed
would unquestionably mean a sacrifice of freedom;
and that for all the risks and probable increase
in our total expenditure there would appear to
be no compensation. I know nothing about the
Chinese Eastern Railway, but I have the impression
that

that the method of control in force is marked
by a systematic elimination of Chinese influence.
It is impossible to say whether or not the
Taoyin has accepted Mr. Ch'e's recommendation in
principle, but even supposing he has done so it
is to be hoped that his views will not be
listened to if expert opinion at this end and
at Harbin succeeds in showing that the main
objection to the plan lies in the fact that it
would make China the direct instrument of a
policy which is entirely opposed to her own
interests. Mr. Ignatieff, so I am given to
understand, is to be opposed at the Conference
by a Mr. Stouris, who served under him in former
days at Blagovestchensk. This man is well-known
in this district as a mob orator, a leading
communist, and a mischievous person. He drank
his way out of his appointment as Director of
the Russian Amur Water Transport and is now retained by the Bolshevist authorities for any odd
job that may turn up. Being a most fluent
speaker, he is regarded as a powerful force. A
great

great amount of preliminary work is now being
done by the Technical Adviser to equip his side
with material for the negotiations and I understand that the case for the Russian side has
also been prepared in its essential features.

**The attitude of the Chinese and Soviet Authorities
towards Mr. Ignatieff, Technical Adviser on Amur
Aids to Navigation.** Mr. Ignatieff has a great
deal to show for his labours, but his task is
a most difficult one for he has to do his work
in the face of a great deal of distrust and
opposition. Some time ago attempts were made
locally to belittle the value of his services to
the Customs. It was thought in Chinese circles
that a Russian-speaking Chinese engineer would be
able to play just as important a part in the
efficient execution of a Technical Adviser's duty
as does Mr. Ignatieff, and there were even those
to be found who insinuated that being Russian Mr.
Ignatieff was bound to be anti-Chinese. The
Soviet authorities have always exhibited towards
Mr. Ignatieff a marked prejudice and personal animus
because they recognise that he is on the other
side

side and busy protecting our pockets against
depredation. Recently there has been an under-
current of better feeling on the part of the
Chinese, and the Taoyin now professes to recognise
the measure of industry and thoroughness that Mr.
Ignatieff brings to the work he undertakes and to
concur in the view that his withdrawal would leave
us without any protecting hand in which to place
our trust. He knows that the estimates prepared
at Blagovestchensk have been on the extravagant
side and that if the local agreement has worked
well, and this it certainly has done, it is because Mr. Ignatieff has been able to effect economies
and take responsibilities. A technical adviser of
Chinese nationality would be easily bamboozled by
the Bolshevists and, of course, it was to avoid
being stung that a comparatively highly paid position
was created. The Soviet people on the other side
of the river are not very friendly to Mr. Ignatieff.
I think that they must resent his intimate knowledge of local facts and the skilful use he makes
of them. They attempt in a half-hearted manner
to disguise their hostility, but really they regret
their

C
C

their inability to subject him to political pressure
and bias of class. If he were to vacate his
appointment in the Customs, it would not be safe
for him to cross the frontier. His freedom would
be short-lived. From some of the Russians with
whom he works, e.g. Mr. Chebisheff, Director of the
Amur Navigation Office, Mr. Feodoroff, his assistant,
and Mr. Schoukin, River Inspector, Mr. Ignatieff
obtains a generous support, but with Mr. Sedoroff,
President of the Russian Water Transport Company,
and Mr. Chebisheff's immediate chief, he finds it
not at all easy to get on. Mr. Sedoroff is a
rabid communist, and a sly, suspicious, and un-
sociable person.

The abolition of the Liangchiat'un Barrier. The officer
formerly in charge of this barrier has been doing
patrol work here, but I have now come to the conclusion that the staff is larger than is required
and I am about to recommend the withdrawal of one
junior officer.

The personal effects of the late Baron von Grot. There
is now a Russian consul at this port and I await
your further instructions.

        Yours truly,

第 46 号半官函   1924 年 12 月 27 日于瑷珲关

尊敬的安格联先生：

　　为道尹邀请航务专门顾问参加即将召开的黑龙江航务会议事（参阅瑷珲关致海关总税务司公署第 193 号及 198 号呈。海关总税务司公署致瑷珲关第 205 号令）。阁下看过呈文后认为，本人本不必对道尹之要求采取否定的态度，而且在当时的情况下应当先向阁下发送电报申请指示。对于未能如此办理以及因此而造成的不便，深表歉意。不过，瑷珲关与道尹公署之间从未产生过敌对之意，恰恰相反，一直是在和谐共事。从道尹的态度可以看出，本人之行为从未令其有过任何的不快。

　　为提议成立联合委员会以管理边境及瑷珲关区内陆水域事：该提议似乎由道尹公署外交顾问兼中国银行大黑河支行经理车席珍先生提出，而且似乎也得到了布拉戈维申斯克（Blagovestchensk）布尔什维克当局一些官员的支持。若果真如此，就苏联官员而言，支持成立联合委员会很有可能只是一种巧言令色的政治手段，是通过干涉中国内政事务来扩大布尔什维克主义在中国的影响力的一个渠道。不过值得一提的是，俄阿穆尔水道局督办且比索夫（Chebisheff）先生却并不支持此提议。其认为，联合委员会这样的机构过于复杂，难以成功运转，而且于苏方而言，此事从任何角度来看都不会易于达成，亦不具有特别的吸引力。其与易保罗（P. I. Ignatieff）先生皆认为，车席珍先生提出这一主张时，并未考虑周全，亦未做过调查。但且比索夫先生的直属上级，俄阿穆尔水运局局长西多霍夫（Sidoroff）先生似乎赞同车席珍先生的提议，而且此二人很有可能已经开始合作。

　　车席珍先生虽然胸有大志，但做事的结果往往都会令人失望，如今其因见曾一起在彼得格勒留学的几位友人都在中东铁路相关部门任职，且薪水丰厚，故认为自己也应有所成就。车席珍先生现已被任命为会议代表，如果其未改变主意，定会利用职务之便在会议上主张成立联合委员会是于中国而言最为有利的决策。所以本人认为，为慎重起见，最好当面告知道尹，航务专门顾问分析后认为成立联合委员会对中国并无益处，与苏联合管辖边境意味着中国的自由将受到侵犯，而且中国方面将承受的风险及可能增加的支出似乎也不会得到相应的补偿。至于中东铁路，虽不了解具体情况，但依本人之见，其内部现行的管理办法就是要逐步削弱中国当局的影响力度。只是不知道尹是否已在原则上接受了车席珍先生的提议。但即便如此，相信只要瑷珲关及哈尔滨关的专业意见能够让各方明晰，成立联合委员会不但无法为中国带来益处，反而会使中国沦为苏联当局的政治工具，因此才会有反对意见,此提议最终便不会被接受。

据悉,在即将召开的航务会议上,易保罗先生很有可能会遭到其此前在布拉戈维申斯克工作时的一名下属的阻扰。此人名为斯图里斯(Stouris),是一名共产主义要员,善于演说,经常招惹是非,在本地区的名声非常不好;据称此前已被任命为俄阿穆尔水运局督办,但因长期酗酒又被撤职,现被布尔什维克当局留任负责各种杂事;此番作为苏方代表出席会议,相信以其能言善辩之能力,定会成为中方强有力的对手。

航务专门顾问已开始为会议的谈判工作做准备,整理出了大量资料以支持其观点。另据悉,苏联方面业已为此次会议做了充分准备。

为中苏两国政府对黑龙江航务专门顾问易保罗先生的态度事:易保罗先生的辛勤工作虽已卓有成效,但在工作过程中总是要面对华人的不信任和俄人的反对,着实艰难。前段时间,地方上还有人试图贬低其为海关所做工作的价值。本地华人大多认为,华籍工程师如果会讲俄文,也同样能够担任航务专门顾问这一要职,而且能够与易保罗先生一样高效;甚至有人暗示,易保罗先生既为俄籍人,定会有反华倾向。而苏联政府方面则因认为易保罗先生站在其对立位置,总是帮助中国政府免受财物损失,而对其始终抱有偏见,充满敌意。不过,华人方面的态度近日已稍有好转,就连道尹都坦承,易保罗先生工作勤恳,细致入微,除其之外,再无可以信任的航务专家。

易保罗先生可以看出布拉戈维申斯克方面制定的预算过高,与实际不符,而且地方协议能够顺利执行亦全赖其在控制预算方面的能力和勇于承担责任的魄力。如果由华人担任航务专门顾问,恐怕很容易就会被布尔什维克当局所蒙骗,但当初设定这一高薪职位,就是为了避免被布尔什维克当局欺骗。而黑龙江对岸的苏联当局对易保罗先生极不友好,相信也一定是因为知道其熟知当地情况,而且还能够有效利用,所以感到愤愤不平。他们一直试图以冷淡的方式掩饰内心的敌意,但却始终无法用政治压力和阶级歧视将其压垮。

于易保罗先生自身而言,如果不在海关任职,重返俄境将会十分危险,人身自由也将受到限制。与其工作有交集的苏联官员中,俄阿穆尔水道局督办且比索夫先生、其助手费奥多罗夫(Feodoroff)先生、俄巡江事务长肖金(Schoukin)先生等人均会对其给予慷慨支持,唯有俄阿穆尔水运局局长,且比索夫先生的直属上级,西多霍夫先生极难相处。西多霍夫先生是一名极端的共产主义者,生性狡猾多疑,且不爱交际。

为裁撤梁家屯分卡事:此前负责此分卡的关员现于大黑河口岸负责巡缉工作。经查,瑷珲关当前关员人数已超过所需,将呈文建议撤掉一名初等关员。

为已故男爵格鲁特（Von Grot）遗物事：大黑河口岸现驻有一名苏联领事，特此申请进一步指示。

您真挚的

贺智兰

28. 贺智兰致安格联函

（第 47 号半官函）

S/O No. 47.

CUSTOM HOUSE,

Aigun 26th. March 1925

Entered in Card-Index.

Dear Sir Francis,

The forthcoming Sino-Russian Conference. This
Conference is to open at Moukden on the 15th.
of next month and Mr. Ignatieff, Technical Adviser
and member of the Heilungkiang Special Advisory
Committee, left here this morning for Tsitsihar.
I have introduced him by despatch to the Harbin
and Moukden Commissioners and I have also given
him copy of your instructions as to the attitude
he is to adopt at the Conference and the nature
of the assistance he is to render. Of all the
people who attend this Conference from Heilungkiang
it is certain that Mr. Ignatieff more than any
can be depended upon to make prudent and workmanlike
contribution to the discussion of the various
questions which will arise concerning navigation on
the Amur and the Sungari, but if he comes into
intimate touch with Comrade-Commissars his position
will in all probability be a somewhat embarrassing
one.   The Chinese here, with one or two
                                        exceptions

Sir Francis Aglen, K.B.E.,

Peking.

exceptions, look for substantial benefits from the
Conference and in my opinion they are over-sanguine
of getting a good Treaty.   The Taoyin thinks
that Chinese merchants should be able to develop
trade with Russia. He sees no reason why results
should not be mutually beneficial and in this view
he is supported by Mr. Ch'ê Hsi-chên, Adviser for
Foreign Affairs and Chairman of the Special Advisory
Committee, and by Mr. Chêng Yen-hsi, Consul-General
at Blagovestchensk.   The Taoyin's argument is that
Russia's commercial relations with other countries
are fast improving and that there are grounds for
considering that the change for the better which is
noticeable is likely to become permanent.   This
is certainly not the experience of foreigners holding
gold-mining concessions in the districts on the other
side of the Amur beyond Blagovestchensk. I have
met a number of these people and they are all
loud in their complaints that they are never given
an opportunity to work their concessions in the
spirit in which they were granted. They protest
that the Soviet authorities are neither honest nor
sincere and that far from improving in their be-
haviour they are developing a progressively destructive
spirit and go out of their way to do all in
                                        their

their power to exasperate, irritate and embarrass.
The result has been the ruination of some under-
takings and if a few companies still hold on it
is because they have sunk their roots so deeply
that they have acquired what is almost a permanent
stake in the country.   An American mining engineer
who has been nearly ten years in this district
tells me that his company's business has become
hopelessly disrupted and that nothing but a smashing
counter-revolution will put it on its feet again.
He says that for years past production has been
very small and very costly and that any idea of
extension of business is utterly out of the
question.   It is interesting to note that there
is a divergence between the Taoyin's theory and
the views held by the Technical Adviser whose
conclusions in regard to probable results of the
Conference are not at all hopeful.   Mr. Ignatieff
argues that the import and export trade in Russia
being no longer left to private enterprise it will
be necessary before any transaction can be completely carried through by a Chinese merchant for
many departments of the Soviet Government to be
consulted and their approval obtained of prices
and conditions of sale.   He thinks that the
                                                    Chinese

Chinese merchant is certain to find the process of
overcoming all the obstacles that are placed in
his way both complicated and costly.   This argument seems very sound, for it is surely not unreasonable to suppose that a country which has
monopolized its foreign trade, eliminated the
middleman, and surrounded every commercial transaction
with red tape, will endeavour, by means of vexatious
commercial ordinances and oppressive taxes and
regulations, to arrange matters in such a manner
as to crush out effectively all competition on
the part of foreign (Chinese) shipping.   And
it also seems to me to be more than over-sanguine
to expect Chinese shipping to succeed in promoting
trade with a country which prevents its ordinary
citizen from acquiring capital and consequently makes
it impossible him for purchase articles either for
import or export.   In the conditions now obtaining
the only cargo available for Chinese vessels at
Russian ports would be the property of the Soviet
and it seems safe to assume that this will be
reserved for the vessels of the Russian Amur Water
Government Transport.   I submit that the Technical
Adviser is right when he says that the Taoyin and
                                                    Mr.

Mr. Ch'ê Hsi-chên draw wrong inferences and that the latter is going to have the shock of his career.

Yours truly,

第 47 号半官函 　　　　　　　　　　　　　　　1925 年 3 月 26 日于瑷珲关

尊敬的安格联先生：

为即将召开的中俄会议事：中俄会议将于 4 月 15 日在奉天召开,易保罗(P. I. Ignatieff)先生作为黑龙江航务专门顾问及黑龙江省特别顾问委员会(Special Advisory Committee)委员,已于今晨离开大黑河前往齐齐哈尔。本人已向哈尔滨关税务司和奉天关税务司发去公文说明易保罗先生的情况,亦已将阁下关于其在参加会议期间所应采取之立场及提供之帮助的令文抄件交与其本人。

相信在讨论黑龙江及松花江航运相关问题时,易保罗先生定会比其他几位黑龙江省参会代表都更值得信赖,更为谨慎,更能够提出专业性的意见。但如果其与苏联政治委员的关系过于亲密,恐怕处境将会略显尴尬。本地华人中绝大多数都希望能够通过此次会议获得切实利益,认为中俄双方可以签订一份互惠互利的条约,但恐怕这一想法过于乐观。道尹甚至认为,嗣后大黑河的华籍商人应该可以开始与俄岸开展贸易,相信此次谈判可以得到一个于双方皆为有利的结果。对此,其外交顾问兼特别顾问委员会主席车席珍先生及中国驻布拉戈维申斯克(Blagovestchensk)总领事郑延禧先生皆表示赞同。道尹有此观点,主要是看到苏联当局正在迅速改善与其他国家的经济关系,因此认为有理由相信这种明显向好的变化趋势将持续下去。

然而,那些已经获得在黑龙江俄岸布拉戈维申斯克以外地区开采金矿特权的外国人却并不这样认为。他们当中有很多人,本人都曾见过,几乎人人都在抱怨苏联当局并未按照约定给予他们使用开采特权的机会,指责苏联当局毫无诚信可言,非但没有改进此前的所作所为,反而利用职权变本加厉地惹恼他们,让他们陷入困境。结果导致一些正在开采的金矿被迫停工。如果还有一些公司仍在坚持,亦是因为投入过多,几乎已与这个国家永远捆绑在一起。一名在本地区工作了近十年的美国矿务工程师告诉本人,其公司的业务现已完全中断,只有进行一场彻底的反革命才能扭转局势,否则再无重新开始的希望;还透露最近几年的金矿产量极低,但开矿费用却极高,想要扩展业务,根本没有可能。

值得注意的是,与道尹所持观点不同,航务专门顾问易保罗先生对此次会议的结果并不抱有乐观态度。其指出,如今苏联私营公司已无权自行开展进出口贸易,华籍商人在实现交易之前,必须向苏联政府各有关部门报备,申请对货物价格及售卖条件的批准。其认为,在此过程中,华籍商人定会遇到种种阻碍,如要克服,亦须耗时耗资,极为复杂。此言论颇有道理,毕竟苏联政府已经垄断了对外贸易,消除了交易的中间商,并将本国所有商业往来都列入了统辖范围,因此面对外国(中国)船运的竞争,必定会以苛刻的商业法令、税则及章程作为手段来实现有效打压。依本人之见,苏联政府连其本国公民购买资产的权利都已剥夺,以致苏联商民根本无法购买商品开展进出口贸易,那么华籍商人若欲与之开展贸易,恐怕更是难以成功。依目前情况来看,华籍船只能够于苏联口岸载运之货物亦仅有苏联政府之财物而已,而这些货物,相信也都是要留给俄阿穆尔国家水运局的船只来运输的。

航务专门顾问还认为,道尹和车席珍先生的推论是错误的,此次会议之结果定会令车席珍先生颇感意外。对此本人表示赞同。

您真挚的

贺智兰

29. 裴德生致泽礼函

（第 51 号半官函）

CUSTOM HOUSE,

S/O No.51.   Aigun/Taheiho, 19th Nov., 192 5

UNSIGNED

Dear Mr. Stephenson,

Lahasusu. I left Lahasusu after an exceedingly busy summer due to the building operations which I am glad to report was practically completed prior to my departure except for a few paths and outdoor building items. One can hardly appreciate the many difficulties of building in an out-of-the-way place such as this unless one has had the experience. No local source for materials - stone from the Lower Amur, lumber from Taheiho and Upper Sungari, fixtures, etc., from Harbin, only bricks made locally, but by an outside brickmaker : no local labour - workmen from Harbin and a truculent lot to deal with : communications very irregular due to low water on the Sungari: and a short time limit due to climatic conditions. I believe the contractor and individuals directly concerned with the enterprise are hardly likely to forget the experience and will wish never to repeat it. Although I have no expert knowledge from which to

J.W.Stephenson,Esquire,

    Officiating Inspector General of Customs,

        Peking.

to speak, I think a very creditable piece of work has been done by the contractor and I hope that next season when the buildings are taken over by the Customs they will be found satisfactory and up to specifications.

The undeserved reputation of Lahasusu as an uncomfortable place in which to live should die. The housing offers everything that any member of the Staff could reasonably require and the extensive garden with its large grove of trees is most attractive. The drawbacks of the port, of course, remain the isolation, very uncomfortable steamer facilities, and the "hutzu" gauntlet down the Sungari and return. For those, however, in whom the adventurous spirit is not yet dead, these drawbacks are subject to discount.

Although Lahasusu is blessed with the absence of schools and the products of higher learning and thus escaped student activities to complicate the situation, not the least of our difficulties, somewhat similar in annoyance, was mosquitoes. What I tell you may sound incredible. So also was the number of mosquitoes last summer. Not a one in sight until the middle of August when the first heavy rains of the season

commenced.

commenced, and then they appeared from the water soaked
earth like a scourge. For a time the workmen refused
to work on the outside building programme. They couldn't.
The only remedy we had was smoke. The compound was
enveloped in an extensive smoke screen day after day from
fires built inside the houses and scattered about the
garden. After six in the evening it was impossible to
remain out-of-doors. Countrymen came to town with netting
around their heads : we wore it in wandering about the
compound: in front of the doors of our dwellings we
kept fires burning and stood in the smoke before entering
to drive the mosquitoes from our clothes : at night the
composite humming and buzzing of these insects sounded
through the windows like the whirr of distant machines.
River captains stated that in thirty years' experience
they had never experienced such a phenomenon. During the
last weeks of September, the mosquitoes gradually disappeared.

Taheiho. It was a pleasure to come to a place where
the good will and local attitude toward the Customs
seemed so genuinely friendly. This is largely due to the
charming personality of my predecessor and his generous
personality. I find entertaining by officials and merchants
here conducted on a lavish scale in spite of most dis-
                                            heartening

heartening business conditions. Whether or not such an
outward show of prosperity on their part is commendable
may be open to argument : that this practice of entertaining, however, on the part of a Commissioner here in
smoothing the path of diplomacy is advantageous seems
undeniable. I find it unfortunately impossible to follow
as far as I would like
/in the footsteps of my predecessor who drew a Commissioner's pay. Official dinners in this nook noted for its
W.C.L., including the obnoxious custom of tipping anywhere
from 20 to 24 "ma pien tzus" who accompany Chinese guests
as coachmen, visiting card dispensers, pistol carriers, coat-
hangers, and what-nots, are in the nature of financial
disasters.

    I find a very comfortable and well furnished house.
I appreciate it. I may mention in passing that this is
the sixth house in which I find myself and my belongings
in a period of less than a year : two houses in Harbin
due to a change of leases and three houses in Lahasusu
in order to accommodate myself to the building operations

Blagoveschensk. My predecessor has given such a full
picture of conditions that little need be added. Taheiho
is dead. Blagoveschensk is dead. The degree of "deadness"
is a matter for argument. I seem to see more hope in
Russia. However mad the present programme across the
                                            border

border may be, there at least is driving force on the part of a few people behind misguided activities: in Taheiho, the atmosphere everywhere is that of passivity and spineless aquiescence to conditions. Smuggling alone seems to keep the latter place alive apart from a little business with goldmines : smuggling from which the police, the military, the officials get their percentage and which the somewhat pitiful efforts of the Customs with a few miles of patrol fails signally to prevent. I intend to report shortly on this preventive and patrol activity if I may . My predecessor seemed to have found it very important : I seem at present, on the one hand,to see only a great expense swelling the large overhead costs of a Customs establishment unable to pay for its own existence, and, on the other, fail to see any great benefits compensating for such expense. One or the other of us must be wrong.

But to get back to Blagoveschenak. After calling on the local officials in Taheiho, I called with Mr. Ignatieff as interpreter on the Russian officials across the river. Some of them had the unmistakeable stamp of Hebraic origin : some seemed still to have the dirt of plowed fields and cattle encampments on their shoes
(figuratively

(figuratively speaking): one was a German or of German origin but he refused to converse with me in his mother tongue because, he explained, I was making an official call on a Russian official. Such a fine distinction of values may perhaps reveal an acute and penetrating intelligence. The Amur Navigation Office with whom it appears that I will have many dealings display-ed a greater percentage of men with intelligence than to be found in the other government departments. Taking them all in all, however, they were very cordial and friendly.

The day I crossed the river (21st October) seemed to herald in the rapid freezing over of the river. A sharp and furious gale from the north froze the spray splashing over the launch and our coats and hats in sheets of ice and icicles. The next day we pulled up the launch for the winter. Whereupon mild weather again set in which, although it prevented the river from freezing over, stopped communications because of floating ice for almost a month. The river eventually froze over on the 17th November, the latest date on record since 1903. Local weather prophets claim that the Japanese earthquake of two years ago has changed the
climatic

climatic conditions of large sections of Siberia. If
true, one can only wish that it might have been still
more accommodating and reduced our winter nights by
six hours.

          Yours truly,

第 51 号半官函　　　　　　　　　　　　　1925 年 11 月 19 日于瑗珲关/大黑河

尊敬的泽礼先生：

为拉哈苏苏事：今年夏季于拉哈苏苏口岸主事期间，一直忙于房屋修建工事。令人欣慰的是，在离开之前，除一些小路及室外建筑，均已完工。然此间所遇之困难，如非亲身经历，断然无法想象。因为拉哈苏苏情况较为特殊，建筑所需材料鲜有可于当地购买者。其中，石料选自黑龙江下游地区，木料选自大黑河及松花江上游地区，固定设施等选自哈尔滨，唯有用砖是由当地提供，而烧砖者又非专业人士。另外，当地并无劳工，所有工人皆须从哈尔滨雇用，十分不易管理；往来轮船受松花江低水位的影响，到达时间极不固定，而工期受气候影响又十分紧迫。凡此繁杂之事，不胜枚举。相信此次修建工事于直接参与其中的承包商及个人而言，必定会是一次难忘的经历，亦是不愿再有的经历。本人虽非专业人士，但从专业的角度来说，承包商所完成的工作质量应该是十分值得称赞的，希望明年航运季，海关接管时，房屋质量可令人满意，达到各项标准。

拉哈苏苏口岸一直被认为是不宜居住之地，但经过此番修建，相信不会再有此类评价。如今房屋内设施齐全，可以满足所有关员的合理需求，室外花园十分宽敞，还栽有茂密树丛，十分喜人。不过，此口岸仍有弊端存在，比如与外界隔离，往来轮船设施陈旧，搭乘时极不舒适，"胡子"（土匪）频繁往来当地与松花江下游之间，等等。然此等问题于仍有些冒险精神的人而言，均不甚紧要。

拉哈苏苏当地缺少学校，亦无受过高等教育之人，因此也无学生活动，但与这些情况相比，夏季出现的大量蚊子同样恼人。下文所述听起来或许有些骇人听闻，但今年夏季蚊子的数量也的确是令人难以置信。8 月中旬之前，并未有蚊子出现，不料一场暴雨过后，被水浸透的地面上开始涌现大量蚊子，如虫灾一般。工人甚至一度拒绝在户外进行工作，实际上，是无法工作。唯一能对付蚊子的办法只有烟熏。每日，无论是房屋内还是花园里，都需要生火，浓烟日日笼罩在海关大院的上空。每日傍晚 6 点过后，便无法于户外逗留。附近村民到镇上时，头上都会围着丝网。我们在大院内行走时，亦会效仿此法，进入住所之前，还需在门前一直点燃的火把旁站立片刻，以便让烟气将衣物上的蚊子驱走。夜间，窗外还会一直传来蚊虫的嗡鸣声，宛如远处有机器在嗡嗡作响一般。松花江上的老船长们都称三十年来从未遇见过此等现象。直到 9 月下旬，蚊子才逐渐消失。

为大黑河事：大黑河的官员及民众对待海关的态度看起来非常友好，这在很大程度上都是受到前任税务司的慷慨大度和人格魅力所影响。能够来此，倍感荣幸。不过，本地商业形势虽令人堪忧，但官商设宴款待本人的排场却依然很大。当然，他们如此显露财富的做法是否值得称赞，还有待商榷，但不可否认的是，此等宴请惯例的确有利于在本口岸任职的税务司促进与当地官商等的关系。然与前任税务司不同，本人领取的并非税务司薪俸，因此无力遵循此惯例行事。大黑河地处偏远，素来以生活成本过高著称，经常举行官宴，无疑会让自己陷入财务危机。而且中国宾客通常会有陪同跟随，他们负责驾车，分发拜帖，为雇主持枪拿衣，还会办理其他杂事。对于这些人，还需付给小费，这已是当地的一种习俗，着实令人厌恶。

税务司住所家具齐全，非常舒适，本人十分满意。顺便说明，这已是本人在不到一年时间之内居住的第六间房屋，在哈尔滨期间，由于租期变更，换了两处住所，在拉哈苏苏期间，为完成房屋修建工事，换了三处住所。

为布拉戈维申斯克（Blagoveschesk）事：关于当地之情形，瑷珲关前任税务司的汇报已经十分全面，于此无须补充。布拉戈维申斯克与大黑河都在经历着如死寂一般的萧条。但"萧条"到何种程度，还有待观察。不过在本人看来，苏联方面恢复的希望更大一些。因为无论当地政府现下推行的政策如何不明智，至少还有人在背后推动，而大黑河处处弥漫着消极的气息，面对现实的窘境，人人皆是低头屈服，毫无骨气可言。现下能够让大黑河保留些许生机的，除了一些金矿生意，便仅有走私一项。而警方、军方乃至地方官员皆会参与其中，并从中获利，因此即使海关日日巡缉数英里，亦完全无法阻止走私活动。关于针对走私活动的防御及巡缉工作，稍后将简要汇报。瑷珲关前任税务司似乎认为此事十分重要，但在本人看来，此项工作一方面只是在不断增加瑷珲关的管理经费，造成入不敷出的后果，另一方面又无法证明海关投入的资金能够有所收益。所以在这一问题上，前任税务司与本人之观点，必有一方存在不合理之处。

重新说回布拉戈维申斯克的情况。在拜访完大黑河地方官员后，本人便过江拜访苏联众官员，并请易保罗（P. I. Ignatieff）先生随行翻译。苏联官员中，有一些可以明显看出是希伯来人，有一些看起来似乎仍有耕种放牧时的样子（打个比方），还有一位应是德国人，或者至少是德裔，但在谈话中，其并不愿使用母语，并表示本人此次访问的是苏联官员，其自应以俄语交谈。此人既能如此坚守原则，相信亦会是敏锐透彻之人。另外，与其他政府部门相比，本人日后需要经常打交道的俄阿穆尔水道局中，有才智和学识者要更多一些。不过，总体来说，苏联官员皆颇为热诚友好。

本人于 10 月 21 日过江时，北风凛冽，汽艇驶过江面溅起水花后，皆会迅速结冰，而我们的衣帽也未能幸免，都结上了冰霜，甚至冰柱。从当日之情形可以看出，江面很快便会冻结。次日，我们便将汽艇拉上岸，准备过冬。之后气温再次回升，虽然江面因此并未完全冻结，但浮冰的出现仍然阻断了船只往来。经过将近一个月的浮冰期后，江面终于在 11 月 17 日彻底冻结，这也是自 1903 年以来封江时间最晚的一次。本地的天气预言家称，西伯利亚大部分地区的气候状况已因两年前的日本地震发生了改变。若果真如此，要是能让气候转变得更加适宜，让此地冬季的夜晚再减少六个小时就好了。

您真挚的

裴德生

第二部分

地方见闻

（1926～1928）

1. 裴德生致安格联函

（第 55 号半官函）

S/O No.55.

Aigun/Taheiho, 18th March, 192 6

REFERRED

Dear Sir Francis,

Customs Patrol and Barriers at Taheiho.

After an observation of five months, I want to
put the following facts as they appear to me before
you with a view to a reconsideration of the value
of maintaining this preventive service. In order to
furnish a background, I beg first to give a few
extracts from my Trade Memorandum for December Quarter,
1925:

".........In the meantime, the Russian demand for
manufactured goods in the region to the north of us
is about 40% higher than the supply. And the stimula-
tion to smuggling and contraband is far too keen to
be resisted by the poverty stricken masses on both
sides of the river, materially aided as such activities
are by a very accessible frontier. Roughly, 50% to 60%
of the business of Taheiho at present rests on
smuggling. The Russian side is either unable to cope
with the problem of evasion of its high tariffs, altho
it has over 300 frontier Customs Stations and a strong
frontier guard, or it tacitly allows such evasion. Contrabandists are generally allowed to cross to China unmolested, but
they are very often captured on their return and their smuggled
goods are seized and sold by a government organisation other
than that of the Russian Customs : and the goods seized are
sold at prices which include the high tariff item in the reck-
oning - an exceedingly profitable activity for the individuals
in control of the ropes. As for the efforts of the Chinese
Authorities to prohibit smuggling, they are stamped with
brilliant failure. Taheiho as a city is in favour of contraband
trade, its very existence depends upon such traffic, as local
demand and Chinese gold mines do not create sufficient business
the local authorities, civil, police, and military, give tacit
approval. The Chinese Customs with a patrol of about 20 miles
attempts to stem the flow outward of native and foreign goods,
but

Sir Francis Aglen, K.B.E.,
Peiping .

but in the face of universal opposition and its limited field of
action finds its activities reduced to 'face pidgin'. It can
do nothing: and if it could do something in the way of effectively prohibiting contraband activities in the type of goods at
present being smuggled, the stronger the efforts, the smaller the
revenues derived from goods imported from southern markets. On
the other hand, it may safely be said that in the contraband
trade, the Customs loses but little revenue as about 80% to 90%
of the goods clandestinely exported is foreign in origin and is
therefore exported free of duty or is Chinese factory products
which have already been given special duty treatment. As for
furs clandestinely imported(practically the only goods smuggled
inwards), they eventually get into Customs hands either at the
Post Office or at Harbin or at a southern port when exported
abroad .... The moment the ice had formed sufficiently
strong to bear weight, the year's season for intensive
smuggling began and it has continued unabated ever since. During
the first week, it was a sight for amazement to see the scores
and scores of black figures scurrying back and forth from one
shore to the other in open view of the guards, police, and
soldiers on both sides of the river. Poorly clad small boys and
women without hats, caps, or shoes, invaded the shops in Taheiho
and then recrossed to the other side in new clothing to be
sold at a profit, the same process being repeated. Then came
stricter instructions from the Russian Authorities : Not so
strict, however, as those of last year when human beings were
suddenly shot down by the Russian frontier guards, a reward of
$15 being paid for each victim. Greater vigilance resulted in
a cessation of contraband activities in the near vicinity, but
they were carried on just as intensively as ever above and
below the two cities beyond the Chinese Customs Barriers which
again are practically powerless to act as goods going overland
up or down river ultimately destined for Russia are almost
invariably declared for places on the Chinese side and remain
on the Chinese side only so long as the Customs patrol is in
sight: and the patrol cannot follow carts for much distance
along an unclosed frontier which extends unguarded on the
Chinese side for hundreds of miles to the east and west......"

The Russian Government Organisation referred to as
making great profits from smuggled goods is the G.P.U.
(Cheka)- the real communists themselves) which controls the
Frontier Guards. Since writing the above Trade Memo, I
have discovered that there is a well organised system
and

and network of smuggling activities co-ordinated on both
sides of the river making profits at the expense of the
Russian Customs and the Government Co-operative Stores.
Such smugglers not connected with the organisation and
working privately are the ones captured as stated and
are deprived of the goods they smuggle which is either
put to private use or sold to swell the profits of the
organisation, the private smugglers until recently being
given a few days' imprisonment and then released. A few
weeks ago, however, shooting of these private smugglers
was resumed, but on the shooting days the word is passed
along to the organised smugglers who remain inactive for
the time being. The Customs Patrol has turned over to
the Local Police as many as 40 individuals per day who
have been caught crossing the river without passports,etc.
The Chinese Police release the Chinese among such captured
and hand the Russians over to the Russian Consul who sends them
in bands across to the other side, where they also are released
after minor penalties.

The important point about this whole business is the
effect on revenue: it is estimated from typical seizure
cases on record and observation in shops that little is
being lost. Fully 90% of smuggled goods is foreign in
origin and would therefore in any case pass free. Smuggling
is not an attempt to evade the Chinese Customs: most
smugglers

smugglers would willingly declare their exports to us
if they did not fear informants causing trouble on the
other side.

It is again to be emphasised that we get no support
from the local Chinese Authorities, that our efforts only
serve to push the activities farther away from the city
to more remote places where they flourish as strongly
as ever.

A few more general aspects of the situation may be
recalled. Prior to the closing of the Liangchiat'un
Barrier, foreign export trade along the entire frontier
bounded by the Argun, Amur, and Ussuri Rivers was rather
effectively controlled at the places of entry to the
frontier and not at the places of exit. By this I mean
to say that

1) In the Harbin District, in summer, Lahasusu collected
revenue on goods distributed by river routes for ultimate
destination across the border.

2) In the Harbin District, in winter, Fukochin (a city 60
miles above Lahasusu on the Sungari growing with astonish-
ing rapidity) was the center for this distribution by overland routes. The Customs lost no revenues on these goods
so distributed as they were shipped during the summer
months by steamer and stored at Fukochin, the duty being
collected by the Harbin Office(no cart traffic between
Fukochin and Harbin in winter to speak of).

3) In the Aigun District, in summer, goods arriving by
steamer was controlled by Aigun and Takeiho afterward
being distributed to Chinese places on the Amur
most of it ultimately destined for Russia.

4) In the Aigun District, in winter, the Customs had
control

control of imports through the Hengchiat'un Barrier
which was the winter port of entry for frontier
goods.

By means of these 4 ports of entry for frontier goods,
the Customs rather effectively controlled foreign export
trade and did not have to worry much about control
of ports of exit of goods for across the border.
Then came the closing of the Barrier, and while it did
not effect (1) and (2) above, it caused a serious
break in the chain of control in the Aigun District
and made it necessary to consider a more effective
control of the ports of exit, - obviously a much more
difficult and expensive undertaking, although in principle
correct. Our control of ports of entry for frontier
export trade had only been possible because it had
in its favour an undeveloped country and a small
number of trade routes.

In the meantime, a patrol within the city limits
of Tahaiho had been established working from the Custom
House as a base. Later it was found necessary to
establish the two Barriers above and below the city
and the patrol was extended with the three points as
bases covering a distance of about 20 miles. Plans
were also being drawn up for an extension of Barriers
to stretch along the river for a distance of about
160 miles. This whole barrier system was being
considered

considered with trade unrestricted and open between
China and Russia. Meanwhile, Russia closed the frontier
to private trading enterprise and tightened its control
of the border by an unbroken line of Frontier Guards
and some 300 Customs Stations. The point I wish to
emphasise is that Russia to all intents and purposes
is now doing the work for us, and consequently so long
as Russian Government control of foreign trade exists
our activities seems largely superflous particularly in
view of the lack of support of the local Chinese
authorities, and merely constitute a bit of "face pidgin"
much more expensive than the situation seems to demand.

It is true as I have stated that smuggling in spite
of the Russian Frontier Guards and Customs Stations is
very active. I estimate that "the work they do for us"
is only about 70% effective but even so our small
system of patrols and barriers supplementing their efforts
so to speak is only about 5% effective and from the
point-of-view of revenue is practially a dead expense.
It might be mentioned also that the Barriers in summer
are of little practical use: the checking of junk
movements past the barriers and keeping of registers of junks
at these points seems a waste of effort as we collect
no "so-called Coast Trade Duty", only River Dues being
collected

collected and these are so much less than the cost of landing cargoes outside the Harbour Limits plus cart transport and general inconvenience, that junks would not find it worth while to indulge in these practices.

As for preventive efforts against contraband and prohibited goods, our efforts in the absence of local support and with the innumerable ways in which the border can be crossed are for the most part wasted: we get nowhere in preventive work.

Under the circumstances outlined above, the question remains as to whether or not for reasons of "face pidgin" we can afford to keep up these barriers and patrols. I need only mention that the revenue of 1925(excluding River Dues and Surtax) was less than any collection since the opening of the station as a subport of Harbin in 1909. There is not much prospect of a larger collection in 1926.

From some points-of-view, there is a value in maintaining this "show" and holding what we have gained, but I believe that this can still be done at less expense. Mr. Baukham, Acting Tidesurveyor, has written me his views of the Patrol and Barriers. I enclose his statement. He is in entire agreement as to the small value of these activities under present conditions. We

have

have estimated that the expense of the patrols and Barriers can be reduced as follows, at the same time maintaing a minimum of "show" as a matter of policy:

1) Maintain the usual patrol of the city limits with the Custom House as a base by keeping two mounted patrols.

2) Withdraw the two Chinese Tidewaiters from the two Barriers to the Head Office to supplement our reduced Staff and give them some real training in Customs work.

3) Take away from the 2 Barriers one Boatman/guard from each to replace 2 employees discharged at Head Office.

4) Leave each station in control of the one remaining Boatman/guard to keep watch of the property and report any unusual activities, these 2 men being changed frequently with other guards to check any possible dishonest practices.

5) Sell 5 horses and thus save the expense of fodder, etc.

The Barriers are at present (excluding the cost of the patrol from the Custom House) costing us yearly approx. Hk.Tls.2425.00 : the reduced yearly expense will be approx. Hk.Tls.319.00(See Tyer's statement). Should the time come when better trade conditions with Russia are established, we can again adapt ourselves to the new conditions.

May I have your sanction to make the charges indicated?

Yours truly,

第 55 号半官函　　　　　　　　　　　　　1926 年 3 月 18 日于瑷珲关 / 大黑河

尊敬的安格联先生：

为大黑河海关关卡及巡缉事：

关于本关的缉私工作，特将这五个月来的观察情况据实汇报，以期总税务司重新考虑此项工作的存续价值。另从 1925 年第四季度贸易报告中截取部分内容，以作背景补充资料：

"……与此同时，大黑河以北的苏联地区对于机制货物的需求量比供应量要高出 40%。黑龙江华俄两岸的贫苦百姓根本无法抵抗走私违禁品等货物所带来的利益诱惑，更何况穿过边境并非难事，这也在无形之中助长了走私之风。粗略估计，大黑河当前有 50% 至 60% 的商业行为都依赖于走私。而黑龙江俄岸，要么是政府无力解决逃税问题，要么就是已经默许，毕竟苏联海关的关税税率极高，而且在边境沿线设有 300 多处关卡，还有强大的边境卫队。走私者在离开俄境要过江至华境时，通常不会受到阻扰，但从华境返回时往往都会被逮捕，走私的货物也会被扣押，并由苏联海关以外的政府机构进行贩卖，售价中还包含了应缴纳的高额关税。这对于掌控此事的人来说，的确是一桩利润丰厚的买卖。而中国政府在禁止走私上所做的努力也一直未见成效。实际上大黑河这个城市是支持走私贸易的，也正是依此才得以存续。因为无论是地方上还是金矿产区的需求，都不足以支撑本地商业的发展，地方政府、商民、警察甚至军队对于走私活动都是默许的态度。中国海关为了遏制洋土各货私自外流，将巡缉范围扩至 20 余英里，但也难以抵挡各方一致的抵抗行径，再加上权力有限，最终也只是徒劳。其实也是无能为力。而且即使有办法对当前走私的货物实现有效阻止，到头来也是越努力，从南部市场运来各货的税收收益越少。另一方面，可以说在走私贸易中，海关的税收损失极少，因为私运出口的货物中有 80% 至 90%，要么是本就得享免税出口待遇的洋货，要么就是已经获得特殊关税待遇的机制之洋式货物。至于暗中走私进口的皮货（几乎是唯一走私进口的货物），无论是通过邮政局运输，还是通过哈尔滨或者南方口岸出口外国，最终还是会经由海关之手……眼下黑龙江的冰面已经十分坚固，可以承受重物，因此又到了每年走私最为盛行的季节，而且此风从未消减。开始的第一个星期，只见江面上人影攒动，人们不断地在两岸之间来往穿梭，而且就在两岸卫兵、警察和士兵的眼皮底下，此等场面令人好生惊讶。俄岸会有许多衣衫褴褛、无帽无鞋的少年和妇人从冰上过江来至华岸,涌入大黑河的店铺中,返回时皆身着新衣,想来是要带回去卖个好价钱。如此往复不断。随后苏联当局便严令禁止私自过江,但与去年相比也并不算严厉。因为去年苏联边境的卫兵突然对往来行人开枪射杀,而且每射杀一人便可得 15 银圆的赏金。人们警觉后,走私活动虽然暂时中止,但在瑷珲及大黑河的上下游地区依旧猖獗。在此等地方,中国海关未设关卡,也基本无力行使职权,因为拟将从上游或下游地区由陆路运至俄岸的货物,报关时都会申报运往华岸各地,而且只要在中国海关的巡缉范围以内,都会老老实实地留在华岸一侧。但是华岸边境沿东西向绵延数百里皆无士兵守卫,海关巡缉队根本无法一直追随货车……"

上述通过贩卖被扣押的走私货物来赚取巨额利润的苏联政府组织就是管控边境卫兵的国家政治保卫局(契卡——共产主义者自己的组织)。自撰写上述第四季度贸易报告以来,渐渐发现两岸的走私活动有一个严密的组织机构,以牺牲苏联海关及政府合作商铺的利益为代价来谋取利润。未加入该组织的走私商人,如上所述已被逮捕,走私的货物被扣押,而扣押的货物要么被该组织的人挪为私用,要么被卖掉以扩充该组织的利益。日前被逮捕的个人走私者在被关押了数日后又获得了释放。然数周前,苏联卫兵又开始射杀这些个人走私者,而组织内的走私者则提前收到了消息,一直未有行动。海关巡缉队抓到未持护照等过江的人员后,均已移交当地警方,每日约有 40 人。中国警方已将被捕华人释放,并将俄人移交给苏联领事,由其送回对岸,苏联警方对此等俄人施以小惩后也已全部释放。

整件事情最重要的一点就是走私对税收的影响。但根据记录在案的缉私案例及对商铺的调查,估计税收损失极小。因为走私货物中有 90% 皆为洋货,无论如何皆会得享免税放行。实际上,这些走私行为并不是为了逃避中国海关,如果不是担心告密者会让他们返回对岸后遇到麻烦,大部分走私者都愿意至中国海关申报出口。

在此还需强调,海关从未得到过中国当局的支持,而自己的努力也不过是将走私活动从城镇驱赶至了更遥远的地方,但在那里走私活动猖獗如初。

由此不禁想到此前的一些情况。梁家屯分卡关闭之前,整条边界河道,即额尔古纳河、黑龙江及乌苏里江上的洋货出口贸易,在进入边境地带时均能得到有效管控,但离开边境时却无法实现。具体情况为:

（1）在哈尔滨关区,夏季,由拉哈苏苏分关对拟由水路运输出境的货物征收关税;

（2）在哈尔滨关区,冬季,富克锦(松花江沿线城镇位于拉哈苏苏上游 60 英里处发展迅速）是陆路贸易集散中心。但因此地之货物皆为夏季期间由轮船运来囤积于此，且当时已由哈尔滨关征税，因此海关在此项贸易上并无税收损失（据悉冬季期间富克锦与哈尔滨之间并无货车运输）。

（3）在瑷珲关区，夏季，由轮船运抵之货物均经瑷珲或大黑河海关稽查征税后再运至黑龙江华岸各地，其中多数最终皆会运入俄境。

（4）在瑷珲关区，冬季，海关通过梁家屯分卡稽查管控运入本关区的货物，该分卡乃冬季期间货物运入边境地带的必经之处。

以上四处关卡均是在货物进入边境地带之前施加管控，因此当货物运出边境过江至俄岸时，海关便不必再费心稽查，但同时也能够保证对出口贸易的有效管控。然而，梁家屯分卡关闭后，哈尔滨关区虽然未受到影响，但瑷珲关区的稽查办法却出现了漏洞，因此不得不考虑在货物运出边境之地实施更为有效的管控。但这显然更加困难，成本也会更高，尽管原则上并没有问题。实际上，海关之所以能够在出口货物运入边境之前实现管控，可能完全得益于本地发展的落后以及十分有限的贸易路线。

于是，瑷珲关成立了巡缉队，并在大黑河镇内以海关办公楼为中心向东西两个方向展开稽查。随后又发现有必要于大黑河上下游再分设两处分卡，并以这三处关卡为中心将巡缉范围扩至20余英里。当时还计划增设分卡，以将沿江巡缉范围延长至约160英里。但这些关卡体系都是基于贸易不受限制，且中俄边境保持开放所做出的考虑。然而，苏联却在此时关闭边境，禁止开展私营贸易，同时加强了边境的守卫，整条边界线上都有卫兵把守，还设立了300余处海关关卡。在此想要强调的是，苏联的举措几乎相当于在为中国而做，因此只要苏联政府继续管制对外贸易，中国海关的巡缉活动似乎就显得十分多余，尤其是在还得不到地方中国官员支持的情况下。可以说，这就像一个"面子工程"，支出的费用远超实际所需。

如上所述，尽管苏联边境守卫森严，同时还设有300余处海关关卡，但走私活动仍然猖獗。估计，"苏联为中国所做的工作"仅起到了70%的作用，但即便如此，中国海关的巡缉制度及所设关卡的职能太过有限，能起到的补充作用也只有约5%，而为此支出的费用，从税收的角度来看，几乎毫无价值。此外，有些关卡在夏季期间几无实际作用，核实往来民船的动向并登记似乎是在浪费精力，因为瑷珲关根本不征收"所谓的土货复进口半税"，仅征收江捐。而所征江捐之数远低于在港口界限以外装卸货物的费用，而且民船在港口界限外装船还需使用货车运输，极不便利，因此也不值得为逃避江捐而私运货物。

至于瑷珲关为缉私违禁品所付出的努力，由于无法得到地方上的支持，而且穿过边境的路线不计其数,大抵也是徒劳了,可以说瑷珲关的缉私工作一无所获。

基于上述种种,目前的问题仍在于,海关是否能够为此"面子工程"负担得起关卡及巡缉工作的支出。在此仅须指出,1925年的税收(不含江捐及附加税)是海关自1909年于瑷珲设关以补充哈尔滨关以来最少的一年。而且预计1926年的税收增幅也不会太大。

当然从某些方面来讲,维持此"门面",守住目前的成果,还是有一定的价值。但即便如此,兹认为也应减少费用支出。特此附上署理头等总巡博韩(G. E. Baukham)先生关于分卡及巡缉工作的书面意见及报表。其亦认为此等工作的价值太过有限。经研究,我们计划将分卡及巡缉工作的费用预算降低,同时出于原则上的考虑,还保留了一定的"门面"。具列体下:

(1)保留两组陆路巡缉队,以继续在大黑河镇内以海关办公楼为中心向东西两向稽查。

(2)将两处分卡的两名华籍稽查员召回大黑河总关,以补充瑷珲关减少的人力,唯须重新培训以便应对海关工作。

(3)从两处分卡各抽调一名水手兼卫兵,以替代大黑河总关裁撤掉的两名关员。

(4)两处分卡各留一名水手兼卫兵负责看管关产,汇报异常状况,该两名关员将与其他卫兵轮值,以查是否有违纪行为。

(5)卖掉五匹巡缉马,以节省草料等费用。目前,分卡的年支出(不含大黑河镇内以海关办公楼为中心向两端巡缉的费用)约为2425.00海关两,调整后,每年将减少约319.00海关两(参阅署理头等总巡的报表)。待与俄贸易的环境有所改善后,海关可相应再做调整。

不知上述举措能否获得总税务司的批准?

您真挚的

裴德生

2. 瑚斯敦致安格联函

（第 57 号半官函）

S/O No.57.   INDEXED

Aigun/Taheiho 31st May,   26

Dear Sir Francis Aglen,

    <u>Commissioner's arrival at Aigun</u>: As reported semi-officially by my predecessor, I arrived here by the first steamer of the season. The trip from Harbin took 15 days, the steamer having had to wait at Lahasusu for a few days until the bulk of the ice in the Amur had cleared away.

    <u>Commissioner visits Chinese and Russian Officials</u>: I have duly called on the local Chinese officials and the gentry, and on the Russian Consul stationed at this port. I have also crossed to Blagoveetchensk and called on the Chinese Consul-General, and on the Governor, the Commissioner of Customs, and the Director of the Amur Government Navigation Office.

    <u>Arrival of new Taoyin and Superintendent of Customs</u>: The new incumbent, Mr. Chang Shou-tseng (張壽增), arrived here on the 30th instant. This is the fourth time that Mr. Chang has been appointed

Sir Francis A. Aglen K. B. E.,
    Peking.

to this port as Taoyin and Superintendent of Customs.

    <u>Commissioner elected vice-President of International Club</u>: Upon my arrival Colonel Wu Shih-chieh (吳士傑), President, asked me whether I would be willing to accept the vice-Presidentship and upon my assenting he called a meeting of the Committee and I was duly elected. The members of the **Club** invited me to dine with them at the Club on the 22nd instant. The evening passed off very successfully.

    <u>Weather</u>: There have been heavy rains during the past two weeks, and the **farmers** are now busily engaged in their fields.

            Yours truly,

            J. A. E. Hourtoun

第 57 号半官函　　　　　　　　　　　**1926 年 5 月 31 日于瑷珲关／大黑河**

尊敬的安格联先生：

　　为抵达瑷珲关事：如前任税务司于半官函中之汇报，本人已乘坐本季航运开通后的首班轮船抵达此地。由哈尔滨至此共用 15 日时间，轮船途中曾于拉哈苏苏停留数日，以等待黑龙江上的浮冰消融。

　　为拜访中俄官员事：抵达本地后已适时拜访了地方官员、乡绅及驻大黑河苏联领事，业已跨江至布拉戈维申斯克（Blagoveschesk）拜访中国总领事、俄阿穆尔州长、俄海关税务司及俄阿穆尔水道局督办。

　　为新任道尹兼海关监督抵达大黑河事：新任道尹兼海关监督张寿增先生已于 5 月 30 日抵达此地，此为其第四次被任命为大黑河道尹兼海关监督。

　　为税务司当选国际俱乐部副主席事：本人到达此地后，吴士杰上校便前来询问是否愿意接受国际俱乐部副主席一职？后经本人同意，其召集了一次委员会议，会上本人如期当选。5 月 22 日俱乐部设宴，本人应邀参加，晚宴颇为顺利。

　　为天气事：过去两周雨势较大，农民现已开始耕种。

您真挚的

瑚斯敦

3. 瑚斯敦致安格联函

（第60号半官函）

S/O. No. 60.

Aigun/Taheiho 7th July, 26

Dear Sir Francis Aglen,

LANDING

Director of the Amur Government Navigation
Office and Mr. P. I. Ignatieff, Technical Adviser
on Amur Aids to Navigation, return from up-river
tour: The Director of the Amur Government Navigation
Office and Mr. Ignatieff returned on the 22nd ultimo
from their tour of inspection on the Upper Amur.
They found that the Aid Signals were in a good
state of repair. Mr. Ignatieff informs me that
all Russian traffic on the upper waters of the Amur
and on the Shilka has ceased, owing to the active
opposition of the Railway Company. He also informs
me that the Amur Navigation Office, having failed
in coming to an agreement with the Chinese Commission
in regard to dredging on the Upper Amur, has now
begun to dredge on the river Zeya, which runs into
the Amur at Blagovestchensk.

Mr. P. I. Ignatieff leaves on tour of
inspection

Sir Francis A. Aglen, K. B. E.,
      Peking.

inspection on the Lower Amur: Mr. Ignatieff left on
the 29th instant on a tour of inspection on the
Lower Amur, and will proceed as far as Lahasusu,
from which place he will return on or about the
14th instant.

Low water in the Sungari: Owing to the
unprecedentedly low state of the water in the Sungari-
the lowest it is said for quarter of a century,
there being less than 2 feet in several of the
channels - no steamer reached here from Harbin between
22nd June and 6th July. The first steamer to
arrive had to transfer her passengers and their
luggage to lighters no fewer than 11 times. The
water in the Amur however, rose 9 feet between the
29th ultimo and the 2nd instant, and consequently
the channels in the Sungari have deepened to such
an extent that steamers have since experienced no
difficulty in reaching this port.

Drought: The long spell of dry weather was
broken on the 27th ultimo, when rain fell to the
extent of 1.35 inches, and crops which would otherwise have perished were revivified.

River Dues Collection: From the beginning
of

of the season until the end of June the River Dues
Collection amounted to $9,600 as against $6,200 for
the same period last year.

Yours truly,

J. D. D. Houston.

第 60 号半官函   1926 年 7 月 7 日于瑷珲关 / 大黑河

尊敬的安格联先生：

为俄阿穆尔国家水道局督办及黑龙江航务专门顾问易保罗（P. I. Ignatieff）先生完成黑龙江上游巡查工作返回事：6 月 22 日，俄阿穆尔国家水道局督办与易保罗先生完成黑龙江上游的巡查工作返回大黑河，据称沿线航路标志状况良好。易保罗先生汇报称，苏联船运方面因受铁路公司的强力阻扰，现已停止往来黑龙江上游及石勒喀河，并称俄阿穆尔水道局因未能与中方委员会就于黑龙江上游疏浚一事达成协议，现已开始在布拉戈维申斯克（Blagoveschesk）汇入黑龙江的结雅河上开展疏浚工事。

为易保罗先生前往黑龙江下游巡查事：6 月 29 日，易保罗先生离开大黑河前往黑龙江下游巡查，此行最远将至拉哈苏苏，预计于 7 月 14 日左右返回。

为松花江低水位事：松花江今年水位极低，据称已创近二十五年来的最低记录，航道中有些地方还不足 2 英尺，以致 6 月 22 日至 7 月 6 日之间无轮船自哈尔滨行至大黑河。首艘抵达此地的轮船，途中因受到低水位的影响不得不将乘客及行李多次转移至驳船上，据悉至少转移了 11 次。不过，6 月 29 日至 7 月 2 日期间，黑龙江水位上涨了 9 英尺，松花江水位随之亦有所上涨，轮船终得以恢复正常航行。

为干旱事：6 月 27 日，历时已久的干旱终于迎来降雨，降水量达 1.35 英寸，枯萎的庄稼获得新生。

为江捐税收事：自航运季开始至 6 月末，共征收江捐 9600 银圆，去年同期征得 6200银圆。

您真挚的

瑚斯敦

4. 瑚斯敦致易纨士函

（第 61 号半官函）

S/O. No. 61.

Aigun/Taheiho. 28th July, 26.

Dear Mr. Edwardes,

INDEXED Mr. P. I. Ignatieff returns from tour of inspection on the Lower Amur: Mr. Ignatieff returned on the 14th instant from his tour of inspection on the Lower Amur. He found the Russians busily engaged repairing such Aids as required attention, and that the Aids as a whole were all in excellent order.

Gold-mining concession obtained by British company: A Commander Pilcher, the representative of some London financiers, and a Mr. Watson, a mining-engineer have arrived here and joined up with a Mr. Luckie, who was formerly in the Salt Gabelle and afterwards had some interest in a gold-mine in the Amur District, in connexion with a gold-mining concession obtained by them from Marshal Chang Tso-lin. They have already been prospecting in several directions in this neighbourhood, and will upon arrival of drills, which are expected within the

next

A. H. F. Edwardes, Esquire,

Peking.

next few days, begin drilling near Mergen (Nunkiang 嫩江).

Crops: Owing to several days' rain during the past fortnight, the wheat, barley, and oat crops have passed the danger-stage, and unless something unforeseen happens the farmers should reap fairly heavy crops.

Yours truly,

J. D. R. Houstoun.

第61号半官函　　　　　　　　　　1926 年 7 月 28 日于瑷珲关 / 大黑河

尊敬的易纨士先生：

为易保罗（P. I. Ignatieff）先生完成黑龙江下游巡查工作返回事：7 月 14 日，易保罗先生完成黑龙江下游的巡查工作返回大黑河，途中亲见苏方正在对航路标志进行必要的维护修理，并称沿线航路标志整体状况极好。

为英国公司获得金矿开采权事：勒基（Luckie）先生曾于盐务总局工作，之后又投身于黑龙江地区的金矿开采事业，如今已从张作霖大帅手中获得一处金矿开采特权，伦敦金融家代表、海军中校皮尔彻（Pilcher）先生及采矿工程师沃森（Watson）先生已来到大黑河与之一起推进此事。他们现已在大黑河周边多方勘探，待钻机过些时日运来后，便开始于墨尔根（嫩江）附近钻井。

为农作物事：过去两周间，接连数日均有降雨，小麦、大麦、燕麦等皆已度过危险期，如无意外情况发生，相信农民今年将会迎来大丰收。

您真挚的

瑚斯敦

5. 瑚斯敦致易纨士函

（第 62 号半官函）

S/O. No. 62.

Aigun/Taheiho, 24th August, 26.

Dear Mr. Edwardes,

Gold-mining concession obtained by British Company (vide
S/O Letter No. 61): Commander Pilcher, Mr. Watson, and
Mr. Luckie left here on the 22nd instant for Mergen
(Nunkiang嫩江) in order to carry out a series of
drilling operations on their concession. A Mr. Brunner,
son of Mr. Brunner of Messrs Brunner, Mond & Co.,
who has been my guest for several weeks past,
accompanied them. If the drilling shows the concession
to be a valuable one, I am of opinion that Messrs
Brunner, Mond & Co. will take a financial interest
in the scheme. The above-mentioned gentlemen will
return to Taheiho in about three weeks' time, when
I shall probably hear as to the value of the
concession.

Mr. P. I. Ignatieff leaves on tour of inspection on the
Upper Amur: Mr. Ignatieff left to-day on a tour of
inspection on the Upper Amur. He will go as far as
Pokrovka, 830 versts above Taheiho, and will return
in

A. H. F. Edwardes, Esquire,
　　Peking.

in about three weeks' time.

Mr. Wang Hsi-ch'ang (王锡昌) Head Manager of the
Tung-pei Steamship Company visits Taheiho: Mr. Wang
arrived here on the 16th instant, and left again on
the 18th instant. He is a very young man for the
position he holds, and has a number of plans for the
improvement of shipping-affairs on the Sungari and the
Amur, such as the abolition of Sansing and Aigun
Customs sub-Stations, in order that vessels of his
Company may be able to work cargo and passengers at
these places at night and on Sundays and Holidays
without payment of special permit fees.

Weather: During the last few days the weather
has been wet and stormy; but the crops, which are
now ripening fast, have not so far suffered any
damage.

Yours truly,

J. D. D. Houstoun.

第 62 号半官函　　　　　　　　　　　　　1926 年 8 月 24 日于瑷珲关 / 大黑河

尊敬的易纨士先生：

　　为英国公司获得金矿开采权事（参阅瑷珲关第 61 号半官函）：皮尔彻（Pilcher）海军中校、沃森（Watson）先生及勒基（Luckie）先生已于 8 月 22 日离开大黑河前往墨尔根（嫩江），以凭其所获开采权开始钻井作业。卜内门洋碱有限公司（Messrs Burnner, Mond & Co.）的布鲁纳（Brunner）先生的儿子也一同前往，在此之前，其已在本人家中做客数周。此次钻井如有成效，相信卜内门洋碱有限公司亦会投资加入。预计他们将于三周之后返回大黑河，届时或许便可知道开采成果。

　　为易保罗（P. I. Ignatieff）先生前往黑龙江上游巡查事：易保罗先生已于今日出发前往黑龙江上游巡查，此行最远将至距离大黑河 830 俄里的波克罗夫卡（Pokrovka），预计三周左右返回。

　　为东北航务局总经理王锡昌先生到访大黑河事：王先生于 8 月 16 日抵达，并于 8 月 18 日离开。其对于总经理这一职位而言，确实非常年轻，但对于改进松花江及黑龙江上的船运事务却有颇多计划，比如废除三姓分关及瑷珲关所辖分关，以使其公司船只能够于夜间、周日及假日在此等地方自由上下乘客及货物，不必再为申领特别准单支付费用。

　　为天气事：过去数日都是狂风暴雨的天气，但农作物并未受损，长势喜人。

您真挚的

瑚斯敦

6. 瑚斯敦致易纨士函

（第 63 号半官函）

S/O. No. 63.   Aigun/Taheiho, 16th September, 1926.

Dear Mr. Edwardes,

    INDEXES Mr. P. I. Ignatieff returns from tour of inspection on the Upper Amur: Mr. Ignatieff returned on the 10th instant from his tour of inspection on the Upper Amur, and reported that the Aids were all in order. He will leave again in a few days time to inspect the Aids on the Lower Amur between this port and Irga.

    Gold-mining concession obtained by British Company: I now learn that this Company will be known in future as the Manchurian Gold-fields Ltd.; Commander Pilcher, and Messrs Luckie, Watson, and Brunner, who left for Mergen (Nünkiang 嫩江) to commence drilling operations, as reported in my last semi-official letter, are expected to arrive back in Taheiho about the 20th instant.

    Weather: During the past two weeks there has been heavy rain almost daily, and the farmers report that a good deal of damage has been done to the standing

A. H. F. Edwardes, Esquire,
  P E K I N G.

standing crops. The roads between here and Tsitsihar are in a very bad state, and the mails from Harbin are consequently arriving several days behind schedule-time.

        Yours truly,

第 63 号半官函　　　　　　　　　　　1926 年 9 月 16 日于瑷珲关／大黑河

尊敬的易纨士先生：

　　为易保罗（P. I. Ignatieff）先生完成黑龙江上游巡查工作返回事：9 月 10 日，易保罗先生完成黑龙江上游的巡查工作返回大黑河，报告称沿线航路标志状况良好。数日后，其将再次离开前往黑龙江下游巡查大黑河与伊力嘎（Irga）之间的航路标志情况。

　　为英国公司获得金矿开采权事：据悉此英国公司日后将更名为满洲金矿有限公司（Manchurian Gold-fields Ltd.）。如瑷珲关第 62 号半官函所述，皮尔彻（Pilcher）海军中校、沃森（Watson）先生、勒基（Luckie）先生及布鲁纳（Brunner）先生已前往墨尔根（嫩江）开始钻井作业，预计将于 9 月 20 日返回大黑河。

　　为天气事：过去两周几乎日日皆有大雨，据农民称，庄稼受损严重。大黑河与齐齐哈尔之间的道路路况极差，邮件自哈尔滨运送至此地的时间会比预计延迟数日。

您真挚的

瑚斯敦

7. 瑚斯敦致易纨士函

（第64号半官函）

S/O.No.64.   Aigun/Taheiho 5th October, 26.

Dear Mr. Edwardes,

     <u>Mr. P. I. Ignatieff inspects the Lower Amur</u>: Mr. Ignatieff left on the 18th September on a tour of inspection of the Lower Amur, and returned again to this port on the 27th September.   He reported that the Aids were all in order.

     <u>Manchurian Gold-fields Ltd.</u>:   Commander Pilcher, and Messrs. Luckie, Watson, and Brunner, returned a few days ago from Mergen, where they had gone to undertake drilling operations.   I gather that they found gold, but in such small quantities that it would not pay to work it.   With the exception of Mr. Brunner, who has left for England, these gentlemen are now prospecting at Taiping-kow（太平溝） some 100 miles below this port.

S/O.No.63

     <u>Mr. R. M. Talbot, appointed in charge of Aigun Customs</u>:   I gather from a telegram I have received from Harbin that Mr. Talbot left that port on or about the 1st instant, in which case he should arrive here by the 9th instant.

                 Yours truly,

                 J. D. T. Houstoun

A. H. F. Edwardes, Esquire,
    PEKING.

第 64 号半官函 　　　　　　　　　　1926 年 10 月 5 日于瑷珲关 / 大黑河

尊敬的易纨士先生：

　　为易保罗（P. I. Ignatieff）先生完成黑龙江下游巡查工作返回事：易保罗先生此前于 9 月 18 日离开大黑河前往黑龙江下游巡查，业于 9 月 27 日返回本口岸，并报告称沿线航路标志情况良好。

　　为满洲金矿有限公司（Manchurian Gold-fields Ltd.）事：数日前，皮尔彻（Pilcher）海军中校、沃森（Watson）先生、勒基（Luckie）先生及布鲁纳（Brunner）先生已自墨尔根返回大黑河，如瑷珲关第 63 号半官函所述，他们之前于墨尔根钻井开采金矿。据悉，他们此番确有采到黄金，但量少不值得继续投资开采。如今，除布鲁纳先生已前往英国，其余几人正于大黑河下游 100 余英里的太平沟勘探。

　　为铎博赉（R. M. Talbot）先生被任命为瑷珲关署理税务司事：哈尔滨关来电告知，铎博赉先生已于 10 月 1 日左右离开哈尔滨，按行程计算，应于 10 月 9 日抵达大黑河。

您真挚的
瑚斯敦

8. 铎博赉致易纨士函

（第 65 号半官函）

S/O. No.65.

Aigun/Taheiho 21st October, 26.

Dear Mr. Edwardes,

　　Assumption of Charge: I wired you on the 13th instant that I had taken over from Mr. Houstoun on the 12th. My first permanent charge coincides with his retirement. I have to thank you for this expression of confidence you have in me and I trust I will be able to carry on to the satisfaction of yourself and Customs interests.

　　I was fortunate in catching the last comfortable steamer from Harbin and arrived on the 10th. As I was familiar with the port Mr. Houstoun was able to hand over at once and returned by the same steamer on the 13th.

　　I have had a very busy week calling on Russian and Chinese officials here and at Blagovestchensk, attending official dinners, etc. I am very pleased to find many old friends amongst the Chinese officials including the Taoyin/Supt. Official entertainment is still as elaborate as that complained of by my predecessors. I have seen nothing like it in other ports of China.

　　Closing of River: Floating ice appeared in

in the River two days ago and navigation has now ceased for the year.

　　Yours truly,

A. H. F. Edwardes, Esquire,
　　PEKING.

第 65 号半官函   1926 年 10 月 21 日于瑷珲关 / 大黑河

尊敬的易纨士先生：

为承担管理责任事：10 月 13 日已向阁下电呈汇报与瑚斯敦（J. H. W. Houstoun）先生于 10 月 12 日完成职务移交一事。巧合的是，本人首次常任一口岸之署理税务司正值瑚斯敦先生退休。感谢信任，日后必将维护海关利益，不令阁下失望。

幸运的是，本人搭乘上由哈尔滨出发的最后一班轮船，并于 10 月 10 日抵达大黑河，且因熟悉本口岸各项事务，抵达后很快便与瑚斯敦先生完成工作交接，使其能够于 13 日搭乘同一艘轮船返回哈尔滨。

本人上任后有一周时间都在不停地拜访大黑河及布拉戈维申斯克（Blagoveschesk）的中俄官员，参加官方晚宴等。令人欣喜的是，中国官员中还有很多旧友，包括道尹兼海关监督。官方宴请一如前任税务司们描述的那般隆重，本人从未在其他口岸遇到过类似之事。

为封江事：两日前，江面开始出现浮冰，今年的航运已经停止。

您真挚的

铎博赉

9. 铎博赉致易纨士函

（第 66 号半官函）

S/O.No.66.

CUSTOM HOUSE.

Aigun , 9th November, 1926.

Dear Mr. Edwardes;

Situation in Blagovestchensk: As I informed you in my last S/O., I paid a visit to Blagovestchensk to make my official calls. It is interesting to compare the town now to what it was 5 years ago. Then there was a little life and hope but there seems to be none now. During the period one substantial office structure has been built but otherwise the appearance of the place is the same. The buildings, however, (mostly of wood) are rapidly deteriorating. They have not been repaired and a paint brush has not touched them. Fences are wobbling and sidewalks shaky. The few people on the street are poorly dressed and seem without morale. The intelligent people have all left and those remaining are content to eke out an exixtance from day to day; living off their gardens in the summer and apparently hibernating like bears in the winter. The only income the place has is

A. H. F. Edwardes, Esquire.

PEKING.

is from the administrative offices which keep a certain percentage going. It appears to me that the inhabitants will gradually revert to nature and will be living in holes in the ground as soon as the present structures topple on their heads. There may be a brain somewhere in the inert mass but it is not apparent here where we can only view the extremities. There are but vague hopes of the opening of the frontier. It seems now that the Bolsheviks object to Chinese labourers entering the country. The attitude seems to be similar to that adopted by the U.S.A. and for the same reasons. With all their outward protestations of friendliness for the Chinese, it would appear that inwardly they are actuated by the same old spirit that existed before the War. The attitude of the local Chinese toward Bolshevik teachings is shown by an incident of last Sunday. The Russian Consul had invited the Chinese Officials including the Customs to a reception at the Consulate at noon to celebrate the 9th Anniversary of the Russian Revolution. In the morning red flags, bunting, etc., were put all over the front of the building together with pictures of Lenin, Trotsky and Sun Yat Sen. The local officials at once ordered them down. I thought at first there would be no function but the pictures were taken down and at the reception all was quite

on

on the surface.

Inspection of Out-Stations: I visited Aigun on the 21st
ultimo and spent the day looking over the place.
There is little trade there, beyond the export of skins, in
the winter. The quarters there are comfortable and
the Officer-in-Charge, Mr. 2nd Class Tidewaiter Eysymontt,
seemed to have everything up-to-date and in order. On
the 2nd instant I visited the former barrier at
Liangchiat'un. The quarters there are in charge of a
boatman/guard and I was glad to find them in good
condition despite the fact that they have been vacant
for some time. I consider they should be kept in
good repair as it is probable they will be required
again on the resumption of normal trade with Siberia
or the arrival of the Railway.

Travelling Expenses between Harbin and Aigun : I am
forwarding Aigun Despatch No. 291 in which I raise the
question of a revision of the present procedure whereby
only a Mess Allowance is issued to members of the
Staff when travelling between Harbin and Aigun. I am
told that Mr. Houstoun wished to take up the matter
but being a bachelor, like his predecessors, he
apparently did not do so. I wish he had because I
do not like to appear as one who immediately tries to
raise new questions on arrival at a port; but in justice
to those who will come after me and to all married
members of the Service who will be transferred to or
from Aigun, I think the question should be referred
to you. Ordinarily there will be no hotel expenses
at Harbin for Commissioners passing through but in
my instance the Commissioner house there was being
repaired.

Brick Building on New Customs Site: I. G. despatch
No. 318/109,988 "hits the nail on the head" exactly.
The brick house does not belong to us, as I have
good reason to know. I was in charge of Aigun at
the time and conducted the negotiations leading up
to the purchase of the property concerned. The
property is now temporarily enclosed by old roofing
boards from demolished shops. I shall go into the
whole matter at once and let you have my recommendations shortly.

Aids to Navigation: This question is occupying a
great deal of my time. The Russian Commission has
written in again asking that joint rules of navigation
be drawn up. I wish to talk to the Taoyin about
this matter on his return from Kirin bearing in mind
the

the Inspector General's instructions in S/O dated the
15th March, 1926, to Aigun that this matter lies outside
the province of the Aids Commission. From what I have
seen of the general situation I don't like it. Our
own position is so vague that the territorial officials
are encouraged to think that they can take over the
entire control of the Amur and Sungari and the
shipping thereon leaving us to collect duty only.
I wish the Coast Inspector could take control at an
early date and regularise things as far as possible.
It seems to me that if a general survey of the
requirements of the Sungari and Amur shipping could
be made by a competent Customs authority and
recommendations made with reference to aids, navigation
rules, pilotage regulations, certificating of officers,
etc., to be submitted to the Ch'n for negotiation
with the Chinese territorial officials concerned, our
position in this part of China might be regularized.
I realize that this question has long been under
consideration by the Inspectorate but the possibility
of early action on the part of Provincial authorities
must now be taken into consideration. I am keeping
in touch with Harbin in these matters.

Taoyin visiting Kirin: The day after my arrival the
Taoyin/Supt.

Taoyin/Supt. left on a journey with the intention
of visiting Kirin and talking over with the authorities
there the question of Aids on the Ussuri and in the
neighbourhood of Habarovsk as well as boundary questions.
He left on telegraphic instructions of the Tsitsihar
authorities to whom he is to report after his Kirin
interview. He may have some important instructions
on his return to Aigun.

Yours truly,

第 66 号半官函   1926 年 11 月 9 日于瑷珲关 / 大黑河

尊敬的易纨士先生：

    为布拉戈维申斯克（Blagoveschesk）局势事：如第 65 号半官函所述，本人已赴布拉戈维申斯克进行了正式访问。城内的景象与五年前相比，萧条不少。当年至少还有些生气与希望，但如今这些都已不复存在。在此期间，除有一座坚固的办公大楼为新建，其他皆是旧时模样。而那些原有的建筑又多为木质结构，且年久失修，甚至都未曾被粉刷过，损毁的速度日益加剧。围栏都已松动摇晃，人行道路更是破败不堪。街上鲜有行人往来，即使有，亦是衣衫褴褛，精神萎靡。有能力的人都已离开此地，留下的都是愿意为了生计勉强度日的人，他们夏季依靠自家的园子过活，冬季则像熊一样开始冬眠。当地唯一的收入来源就是还在维持运转的政府部门。当地居民看起来似乎要逐渐回归原始生活，现在居住的房屋一旦倒塌，他们很有可能就会住进地下的洞穴里。也许这些毫无行动力的人中也有智者，但在这个满眼都是行尸走肉的地方，的确看不出来。边境开放的希望十分渺茫。目前这些布尔什维克党反对华籍劳工进入俄境，美国方面的态度亦是如此，背后的原因也基本相同。他们表面上宣称对中国友好，但实际行动仍然受战前旧思想的影响。而大黑河中国官员对布尔什维克主义的态度，亦可从上星期日的事件中窥得一二。当日驻大黑河苏联领事邀请中国官员，包括海关人员于中午到领事馆，参加苏联革命 9 周年庆典。清晨，领事馆前便挂满了红旗、彩旗及列宁（Lenin）、托洛茨基（Trotsky）和孙中山的画像。中国官员见状，立即命之取下。起初还以为不会有何作用，但最终画像还是都撤下了，庆典招待会上，一切都十分流于表面。

    为视察分关事：10 月 21 日至瑷珲口岸视察一日。当地除冬季有皮货出口，几无贸易往来。宿舍状况良好，居住环境舒适。负责关员二等铃子手伊思孟（V. A. Eysymontt）先生似已将各项事务都安排得井井有条。11 月 2 日又至梁家屯分卡旧址视察。当地宿舍现由一名水手兼卫兵负责看管，虽已闲置多时，但状况依然良好。兹认为应一直对此处房屋进行维护，以备将来与西伯利亚恢复贸易或者铁路修建完成后再投入使用。

    为来往哈尔滨关与瑷珲关之间的旅费事：11 月 6 日发出的瑷珲关第 291 号呈中指出，按照现行惯例，关员来往哈尔滨与瑷珲两地时，仅得享膳食津贴，建议调整。据悉，瑚斯敦（J. H. W. Houstoun）先生亦有此意，只是因为与其上一任税务司一样皆是未婚，所以最终并未采取行动。真心希望其已有所行动，因为实在不愿给人以上任之初便提出新问题的印象。只是考虑到之后上任的税务司，以及调至或调离瑷珲关的已婚关员，兹认为还是应向总税务司提请指示。通常情况下，税务司经过哈尔滨时都不会产生旅店费用，但本人停留期间，税务司住所正在维修。

为新海关关址上的砖房事：海关总税务司公署第 318/109988 号令全然"切中要害"。此前在瑷珲关任职期间恰好在商议购买此房产，因此可以确定，此砖房并不属于海关。目前已使用此前拆除商铺时留下的屋顶板为该关产修建了围栏。具体情况，将即刻着手调查，以尽快提出建议。

为航路标志事：此事占用了本人大量的时间。苏联水道委员会再次来函要求起草航行章程。对于此事，希望等道尹从吉林返回后可与之商议，当然亦不会忘记总税务司 1926年 3 月 15 日半官函已指示此事不在水道委员会的职权范围内。综观大局，当前的形势并不乐观。海关的定位十分模糊，以致地方关员以为他们能够接管松黑两江及往来船运，而海关则仅需负责征收关税。希望巡工司能够尽早接管航务相关事务，并让这一职能尽量合法化。如果能够由有能力的海关机构对松黑两江上的船运需求做出全面调查，并针对航路标志、航行条例、引水章程、驾驶员证书等向税务处呈交建议，以与相应地方官员进行协商，那么海关在本地区的身份或许可以实现合理合法化。本人当然知道，总税务司一直都在考虑这一问题，只是现在还需考虑的是省政府方面很有可能会提早行动。相关各事，将及时与哈尔滨关沟通。

为道尹赴吉林公干事：在本人到达瑷珲关后的第二日，道尹兼瑷珲关监督便动身前往吉林，与当地政府商议乌苏里江及哈巴罗夫斯克（Habarovsk）附近的航路标志事宜以及边境问题。其此番前往，是奉了齐齐哈尔政府的电令指示，返回后亦会向齐齐哈尔政府报告，届时或许会带回重要指示。

您真挚的

铎博赉

10. 铎博赉致安格联函

（第 67 号半官函）

S/O. No.67.

Aigun/Taheiho,17th December, 26.

Dear Sir Francis,

FRONTIER RELATIONS: Prospects for the opening of the frontier do not improve. The other day the newly appointed President of the Amur Province (Loboda) called on me. I received him at my house and found him a very decent sort. Were he in a different environment he would probably soon forget his Bolshevik ideas. He was quite frank in saying that the authorities at Blagovestchensk had no authority to open the frontier and its closure was due to part of a general scheme of those higher up. A statement of this sort is more conductive to an understanding than the promises that have been made so long. To my mind were the Kuomingtang in control of the three Manchurian provinces the frontier might have been opened long ago and trade carried on as it is now between Vladivostock and Canton. With the passing of time the relations between the Chinese and Russians of this part of Asia seem to become more strained - the Chinese officials here are quite open in their expressions of distrust and dislike of those in control on the Soviet side of the river. A new Consul named Melamet (a Jew) has

Sir Francis Aglen, K. B. E.,
 Peking.

has been appointed here by Moscow in place of Toropoff who returns to the capital. The change seems to be of a routine nature but in many instances it is said that Russian Consuls now being sent to China are men of military experience. This is also true of the newly appointed Vice President of the C.E.R. Yesterday I returned the call of the President at Blagovestchensk and was received very hospitably. The omnipresent question of the opening of the frontier was again brought up casually. This time the president said that one of the drawbacks would be the great influx of "Whites". When it was pointed out that these were now negligible in number along the frontier he said that the Chinese themselves were adverse to resuming trade relations. As I know this is untrue the question was dropped and subjects of a more general nature discussed. Whilst proceeding to the Government's House we passed a crowd of some 100 contrabandists under escort who had been captured the night before by armed patrols whilst trying to smuggle goods across the ice from China. It is said that this number is the daily "grist of the mill". The punishment meted out is confinement in jail but as there is no food to spare they rarely remain therein more than three days. As to the nature of the goods smuggled over from the Chinese side

I.

I, myself, have visited several of the Chinese shops which deal
in contraband along the river above and below Taheiho and, with
the exception of spirits, the goods displayed are almost without
exception of cheap foreign origin which presumably have paid duty
on entry into China.

UNDERED   AIDS TO NAVIGATION: At my instance the Taoyin/Supt.
recently called a meeting of the Chinese Aids Commission to
consider the new agreement.   Mr. Ignatieff and myself had been
working for some time getting together the details necessary for
the consideration of the renewal of the old agreement which
expired on the 30th November, 1926.   As I wrote in my last S/O
the Taoyin had been summoned by the Kirin authorities to discuss
the Aid's question principally with regard to the Ussuri and the
boundary at Habarovsk.   As he was returning via Tsitsihar it
was felt that he might have something important to communicate.
If he did receive any instructions he must be keeping them up
his sleeve for he disclosed very little beyond saying that in
discussing the question of maintenance of Aids at Moukden both
Marshall Chang and Admiral Sheng said that financial aid from
the provinces concerned was out of the question at present.
The Tsitsihar authorities favoured raising the rates of River
                                                        Dues.

Dues.   To this suggestion I was not at all sympathetic and
told the Taoyin that I thought the merchants were already
paying heavily and that the Government ought to subsidize
a bureau like the Aids which was promoting communication
between distant parts of the Empire and was making transport
possible in case of military necessity.   Written requests
were submitted from the Russian Aids Commission for permission
to remove stones from the Argun River fairway at their own
expense and for co-operation in restoring Aids on the Ussuri.
The Taoyin said he would have to wire the authorities at Kirin
and Tsitsihar for instructions on these points but he may be
merely putting off the exposure of his instructions as it was
to settle just such questions that he made his recent trip.
MR. IGNATIEFF HAD DRAWN UP ESTIMATES based on the figures of
last year and providing for improvement of the Ussuri as
follows:

                    INCOME FOR THE YEAR 1927.
River Dues Collection: about $35,000.00
Advances from Sungari Aids Account: $20,000.00
Balance from 1926:   about $ 3,000.00
                                            $58,000.00
                                            EXPENSES

EXPENSES FOR THE YEAR 1927.

Share of Amur Aids:	about	$35,000.00
Share of Ussuri Aids:	about	$ 7,000.00
Taoyin's Office:		$ 2,000.00
Technical Adviser's Office:		$ 8,500.00
10% to Customs for collection:		$ 3,500.00
Loss on exchange:		$ 2,000.00
		$58,000.00

The Russian estimates for 1927 are considerably larger than
those of Mr. Ignatieff for the same work.   Inasmuch, however,
as we are prepared to supply the Russians with workmen and
materials as per our estimates they are prepared to reduce
theirs but it remains to be seen by how much.   As has been
stated before they have some Rbls. 1,200,000.00 to spend on
the Amur basin and are somewhat at a loss as to what to do with
so much money.   It is possible that they will offer to pay
more than their share in the maintenance of lights and beacons
(the number of which they claim should be increased) but I am
against this in principle and think we should pay our way
though it is a sad reflection on China that she can spare only
$42,000.00

$42,000.00 towards Aids on such a great length of navigable
frontier waters.   I should like your instructions on this
point.   Would it be a question to be left to the Provincial
authorities as would that of whether dredging could be done
wholly at the expense of Russia?   It will be seen that the
Russians have now raised the question of renewing the AIDS ON
THE USSURI (to Hulin) which were formerly maintained by her.
River Dues are now collected at Lahasusu on cargo destined for
points on the Ussuri and proceeding thereto via the lower Amur
and the Kasakevich waterway.   For 1926 this collection
amounted to some $10,000.00 as compared with the total
collection of some $35,000.00 shown above, while some 60
Chinese steamers (of smaller tonnage than those proceeding to
Taheiho) navigated the Ussuri as compared with 74 on the Amur.
Under these circumstances both the Technical Adviser and myself
approve the offer of the Russian Aids to improve navigation on
the Ussuri and it will be seen in the above estimate that
$7,000.00 is set aside for the Chinese share.   As a separate
agreement would have to be drawn up in which the Taoyin would
represent the Kirin government an impasse was reached when it
came to the proposed wording of this agreement as a formula
could

could not be found that would not bring up the question,
inferentially or otherwise, of the disputed boundary at
Habarovsk.   As a possible solution I finally suggested that
the Chinese Commission offer to maintain the upper section on
<u>both sides</u> of the Ussuri from Hulin to Jaohohsien (a point about
half way to Habarovsk) and that the Russians maintain the lower
section.   This would allow the Russians a free hand in their
section and the question of the boundary would not be raised.)
Mr. Ignatieff says that the Kasakevich waterway of about 30
versts in length (most deeply involved in the dispute) can
continue to remain uncared for as it is not difficult to
navigate.   In making this suggestion I had in mind your
instructions in I.G. Despatch No.106/93,388 to Aigun in which
you say that as the Commissioner and the Superintendent both
strongly approve the idea of operating the Amur Aids by sections
that the Superintendent should lay his views before the Ch'u.
The Taoyin at once approved this way out of a difficult situation
and has telegraphed Kirin for instructions.   It should be
remarked here, however, that it is not at all certain that the
Russian Aids will approve of this modus operandi in which case
it may happen that nothing will come of the proposal to improve
the

the Ussuri this year.   In connection with the proposal to
undertake the improvement of the Ussuri I have carefully read
Mr. Petterson's S/O No.54 and the Harbin Commissioner's comments
thereon.   Also Aigun Despatch No.230 to I.G. which relates
the discussions that took place between the two Commissions
about Aids on that waterway.   I cannot find that you have
placed on record an expression of opinion as to whether the
Ussuri Aids should be administered from Aigun or Harbin.   From
my study of the situation and from talks with Mr. Ignatieff it
seems to me that Aigun is the logical center for the control of
Aids on the frontier rivers.   Kirin Provincial authorities
would also appear to be of the same opinion.   As to the
complete control of the upper section of the Ussuri as outlined
above Mr. Ignatieff says he is prepared to do this cheaply and
effectively.   A Russian Foreman of long experience is available
as well as Chinese workmen who understand what is required.
While the expenditure of 1927 might be from $5,000.00 to $7,000
it should be less next year as the initial cost of putting the
old beacons in repair and resetting them will be considerable.
Another question that was brought up was the Russian <u>PROPOSAL
TO FORMULATE JOINT RULES OF NAVIGATION</u>.   I told the Taoyin
of

of your attitude in the matter and that it would seem a question
for negotiation in Peking.   I further was able to tell him
that I had heard that the Russian Ambassador at Peking had just
wired the Russian Consul at Tahaiho for all available information
on the subject.   This may mean that the question is being taken
up again there.   It was suggested that in lieu of complete
rules involving judicial and political questions a set of simple
rules might be agreed on (and approved by the higher authorities)
to prevent collisions.   Will you please let me know whether
you think this feasible and whether it lies within the province
of the Aids to negotiate.   The meeting closed with the
understanding that the Taoyin would reply as Taoyin to the
communications regarding the removal of stones on the Argun
and the proposal to draw up an agreement as to navigation rules.
On the occasion of the call of the President alluded to above
he expressed particular concern that there should be no hitch
in drawing up a new agreement.   The present Taoyin/Supt.
Chang Shou-cheng is a very clever man of strong and independent
character and where, heretofore, the Taoyin concerned was content
to sit back and let the Customs do all the work the present man
is very alive to all the ins and outs of the question and

                                        inclined

inclined to lead rather than trail.   So far, however, I have
no cause to complain and welcome his initiative and interest.
Since the above mentioned meeting, however, there have been
no developments and he seems to be playing a waiting game of
some sort.   I shall call on him to-day and propose that we
conclude the Amur agreement at once and settle the other
questions later.   It will be seen that the Aids question is
broadening in scope and becoming more involved.   With the
precedents established and the principles laid down by yourself
as guides, however, I think agreements satisfactory to yourself
will soon eventuate.

        I am sending a copy of this S/O to the Harbin
Commissioner for his information and possible comment.   It
occurs to me that if the Chinese Commission does take over the
maintenance of Aids on one section of the Ussuri that this
might be done by the Sungari Aids at our expense or with a
reduction in the sum to be advanced by them.

                    Yours truly,

第 67 号半官函　　　　　　　　　　　　　1926 年 12 月 17 日于瑷珲关 / 大黑河

尊敬的安格联先生：

为边境关系事：边境开放的前景不容乐观。12 日前俄阿穆尔省新任主席罗伯达（Loboda）前来拜访，本人于家中招待，发现其为人十分有礼。如果身处其他环境，其可能很快便会将布尔什维克思想抛之脑后。其坦承布拉戈维申斯克（Blagoveschesk）政府无权开放边境，关闭的决定也是在上层政府的整体计划之内。相较于苏联政府长期以来的承诺，这样的言论让人更容易理解。兹认为，如果由国民党控制东北三省，边境或许早已开放，贸易也能如符拉迪沃斯托克（Vladivostok）与广东之间那样如常开展。随着时间的推移，亚洲这一地区的中苏关系日益紧张，本地中国官员已经公开表达了对黑龙江对岸苏联当局的不信任与不满。莫斯科方面已派来新任驻黑河苏联领事默拉美德（Melamet）先生（犹太人），其前任多罗波夫（Toropoff）先生将返回首都。此番人事变动看似例行调任，但据了解如今调任至中国的苏联领事大多皆有军方背景。新任命的中东铁路副主席也是如此。昨日前往布拉戈维申斯克回访俄阿穆尔省主席时，受到了热情款待，不经意间又提到了边境开放问题。这次其表示，开放边境的弊端之一是会有大量的"白俄人"涌入，对此本人指出边境一带的白俄人数量实属微不足道，其又辩称是华人自己不愿继续与苏联维持贸易关系。本人当然知道此非事实，于是便停止讨论边境开放一事，又继续探讨其他更为普遍的问题。在前往政府大楼的途中，还遇见了 100 余名被押送的违禁品走私者。据了解，他们是在昨晚试图将货物从华岸运输过江时被武装巡缉队逮捕的。据说每日逮捕的人数都有这么多。惩罚办法通常为收监，但由于监狱中也没有多余的粮食，关押时间一般不会超过三天。至于从华岸走私过江的货物，本人已亲自走访大黑河上下游沿岸的违禁品商铺，发现除酒类，几乎皆为廉价洋货，而这些洋货在进入中国时应已支付了关税。

航路标志：在本人的坚持下，道尹兼海关监督近日召集了中国黑龙江水道委员会的委员们商议新协议之事。易保罗（P. I. Ignatieff）先生及本人经过一段时间的研究，已经汇总了续签协议时需要考虑的各项问题，旧协议将于 1926 年 11 月 30 日期满。如上一封半官函中所述，道尹被吉林省政府召去商议航路标志的相关事宜，主要涉及乌苏里江及哈巴罗夫斯克（Habarovsk）的边界问题。鉴于其在返程途中经过了齐齐哈尔，相信应该会有重要指示传达，但其返回后仅透露在奉天商讨航路标志的维护问题时，张作霖大元帅及海军上将沈鸿烈先生均表示目前有关地方政府无法提供资金援助。据此推断，如果其果然收到了某些指示，也早已将之收为锦囊妙计。齐齐哈尔政府支持提高江捐税率。对此提议，本人完全无法赞同,并向道尹指出商人承担的税赋已经很重,政府应当对像水道委员会这样能够改善边远地区交通状况,实现军需运输要求的机构提供资助。苏联黑龙江水道委员会已经来函请求允许其独自出资清理额尔古纳河河道的礁石,同时由华俄双方联合修复乌苏里江上的航路标志。道尹表示需要向吉林省政府和齐齐哈尔政府提请指示,但也很有可能是其想要暂缓传达日前返程时所收到的相关指令。

为易保罗先生拟订预算事:下列预算乃基于去年数据所拟,乌苏里江航路标志的维护预算亦包含在内:

1927 年收入	
	银圆
江捐税收	(约)35000.00
松花江航路标志账户预支款	20000.00
1926 年结余	(约)3000.00
总计	58000.00
1927 年支出	
黑龙江航路标志摊款	(约)35000.00
乌苏里江航路标志摊款	7000.00
道尹公署办公经费	2000.00
航务专门顾问办公经费	8500.00
10% 海关征税佣金	3500.00
汇兑损失	2000.00
总计	58000.00

对于上述工事,苏方 1927 年的预算远高于易保罗先生所拟数据。尽管如此,中方仍将按照自己所拟预算为苏方提供工人和物料,苏方将须削减预算,不过最终会削减多少,还有待商定。如此前所述,苏方对黑龙江流域的预算约有 1200000.00 卢布,但究竟如何使用,还不甚明了。他们很有可能会提出要为维护灯罩标杆(数量应比他们提出的要多)支付超过其摊款份额之数。对此,本人原则上持反对意见,认为中方应量入为出。只是比较可悲的是,中方仅能为如此绵长的边界河道上的航路标志维护工作拿出 42000.00 银圆。对此还请总税务司示下。由苏方独立出资完成疏浚工事的问题是否应交由省政府解决?

苏方现已提出要对此前便由其维护的乌苏里江至虎林河段的航路标志进行更换。拉哈苏苏海关现对运往乌苏里江沿岸各地及经黑龙江下游及嘎杂克维池（Kasakevicheva）水道运来之货物征收江捐。1926 年此项征收数额约有 10000.00 银圆，当年江捐税收总数如上所示为 35000.00 银圆。乌苏里江上约有 60 艘华籍轮船（吨位较前往大黑河的轮船小）往来航行，黑龙江上有 74 艘。有鉴于此，航务专门顾问及本人均赞同由苏方对乌苏里江的航路状况进行改善，而对于此项工事，中方的摊款如上所示为 7000.00 银圆。

此外，华俄双方还须为此单独起草一份协议，而在此协议中道尹所代表的是吉林省政府。但在商定协议文本时，无论怎样均无法绕过存有争议的哈巴罗夫斯克边界问题，双方因此陷入了僵局。最终本人建议，由中国黑龙江水道委员会负责乌苏里江上游自虎林至饶河县（位于虎林与哈巴罗夫斯克两地中间）河段华俄两岸的维护工作，下游河段则全由苏方负责维护。如此一来，既能让苏方在其河段内自由行动，又可避免涉及边界问题。易保罗先生还指出，嘎杂克维池水道（争议最大）长约 30 俄里，轮船于此航行并无困难，因此可以继续不予维护。

在提出上述建议时，一直牢记海关总税务司公署致瑷珲关第 108/93388 号令的指示，即如果税务司与海关监督均强烈赞成通过划分江段来开展黑龙江上的航路标志工作，则应由海关监督向税务处呈报说明。道尹立即赞成借此办法摆脱当前困境，并已向吉林省政府发送电报提请指示。但需要补充说明的是，现在完全无法确定苏联黑龙江水道委员会是否会赞成这一折中方案，如果不赞成，最终结果很有可能是今年不会对乌苏里江航道进行改善。

关于对乌苏里江的维护建议，在研究过程中，已经仔细阅读了裴德生（C. M. Petterson）先生致总税务司第 54 号半官函，及哈尔滨关税务司对此半官函的意见，以及瑷珲关致海关总税务司公署第 230 号呈（汇报黑龙江水道委员会华俄双方关于乌苏里江航政工作的协商过程）。从中并未发现总税务司对乌苏里江航政工作究竟应由瑷珲关还是哈尔滨关负责给出过明确意见。经研究及与易保罗先生商议，最终认为瑷珲关应为管理边界河道航路标志的中心。吉林省政府似乎亦持此观点。对于上述由中方全权负责乌苏里江上游河段的维护工作一事，易保罗先生表示将会在降低成本的同时实现有效管理。现在能够雇用到一名经验丰富的俄籍工长，以及一些熟悉此项工作的华籍工人。如此一来，1927 年的支出可能会由 5000.00 银圆增加至 7000.00 银圆，但下一年应会更低一些，因为修复及更换旧标桩的初期经费会很高。

为苏方提议拟订联合航行章程事：已将总税务司对此事的意见告知道尹，并说明该问题似乎将由北京方面商定，还透露有消息称苏联驻北京大使已向驻大黑河领事发送电报索要所有相关信息。如此则意味着,此问题将再次由北京方面解决。有建议称,为避免冲突,或许可以拟订一套简单的条例(由高级政府审批),不必涉及司法及政治两方面的所有问题。烦请告知此建议是否可行,水道委员会是否有权协商。最终与道尹商定,将由其以道尹的身份就额尔古纳河上的礁石移除工事及起草航行章程的提议向苏方做出回复。与上述俄阿穆尔省主席会面时,其曾特意表示新协议的起草工作应不会遇到任何阻碍。

现任道尹兼海关监督张寿增先生为人非常精明,处事风格强硬且独立。前任黑河道尹习惯待在后方,让海关处理所有事情,而张寿增先生对于所有事情都十分积极,不愿被动接受,更倾向主动领导。不过迄今为止,对于他的主动与关心,本人并无抱怨之处,反倒十分乐于接受。自上述会谈结束以来,事情便再无任何进展,道尹似乎在故意等待伺机而动。今日将再次前去拜访,计划建议尽快签订黑龙江航路标志协议,其他问题稍后再议。可以看出,航路标志问题所涉范围越来越广,亦更加耗时耗力。不过,有此前先例及总税务司规定的原则作为指导,相信很快即可签订令人满意的协议。

已将此半官函抄件发送给哈尔滨关税务司,以供其参考并给出意见。兹认为,如能由中国黑龙江水道委员会接管乌苏里江一段河道上的航路标志维护工作,具体实施或许可由松花江航路标志机构负责,费用可由海关支付或者从松花江水道委员会预支的款项中扣除。

您真挚的

铎博赉

11. 铎博赉致易纨士函

（第73号半官函）

CUSTOM HOUSE.

Aigun/Taheiho, 29th March, 1927.

S/O No.73.

Dear Mr. Edwardes,

Work in conjunction with the proposed Rules of Navigation, which were sent off to you in my preceding S/O, an investigation into irregular practices and the preparation of my Annual Trade Report has prevented me from writing you for some time about current affairs in the port.

FRONTIER RELATIONS: the relations between the officials on the two sides of the Amur have not improved since my last letter. The Taoyin now openly ignores the local Russian Consul and goes over his head in communicating with the Soviet officials in Blagovestchensk. He distrusts the Consul, rightly or wrongly I cannot say, and prefers to have nothing to do with him. On the other hand this policy may be dictated by Moukden. Personally I find the Consul not a bad sort. On the occasion of the recent taking of Shanghai by the Southerners a half holiday was declared in Blagovestchensk and given over to parades and

A. H. F. Edwardes, Esquire,
Peking.

and speeches. The situation in China is followed very closely by the Soviet officials and there is no doubt but that the political and economic future of Taheiho rests largely on the outcome of the struggle now going on between the pro-and anti-Bolsheviks there. I have yet to hear of any military preparations being made on the other side with a view to an offensive against China.

RULES OF NAVIGATION: In my S/O No.72 in which I submit a draft of the proposed new Rules I forgot to mention that Mr. Boezi appears to have forwarded a version of such Rules in his S/O No.11 of 5th April, 1922, which the I. G. commented on in his S/O of the 24th May, 1922. I have made a thorough search here but I cannot find the Rules in question - perhaps a copy was not kept. It will undoubtedly be found on file in the Inspectorate, together with the original Rules submitted by the Russian authorities, but I do not anticipate that either can differ much from the draft now submitted.

LONG LEAVE FOR FOREIGN OUTDOOR STAFF: I wired you on the 2nd March that for financial reasons

Mr.

Mr. Baukham, Acting Tidesurveyor, had had to cancel his leave. In my despatch No.305 I submitted his application officially and in your despatch No. 337/111,707 in reply it was cancelled. It is too bad that his plans should have been interrupted in this manner and I must remark in passing that there is no hospital in Taheiho to accommodate foreigners and a serious illness in a family, which requires an operation or professional nursing, necessitates a very expensive trip to Harbin. Mr. Baukham has now been in Taheiho some six years and there is no doubt but that a change after such a long period in one port would be desirable. He would like to remain on here, however, and has given up all present intentions of going home. This might mean the easiest solution of the awkward problem of finding a suitable Russian speaking non-Russian to replace him.

In my despatch No. 306 I forwarded Mr. Dreggs' (Assistant Examiner B) renewal of application for Long Leave to date from the close of navigation this autumn. In this despatch I state that he need not be replaced until the opening of navigation the

following

following spring. I feel that one Examiner will be enough in the winter to keep up the records, attend examination work at the Post Office, etc. Should he be ill we can still manage.

DISHONESTY IN THE NATIVE OUTDOOR STAFF: I now come to a very disagreeable subject. Some time ago, at the time of the examination of Watcher Yü Fu-shou for possible promotion to the rank of Chinese Tidewaiter - (my despatch No. 301 submitting his papers and I. G. despatch No.332/111,421 in reply saying that his showing was satisfactory) - I received an anonymous letter saying that he had received assistance during his examination and that, furthermore, he had been guilty of demanding bribes at the Lower Barrier. Though the letter was anonymous and probably written by some jealous member of the local Staff I considered it only fair that he should be given a chance to clear his name and I prepared two more papers for him. This time I gave the Tidesurveyor instructions not to leave his office, where the test was being held, until it was completed. As the results were as good as on the occasion of his original examination and there was no

proof

proof of his having taken bribes and as, moreover, his
record for the past 9 years was clear, I sent up his
papers with my favourable recommendation. On the 15th
ultimo the Watcher at the Upper Barrier, Hsing Chin-shan
(邢 峻 珊) by name, sent in a Boatman/Guard by the
name of Kao Yung-chêng (高 永 禎) with the charges
that he had disobeyed orders and had been demanding
bribes. On questioning the accused he denied them but
said that the Watcher himself had been receiving
squeezes from the neighbouring contraband shops and that
he would produce a shopkeeper to verify what he said.
I thereupon sent the Tidesurveyor and a Clerk to the
shop, obtained his account books and called him to my
office. Investigation of the books showed payments to
Customs employees at the Upper Barrier at various times
and the shopkeeper said these were made to both Kao and
Hsing. I then suspended these two from duty and
requested the cooperation of the Taoyin in appointing a
deputy to accompany one of my Clerks in the investigation
of the account books of all the shops near the two
Barriers. Several days were spent in doing this and
much opposition was encountered as both the employees
                                                    and

and the shops concerned had got the wind up. Eventually
some six sets of books were obtained all of which had
entries showing that irregular payments had been made.
In most cases the entries had been changed and falsified
but it was possible to still read what had originally
been written. It was plain that systematic payments
had been made to our Staff by all the contraband shops
in the vicinity of the two Barriers since they were
opened and only ceasing when the latter were recently
closed. These payments were made by the shops to
secure protection for their clients who bought their
merchandise for smuggling across the river. As to how
much was collected from the smugglers themselves, of
which there was no record, only conjecture can be made
but the amount must have been large. My first
inclination was to dismiss all directly concerned, who
proved to be:

Li Yuan Ching (李 元 慶) 3ºCl.Chi.Twtr.
Kung Chun Lin (龔 春 霖) 4º   "   "   "
Yü Fu-shou   (于 福 壽) Watcher
Hsing Chin-shan (邢 峻 珊) Watcher
Kao Yung-chêng (高 永 禎) Boatman/Guard
Sun Shou-chen (孫 守 臣)   "   "
Yü Teh-yuan (于 德 元)   "   "
                                    However

However I eventually decided that this would not be
good policy, under existing conditions, for the
following reasons: in addition to the entries of
payments to Customs employees there were similar records
of bribes to soldiers and police and I soon learned
indirectly that the officials concerned, who knew of
these extortions, were greatly chagrined that they
should have been brought to light by myself.   The
Supt.'s sentiments were that it was a great loss of face
to the Chinese to have such disclosures made at this
time when Chinese institutions were on trial and "they
were taking steps to assume control of the Customs".
On learning of this state of mind amongst the local
officials I called on the Supt. and finally brought up
the subject of the recent disclosures of dishonesty
amongst my Staff, as shown by the shops' records, and
asked what he thought their punishment should be.   He
was rather non-committal and ventured the remark that
possibly the matter had better be kept out of the
courts.   I told him I had no intention of making the
scandal public and said that I had decided on dismissal
in two or three cases and on lighter punishment in
                                           others.

others.   This appeared reasonable to him so I let the
matter drop there.   In the meantime Chinese Tidewaiter
Kung had come to me and made a confession, which he
later confirmed in writing, and asked for mercy.   As
the evidence in connection with his name pointed not
only to the acceptance of bribes but of certain sums
entered in the accounts of one shop as payments of
duty, I informed him that I had no option but to
dismiss him.   Later on after considerable pressure
from the Chinese Staff and taking into consideration
the fact that these irregular payments were commonly
accepted by the military and police and were looked on
as natural transactions by all concerned, I commuted
the sentence to "Permitted to Resign".   All the other
employees stoutly declared their innocence.   Watcher
Hsing was dismissed as the evidence against him was
quite clear.   That against Chinese Tidewaiter Li was
more circumstantial and I decided to let him off with
a warning in the Order Book that a repetition of such
an offence would entail his prompt dismissal and that
a Memo containing a copy of the Order would be enclosed
in his next transfer despatch.   Watcher Yü Fu-shou also
                                           denied

denied that he had received bribes and in his case, as
in others, matters were complicated by the fact that
certain shops seemed to have acted as "bankers" for
different employees at the two Barriers while goods
were honestly bought from time to time on credit,
though payment could not always be proved. However
there was enough evidence to make me believe that
Yü Fu-shou was incriminated to such an extent that I
would have to withdraw the recommendation I had made to
you that he be promoted to the rank of Chinese
Tidewaiter.   I recorded this in the Order Book with
the additional remark that further complaints of a
similar nature would result in his instant dismissal.
Boatman/Guard Kao had disappeared.   Boatmen/Guards
Sun and Yü were warned against a repetition of such an
offence in the Order Book.   All whose connection with
the Service had not ceased were restored to duty and I
wrote the Taoyin saying that I had punished the Customs
employees concerned in taking bribes from the
contraband shops, pointing out on the other hand that
the shops were equally guilty, and asking him to take
such steps as he considered sufficient to prevent them
from

from continuing such practices.   I am submitting the
whole affair to you by despatch and hope you will
approve of what I have done.   In the meantime I can
carry on with a shortage of one Chinese Tidewaiter
(the other vacancies have been filled) until the
opening of navigation.   I shall mention in my despatch
that Chinese Tidewaiter Kung is hoping for the refund
of his contributions and one of the factors that led
me to soften his sentence of dismissal is the fact that
he will be under heavy expense for the return to his
native home in Foochow and he is apparently without
means.

MANCHURIAN ALLOWANCE TO OUTDOOR STAFF: in
my despatch No.298 of 12th January, 1927, I submitted
tables showing that the cost of living in Taheiho was
higher than last year and venturing to recommend that
the Manchurian Allowances be continued to the Foreign
Outdoor Staff.   Up to now no reply has been received
from the Inspectorate and the Allowances in question
have been withheld since the 1st January.   Beginning
with March the enhanced salary paying rate will make
up to a certain extent for the loss of the Allowances.
At

At the rate of 175 the two may be compared as follows:

	Allowance: @ 156.65	Gain by Exchange: @ 175
Messrs Baukham:	$78.33	$52.30
Mikulin:	62.66	34.50
Dreggs:	47.00	26.74
Klimenko:	31.33	21.10
Eysymontt:	31.33	19.84
Lankin:	31.33	15.52

If you do not consider that you can continue the allowances in question it may be possible to issue them for January and February.

RAISING OF COLLECTION RATE: On the 24th inst. I telegraphed you asking your permission to sell a Sh.Tls. cheque covering the salaries of the Foreign and Chinese Staffs and to pay them the proceeds. You agreed to this and their pay worked out at the rate of 180.47. You also instructed me to inform you of the progress of negotiations for the raising of the rate by despatch. I encountered a certain amount of objection at first to my proposal and was rather nervous that it might not be adopted and that if it was turned down the refusal would react on the situation

in

in Harbin. I am pleased to say, however, that a despatch has now been received from the Supt. approving the intended action and I am issuing a notification tomorrow that the rate will be raised as from the 15th April, giving two weeks warning as directed in I. G. despatch No.333/111,451. I presume that the Office Allowance for the first half of April will be drawn at the old rate of 156.65 and that for the balance of the month at the new rate (175) and the Official and Revenue balances will be written down on that date. Also that all such balances will have to be written up or down at the end of each month hereafter, if the rate changes. I shall write the Harbin Commissioner asking him for his accounts procedure as he has similar questions to contend with.

Yours truly,

第 73 号半官函　　　　　　　　　**1927 年 3 月 29 日于瑷珲关 / 大黑河**

尊敬的易纨士先生：

　　近来需要处理之事较多，包括上一封半官函汇报的航行章程相关工作、关员违纪行为的调查工作以及瑷珲关年度贸易报告的编撰工作等，以致未能及时汇报本口岸的局势发展。

　　为边境关系事：自发送上一封半官函以来，黑龙江华俄两岸地方官员的关系依然未得到改善。道尹现已公然无视苏联驻大黑河领事，直接与布拉戈维申斯克（Blagoveschesk）的苏联官员对接。道尹不信任苏联领事，不愿与之有任何瓜葛，但对错与否，殊难评判。不过此做法或许也是受到了奉天方面的指示。就个人意见，本人觉得苏联领事并非恶人。目前上海被南方部队占领，布拉戈维申斯克全城休假半日，举行游行演讲。苏联官员一直密切关注着中国的局势，因此大黑河地区日后的发展，无论是在政治上，还是在经济上，都必然会受到对岸布尔什维克党拥护者与反对者双方斗争结果的影响。但迄今仍未听闻对岸有要动用军队侵犯中国的准备。

　　为航行章程事：第 72 号半官函呈交新航行章程草案时，忘记提及包安济（G. Boezi）先生似乎曾于 1922 年 4 月 5 日第 11 号半官函中附寄过一版航行章程，而且总税务司于 1922 年 5 月 24 日回函时也给出了意见。但查遍本关档案，都未能找到半官函中所述的航行章程，或许是当年抄件并未存档。但相信海关总税务司公署一定有存档，包括苏联政府递交的条例原件。估计存档的航行章程与当前所呈交的草案在内容上不会有太大差异。

　　为洋籍外班关员休长假事：已于 3 月 2 日电呈汇报署监察长博韩（G. E. Baukham）先生因资金问题不得不取消休假，并于瑷珲关第 305 号呈中正式提交此申请，最终由海关总税务司公署第 337/111707 号令批准取消。博韩先生原定的休假计划以此种方式取消，实为遗憾。但还需提及的是，大黑河并无可以安置外国人的医院，如果外籍关员的家人得了重病，需要手术或者专业护理，还要花重金前往哈尔滨接受治疗。博韩先生至今已于大黑河口岸服务 6 年之久，按理在一个口岸工作了如此长的时间，定会希望调任他处，但其仍愿意继续于此任职，而且现下已经放弃了返回家乡的想法。因此，需要另派一名通晓俄文的非俄籍关员接替其职位的尴尬问题也相当于提早解决了。

　　瑷珲关第 306 号呈中汇报称三等验货后班德里格（C. O. Dreggs）先生再次申请自今年秋季航运结束起开始休长假，同时说明在明年春季航运开通之前无需另派关员接替其职位。相信一名验货员应足以应对冬季期间的记录工作及邮政局的验货工作等。即使其生病休假，关务亦不会受到影响。

为华籍外班职员违纪事：以下汇报之事令人十分不快。前段时间,华籍巡役于福寿为晋升华籍稽查员参加考试(答卷已由瑷珲关第 301 号呈递交并由海关总税务司公署第 332/111421 号令批示结果满意)。随后本人便收到一封匿名信,内称于福寿先生在考试期间有他人襄助,而且在图东分卡任职期间还曾索取贿赂。尽管信件为匿名,也很有可能是本关职员中有人因嫉妒而写,但为公平起见,还是给了于福寿先生一次正名的机会,又发给其两份试卷。此次考试在监察长办公室内进行,特命监察长监督考试过程,并要求其结束之前不得离开。最终考试结果与第一次一样优秀,而且也无证据证明其曾收受贿赂,更重要的是,其过去 9 年间记录清白,因此本人便向总税务司呈交其答卷,并推荐晋升。

2 月 15 日,图西分卡巡役邢峻珊实名举报水手兼卫兵高永祯不服从命令且收受贿赂。面对此控告,高永祯矢口否认,反指控巡役邢峻珊一直压榨图西分卡附近的违禁品商铺,并称有商铺店主可为其作证。本人遂命监察长及一名税务员前往该商铺调查,并将店主及商铺账簿一并带回。经查,账簿中有店主在不同时期向图西分卡海关职员交款的记录,店主表示邢峻珊和高永祯均为受益者。本人随即将此二人停职,并请道尹派遣一名代表与本关一名税务员一同前去调查图西图东两处分卡附近的所有商铺的账簿。

调查之事历经数日,且因职员和商铺都担心受到牵连,进展得并不顺利。最终带回六本账簿,均载有不合常规的支付记录。其中大多记录都有涂抹篡改的痕迹,但最初的笔迹仍然依稀可辨。显然自两处分卡开设以来,周边所有的违禁品商铺一直都在向本关职员行贿,直到近期两处分卡关闭后才得以终止。商铺行贿旨在保护其顾客在购买商品走私过江时免受海关稽查,至于他们会向走私商人收取多少,账簿中并无记录,只能猜测,但相信数额不会太少。最初对于所有直接参与此事的职员,本人原打算全部解除职务,人员有:

李元庆：华籍三等一级稽查员

龚春霖：华籍四等一级稽查员

于福寿：华籍巡役

邢峻珊：华籍巡役

高永祯：水手兼卫兵

孙守臣：水手兼卫兵

于德元：水手兼卫兵

但考虑到当前的情况,最终还是认为此非良策,因为商铺账簿中的行贿记录除涉及海关职员,还有士兵和警察,而且不久前还间接了解到,知悉此等索贿行为的有关官员在得知本人要将此事公之于众时,十分震怒。海关监督认为,现下中国的制度还在试运行阶段，"他们还企图接管海关"，值此之际披露索贿之事，会使中国官员颜面尽失。知悉地方官员有此想法后，本人便前去拜访海关监督，最终提及日前经翻查商铺账簿发现本关职员有违纪行为一事，并向其征询惩罚意见。海关监督并未表明态度，只是提出最好私下解决。对此，本人表示亦不希望公开此事，已决定仅解雇两三名关员，其他涉事关员一概从轻处罚。此决定在其看来，亦颇为合理，因此当时便未再继续讨论。

此外，华籍稽查员龚春霖先生已向本人主动承认索贿之事，请求宽大处理，随后又以书面确认。然鉴于与其相关的记录不仅涉及收受贿赂，还有一家商铺的账簿中载明其曾以关税的名义收款。因此已告知只能将其解雇。但之后迫于华籍职员方面的压力，又考虑到此等收贿行为在军方及警方看来十分平常，而且已被有关各方视为寻常交易，最终决定将对其的处罚改为"准许辞职"。但所有其他涉事关员均坚决否认指控，宣称清白。巡役邢峻珊因证据确凿已被解雇。华籍稽查员李元庆，考虑到对其的指控多为间接推测，已决定从轻处罚，仅于谕令簿中警告其如有再犯，将立即解雇，日后调离本关时亦会于其调任公文随附的关员履历表中加入此谕令抄件。巡役于福寿同样拒不承认有收贿行为，而且与其他涉事关员一样，情况的复杂之处在于，有些商铺似乎是充当了"银行"的角色，允许两处分卡的职员赊账购买商品，尽管账簿记录中并不是所有的欠款都已偿清。无论如何，当前证据足以证明于福寿确有收贿嫌疑，因此只能撤回此前推荐其晋升华籍稽查员的申请，并将此记入谕令簿，备注说明如再收到类似指控，将立即将其解雇。水手兼卫兵高永祯已经消失。水手兼卫兵孙守臣和于德元亦处以警告，命之不得再犯，并记入谕令簿。所有未与海关解除关系的职员均已复职。随后已致函道尹说明所有涉嫌从违禁品商铺收受贿赂的关员均已受到处罚，指出涉事商铺同样负有责任，请其采取必要措施加以约束，以避免此类不当行为的再次发生。

同时已呈文汇报整件事情，希望所做决定能得总税务司批准。此外，在航运开通之前，缺少一名华籍稽查员（另一空缺已由人补上），关务不会受到影响。呈文中还将汇报华籍稽查员龚春霖申请退还其养老储金。实际上，本人最后决定将对其的处罚从解雇减轻为准许辞职，还因考虑到于其而言，返回福州老家所需的费用将是一笔巨款，而且其显然已没有钱银。

为外班关员的满洲津贴事：1927年1月12日瑷珲关第298号呈中递交了一份大黑河物价表，从中可以看出，与上年相比本地的生活成本已大幅上涨，因此建议继续为洋籍外班关员发放满洲津贴。然而迄今为止，仍未收到总税务司的回复，且自今年1月1日起已停止发放满洲津贴。但3月初以来，随着薪俸支付汇率的提高，关员因停止发放津贴所遭受的损失将会在一定程度上得到弥补。以 100 海关两兑换 175 银圆的薪俸支付汇率为例,津贴与汇兑盈余的金额对比如下:

	津贴 (100 海关两 1=156.65 银圆)	汇兑盈余 (100 海关两 =175 银圆)
	银圆	银圆
博韩(G. E. Baukham)	78.33	52.30
密库林(S. E. Mikulin)	62.66	34.50
德里格(C. O. Dreggs)	47.00	26.74
葛满阔(W. G. Klimenko)	31.33	21.10
伊思孟(V. A. Eysymontt)	31.33	19.84
蓝金(V. Z. Lankin)	31.33	15.52

　　总税务司如未考虑继续发放满洲津贴,不知能否仅为上述关员发放 1 月 2 月的津贴。

　　为提高海关征税汇率事:3 月 24 日曾电呈总税务司申请将为支付华洋外班关员薪俸的一张上海规元支票卖出,并将售卖收益一并发给关员。获得批准后已照办,最终薪俸支付汇率为 100 海关两兑换 180.47 银圆。总税务司还指示要求通过呈文汇报提高海关征税汇率的协商进展。提议之初,确实遭到了一些反对,当时很担心提议最终可能不会被采纳,也担心万一遭到拒绝,哈尔滨方面可能也会受到牵连。不过,海关监督现已来函告知同意此项提议。明日将发布海关公告,宣布自 4 月 15 日起提高海关征税汇率。如此亦是遵照海关总税务司公署第 333/111451 号令指示提前两周发布预告。预计 4 月上半月的海关经费仍将按照 100 海关两兑换 156.65 银圆的旧汇率支领,下半个月再按照新汇率支领,即 100 海关两兑换 175 银圆。调整后,自调整日起将对海关经费及税收的账面余额进行减记,此后如遇汇率调整,无论需要增记,或是减记,均将于每月底进行。鉴于哈尔滨关税务司亦需处理类似问题,将向其致函询问哈尔滨关的入账手续。

您真挚的

铎博赉

12. 铎博赉致易纨士函

（第74号半官函）

S/O No.74.

CUSTOM HOUSE,

Aigun/Taheiho. 3rd May, 1927.

Dear Mr. Edwardes,

FRONTIER CONDITIONS: there has been little communication with Blagoveschensk for many days owing to the breaking up of the ice on the Amur. From what I can gather, however, everything is quiet and there is no undue excitement over the situation in China. On the 1st May there were big demonstrations against Chang Tso-lin during which his effigy is said to have been publicly burned and at another place stuffed figures supposed to represent him were set up and had their heads cut off by mounted soldiers riding at full tilt. It is to be hoped that these bloodthirsty acts will satiate their thirst for gore! The Taoyin/Superintendent left the port on the 3rd April with the ultimate intention of visiting Peking (when he would have called on the Inspectorate) but on arriving at Changchun he got the news of the searching of the Russian Legation and at once started back

A. H. F. Edwardes, Esquire,
Peking.

back for Taheiho. The last few days of his journey were pluckily spent in a cart as the road from Tsitsihar to Taheiho was impassable for motor cars. He arrived here on the 26th ultimo and at once called on the Russian Consul telling him, so he informed me, that as he had received no instructions from the Central Government indicating any change in their relations, that he hoped things would carry on as usual and that, especially, the Amur Aids Agreement would not be interfered with. The Consul assured him that as far as he knew there was to be no change. The Consulate Staff has been very nervous of late and I take it that they have little reason to expect any assistance from the Soviet authorities if they are eventually asked to leave. Should there be a break in local official relations I hope that the two Aids Commissions will be able to carry on as before.

USSURI AIDS: In my S/O No.71 of the 2nd February, I report that, as an impasse had again been reached in the negotiations concerning Aids on the Ussuri, owing to the boundary question in the vicinity of Harbarovsk, the whole matter was being referred to the Sino-Russian Conference, Peking, by the Chinese and

Russian

Russian authorities concerned. On the 11th March the
Taoyin sent a despatch to the Amur Navigation Bureau
that he was in receipt of instructions from the Kirin
authorities to the effect that as the question of Aids
on the Ussuri had been referred to Peking that neither
Commission should do any work on that river pending a
decision. In talking the matter over with the Taoyin
later I informed him that I had reason to believe that
the Russian Commission would not agree to this as the
boundary on their side of the river was not in dispute
and they would naturally expect a free hand to
establish Aids on their side of the Ussuri at their
own expense. I further pointed out that under
present conditions we might have to wait for years for
a decision from the so-called Sino-Russian Conference.
At a later meeting of the two Commissions the Taoyin
executed a complete volte face and requested the
Russian Commission to reply to his letter in a manner
that would permit the reopening of the question. A
suitable reply was received shortly afterwards but the
Taoyin took no further steps. On my calling on him
yesterday, however, he seemed very anxious to go ahead
with the matter and I am in hopes that we may be able
to

to conclude an early agreement.

RULES OF NAVIGATION: I have not been
pushing this question as I have been waiting for an
expression of opinion from you as to the draft Rules
submitted in my S/O No.72 of the 25th March. This
draft was given to the Russian Commission for comment
and it has been returned with suggested alterations
and additions of only a slight, and acceptable, nature.
It is probable that the Taoyin will begin to press that
an Agreement be drawn up shortly. In connection with
the point I made in my S/O No.72 that the Customs take
over the enforcement of the Rules when adopted I am
glad to say that the Taoyin has now expressed himself
clearly to the same effect without knowing my ideas on
the subject.

DIGGING OF CHANNEL IN THE HARBOUR: this
work has been brought to a successful conclusion at an
expenditure slightly under $2,000. The Tungpei S/S
Co. have also been induced to do considerable work
around their jetty in the way of the removal of stones,
etc. to accelerate the current through the new channel.
In connection with the repayment of the loan of $2,000
I understand that there is now a possibility (probably
slight) of the Tungpei S/S Co. assuming this liability.
In

In the meantime I am hoping that you will authorize me
to repay the loan of $2,000 from the Bank of China (
which expires 6th May) as an advance from Aids funds -
my despatch No.311.

    INCREASE IN RIVER DUES: in my despatch No.
311 I mention the receipt of the Taoyin's instructions
that the River Dues Tariff be raised for the purpose of
providing the Aids Commission with more funds. The
negotiations with the local Chamber of Commerce in this
connection have been satisfactory and an early
agreement will be reached. I propose to tax the
export of gold, which is not considered economically
justifiable in the ordinary way. However I consider
gold to be of the same nature as any other local
product as it is mined in this vicinity and is not
being shipped out to pay for cargo imported.

    DISHONESTY AT THE BARRIERS: In my despatch
No.310 reporting dishonesty amongst the Staff at the
Barriers, the enclosure thereto, containing
incriminating extracts from the account books of various
firms, showed certain payments by the firm Fu Sheng-
hsing to Hwong Ta-ch'ing (黄 達 鄉). 3rd Class
Chinese Tidewaiter, since transferred to Kiukiang.

                              Though

Though the shopkeeper maintained that these items were
for purchases in the ordinary way that had not yet been
paid for I cannot but believe that they were "squeezes"
and it is probable that had the investigation gone
deeper into the time he served at the Barriers that more
evidence of a similar nature would have been found
against him. I did not mention this matter in my
despatch referred to above as I thought it better to
refer it to you by S/O for your information.

    MR. WOO YU CHANG. 2ND CLERK C. REQUESTS
REFUND OF TRAVELLING EXPENSES ON HIS APPOINTMENT TO
TIENTSIN FROM LEAVE: I have received a letter from
Mr. Woo to the effect that his leave has been curtailed
and he has been appointed to Tientsin. To quote from
his letter: "Now I am given to understand that recently
"a Chinese Assistant who was granted Inspectorate leave
"from Lungchingtsun and reported for duty at Tientsin
"was issued first class mileage from Lungchingtsun to
"Tientsin by Tientsin office as a result of the
"Commissioner's recommendations of the former port with
"the I. G.'s sanction. This time I suffered a great
"deal, I don't know if I can claim my travelling
"expenses from Taheiho to Harbin and mileage from
"Harbin to Tientsin." Mr. Woo served in Aigun for two
                              years

years and his leave was overdue. I do not know the
circumstances under which the travelling expenses of
the Chinese Assistant referred to were paid but if
Mr. Woo has any claim from the fact that Aigun/Taheiho
is a frontier port may I forward it officially?

COLLECTION OF WASHINGTON SURTAX: On the
17th March I wired you that the Superintendent had
started the collection of surtax as from the 16th and
asking whether the booth occupied by the Bank, which
was too small to accommodate the Supt's Deputy too,
should be enlarged. Your reply was to the effect that
the Bank should be removed to the brick building on the
New Custom House Site. Shortly after the receipt of
your instructions both the Supt. and the Manager of the
Bank of China left for Peking so I was unable to do
anything. The former has now returned and I shall
take up the matter before the opening of navigation.
As a matter of fact a little delay in the matter has
done no harm for to have requested an immediate removal
on the beginning of the surtax collection would have
caused the Superintendent to lose face. In your instructions regarding the collection of surtax you
emphasise the point that the Duty Memos are in reality

the

the Superintendent's documents as they are issued by
him. I presume that the Harbin Office has already
pointed out that in this district we print our own
receipts - in Russian and Chinese, and as I have heard
nothing from that office about this technicality, I
have considered that we are to carry on as in the rest
of China. The Bank of China are pressing for a new
agreement re Collection of Revenue and say that one
has been concluded at Harbin. I shall take up the
matter on the return of the Manager. Personally I
should like to see the collection given to the Bank
of Communications, though it might not be politic or
convenient to do so.

BRITISH MEMBERS OF THE STAFF RECEIVE NOTICE
TO EVACUATE: Messrs Baukham and Dreggs of this Staff
are in receipt of a Circular from the British
Consulate, Harbin warning them to withdraw to places
of safety at open ports. I presume the same notice
has been sent to all Britishers in North China. At
the same time I received a private letter from Mr.
Porter containing the paragraph - "I do not know if
"it will be possible for them to leave without
"embarassing the Customs Administration but I have no

"alternative

"alternative but to issue the warning". I am replying
to the above that there is no means of evacuating, if
the two Britishers concerned and their families wished
to go, pending the opening of navigation and that in
the meantime I am referring the matter to you. At the
same time I am saying that I can see no present local
reason why they should leave and if they did so now it
will be on their own responsibility. Of late the news
from the South seems more reassuring but there is no
overlooking the fact that should communications be cut
between here and Darien that we would be in a difficult
position unless we could leave via Blagovestchensk for
Europe or Vladivostock. Whether we could go that way
would be doubtful for it might mean "out of the frying
pan into the fire" - at Taheiho we might be between two
fires. As I have just said, however, at present there
seems no cause for uneasiness. Telegraphic
communication is very uncertain now on account of the
poor condition of the lines but if it is necessary to
send any urgent messages warning me of a change in
conditions it would be possible to send it through the
Great Northern Telegraph Co. to their Agent at
Blagovestchensk (a friend of mine) whose name is Dechler

He

He could get it over to me in a few hours.
                    Yours truly,

第 74 号半官函 　　　　　　　　1927 年 5 月 3 日于瑷珲关 / 大黑河

尊敬的易纨士先生：

　　为边境局势事：自黑龙江上的冰层开始破裂以来，大黑河与布拉戈维申斯克（Blagoveschesk）已许久未有交通往来。据悉，俄岸并无异常，对于中国局势的变化也没有表现出异常的兴奋。5 月 1 日多地爆发了抗议张作霖的示威活动，其画像被当众烧毁，还有地方竖立了很多代表其的人像，并由骑兵急速驶过，将人像的头砍掉。希望这些暴力行为能够到此为止。4 月 3 日，道尹兼海关监督离开大黑河，欲前往北京（届时将至海关总税务司公署拜访），但到达长春时便得到消息称苏联公使馆遭到搜查，于是又启程返回。回程时，由于齐齐哈尔至大黑河的道路难行，其无法乘坐汽车，最终只得搭乘马车，并于 4 月 26 日抵达，随后立即拜访了苏联领事。据其所述，其已告知苏联领事，中央政府并未下达关于改变双方关系的指示，希望一切照旧，尤其希望黑龙江航路标志协议不要受到影响。苏联领事亦明确表示，据其所知也不会有何变化。近日来，领事馆的职员颇为紧张，但相信即使他们最终被遣返回国，应该也无理由期待苏联政府会施以援手。万一地方关系破裂，希望中俄黑龙江水道委员会还能如常开展工作。

　　为乌苏里江航政事：之前已于 2 月 2 日第 71 号半官函中汇报，乌苏里江航路标志的相关谈判，因涉及哈巴罗夫斯克（Habarovsk）附近的边界问题，再次陷入僵局，将由中俄有关当局在北京召开的会议上解决。3 月 11 日，道尹向俄阿穆尔水道局致函说明已收悉吉林省政府指示，即乌苏里江航路标志的相关事宜既已提交北京方面，在有决议之前，双方均不得于乌苏里江上开展任何工事。本人随后与道尹商议此事时表示，苏联境内的乌苏里江并不存在边界争议，苏联水道委员会根本不可能同意按照吉林省政府的指示办理，定会希望可以自由地在乌苏里江苏联一侧安设航路标志，当然费用亦由其自行承担，同时还指出按照当前的局势发展，恐怕要等上数年，才能等到所谓的中俄会议给出决议。在之后的中俄黑龙江水道委员会会议上，道尹彻底转变了态度，希望苏方委员可以回函说明同意重新商议此事。不久后道尹便收到了苏方的回函，但并未采取进一步行动。昨日拜访时可以看出，道尹迫切希望此事能够有所进展，相信双方或许可以很快达成协议。

　　为航行章程事：自通过 3 月 25 日第 72 号半官函递交了航行章程草案以来，一直在等待总税务司批示，因此其间并没有推进此事。之前也将此草案发给了苏联水道委员会征询意见，如今已收到反馈，增改之处较少，已基本接受。道尹可能很快便会开始催促起草协议。72 号半官函中曾表示希望待航行条例实施时，可由海关负责。道尹现在亦表明此意,而且其并不知本人有此想法。

为疏浚港口河道事:此项工事已顺利完成,费用不到 2000 银圆。经引导,东北航务局也参与了大量工作,主要负责其码头周围的礁石移除等工事,以加快水流通过新河道的速度。关于上述 2000 银圆的偿付问题,据了解,或许可以由东北航务局承担,但希望或许也很渺茫。与此同时,特此申请批准暂预支航路标志资金(参阅瑷珲关第 311 号呈)偿付中国银行的 2000 银圆贷款(到期日为 5 月 6 日)。

为提高江捐税率事:瑷珲关第 311 号呈中汇报道尹要求提高江捐税率,以为水道委员会提供更充足的资金。与地方商会的谈判也比较顺利,相信很快便可达成协议。建议对出口黄金收税,虽然通常从经济的角度来看,此举并不合理,但黄金与地方生产的其他土货本质相同,既在本地区开采,运出时又不缴税。

为分卡职员渎职事:瑷珲关第 310 号呈中汇报了图西、图东分卡职员中存在渎职行为,附件中还有各商行账簿的摘录。其中显示,华籍三等钤子手黄达卿曾接受过福盛兴商行的贿赂,但之后其已调任九江关。尽管店主坚称,这些都是平时购买所产生的费用,只是还未结款而已,但本人还是认为这些都是"压榨"之款,而且如果继续深入调查其于分卡任职期间的情况,相信还会找到更多类似的证据。未将上述情况于呈文中说明,主要考虑到还是以半官函的方式汇报更为适宜。

为二等同文供事后班吴煜章先生申请为其休假结束调任津海关之行程报销旅费事:吴煜章先生来函表示其假期提前结束,将调任津海关。函中称:"得知近日龙井村关的一名华籍帮办休假结束至津海关上任时,经龙井村关税务司的推荐,已获总税务司批准由津海关为其自龙井村至天津一段行程发放一等里程津贴。本人此行已经受诸多困难,不知能否同时申请大黑河至哈尔滨一段的旅费及哈尔滨至天津一段的里程津贴。"吴煜章先生在瑷珲关任职两年,假期还未休完。虽不知上述华籍帮办的旅费报销依据为何,但如果吴煜章先生以瑷珲关(大黑河)乃边境口岸为依据申请报销旅费,可否提交正式申请?

为征收华盛顿附加税事:3 月 17 日曾电呈说明海关监督已于 3 月 16 日起开始征收附加税,但中国银行使用的收税亭过于狭小,再安置海关监督副手则显得十分拥挤,因此询问是否需要扩建。总税务司指示将银行办公地点移至新海关关址上的砖房内。收悉该指示后不久,海关监督及中国银行大黑河支行行长便离开大黑河前往北京,因此一直未能有所行动。海关监督现已返回,在航运开通前将与之说明此事。实际上,拖延一段时日亦非坏事,因为如果刚开始征收附加税,便提出搬离要求,会有损海关监督的颜面。关于征收附加税一事,总税务司指示中强调税款缴纳证实际上是海关监督的凭证,因为皆是由其签发。相信哈尔滨关税务司已经说明本关区皆是自行印制俄文及汉文完税收据，但因之前一直未从哈尔滨关方面收到过相关消息，因此还以为应遵循其他口岸的惯例。中国银行希望尽快重新签订收税合同，并称已与哈尔滨关完成签订。待中国银行大黑河支行行长返回后，将着手处理此事。就个人意见，本人更希望由交通银行为海关代收关税，但或许并非上策，也不会方便。

为英籍关员收到撤离通知事：博韩（G. E. Baukham）先生及德里格（C. O. Dreggs）先生收到英国领事馆通令，提醒他们撤离至通商口岸的安全地点。相信所有在中国北部的英籍人员都已收到此通知。与此同时，波特（Porter）先生还发来一封私人信函，其中有一段内容为"虽不知他们能否在不使海关当局为难的情况下离开，但目前除了签发撤离通知，已别无选择"。对此，本人回复当前无法撤离，如果该两名英籍关员及家人希望离开，只能等待航运开通，而且还须向总税务提请指示，此外还说明当前地方上的形势还没有到必须撤离的地步，如果他们现在撤离，一切后果将需自行承担。近来，南方传来的消息倒是令人宽慰不少，但不容忽视的是，一旦大黑河与大连之间的交通被阻断，本地关员的处境将会十分艰难，若想离开，则只能经布拉戈维申斯克前往欧洲或者符拉迪沃斯托克（Vladivostok）。但这条路线是否可行，还很难说，因为这很有可能意味着"跳出油锅又落火坑"，而留在大黑河又很有可能是受到两面夹击的境况。无论如何，如上文所述，地方上的形势似乎还没有造成令人不安的局面。本地的电报通信因线路问题极不稳定，如果情况有变，需要发来紧急警告，可通过大北电报公司在布拉戈维申斯克的代理人发送电报。此代理人为本人的朋友，名叫德克尔（Dechler），其收到电报后，数小时之内便可将消息送达本人手中。

您真挚的

铎博赉

13. 铎博赉致易纨士函

（第76号半官函）

S/O No.76.

Aigun/Taheiho 15th June. 27.

Dear Mr. Edwardes,

INCREASE IN RIVER DUES TARIFF: In my last S/O I reported that the increase in River Dues Tariff had been put in force and that the fact would be reported to you officially. I further stated that the last increase had been made without reference to Peking and that the same procedure was being followed in the present instance. A few days later I received your despatch No. 350 directing that the Taoyin must secure the approval of the Ch'u before the increase could be put into effect. Before relating my interview with the Taoyin subsequent to the receipt of this despatch, and previous to the sending to you of my telegram of the 2nd instant, I wish to explain my reasons for assuming that a precedent had been formed for putting such an increase into effect on the instruction of the Provincial Authorities only. Aigun despatch No.54 of 10th June, 1922, submitted the original River Dues Tariff as approved by the Ch'u. Paragraph 4 is liable to convey the wrong impression

that

A. H. F. Edwardes, Esquare.

Peking.

that it was altered to meet the wishes of the local Chamber of Commerce after the approval of the Ch'u. Reference to the Chinese enclosure shows, however, that the recommendation of the Chamber, that the Amur be divided into an upper and lower section and that half the tariff be levied on goods travelling in each, was included in the tariff regulations before they were submitted to the Ch'u. Aigun despatch No. 230, §6, reporting the raising of the tariff to "full rates" is also ambiguous. Mr. Hedgeland says in the opening sentence of that paragraph: "In my despatch No. 218 "I submitted that as the collection of River Dues at a "half tariff rate no longer provided sufficient funds "to meet current expenditure the proper course was to "collect at the full rate". Reference to Aigun despatch No. 218, §5, discloses the following explanation of the terms "full rate" and "half rate": "My first proposal was to collect River Dues at a full "tariff rate. At present, for the purpose of assessing "River Dues, the Amur is divided into two sections, an "upper section from Taheiho to Pokrovka and a lower "section from Taheiho to Kasakevich, and for each "section one half of the tariff only is paid. The "Russians, on the other hand, collect a full rate

"irrespective

"irrespective of distance travelled". It will thus
be seen that when Mr. Hedgeland spoke of a "full
tariff" rate he meant in reality a doubling of the
existing rates. For example, grain under the original
tariff paid ½ cent per pood from Lahasusu to Taheiho
and if then transhipped to up-river it paid another ½
cent. Aigun despatch No. 230, just referred to,
reports that the collection of "full tariff rates"
commenced on the 9th June, 1925. In other words,
using the same example, grain from Lahasusu to Taheiho
in future would pay one cent per pood from Lahasusu to
Taheiho and an additional cent if then transhipped for
up-river. Further, to quote Mr. Hedgeland's order to
the General Office in this connection:

PRACTICE ORDER NO.95.

Custom House,
Aigun/Taheiho,9.June,25

AMUR RIVER DUES:

With reference to Practice Order No.14;

Provisional Regulations for
collection of Amur River Dues for
1922, notifying:

it has now been decided that Amur River Dues on
cargo will be collected from this date and until
further orders at double the rates laid down in
the above order, as the result of arrangements
made with the Heiho Taoyin and the Chamber of
Commerce. Dues on passenger tickets will be
levied

levied at 5 per cent as hitherto.

(signed): R. F. C. Hedgeland
Commissioner.

In view of the above I considered that it was not
necessary, from a Customs standpoint, to refer the
present increase, which was not so great as the former
one, to the Ch'u for approval. This decision of mine
was arrived at independently of the attitude of the
Taoyin although he had maintained during the preliminary
discussions about the increase that the Provincial
Authorities only were concerned in fixing the amount
that should be collected for River Dues. After the
receipt of your despatch No. 350 I told the Taoyin of
your instructions to myself and asked him, in view of
the fact that the increase had already been put in force,
to wire the Ch'u for permission to levy the increase.
He again declared his inability to do so maintaining
that as the Ch'u had sanctioned the collection of River
Dues by the Customs it was no longer concerned or
interested in how much or how little was assessed and
that such matters lay entirely in the hands of the
Provincial Authorities concerned. I did not wish to
argue about the relative amount of authority the
Inspector General (Shui-wu Ch'u) and the Heilungchiang

Authorities

Authorities had over the River Dues collection but I
pointed out that as a matter of courtesy (and mere
formality) the I. G. should be informed of the increase
through the Ch'u and that, moreover, his present
position was tantamount to giving me orders over the
head of yourself.   The interview was conducted in the
usually friendly manner but the Taoyin at one time
went so far as to say that if the Aigun Customs was
not prepared to follow the instructions of the
Provincial Authorities in this instance he would have
to consider some other system of collecting River Dues.
Such "sabre rattling" has occurred before in former
years.   I do not know how far the present Taoyin would
go in the direction of assuming full control of the
machinery for the collection and administration of
River Dues but he is a man of very independent views
and action and now that he is collecting the Washington
Surtax he probably believes that River Dues could be
collected as easily.   In this connection I might say
that I had pointed out to him only a few days before
that, whereas the running expenses of the Aigun
Customs was some $4,500 per month, about 2/3rds of this
expense or (say) $36,000 per year was for the
collection of River Dues while the Customs only

received

received $3,500 as 1/10th of the collection.   Further
that the Lahasusu Staff was also largely employed in
the collection of River Dues.   Considering, however,
that we must maintain a Staff in Aigun anyway these
figures may be a little exaggerated but a control over
the collection as effective as ours would cost the
Aids Commission nearly as much as that if they were to
set up an independent bureau.   The interview wound up
by the Taoyin requesting me to wire you stating his
position and requesting that the matter of the increase
be left entirely in the hands of the Provincial
Authorities as on the occasion of the previous increase.
This I accordingly did in my telegram of the 2nd inst.
Your reply of the 3rd inst. instructed me to continue
the collection of the increase as it had already been
put in force and to obtain in writing the instructions
of the Taoyin for the increase.   Such instructions had
already been received and will be forwarded officially
as directed.   I am also requesting the Taoyin as
Superintendent to acquaint the Ch'u with the fact that
the River Dues Tariff has been increased under
instructions of the Provincial Authorities.   I have
gone into this question at length as I have felt that
you consider the manner of instituting this increase

as

as somewhat irregular. I hope that I have made my
position clear; also that I was acting on precedent.
At the same time I must record that the questions
concerning the frontier rivers are very complicated and
it is becoming increasingly difficult to steer a course
between the Chinese authorities (acting under the
influence of the growing national spirit in China) and
the Russian authorities (animated by a desire to worst
Chang Tso-lin where possible and to further their own
nefarious ends).

USSURI AIDS: The signing of the agreement
for the joint upkeep of Aids on the Ussuri from Hulin
to Kasakevich at an estimate of Gold Roubles 8,600
(Chinese share G.Rbls.4,300) has been arranged for for
tomorrow. The negotiations for this work have extended
over the past few years and it will be gratifying to be
able to report their favourable completion in view of
the difficulties that have been surmounted. The Taoyin
has agreed to request the Kirin Authorities to inform
the Ch'u of the signing of the agreement.

MANCHURIAN ALLOWANCE: I. G. despatch No.
344/112,252 to Aigun instructs the discontinuance of
the Manchurian Allowance to the local Foreign Outdoor
Staff. I am now informed that such an allowance is

being

being issued at Harbin to both Native and Foreign
Staff of certain ranks. The Staff here are pointing
out to me that this hardly seems right as they have
to pay the same price for goods as the Harbin Staff
plus the cost of freight and duty on same from Harbin.
I must say that I sympathize with them to a certain
extent though I have held out no encouragement that
you would be able to reconsider your decision to stop
the allowance.

FRONTIER RELATIONS: The press of Blagovestchensk is now taken up with vilifying the British
as a result of the breaking off of trade relations by
the latter. The attacks are so violent and the
actions attributed to the British so absurd that the
propaganda would seem to defeat its own ends. It
cannot be seen as yet that there is any increasing
reaction on the other side of the river to the growing
influence of the Cantonese. In the negotiations
attending the drawing up of an agreement for Aids on
the Ussuri, however, the tone assumed by the Russian
Consul has been at times very truculent and even
impolite in contrast to his previous attitude. It is
known, however, that the Taoyin and the Consul are on

anything

anything but friendly personal relations.

LOCAL CONDITIONS: There seems to be a
large element amongst the local Chinese imbued with
the "nationalist" spirit.   Amongst the labourers (who
have been badly exploited by the mine owners) there is
even a spirit of Communism.   I have seen very little
evidence as yet of anti-foreign or anti-Customs spirit.
The local authorities have matters well in hand but it
would be difficult and a long process to reestablish
order in this remote district were the power of the
local authorities to come to an end.   Such a condition
would be taken advantage of quickly by our Soviet
neighbours.   The local Japanese have received
instructions to be ready to evacuate on receipt of
telegraphic instructions.   Such uncertainty is
reflected in local trade conditions which are becoming
more and more depressed.   Only three or four steamers
per week ply between here and Harbin now as compared
with three or four a day in 1922-23.   The Tungpei S/S
Co. is also discriminating against this port in favour
of Sungari river trade which can be hauled at greater
profit.   The hoped for influx of immigrants did not
eventuate though an unprecedented number are reported
to have settled on the Sungari.   A long dry spell was
                                                                    broken

broken by a very welcome rain last night.
                        Yours truly.

第 76 号半官函 1927 年 6 月 15 日于瑷珲关／大黑河

尊敬的易纨士先生：

为提高江捐税率事：上一封半官函中汇报了已经开始施行新税率一事，并说明稍后将呈文正式报告此事，还指出因上一次提高江捐税率时并未提前向北京方面呈报，故此次也照此先例办理。数日后收悉海关总税务司公署第 350 号令指示，内称道尹应于施行新税率之前提请税务处指示。随后已与道尹会面商谈，但在汇报此次商谈及本人 6 月 2 日至总税务司的电报内容之前，希望先对为何会认为此前已有仅凭省政府指示便提高江捐税率之先例的原因加以说明。

1922 年 6 月 10 日瑷珲关第 54 号呈中汇报了由税务处批准的初始江捐税率。但呈文第 4 项的措辞容易让人误以为江捐税率经税务处批准后又为满足本地商会意愿而做出了调整。但随附汉文附件中显示，其实是商会关于将黑龙江分为上游下游两个江段并对经由每个江段的货物征收半价江捐的建议在提请税务处指示之前被纳入了江捐税率章程。

瑷珲关第 230 号呈第 6 项汇报将税率提高至"全价"时的表述亦不甚明确。贺智兰（R. F. C. Hedgeland）先生在此段开篇处指出："瑷珲关第 218 号呈中已说明，若继续按照半价税率征收江捐，实难以负担目前各项开支，应当按全价税率征收。"而瑷珲关第 218 号呈第 5 项对"全价税率"及"半价税率"的解释为："一是建议按照全价税率来征收江捐。目前，为计征江捐，已将黑龙江划分为两个江段，自大黑河至波克罗夫卡（Pokrovka）为上游江段，自大黑河至嘎杂克维池（Kasakevich）为下游江段，每段仅按半价税率征收，而苏方则不论航行里程，一律按照全价税率征收。"

由此可见，贺智兰先生谈及"全价"税率时，实际上指的是将当前税率增加一倍。例如，按照初始税率，谷物自拉哈苏苏运至大黑河时，每普特收税 0.5 分，如继续自大黑河运往上游，则每普特再收 0.5 分。上述瑷珲关第 230 号呈中报告称"全价税率"自 1925 年 6 月 9 日起开始施行。换言之，同样以谷物为例，以后自拉哈苏苏运至大黑河时，每普特将收税 1 分，如继续自大黑河运往上游，则每普特再收 1 分。

此外，将贺智兰先生就此事向征税汇办处下达的指令列下：

第 95 号办法

瑷珲关／大黑河，1925 年 6 月 9 日

为黑龙江江捐事：

根据瑷珲关第 14 号办法：

"为通知 1922 年黑龙江江捐征收临时章程事。"

经与黑河道尹及商会协商,现决定：即日起按照上述办法规定之税率的两倍对黑龙江上的往来货物征收江捐,如有调整,将另行通知。但客票捐仍按值百抽五的税率征收。

贺智兰

瑷珲关税务司

基于上述种种,兹认为此次提高江捐税率的额度远不及从前,因此从海关的角度来看,并无提请税务处批准之必要。但此仅为本人自己的决定,并未受到道尹态度的影响,尽管初期讨论时,道尹坚持认为江捐税率的制定仅应涉及省政府层面。

收悉海关总税务司公署第 350 号令后,已将令文指示告知道尹,并请其电呈税务处申请批准继续按照已付诸实行的新税率征收江捐。道尹再次表示无法照此行事,坚称税务处既已批准由海关负责江捐的征收事宜,便不会再关注计征税率的多少,而且此等事宜应由相应的省政府全权决定。虽不愿与之争辩在江捐征收一事上,总税务司（税务处）与黑龙江省政府的权力究竟孰高孰低,但还是指出,即使出于礼节（或者仅为例行公事）,提高江捐税率一事也应通过税务处知会海关总税务司,而如今之情形,道尹无异于是越过总税务司直接向本人下达了命令。此次会谈氛围一如既往地友好,只是期间道尹突然表示如果瑷珲关不愿遵照省政府指示施行新税率,其将考虑由其他部门征收江捐。早年间也曾有过类似的"武力威胁"。虽不知现任道尹在全权掌控江捐征收及管理制度上能做到何种程度,但必须承认的是,无论是在思想上,还是在行动上,其都非常独立,而且其现已开始征收华盛顿附加税,很有可能会认为征收江捐亦非难事。

此外,数日前已向道尹指出,瑷珲关每月办公经费约有 4500 银圆,其中的三分之二皆为江捐征收工作的支出,即每年 36000 银圆,但海关实际上仅扣留江捐税收的 10% 作为征收佣金,即 3500 银圆,而且拉哈苏苏海关的职员大多亦是为江捐征收工作所雇用。然而,考虑到无论如何瑷珲关都须维持一定的人员配置,这一数据可能有所夸大。但如果成立独立的航务局,且要对江捐征收工作实现与瑷珲关一样的有效管理,水道委员会需要承担的支出将与上述金额相差无几。

会谈结束时,道尹请本人电呈总税务司说明其立场,并提出提高江捐税率之事应与此前先例一样仍由省政府全权决定。对此,已于 6 月 2 日电呈汇报。总税务司 6 月 3 日电令回复指示新税率既已开始施行,可继续照此征收,但须向道尹索要书面指令。书面指令现已收悉,将遵照指示正式呈交。另已请道尹以海关监督的身份向税务处说明已奉省政府指示提高江捐税率。

因查总税务司认为此次提高税率的办法有些不合规矩,特于此详述此事的来龙去脉。希望已将自己的立场阐明,也希望总税务司能够理解本次施行新税率的确是依照先例办理。另需提及,边界河道的问题尤为复杂,华俄两国地方政府之间的协商越来越难以开展下去。中国地方政府方面深受国内涌起的爱国热潮所影响,而苏联地方政府方面则意图伺机打垮张作霖,以进一步达到自己龌龊的目的。

为乌苏里江航政事:华俄双方已商定于明日为联合维护乌苏里江自虎林至嘎杂克维池河段的航路标志工作签订协议,工程预算共计 8600 金卢布(中方摊款 4300 金卢布)。双方为此项工事协商谈判历时数年之久,如今克服重重困难,终将达成圆满协议,着实令人欣慰。道尹已同意请吉林省政府向税务处说明签订协议一事。

为满洲津贴事:海关总税务司公署致瑗珲关第 344/112262 号令指示停止向地方洋籍外班职员发放满洲津贴。但现得知,哈尔滨关仍在对一定职级的华洋职员发放此津贴。本关职员已提出,他们不仅要负担与哈尔滨关职员一样的物价,还要额外承担货物自哈尔滨运来的运费及关税,如此还不能同享满洲津贴,似乎不公。须承认,对于他们的遭遇,本人的确深感同情,但并未给他们以总税务司会重新考虑发放满洲津贴的希望。

为边境关系事:英国中断与俄贸易后,布拉戈维申斯克(Blagoveschesk)的报章杂志已经开始发文诋毁,言语攻击十分猛烈,但归咎于英国的行为着实有些荒谬,此番煽动最终可能会以失败告终。然而,迄今仍未看出黑龙江对岸在广东方面日趋增长的影响下有何变化。不过在协商草拟乌苏里江航路标志协议的过程中,苏联领事有时候的态度与之前相比显得十分粗暴,甚至无礼。据了解,道尹与苏联领事的私人关系一点也不友好。

为地方局势事:当地华人中满怀"民族主义"精神者似乎大有人在,饱受矿主剥削的工人们甚至还怀有共产主义精神。不过迄今还未发现当地人有反洋人或者反海关的情绪。目前地方政府仍能实现有效管控,但万一政权被推翻,此偏远之地再想重建秩序便会十分困难,且非短期之内所能实现,也会让对岸的苏联政府有机可乘。本地的日籍人士已经接到指示等候撤离电令。局势的不稳定已对贸易造成影响,地方经济日益萧条。每周仅有三四艘轮船往来大黑河与哈尔滨两地之间,但 1922 年至 1923 年间,每日便有三四艘轮船往返。东北航务局也对本口岸区别对待,更重视获利更多的松花江船运贸易。本关区最终也未能实现移民涌入的愿望,反倒是松花江沿岸定居的人数出现了激增。长期的干旱终于被昨晚的一场降雨打破。

您真挚的

铎博赉

14. 铎博赉致易纨士函

（第 77 号半官函）

S/O No.77.

Aigun/Taheiho 24th June, 27.

Dear Mr. Edwardes,

USSURI AIDS: The Agreement for the joint upkeep of Aids on the Ussuri from Hulin to Kasakevich was signed at a meeting of the Sino-Russian Aids Commission at the Taoyin's yamen on the 17th instant. This Agreement follows the lines of the 1923/24 Amur Aids Agreement and contains a reservation by the Chinese to the effect that, as the boundary from Kasakevich to Harbarovsk is in dispute, Aids will not be placed in that section (jointly) at present. Work on the Ussuri is to commence at once. The estimate for the remainder of the year has been fixed at Gold Rbls.8,600 of which sum we pay half. The negotiations almost broke down several times the past few months but with the able assistance of the Technical Adviser I have been able to prevent the matter being dropped

entirely

A. H. F. Edwardes, Esquire.

Peking.

entirely and it is with considerable satisfaction that I can record the definite conclusion of this long outstanding question. As soon as I receive the official copies of the two versions of the Agreement I will report the matter officially.

RIVER DUES COLLECTION: the collection of River Dues for May of this year, taking the increased tariff into consideration, was up to expectations. The figures compare with those of last year as follows:

	May, 1926	May, 1927
Taheiho:	$2,560	$3,980
Lahasusu:	2,740	6,220
Total:	5,300	10,200

I do not look for such a large increase for June, however. It will be seen that Lahasusu is now collecting considerably more than Taheiho. The fact that a large part of its collection has been on Ussuri cargo has served as one of my strongest arguments in inducing the Taoyin to improve conditions on the Ussuri and to sink political differences in drawing up what

should

should be a purely technical agreement for that river.

INSPECTION OF THE LOWER AMUR AND USSURI: it is the intention of the Russian Commission to leave on their own steamer about the middle of July for an inspection of the lower Amur and the Ussuri. They have invited the Taoyin/ Superintendent, the Russian Consul, the Technical Adviser and myself to accompany them. The trip will last about ten days and a stop will be made at Harbarovsk. Such a journey will enable me to gain first hand knowledge of the complicated situation involving the boundaries and navigation in that vicinity. It would also enable me to gain a practical knowledge of what is required in the upkeep of Aids; while my presence would complete the personnel of the two Commissions. Mr. Boezi, in September, 1922, left on a similar tour of the upper Amur being gone about ten days. During his absence the Tidesurveyor was put in charge of the Outdoor Staff and the Chinese Assistant of the Indoor (Aigun S/O No. 16 to I. G. of 8th July, 1922, and I. G. S/O in reply of 28th July, 1922).

1922). At present I can see no reason why the port could not carry on without me for a period of ten days, and with your permission I should like to absent myself for that length of time.

SERVICE MONEY THAT MAY BE DUE THE ESTATE OF THE LATE ASSISTANT EXAMINER A, MIKULIN: Mr. S. E. Mikulin, Examiner B, of this Staff inquires whether he may claim officially from the Service whatever moneys that may be due the estate of his brother, the late Mr. G. S. Mikulin, Assistant Examiner A, who was killed in Chita the 18th June, 1922, together with his wife. He has only just been able to establish his right as the lawful heir of his brother in the Shanghai courts and has been paid a fairly large sum to the account of the latter in the Hongkong and Shanghai Bank there, at the order of the Provisional Court. He does not know what was due his brother in the way of Retiring Allowance and Contributions. I have told him I would refer the matter to you first semi-officially for your instructions.

STUDY OF RUSSIAN: I am pleased to record

record the exceptional interest taken by the
three newly appointed employees Messrs Li Pung-
tseh, 2nd Clerk C, Chang Yuan Yang, 3rd Clerk C,
and Wang Liang, 4th Class (Chi.) Tidewaiter B,
in acquiring a knowledge of Russian. A bonus
of Hk. Tls. 5 p. m. and a teacher's allowance of
$15 p. m. is being issued to each in accordance
with standing Inspectorate authority. I have
secured a good teacher for them and shall
examine them regularly.

FRONTIER RELATIONS: It is reported
that a partial mobilization is taking place at
Blagovestchensk and that many are escaping to
this side as a consequence. In talking to an
old lady who came from an interior village, she
asserts that the Communists are hated there and
have all been chased out. She also says that
they are only waiting for mobilization of the
older men to get guns and ammunition into their
hands when they will upset the present regime.
If a turnover doesn't come soon it may never
happen as there can be little doubt that with
the passing of the ten years since the
Bolsheviks took control, the rising generation

knows

knows nothing better and is pumped full of
Bolshevik ideas. The "reign of terror" in
Russia, following the breaking off of relations
with Great Britain, has its echo in Blagovestchensk. All prominent whites have been seized
and imprisoned and some ten are reported to have
been shot. A good friend of the Customs, the
Manager of Churin & Co., had his house searched
from 2 to 6 a. m. and, though nothing was found,
he is still in prison. The searching takes place
at night without warning and those who are not
Communists pass the nights in terror for fear
they will be visited.

Yours truly,

第 77 号半官函　　　　　　　　　　　　　**1927 年 6 月 24 日于瑷珲关／大黑河**

尊敬的易纨士先生：

为乌苏里江航政事：6 月 17 日，中俄黑龙江航路标志联合委员会在道尹公署召开会议，会上双方就联合维护乌苏里江自虎林至嘎杂克维池（Kasakevich）河段上的航路标志工作签订了协议。协议内容主要依据 1923 年和 1924 年黑龙江航路标志协议的各项条款拟订，另增加中方保留权利一项，即鉴于乌苏里江自嘎杂克维池至哈巴罗夫斯克（Habarovsk）一段的边界问题仍存有争议，华俄双方暂时将不会于此段开展航路标志的联合维护工作。协议签订后，将立即于乌苏里江开展相应工作。今年余下时间的预算为 8600 金卢布，由中方摊付半数。在之前数月的谈判期间，双方多次陷入僵局，幸好有航务专门顾问易保罗（P. I. Ignatieff）先生的大力相助，本人才能够让事情有了转圜的余地，不至半途而废。拖延良久的乌苏里江维护问题如今终得解决，着实令人欣慰。待收到协议汉俄文本的官方抄件后，将正式呈报此事。

为江捐税收事：今年 5 月的江捐税收已达到提高税率后的预期。与去年同期数据对比如下：

	1926 年 5 月	1927 年 5 月
	银圆	银圆
大黑河口岸	2560	3980
拉哈苏苏口岸	2740	6220
合计	5300	10200

但估计 6 月可能不会有如此大幅的增长。可以看出，拉哈苏苏如今征收之数已远超大黑河。其中大部分皆为对乌苏里江上往来货物所征收的捐款，此亦为本人力荐道尹改善乌苏里江航路状况，摒弃政治分歧，拟订单纯的工程协议的最为有力的理由之一。

为巡查黑龙江下游及乌苏里江事：苏联黑龙江水道委员会计划于 7 月中旬乘坐其自己的轮船前往黑龙江下游及乌苏里江进行巡查，并邀请道尹兼海关监督、驻大黑河苏联领事、航务专门顾问及本人共同前往。此次行程约需 10 日，途中会于哈巴罗夫斯克停留。借此机会，不但可以亲身了解复杂的边界问题及附近一带的航运情况，还能够看到航路标志维护工作的实操过程。本人如能随行，此次巡查便是中俄黑龙江航路标志联合委员会的全员之旅。包安济（G. Boezi）先生曾于 1922 年 9 月前往黑龙江上游巡查，行程用时共约十日。其间瑷珲关外班关员皆由头等总巡管理，内班关员则由华籍帮办负责（参阅1922年7月8日瑷珲关致总税务司第16号半官函及总税务司1922年7月28日回复之半官函）。有鉴于此，相信本人离开十日，亦不会影响关务，如获批准，将答允前往。

为海关或应支付已故三等验货前班密库林（G. S. Mikulin）先生钱款事：瑷珲关二等验货后班密库林先生询问，其能否正式向海关申领其已故兄弟三等验货前班密库林先生应得享之钱款。1922年6月18日，密库林先生与妻子于赤塔（Chita）遇害。而直到最近，密库林先生才被上海法院宣判为其兄弟的合法继承人，在临时法庭的判决下获赔了大笔钱款，已存入其兄弟在汇丰银行上海分行的账户。他想知道其兄弟在海关是否有应得享的酬劳金或者养老储金。本人已表示将先以半官函的形式提请总税务司指示。

为俄文学习事：值得一提的是，二等同文供事后班李鹏泽先生、三等同文供事后班张远扬先生及四等华籍铃子手后班王良先生三名新任关员学习俄文的兴致极高。现已按照总税务司常规授权，为三人发放奖金每人每月5海关两，教师津贴每人每月15银圆。另已为他们找到合格教师一名，可定期检查学习成果。

为边境关系事：据报，布拉戈维申斯克（Blagoveschesk）已开始局部动员，很多民众因此逃至华岸。从一位自内地村落逃来的老妇人口中得知，共产主义者在当地备受痛恨，已被全部驱逐出去，他们正在伺机动员老人交出枪弹以帮助推翻当前的政权。但近期内如果不能出现转机，相信以后也不会再有机会，因为布尔什维克党掌权后的十年间，新崛起的一代除了布尔什维克思想一无所知。苏联自与英国断交以来，便被"恐怖统治笼罩"，布拉戈维申斯克也深受影响。白卫军的重要人物都已被逮捕入狱，据报告还有十多人已被枪决。海关的友人秋林公司经理的家中亦遭到搜查，整个过程从凌晨2点一直持续到清晨8点，尽管并未搜出任何证据，但其也被关押了起来，而且至今还在狱中。搜查行动基本都是在夜间开展，毫无预警，非共产主义者夜夜胆战心惊，害怕会被突然搜查。

您真挚的

铎博赉

15. 铎博赉致易纨士函

（第 78 号半官函）

S/O No.78.

Aigun/Taheiho 26th July, 27.

Dear Mr. Edwardes,

      RULES OF NAVIGATION: nothing has been heard from the Russian side for some time about drawing up Rules of Navigation and, as the Director of the Amur Navigation Bureau has left for an inspection trip down river and will be gone some three weeks, the matter will probably not be taken up before his return.

      INSPECTION TRIP ON LOWER AMUR AND USSURI: I was pleased to receive your wire of the 14th inst. granting me permission to proceed on what should be a very interesting inspection trip. Our plans were changed at the last minute and our departure postponed. By mutual consent, it would seem, the Russian and Chinese sides of the Commission decided to go separate ways and the Taoyin, Mr. Ignatieff and myself are leaving on the 3rd August by a Chinese steamer that has been placed at our

disposal

A. H. F. Edwardes, Esquire,
      Peking.

disposal by the Tung Pei S/S Co. as far as Lahasusu, where another will be waiting to take us up the Ussuri and where we expect to meet Mr. Barentzen and the Ilan Taoyin.

      FINES FOR EVASION OF RIVER DUES: heretofore fines inflicted for evasion of River Dues have always been brought to account in the ordinary way as though Revenue was involved. It would appear to me more regular if they were credited to River Dues account and a system of rewards arranged with the Taoyin to be paid from that account.

      TRAVELLING EXPENSES FOR CLERK'S FAMILY: at the time Mr. Li Pung-tseh, 2nd Clerk C, was appointed to this port from Shanghai (he arrived here on the 29th May) he states that his wife was too ill to accompany him. She has now arrived and Mr. Li has handed in a statement showing an expenditure of some $130, from Harbin to Taheiho, incurred on her behalf. I cannot find Circular instructions as to the treatment of such cases and venture to refer the question of any refund to you in this manner and to inquire if I may report the matter officially. In-as-much as the presence of wives in this remote port increases the contentment of the employees

concerned

concerned their coming is to be encouraged.

MANCHURIAN ALLOWANCE, ETC.: the Chinese
Staff is dissatisfied that the Harbin Staff is issued
a Manchurian allowance, that they have to pay doctors'
fees while the Foreign Staff doesn't and with the
allowances allowed on transfer as applying to the
journey from Harbin to Taheiho. The petition is a
long one and will be forwarded in a few days. That
part relating to allowances on transfer was dealt with
in my despatch No.324 asking for more lenient
treatment for families on the journey from Harbin to
Taheiho. As to whether or not a Manchurian Allowance
is still issued to the Harbin Staff I have not
inquired.

HARBIN AMERICAN CONSUL VISITS TAHEIHO:
Mr. Hanson, American Consul at Harbin, arrived in this
port as my guest on the 5th July and departed on the
8th. Though Taheiho is in the Harbin Consular
district this is the first time an American Consul has
visited the place. He was well received by the local
officials and should be able to write a very
interesting report.

LOCAL CONDITIONS: the local financial
condition is getting worse from day to day. The
staffs

staffs of the Bank of China and the Bank of
Communications have been greatly reduced. The
reduction includes the Manager of the Bank of China -
Ch'e P'ing-shan - who, as "Diplomatic Adviser" to the
Taoyin and member of the Amur Aids Commission, has
often advocated the reorganization of the system of
collecting and administering River Dues including the
employment of a Chinese instead of a Foreign Technical
Adviser. As has been said before the one hope of this
region (the prospect for the resumption of trade with
Russia appears very remote) seems to be the connecting
of Harbin and Taheiho by rail, which would reduce the
time required for the journey between the two places
from some 12 days to almost as many hours, and would
promote immigration to this district.

CONDITIONS IN BLAGOVESTCHENSK: the
prisons are now said to be full of farmers who are
being squeezed dry. There now being no place to
confine contrabandists they are being brutally beaten
when caught and their goods confiscated. Shipping on
the Russian side of the Amur may be said to be dead.
As I write this I can see the long water front of
Blagovestchensk with its fine godowns, pontoons, etc.,
but no sign of life either ashore or afloat. What few
steamers

steamers do ply carry mail only and have few passengers
and parctically no freight.　Traffic on the Salimja
River, an affluent of the Zeya River, that runs up into
a rich gold producing country, furnishes a good example
of the extent to which Bolshevism has paralysed trade
and industry in Siberia.　Formerly some 15 steamers
plied on the Salimja, last year there were 2 and this
year one went up on the opening of navigation since
when there have been no more.

Yours truly,

第 78 号半官函　　　　　　　　　　　1927 年 7 月 26 日于瑷珲关／大黑河

尊敬的易纵士先生：

为航行章程事：关于起草航行章程一事，苏方已许久未有消息。但俄阿穆尔水道局局长已经前往黑龙江下游巡查，将会离开三个星期左右，在其返回之前此事可能不会有何进展。

为巡查黑龙江下游及乌苏里江事：很高兴收到总税务司 7 月 14 日批准本人前去巡查的电令。此行应会十分有趣，但最后计划有变，行程推迟。黑龙江水道委员会华俄双方委员最终商定分开行动。道尹、易保罗（P. I. Ignatieff）先生及本人拟于 8 月 3 日搭乘东北航务局提供的华籍轮船前往黑龙江下游至拉哈苏苏河段巡查，再于拉哈苏苏换乘另一艘轮船前往乌苏里江，届时可能会与巴闰森（P. G. S. Barentzen）先生及依兰道尹会面。

为逃避江捐罚金事：在此之前，针对逃避江捐行为处以的罚金，尽管与税收有关，仍一直按照普通办法入账。兹认为，如能将此等罚金收益记入黑龙江江捐账户项下，并与道尹商定由此账户向关员支付缉私奖金，应当更为合理。

为同文供事家人旅费事：二等同文供事后班李鹏泽先生自江海关调任本口岸时（抵达时间为 5 月 29 日），报告称其妻子有恙在身不能随行。如今其妻子已抵达本口岸，李鹏泽先生代为呈交了一份自哈尔滨至大黑河的旅费报销单，金额为 130 余银圆。然经查，并未找到针对此等情况处理办法的通令指示，故以此半官函的形式询问报销办法。另请告知能否呈文正式申请。在此偏远口岸，有妻子随行，关员满意度可大大增加，应当鼓励。

为满洲津贴等事：华籍关员请愿指出，哈尔滨关关员得享满洲津贴，但他们没有，洋籍关员可以免费就医，但他们需要付费，他们可以为调任期间由哈尔滨至大黑河一段申请的津贴标准偏低。请愿书篇幅较长，稍后将予呈送。与调任津贴有关的部分已由瑷珲关第 324 号呈汇报，当时已申请为关员家人由哈尔滨至大黑河的旅程制定更为宽容的报销办法。至于哈尔滨关是否仍在为关员发放满洲津贴，还未询问。

为美国驻哈尔滨领事到访大黑河事：7 月 5 日，美国驻哈尔滨领事韩森（G. C. Hanson）先生接受本人邀请来至大黑河做客，并于 8 日离开。大黑河虽然属于哈尔滨领事辖区，但这还是第一次有美国领事到访。韩森先生在此期间受到了地方官员的热情款待，相信返回后应会写出十分有趣的报告。

为地方局势事：地方经济形势每况愈下，中国银行及交通银行都已大幅裁员。其中包括中国银行大黑河支行行长车平山先生，其亦为道尹的"外交顾问"，也是黑龙江水道委员会的委员，之前总是提议要整改江捐征收及管理体制，还曾提出要将洋籍航务专门顾问换成华人。如此前所述，本地区经济恢复的希望似乎只能寄托于哈尔滨至大黑河铁路的开通，毕竟重新开展与俄贸易的希望十分渺茫。此段铁路开通后，两地之间的单程时间将从 12 日缩短至数小时，同时还可以促进移民来此地区发展。

为布拉戈维申斯克（Blagoveschesk）局势事：据悉，当地监狱已经关满了饱受压迫的农民，再无关押违禁品走私者之地。因此走私者一旦被捕便会遭受毒打，货物也会被充公。可以说，黑龙江俄岸的轮船运输已经停滞。撰写此函时，布拉戈维申斯克绵长的江岸上只能看到仓库、浮码头等设施，江上、岸上均不见人影。即使偶尔有轮船往来，亦仅是为运送信件，鲜有乘客，亦无货物。谢列姆贾河是结雅河的一条支流，流经一个产金丰富的村落。这条河上的船运情况足以说明布尔什维克政府已将西伯利亚地区的贸易与工业打压到何种程度。谢列姆贾河上此前约有 15 艘轮船往来，去年只有 2 艘，今年自航运开通以来便只有 1 艘。

您真挚的

铎博赉

① 原文为 Ch'e P'ing-shan，车平山为音译，根据身份等信息推测应为车席珍。

16. 铎博赉致易纨士函

（第 84 号半官函）

S/O No.84.

Aigun/Taheiho 7th December, 27.

Dear Mr. Edwardes,

MR. BAUKHAM, ACTING TIDESURVEYOR, AND LONG
LEAVE: Chief Secretary's Memo No.1280 of the 3rd
November, 1927, directs me to state officially Mr.
Tidesurveyor Baukham's intentions about applying for
long leave and to accompany my despatch by a semi-
official letter if necessary. In my despatch No.340
I report that Mr. Baukham would like to shelve the
question of long leave for the present as he would
like to put his two eldest sons in school in China
which would take up all his resources. With regard
to Mr. Baukham's retention in this port I wrote the
Staff Secretary on the 31st January, 1927, before
Mr. Baukham cancelled his application for long leave,
regarding the type of man needed to replace him. He
has now been in the port for six years, and in

Manchuria

A. H. F. Edwardes, Esquire,
Peking.

Manchuria for a longer period, which is too long to be
out of touch with China proper. At the same time I
realize the difficulties of finding a Russian speaking
foreigner to replace him. He performs his services
satisfactorily here.

AMUR AIDS: the Russian Consul, as President
of the Russian Aids Commission, has been pressing again
for permission to dredge the upper Amur, either by
themselves or jointly. The Taoyin is of the same
opinion as Mr. Ignatieff and myself that it would be
absurd to spend some $120,000 in dredging a stretch
of river navigated by only one Chinese and two or
three Russian vessels, the collection of River Dues
on account of which is very small. The manner in
which this question is being brought up this year
rather inclines me to a theory Mr. Ignatieff has - that
the U.S.S.R. desires to improve the river to secure
better communication in the rear in case of war with
some European country.

ARGUN AIDS: the Soviet authorities are again
applying for permission to remove stones from the
channel of the Argun at their own expense as was done

last

last year. They also wish to erect Aids on both banks
of that river from their own funds but the Taoyin,
having partly opened the door in allowing them to remove
stones on their own, is trying to prevent its being
opened any wider by refusing permissions to erect Aids
on the Chinese side. I have suggested that he grant
their request on condition that they give us permission
to erect Aids on both sides of the disputed Kasakevich
Waterway - a quid pro quo.

USSURI AIDS: this office has received a
report from the Amur Navigation Bureau of the sinking
of the Chinese steamer "Hu-chiang" belonging to the
Tungpei S/S Company at a point just below Hulin on the
Ussuri. The accident occurred on the 15th October,
1927, and according to the report was caused by the
vessel striking a large submerged tree trunk. As the
workmen placing new Aids report that they arrived on
the scene only two days after the incident it cannot be
said that the channel had yet been marked and no blame
would seem to attach to the Aids Commission. In
response to a telegram from the Manager of the Tungpei
S/S Company a report of the wreck has been sent to the
Head Office of that company by the Technical Adviser.

There

There seems to have been no loss of life or cargo.
The vessel can be refloated (she is now grounded on a
sandspit) but not easily or cheaply.

The Ilan Taoyin and the Harbin Superintendent
have suddenly awakened to the fact that River Dues
have been collected on Ussuri traffic for several years
by the Lahasusu Customs on behalf of the Amur Aids
Commission and they have had no finger in the pie. I
have recently had some correspondence with the Harbin
Commissioner about the matter forwarding him copies of
the local Taoyin's replies to the Harbin Supt.'s
queries. The Kirin Authorities have also been
addressing the Heihe Taoyin direct until the latter
now says he is very fed up about the whole matter and
wishes he could be rid of the responsibility of the
Ussuri Aids. Kirin seems to feel that he must be
making a good squeeze from the Aids collection. I
am pressing him to carry on as otherwise it will be
awkward if separate Agreements will have to be made
between the Soviet and Heilungchiang and Kirin
Authorities for the Amur and Ussuri respectively and
if separate accounts, etc., have to be rendered by
this office.

ADVANCES

ADVANCES ON ACCOUNT OF MR. GARDEN'S
INSPECTION TRIP: in my last S/O I went into detail
regarding the negotiations I have been carrying on
with the Taoyin for permission to include in Aids
Account the amount formerly outstanding in Harbin
Suspense A/c as expended by Mr. Garden on his
preliminary inspection of the Amur Aids.   I now learn
that my last despatch to the Taoyin has been forwarded
by him to the Provincial Authorities with
recommendations to the effect that as there is no
information on file in his office regarding the matter
it should be referred to the Shui-wu Ch'u.   The
Civil Governor's reply should be received shortly.

FRONTIER CONDITIONS: I recently received
instructions from the Superintendent to pass 10,000
cases of kerosene from Blagovestchensk.   In a
conversation with the Russian Consul I inquired if
this meant that trade was to be resumed.   He stated
that he now had hopes that some arrangement would be
arrived at soon. Personally I think this is eye-wash
and don't expect any changes to be made in the present
policy of the Soviet.   The necessities of life are
daily becoming more scarce in Blago and rice, tea,

coffee,

coffee, sugar, dress goods and suitings, etc., are
hardly to be had.   On the other hand I understand that
for some reason conditions are better there than in
most other parts of Russia.   It is a sad commentary
on the system of government of the U.S.S.R. that
despite 10 years of effort economic conditions have
fallen to such a low ebb that tea, the most important
item (next to bread) of the Russian diet, is hardly
to be had and a beverage is now being resorted to
brewed from the leaves of a wild strawberry plant!

LOCAL CONDITIONS: the crops the last season
were excellent and everywhere one can see that
improvements have been made by farmers to their
buildings and fences.   The agricultural resources of
this region are more important than the mineral or the
possibilities of renewed trade with the U.S.S.R.   The
one thing that is required is a railroad from Tsitsihar
in order to break up the shipping monopoly and secure
cheaper transportation rates for passengers and cargo.
The Taoyin tells me that he has urged this scheme on
the authorities at Tsitsihar but they have no
sympathetic interest in the project and seem to regard
the Taoyin's idea as one out of which he desired to

line

line his own pocket.   Economic interests will
eventually force the building of the road but stupid
officials can delay the event.   I know the Japanese
are watching the situation carefully, and if there
is any loose capital in Peking I don't know of a
better means of employing it in China.

Yours truly,

第 84 号半官函　　　　　　　　　　　1927 年 12 月 7 日于瑷珲关／大黑河

尊敬的易纨士先生：

　　为署监察长博韩（G. E. Baukham）先生长假申请事：1927 年 11 月 3 日总务科税务司第 1280 号通函要求正式汇报署监察长博韩先生的长假申请情况，并指示如有必要，可发送半官函，以作呈文的补充内容。瑷珲关第 340 号呈中报告称，博韩先生因资金有限无法同时负担休假和两个儿子在中国入学的费用，希望暂缓休长假。在博韩先生取消长假申请之前，本人曾于 1927 年 1 月 31 日就其于本口岸的留任事宜向铨叙科税务司致函说明接替其职位之人应具备的各项条件。如今其已于瑷珲关任职 6 年之久，在满洲任职的时间还要更长一些，对于中国内陆的情况已经不再了解。与此同时，于本关而言，也很难再找到一位通晓俄文的洋籍关员来接替其职位。博韩先生在此任职期间的工作表现令人十分满意。

　　为黑龙江航政事：驻大黑河苏联领事以黑龙江水道委员会苏方委员长的身份再次提出，希望可以对黑龙江上游河道进行疏浚，无论是由苏方单独负责，还是由华俄双方联合开展，均无意见。道尹与易保罗（P. I. Ignatieff）先生及本人一致认为，黑龙江上游仅有一艘华籍轮船和两三艘俄籍轮船往来航行，为此花费 120000 银圆疏浚河道，着实荒谬，而且在此河段能够征收的江捐数额极少。苏方今年一再提及此事，不禁让本人想到易保罗先生提出的观点，即苏联希望改善此段河道，是为了确保万一与欧洲某国发生战争，后方交通能够畅通无阻。

　　为额尔古纳河航政事：苏方再次提出希望可如去年一般允许其自行出资于额尔古纳河上开展礁石移除工作，还希望可于此河道华俄两岸安设航路标志，费用亦由其承担。道尹已同意苏方自费清理礁石，但为避免其得寸进尺，拒绝了他们于华岸安设航路标志的申请。本人已向道尹建议，可同意此请求，但前提条件是，苏方须允许我方于存有争议的嘎杂克维池（Kasakevich）水道两侧安设航路标志。

　　为乌苏里江航政事：俄阿穆尔水道局发来消息称，东北航务局的华籍轮船“沪江（Hu-chiang）”号在乌苏里江虎林下游处沉船。事故发生于 1927 年 10 月 15 日，据报告当时是因轮船撞到了水下一根巨大的树干。据负责安设航路标志的工人所述，他们抵达现场时，事故刚好发生了两日。由此可知，事发当时河道尚未标注，因此这次事故似乎也就不能归咎于黑龙江水道委员会。为回复东北务局经理的电报，航务专门顾问已将沉船事故报告发送至该公司总部。目前看来，似乎并无人员伤亡，亦无货物损失。事故船只现搁浅在一处沙洲上，如要再次浮起来，将会十分困难，费用也不会太低。

近来，依兰道尹和哈尔滨关监督突然意识到，拉哈苏苏海关代表黑龙江水道委员会对乌苏里江上的往来运输征收江捐已有数年时间，但他们却没能分到一杯羹。本人已就此事与哈尔滨关税务司通信，并将黑河道尹回复哈尔滨关监督询问的信函抄件发去。吉林省政府也一直在向黑河道尹致函询问此事，直到道尹回复表示不愿再被此事牵涉，甚至希望摆脱乌苏里江航路标志的责任后，询问才算告一段落。吉林省政府似乎认为道尹定是在为航路标志工作征收江捐的过程中捞到了好处。本人正在劝说道尹坚持下去，因为一旦放弃，便须由苏联方面与黑龙江省和吉林省分别就黑龙江及乌苏里江上的事宜单独签订协议，本关也须分开呈交账目，届时局面将会非常尴尬。

为贾登（H. G. Garden）先生巡查旅费预支款事：上一封半官函中详细汇报了与道尹就将哈尔滨关暂付款账中为贾登先生预支的初次巡查黑龙江航路标志的未结款项记入黑龙江航路标志账户一事进行商议。现得知，道尹已将本人发给他的上一封函文转呈给省政府，并指出因道尹公署并无信息记录在案，建议将此事呈报税务处。相信不久便可收到省长回函。

为边境局势事：日前海关监督指示本关为运往布拉戈维申斯克（Blagoveschesk）的10000 箱煤油放行。随后在与苏联领事交谈时，本人便询问此事是否意味着两国即将恢复贸易，其表示相信应该很快便可达成某种协议。但就个人意见，恐怕这只是一句空话，相信苏联政府不会对其当前的政策做出任何改变。如今，布拉戈维申斯克的生活必需品日益紧缺，稻米、茶叶、咖啡、糖、衣物等更是难以获得。但据了解，与苏联境内的大多地区相比，远东地区的情况已经要好很多，尽管也不知是何原因。苏联人的饮食中除了面包，最为重要的便是茶，但现在都已很难购买到，饮品也要用野生草莓的叶子来酿造。苏联政府经过十年的时间，竟让经济下滑得如此厉害，足以说明其体制存在问题。

为本地局势事：今年秋季粮食大丰收，农民纷纷开始修缮房屋和篱笆。本地区的农业资源比矿产资源，甚至是与苏联重开贸易之事，都更为重要。但最好能与齐齐哈尔开通铁路，以打破船运的垄断局面，让乘客及货物的运费更加低廉。道尹告知，其已向齐齐哈尔政府提出此事，但并未得到支持，反而被误认为是他自己想要借此中饱私囊。从经济利益的角度考虑，修路是迟早的事，但这些愚蠢的政府官员只会一味拖延。据了解，日方正在密切关注局势的发展，北京方面如有流动资金，在中国除了用于修路，本人实在想不出还有什么更好的用处。

您真挚的

铎博赉

17. 铎博赉致易纨士函

（第 85 号半官函）

S/O No.85.

Aigun, 19th December, 27.

Dear Mr. Edwardes,

A CHINESE BUREAU OF NAVIGATION: on the 12th instant Mr. Ignatieff received a letter from a friend who was formerly under him in the Amur Navigation Bureau saying that he had met the Russian adviser of the Tungpei S/S Co., a Mr. Bigaieff, formerly a River Inspector in the same Bureau, on the street in Harbin and Bigaieff had told him that the Tungpei Co. were intending to dredge the Sansing Shallows and asking Mr. Ignatieff's informant whether he was free to accept an appointment in that connection. Further that a Bureau was being formed in Harbin similar to the Amur Navigation Bureau, presumably to take over Aids on the Sungari (and possibly on other rivers in Manchuria). It is known that Mr. Wang, formerly manager of the Tungpei Co., is out of a position and it is probable that he

is

A. H. F. Edwardes, Esquire,
        Peking.

is behind any such scheme. He would probably associate himself with Ch'e Hsi-chen（車席珍）the former Manager of the Taheiho Bank of China and member of the Chinese Aids Commission who is also in Harbin out of a job. In Aigun S/Os Nos. 50, 72 and 78 of 26th August, 1925, 25th March and 26th July, 1927, respectively, it was reported that this meddlesome individual was doing his best to upset the personal of the Chinese Aids Commission and to form one purely Chinese along the lines of the Amur Navigation Bureau. Not long ago, too, the local agent of the Tungpei Co. sent a Russian member of his staff to Mr. Ignatieff asking the latter to make out an outline showing the organisation of that Bureau. Mr. Ignatieff evaded the request knowing the use to which such information would probably be put.

AMUR AIDS: DREDGING THE UPPER AMUR: on the 12th instant, at a dinner given by the Taoyin on the occasion of his birthday, the Russian Consul became very communicative. During the course of the evening he confided to Mr. Ignatieff that he had been discussing with the Chinese Consul at Blagovestchensk the

necessity

necessity of dredging the Upper Amur and that the
Consul saw the matter in the same light and was prepared
to take it up with Moukden. When Ignatieff expressed
his surprise to the Consul that he and the Chinese
Consul should discuss the dredging question without
reference to the Taoyin and the Chinese Aids Commission
he passed the matter off in an airy sort of way as
though the Commission was of no importance. He went
on to say that he himself had also written to the Soviet
Consul General at Moukden asking him to take up the
question direct with the Higher Authorities. Mr.
Ignatieff reported the Consul's indiscreet admissions
to me and as it would appear that the Soviet and Chinese
Consul were playing a game that would undermine the
authority of the Chinese Aids Commission I decided to
call on the Taoyin with Ignatieff. I told him what
Ignatieff had heard from the Consul, and also of the
letter received from Harbin about the establishment of
a Navigation Bureau there. The Taoyin was greatly
surprised at the information imparted and kept us some
two hours in discussing the situation. When we left
he said he intended sending a telegram to Moukden
requesting that no decision be made about dredging until
they

they had his full report and that he would proceed to
Moukden himself within the next two weeks and see what
was being done. The present Chinese Consul in
Blagovestchensk, a Mr. Tsou Shang Yu (邹 尚友),
has only been there a short time and is quite
inexperienced. He has been guilty of letting the
Taoyin down a couple of times already and is now in
Moukden or Peking on some unknown errand. The Taoyin
quite believes that he is capable of conspiring with
the Soviet Consul to go over the heads of himself and
the Chinese Commission. To make the situation
clearer it should be explained that the Chinese
Consul's authority in Blagovestchensk has heretofore
always been considered as subordinate to that of the
Heiho Taoyin - as the Chinese might say, the relation
of the Consul to the Taoyin is as "the lips to the
teeth". The Taoyin also considered that it was
possible that the formation of a Navigation Bureau
was being considered at Moukden to correspond with the
Amur Navigation Bureau. His feeling was that the
intention of such a Bureau to absorb the Amur/Ussuri
Aids Commission should be nipped in the bud for the
following

following reasons:-

1. We are operating at a minimum of expense
   and carefully watching the expenditure of
   every dollar whereas were Aids funds to be
   saddled with a costly overhead expense both
   ends could not be made to meet.

2. The contact between the Soviet and
   Chinese Aids authorities is at Taheiho/
   Blagovestchensk and it would not be
   practicable to have a Navigation Bureau
   with its head office at Harbin.

3. The questions involved in the drawing up
   of the Aids Agreements are largely
   diplomatic and should only be dealt with by
   the Taoyin - that the Bureau could not have
   a "diplomatic" standing.

4. The Customs is now functioning efficiently
   and honestly and it would be a mistake to
   take the collection and expenditure of
   River Dues out of their hands.

The Taoyin further states that on his visit to Moukden
(and Tsitsihar and Harbin) he would also inquire into
this question of the formation of a separate Navigation
Bureau along with that of dredging the Amur.

After my call on the Taoyin, Ignatieff
met the Soviet Consul and the latter asked him just
what he said at the Taoyin's dinner! On being told,
the Consul said it was true that he had been in
consultation with the Chinese Consul at Blago. and
that the latter, on his appointment, had been told in
Moukden to prepare a report on Aids on the Amur. A

joint

joint trip of inspection of Aids on the Amur by the
two Consuls had been arranged to take place last autumn
but had been postponed until this spring! The Soviet
Consul went on to say further that the Chinese Aids
Commission as now constituted had no "official status".
"What is required", he continued, "is a regularly
appointed Bureau like the Amur Navigation Bureau which
would represent a central authority as the Amur
Navigation Bureau represented Moscow and with whom we
can deal on equal terms". Ignatieff's reply was that
the Chinese Aids Commission was known to be but a
temporary institution functioning pending settlement
of frontier river questions by the Sino-Soviet
Conference and that as now constituted it had sufficient
authority for present purposes and, as far as he could
see, was quite competent to deal with questions now
being considered. He might have added that it would
seem futile to establish a new Bureau with authority
from Peking to settle frontier river disputes with
Soviet authorities in the face of abortive attempts by
the Sino-Soviet Conference to arrive at any modus
vivendi for the consideration of such complicated
questions.

It would also appear that if a new

Bureau

Bureau of Navigation is being formed for Manchuria that
Soviet interests will probably do everything possible
to promote it at the expense of the Chinese Aids
Commission.   Their aim in doing this would be to get
rid of the influence of the Customs including Ignatieff.
They do not like us for two reasons, first, that we
represent the "imperialists", second, there is no
chance to pull the wool over the eyes of the Chinese
as long as we are watching their interests.   Were the
control to be taken out of the hands of the Taoyin and
ourselves and vested in a purely Chinese Bureau with
headquarters at Harbin they probably believe there
would be everything to gain and nothing to lose.

In addition to a desire to wreck the
authority of the present Commission it would appear that
there is the further motive of an attempt to get the
approval of the Chinese authorities to the dredging of
the Amur which we discourage as being a useless waste
of money.   As reported in my last S/O such determined
methods would seem to indicate that the local Soviet
officials are being pressed by their higher authorities
to undertake a work that can only be useful for strategic
purposes.

purposes.
What I have reported above may, of
course, lead to nothing.   I have had no intimation
from Mr. Barentzen of the formation of a separate
Navigation Bureau and am sending him a copy of this
S/O that he may comment on the foregoing.

ARGUN AIDS: I stated in my last S/O
that the Taoyin intended to refuse the Soviet
Commission permission to instal Aids at their own
expense on the Chinese side of the Argun.   It now
transpires that the Chinese Consul at Blagovestchensk
supports the Soviet's position; a further point for
the Taoyin to take up at Moukden.   There is now no
shipping on the Argun and little likelihood of any
even with Aids.

AMUR/USSURI AIDS AGREEMENTS: the Amur
Navigation Bureau has requested that the renewal of
the two Aids Agreements, which expired the 30th
November, be postponed until January when their
estimates will be ready.   It now appears probable that
the old Agreements will be extended another year
without any material changes.

AMUR/USSURI AIDS FINANCES: I am now
able

able to supply the total collection of River Dues for
1927 - $50,427.53 as compared with $35,469.42 for 1926.
After paying all sums due the Amur Navigation Bureau
for the year and the Taoyin's allowances of $2,000 for
Amur Aids and $600 for Ussuri Aids expenses for the
half year there is a balance of some $5,000 to cover
expenditure from the 1st December to 1st May of next
year.   By careful management I believe this can be
made to suffice until collection is resumed as reported
in my despatch No.336 to I.G.   Losses by exchange are
now becoming a not inconsiderable item owing to the low
value of the medium in which River Dues are paid.   It
would be better if the tariff were fixed in Hk.Tls.,
payment being made at the Customs collection rate.

RULES OF NAVIGATION: rough copies of
the proposed Rules of Navigation on Frontier Rivers
have been accepted by both Commissions.   The Taoyin
is rushing the Chinese version of the Agreement and
Rules in hopes of getting the Agreement signed before
he goes to Moukden.   He will then have something
concrete to offer at the time he discusses the
questions mentioned above.   The alterations suggested
by the Coast Inspector in his comments on my S/O No.
72 to you are of a minor nature.   They have been

adopted

adopted where possible but it is the desire of the
Soviet Commission to make no changes in the old Rules
which Russian and Chinese Masters have followed on the
Amur and Ussuri (and Sungari) for many years.   Several
of the Rules are mere repetitions of the same thing but
they prefer it that way.

WEATHER: the thermometer touched -25°
Reamur last night.   Luckily there has been no wind.

Yours truly,

第 85 号半官函   1927 年 12 月 19 日于瑷珲关

尊敬的易纨士先生：

　　为中国航务局事：12 月 12 日，易保罗（P. I. Ignatieff）先生收到其之前在俄阿穆尔水道局任职期间的一名下属的来函，内称在哈尔滨街头偶遇阿穆尔水道局前任巡江事务长比盖夫（Bigaieff）先生，并说明此人现在为东北航务局的俄籍顾问，通过交谈得知东北航务局正在计划疏浚三姓浅滩，并已从旁打听易保罗先生是否有时间参与此事，还获悉哈尔滨正在筹建一个类似于俄阿穆尔水道局的机构，拟将接管松花江上（甚至可能还有满洲其他河道）的航路标志工作。据了解，东北航务局前任经理王先生已经离职，其很有可能是此事的幕后推手，也可能会与失业待在哈尔滨的车席珍先生联合。车先生此前任中国银行大黑河支行行长，亦为中国黑龙江水道委员会的委员。瑷珲关 1925 年 8 月 26 日第 50 号半官函、1927 年 3 月 25 日第 72 号半官函及 1927 年 7 月 26 日第 78 号半官函中皆对车席珍先生的干预行为有所汇报，称其一直在竭力打乱中国黑龙江航路标志委员会的人员结构，企图按照俄阿穆尔水道局的架构成立一个纯华人的组织。就在不久前，东北航务局大黑河办事处还派遣一名俄籍雇员向易保罗先生询问俄阿穆尔水道局的组织结构。但易保罗先生洞悉到了他们的用意，并未相告。

　　为黑龙江航路标志及黑龙江上游疏浚事：12 月 12 日，道尹借生日举办了一场晚宴，宴会上苏联领事显得十分乐于交流，其间还向易保罗先生透露，其已与中国驻布拉戈维申斯克（Blagoveschesk）领事讨论了黑龙江上游疏浚工事的必要性，并称中国领事与其意见一致，已经准备提请奉天方面的指示。易保罗先生对此表示惊讶，指出其不应在未告知道尹及中国黑龙江水道委员会的情况下与中国领事商讨疏浚问题。但其不以为然，语气中似乎认为黑龙江航路标志委员会无足轻重，还称自己亦已致函苏联驻奉天总领事，请之与上级政府直接商议此事。

　　易保罗先生随后便汇报了苏联领事鲁莽承认之事，本人听罢察觉苏联领事与中国领事似乎是要密谋削弱中国黑龙江水道委员会的权力，于是决定与易保罗先生一同前去拜访道尹。会面后除了将易保罗先生从苏联领事处获悉之事相告，还提到已收悉哈尔滨要成立航务局的消息。道尹对此极为震惊，并就当前的局势与我二人讨论了两个多小时，最后表示会尽快向奉天方面发送电报请求在收到其全面报告之前不要对疏浚工事下达任何决定，两周之后再亲自前往奉天一探究竟。

　　现任中国驻布拉戈维申斯克领事是邹尚友先生，上任时间较短，缺乏经验，而且迄今已让道尹失望数次，目前正在奉天或者北京公出。道尹坚信中国领事很有可能会与苏联领事合谋越过自己和中国黑龙江水道委员会。为使局面更加清晰，需说明，在此之前中国驻布拉戈维申斯克领事的权力一直从属于黑河道尹，用中国人的话说，中国领事与道尹的关系就是"唇齿相依"。道尹还认为，奉天方面很有可能也在考虑成立航务局，以与俄阿穆尔水道局直接对接，同时吞并黑龙江（乌苏里江）水道委员会，并表示应将此等意图扼杀在萌芽状态，原因如下：

1. 黑龙江航路标志委员会始终致力于将费用预算控制在最低限度，还会仔细监管每一笔支出。如果让航路标志资金负担上高昂的管理费用，最后恐怕难以实现收支平衡。

2. 中俄黑龙江航路标志管理机构的会面地点都是在大黑河或者布拉戈维申斯克，如果成立航务局，并将总部设于哈尔滨，恐怕不会切实可行。

3. 航路标志协议的草拟工作所涉问题大多都属于外交范畴，仅应由道尹出面交涉，拟将成立的航务局并不具备"外交"资质。

4. 海关工作有效且忠诚，如果不让海关继续负责江捐的收支管理工作，将是一大错误。

道尹还告知，抵达奉天（及齐齐哈尔和哈尔滨）后，将会调查成立航务局及黑龙江上游疏浚工事等问题。

与道尹会面结束后，易保罗先生又遇到了苏联领事。苏联领事反倒问起自己在道尹生日宴会上都说过些什么！被告知后便坦承的确曾与中国驻布拉戈维申斯克领事商议过相关事宜，并称中国领事在获得任命时，便接到了奉天方面要求呈交黑龙江航路标志报告的指示。而且两位领事上个秋季便计划共同前往黑龙江巡查航路标志的情况，只是最后因故才延迟到了今年春季！苏联领事还表示，当下成立的中国黑龙江水道委员会并无"官方身份"，"需要的是像阿穆尔水道局那样正规任命的机构，能够代表中央权力，就像阿穆尔水道局代表莫斯科方面一样，要能够让两边的机构处于平等地位"。易保罗先生对此指出，中国黑龙江水道委员会成立之初便说明了是临时机构，只待中俄两国会商解决界河问题，但所得授权已经足以应对当前需要处理的各项事宜，也有足够的能力去解决现下的所有问题。此外，其还补充道，边界问题极其复杂，中俄会议尚未能做出决议，成立一个新的航务局，即使有北京方面的授权，似乎亦是徒劳。

另外，如果要于满洲成立新的航务局，苏联有关利益方很有可能会想尽一切办法促成此事，并以牺牲中国黑龙江水道委员会为代价。他们此举的目的就是要摆脱海关乃至易保罗先生的影响，背后的原因主要有两方面：一则因为我们代表的是"帝国统治拥护者"，二则因为只要有我们的监管，他们便没有机会蒙骗华人。倘若监管之权由道尹及海关手中转移到一个纯华人且总部设于哈尔滨的机构,在苏联有关利益方看来,可能是百利而无一害的。

除了削弱中国黑龙江水道委员会的权力,苏联方面似乎还希望借此机会让中国当局同意其开展已被地方以无用且耗资为由否决的黑龙江上游疏浚工事。如上一封半官函中所述,苏联地方官员似乎是迫于上级政府的压力,才会一再提出要开展此项仅于战略有利的工事。

当然以上所述各事最终也许不会有任何结果,而且巴润森(P. G. Barentzen)先生也从未透露过哈尔滨要单独成立航务局的消息。但已向其发送此半官函的抄件,希望能够获得相关意见。

为额尔古纳河航政事:上一封半官函中已经汇报,道尹决定拒绝苏联黑龙江水道委员会要自行出资在额尔古纳河华岸一侧安设航路标志的申请。如今既已知悉中国驻布拉戈维申斯克领事支持苏方立场,道尹抵达奉天后亦将调查此事。目前额尔古纳河上并无船只往来,即使安设了航路标志,似乎也无可能。

为黑龙江及乌苏里江航路标志协议事:黑龙江航路标志协议及乌苏里江航路标志协议均已于 11 月 30 日期满不生效力,俄阿穆尔水道局已提出希望可将续签日期延迟至 1928 年 1 月,即预算完成之时。目前看来,旧协议再展期一年时,应不必做出重大改动。

为黑龙江及乌苏里江航路标志资金事:1927 年共征收江捐 50427.53 银圆,1926 年共征收 35469.42 银圆。1927 年的支出款项包括,向俄阿穆尔水道局摊付的工程款、道尹的黑龙江航路标志办公经费 2000 银圆及乌苏里江航路标志工作的半年摊款 600 银圆。全部付清后,还有结余约 5000 银圆,需要应对 1927 年 12 月 1 日至 1928 年 5 月 1 日期间的支出。相信只要精心管理,此笔经费应足以支撑到下次征收江捐之时(参阅瑷珲关致海关总税务司公署第 336 号呈)。但因征收江捐所用的货币一再贬值,汇兑损失也不容小觑。如能以海关两制定税率,并按照海关征税汇率交付税款,结果也许会更为有利。

为航行章程事:黑龙江水道委员会的华俄双方都已通过了拟于边界河道上施行的航行章程草案。道尹正在加紧完成协议及航行章程汉文文本的编制工作,以期在前往奉天之前完成签订事宜,如此便可于提出上述问题时,有确实的依据。至于巡工司在其关于瑷珲关致总税务司第 72 号半官函的意见中提出的修改建议,虽非紧要,但凡有需要之处,皆已相应采纳。只是苏方委员认为,黑龙江及乌苏里江(乃至松花江)上的华俄船长已遵照旧版航行章程行船多年,不希望做出改动。实际上,条例中有数条规定的内容都相互重合,但苏方委员倾向如此。

为天气事：昨晚温度计显示为零下 25 摄氏度,幸运的是一直无风。

您真挚的

铎博赉

18. 铎博赉致易纨士函

（第 88 号半官函）

S/O No.88.

Aigun   10th March.   28.

Dear Mr. Edwardes,

RUMOURED CHINESE BUREAU OF NAVIGATION: I am in receipt of a copy of Mr. Barentzen's S/O No.735 to you in which he reports that it had been given out both to his Superintendent and to himself by Admiral Sheng that it was the intention to establish a Conservancy Board for the eventual control of Aids, etc., matters on the North Manchurian rivers.   Since writing you in my S/Os Nos.85 and 86 that I understood such a scheme was in the air I have heard nothing further.   I succeeded in arousing the Taoyin's resentment toward the plots of the Tungpei clique to the extent that he left here sometime ago for Moukden with the express purpose of "scotching" the idea if possible.   He continued on from Moukden to Peking with General Wu, Military Governor of the Three Provinces., to stay with the latter in Peking and to be

A. H. F. Edwardes, Esquire,
        Peking.

be present at Chang Tso Lin's birthday ceremonies. I understand he is now on his way back to Moukden with General Wu.   On account of his close personal relations with the latter I have hopes that he will be able to squash the nefarious scheme.   With reference to the memorandum Mr. Barentzen proposed submitting to his Superintendent on the Sungari Aids to Navigation Service, I submitted such a memorandum to the Heiho Taoyin at his request, and in connection with a report on Amur Aids by the Technical Adviser,pointing out the efficient and inexpensive manner in which Aids was now jointly administered by the Customs and himself.   The Taoyin proposed to base recommendations to the Heilungchiang and Kirin Governments on my memorandum to the effect that the present control of Aids on the frontier rivers be not disturbed.

LEAVE GRANTED TO MR. LIU WEN KUEI. 3RD CLERK B: I. G. despatch No. 390/116,060 to Aigun grants Mr. Liu 3 months' leave to date from the 1st October whereas it was applied for to begin this Spring.   This despatch also states that it is
                                    presumed

presumed that Mr. Liu need not be replaced during the
Winter season.   I trust that you will not take it
amiss if I ask you to reconsider your decision not
to replace Mr. Liu.   While it is true that the
closing of the navigation season releases one Clerk
from work in the General Office his time is wholly
employed in the Secretary and Accountant's Office
where a Chinese Assistant carries on during the
Summer without help.   While the latter can manage
in the Summer by working very long hours he cannot
carry on alone in the Winter when annual reports, the
Trade Report, the long despatches and enclosures
reporting the signing of the various Aids Agreements,
the Technical Adviser's Annual Report, the Annual
Statement of Aids Expenditure, etc., etc., have to be
prepared.   The remaining Clerk in the General Office,
Russian speaking, is likewise engaged in carrying on
the curtailed routine of that office, in making
translations in connection with Customs and,
especially, Aids matters, etc.   As a matter of fact
the demands on the Staff by the Aids Commission is
growing greater each year and it is now a case of the
"tail wagging the dog".   I trust, therefore, that a

further

further reduction of the Chinese Indoor Staff may be
postponed for the time being.   With your permission
I will address you officially on the subject.

EXPENDITURE FROM A/C. A: It is interesting
to record the steady decline in expenditure from A/c.
A due to economies that have been effected:

Total net expenditure in A/c.A:

1924:	Hk.Tls.56,218.09
1925:	53,189.88
1926:	49,280.45
1927:	44,394.06

The Office Allowance is Hk.Tls.60,000 per annum.

MR. BAUKHAM, ACTING TIDESURVEYOR AND
HARBOURMASTER, AND SOVIET AUTHORITIES: every year it
becomes increasingly difficult to get passes to
proceed at any time to and from Blagovestchensk.   I
understand that at present only eight regular passes
are issued for all of Taheiho of which four are given
to the Customs, i.e. Commissioner, Chinese Assistant,
Tidesurveyor and Technical Adviser.   These passes
are issued quarterly.   When I applied as usual last
January Mr. Baukham's was not issued, the Soviet

Consul

Consul explaining to me privately that some objection
had been made by the Blagovestchensk authorities and
hinting at his being British, etc. After waiting
for a time for a written refusal to issue Mr. Baukham
a pass I wrote again pointing out that as the harbour
was "common" to the two communities it was essential
that the Harbour Authorities have permission to
communicate freely. I have received no reply to
this last letter but I have learned indirectly that
a pass will not be issued to Mr. Baukham. I do not
know what is behind it all but cannot think it is a
matter of nationality. It would appear that,
probably unknowingly, he has made himself unpopular
with the Consul or some of the Soviet Officials on
the other side the susceptibilities of whom are
easily offended. The situation is rather
embarassing. I shall submit his name again when I
apply for June Quarter's passes this month and if
issuance is again refused I am considering demanding
a written explanation. If they have charges against
Mr. Baukham that are not consistent with the manner
in which he should discharge his duties as an official
of a Chinese Service I believe that I should know them
and if they cannot give any reasons for their attitude

                                                   I

I feel that a pass must be issued to him in his
official capacity.

     REVENUE COLLECTION: our principal source
of revenue in the winter has always been the duty on
furs sent by post. These furs are considered to be
smuggled from Russia (though we have no proof) and
therefore are charged 5% ad valorem as foreign
imports. Were they charged duty as native exports
the amount of duty leviable would be very small. By
an anomaly that has often been pointed out, the
Tientsin Superintendent issues San Lien Tan on
Taheiho which is virtually an open port. In the
case of furs, the foreign dealers in Tientsin have
followed the practice of obtaining San Lien Tan for
furs as native goods to be purchased at Taheiho and
brought to Tientsin. Hitherto the local agents of
these Tientsin dealers, as just stated, have passed
the furs through the Customs at the C.P.O. and have
paid import duties as foreign goods. When sent by
mail carts afterwards to Tsitsihar they passed as
native goods under Outward Transit Pass. However
that was no concern of ours. This year the furs in
question are being sent by cars overland and are not
being presented to the C.P.O. at all. The local

                                                   Tax

Tax Office accepts them as native goods and passes them under San Lien Tan without duty. As we no longer have jurisdiction over overland traffic and I would hesitate before searching a car proceeding to Tsitsihar that did not report first at the Custom House. Moreover our position is very weak when we assume that all furs are smuggled and therefore foreign goods. If a test case were made of this we might lose especially if the foreign dealers were to appeal to their Consuls on the plea that the goods are native. The Taoyin/Supt. is away at present so I can do nothing beyond warning the dealers concerned that they are taking chances when they thus suddenly change the old practice of the port. The remedy seems to me in the Supt. arranging through the Ch'u to stop other ports from issuing San Lien Tan on Taheiho. He can then control their issue from here and refuse to issue them for furs as foreign goods. Since a Supt. was appointed to Aigun/Taheiho this question has been continually shelved as it would appear that there has been nobody in the Supt.'s office who understood the question sufficiently to write the Ch'u about it and

and obtain San Lien Tan forms and Regulations.

ACTING COMMISSIONER AND SHORT LEAVE: I am expecting the American Consul and Mr. Bradley from Harbin shortly. They will be my guests for a few days and on their return to Tsitsihar I desire to go with them in their motor car. I have long wished to make this interesting trip (which can only be done in the winter) in order to broaden my knowledge of the Province. As Mr. Hanson and Mr. Bradley may return before I can receive a reply to this it is probable that I will wire you for permission to be absent six days (allowing one day for rest in Tsitsihar and one for eventualities). If my application is approved I shall follow the instructions of I.G. despatch No.366/114,208 to Aigun and leave Mr. T'u Shou Chen, Chinese Assistant, in charge.

ANNUAL TRADE REPORT: My annual Trade Report has been forwarded. As the trade of the port has diminished to such uninteresting proportions I have taken up most of the Report by a history of the causes leading up to the present depression. I was led to do this because Aigun was made a separate port after the last Decennial Reports were written; as

as there is very little of the sort on record, it
seemed to me that a short historical sketch would
be more interesting and useful than comments on
trade that barely exists.   I have made a departure
in adding as an appendix a summary of the year's
Aids activities; something on the style of the
Conservancy Boards' reports at Shanghai, Foochow
and Canton appended to the Annual Trade Reports of
those places.   Political issues have been avoided
and I trust you will approve of its publication.

Yours truly,

第 88 号半官函　　　　　　　　　　　　1928 年 3 月 10 日于瑷珲关

尊敬的易纨士先生：

为中国航务局的传闻事：巴闻森（P. G. S. Barentzen）先生致总税务司第 735 号半官函抄件已收悉，内称其与哈尔滨关监督均已从海军上将沈先生处得知地方政府计划成立管理机构以接管北满洲河流的航路标志等事务。自通过第 85 号及 86 号半官函向总税务司汇报相关传闻后，便再未收到相关消息。听完本人的分析，道尹亦开始对东北水道局等方面的阴谋感到不满，数日前已离开大黑河前往奉天，明确表示要尽可能"阻止"此事，抵达奉天后又与东三省军事长官吴司令一同奔赴北京参加张作霖的寿宴。据了解，此二人现已在返回奉天的途中。道尹与吴司令私下相交甚好，希望其能够借此粉碎成立航务局的计划。

参考完巴闻森先生拟就松花江航路标志机构向哈尔滨关监督递交的报告后，本人已应黑河道尹要求发给他一份相类似的报告，内容以航务专门顾问所拟的黑龙江航路标志报告为依据，并指出黑龙江航政工作如今在他与海关的联合管理下，正在有序进行，成本亦相对较低。道尹提出要以此报告为基础向黑吉两省政府提议不要干预边界河道航路标志的管理工作。

为三等二级税务员刘文湛先生休假事：刘文湛先生原申请于今年春季开始休假，但海关总税务司公署第 390/116060 号令批准其自 10 月 1 日起休假三个月。令文中还说明今年冬季期间应无须另派关员接替其职位。关于此项决定，还请总税务司重新考虑。有此请求，万望勿怪。航运季结束后，的确有一名税务员可以从征税汇办处的工作中抽离出来，并全身心地投入到会计课及文案房的工作当中去。而这些工作在夏季期间也确实是仅由一名华籍帮办负责，但每日也需要工作很长时间才能够完成。冬季期间除日常工作，还需要编制年度报表、贸易报告，为汇报航路标志协议的签订事宜编写长篇呈文及各种附件，此外还有航务专门顾问的年度报告、航路标志年度支出报表等等，绝非一人之力可以完成。而留在征税汇办处的税务员，因通晓俄文，除日常公务，还负责与海关有关，尤其是与航路标志等方面有关的翻译工作。实际上，黑龙江水道委员会的工作对关员的需求正在逐年增多，现在看来大有"喧宾夺主"之意。故此认为冬季裁减华籍内班关员一事，应暂缓执行。如蒙允许，将正式呈报此事。

为瑷珲关 A 账户支出事：实行节约政策后，A 账户的支出已稳步下降，具体如下。

A账户净支出总计	
年份	海关两（两）
1924	56218.09
1925	53189.88
1926	49280.45
1927	44394.06

海关经费为每年 60000 海关两。

为瑷珲关署监察长兼理船厅博韩（G. E. Baukham）先生及苏联当局事：如今无论何时往来布拉戈维申斯克（Blagoveschesk），想要获得过境小票，都十分困难，且困难程度逐年增加。据了解，目前整个大黑河，常规签发的过境小票仅有 8 份，有 4 份发给海关人员，包括税务司、华籍帮办、监察长及航务专门顾问。这些过境小票均按季度签发。但 1 月照例申请时，博韩先生却未获签发。苏联领事私下告知是布拉戈维申斯克地方政府有反对意见，并暗示是因其为英籍人士之故。在等待苏方下达拒绝为博韩先生签发过境小票的书面文件期间，本人再次致函指出，港口为两岸民众所"共用"，港务当局应当获准自由往来。但这次并未收到回复，只是后来间接了解到苏方不会再为博韩先生签发过境小票。虽不清楚这背后的原因究竟为何，但相信绝非与国籍有关。有可能是博韩先生不知何时得罪了苏联领事或者是对岸的苏联官员，毕竟他们都十分敏感，一不小心就容易冒犯到。如今局面十分尴尬。无论如何，申请第二季度过境小票时，递交名单上还是会加入博韩先生，如果再遭拒绝，本人将考虑要求他们提供书面解释。如果他们指控博韩先生未能履行作为中国海关关员的职责，是否属实，相信本人自能分辨；但如果他们无法给出合理解释，则须照例为博韩先生签发过境小票。

为税收事：瑷珲关冬季主要的税收来源一直都是通过中国邮政局运输的皮货。这些皮货因被认定为是从俄境走私运至大黑河（但并无实据），本关一直将之视作进口洋货按值百抽五的税率征收关税。如果将之视为出口土货，应税金额将会非常之少。但有一个反常情况，此前亦常有提及，即津海关监督签发大黑河（相当于通商口岸）的三联单。以皮货为例，天津的洋籍商人按照惯例在当地申领于大黑河购买皮货的三联单，采买后再运回天津，但三联单上将皮货注明为土货。在此之前，上述天津经销商在大黑河的代理商们一直通过中国邮政局运送皮货，运出时皆由邮政局的海关办事处放行，并相应完纳洋货进口关税。之后再由邮政局的货车运送至齐齐哈尔，在当地以土货凭出口过境单通行。当然这与瑷珲关无关。今年，上述皮货通过汽车由陆路运出，根本未至中国邮政局报明。地方税捐局遂将之视为土货凭三联单免税放行。然鉴于陆路运输已不在海关管辖范围以内，如有运输货物的汽车未先至海关报明即前往齐齐哈尔，是否应予搜查，本人也有所疑虑。更何况，假定所有皮货皆为自俄境走私而来并将之视为洋货的理据也十分薄弱。如果前去搜查，万一洋籍商人向本国领事申诉皮货为土产，海关很有可能会得不偿失。而且目前，道尹兼海关监督不在大黑河，除了警告这些洋籍商人不要贸然改变本口岸的旧惯例，本人别无他法。至于补救措施，兹认为可由海关监督向税务处呈请不再让其他口岸签发大黑河的三联单。如此海关监督便可于本地控制此事，并拒绝为洋产皮货签发三联单。但自从有海关监督被任命至瑷珲关（大黑河）以来，此问题便一直搁置，因为海关监督公署似乎没有人能够充分了解此事，能够禀明税务处申领三联单表格及相关章程。

为瑷珲关署理税务司申请短期休假事：美国领事韩森（G. C. Hanson）先生和哈尔滨关署副税务司柏德立（H. W. Bradley）先生不日即将到访，届时将至本人家中做客数日。待他们驱车返回齐齐哈尔时，希望可与之同行。实际上，本人很早就希望能够有此一行（只能在冬季实现），以丰富自己对黑龙江省的了解。但考虑在收到总税务司回复之前，韩森先生和柏德立先生很有可能已经踏上归程，因此稍后可能会通过电报申请休假6日，其中1日用于在齐齐哈尔停留休息，1日用于应对突发事件。如获批准，本人将依照海关总税务司公署致瑷珲关第366/114208号令指示休假，并令华籍帮办屠守鑫先生暂代关务。

为年度贸易报告事：瑷珲关年度贸易报告已经呈交。但因本口岸贸易萧条至极，值得汇报之事极少，报告大部分内容皆是在叙述造成当前萧条局面的原因。如此撰写，还因为瑷珲关成为独立口岸时，上一份《各口海关十年报告》刚好完成。考虑本关档案中相关资料甚少，在报告中加入史料概述，相信应比评述几乎不存在的贸易要更为实用有趣。此外还于报告后增加附录一份，总结了今年的航路标志活动，形式上类似于江海关、闽海关及粤海关于其年度贸易报告后附加的河流管理报告。报告中已规避政治问题，相信总税务司应会批准刊印。

您真挚的

铎博赉

19. 铎博赉致易纨士函

（第 90 号半官函）

S/O No.90.

Aigun   4th May,   28.

Dear Mr. Edwardes,

  OPENING OF THE FRONTIER: in my last S/O
I mentioned that the Soviet Authorities were
negotiating with the local merchants for the purchase
of large quantities of grain, and the latter were
bringing pressure to bear to compel the Taoyin to
allow grain so bought to be exported.   In this
connection the Soviet Consul called on me and asked
me to use my influence with the Taoyin.   He explained
to me that they wished to purchase some 300,000 poods
of wheat besides large quantities of oats and beans
involving an expenditure of about $1,000,000; that
other things which the local community might have to
sell such as piece goods and sundries could be
purchased more cheaply in Harbin and elsewhere.   At
the same time he wished permission from the Chinese
Authorities to send to Tahsiho for sale such articles
           as

A. H. F. Edwardes, Esquire,
  Peking.

as dried fish, butter, kerosene oil, benzine, etc.
All trading was to be controlled by the Soviet
Government trading society known as the "Golstork".
The Consul's proposal seemed very reasonable to me.
The prices to be paid for grain was higher than the
farmers could obtain in Harbin and they could use the
money to increase their holdings and to buy more
modern implements.   Incidentally Customs revenue
would benefit greatly.   Although the Consul gave no
reason as to why the grain was wanted it seemed clear
to me that they wished to ship it abroad to establish
gold credits.   The grain could be purchased here with
paper roubles that must be worth very little in other
countries.   I called on the Taoyin soon after this
interview and told him what the Consul had in his mind.
He at once took the position that until the frontier
was opened by the Soviet so that trade could be
carried on as before he would not allow any grain to
pass the frontier.   I presume he is acting on the
instructions of the Tsitsihar Authorities.   I pointed
out that I thought he was asking for the impossible;
that the frontier of Russia was closed to all the
          world

world and it could not be opened at this small spot;
that private trading was forbidden in Russia and even
were the frontier to be opened trading could only be
carried on with Soviet Government buying agencies as
was now proposed; that if the grain was not bought here
it could be had in Harbin from where goods passed
freely on the C.E.R. through Suifenho and Manchouli and
that countries like Great Britain and the United States,
who had no diplomatic relations with the U.S.S.R.,
permitted the latter to make very large purchases in
their respective countries.   The Taoyin, however, was
not to be moved and it would now seem that he has won
some of the more influential merchants to his way of
thinking, i.e. that the Soviet will open the frontier
as a <u>quid pro quo</u> for the export of grain.   Japanese
interests have also sought to influence him (indicating
that the grain is probably intended for that country)
but this has only made him the more suspicious.   The
desire of the U.S.S.R. to buy grain in China indicates
the shortage in Siberia.   It is now well known that
Soviet farmers will only raise enough for their own
personal use.   They argue that there is no advantage

in

in raising a surplus of grain to be sold for cash when
there is nothing to buy with money and it is dangerous
to hoard it either from fear of confiscation or of its
eventual repudiation.

CONSERVANCY BUREAU, HARBIN: Mr. Barentsen
has sent me a copy of that part of his S/O No.793 to
yourself which touches on the new Conservancy Bureau.
It is of some significance that the American Consul,
Harbin, wrote a local mining engineer experienced in
dredge work, who had asked the Consul's assistance in
procuring a position on the dredge that was to be
bought, that no dredge was likely to be purchased
unless the Customs guaranteed its payment.

KIRIN AUTHORITIES AND USSURI AIDS: an
article has appeared in the 國際協報 a Harbin
Chinese daily, saying that the Kirin Authorities and
the Soviet Consul to Harbin have formed a joint
commission consisting of six members, 3 Russian and
3 Chinese, to take over Aids on the Ussuri.   The
Taoyin appears to have no official news of the matter
and has wired the Kirin Authorities asking if the
report is true.   It is possible that they (the Ilan
Taoyin) wish to take over the expenditure of the

River

River Dues now collected by the Lahasusu Customs.
What they will do for technical advice in such an
event remains to be seen.   The Amur Commission can
ill afford to lose the Lahasusu River Dues collection
and I shall do all I can through the Heiho Taoyin to
prevent the separation.   If the report is true it is
probable that those concerned got their cue from the
organizers of the new Conservancy Bureau in Harbin.

INSPECTION OF THE UPPER AMUR AIDS: the
Taoyin has expressed the desire that the Technical
Adviser and myself accompany him on a trip up-river
to examine the necessity of dredging certain shallows
(my despatch No.362/I. G.) a work the Soviet
Authorities have long wished the Aids Commission to
take in hand.   The trip would necessitate my being
absent some 10 to 14 days and would be made in July.
I will refer to the matter again when the proposal
takes more definite form.

TUNGPEI JETTY: as a result of my
representations to the Director of the Kuang Hsing
Bank (廣信公司), whose guest I was while in
Tsitsihar, permission has been given the Tungpei S/S
Company to lift temporarily the ice breakers protecting
the

the Government gold dredge lying behind the Tungpei
jetty.   With the ice breakers removed it has been
possible to finally take away the remainder of that
objectionable part of the jetty described in Aigun
despatch No.311.   As a result of this improvement a
much stronger current is now flowing through the
harbour and I have reason to believe that the silting
which was endangering its existence will be arrested.

PUBLIC PARK AT SSŬ CHIA TŬU (四家子):
a little less than half way between Taheiho and Aigun
there is a small stretch of forest through which winds
a small stream of most excellent drinking water.   The
natural beauty of the place is most refreshing (in
China) and of late, with the introduction of motor
buses, it has become increasingly popular with both
Chinese and Foreigners.   With a view to increasing
this popularity and attractiveness the Taoyin, Mr.
Ignatieff and myself visited the grounds recently and
laid out walks and drives, to be lined with trees
procurable on the spot, decided on the erection of a
rustic bridge, of a summer house, pai lou, tables for
picnics, benches on suitable spots, brick stoves for
heating water for tea, hitching posts for horses, etc.
etc.   At the same time the place is to be treated as

a reserve and the cutting of trees is to be forbidden.
The necessary funds are to be raised partly from public
sources and the balance by private subscription.

TUNGPEI FREIGHT RATES: despite the
complaints made by the public last year that the high
freight rates of the Tungpei S/S Company were strangling
the development of settlements along the frontier rivers
and in the face of a profit shown by the company of some
$4,000,000 for the year, the rates have been increased
again this year. Under such conditions immigrants will
not come to this part of Manchuria. Protests have been
made by the local Chamber of Commerce to the Provincial
Authorities and it is understood that some slight
reductions have been made but nothing commensurate with
the demands of the occasion.

INDEXED OPENING OF NAVIGATION: Spring has been
rather backward but a warmer spell has set in. The ice
first shifted on the 22nd April but moved slowly until
today when the river began to rise with exceptional
rapidity. The up-river ice is now passing down with
a rush that makes an impressive sight. It is reported
that seven steamers are already waiting at Lahasusu for
the Amur to clear itself of ice. The present prospects
are

are that the first steamer will arrive about the same
date as it did last year - the 6th May.

Yours truly,

第 90 号半官函   1928 年 5 月 4 日于瑷珲关

尊敬的易纨士先生：

为边境开放事：上一封半官函中提及苏联政府正与本地商人协商要购买大量谷物，商人因此力请道尹允许苏联政府拟将购买的谷物出口。苏联领事亦针对此事前来拜访，希望可借本人之力说服道尹，并说明苏联政府此次希望购买 300000 普特小麦，还有大量的燕麦及豆类，购买预算总计约达 1000000 银圆；还指出本地商人出售的其他货物，如按件货物及杂货等，于哈尔滨等地购买，价格更为低廉。同时，其还希望中国政府可准许鱼干、黄油、煤油、轻质汽油等货物运至大黑河销售。所有贸易都将由苏联政府贸易机构"苏联远东国家贸易局"负责管理。在本人看来，苏联领事的提议十分合理。他们为谷物开出的价格比农民在哈尔滨销售的价格要高一些，农民可以利用这笔钱扩大租地面积，采买更为先进的设备。而且海关的税收也可以随之大幅增加。虽然苏联领事并未说明为何要采购谷物，但相信苏联政府应该是希望将这些谷物出口外国以建立良好的声誉。毕竟卢布纸币在大黑河还可以用来购买谷物等，但在其他国家却没有什么购买能力。

此次会谈后不久便与道尹会面，并转述了苏联领事的想法。道尹听罢，立即表示在苏联方面重新开放边境以使贸易恢复如常之前，不会允许谷物运输出境。相信道尹此举应是受到了齐齐哈尔政府的指示。对此，本人指出，这样的要求根本无法实现，苏联对全世界都封锁了边境，不可能单单在大黑河这个小口岸开放，更何况私人贸易已遭禁止，即使将来开放边境，亦仅能如上述提议那般与苏联政府贸易机构进行贸易。此外，苏联政府即便无法于大黑河购买谷物，亦可于哈尔滨购得，而且还能通过绥芬河及满洲里由中东铁路免税运输；而且像大不列颠和美利坚合众国那样未与苏联建立外交的国家，都允许苏联在其国内大量采购。经此番劝说，道尹仍无动于衷，目前看来其应该是已经得到了一些更具有影响力的商人的支持，他们都认为作为谷物出口的回报，苏联政府应当开放边境。日本相关利益方也开始试图影响道尹，表示谷物可出口至日本，但道尹因此反而对这件事更加疑心。苏联希望从中国购买谷物的举动表明西伯利亚地区粮食紧缺。现在众所周知，苏联农民将仅种植供自己食用的粮食。他们认为种植过多的谷物，即便卖掉换成现钞，也买不到什么，而且储藏现钞还要担心被充公，或者被废弃。

为哈尔滨管理局事：巴闯森（P. G. S. Barentzen）先生已将其致总税务司第 793 号半官函的部分内容抄件发来，其中提到哈尔滨新成立的管理局。此前，大黑河一名疏浚经验丰富的采矿工程师曾请求驻哈尔滨美国领事帮助他在拟将购买的挖泥船上谋一个职位，现在收到的回复是如果海关不负责费用,采购挖泥船之事将不会实现。

为吉林省政府及乌苏里江航路标志事:据《哈尔滨国际协报》(汉文日报)上的一篇文章报道,吉林省政府与驻哈尔滨苏联领事已成立了联合委员会以接管乌苏里江上的航路标志工作,共有六名委员,华俄双方各有三名。但道尹似乎并未收到官方消息,已向吉林省政府发送电报询问此报道是否属实。很有可能是依兰道尹想要接管拉哈苏苏海关所收江捐的支出事宜。但他们在寻求技术支持方面会怎样做,还要拭目以待。黑龙江水道委员会无法承受失去拉哈苏苏海关的江捐税收,本人将竭尽所能通过黑河道尹阻止此事的发生。如果报道属实,很有可能是相关方面从哈尔滨新成立的管理局的组织者那里得到了启发。

为巡查黑龙江上游航路标志事:道尹已表明希望航务专门顾问及本人陪同其前往黑龙江上游巡查,以确定是否有必要对某些浅滩进行疏浚(参阅瑷珲关致海关总税务司公署第 362 号呈),苏联政府一直希望黑龙江水道委员会可接手此项疏浚工事。此次巡查将于7 月开始,需要 10 至 14 日时间。待得到更为确切的消息后,将再次呈报此事。

为东北航务局码头事:日前在齐齐哈尔停留期间曾到访广信公司,并与其负责人交涉了移走破冰船一事,如今东北航务局已获准暂将用于保护停靠其码头后身的政府采金船的破冰船移走。破冰船移走后,终于可将码头剩余部分拆除,具体参阅瑷珲关第 311 号呈。经此番改善,通过港口的水流流势更强,相信此前对港口造成威胁的淤塞情况亦将不复存在。

为四家子公园事:大黑河与瑷珲两地中间不到半程处有一片森林,林间有一条小溪蜿蜒流过,溪水甘甜,可以饮用。这里的自然美景最是令人心旷神怡,尤其对于中国来说。近来随着往来汽车的增多,此处吸引了越来越多的华洋人士。为增强这片森林的吸引力,道尹、易保罗(P. I. Ignatieff)先生和本人已于近日前去视察,并铺设了人行和车行道路,道路两旁皆是森林原有的树木,除此之外还决定搭建木桥、凉亭、牌楼、野餐桌、长凳、用于烧水烹茶的砖炉、马厩等。与此同时还会将此地设为自然保护区,严禁砍伐树木。所需资金将向公众募集一部分,余下之款将由私人定期募捐。

为东北航务局运费事:尽管商民去年已开始抱怨东北航务局的运费过高,限制了边境流域村落的发展,而且该公司去年的收益额已高达 4000000 银圆,但今年的运费还是再次被提高。如此一来,将不会再有民众迁移至满洲此地。地方商会已向省政府提出抗议,据悉运费已有所下调,但根本无法满足实际需求。

为航运开通事:今年春季来得较晚,但天气已逐渐回暖。4 月 22 日开始有浮冰移动,只是速度一直比较缓慢。直到今日，江水开始迅速上涨。黑龙江上游的浮冰已开始急速漂流而下，场景十分壮观。据报告，现已有七艘轮船停靠在拉哈苏苏准备在浮冰消失后驶入黑龙江。照目前的情况来看，第一艘抵达大黑河的轮船在时间上应与去年大致相同，即5月6日。

您真挚的

铎博赉

20. 铎博赉致易纨士函

（第 91 号半官函）

S/O No.91.

Aigun   31st May, 28.

Dear Mr. Edwardes.

OPENING OF THE FRONTIER: contrary to my
predictions in my last S/O. but in line with the
arguments I used with the Taoyin/Superintendent,
the latter has decided to allow the export of grain
to Siberia and has sent me a despatch instructing
me to pass 200,000 poods. It is proposed to export
parts of the purchase from Taheiho and Aigun but the
greater part will be shipped from Chikote a village
some 350 li below here and not under Customs control.
I consulted the Superintendent as to the control of
wheat shipped (by Russian vessels) at Chikote and he
was of the opinion that grain should only be exported
at Aigun and Taheiho. I understand that the Chamber
of Commerce, who are handling the business, will
appeal to the Superintendent to alter his decision
                                                    and

A. H. F. Edwardes. Esquire,
        Peking.

and allow export at Chikote. In event the Supt.
grants the appeal I propose that any Russian vessels
proceeding to places outside of Customs control shall
first enter at Taheiho then clear for her destination
with a Customs officer on board (paying the required
fees) and return here for clearance to the other side
of the river. I cannot say whether it is the
intention of the Superintendent to allow further
export of grain. I understand, however, that he is
not allowing the Soviet authorities the return
privilege of bringing goods to Taheiho until they
declare the frontier open.

ASSISTED PASSAGE TO CHINESE STAFF PROCEEDING
ON LEAVE: In my despatch No. 371 I forward the
application of Mr. T'u Shou Chen (屠 守 宸).
4th (Chinese) Assistant B. for four months' leave
with his further request that the Service pay his
passage back to China proper. I. G. despatch No.
362/113,916 lays down that members of the Chinese
Staff who have served three years in Aigun will have
their return passage paid when proceeding on
Inspectorate leave. Mr. T'u will have served here
but little more than two years if his leave is
                                                    granted

granted but he hopes that as his leave is now due that
it will not be necessary for him to postpone it for
another year in order to enjoy a privilege that would
have been his had he been appointed to the port one
year earlier.   If Mr. T'u's leave is granted a
capable, discreet and experienced Chinese Assistant
will be needed to replace him.   There is no Foreign
Assistant at Aigun and the Chinese Assistant has the
responsibility of Accounts and Secretary's work,
supervision of the General Office and is in charge
during temporary absences of the Commissioner.   I
take the occasion to mention that, while lacking
somewhat in experience, Mr. T'u has fulfilled his
duties very satisfactorily on the whole.

INDEXED   AIDS NOTES: Mr. Ignatieff has returned from
his trip of inspection of the Upper Amur where he
found all in order and is now absent on the Lower Amur
and Ussuri.   The recently adopted Rules of Navigation,
printed bilingually in Chinese and Russian and kindly
seen through the press by the Harbin Commissioner,
have arrived and are being given out to Chinese
steamers plying the Amur and Ussuri.   At the same
time the Soviet Authorities are putting the Rules into
effect

effect as applying to Russian vessels plying the
frontier rivers.   With the arrival of the printed
versions of the Rules I am now able to report their
adoption officially to you and the necessary despatch
is being prepared.   The Taoyin is likewise now
sending the first copies of the Rules to the Wai-chiao
Pu, Chiao-tung Pu and Shui-wu Ch'u through the
Tsitsihar Authorities though the latter have already
reported their being signed to these Boards.   In
accordance with your attitude in the matter I am
carefully refraining from associating the Customs with
the enforcement of the Rules pending the receipt of
further instructions from you.   To date River Dues
Collection has held its own with that of last year.
I understand that there will be an increase on the
Ussuri.   In my last S/O I spoke of a rumour to the
effect that Kirin and Soviet Authorities were forming
a joint commission to take over Aids on the Ussuri.
The Taoyin wired to Kirin to find out if the report
was authentic and received the reply that it was not.
I am greatly relieved to hear this.

INDEXED   TS'AI-CHENG PU REQUESTS FIGURES OF REVENUE
COLLECTION AND OFFICE EXPENDITURE: I have received a
despatch

despatch from the Superintendent enclosing copy of a
Ts'ai-chêng Pu despatch No.486 with form to be filled
out showing collection figures for imports, exports,
etc., for the first 15 years of the Republic; at the
same time details of office expenditure are also called
for.　As the figures demanded are supplied to the
Superintendent monthly and quarterly for collection and
quarterly (after accounts are passed by the Audit
Secretary) in the case of office expenditure, and as I
had not received any instructions from you in the matter
I inquired of Mr. Barentsen if he had been requested to
furnish any such statistics.　His reply was in the
negative.　I enclose an abbreviated copy of the form
to be filled out and would appreciate your telegraphic
instructions as to what reply to make to the Taoyin.
In the Ts'ai-chêng Pu despatch it says that the figures
called for have not been supplied before but the
Superintendent's office denies this.　At the same time
it seems to me that the Superintendent might supply the
desired information from his own archives.

　　　SHIPPING AND TRADE:　shipping and trade
conditions are not improving and are getting worse if
　　　　　　　　　　　　　　　　anything.

anything.　The purchase by the Soviet of 200,000 pood
of wheat at $1.65 per pood has meant the distribution
of some $370,000 in the neighbourhood which is all to
the good.　Duty collected on cargo carried by steamer
is about the same as last year.

　　　Yours truly,

第 91 号半官函　　　　　　　　　　　　　**1928 年 5 月 31 日于瑷珲关**

尊敬的易纨士先生：

为边境开放事：与上一封半官函的预测相反，道尹兼海关监督最终听取本人的意见，决定允许谷物出口至西伯利亚，并已来函指示海关放行 200000 普特。有建议称，苏联政府购买的谷物中，仅有部分应从大黑河及瑷珲口岸运出，大部分将从大黑河下游约 350 里处的奇克特村运输过江，而此地并不受海关稽查管控。为此已向海关监督询问对于由俄籍船只从奇克特运输的小麦应如何管控，其表示这些货物仅应通过瑷珲及大黑河口岸出口。然而据了解，此次贸易皆由商会负责，他们会劝说海关监督改变此项决定，以允许从奇克特出口。万一海关监督批准了此项诉求，建议规定，凡是前往海关稽查范围以外各地的俄籍船只，均须先至大黑河口岸办理相应手续，然后才允许前往目的地，同时须由海关关员登船随行（支付必要费用），最后在过江之前还须返回口岸办理结关手续。虽然不确定海关监督日后是否会继续允许谷物出口，但据了解，其坚持在苏联政府宣布开放边境之前，不允许他们向大黑河出口货物。

为华籍关员休假旅费事：瑷珲关第 371 号呈中递交了华籍四等帮办后班屠守鑫先生休假四个月的申请，他还请求海关为之报销返回中国内地的旅费。海关总税务司公署第 362/113916 号令指示，华籍关员如已于瑷珲关任满三年，奉总税务司指令休假时，可申请报销返程旅费。屠守鑫先生的休假申请如获批准，届时他将仅于本关任职两年多一点。但他认为，对于此项旅费报销特权，自己如能提早一年被任命至瑷珲关，即应得享，现不愿为此将假期推迟一年，希望能按时休假。其休假申请如获批准，还需为瑷珲关任命一名有能力、谨慎且有经验的华籍帮办，以接替其职位。瑷珲关现无洋籍帮办，华籍帮办不仅需要负责会计课及文案房的工作，还需要监管征税汇办处，税务司临时外出期间还要代行管理之责。另需提及，屠守鑫先生除了经验稍有不足，整体履职情况令人十分满意。

为航路标志事：易保罗（P. I. Ignatieff）先生已完成对黑龙江上游的巡查工作，汇报称一切正常，现又赴黑龙江下游及乌苏里江巡查。日前采用的航务章程，已通过哈尔滨关税务司印制完成，为汉俄双语，收到后已分发给黑龙江及乌苏里江上往来的华籍轮船。与此同时，苏联政府也开始对边界河道上的俄籍轮船施行此章程。收到航务章程的印刷版本后，终于可正式向总税务司汇报章程的施行一事，相关呈文已在编写当中。道尹也开始通过齐齐哈尔政府将航行章程的首批抄件发送至外交部、交通部及税务处。不过齐齐哈尔政府早已向上述各部汇报了航行章程的签订事宜。考虑到总税务司对于此事的态度，在收到进一步指示之前，定会谨慎行事，不会让海关参与航行章程的施行工作。截至目前，江捐税收与去年的数额持平。据了解，乌苏里江上的江捐税收今年将会有所增加。上一封半官函中提到有传言称吉林省政府与苏联政府已成立联合委员会以接管乌苏里江上的航路标志工作。道尹为此还向吉林省政府发送电报询问是否属实，如今收到的回复是并不属实。听闻此消息，着实松了一口气。

为财政部要求呈交海关税收及办公支出数据事：刚收悉海关监督函文一封，其中随附了财政部第486号令抄件及表格一份，要求填具中华民国前十五年间的进出口等关税的征收数据及办公支出明细。鉴于税收数据均是按月、按季度报给海关监督，而办公支出明细（经会计科税务司审查）也会按季度呈报，再者也未收到总税务司相关指示，因此已询问巴闰森（P. G. S. Barentzen）先生是否亦收到了此等要求。但他告知并未收到。特此附上要求填具之表格的简要抄件一份，请求电令指示如何回复道尹。财政部令文中还说明此次要求的数据，之前从未收到过，但海关监督公署方面已予否认。兹认为，海关监督应当可以在其档案中找到所需数据并发给财政部。

为船运及贸易事：船运及贸易的情况仍未有改善，甚至可以说是每况愈下。苏联政府购买的200000普特小麦，每普特1.85银圆，总价约合370000银圆，均是周边地区所售，如今看来也不失为一件好事。今年对船运货物所收税额与去年基本相同。

您真挚的

铎博赉

21. 铎博赉致易纨士函

（第92号半官函）

S/O No.92.

Aigun   28th June,   28.

Dear Mr. Edwardes,

SUPERINTENDENT'S OFFICE ALLOWANCE: the Superintendent has transmitted the instructions of the Ts'ai-chêng Fu that his allowance is to be paid at the Banks' rate of the day for big dollars as from the 1st April.   I am now awaiting your instructions - it would simplify matters if the payment could be made at the collection rate of the day, i.e. his present allowance of $400 @ 150 = Hk.Tls. 266.67 @ the collection rate of the day.

REDUCTION OF NATIVE INDOOR STAFF DURING WINTER SEASON: in granting an application for leave from Mr. Liu Wen Kuei, 3rd Clerk A. Inspectorate despatch No. 390/116,060 stated that he would not be replaced this winter.   On my appealing from this decision in my S/O No.88 you replied in your S/O of 3rd April that I would have to put forward strong reasons if I wanted the Native Indoor Staff kept at full strength during the

non-navigation

A. H. F. Edwardes, Esquire,
        Peking.

non-navigation season.   At the same time you mention that Aigun despatch No.272 states that the services of one Clerk might be dispensed with in the winter.   I find that that despatch was written by Mr. Houstoun who was here only during one summer and must have known very little of conditions in the winter.   Moreover Aids activities have expanded greatly of late practically all the clerical work in connection therewith falling on the Staff in the winter.   For the 1/10th of Aids Collection paid over for our trouble in collecting River Dues we received $5,000 last year.   However it is possible that, by working long hours, Mr. Liu need not be replaced and I shall give the experiment a trial.

DREDGING THE UPPER AMUR: a short and simple Agreement was signed on the 19th instant for joint dredging of the Upper Amur.   The estimate agreed to was G.Rbls.6,000 of which sum China is to pay half. The estimate is ridiculously small and there can be no doubt but that the Soviet Authorities must spend much more than will appear in the accounts.   As mentioned on previous occasions I have given the Taoyin to understand that he must find the additional funds required.   He now tells me that the Tung Pei Navigation

Bureau

Bureau have been asked to supply the required G. Rbls. 3,000 (equal to about $2,000 at the present rate) as their steamers only will be benefitted. I regret this step as it may give the Tung Pei crowd an excuse for mixing in the affairs of the Aids Commission as they did in those of the Sungari Aids at Harbin. I think it would be better for the Customs if we were to get another advance from Sungari Aids funds of $2,000. There is still an authorised balance due from that source of $15,000 which we have not drawn on. With the signing of the Agreement for the dredging of the Upper Amur all outstanding Aids questions have been arranged, temporarily at least.

RIVER DUES COLLECTION: I have just received a memo from Ignatieff, who has arrived back at Lahasusu after an inspection of Ussuri Aids. He states that the river is again flooding its banks and is almost as high as during the record flood of last year. The consequence is that steamers with cargo are not proceeding to that district and River Dues Collection is falling off badly. This is discouraging news as the Aids Commission is already "scraping bottom" as far as finances are concerned.

LOCAL

LOCAL POLITICAL CONDITIONS: the news of the death of Chang Tso Lin and Wu Tuchün has been received quietly here. There is, naturally, a certain amount of uneasiness on the part of the Civil and Military officials as to their future. General Wu has been Tuchün of Heilungchiang for some eight years and though there has been much to criticise in his administration he kept a firm grip on all elements. It seems to me that politically conditions in Peking must be very uncertain at present and that the problems you will be called on to face will be numerous and without precedent.

Yours truly,

第 92 号半官函 　　　　　　　　　　　　　　1928 年 6 月 28 日于瑷珲关 / 大黑河

尊敬的易纨士先生：

　　为海关监督办公津贴事：海关监督已传达财政部指令，即自 4 月 1 日起按照当日银行汇率以大洋为本位为之发放每月津贴。特此申请指示。如能按照当日海关征税汇率进行支付，事情会简单很多。也就是说，海关监督当前办公津贴为每月 400 银圆，按照 150 银圆兑换 100 海关两的征税汇率计算，即为 266.67 海关两。

　　为冬季期间华籍内班关员减员事：海关总税务司公署第 390/116060 号令在批准三等一级税务员刘文湅先生的休假申请时指出，今年冬季将无须另派关员接替其职位。对此，本人曾于第 88 号半官函中请求暂缓执行冬季裁员之决定，但总税务司于 4 月 3 日第 79 号半官函中回复时提出如要在非航运季期间保持华籍内班职员的原定人数，则需提出极具说服力的理据。函中还提到瑷珲关第 272 号呈中曾汇报冬季期间或许可以减少一名税务员。经查，此呈乃由瑚斯敦（J. H. W. Houstoun）先生提交，但其在本口岸任职期间，仅仅经历了一个夏季，因此对于冬季的情况知之甚少。此外，近来航路标志活动大幅增多，相关的文书工作都落在了冬季职员的肩上。为航路标志工作所收之江捐的十分之一为海关的征收佣金，去年收到 5000 银圆。不过如果延长工作时间，或许可以不必另派关员接替刘文湅先生的职位，将予一试。

　　为黑龙江上游疏浚作业事：6 月 19 日华苏双方就黑龙江上游的联合疏浚工事签订了一份简短的协议。协定支出预算为 6000 金卢布，由中国摊付半数。此项预算过低，相信苏联政府的实际支出定会高于账面金额。如此前所述，已向道尹指出应想办法获得该笔额外所需资金。如今道尹前来告知已要求东北航务局提供所需的 3000 金卢布（按照当前汇率计算约合 2000 银圆），因为此项疏浚工事的受益方为其所有之轮船。但恐怕东北航务局等会借此插手黑龙江水道委员会的工作，正如他们在哈尔滨对松花江航路标志工作所做的那样。兹认为，如能从松花江航路标志资金中预支 2000 银圆，于海关应更为有益。此前批准预支的 15000 银圆中还有一部分未支领。黑龙江上游疏浚协议签订后，航路标志相关的所有未结问题都已安排妥当，至少暂时如此。

　　为江捐税收事：易保罗（P. I. Ignatieff）先生已完成对乌苏里江航路标志的巡查工作，并从拉哈苏苏返回，相关报告业已呈交。据其所述，乌苏里江爆发洪水，再次淹没了江岸，水位几乎已达到去年洪水期间的最高记录。轮船因此无法载运货物前往该地区，江捐税收也随之大幅下降。黑龙江水道委员会的资金状况已是捉襟见肘，得此消息，更是令人灰心丧气。

　　为地方政治局势事：张作霖和吴俊升督军的死讯悄然传来，地方文武各官难免会对自己的前程有所担忧。吴俊升司令任黑龙江省督军八年之久，尽管在执政上可批之处甚多，但不得不承认其对各方面的掌控的确十分牢固。相信北京当前的政治局势定然是动荡不安，总关税务司需要应对的问题也将是前所未有，纷繁复杂。

您真挚的

铎博赉

22. 铎博赍致易纨士函

（第 95 号半官函）

S/O No.95.

Aigun   25th August,   28.

Dear Mr. Edwardes,

FLOODS IN THE AMUR AND ZEYA RIVER VALLEYS:
the regions of the valley of the Amur from Taheiho to
the sea and the Zeya River valley have just experienced
a very serious flood.   At Taheiho the river began to
rise appreciably on the 15th July when it stood at
10.1 feet above low water mark.   On the 16th it rose
4'6" and by the 30th the maximum was reached at a
point 28.1 feet above zero.   The rise was due to
heavy local rains and to the effects of the
unprecedented discharge of water from the Zeya river,
which empties into the Amur just below Taheiho,
serving as a dam to back up the Amur waters onto
Taheiho and Blagovestchensk.   The great rise only
extended a short distance above Taheiho.   For two or
three days at the end of July it appeared as if
Taheiho might be covered to a depth of several feet
and many people moved to higher ground at the back

of

A. H. F. Edwardes, Esquire,
        Peking.

of the town while steamers and barges stood by in case
of an emergency.   Miraculously the rise stopped short
by about a foot from topping the bund in several places
though the lower end of the town, including the Public
Garden, Sau Ling Pu and the Native Indoor Staff Quarters,
was flooded.   The water also backed up the second street
from the bund until the old Customs compound was covered
to a depth of over 1 foot in many places while a rise of
another 6" would have covered my compound - as it was I
lost a flourishing vegetable garden near the public
park.   All private ice cellars of the place, where the
summer supplies of ice are kept, were flooded and the
ice melted.   On the 26th those members of the Staff
occupying the Native Indoor Staff Quarters were forced
to evacuate.   I authorised them to move their effects
to such temporary quarters as they were able to engage
on such short notice; it remains to be seen if they will
be able to reoccupy the old building.   This matter will
be reported on officially.

A short distance below Taheiho where Zeya and
Amur river currents met the whole region was flooded for
miles and resembled a great sea.   Many villages were
destroyed and all crops ruined.   Fortunately, owing to

the

the slow rise of water, there was little loss of life.
The inhabitants were taken off in junks and steamers.
The Customs motor boat made one trip to that area
and brought back 16 old people and babies but as it
was the only dependable motor boat in the harbour I
kept it at hand for emergency purposes. Further down
the Amur, on the Chinese side of the river, several
communities were flooded and houses and crops ruined
but there was little loss of life. In this connection
I have written the Taoyin calling his attention to
the praiseworthy manner in which several of the Tungpei
S/S Co.'s steamers stood by distressed villages and
aided the inhabitants to get to higher grounds with
their effects.

It is difficult to get reliable reports as to
what happened up the Zeya river and along the Soviet
side of the lower Amur. All information, for some
inexplicable reason, has been suppressed. I am told
that some 50 villages on the Zeya, including some of
large size, were almost completely destroyed. The
rise on that river was the highest since 1822 - a period
of 56 years. The loss of life must have been considerable. One of the most serious effects will be the
destruction

destruction of crops as the Zeya valley is very fertile.
For a distance of some 400 miles the river spread out to
a width varying from 20 to 30 miles. Just at this
juncture the loss of wheat involved will greatly aggra-
vate the grain shortage already felt. It is said that
the Soviet Authorities are withholding aid until the
farmers of the different stricken districts agree to
form communes, to raise stipulated amounts of grain, and
to dispose of their crops as the Soviet directs. They
are now "between the devil and the deep sea".

At one stage of the rise a break in the bund
formed just above our bunding and had it extended
behind our bund the effect would have been serious.
Quick action was necessary and I had a row of piles
driven at the threatened point and the embrasure filled
in with sand bags. The cost was $100 which I took upon
myself to advance from Suspense A/c and am now claiming
from the Chamber of Commerce. The drains along our
property in some places were seriously damaged and a
certain amount, to be reported officially, will be
required to put them right. The basement of the Custom
House was flooded to a depth of some 3 feet but has
been pumped out and the building seems none the worse
for

for it. The guard had to be withdrawn from the Lower
Barrier but he has since returned. The premises there
were flooded but no damage was done. Taking it all in
all the Customs and the community in general got off
very lightly though for three days and nights we were
in anxious suspense lest the narrow margin separating
the place from disaster might be wiped out. In the
interior the heavy rains damaged the crops badly in
low lying places but on the higher levels they seem
to have been benefitted. The rainfall for the month of
July was 11.02 inches with 4.22 inches on the 27th.
Both these figures seem to have been records for Taheiho
and can better be appreciated when it is stated that
the rainfall for July last year, a normal one, was
3.62 inches, less than that of the 27th July this year.
The local Staff have contributed generously from their
pay for relief to the flooded area.

RENEWAL OF THE CONTRACT OF THE TECHNICAL
ADVISER TO THE AMUR AIDS COMMISSION: In my despatch
No. 386 I recommended that Mr. Ignatieff's contract,
which expires on the 15th September, be renewed. The
Taoyin shares the confidence he has always received
from the Customs and all talk of his being replaced by
a Chinese Adviser at a lower salary seems to have died
down

down for the present. It is pertinent to record in
this connection that the newly formed Sungari Aids
Commission seems unable to obtain a satisfactory foreign
expert at a salary of Hk.Tls.1,000 per month whereas
Ignatieff receives only Hk.Tls.400.00.

ADVANCE TO ASSIST MR. 4° ASSISTANT T'U SHOU
CHEN TO MEET HIS TRAVELLING EXPENSES WHEN PROCEEDING
ON INSPECTORATE LEAVE: Mr. T'u is proceeding on
Inspectorate leave the 1. September and the sum required
to move himself and family from Taheiho via Harbin and
Dairen to Shanghai will amount to some $600. This is
a large amount for a man of his seniority and it seemed
to me that, while his expenses cannot be paid by the
Service as would be the case had he served another
year in the port (I.G.Despatch No. 413/117,396), some
assistance might be given and as Accounts Instructions
forbid the advancing of pay I wired you on the 21st
inst. asking if an advance might not be made to be
recovered from the pay that will be issued to him by this
office the first two months of his leave. Mr. 4°
Assistant Lee Peng Sheo has arrived to replace Mr. T'u
and is now learning the duties he is to assume on the
latter's departure. His family was not able to travel
with

with him and is expected later when Mr. Lee will
present a claim for their travelling expenses.

Yours truly,

第 <u>95</u> 号半官函   1928 年 8 月 25 日于瑷珲关

尊敬的易纨士先生：

为黑龙江及结雅河流域爆发洪水事：黑龙江自大黑河至入海口一段流域及结雅河流域刚刚经历了极其严重的洪灾。在大黑河,江水自 7 月 15 日开始有明显上涨,当时水位显示高出低潮线 10.1 英尺。16 日又上涨 4 英尺 6 英寸,到 30 日最高水位已涨至 28.1 英尺。江水上涨主要是因近来本地连降暴雨,结雅河又同时发生前所未有的泄洪,河水全部涌入大黑河下游的黑龙江河段,如同水坝一般将黑龙江水拦回大黑河及布拉戈维申斯克（Blagoveschesk）河段。但洪水仅蔓延至大黑河上游不远处。7 月最后的两三日,大黑河镇内也被洪水覆盖了数英尺,许多人都迁移到镇子后面的高地上,轮船和驳船均在一旁待命,以防有紧急情况。幸运的是,江水在离数处堤岸顶面仅有一英尺的距离时,突然停止上涨,不过镇内地势较低的一端,包括公园、司令部及华籍内班职员宿舍在内,还是遭到了洪水的侵袭。江水停止上涨后,与堤岸相隔一条街道街区的洪水也开始消退,当时旧海关办公楼大院内多处地方的水深都已超过了 1 英尺,再上涨 6 英寸,税务司住所大院也将被洪水淹没,但公园附近长势喜人的蔬菜园确已不复存在。所有私人冰窖（为夏季储存冰块）都被洪水淹没,冰块也全部融化。7 月 28 日,在华籍内班职员宿舍居住的关员被迫撤离。本人已批准他们暂将私人财物转移至在如此短时间之内能够找到的临时宿舍内,至于原宿舍之后能否继续居住,还很难说。此事稍后将由呈文正式汇报。

就在大黑河下游不远处,黑龙江与结雅河合流一带,洪水蔓延数英里,犹如一片汪洋。许多村庄都被冲毁,所有庄稼都被吞没。幸运的是,水位上涨速度缓慢,几乎没有造成人员死亡。当地居民已被民船及轮船转移。海关摩托艇也曾前去营救过一次,运回 16 名老人和婴孩,但由于港口内仅有这一艘摩托艇可用,为应对紧急需求,之后便没有再派出。更远处的黑龙江下游华岸沿线,有数处村落被洪水淹没,房屋、庄稼尽数被毁,但几乎没有人员死亡。此次洪水期间,东北航务局派出数艘轮船支援受难村庄,帮助将居民及其财物转移至地势较高的地方,值得称赞。为此已向道尹致函请其关注。

至于结雅河上游及黑龙江下游俄岸的情况,很难获得可靠情报。而且不知为何,苏联方面的消息都被封锁了。据了解,结雅河沿线有 50 多处村落几乎全部被冲毁,其中不乏一些规模较大的村庄。洪水期间,结雅河的水位已达到自 1872 年以来 56 年间的历史最高点。相信定已造成了大量的人员伤亡。最严重的后果还应包括庄稼的损毁,毕竟结雅河流域十分富饶,有 400 英里的河段宽度都能达到 20 至 30 英里。而此时爆发洪水,造成的谷物损失势必会加剧当前的粮食短缺情况。据悉，苏联政府已经下令，在受灾地区农民同意重新建设村庄，按规定提高谷类的种植量，并依政府指示处理粮食之前，不会为之提供援助。农民目前是"进退维谷"。

洪水上涨期间，海关办公楼上游堤岸出现了一个裂口，一旦扩大，便会殃及海关所筑堤岸，后果不堪设想，须立即采取补救措施。本人当即命人在裂口处打入一排木桩，并以沙袋填充。费用共计 100 银圆，已从暂付款帐中预支，现正在向商会索款。海关关产四周的排水沟多处受损严重，修复需要一笔费用，具体情况将呈文正式汇报。海关办公楼地下室亦遭水淹，当时积水深约 3 英尺，但后来已全部抽出，房屋整体似乎并未受到影响。图东分卡的卫兵已被召回，当地关产亦被洪水侵蚀，所幸并未造成损失。总的来说，海关及大黑河镇上的居民受损情况较轻，尽管有三日，日夜悬心，担忧堤坝会被冲毁，整个镇子会被洪水吞没。至于内陆地区，地势较低处的庄稼因暴雨影响受损严重，但地势较高处的庄稼反倒因此受益。7 月的降雨量有 11.02 英寸，其中 27 日有 4.22 英寸，应已打破了大黑河月降雨量及单日降雨量的记录。据记载，去年 7 月的降雨量较为正常，仅有 3.62 英寸，还没有今年 7 月 27 日单日的降雨量高，由此更能看出今年的雨量之大。本关职员纷纷慷慨解囊，拿出部分薪俸为受灾地区提供救济。

为黑龙江水道委员会航务专门顾问的合同续签事：瑷珲关第 386 号呈中已汇报易保罗（P. I. Ignatieff）先生的合同将于 9 月 15 日期满，建议续签。如今道尹与海关相互信任，所有关于由薪俸较低的华籍航务专门顾问代替易保罗先生的言论也已逐渐平息。另外值得提及的是，新成立的松花江航路标志委员会以 1000 海关两的月薪标准都未能雇用到一名令人满意的洋籍顾问，而易保罗先生每月薪俸仅有 400.00 海关两。

为四等帮办屠守鑫先生休假预支旅费事：屠守鑫先生将于 9 月 1 日开始休假，其与家人自大黑河经由哈尔滨和大连至上海的旅费共计 600 余银圆。这对于他这个职级的关员来说也是一笔不小的费用，但海关又不能为之支付，除非其再于本口岸任满一年（参阅海关总税务司公署第 413/117398 号令）。尽管如此，本人还是认为应当为其提供一些帮助。鉴于账目通令早有指示不得预支薪俸，因此已于 8 月 21 日电呈总税务司询问能否先为其预支本关将为之发放的休假期间前两个月的薪俸。接替其职位的四等帮办黎彭寿先生已抵达瑷珲关，正在学习相关业务，以在其离开后接手相应工作。黎彭寿先生的家人未能随行，预计过些时日会来此地，届时其将为家人申请报销旅费。

您真挚的

铎博费

23. 铎博赉致易纨士函

（第 96 号半官函）

S/O. No. 96.

Aigun/Taheiho, 21st September 28.

Dear Mr. Edwardes,

       <u>Rules of Navigation</u>: On the return of the Taoyin from Moukden and Harbin early in August he told me that he had discussed the newly adopted Rules of Navigation for Frontier Rivers with the Head Office of the Tungpei Steamship Company at Harbin and they had expressed themselves as desirous of issuing the Rules to the Masters of steamers plying on the Sungari, saying that to have one set of Rules for the Amur and Ussuri rivers and another for the Sungari would be very confusing and unnecessary. Shortly after my conversation with the Taoyin the Tungpei Steamship Company wired him asking for 60 copies and he told me to supply them (the Rules are stored in the Custom House). On the 23rd ultimo I sent the 60 copies but suggested in my letter that they be sent instead to the Harbin Superintendent (concurrently a member of the Sungari Conservancy Board) who

A. H. F. Edwardes, Esquire,

    Peking.

who could pass them on to the Tungpei Company with such instructions as he saw fit to issue. It seemed to me that this procedure would be more regular and might even lead to the official promulgation by the Harbin Superintendent of the Rules on the Sungari. I have informed Mr. Barentzen of these developments.

    <u>Fire-wall between Kunst & Albers property and the old Custom House site</u>: The firm of Kunst & Albers, whose property adjoins our old Custom House site, has requested the cooperation of the Customs in erecting a common fire-wall. The cost would be some Harbin $1,300 = Hk.Tls.650, of which the Customs share would be Hk.Tls.325. While the Customs buildings to be protected are of no great value the Kunst & Albers compound contains two garages that are dangerous fire risks and large quantities of firewood are stored each year in our compound. I have told Kunst & Albers that I doubted very much if the Customs would undertake such an expenditure at this time. If funds are available, however, I should like to submit the matter officially as the cost of the proposed wall is not much and it

would

would add considerably to the value and safety of our
compound.

     Repairs necessitated by the flood: The
weather continues to be atrocious with heavy rains
nearly every day and the river continues at an abnormal
though not dangerous height. The repairs to street
drains along our property, which I mentioned in my last
S/O. have been taken in hand as to delay only meant
heavier expenditure; once a break is made in the walls
of a drain the continuous rains rapidly enlarge it. The
amount involved is some Harbin \$350 = Hk.Tls.175. During
the past week the ice cellar of the Tidesurveyor's
compound collapsed owing to the heavy rains and the
rotten condition of the structure. As it must be
reerected before cold weather sets in and as it now
takes some six weeks to get a reply to a communication
to the Inspectorate (both the mail and telegraph services
are hopelessly out of order) I have also taken the
liberty of putting this work in hand at a cost of Harbin
\$150 = Hk.Tls.75. I shall report these expenditures
officially and trust that my action will meet with your

                approval

approval.

     River Dues Collection: The collection
of River Dues to date is practically the same as that
of last year. There has been a gain by exchange,
however, of some \$8,731 in making our Rouble payments
to the Amur Navigation Bureau whereas my estimate in
Aigun despatch No.373 of Aids expenditure for the
present season allowed for a gain of only \$2,000. If
present conditions continue, Aids will show a comfortabl
balance to the good at the end of the year.

     Possible famine in Siberia: For some
time I have noticed cues in front of the bakeries in
Blagovestchensk waiting for a small allowance of bread
and today the Japanese Consul from there tells me that
only a small dole of black bread is now being issued
with every prospect of conditions getting worse instead
of better. Crops in the adjoining part of Siberia
have practically been ruined by floods and continuous
rains while there is no reserve to fall back upon. The
Japanese Consul reports the outlook as very serious. I
have every reason to believe that conditions in the

                interior

interior of Siberia are even worse than they are here
on the frontier.   Some grain was shipped to Blagovestchensk from this side earlier in the season but no more
can be spared under the exsisting adverse crop conditions
However the Soviet authorities have no money even if
they wished to purchase grain from Harbin where, I
believe, there is plenty.   The so-called "government"
in Russia (Siberia) is getting itself deeper and deeper
into the mire.

　　　　Mail and telegraphic communications: As
stated above the mail and telegraph services between
Harbin and Taheiho are badly disrupted owing to the
continuous rain.   The telegraph lines have not been
repaired for many years and both poles and wires can no
longer bear their own weight.   No present prospect is
held out for the resumption of the telegraph service but
a wireless station has been installed by the military
and is functioning fairly well with Harbin.   Under these
conditions I thought it best to ask Harbin to wire the
Inspectorate to send all Aigun messages there for
relaying by wireless to Taheiho.

　　　　　　Yours truly,

第 96 号半官函　　　　　　　　　　**1928 年 9 月 21 日于瑷珲关 / 大黑河**

尊敬的易纨士先生：

　　为航行章程事：道尹于 8 月初自奉天经哈尔滨返回后前来告知，其已与东北航务局哈尔滨总公司讨论了边界河道上新施行的航行章程，该公司希望能向松花江上往来的轮船船长颁布此章程，认为如果松花江与黑龙江及乌苏里江所施行的航行章程不能统一，将会对往来轮船造成不必要的困扰。此次会面后不久，东北航务局便向道尹发送电报申请 60 份航行章程抄件。本人随后应道尹要求于 8 月 23 日发给他 60 份抄件（章程文本均存放于海关），并于信函中建议将抄件发送给哈尔滨关监督，亦为松花江管理局（Sungari Conservancy Board）的成员，再由其转交东北航务局，同时还可由其下达相应指示。兹认为，如此办理更合乎规矩，甚至可以让哈尔滨关监督正式宣布松花江上将施行此航行章程。上述进展已转达哈尔滨关税务司巴闰森（P. G. S. Barentzen）先生。

　　为孔士洋行房产与旧海关办公楼关址之间的防火墙事：孔士洋行因其房产与旧海关办公楼关址相邻，提出希望海关能够与其合作搭建一堵共用的防火墙。费用预计约为哈大洋 1300 元，约合 650 海关两，将由海关摊付 325 海关两。实际上，海关此处房产并无太大价值，但大院中每年都会存放大量的薪柴，而且孔士洋行大院中的两个车库存有火灾隐患。现已回复孔士洋行不确定海关此时能否承担这笔支出。但如果资金方面允许，希望可以正式呈报此事，一来因拟建防火墙的费用并不是很多，二来建成后也将大大提高海关关产的价值及安全性。

　　为洪水过后的修缮事：本地天气一直十分糟糕，几乎日日暴雨，黑龙江水位持续高涨，不过幸运的是，暂时还未达到危险的高度。上一封半官函中汇报的修缮关产街边排水沟一事已经着手办理，毕竟拖延只会增加费用支出，因为排水沟壁一旦出现缺口，便会因连续的降雨迅速扩大。修缮费用约为哈大洋 350 元，合 175 海关两。上周，监察长住所院落内原本就破败不堪的冰窖被大雨冲塌。鉴于重建工作需要在天气转冷之前完成，而且本地的信件及电报服务都已出现故障，从呈报到收到总税务司的回复至少需要 6 个星期左右的时间，因此已提前动工，费用为哈大洋 150 元，合 75 海关两。嗣后将呈文正式汇报上述支出，相信总税务司定会予以批准。

　　为江捐征收事：截至今日，江捐征收数额与去年同期基本持平。但在以卢布向俄阿穆尔水道局支付航路标志摊款一项上已得汇兑盈余约 8731 银圆，而瑷珲关第 373 号呈汇报的航路标志工作支出预算中，本季度的汇兑盈余仅有 2000 银圆。照此发展，年底时黑龙江航路标志资金应会有充足的盈余。

为西伯利亚或将遭遇饥荒事：据观察，近来布拉戈维申斯克（Blagoveschesk）面包房门前日日排有长队，但每人能够得到的量却十分有限。今日从当地日本领事口中得知，现在仅发放少量的黑面包，如此则意味着，情况可能只会愈发糟糕，难以好转。西伯利亚邻近地区连降暴雨，洪水泛滥，庄稼几乎已全部被冲毁，而且也无储备粮食可供维持生计。日本领事认为当地前景非常严峻。因此完全有理由相信西伯利亚内陆地区的情况比边境地区还要更糟。航运季初期，还有一些谷物自大黑河运至布拉戈维申斯克，但如今庄稼受损，华岸各地也无富余。虽然哈尔滨地区应该还有大量粮食，但苏联政府财政空虚，即使有意购买，资金上也无力支持。苏联（西伯利亚）所谓的"政府"如今在泥潭中已是越陷越深。

为信件及电报通信事：如上所述，哈尔滨与大黑河之间的信件及电报服务已因连绵不断的降雨严重受阻。电报线路年久失修，无论是电线杆还是线缆都已无法承担自重。目前看来，电报服务已无恢复希望，不过军方已经安装了无线电台，与哈尔滨收发电报的效果很好。有鉴于此，兹认为，如能请哈尔滨关税务司电呈总税务司申请将与瑷珲关有关的消息均发送给他，再由他通过无线电台转发至大黑河口岸，应更为妥当。

您真挚的

铎博赉

24. 铎博赍致易纨士函

（第 99 号半官函）

S/O No.99

CUSTOM HOUSE,

A I G U N. 13th December, 19 28.

Dear Mr. Edwardes,

ACTING COMMISSIONER RETURNS FROM HARBIN:
in my last S/O I reported that I was proceeding to Harbin
by rail via Blagovestchensk and Vladivostock as motor cars
would not start running soon enough to permit me to travel
via Tsitsihar and arrive in Harbin for my Chinese Examination by the 15th November. I left here on the 8th ultimo
while I was still able to cross to Blagovestchensk by
small boat through the floating ice, waited there two days
for the express to Vladivostock and after a tiresome
journey arrived in Harbin on the 15th. Mr. Alabaster
did not arrive until the 21st, two days were then taken
up with my examination after which I proceeded to Tsitsihar
obtained transportation in a motor car on the 26th and
arrived back in Taheiho on the 29th. I was met at
Tsitsihar by my servant, who had taken the first available
car, with warm coat, camp bed, etc., so I was able to

keep

A. H. F. Edwardes, Esquire,
Peping.

keep warm on the return trip but the road was indescribably
rough in places. On my return I found that the Customs
had functioned without incident under the direction of
Lee Peng Sheo, 4th Chinese Assistant B. who had been in
charge during my absence. As I have said the trip was
a trying one and I trust due allowance will be made for
the fact in the consideration of the results of my
examination.

CHARGE ALLOWANCE FOR AIGUN SUB-STATION: in my S/O No.97
I inquire whether or not a Charge Allowance of Hk.Tls.10
per month may not be issued to the Officer-in-charge at
Aigun. In your S/O of the 7th November in reply you ask
if such an allowance is justified in view of my statement
that there was little to do there aside from routine and
simple examination work at the Chinese Post Office. In
minimizing the importance of the work to be done I was
thinking of the requirements of the winter season. while
navigation is open all steamers call at Aigun, land and
ship cargo and passengers and are regularly entered and
cleared. The steamers are searched, cargo examined and
duty assessed. Aigun is really the port while Taheiho
is the sub-station although it has now become the head

office

office. At the same time considerable prestige obtains at Aigun, a great deal of tact is required in dealing with local merchants who are a troublesome lot and a certain amount of face must be maintained with the local officials. While it is true that there is not so much to do at Aigun during the winter months the average exactions of the place for the year are not light and I consider that the Officer-in-charge there should have an extra allowance over and above what he would receive were he stationed at the head office. The station is some 25 miles down river from Taheiho and supplies, other than those locally produced, must be obtained from here at added expense.

APPOINTMENT OF ACTING TIDESURVEYOR AND ACTING HARBOURMASTER in my S/O No.97 under STAFF MOVEMENTS I informed you that, acting on the spirit of your wire transmitted by the Harbin Customs under date of 24th September inquiring if Snow could carry on if Smith did not take up the appointment of Tidesurveyor, I had turned over the duties of the Tidesurveyor's office to Snow. Until now I have received no specific instructions from the Inspectorate to do this and accordingly have not issued him an acting allowance, to which, presumably, he is entitled. I should be glad if you would inform me whether any official instructions will

be

be sent in the matter. H. W. Snow, Assistant Examiner B, has carried on the duties of Acting Tidesurveyor and Acting Harbourmaster as from the 16th October, 1928.

METEOROLOGICAL READINGS: I am in receipt of a despatch from the Institute of Meteorology, Nanking, (copy enclosed in Summary of Non-urgent Chinese Correspondence for November) to the effect that since the matter was sanctioned by the Ts'ai-chêng Pu no daily meteorological telegrams had been received from Aigun. This is the first I have heard of the question; at the same time the statements containing copies of daily meteorological telegrams sent during October and November to the Central Observatory, Peking, have been returned by the Post Office with the remark that the addressee could not be found. Daily telegrams for the Central Observatory, Peking, are still being accepted by the local telegraph office, however, and they express their willingness to forward similar telegrams to the new Nanking Institute of Meteorology, I should be glad to know if I am to make any immediate change in the present procedure of sending daily readings i.e. to the Peking Observatory, Sikawei Observatory and Kiaochow Observatory.

CONDITIONS

CONDITIONS IN SOVIET SIBERIA: from time to time I have
commented on the increasing difficulty the people in
Siberia are having in obtaining the common necessities of
life. On my recent trip to Harbin by rail via Blagovestchensk and Vladivostock I was able to see still more of
conditions that exist. Everywhere there is a shortage of
bread and long cues are daily formed to receive the day's
supply. Owing to the lack of hay, etc., dairy cows are
being killed and sold for meat with the result that butter
and milk is becoming very scarce. Materials for clothing
have only been obtainable in very limited quantities for
some years so that the population have the appearance of
being in rags. Only in Vladivostock did I see white
collars and any attempt to keep up appearances. Even
fuel is very scarce though all communities have large
forests at no great distance. As in everything else,
there is a lack of organization and the people sit with
folded hands waiting for things to be done for them. Farmers
are producing less every year, the rouble is falling,
manufacturing is at a standstill and unless something
radical is done, such as throwing the country open to

                                        foreign

foreign enterprise and private trading, the whole Soviet
system is doomed to an early collapse. There is little
evidence, however, that this will come about through any
organized effort from without or within.

        Yours truly,

第 99 号半官函   1928 年 12 月 13 日于瑷珲关

尊敬的易纨士先生：

为署理税务司由哈尔滨返回事：上一封半官函中已汇报，为于 11 月 15 日抵达哈尔滨参加汉文考试，本人计划取道布拉戈维申斯克（Blagoveschesk）和符拉迪沃斯托克（Vladivostok）由铁路前往，因为如果搭乘汽车经齐齐哈尔前往，时间上恐怕会来不及。11 月 8 日离开大黑河时，黑龙江上虽已有浮冰，但仍能够搭乘小船过江至布拉戈维申斯克，在当地等了两日后便搭乘直通列车至符拉迪沃斯托克，最后终于在经历了一段烦劳的旅程后于 15 日抵达哈尔滨。但直到 21 日，阿拉巴德（E. Alabaster）先生才到来。考试用时两日，结束后本人便只身前往齐齐哈尔，26 日在当地搭乘上汽车，并于 29 日抵达大黑河。在齐齐哈尔时，幸好有仆人接应，不仅提前订好车辆，还准备了棉衣棉被等，以使返程途中不至那么寒冷，不过很多地方的路况确实非常糟糕。返回后发现离开期间，关务在四等二级帮办黎彭寿先生的代管下一切正常，并无意外发生。如上所述，此行舟车劳顿，相信在评判本人考试成绩时，应会将此实际情况考虑在内。

为瑷珲口岸负责关员的职务津贴事：此前于第 97 号半官函中询问能否为瑷珲口岸的负责关员发放每月 10 海关两的职务津贴。总税务司于 11 月 7 日半官函中回复时指出，既然除日常公务及中国邮政局处简单的验货工作，瑷珲口岸几无需要处理之事，此份职务津贴的发放是否合理。对此，需说明，在叙述口岸工作时，只是考虑到冬季的需求，负责关员的职务实际上要比之前所述重要的多。航运开通后，所有轮船都会停靠瑷珲口岸，上下客货，照常办理报关结关手续。关员也需要登船检查、验货、计税。更何况事实上瑷珲才是真正的口岸，大黑河原本不过是分关，只是后来才成了总关。另外，海关需要在瑷珲口岸赢得声望，因为当地商人很难应付，与之打交道时很需要技巧，同时还要与地方官员维持面子上的往来。瑷珲口岸冬季的工作确实没有很多，但全年平均的任务量并不少，故此认为当地负责关员得享的津贴额度应当高于其在总关任职所应享有之数。此外，瑷珲位于大黑河下游约 25 英里处，一应供给，除当地所产，均须从大黑河购买，如此还需一笔额外费用。

为代理监察长兼代理港务长的任命事：已于第 97 号半官函人事调动一项中报告称 9 月 24 日哈尔滨关通过无线电报传达总税务司指示，询问如果施密（H. A. Smith）先生无法接受监察长的任命，今年冬季能否暂由思诺（H. W. Snow）先生接任此职，并说明根据该电令的指示精神，已将监察课的工作交由思诺先生负责。然鉴于迄今仍未收到海关总税务司公署关于此事的明确指示，因此还未向他发放代理津贴，不过想来其应有权得享。还望告知是否会就此事正式下达指示。二等副验货员思诺先生已自 1928 年 10 月 16 日起就开始担任代监察长兼代理港务长之职。

为气象记录事：已收悉南京北极阁气象研究所来函（抄件随附于 1928 年 11 月非紧急中文往来函摘由簿），内称自财政部批准由各口岸发送每日气象电报以来，还未收到过瑷珲关的气象电报。实际上，此为本人第一次知悉此事。至于函中索要的 10 月 11 月发送给北京中央研究院气象研究所的气象电报抄件，按照要求发送后已被邮政局以未找到收信人为由退回。但大黑河电报局仍同意每日向北京中央研究院气象研究所发送气象电报，还表示愿意将此类电报转发给南京北极阁气象研究所。目前本关每日须向北京中央研究院气象研究所、南京气象研究所及胶州气象研究所发送气象电报，还望指示是否应立即做出调整。

为西伯利亚局势事：关于西伯利亚地区的居民愈来愈难获取生活必需品的情况，此前已有所汇报。日前经布拉戈维申斯克和符拉迪沃斯托克由铁路前往哈尔滨时，发现实际情况要更为糟糕。各地面包都十分紧缺，日日皆有居民排成长队领取当日的供给。由于干草等短缺，奶牛都被宰杀卖肉，以致奶油和牛奶已成为稀有之物。数年来，当地布料的供应量一直非常有限，人们如今都是衣衫褴褛的模样。只有到符拉迪沃斯托克时才看到有白领人士，人们也都尽量保持着装。但在整个地区，就连燃料都极为稀缺，尽管所有村落的不远处就有大片的森林。当地各行各业都缺少组织，人人都是两手一摊，想要坐享其成。农民的粮食产量逐年减少，卢布一再贬值，制造业也都停滞。如果不能彻底改变，比如对洋企及私人贸易实行开放政策，整个苏联体制注定会很快崩塌。但目前并无迹象表明苏联体制内外有什么组织在试图做出改变。

您真挚的

铎博赉

第三部分

地方见闻

（1929～1932）

1. 铎博赉致梅乐和函

（第 102 号半官函）

S/O No. 102

CUSTOM HOUSE,

Aigun   18th February, 1929.

Dear Mr. Maze,

INTRODUCTION OF THE NEW IMPORT TARIFF: various telegrams were received from yourself regarding the introduction of the new tariff in time to put it in force on the 1st February.   A joint notification had previously been issued by the Superintendent, and myself on the 14th January preparing the public for the innovation. Where points were not clear, due to the late receipt of certain telegrams, I wired the Harbin Commissioner as to what procedure he was following rather than to bother you at a time when I knew you must be very busy.   It happens, too, that the local collection is small at this time of the year, due to the closed navigation season, so that new points raised have not been so pressing as they must have been at the larger ports.   The arrival of Circular instructions mentioned as having been sent in your telegram

of

F. W. Maze, Esquire,
      Shanghai.

of the 1st February will undoubtedly make everything clear. The public seem to have taken the increase calmly with the exception of the fur merchants whose complaints I speak of below.

SURTAXES ON FOREIGN IMPORTS, AND ON NATIVE EXPORTS AND COASTWISE TRADE: in my S/O No.100 of the 19th January, 1928, supplemented by my telegram of the 25th January, I reported the receipt of instructions from the Superintendent to the effect that that part of the collection on Foreign Imports which represented the increase in the new tariff instead of the old should be remitted to the Pao An Tsung Seu Ling Pu, Moukden, if the Surtax on Foreign Imports was discontinued, and that I was in touch with the Harbin Commissioner and proposed to follow the instructions you issued him.   I have since received a telegram from him dated the 1st February to the effect that his instructions from you are to retain all collection under the new tariff and to make no remittances to Moukden. I shall act accordingly; at present no revenue remittance is required, owing to the small collection, so the question need not be raised.   The Superintendent now informs me verbally that he has received telegraphic instructions to

continue

continue the collection of the Surtax on imports. I have
instituted the collection of the 2½% Surtax on Native
Exports and 1½% on Coastwise traffic. As the Superintendent has received no instructions on the point I wrote him
officially of the step I was taking. He made no comment
beyond suggesting in an interview that a joint notification
be issued.

CUSTOMS TO TAKE OVER THE LOCAL TAX BUREAU AND
KEROSENE TAX OFFICE: whilst calling on the Superintendent
on the 1st February he showed me a telegram from T. V.
Soong directing the Customs to take over the local tax
bureau and Kerosene Tax Office. He informed me that he
was referring the matter to Moukden. I presume Mr. Soong
hardly expects any immediate notice being taken of these
instructions by Manchurian officials.

DUTY TREATMENT OF FURS: it has been port
practice in the past to consider all furs, with the
exception of cat and dog skins, as foreign imports on the
presumption that they were smuggled across the Amur from
the Russian side and therefore were foreign goods that
had not paid duty. In my S/O No.88 of 10th March, 1928,

under

under REVENUE COLLECTION I raise the question of whether
such furs should not be treated as native goods and say
that our position is very weak when we assume that all
furs are smuggled and that were one of the foreign fur-
exporting firms to make a test case and appeal to their
Consul we would have difficulty in justifying our practice.
With the introduction of the new tariff increasing the
import duties on furs (dressed or tanned) to 22½% all
local fur dealers are preparing to close stating that with
this increase, the Superintendent's Surtax and a 25% tax
by the local tax bureau, business is impossible. I have had
some conversation with the Superintendent about the matter
and he informs me that he will shortly address me officially
requesting that furs be treated as native goods hereafter
that they may pay according to the export tariff. My
information is to the effect that a very small percentage of
the furs dealt with in this region are smuggled from Russia.
Certain kinds such as sable and white fox obviously are, but
they are rare. Under the circumstances, therefore, and
in view of the likelihood of the new tariff rate killing
what is practically the only industry flourishing in this

place.

place, I would advocate changing the local practice (with
the exception of that applied to sables, white fox and
similarly obviously Russian skins) and treating furs as
native exports. The fact that the Superintendent is
willing to lose practically his only revenue in the way
of surtaxes by the change argues for its justice. I
shall submit the question officially on receipt of the
Superintendent's communication on the subject but in view
of the hardship now being felt by local dealers and their
preparations to close down I should be glad if you would
advise me semi-officially to change the local practice at
once on my receipt of the Superintendent's letter asking
me to do so. I should add that under the export tariff
many of the furs exported will have to pay 5% the same
as they paid under the old import tariff so that our
revenue will be little less than formerly from this source.
Furs smuggled overland to Harbin without being declared at
the Aigun Customs are treated as native by the Harbin
Customs when exported by parcel post from there. If I
receive your sanction to consider furs as Native Exports
I shall point out to the Superintendent that more favourable
treatment should also be allowed by the local tax office.

AUDIT

AUDIT BUREAU OF THE THREE EASTERN PROVINCES
(東三省財務稽核處), AND THE CUSTOMS: I am in receipt of
three despatches from the superintendent transmitting
instructions from the Pao An Tsung Ssu Ling Pu (奉天保安總司
令部), Moukden, as follows:

    (1) notifying the establishment of an
        Audit Bureau at Moukden for the
        scrutinizing of the accounts of all
        tax collecting bureaux, not directly
        under the officials of one of the
        Three Eastern Provinces, such as the
        Customs, Telegraphs, Posts, etc. The
        tax collecting offices concerned are
        to submit statements at regular
        intervals of their accounts and all
        moneys collected must be forwarded
        to the Audit Bureau,

    (2) calling for the despatch within ten
        days to the Audit Bureau of the
        Three Eastern Provinces of statements
        showing an estimate of receipts and
        expenditures, tariffs, rules and
        regulations, etc.,

                        (3)

(3) instructing that Service records of
all employees together with details
as to their birth, parentage, etc.,
be submitted to the Audit Bureau
within ten days.

The dates of the three despatches are, respectively, 26th,
28th and 28th January, 1929. Directly after their receipt
I interviewed the Taoyin/Superintendent in order to obtain
more details and asked whether the particulars now furnished
him, as Superintendent, of collection and remittance were
not sufficient. At the same time I explained that I could
not supply the information desired by the Audit Bureau
without first consulting you, and acting in conformity with
the other Custom Houses functioning in Manchuria. He stated
that as far as the Customs was concerned he saw no necessity
of any immediate notice being taken of the instructions in
question whereupon I told him I would refer them to you.
No doubt this matter has already been reported to you by the
various Manchurian ports and I should be glad if you would
inform me what reply, if any, I am to make to the above

x communications

communications. If you think an urgent reply is necessary
I should be glad if you would transmit the instructions by
telegraph.

I am sending a copy of this S/O to the
Harbin Commissioner for possible comment.

Yours truly,

第 102 号半官函　　　　　　　　　　　1929 年 2 月 18 日于瑷珲关

尊敬的梅乐和先生：

为实行新进口税则事：

阁下关于自 2 月 1 日起开始实行新进口税则之电报均已收悉,瑷珲关海关监督与本人业于 1 月 14 日发布联合公告,以便商民有所准备。之前因阁下发来之电报有延迟送达之情况,本人对有些具体事项不甚明确,但考虑阁下当时事务繁忙,故已向哈尔滨关税务司发送电报询问其遵循的办事手续。此外,本口岸每年此时皆因受航运关闭影响而仅能征收少量税款,今年亦无例外,因此新税则之实施并未如规模较大之口岸那般紧迫。收悉阁下 2 月 1 日电报发来之通令指示后,一切疑问都将迎刃而解。对于此次提高税率一事,大多商民似已平静接受,唯有皮货商人有抱怨之言,详见下文。

为洋货进口、土货出口及复出口附加税事：

本人此前于 1928 年 1 月 19 日第 100 号半官函及 1 月 25 日电报中汇报称:"海关监督已指令待有明确指示要求停止对进口洋货征收附加税时,海关须将按照新税则多征收之税款汇至奉天保安总司令部"。本人随后已与哈尔滨关税务司取得联系,提议瑷珲关依照阁下对哈尔滨关下达之指示行事。嗣后哈尔滨关税务司于 2 月 1 日发来电报称,按照当前指示,凡按照新税则征收之税款,均需留存,不必汇至奉天。本人便遵照办理。目前,瑷珲关所收税款较少,并无汇出之需要,因此暂不必对此提出问题,且现今海关监督又口头告知,其已收到电令指示将继续对进口货物征收附加税。此外,本人已开始下令对出口土货征收 2.5% 的附加税,对复出口土货征收 1.25% 的附加税。鉴于海关监督尚未收到土货附加税相关指示,本人已正式向其致函说明已采取之措施,对此他并无意见,只是于见面会谈时建议发布联合公告。

为海关将接管各地税捐局及煤油特税局事：

本人于 2 月 1 日与海关监督会面时,他出示了一份宋子文发来的电报,内称将由海关接管各地税捐局及煤油特税局。海关监督表示他已将此事汇报给奉天方面。本人猜测宋先生并不指望满洲官员立即注意到其发出的指令。

为皮货征税办法事：

按照本口惯例,除猫皮狗皮,所有皮货均假定自黑龙江俄岸走私而来,未曾完税,因此均归为进口洋货一类。本人曾于 1928 年 3 月 10 日第 88 号半官函税收一项中提出可否将皮货归为土货一类,因为目前将所有皮货均视为走私而来之办法并无强力证据,倘遇外国皮货出口公司提出质疑并向该国领事申诉,海关恐怕难以力证此惯例之合理性。

实行新税则后,皮货进口税率已增长至22.5%,当地皮货经销商均已准备歇业关张,并称海关提高进口税率,海关监督征收附加税,地方税捐局又征收25%的税费,皮货生意根本无法继续经营。关于此事,本人已与海关监督进行多次交流,他表示将于近期正式向本人致函要求将皮货归为土货一类,并按照出口税则缴纳税款。

据悉,本地区所交易的皮货中仅有极小一部分是自俄岸走私而来。其中诸如紫貂皮和白狐皮之类的皮货自然可以确定是走私而来,但此类皮货极为稀少。基于上述种种,鉴于新税则可能会将本地区唯一兴盛之贸易扼杀,特此提议,更改瑷珲关现行惯例,将皮货归为出口土货一类,但紫貂皮、白狐皮等明显为俄岸所有之皮货的征税办法不变。事实上,海关监督亦表示愿意为此放弃征收其唯一税收来源的附加税,由此可见,本关更改惯例亦属公平之举。

待收到海关监督相关函文后,本人将正式呈报此事,但鉴于当地经销商当前处境艰难,甚至有关门停业之打算,故此请阁下于本人汇报海关监督来函示意之事后,以半官函之形式下达更改惯例之指示。此外,按照现行出口税则,大部分出口皮货仍需支付5%的税费,与此前旧进口税则规定之税率相同,因此,此类皮货的税收将与此前相差无几。

对于未至瑷珲关报关经陆路私运至哈尔滨的皮货,若通过邮政包裹自哈尔滨关出口,哈尔滨关则将之归为土货一类。若阁下批准瑷珲关将皮货归为出口土货一类,本人将向海关监督指出,地方税捐局亦应出台更为有利的征税办法。

为东三省财务稽核处与海关事:

本人已自海关监督处收悉奉天保安总司令部下发的三份公文指令,内容如下:

（1）通知：东三省财务稽核处已于奉天成立,将负责对海关、电报局、邮政局等不在东三省任一省级官员统辖范围内的收税部门的账簿进行审查。各相关收税部门日后须定期呈交账簿及所收税款。

（2）各相关收税部门须于十日内将收支预算报表、税则、条例规章等呈交至东三省财务稽核处。

（3）各相关收税部门须于十日内将职员清册,附注生日、出身等信息,呈交至东三省财务稽核处。

第一份公文的下发日期为1929年1月26日,后两份的下发日期为1929年1月28日。收悉三份公文后,本人立即与道尹兼海关监督会面,以期了解更多详情,同时询问其作为海关监督所收到的税收及汇款信息是否足够呈报,并表示对于东三省财务稽核处所要求之信息,若无总税务司批准,本人无权提供,而且在此事上,瑷珲关须与满洲其他海关统一行事。海关监督认为海关无须立即对东三省财务稽核处之指示做出回应。本人随即说明会将此事呈报总税务司。相信满洲其他各口应已呈报此事,烦请告知应如何回应。若阁下认为本人需及时做出回复,还请以电报下达指示。

此函抄件亦发送给哈尔滨关税务司,以征询意见。

您真挚的

铎博赉

2. 铎博赉致梅乐和函

（第 103 号半官函）

S/O No.103.

CUSTOM HOUSE.

INSPECTED

Aigun 18th March, 1929.

Dear Mr. Maze.

 I. "WASHINGTON SURTAXES": though the
Superintendent was without instructions until the 9th
March as to whether he should cease the collection of the
2½% Surtax he wrote me on that date that the collection
ceased as from the 1st February. There were no dutiable
imports during February.

 II. CONTINUED COLLECTION OF RIVER DUES ON OLD
BASIS: your Circular No.3867 transmits the instructions
of the Kuan-wu Shu that such Wharfage Dues, Conservancy
Dues, etc., as have previously been authorized by the
Central Government are to continue to be collected at the
rate previously sanctioned and that a joint notification
was to be issued to that effect in consultation with the
Superintendent. I have proposed to the latter that such
a notification be issued but he is of the opinion that

aa

P. W. Maze, Esquire,
 SHANGHAI.

as the local River Dues Tariff is not based on the old
Tariff such a notification is not necessary at Aigun.
In-as-much as the Amur Aids Commission proposes to raise
the River Dues Tariff on some items shortly, on instructions
from the Higher Authorities, it would seem best to defer
to the Superintendent's opinion and not press for the
issuance of the joint notification in question.

 III. REMITTANCE TO MOUKDEN OF PORTION OF REVENUE
COLLECTED UNDER NEW IMPORT TARIFF: early in the week I
had an interview with the Superintendent during which he
said that he had received a sharp telegram from the
Tao An Tsung Sau Ling Pu, Moukden (奉天保安總司令部),
inquiring why no response had been received to the
instructions of that Bureau regarding the remittance to
Moukden of that part of the revenue desired as collected
under the new Import Tariff. I explained that in the
first place there had been no collection under the new
Tariff and that, moreover, I was just in receipt of
instructions from yourself (copy of I.G. despatch No.
2718/119,931 to Antung) to the effect that the Kuan-wu
Shu had ruled that no funds were to be appropriated by
Commissioners without authority. The Superintendent

complained

complained of the unreasonable attitude of Moukden but
wished for a reply to his original despatch to the effect
that I could remit no funds to Moukden on my own authority.
A day or two later, however, he sent word that he had
received instructions to drop the question and that no
reply was required from me.   I take it that some
compromise has been arrived at between Moukden and Nanking.

AUDIT BUREAU OF THREE EASTERN PROVINCES AND
CUSTOMS: I have received your telegram of the 4th March
in response to the request in my S/O No.102 that I be
informed as to whether certain information as to
collection and accounts figures should be supplied to the
above Bureau, as directed, through the Superintendent.
In accordance with the spirit of your instructions I have
agreed to supply the latter, unofficially, with extra
copies of the Chinese versions of B-6 and B-6ᵃ.   He
states that the other information required, i.e., Service
records of employees, statements of accounts and office
expenditure, etc., need not be supplied for the present.

ACTING TIDESURVEYOR POSTPONES APPLYING FOR
LONG LEAVE: Aigun despatch No.411 forwards a statement
from Mr. H. W. Snow, Acting Tidesurveyor (Assistant
Examiner B) stating that he is compelled to postpone his
application

application for long leave owing to financial reasons.
In his statement he requests information as to whether
the passage of his wife and child can be paid to Shanghai
if they precede him to that port this autumn in
anticipation of his going on long leave later.   She has
found the past winter very trying on her health and feels
that it would be unwise to try and spend another here.
At the time he was appointed to Aigun she was not well
enough to accompany him but came up here later when her
travelling expenses were paid separately (Aigun despatch
No.391 to I.G. and I.G. despatch No.430/118,507 in reply
sanctioning the claim).   In the present instance I
would recommend the payment of her passage back to
Shanghai subject to readjustment if he is transferred
before his leave is granted.

ACTING COMMISSIONER APPLIES FOR LONG LEAVE:
in my despatch No.410 I apply for one year's long leave
to date from the 16th October of this year. By that time
I will have spent three years in this port. My application
states that I should like to be relieved from duty on
or before the 1st October on the presumption that the
Staff

Staff at Aigun should have the privileges of that of a
distant port.   The journey to Shanghai, my port of
embarkation, would require a minimum of three weeks and
I should like to book from there on the first steamer
sailing after the 16th October if my leave is granted.

Yours truly,

第 103 号半官函　　　　　　　　　　　　　　**1929 年 3 月 18 日于瑷珲关**

尊敬的梅乐和先生：

为"华盛顿附加税"事：

截至 3 月 9 日，海关监督依然未收到是否应停止征收 2.5% 附加税之指令，但其已于当日来函告知自 2 月 1 日起停止征收附加税。此外，瑷珲关 2 月间并无进口税可征。

为继续按照此前税率征收江捐事：

根据海关总税务司公署第 3867 号通令，内称关务署指令此前由中央政府批准征收的码头捐、滩捐等税项继续按照此前批准之税率征收，各关税务司须与海关监督协商后发布联合公告，本人已向瑷珲关海关监督提及此事，但他认为大黑河地区并未按照此前税率征收江捐，因此无须发布此联合公告。鉴于黑龙江水道委员会不日将奉上级政府之命提议增加部分货物的江捐税率，因此还是遵从海关监督的意见为宜，暂缓发布联合公告之事。

为将按照新税则多征收之税款汇至奉天事：

本周初与海关监督会面时，其称奉天保安总司令部发来电报质问为何未对按照新进口税则多征收之税款汇至奉天之指示做出回复。本人解释称，自实行新税则以来，瑷珲关并未征收到任何税款，而且总税务司已下令（海关总税务司公署致安东关第 2718/119931 号令抄件）告知，关务署规定海关税务司未经批准不得擅自动用税款经费。海关监督对奉天方面来电的无理态度也颇有微词，但还是希望本人可向其回函说明税务司无权自行汇寄税款。然时隔一两日后，海关监督又发来消息称已接到指示此事不必再议，亦不需要本人回函说明。本人猜想奉天当局和南京当局应已达成某种妥协。

为东三省财务稽核处与海关事：

3 月 4 日电报收悉，内开对本人第 102 号半官函所提是否可以按照指示通过海关监督向东三省财务稽核处呈交税收账簿等数据一事之回复，特此说明，本人已遵照电令指示精神，同意以非官方形式为海关监督提供（B.–6）和（B.–6a）汉文版抄件。海关监督表示，财务稽核处要求的职员清册、收支报表等信息暂且不必提交。

为瑷珲关署监察长推迟申请休长假事：

本人已于瑷珲关第 411 号呈中汇报署监察长思诺（H. W. Snow）先生（二等副验货员）由于经济原因推迟申请休长假一事。思诺先生于附录报告中提出，其妻儿如果先于他在今年秋季前往江海关，不知至上海的旅费是否可以在他之后休假时予以报销。其妻子称去年冬季自己的身体状况已受到严重影响，不宜于此再停留一个冬季。思诺先生最初调任瑷珲关时，其妻子便因身体问题未能一同前来，之后独自前来的旅费已由海关单独报销（参阅瑷珲关致海关总税务司公署第 391 号呈及海关总税务司公署致瑷珲关第 430/118507 号令）。有鉴于此，兹建议，其妻子返回上海的旅费的报销办法视思诺先生是否会于休假获准前被调离而定。

为瑷珲关署理税务司申请休长假事：

本人已于瑷珲关第 410 号呈中申请自 1929 年 10 月 16 日起休假一年，届时本人将于本口岸任满三年。本人在休假申请中提出，考虑瑷珲关为偏远口岸，职员应享有特殊待遇，希望可于 10 月 1 日或之前解除职务，因自大黑河至上海至少需要三周时间，故计划待休假申请获准后，预订 10 月 16 日后自上海出发的最早一班轮船。

您真挚的

铎博赉

3. 铎博赉致梅乐和函

（第 105 号半官函）

S/O No.105.　　　　　CUSTOM HOUSE,

　　　　　Aigun　　15th April, 19 29.

Dear Mr. Maze,

TUNGPEI NAVIGATION BUREAU IMPROVES LOCAL GODOWN FACILITIES: after my arrival in Taheiho I had requests from the Tungpei Navigation Bureau (东北航务局) to allow steamers arriving out of Office hours to discharge cargo on the bund pending examination and release. I refused to allow this but said that if it was discharged into a godown controlled by the Customs the matter would be considered. At the same time I suggested to the Bureau that it enclose a part of its wharf which could be used conveniently for the purpose. The local Manager applied for an appropriation to carry out my suggestion but it was refused despite the fact that the profits of the Bureau for that year (1927) were some $4,000,000. This year funds have been secured and a godown will be built which will function under Customs regulations

F. W. Maze, Esquire,
SHANGHAI.

regulations as to control. It will greatly facilitate the quick return of steamers from this port to Harbin, and remove the cause of a certain amount of friction that has existed between the Customs and this semi-official concern.

WRECK OF THE "HUNGTAI" AND SOVIET INTERFERENCE: last September a Chinese steamer, the "Hungtai", went aground some 100 miles below Taheiho on the Konstantinovska Shallows. She was on the Russian side of the channel and the owner was not permitted to employ Chinese workmen to move her to the channel but was compelled to employ Russian labour by the Soviet Unions of the place. They failed to float her. This spring, when the question came up again, neither the owner nor other Chinese were allowed to go near the wreck without passports and until they had again agreed to employ members of the Soviet unions to continue the work of salvage. I sent the Technical Adviser to the Taoyin to suggest that a strong protest be lodged with the local Russian Consul against this assumption of authority over the Amur by Soviet labour unions. I asked Mr. Ignatieff to point out that if a precedent of this sort were established we would have infinite trouble in the future (possibly involving boundary questions)

questions) whenever a Chinese steamer went aground, and to
remind the Taoyin that according to the Joint Rules of
Navigation the owners of a wrecked vessel and the River
Authorities of the nationality of the steamer concerned
were responsible for its removal.   The Russian Consul and
the Blagovestchensk river authorities admitted the injustice
of the unions' position but it was only after constant
pressure for several days, when every day was valuable if
salvage operations were to be completed before the ice-
drift set in, that the unions agreed to give the Chinese
owner a free hand.   They seem to lack the rudimentary
knowledge of the courtesy that should be shown a vessel
of a friendly nation in need of help.

AN AGREEMENT IS PROPOSED REGARDING THE
ASSISTANCE THAT IS TO BE RENDERED TO STEAMERS IN DISTRESS
ON SINO-SOVIET FRONTIER RIVERS: the incident in connection
with the salvaging of the S/S "Hungtai" just referred to
showed the necessity of supplementing the Joint Rules of
Navigation by a more complete understanding as to the
assistance to be rendered vessels in distress on the Amur,
Argun and Ussuri rivers by passing steamers, and by the
local authorities under whose jurisdiction the wreck lies.
                                                        The

The Tungpei Navigation Bureau has submitted a memorandum
regarding the matter and a suggested scale of fixed charges
to be paid per hour to Chinese and Soviet steamers standing
by to give assistance when requested to do so.   The Taoyin
tells me that he intends to reconvene the Commission that
drew up the Rules of Navigation and request it to draft a
suitable Agreement regarding the matter.   I would propose
for your approval that Mr. Ignatieff and myself be allowed
to sign such an Agreement as members of the Aids Commission
only, and not as representatives of the Customs, as was
done in the case of the adoption of the Joint Rules of
Navigation (vide S/O of 22nd January, 1927, from O. I. G.).

EXAMINATION FOR CUSTOMS TRAVELLING SCHOLARSHIPS:
in accordance with the instructions of your Circular No.
3,857 the examination of candidates for a Customs Travelling
Scholarship was duly held on the last two Sundays of March
and the results have been forwarded to the President of the
Customs College.   Only one applicant, Mr. Lee Peng Sheo,
4th (Chinese) Assistant B, presented himself in this port.

ACTING COMMISSIONER APPLIES FOR LONG LEAVE: in
my last S/O I mentioned that I had applied for long leave
and requested that I be relieved from duty if possible in
time to catch a steamer in Shanghai soon after the 15th
                                                    October.

October. Since then I have ascertained that, if my Leave
is granted, a steamer can be had from Dairen about the 3rd
November (Shanghai the 12th November) so that I need not
leave Taheiho before early in October.

ACTING COMMISSIONER'S ALLOWANCE: I was
pleased to receive a despatch today granting me Hk.Tls.50
as Special Allowance in addition to the Hk.Tls.100 I
receive as Acting Allowance under the instructions of your
Circular No.3,880. I find Aigun to be the most expensive
port of my experience. The intimate relations the
Commissioner has with all the officials in this small
place means a heavy drain on his resources for official
banquets, wedding and birthday presents, etc., etc. Added
to this is the necessity of entertaining Soviet officials,
in connection with the position of Vice President of the
Amur Aids Commission.

CONDITIONS IN NEIGHBOURING SIBERIAN DISTRICTS:
I recently had occasion to visit Blagovestchensk and find
that living conditions there are daily becoming more acute.
Long disorderly bread lines now form in front of the
bakeries every day and small amounts of bread are doled out
to those holding cards. These cards are only issued to
members of unions, who constitute one fifth of the
population.

population. The rest have been able to carry on so far
by the purchase of bread at higher prices without cards
and by buying flour from farmers at high rates at the
bazar. Meat is daily becoming more dear and more difficult
to obtain. It can be said without exaggeration that the
gaunt spectre of hunger will make its appearance shortly
in what was one of the richest agriculture centres in
Siberia! In other parts of Siberia and Russia conditions
are said to be much worse. For example, in the large city
of Irkutsk there is a scarcity of fuel so that electric
lights are not turned on until 10p.m. A Soviet Commissar
recently crossed the Amur to a small Chinese village and
when questioned admitted that the grain situation was
serious. "But what will you do next year"? "Farmers
who grow a surplus over their own needs will have the
surplus taken over; those who do not grow more than they need
will have all they grow taken from them", was the answer.
"But that will mean starvation for most of the farmers for
they will have no surplus wheat for planting", said the
Chinese. "All the better", replied the Commissar, "there
will be so many less mouths to feed". Illogical and
heartless reasoning but typical of the Communists in control.
Still there is no indication of any counter-revolution.

Yours truly,

第 105 号半官函　　　　　　　　　　　**1929 年 4 月 15 日于瑷珲关**

尊敬的梅乐和先生：

为东北航务局于大黑河修建货栈事：

自本人至大黑河任职以来，东北航务局已多次提出希望可允许在非海关办公时间抵港的轮船暂将货物卸在堤岸上以待查验放行。对此，本人已回绝，但表示如果货物可暂存于由海关监管的货栈中，此事可重新考虑，同时建议其可在东北航务局码头围建一处货栈，以便卸货查验等。东北航务局大黑河经理遂据此申请拨款，但未获批准，尽管当年（1927 年）东北航务局的利润高达约 4000000 银圆。今年所需资金已经到位，东北航务局将于此修建货栈，并依照海关章程管理运作。建成后，轮船可在更短的时间内自本口岸返回哈尔滨，海关与东北航务局这一半官方机构之间的摩擦亦可逐渐消除。

为"鸿泰（Hungtai）"号轮船搁浅苏联当局干预事：

去年九月，中国"鸿泰"号轮船在大黑河下游约 100 英里处的康斯坦丁诺夫斯基（Konstantinovska）浅滩搁浅。由于轮船搁浅地点位于苏方一侧航道，苏联工会不允许船主雇用华籍工人将其拖回，强迫其于当地雇用俄籍劳工，但最终并未能让轮船重新漂浮起来。今年春季，再次提及此事时，苏联工会却提出，无论是船主或是其他华人，只要未持有护照，均不得接近搁浅轮船，而且只能雇用工会的俄籍劳工救援轮船。

本人随即派遣黑龙江航务专门顾问易保罗（P. I. Ignatieff）先生前去面见道尹，一来建议道尹向驻大黑河苏联领事强烈抗议苏联工会于黑龙江上的越举行为，二来向道尹指出若开此先例，日后再有中国船只在黑龙江上搁浅，麻烦恐会无休无止（甚至可能涉及中苏边境问题），而且根据联合航行章程，轮船于边界河道失事后，应由船主和船只所属国家的航路厅负责转移工作。随后，苏联领事和布拉戈维申斯克（Blagovestchensk）航路厅亦承认苏联工会此事处理不当。此次救援工作若欲于浮冰出现之前完成，则必须尽快开始，中方据此不断向苏联方面施压，数日后，苏联工会终于同意让中国船主自行处理此事。苏联方面似乎连应对友好邻国失事船只施以援手此等最基本的礼仪都不甚知晓。

为拟订中苏边界河道轮船遇险救援协议事：

通过上述"鸿泰"号轮船救援事件可以看出，中苏双方有必要对联合航行章程增加补充条款，拟订黑龙江、额尔古纳河及乌苏里江上有轮船遇险时，往来轮船及遇险地点所在辖区的政府机构应提供的救援办法。东北航务局已就此事递交了一份报告，建议对按照要求提供救援的中苏两国轮船按小时支付一定费用。道尹告知，其计划重新召集拟订航行章程的中苏联合委员会,就救援之事拟订协议。特此申请批准易保罗先生和本人以黑龙江水道委员会委员之身份,并不代表海关,签署此协议,与此前签订实施联合航行章程相关协议时所采取之办法相同(参阅代理总税务司 1927 年 1 月 22 日半官函)。

为海关行政考察员考试事:

根据海关总税务司公署第 3857 号通令指示,海关行政考察员考试已于 3 月的最后两个星期日举行,考试结果业已发送给税务专门学校校长。本口岸仅有一名关员参加考试,即华籍四等二级帮办黎彭寿先生。

为瑷珲关署理税务司申请休长假事:

本人曾于上一封半官函中提及申请休长假一事,并说明希望可尽快解除职务,以便及时抵达上海搭乘 10 月 15 日后最早一班轮船离开,但随后获悉,若休假申请得以批准,本人亦可搭乘大连 11 月 3 日左右出发的轮船(上海发船时间为 11 月 12 日),因此无须在 10 月初之前离开大黑河。

为瑷珲关署理税务司津贴事:

今日收悉令文批准本人除可按照海关总税务司公署第 3880 号通令指示得享代理津贴 100 海关两外,还可得享特殊津贴 50 海关两,得此消息,甚为欢喜。不得不说,瑷珲关是本人任职口岸中开支最大的一处。大黑河地方虽小,但作为税务司,为了与所有地方官员维系关系,不得不在官方宴会、婚礼、生日礼物等方面投入大量金钱,同时作为黑龙江水道委员会副委员长,又要不时宴请苏联官员,如此这般,开支着实不小。

为西伯利亚地区局势事:

本人近日到访布拉戈维申斯克时发现,当地生活条件每况愈下。面包房门前日日排满毫无秩序的长队,但面包数量有限,只有手持面包票的人可以领到。这些面包票只发放给各工会成员,而这些人只占当地总人口的五分之一。没有面包票的人只能以高价购买面包,或是在街市上从农民手中购买面粉,但价钱依然十分高昂。肉类的价格日趋上涨,亦更加难以购买。毫不夸张地说,昔日西伯利亚地区最富庶的农业中心不日即将迎来大饥荒!据悉,西伯利亚其他各地的情形更为糟糕。例如,大城市伊尔库茨克(Irkutsk)因燃料匮乏,已下令晚上 10 点之前不得使用电灯。

一名苏联政治委员近日到访黑龙江华岸的一个村庄时,坦言粮食问题已十分严重。当地中国居民问道:"明年有什么计划?"政委回答:"凡农民所收粮食扣除己需仍有剩余者,均须将剩余粮食上交,如果没有余粮,则须将所有粮食上交。"中国居民又问:"农民没有余粮,明年就没法播种,大多数人就会面临饥饿,到时候怎么办?"政委答道:"全都饿死才好，这样就不会有那么多人抢粮食了。"该名政委的话不合逻辑且毫无人性，但这恰恰是掌权的共产主义者的典型风格。此外，西伯利亚地区暂未出现反革命活动的迹象。

您真挚的

铎博赉

4. 铎博赉致梅乐和函

（第106号半官函）

S/O No.106.

CUSTOM HOUSE,

Aigun   20th April, 1929.

Dear Mr. Maze,

NEW HARBIN CONSERVANCY BUREAU AND AMUR AIDS COMMISSION: at the time of the formation of the new Harbin Conservancy Bureau, in the spring of 1928, the Amur Aids Commission was concerned lest the former's control be extended to frontier rivers.   The Taoyin proceeded to Moukden at the time (my S/O No.88) to forestall any such move and succeeded in postponing action for the time being detrimental to our interests. This spring he was in Moukden again when, he informs me, he had a long talk with Admiral Sheng.   It appears that during the past year the Harbin Conservancy Bureau carried out very little of its ambitious programme and he took the occasion to contrast its inactivity with what the Amur Aids Commission was accomplishing with very little show.   Admiral Sheng acknowledged the good work we had done and complimented the Taoyin on the

manner

F. W. Maze, Esquire,
    Shanghai.

manner in which the Commission had carried on its relations with the Soviet Authorities.   On the Taoyin's return from this Moukden visit he addressed Admiral Sheng officially inquiring whether action was contemplated in the way of curtailing the activities and authority of the Aids Commission.   He now informs me that he is in receipt of a despatch from Moukden that aids and conservancy work on frontier rivers must continue to be controlled from Taheiho and that there was no intention of amalgamating the Aids Commission and the Harbin Conservancy Bureau.

NEW PROVISIONAL REGULATIONS TO GOVERN THE TREATMENT OF ARTICLES FOR MILITARY USE: in accordance with the instructions of your Circular No.3861 I consulted with the Superintendent regarding the putting into force locally of the new Regulations governing the treatment of arms and munitions of war.   He declared himself ready to do what he could to enforce them but said that if the local military authorities chose to ignore them he could do nothing in the matter and that, moreover, he did not wish to put himself in a position whereby he might lose face in trying to impose regulations which might not be obeyed.   I believe that the position of the military in

this

this remote place is possibly more independent than
in most ports under the control of Moukden. As
instructed I shall carry on the old procedure if
objections are raised to the new by the military and
I am not backed up by the Superintendent but I should
like to inquire if I am to say definitely, now, by
despatch, whether the Superintendent is prepared to
put the new Regulations into force or whether I shall
await a test case.

DUTY TREATMENT OF FURS: I duly received
your telegraphic instructions, in answer to the
representations made in my S/O No.102, to the effect
that certain furs might be treated as exports instead
of imports on receipt of a letter from the Taoyin that
local procedure be changed. I sent word to the Taoyin's
office of your instructions but was informed that the
matter had been referred to Tsitsihar and the Kuan-wu
Shu. It will probably be some time before replies are
received.

PROPOSED INCREASE IN RIVER DUES: on the
opening of navigation in May last year, River Dues were
considerably increased by the Amur Aids Commission on
instructions of the Provincial Authorities. The increase
was

was put into effect without first notifying the Inspector
General. He was first informed of the intention to
increase the River Dues Tariff in Aigun despatch No.311.
In his despatch No.350/112,642 in reply he instructed
that the collection of the increased River Dues by the
Customs should not begin until the Ch'u's authority had
been obtained. In my S/O No.76 I explained that the
increase had already been put into effect on the
instructions of the Heilungchiang Authorities, acting
on a former precedent when the original River Dues Tariff
was doubled without previous reference to the Ch'u, and
that the Taoyin was now moving the Authorities to report
the increase. I.G. S/O of 6th July, 1927, in reply states
that I elucidate some points on which the records were
not clear but that the Territorial Authorities should
accept the responsibility for action taken on their
behalf by the Customs and that the Ch'u should be notified
to that effect. The above is introductory to my informing
you that I have received veral instructions from the
Taoyin to go into the question of increasing the Tariff
on timber and firewood to begin with the opening of
navigation. It has been found that the increase on
these two articles introduced last year, was not enough
and

and not proportionate to the value of the cargo concerned
(the increase will not amount to more than some $2,500 per
year, based on last years figures, and will be largely
borne by the Tungpei Navigation Bureau). When the new
rates have been decided on the Taoyin, as President of the
Commission, will presumably instruct me to put them into
effect on the order of the Provincial Authorities. I
should be glad if you would instruct me as to whether I
may follow the precedents established in August, 1925.
(Aigun despatch to I.G. No.230, §6) and last year, of
again increasing the tariff (on timber and firewood) on
the instructions of the Heilungchiang Government the
Kuan-wu Shu to be notified by the latter of the action
taken on its behalf by the Aigun Customs. As navigation
will open the first week in May, when the increase would
be put into effect, I beg to solicit your instructions by
wire. I shall report the matter officially when I get
the Taoyin's official instructions.

BUNDING THE FORESHORE: I am in receipt of a
despatch from the Taoyin/Superintendent, as President of
the Amur Aids Commission, instructing me that $5,000 is
to be appropriated from Aids funds for the bunding of the
local foreshore. This question was first taken up by

myself

myself in 1921, when the need was apparent and when, by
a coincidence, the present Taoyin was acting in the same
capacity as now. At that time I drew up a complete
scheme for conserving the entire foreshore to be paid for
by a wharfage dues system adapted after that of Wuhu.
This project was submitted to the Taoyin and to the Harbin
Commissioner (Aigun was then a sub-office) but I was
shortly afterwards transferred and nothing further was
done then or after about a scheme of wharfage dues for
local conservancy work. In 1923 permission was requested
in Aigun despatch No.121 to bund the foreshore in front
of the Custom House at Customs expense, at a cost of $250,
as the erosion to the bund was such that the foundations
of that building would eventually be weakened. The
expenditure was authorized in I.G. despatch No.133/ 94,724.
At the same time $500 was spent from Aids funds, on the
Taoyin's authority, only, it would appear, for bunding a
short stretch of adjacent foreshore. The work was carried
out under the supervision of the Technical Adviser. The
material used in both jobs was first a layer of coarse
gravel and then one of broken stone kept in place by
parallel rows of stakes driven into the face of the incline
and joined together by weaving long willows between them.

willows

Willows were subsequently planted over the surface of the bunding. These have flourished and the whole structure is now bound together by a mass of roots. This form of bunding has stood the test of time admirably and the width and condition of the Customs bund is now in marked contrast with the rest of the foreshore. The great flood of last year, which rose to the top of the bund, did not effect our stretch but made great inroads on what is left of the bund in other places and another such rise will erode it back to the building line at certain points, destroying its continuity and usefulness and endangering the structures along it.

With the subsidence of the flood of last autumn it could be seen how critical the condition of the bund had become; had a strong north wind set in when the waters were at their highest practically the whole bund would have disappeared under the action of the waves. The Taoyin consulted with myself and the Technical Adviser as to what should be done at the same time instructing that a short stretch of foreshore should be taken in hand at once. This work included the bunding of the foreshore just below the Custom House, part of the frontage concerned being our property - the Tidesurveyor's residence. The

cost

cost was $406 and was advanced from Aids funds. I proposed at the same time, as I did in 1921, that a system of wharfage dues be introduced to pay for any further bunding but the Taoyin would not agree to my proposal pointing out the local merchants already paid River Dues and the trade of the port is at such a low ebb that it will not stand any other form of taxation. He maintained that the expenditure should and could come from River Dues and instructed the Technical Adviser to go into the matter and report. This the latter did emphasizing in his recommendations the necessity of putting the work in hand as early as possible this spring. The Taoyin thereupon instructed me as reported above. It would appear, however, that he has the idea that $5,000 (which at the collection rate of the day would equal some Hk.Tls.2,300) will be enough to complete the entire bund from the Custom House to the Tungpei Navigation Bureau but the Technical Adviser says he has a wrong impression and that $2,000 or $3,000 additional would be required to extend the bunding so far. However the most urgent work could be completed this year for $5,000. The form of bunding would be the same as that described above.

In addressing me as he has done I take it

that

that the Taoyin recognizes that the conservancy of the
Harbour is a matter that concerns the Customs and not
the Aids Commission - a view he has expressed verbally.
The work could be carried out under the supervision of
the Harbourmaster with the assistance of the Technical
Adviser who has had much experience in such work.

There is a surplus in Aids funds this year
of some $8,000 so that $5,000 could be spared to meet the
demands of the situation. The question arises, however,
of whether a surplus in Aids funds should not be employed
toward repaying the money ($15,000) the Amur Aids
Commission has borrowed from Sungari Aids. I have taken
every opportunity of reminding the Taoyin of this (vide
I.G. despatch No.350/112,642 to Aigun in reply to my
despatch No.311) but I venture to propose that the question
of repayment be again postponed for another year in
consideration of the urgent nature of the work required,
of the fact that local trade cannot bear a special tax
for the project, and of the taking over of the Sungari
Aids River Dues Collection, and the trebling of the River
Dues Tariff of the Sungari, which would appear to make
the repayment of the money owed the Sungari Aids no longer
pressing. For the Customs to refuse consent for the

work

work to be done would create a difficult situation. The
question is being reported to you officially by despatch,
enclosing copies of the Taoyin's instructions; in the
meantime I should be glad of your telegraphic instructions
in this case also as the work should be put in hand
immediately with the opening of the river.

A copy of this S/O is being sent to the Harbin
Commissioner for his information and possible comment,
especially on the subject of the repayment of the money
due the Sungari Aids.

Yours truly,

第 106 号半官函   1929 年 4 月 20 日于瑷珲关

尊敬的梅乐和先生：

为新设哈尔滨管理局（Harbin Conservancy Bureau）与黑龙江水道委员会事：

1928 年春哈尔滨管理局设立之初，黑龙江水道委员会担忧该局对河流的管制会扩展至界河，为此道尹当时还曾前往奉天预先阻止，成功使得有损海关及黑龙江水道委员会利益的行动暂缓进行（参阅本人第 88 号半官函）。道尹告知，今春他再次前往奉天时与沈鸿烈上将进行了长谈。哈尔滨管理局初设时便制定了宏伟规划，但过去一年间似乎并未有何行动，道尹借机将该局的无所作为与黑龙江水道委员会的工作成果进行对比说明，而且并无半点夸张的成分。沈鸿烈上将对黑龙江航路标志委员会的工作表示认可，称赞道尹在航路标志委员会与苏联当局的关系维系问题上处理得当。道尹自奉天返回后立即向沈鸿烈上将致函询问当局是否计划限制黑龙江水道委员会的行动及权利。如今其告知已收到奉天方面的回函，内称边界河道的航路标志及管理工作仍继续由大黑河方面负责，而且并无将黑龙江水道委员会与哈尔滨管理局合并之计划。

为实施新军用物资管理办法暂行章程事：

根据海关总税务司公署第 3861 号通令指示，本人已与海关监督商议于大黑河实施新战备物资管理办法暂行章程事。海关监督表示，其愿意一试，但如果地方军队不予遵守，其亦无可奈何，更不希望因强制实施军方可能不会遵从的章程而有损颜面，陷入窘境。兹认为，大黑河地理位置偏远，此地的军队与奉天辖区内其他大多口岸的军队相比可能更加独立。按照指示，如果新章程招致军方反对，海关监督又不予支持，本人将继续按照旧章程办理。特此询问，本人现下是否可以正式呈文说明海关监督已准备实施新章程，抑或说明需要先试行新章程。

为皮货物征税办法事：

根据阁下为回复本人第 102 号半官函所发出的电令指示，即如果海关监督正式致函要求将部分皮货视为出口土货征税，则可遵照办理，特此汇报，本人已将该指示传达至道尹公署，但收到回复称，此事已呈报齐齐哈尔当局及关务署。因此可能还要过些时日，方能收到答复。

为拟将提高江捐税率事：

去年 5 月航运开通之初，黑龙江水道委员会便奉省政府指示大幅提高江捐税率，但总税务司并未提前收到通知。总税务司通过瑷珲关第 311 号呈中首次知悉江捐税率或将提高一事，之后于海关总税务司公署第 350/112642 号令中回复称，在收到税务处批准之前，海关不得按照新税率征收江捐。嗣后本人于第76号半官函中解释称,因1925年曾有未提请税务处批准便增加江捐税率之先例,故此次已奉黑龙江省政府之指示实行新税率,而且道尹已请省政府向税务处说明此事。总税务司于1927年7月6日半官函中回复称,虽然有些记录不明之处现已解释清楚,但省政府应为海关代其按照新税率征收江捐之行为承担责任,亦应将此事告知税务处。

根据以上内容,特此告知,道尹已下达口头指示,要求开始研究航运开通后提高木料和木样税率一事。虽然该两项货物的税率已于去年有所增加,但在实际过程中发现增幅不够,而且与货价不成比例(以去年所征税收之数计算,嗣后每年增加的税收金额将不超过2500银圆,且主要由东北航务局承担)。新税率一经裁定,道尹兼黑龙江航路标志委员会委员长很有可能会指令本人按照黑龙江省政府指示予以实施。

届时本人是否应遵从1925年8月(参阅瑷珲关致海关总税务司公署第230号呈)及去年的先例,再次奉黑龙江省政府之指令提高木材及木样的税率,之后再由省政府向关务署说明,还请予以指示。鉴于5月第一周航运开通后,新税率便将开始实行,特请阁下通过电报发送指令。待收到道尹官方指令后,本人将正式呈报此事。

为修筑前滩堤岸事:

日前,道尹兼海关监督以黑龙江水道委员会委员长的名义来函指令本人从航路标志经费中拨款5000银圆用于修筑大黑河前滩堤岸。

1921年,本人曾因大黑河堤岸亟待修缮,首次提出修筑之事,并草拟了一份完整的筑堤方案,计划效仿芜湖关的做法,使用码头捐支付修筑整个前滩堤岸的费用。本人当时已将此方案呈交道尹(恰巧亦为现任道尹)和哈尔滨关税务司(瑷珲关当时为哈尔滨关分关),但不久之后便被调离此地,使用码头捐支付地方保护管理工作费用一事亦就此搁置。

1923年,瑷珲关第121号呈汇报称,整个大黑河堤岸均存在被水流侵蚀之危险,新海关办公楼的地基亦会受此影响,申请批准由海关支出250银圆以修筑新海关办公楼前的堤岸。海关总税务司公署第133/94724号令批准了此项支出。与此同时,道尹批准自黑龙江航路标志经费中支出500银圆用于修筑相邻一段堤岸,只是距离较短。此次筑堤工程在航务专门顾问的监督下完成。两段工程使用的是同一种筑堤办法,即先于堤岸斜面铺设一层粗砂砾,再铺设一层碎石,同时成排插入木桩固定位置,使用柳条编制成网将木桩连接起来,最后再种上柳树。如今,柳树生长茂密,地下的树根相互盘缠,已将整个堤面牢牢固定在一起。以此法筑堤经得起时间的考验,现在海关办公楼前的堤岸无论是整体状况还是宽度均与其他前滩堤岸形成鲜明对比。

去年大黑河地区爆发大洪水，水位一度涨至堤岸顶面，海关办公楼前方堤岸未受影响，但其他河段堤岸却受到严重侵蚀。如此大洪水若再次来袭，有些堤岸必会受损，甚至退至建筑红线，无法继续使用，同时也会殃及沿线建筑。去年秋季洪水退去后，大黑河堤岸的情况已十分严重。而且如果洪水达到顶峰时，再遇上强劲的北风，这些堤岸可能早已被海浪冲毁。

道尹随后邀本人和航务专门顾问共同商议解决办法，同时下令立即着手修筑一小段前滩堤岸，海关办公楼下游监察长住所前面的堤岸亦在此次修筑之列。此次费用为406银圆，由航路标志资金支付。同时本人提议可使用码头捐支付筑堤费用（如1921年所提建议），但道尹表示反对，并指出当地商人已缴纳了江捐，大黑河地区的贸易又处在低潮期，恐怕无法再负担其他税捐。道尹坚持认为应使用江捐支付，并命航务专门顾问研究此事呈交报告。航务专门顾问强烈建议应尽早于今年春季动工。道尹随后便向本人下达了上述指示。

道尹似乎认为5000银圆（按照当日税收汇率相当于2300海关两）应足以完成自海关办公楼至东北航务局整个前滩的筑堤工程，但航务专门顾问指出，若要完成整个筑堤工程，额外还需2000或3000银圆。不过该5000银圆足够完成今年最为紧急的工程，而且还将采用上述筑堤办法。

从道尹来函中可以看出，他似乎认为保护港口乃为海关之职责，与黑龙江水道委员会无关，他此前亦曾口头表达过此观点。因此此项工程可由港务长负责监督，由经验丰富的航务专门顾问从旁协助。

今年航路标志经费尚有余额约8000银圆，完全可以支出5000银圆应对当前所需，但现在的问题是，此余额是否应用于归还此前黑龙江水道委员会从松花江航路标志账户借用的款项（15000银圆）。一直以来，本人一有机会便会提醒道尹归还借款一事（参阅海关总税务司公署回复瑷珲关第311号呈的第350/112642号令），但鉴于今年大黑河筑堤工程亟待开展，当地贸易又过于萧条难以承担额外税款，而且松花江江捐税率提高了两倍，税收增多后，还款之事应不会特别紧迫，再加上松花江江捐税收已被接管，因此建议还款一事暂缓一年。此外，瑷珲关若不同意此次筑堤计划，恐将陷入尴尬境地。本人已正式呈文汇报此事，并附道尹令文抄件。鉴于筑堤工程将于黑龙江开江后立即开展，特请阁下通过电报发送指令。

此函抄件已发送至哈尔滨关税务司，以供其参考并给出意见，尤其是关于归还松花江航路标志账户欠款一事。

您真挚的

铎博赉

5. 铎博赉致梅乐和函

（第 109 号半官函）

S/O No. 109.

CUSTOM HOUSE,

Aigun   19th June,   29.

Dear Mr. Maze,

PROVINCIAL AUTHORITIES REQUEST APPOINTMENT BY AIGUN CUSTOMS OF INSPECTOR TO ENFORCE JOINT NAVIGATION RULES: in my comments on Harbin despatch No.3,835 to I.G., wherein you are informed of the receipt by the Harbin Customs of the new Provisional Regulations governing the control of merchant shipping in the Three Eastern Provinces, I state that I have conferred with the Taoyin and at his request had written him inquiring whether these new Regulations would modify the instructions of the Kirin and Heilungchiang Provincial Authorities that the Customs appoint an inspector for frontier rivers. Since then I have heard nothing further from him about the matter.   In the Coast Inspector's comments on my despatch No.414, transmitting the instructions of the Provincial Authorities that the Customs appoint a frontier rivers inspector, the opinion is expressed that the

F. W. Maze, Esquire,
    Shanghai.

the enforcement of the Joint Rules of Navigation is a matter that should be left to the Central Authorities and that, further, one inspector could not exercise the necessary control and a large staff would be required. While I agree that the Rules could better be enforced by the Central Government its control in the two Provinces concerned is very limited and is perhaps best represented by the Customs.   If my suggestion is adopted of appointing Mr. Ignatieff as inspector, half his salary to be paid by the Customs and half by the Aids Commission, his authority would have the backing of the Kirin and Heilungchiang Governments through the Taoyin, as President of the Amur Aids Commission, and of the Customs, which would seem to be sufficient to enforce any disciplinary action deemed necessary.   It is also true that several inspectors would be preferable to one but this seems to be a case of "half a loaf being better than none".   During the navigation season the Technical Adviser is continually on tours of inspection of Aids on the frontier rivers.   At present he has no authority to criticise in any way the navigation of Chinese shipping though he is a member of the Commission that drew up the Joint Rules of Navigation, and of the Amur

Aids

Aids Commission. Had he the requisite authority the practical and moral effect would be great. Masters would know that their movements might be under supervision at any time and though the inspector could not be everywhere at the same time it would not be known at what place or at what time he might make an appearance. As the situation is now no attempt has been made to enforce the Regulations since their adoption which puts the Aids Commission and Chinese Authorities in a queer position vis-a-vis the Soviet Authorities who are carefully enforcing them. At the same time I quite realize that questions of policy, limitations of Staff, etc., etc., may compel you to decide that the Customs should not take on this added responsibility.

BUNDING THE FORESHORE: the bunding of the foreshore, your telegraphic approval of which was received on the 5th May, is practically completed. The work was carried out under the supervision of the Technical Adviser and was done thoroughly, expeditiously and cheaply. It will be reported on officially as soon as the accounts for the scheme are closed. It would now seem that the improvement was undertaken none too soon as the summer is starting in with rain every day as it

did

did last year when it culminated in the big flood.

INCREASE IN RIVER DUES TARIFF: with your telegraphic approval, received on the 5th May, the increase in the River Dues on timber and firewood was put into effect without protest. This increase will also be reported officially as a matter of record. A great deal of firewood is arriving this year and for the first time for many years it is cheaper than the year preceding - $8.10 per sajen as compared with $9.574.

SPECIAL MANCHURIAN ALLOWANCES: I. G. despatch No.456/181.166 was duly received granting members of the Staff a double Mileage Allowance for travel on the South Manchurian Railway, a Winter Outfit Allowance and gradually doing away with the Special Manchurian Allowance. While the Foreign and Native Outdoor Staff, who continue to draw all or half of their former Manchurian Allowance, are satisfied with the new arrangement, those members of the Chinese Indoor Staff, who were in the port at the beginning of the year, feel that they have been over-looked and they have approached me with the request that their situation be placed before you in the hopes that some relief can be had. They represent that, while it is true that their pay has been

increased.

increased, they have asked for no increase in rent
allowances which are already at a minimum, (vide Aigun
despatch No.424 to I.G.), their Special Manchurian
Allowances have been automatically cancelled and they
will draw no Outfit Allowance; and that their income
from the Service is, therefore, no greater than that
of the Chinese Indoor Staffs in the cheapest ports of
China whereas Aigun is one of the most expensive. They
further point out that, being on the frontier, most
of them have been compelled to leave their families in
China, at additional expense, for educational and climatic
reasons.   Their idea is that a temporary "Frontier
Allowance" might be issued to them to differentiate
their position from that of similar employees in other
ports in China where the cost of living may be said to
be normal.   If you approve of the idea in principle I
will submit proposals officially; at the same time I
have explained to them that in the introduction of new
allowances there were nearly always inequalities at the
beginning that were unavoidable.   The case of Mr. Lee
Peng Sheo would seem to be especially deserving.
Considering his responsibility as the only Assistant on
the Staff and the cost of living here, his income is

small

small, while he is called on to assume a prominent
position in Chinese Official circles entailing heavy
expenditures though they are kept at a minimum.   The
Harbin Commissioner in his despatch No.3,840 to I.G.
raises the question as to whether the issue of the
double Mileage Allowance is to apply to travel on the
South Manchurian Railway only.   I am awaiting your
ruling on the point before issuing the Allowance to
two recent appointees to the Staff - one from Chinwangtao
and one from Newchwang.

LOCAL: the Taoyin has been absent from the
port for a month on a trip to Harbin and Tsitsihar. His
return was undoubtedly hastened by the strained relations
between local and Blagovestchensk Chinese and Soviet
officials caused by the searching of the Soviet
Consulate in Harbin.   The local Consulate was not
searched but the Chinese Authorities threatened to close
it if an interpreter of the Taoyin's yamen, who had
gone to Blagovestchensk on official business, was not
permitted to return.   He was allowed to come back at
once.   The officials of the Chinese Consulate in
Blagovestchensk, however, are not allowed to come to
Taheiho while the Chinese Authorities will only allow
bona fide Soviet officials to come to Taheiho -

representatives

representatives of commercial organizations are being
excluded at present. The boycott against the Tungpei
Steamship Bureau has been raised the Bureau apparently
having cancelled their new and, to the merchants,
obnoxious regulations. Cargo is now arriving from
Harbin in considerable quantities and as it is being
passed there without examination, owing to the rush of
export cargo, the Examining Staff is very busy here.
Unfortunately for our revenue the cargo is practically
all duty paid. River Dues collection, on the other
hand, is fairly satisfactory.

Yours truly,

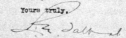

第 109 号半官函   1929 年 6 月 19 日于瑷珲关

尊敬的梅乐和先生：

为省政府要求瑷珲关委派专员负责联合航行章程的执行事：

本人在关于滨江关致海关总税务司公署第 3835 号呈的意见中说明,已就呈中所报滨江关收到东三省商船管理办法暂行章程一事与道尹商议,并按照道尹要求向其致函询问黑龙江和吉林两省政府关于要求瑷珲关委派专员至边界河道稽查管理之指示是否会受此新章程的影响。但至今道尹仍未有回复。

海务巡工司在关于瑷珲关致海关总税务司公署第 414 号呈的意见中表示,对于省政府要求海关委派专员至边界河道稽查管理一事,其认为联合航行章程应由中央政府审批,而且稽查管理工作非一名专员可以应对,如果应承此事,还需加派人手。

本人亦赞同联合航行章程最好由中央政府下令实施,但中央政府对黑吉两省的管制十分有限,或许由海关代为执行方为良策。本人此前建议任命易保罗（P. I. Ignatieff）先生为专员,由海关和黑龙江水道委员会各为其支付半数薪俸,若该建议获得批准,易保罗先生不仅可以获得海关的支持,还可通过作为黑龙江水道委员会委员长的道尹获得黑吉两省政府的支持,如此一来,其手中的权力应足以实施必要的管理措施。另外,如果条件允许,能够派遣数名专员自然最好,但于此事而言,一名专员亦聊胜于无。

航运季期间,航务专门顾问易保罗先生经常往来边界河道巡查航路标志的情况,然而尽管他为起草联合航行章程委员会的成员,亦为黑龙江水道委员会委员,但目前并无权力规范中国船只的航运。若可授予他必要的权限,相信稽查管理工作在实际操作和思想规范方面均会取得不错的成果。因为船长们将意识到,航行中的一举一动都会受到专员的监督。虽然专员不会同时出现在所有航道,但船长们亦无法得知其将于何时何地出现。

鉴于当前之情形,自通过联合航行章程以来,中方尚未采取措施予以执行,但苏联当局已开始严格遵照条例行事,以致黑龙江水道委员会和中国政府的处境略显尴尬。但同时本人也意识到,出于对政策、职员等方面的考虑,阁下或许只能决定海关暂且不应承担此事。

为修筑前滩堤岸事：

阁下关于批准修筑前滩堤岸的电令已于 5 月 5 日收悉,现已基本完工。此次工程由航务专门顾问负责监督,完成质量较好,做到了经济高效。待工程账目结算完毕,本人将正式呈文汇报。现下已开始进入夏季,日日降雨,去年夏季便是如此,最终导致大洪水来袭，如此看来，此项修筑工程完成得恰逢其时。

为提高江捐税率事：

阁下关于批准提高木料和木桦江捐税率的电令已于 5 月 5 日收悉，自实行新税率以来尚未有抗议之声。本人亦将正式呈文汇报此次提高税率一事，以便记录备案。今年已有大量木桦运抵大黑河，多年来首次出现价格下跌的情况：今年每俄丈为 8.10 银圆，去年每俄丈为 9.574 银圆。

为满洲特殊津贴事：

海关总税务司公署致瑷珲关第 456/121166 号令已如期收悉，内称批准为经南满铁路往来的关员发放双倍里程津贴，为所有关员发放冬季置装津贴，逐步废除满洲特殊津贴。对于此项新安排，可继续申领全额或半额满洲特殊津贴的华洋外班关员均已欣然接受，但自今年年初便在瑷珲关任职的华籍内班关员认为已被海关忽视，请求本人将其境遇告知阁下，希望可以获得一些补助。

华籍内班关员表示，虽然其薪俸的确有所增长，但其房租津贴已为最低标准（参阅瑷珲关致海关总税务司公署第 424 号呈），满洲特殊津贴业已自动取消，置装津贴又无权申领，综合计算，其于海关所得之收入比在中国消费水平最低口岸任职的华籍内班关员还要低，而瑷珲关区却是中国物价最高的关区之一。此外，他们还指出，瑷珲关区地处边境，他们大多被迫与家人分离，在子女教育和应对气候变化等方面，还要有额外支出，因此提出或可为他们发放临时"边境津贴"，以此显示出他们与在中国其他物价正常的口岸任职的同级关员的区别。如果阁下原则上同意他们的请求，本人将正式呈交提议。与此同时，本人已向他们解释，新津贴发放之初出现不均等的情况亦是无法避免之事。

值得一提的是，黎彭寿先生为瑷珲关唯一帮办，时常要与中国官员打交道，亦需为此投入钱财，虽然他已竭力将此项花费控制在最低标准，但数目依然很大，再加上本地物价高昂，其收入便显得十分微薄。

滨江关税务司在其致海关总税务司公署第 3840 号呈中询问双倍里程津贴是否只对经南满铁路往返的关员发放。本人亦在等待阁下关于此事之回复，待收到指示后再向两名近日调任本关的关员发放津贴，一名自秦皇岛关调来，一名自牛庄关调来。

为地方局势事：

道尹离开大黑河前往哈尔滨和齐齐哈尔已有一月。目前，大黑河与布拉戈维申斯克（Blagovestchensk）的中苏官员因苏联驻哈尔滨领事馆被搜查一事，关系变得十分紧张，相信道尹定会因此提早返回。中国政府虽未搜查苏联驻大黑河领事馆，但威胁称，如果苏联政府不将此前至布拉戈维申斯克处理公务的黑河市政筹备处翻译人员安全放回，则将关闭该领事馆。随后，该名翻译立即被放回。但中国驻布拉戈维申斯克领事馆的官员却不被允许返回大黑河，中国政府亦仅允许真正的苏联官员来至大黑河，因此商业组织的代表们现已不得过境来此。

东北航务局因遭到抵制已取消了针对商人制定的苛刻新规定。如今已有大量货物自哈尔滨运抵大黑河，滨江关因货物急需出口未能查验便予放行，本关的验货员现下十分繁忙，但因货物均已完纳税款，本关并无税款可征。不过江捐税收还较为可观。

您真挚的

铎博赉

6. 铎博赉致梅乐和函

（第 110 号半官函）

S/O No.110.

CUSTOM HOUSE,

Aigun   28th June, 19 29.

Dear Mr. Maze,

PROPOSED TRIP OF INSPECTION OF AIDS ON THE
UPPER AMUR: I duly received I.G. S/O of the 30th May, 1929,
to the effect that the Taoyin could be informed that I
would be able to join the Chinese Aids Commission in an
inspection of the Upper Amur.   It was planned to leave
on the 1st July but the non-return of the Technical Adviser
on a long inspection of the lower Amur and Ussuri,
complicated by recent activities of hunhutze about 200
miles above Tahsiho culminating in the sack of a large
town named Humaho (呼 玛 河), will delay our departure
somewhat.   As soon as plans are definitely fixed I will
wire for formal permission to be absent from the port.

ANNUAL AIDS DESPATCHES REPORTING RENEWAL OF
AGREEMENTS, BUDGET, ETC.: these despatches are generally
sent off toward the end of May.   This year their
preparation has been held up by the absence of the Technical
                                                    Adviser

F. W. Maze, Esquire,
SHANGHAI.

Adviser on an inspection of the lower Amur and the Ussuri
since the middle of May, and a consequent delay over
estimates and certain specifications.   The despatches
will be sent off on his return which is expected shortly.

SOVIET CONSUL CROSSES AMUR TO BLAGOVESTCHENSK
WITHOUT REPORTING TO CUSTOMS AND PASSPORT OFFICE: two or
three times of late the Soviet Consul, on proceeding to
Blagovestchensk in his motorboat, has crossed the Amur
direct from the Consular steps without reporting at either
the Customs pontoon or the Passport Office.   On this
being reported to me I sent a Clerk to the Consulate to
say that I did not wish to write in officially about the
matter and requesting them to report at the Customs in the
future when crossing the Amur.   My clerk saw the Consular
Secretary (a sort of Vice Consul) who said that where
lower employees of the Consulate were concerned, they should
report but that, in the case of the Consul and himself,
it was not considered necessary.   He went on to say that
a Consul was not liable to search and that for him to
report to the Customs was a loss of face!   I had not
expected this stand to be taken and sent the Clerk to the
Superintendent to report the interview.   The latter,
                                                    without

without informing me, wrote to the Consul that he must
report at the Customs (ignoring the question of the Passport
Office) whereupon the Consul called on him to protest
against the letter and against reporting. Eventually,
however, he agreed to report but said he would send in a
protest. The Superintendent thereupon told him to go
slow until he could talk the matter over with me. The
latter called yesterday and asked my opinion about the
position he had taken up. I told him I thought he was
quite right, that no country would permit any Consul to
cross the frontier without reporting and suggesting that
he point out that the Chinese Consul at Blagovestchensk
was allowed no such privileges in passing the Soviet
Customs to come to Taheiho. It was understood that the
Chinese Customs does not intend to search the Consul or
his launch but the Superintendent agreed with me that he
must come to the pontoon for a cursory inspection to
determine that quantities of arms or propaganda were not
being carried. I consider that the Consul's stand in the
matter is unreasonable and untenable and I do not expect
him to maintain it.

MR.

MR. CHANG YUAN YANG, 3RD CLERK B, APPLIES FOR
INSPECTORATE LEAVE: Aigun despatch No.431 to I.G. encloses
the application of Mr. Chang Yuan Yang, 3rd Clerk B, for
3 months' Inspectorate leave from the 16th October, 1929.
In my S/O No.107 I report that Mr. Li P'éng-tse, 2nd Clerk B,
was applying for 4 months' leave from 1st August (Aigun
despatch No.417) but that if necessary his going away might
be postponed until the end of the navigation season when
he need not be replaced, if the Service is short-handed,
until next spring. The application of Mr. Chang for leave
to date from the close of navigation rather alters the
situation and if it and the application of Mr. Li are both
to be granted I would now recommend that the leave of Mr.
Li date from the 1st August (or 1st September according to
Circular No.3,905) as he requests, that he be replaced
before his departure, and that, if necessary, Mr. Chang be
not replaced until next spring. The successor of Mr. Li
should be a good typist.

PROPOSED ESTABLISHMENT OF A SEMI-OFFICIAL
CHINESE COMMERCIAL AGENCY TO DEAL WITH SIMILAR SOVIET
ORGANIZATIONS: in a recent conversation with the Superintendent, formerly Taoyin and now known as Mayor under the new
order of things, he informed me that he had submitted to the

Heilungchiang

Heilungchiang and Moukden Authorities a scheme for the
establishment of a semi-official Chinese commercial agency
with head office in Taheiho and branches along the
Heilungchiang-Soviet frontier which would have the authority
to deal with Soviet mercantile agencies of a similar nature
and to carry on trade with them along the Amur. At present
the frontier is closed and no goods of any kind are allowed
to pass by either the Chinese or Soviet Authorities, an
exception having been made in May, 1928, when the latter
bought 200,000 poods of wheat and 10,000 poods of flour.
All buying and selling in this region by the Soviet would
be done through the newly established agency. In my S/O
No.90 of 4th May, 1928, I report calling on the Taoyin and
recommending that the purchase of grain, mentioned above,
be allowed in view of the facilities given for the purchase
of goods by the Soviet in Harbin and subsequent shipment via
Suifenho and Manchouli. At that time he expressed himself
as strongly opposed to any commercial intercourse with the
Soviet. Later, in S/O No.91 of 31st May, 1928, I reported
a change in his attitude and his approval of the grain
deal. I understand that this was brought about by local
merchants going over his head to the Tsitsihar Authorities.
That he now contemplates the establishment of an agency for

open

open trade with the Soviet indicates a complete reversal of
his attitude. If his recommendations are approved by his
Higher Authorities it may mean a revival of trade on a
considerable scale with Siberia. Grain, for example, with
merely the cost of transportation across the Amur, could
probably be landed more cheaply in Russia from here than
from any other place. In connection with the present project
the Taoyin raised the question of duty treatment of cargo
passing the frontier at points on the Amur distant from
Taheiho where we have no stations. I told him I would
submit the question to you as soon as he could put it in
a concrete form. I do not find that the limits of control
of the Customs along the frontier have ever been defined
but the tendency in the past has been to consider that goods
crossing the Amur should eventually pay duty at Aigun/Taheiho
otherwise they would be considered as smuggled.

Yours truly,

第 110 号半官函   1929 年 6 月 28 日于瑷珲关

尊敬的梅乐和先生：

为拟将前往黑龙江上游巡查航路标志事：

1929 年 5 月 30 日总税务司半官函收悉，内称可告知道尹本人将代表黑龙江水道委员会前往黑龙江上游巡查。本次行程原计划于 7 月 1 日出发，但航务专门顾问前往黑龙江下游及乌苏里江巡查尚未返回，而且大黑河上游约 200 英里处的呼玛河镇近来土匪活动猖獗，出发时间因此会有所延迟。待具体时间确定后，本人将立即发送电报请准暂离口岸。

为呈报航路标志协议续约及预算等事：

航路标志相关呈文通常于 5 月末呈送，但今年因航务专门顾问于 5 月中旬前往黑龙江下游及乌苏里江巡查，而有所延误，相关预算报表等亦因此而未能及时呈报。航务专门顾问不日即将返回，届时将尽快呈送。

为苏联领事未经海关和护照检查处（Passport Office）擅自跨江返回布拉戈维申斯克（Blagovestchensk）事：

近日，苏联领事已有两三次未经海关码头和护照检查处直接自领事馆乘摩托艇前往布拉戈维申斯克。收到相关报告后，本人立即命税务员前去苏联领事馆说明，本人并不愿正式呈文汇报此事，但请领事馆官员日后过江之前先至海关报明。当时与税务员会面的是苏联领事秘书（相当于副领事），他回复称，凡领事馆低阶官员需要过江者均会至关报明，但他与苏联领事二人应无此必要，还宣称，领事不应被搜查，至海关报明于其而言实为有损颜面之举！本人从未料到会收到此等回应，遂命税务员向海关监督报告此次会面之事。于是海关监督在未告知本人的情况下直接向苏联领事致函要求其日后必须至关报明（未提及护照检查处）。苏联领事随后面见海关监督，对此信函和报明之事提出抗议，不过最终还是同意在过江之前至关报明，但表示仍会提交抗议。海关监督遂让他稍安勿躁，表示会与本人商议此事。

昨日，海关监督前来询问本人对他处理此事的态度有何意见。本人对其表示赞同，指出没有国家会允许外国领事未经报明便擅自离境，建议其向苏联领事说明中国驻布拉戈维申斯克领事在通过苏联海关过江来至大黑河时从未享此特权。最终海关监督与本人达成共识，商定中国海关不会对苏联领事及其摩托艇进行搜查，但须于海关码头对其进行粗略检查以确保其未携带大量军火武器或政治宣传手册。兹认为，苏联领事之观点并不合理，无法立足，相信不会坚持太久。

为三等二级税务员张远扬先生申请休假事：

本人此前于第 107 号半官函中汇报称，二等二级税务员李鹏泽先生申请自 1929 年 8 月 1 日起休假四个月（参阅瑷珲关致海关总税务司公署第 417 号呈），届时若公务需要，可命其至航运季结束后再行离职，待明年春季，若出现人手不足之情况，再委派关员接替其职位。而今三等二级税务员张远扬先生又申请自 1929 年 10 月 16 日起休假三个月（参阅瑷珲关致海关总税务司公署第 431 号呈），情况则有所改变。

鉴于张远扬先生将于航运季结束时离职，故此建议，若两人之休假申请均获批准，则允许李鹏泽先生自 8 月 1 日起（或按照海关总税务司公署第 3905 号通令指示自 9 月 1 日起）休假，接任者须在其离职之前到任。至于张远扬先生之职务，如有需要，可至明年春季再委派关员接任。李鹏泽先生的接任者须有熟练的打字技术。

为拟设半官方中国贸易机构以接洽相应苏联贸易公司业务事：

日前与海关监督兼黑河市政筹备处处长（前道尹）会谈时，其透漏已向黑龙江省政府和奉天当局提议设立半官方中国贸易机构，以便与类似性质的苏联贸易公司开展黑龙江沿岸贸易，并建议将该机构总部设于大黑河，沿中苏边境设立多个办事处。如今中苏两国政府已封锁边境，禁止一切跨境贸易，唯 1928 年 5 月有一特例，苏联方面于此收购了 200000 普特小麦，10000 普特面粉。嗣后苏联方面于本地区的贸易都将通过该新设立的贸易机构完成。

关于苏方于去年 5 月收购小麦面粉一事，本人曾于 1928 年 5 月 4 日第 90 号半官函中汇报称，因考虑苏方可于哈尔滨进行购买再通过绥芬河和满洲里运出，故向道尹提议允许苏方于本地区收购。但道尹当时坚决反对一切与苏贸易。嗣后本人又于 1928 年 5 月 31 日第 91 号半官函中汇报，道尹已改变态度批准此项贸易。据悉，道尹后来转变态度是因为大黑河地区的商人越过其直接向齐齐哈尔当局汇报了此事。如今道尹既能主动提出设立贸易机构与苏方开展贸易，足以看出其态度已完全转变。若其建议可获上级政府批准，本地区与西伯利亚地区的贸易或将迎来复兴。以粮食为例，从大黑河地区跨江运入苏联境内虽需支付少量运费，但总体费用可能仍然比从苏联其他任何地区收购都更为低廉。

关于设立贸易机构一事，道尹还指出，海关于黑龙江沿岸距离大黑河较远之地并未设立税卡，对于经此等地方过境之货物将如何征税。本人表示将于设立贸易机构一事确定后提请总税务司指示。经查，海关对于边境沿线的管控从未受到限制，只是按照惯例，凡跨江运输之货物最终均须至瑷珲或大黑河口岸完纳税款，否则即被视为走私。

您真挚的

铎博赉

7. 铎博赉致梅乐和函

（第 111 号半官函）

S/O No.111.　　　　　　　CUSTOM HOUSE,

　　　　　Aigun　10th July, 1929.

INWARD

Dear Mr. Maze,

　　　TRAVELLING SCHOLARSHIP EXAMINATION: I am in receipt of your wire of the 1st July instructing Mr. Lee Peng Sheo, 4th Assistant A. to report at the Inspectorate on the 3rd August for an oral examination. This means that he will have to leave here not later than the 10th and that he cannot arrive back before the 1st September. If he is successful in his oral examination I presume he will not return at all. His absence will make this port very short-handed and will leave me with only four Clerks to carry on the work of the General Office, Returns, Secretary's and Accounts offices. And of these four none of them have had experience in accounts. As we are very busy just now with a rush of cargo from and to Harbin following the lifting of the boycott against the shipping companies I could see no other course open than to wire you for assistance, temporary or otherwise,

　　　　　　　　　　　　　　　　pending

F. W. Maze, Esquire,
SHANGHAI.

pending the return or replacement of Mr. Lee; a wire to this effect was sent off on the 5th instant. It is possible that a Clerk or Assistant may be detailed from the Harbin Staff to tide over the emergency. The accounts for June quarter have just been closed but it seems doubtful if Mr. Lee will have time to make up the abstracts before he goes though he is endeavouring to do so.

　　　PROPOSED TRIP OF INSPECTION OF AIDS ON THE UPPER AMUR: it has been decided that the Aids Commission (Chinese) will leave here for up-river on the next trip of the s.s. "Aigun" which should leave in about a week. However, in view of the unexpected absence of Mr. Lee Peng Sheo, spoken of in the preceding paragraph, I have informed the Taoyin that I do not see how I can get away at this time.

　　　CHART OF AMUR RIVER AND MAP OF EASTERN SIBERIA BOUGHT WITH SERVICE MONEY AND NOW IN AIDS ARCHIVES: I.G. despatch No.12/87,064 sanctioned the purchase of a navigation chart of the Amur from Moho to Ekaterino - Nikolsk and a map of Eastern Siberia and Northern Manchuria on a very large scale for $120 to be charged

　　　　　　　　　　　　　　　　to

to A/o. A: 7/2. Since their purchase (1921) they have
rested in the archives of the Technical Adviser's office
where, in my opinion, they should remain and I would
propose, with your consent, to request the Taoyin for
authority to refund their cost to the Service from Aids
funds.

AMUR RIVER IN FLOOD: in my last S/O but
one (No.109), in describing the bunding that had been
done to the foreshore, I mentioned that the work was
completed none too soon as heavy rains every day indicated
another flood such as we had last year. Since the first
of June a very large amount of water has fallen in this
and the region of the upper part of the Amur with the
result that the river has risen steadily. On the 4th
instant it touched 426.35 as compared with 427.5 last
year which was a record since 1872. Since then it has
gradually fallen. Luckily the Zeya river which empties
into the Amur a short distance below here, and which
caused all the damage last year by backing up the Amur,
did not rise this time. Had the two rivers risen
together great damage would have been done to Taheiho
and Blagovestchensk. The drainage system of the country
back of Taheiho has become changed and the last two heavy
rains

rains precipitated a flood on the town from the hills.
Streets were washed out and many houses collapsed while
heavy damage was done to countless others. Unprecedented
rains and floods two years in succession have cast a
gloom over the populace. Crops, however, may be alright
with a little sunshine and not so much damage was done
to riverine villages below Taheiho as last year. Many
rafts broke loose from their moorings. As they consisted
of heavy logs they were a potential menace to shipping
along the foreshore. The Customs motorboat was kept
ready all the time and whenever a raft was seen to be
adrift it was pushed into the channel until clear of the
harbour and then beached. In this manner practically
no rafts got out into the open Amur where they would have
been lost and it may be said that the Customs saved the
raft owners many thousands of dollars the last two weeks.
Parts of two street drains along Customs property gave
away during the flood and will have to be repaired, at
a cost of some $120. Official sanction will be requested
for the expenditure required later. As I said above, the
bund was completed just in time and held splendidly. The
water rose to within two or three feet of its top so that
it was subject to an unusual test at once.

Yours truly,

第 111 号半官函   1929 年 7 月 10 日于瑷珲关

尊敬的梅乐和先生：

为海关行政考察员考试事：

7 月 1 日电报收悉,内称命四等一级帮办黎彭寿先生于 8 月 3 日至海关总税务司公署参加口试。如此则意味着,黎彭寿先生须于 7 月 10 日之前动身出发,至 9 月 1 日以后方可返回,但若通过口试,相信亦不会再返回瑷珲关任职。其离开后,瑷珲关的人手将更加紧张,总务课、统计课、文案房及会计课的公务只能交由四名税务员处理,而他们当中并无拥有会计经验者。自从本地商民对航业公司的抵制停止后,每日都有大批货物往来哈尔滨,以致本关业务日益繁忙,故此只得于本月 5 日向阁下发送电报请求黎彭寿先生返回或接任者到来之前,暂时提供支援。本人认为或许可从滨江关选派一名税务员或帮办帮助瑷珲关度过这一紧急时期。第二季度账目已结,黎彭寿先生业已在竭力编制报表,只是不确定能否于离开之前完成。

为拟将前往黑龙江上游巡查航路标志事：

中国黑龙江水道委员会已决定乘坐下一班"瑷珲 (Aigun) "号轮船前往黑龙江上游,发船时间预计还有一周左右。但因如上所述,黎彭寿先生将要离开,本人已经告知道尹此时恐怕无法离开瑷珲关。

为由海关经费购买但归入航路标志档案的黑龙江航图及东西伯利亚地图事：

海关总税务司公署致瑷珲关第 12/87064 号令曾批准购买一份黑龙江航图,覆盖范围自漠河延伸至叶卡捷琳堡 – 尼科利斯克 (Ekaterino-Nikolsk),及一份北满洲和东西伯利亚地图,并指示将购买所用的 120 银圆记入瑷珲关 A 账户 (费用项目 7/2)。但自购买以来 (1921 年),两份地图便一直存放于航务专门顾问办公室的航路标志档案之中。兹认为,可继续如此归档,但建议请道尹批准使用航路标志经费偿还海关此笔款项,还请予以批示。

为黑龙江发生洪水事：

本人于第 109 号半官函中汇报完成筑堤工程一事时,曾提及进入夏季后每日皆有降雨,很有可能会与去年一样再次遭遇洪水,因此此项工程完成得恰逢其时。自 6 月 1 日起,大黑河及黑龙江上游地区便连降暴雨,黑龙江水位逐步上涨。至本月 8 日,水位已达到 426.35 (去年为 427.5,是 1872 年以来的最高水位),但之后便开始逐渐回落。结雅河在大黑河下游不远处汇入黑龙江,去年爆发洪水时造成了不小的损失,所幸今年水位并未上涨。如果黑龙江与结雅河同时爆发洪水,大黑河和布拉戈维申斯克 (Blagovestchensk) 地区必将遭受巨大损失。

　　大黑河背面村庄的排水系统已发生变化，最近两场暴雨过后，洪水开始从山上倾泻至城镇之中。街道遭到洪水冲刷，许多房屋被冲毁，其他地区的损失也不计其数。连续两年史无前例的强降雨和大洪水让当地百姓的生活蒙上了一层阴影。不过粮食方面，如果多一些日照，产量或许不会受到影响，而且大黑河下游沿江村落的受灾情况并未如去年那般严重。很多木筏都于系泊时被洪水冲散，木筏上载有大量木料，于前滩一带的船运而言，十分危险。瑷珲关摩托艇时刻待命，一旦发现漂流的木筏，便会立即行驶入航道将之清除。因此，几无木筏漂入黑龙江航道。可以说，在过去两周内，瑷珲关已为木筏船主挽回了数千银圆的损失。发洪水期间，海关关产周围的两处街道排水沟被冲毁，需要修缮，费用预计120银圆。稍后将正式呈请批准此项支出。如上所述，筑堤工程完成得恰逢其时，非常有效。黑龙江水位最高时距离堤岸顶面仅有两到三英尺，堤岸修筑完毕，便立刻接受了一次不同寻常的考验。

您真挚的

铎博赉

8. 铎博赉致梅乐和函

（第 112 号半官函）

S/O No.112.

CUSTOM HOUSE,

Aigun ____ 27th July, 19 29.

Dear Mr. Maze,

    SINO-SOVIET CRISIS: on the 12th July I learned that the Chinese Authorities at Harbin had taken steps that indicated their intention of taking over the Chinese Eastern Railway and on the 15th that the U.S.S.R. had sent an ultimatum to China and had stopped the trains from passing at Suifenho and Manchouli. On the 17th I had a wire from Barentzen saying that the situation was tense and that he had authorized the evacuation of the Staffs of his different frontier stations if circumstances demanded it. As the trend of the situation was so serious I decided to send my wife, child and governess to Harbin at once; they were on the point of going anyway as our child (of 7 years) was ill and the doctor had ordered a change of climate. They left on the S/S "I Hsing" on the 18th. The day before I had wired you that all was quiet so far but that the Soviet troops were on the move.

        On

F. W. Maze, Esquire,
  Shanghai.

    On the 20th I met the Taoyin early in the morning coming from the Soviet Consulate. He informed me that he had just received a telegram from down river that the S/S "I Hsing" had been seized by the Soviet and was being escorted back toward Blagovestchensk. I called on the Soviet Consul at once reporting that my family was on board the seized steamer and requesting his assistance. He promised to see what could be done and left for Blagovestchensk. An hour later he returned and assured me that my family would be looked after and that I need not worry.

    A little later in the day I learned of the seizure of another steamer the S/S "Haicheng" whereupon I wired you (on the 20th instant) informing you of the seizure of the two steamers without warning or explanation, that the local situation appeared tense, that the local populace was in a small panic for fear of being cut off entirely, that the local Soviet Consul was still functioning and that I was making arrangements to evacuate the Russian Staff. At the same time I wired Barentzen that the Taoyin, on instructions from Moukden, had ordered all White Russians to concentrate at Mergen (half way to Tsitsihar) and that as I was in the dark about the

        situation

situation in general would he advise me as to whether he
considered that my Russian Staff should be evacuated. He
replied on the 21st instant that his Russian Staff was
being withdrawn from all frontier stations and the Chinese
Staff from Suifenho and Manchouli.

Later in the same day I had a letter from the
Soviet Authorities that my family was awaiting transportation to Taheiho. I crossed to Blagovestchensk where I
got in touch with them after considerable formality. My
wife told me that they had been very well treated on board,
as had all Chinese passengers, that the Governor had called
on her on their arrival and a motor car had been provided
by the G. P. U. to take them to the hotel. Our daughter,
however, had developed considerable of a temperature and
on a doctor's advice, and with the consent of the
Authorities, she decided to remain in Blagovestchensk until
the child was better. Had she come to Taheiho the only
means of evacuating them would have been by cart along the
big road to Tsitsihar which is now well nigh impassable
owing to the heavy rains which have occurred almost daily
this summer, as they did last year at this time. Under
present conditions some two weeks would be required for
the journey and the road is equally dangerous from

hunghutze

hunghutze and Chinese soldiers. There is also the further
uncertainty of who will be in possession of Tsitsihar on
arrival and the probable difficulty of travelling on the
railway from Tsitsihar to Harbin.

As a result of the lack of news and the
beligerent attitude of the Soviet Authorities across the
river the Chinese populace had begun to flee and price of
carts to Mergen rose to $400 and $700 to Tsitsihar. As
I now felt that it was not safe for White Russians to
remain in the vicinity of the frontier, and as the only
direction in which they could proceed was toward Tsitsihar,
I told them to engage carts and prepare to proceed along
that road despite the hardships I have just described. Carts
were accordingly arranged for and secured in the Customs
compound. I succeeded in getting lower terms than those
just stated an arrangement being made to pay $4 per day
to each cart while awaiting orders, $25 per cart to
Liangchiat'un and $90 if they went to Mergen.

On the 22nd I received your wire through the
Harbin Commissioner directing me to take such steps to
secure the safety of the Staff as I thought best. In the
morning, at the request of the Taoyin, the frontier having
been closed by now by the Soviet Authorities, I took a

representative

representative from his office to Blagovestchensk. The
latter had three telegrams for the Chinese Consulate there
and wished to see the Governor about the return of the
Chinese passengers on the two seized steamers - some 600
in all. The Taoyin's man was not allowed to pass the
frontier but I was permitted to pass and was authorized to
take the telegrams to the Chinese Consulate. On arrival
there I found they had packed up ready to move but that
final orders had not arrived. They also told me that
several hundred Chinese of all classes had been arrested
during the night. This was possibly with a view to
internment.

I then proceeded to the hotel and called on
the Taheiho Soviet Consul who had taken rooms there. I
should have said above that he evacuated from Taheiho on
the 21st instant being given every assistance by the Chinese
authorities who treated him very politely. I told the
Consul of the Taoyin's anxiety for the safe return of the
passengers on the two Chinese steamers but was informed that
nothing could be done until a reply was received from Moscow
to a telegraphic request that had been sent requesting
instructions. On my return to Taheiho I was told by the
Soviet Authorities that I could not cross again unless I

was

was sent for.

The Russian Staff to be evacuated consisted of
Mr. T. Ivanoff, Examiner A, with wife and two small children,
Mr. V. V. Pravikoff, 1st Class Tidewaiter, with wife and
mother, and Mr. V. Z. Lankin, 2nd Class Tidewaiter, with
wife and mother-in-law. At Aigun they would be joined by
Mr. S. M. Bulgakoff, 1st Class Tidewaiter, and wife. At
the last minute it was decided to attempt to use a motor
car along with the carts several days of fair weather having
intervened. Kunst & Albers agreed to supply an open truck
on condition that the women of their Staff were also taken -
5 in all - and that the Customs furnish the benzine and
chauffeur. 3 carts were to be taken for transporting the
baggage and food. It also became necessary to relieve Mr.
Bulgakoff at Aigun by a Chinese Tidewaiter which would require
another motor car and finally the services of a third were
engaged (a small one) to show the road long detours being
necessary because of the bad going. I had expressed to
Messrs. H. A. Smith and H. W. Snow, respectively Acting
Tidesurveyor and Assistant Examiner A, and American and
British, that I should like to see their wives and families
leave also that our future movements would not be handicapped
but at the last moment they decided not to let them go. I

did

did not feel at the time that circumstances warranted my
ordering the evacuation of other than Russians.

The cavalcade started out with every prospect
of getting at least to Aigun by motor car but after two hours
on the road they had the misfortune to be overtaken by a
violent downpour which necessitated their returning to a
Chinese village for the night.   The next day the uncertainties
of the road were such that only Messrs. Ivanoff and Lankin
(the latter was acting as chauffeur to the Kunst & Albers car)
and their families decided to try and reach Aigun.   Mr.
Pravikoff and family and the Kunst & Albers families remained
behind to see if the others got through.   The other two cars
with the Chinese Tidewaiter returned to Taheiho after a 5
hours struggle with the roads.   The car that went on to Aigun
arrived there at 3 p.m. and reported that it would be
impossible to use the car further and extremely difficult to
proceed by cart.

The Chinese Consul was expected from Blagovestchensk
during the afternoon of the 25th as the Soviet authorities had
sent over a request that transportation be supplied.   A
deputation of Chinese official, civil and military, waited on
the bund to welcome him.   After a long wait, however, it was
seen that something must be wrong and that the launch and

junk

junk sent from here were being detained.   They eventually
arrived at 5 a.m. the next day (26th).   I have been told
since by the Taoyin that a rigorous search of the Consular
effects had been made lasting the whole night and that many
rifles, gold roubles and some other contraband had been
found.   The rifles were part of the Consular armament but
should have been left behind.   The gold was contraband.   It
was also reported that the Soviet Officials claim to have
found evidence of Japanese-Chinese cooperation in the present
crisis.   As a result of the discoveries made the Chinese
Consul and Vice Consul have been detained in Blagovestchensk
their families and effects being released.   A Chinese
motorboat used as a ferry between Taheiho and Blagovestchensk
was also detained there at the same time with no explanation
and a third steamer, the "Aigun", which has been tied up to
the Chinese side of the Amur near Moho since the trouble
began, was brought to Blagovestchensk by the Soviet troops
who had crossed over to the Chinese side and seized her.

After the seizure of the first two Chinese
steamers I wrote to the Governor at Blagovestchensk asking
if he would please send over all Customs mail through the
Chinese Consul but it was not done.   There was apparently
a large mail on the "Haicheng" from Harbin and it is probable

that

that many official covers were in it as I have had only one
mail in several weeks owing to the bad roads. I am asking
Harbin to make inquiries of the Post Office there to see if
any record was kept of the Customs mail forwarded by that
steamer.

   To return to the subject of the evacuation of
the Russian Staff, Messrs. Ivanoff and Lankin with families
are leaving Aigun today by cart, the truck remaining in the
Custom House there to be sent for by Kunst & Albers. Mr.
Bulgakoff, Officer-in-Charge at Aigun, is awaiting a
remittance I am sending him by military messenger before he
evacuates for Liangchiat'un. Mr. Pravikoff, who was left
behind in the small village, will also proceed by cart today
and the four families should foregather in the station at
Liangchiat'un tonight. There they will remain with their
carts for the time being arrangements having been made to
send a messenger from Aigun to warn them in case of danger,
when they can continue towards Tsitsihar. They are carrying
documents issued by the Taoyin and Garrison Commander to
protect them enroute and are armed with revolvers.

   The Chinese Staff were fairly at ease until the
departure of the Russian Staff when I authorized them to
       procure

procure carts to be retained in the Customs compound at $5
per day until it is seen if they will be needed. To obtain
them at the last moment will be impossible. I am making
no arrangements for the evacuation of the Chinese Miscellaneous
Outdoor Staff as they are natives of the place and should be
able to look after themselves.

   Personally I shall stay on as long as possible as
will Messrs. Smith and Snow. Should the Soviet forces cross
the river, however, it may be necessary to evacuate during
the bombardment as their discipline is uncertain as well as
their ability to distinguish between White Russians and
foreigners. After the first excitement is over I should be
able to get in touch with the officer in command and secure
protection for the Customs; this in event that the Soviet
troops do try to cross.

   Needless to say all trade has stopped and Customs
business is at a standstill. To make matters worse
telegraphic communication has been interrupted the last two
days so that we are absolutely in the dark as to what is
going to happen. Added to this uncertainty is the bad
weather. The Amur is rising again and swollen streams are
washing out the roads between here and Tsitsihar. However
those of us remaining are at present better off than the
       unfortunates

unfortunates that had to evacuate and there is always the
possibility that nothing will happen after all.

I apologize for the length of this S/C - I
could have condensed it greatly but it seems to me best to
have a full record of what has transpired in case a similar
crisis arises in the future.

Yours truly,

第 <u>112</u> 号半官函 　　　　　　　　　　　　　　　　　1929 年 7 月 27 日于瑷珲关

尊敬的梅乐和先生：

为中苏危机事：

本人于 7 月 12 日获悉，哈尔滨中国当局已采取行动，计划接管中东铁路。7 月 15 日苏联方面向中国发出最后通牒，并阻止火车经过绥芬河和满洲里。7 月 17 日，巴闰森（P. G. S. Barentzen）先生发来电报称因局势紧张，其已批准滨江关各边境分关在必要时撤离。鉴于局势发展日趋严峻，本人决定将妻儿及保姆立即送往哈尔滨避难，不过即便事态未如此严重，他们亦须离开，因为本人七岁的孩子正在病中，医生已告知须到气候适宜之地调养。随后他们于 7 月 18 日乘坐 "宜兴（I Hsing）" 号轮船离开大黑河。就在他们离开的前一天，本人还曾向阁下发送电报汇报称大黑河地区局势尚且平稳，但苏联军队已开始行动。

7 月 20 日清晨与道尹会面时，道尹刚从苏联领事馆返回。其告知刚刚收到黑龙江下游地区发来的电报，内称 "宜兴" 号轮船遭遇苏联方面拦截，已被押至布拉戈维申斯克（Blagovestchensk）。本人立即拜访苏联领事，说明家人亦在被拦截的轮船上，望其相助。苏联领事答允后便动身前往布拉戈维申斯克，一小时后返回告知，本人家人会有人照料，不必担忧。

当日稍晚时候收到消息，"海澄（Haicheng）" 号轮船又遭苏方扣押。本人随后于 7 月 20 日向阁下发送电报汇报称，两艘中国轮船被苏方无故扣押，当地局势开始紧张，民众已开始恐慌担心会与外界完全隔离，但驻大黑河苏联领事依然在此办公，本人已着手安排俄籍关员撤离之事。同时本人亦向巴闰森先生发送电报告知，道尹已按照奉天当局指示命所有白俄人至墨尔根（在前往齐齐哈尔半途中）集合，但本人对整体局势全然不知，望其对瑷珲关俄籍关员撤离一事给出意见。巴闰森先生于 7 月 21 日回复称，滨江关边境分关的俄籍关员已全部撤离，绥芬河分关和满洲里分关的华籍关员业已撤离。

当日晚些时候，苏联当局来函告知，本人家人正在等待轮船返回大黑河。本人随即前往布拉戈维申斯克，在办理了烦琐的手续后，得以与家人见面。妻子告知，她们在船上得到了的礼遇，其他中国乘客也未受到苛待，轮船抵达后，阿穆尔州州长便与其会面，政府政治部还提供了一辆汽车将她们送至旅店。但因女儿发高烧，妻子决定按照医生的建议在女儿情况好转之前暂时留在布拉戈维申斯克，苏联当局业已批准。倘若他们返回大黑河，撤离的唯一办法便是乘车经大路前往齐齐哈尔，但是由于夏季以来几乎每日都有大雨，与去年此时之情形一样，道路泥泞难行。据现有路况估计，前往齐齐哈尔约需两周时间，而且途中既有强盗土匪出没，又有中国士兵往来，抵达齐齐哈尔后，主事者是何人亦无法确定，乘火车前往哈尔滨或将十分困难。

大黑河地区消息闭塞，苏联方面又虎视眈眈，当地中国百姓已开始逃难。运货马车至墨尔根的费用已涨至 400 银圆，至齐齐哈尔的费用已涨至 700 银圆。考虑白俄人继续留在边境地区恐不安全，而唯一能够逃难的去处就是齐齐哈尔，本人遂命他们雇用运货马车，做好前往齐齐哈尔的准备，尽管此行如上所述会有诸多艰难。运货马车雇好后便停放于海关办公楼大院。此次雇用运货马车的费用较上述低廉许多，待命期间，每辆每天 4 银圆，至梁家屯每辆 25 银圆，至墨尔根每辆 90 银圆。

7 月 22 日收到由滨江关税务司转发的阁下电报，指令本人采取措施确保关员安全。当日早晨，因苏联当局已封锁边境，道尹命本人携道尹公署的一名代表共同前往布拉戈维申斯克。该名代表手中持有要交给驻布拉戈维申斯克中国领事的三封电报，希望可与阿穆尔州州长会面商谈释放两艘被扣押轮船上的 600 余名中国乘客，不过最终未能获准通过边境。所幸本人获得过境许可，并获准将电报带给中国领事。本人抵达中国领事馆后发现，中国官员已打点好行装准备离开，只是还未收到最终撤离指令。据其所述，夜间已有上百名中国各阶层民众被捕。不过苏联当局此举可能只是为了关押中国人。

本人随后前去驻大黑河苏联领事居住的旅店拜访。关于此事，本人应已汇报过，苏联领事已于 7 月 21 日在中国政府的友好帮助下自大黑河撤回布拉戈维申斯克。本人向苏联领事说明，道尹急切希望两艘被扣押轮船上的中国乘客可以尽快安全返回中国，但苏联领事告知关于此事已向莫斯科方面发送电报请求指示，如今只能静待回复。本人返回大黑河时，苏联当局告知日后若无邀请，不得过境。

需要撤离大黑河的俄籍关员有：一等验货员艾华诺（T. Ivanoff）先生及妻子和两名幼童、一等稽查员帕维各夫（V. V. Pravikoff）先生及妻子和母亲、二等稽查员蓝金（V. Z. Lankin）先生及妻子和岳母，待至瑷珲后，一等稽查员卜乐喀郭夫（S. M. Bulgakoff）先生及妻子亦会加入到撤离队伍当中。

经过几日晴好天气后，最终决定使用一辆汽车和几辆运货马车运送上述人员撤离。孔士洋行同意提供一辆敞篷卡车，条件是其职员的女性家眷（共有 5 人）亦须随行，并由瑷珲关雇用司机，提供汽油。除此之外还有三辆运货马车运输行李和食物。另外，一等稽查员卜乐喀郭夫先生撤离后，须由一名华籍稽查员至瑷珲口岸接替其职位，因此还需为华籍稽查员准备一辆汽车，另因道路崎岖难行，又雇用了一辆小汽车在前面引路。

此外，本人已告知代理监察长施密（H. A. Smith）先生（美籍）和一等副验货员思诺（H.

W. Snow）先生（英籍），其家属亦可跟随此次撤离队伍离开，同时说明日后撤离亦不会受到阻扰，二人最终决定让家人继续留在此地。兹认为，按照当时的情况，还没有到一定要让非俄籍关员撤离的地步。

撤离队伍出发时计划至少先驱车抵达瑷珲，然两小时后突遇倾盆大雨，他们不得不返回到一处中国村庄过夜。次日，因路况不明，只有艾华诺先生和蓝金先生（驾驶孔士洋行卡车）两家人决定继续启程前往瑷珲。帕维各夫先生一家和孔士洋行职员家眷留在原地等待消息。与华籍稽查员同行的两辆汽车在路上挣扎 5 个小时后返回了大黑河。前往瑷珲的汽车（孔士洋行卡车）于下午三时到达，但据称已无法继续使用，运货马车亦难以前行。

原以为驻布拉戈申斯克中国领事可于 7 月 25 日下午返回大黑河，因为苏联当局已传来消息要求提供交通工具，当地中国文武各官皆至堤岸迎接，但等待良久仍未见踪影，方觉此事有异，稍后才知过江迎接的摩托艇和民船已遭苏方扣留。摩托艇和民船最终于次日（7 月 26 日）早五时返回大黑河。嗣后道尹告知，25 日晚苏方严查了中国领事的物品，搜出大量步枪、金卢布及其他违禁品。其中步枪虽为中国领事的武器，但本不应携带，而黄金则属于违禁品。此外还有报告称，苏联官员宣称已找到证明日本与中国在此次危机中合作的证据。因此中国领事和副领事被扣留在布拉戈申斯克，其家人及财物获得放行。与此同时，往来于大黑河与布拉戈申斯克之间充当轮渡的中国摩托艇被苏方无故扣留，自中苏危机开始以来一直系泊于黑龙江华岸漠河附近的"瑷珲（Aigun）"号轮船亦被苏联军队跨江劫走，拖至布拉戈申斯克。

前两艘轮船遭到扣押后，本人曾向驻于布拉戈申斯克的州长致函，请他通过中国领事将所有海关邮件返还给瑷珲关，但并未有任何结果。"海澄"号轮船上有哈尔滨寄来的大批邮件，甚至可能有很多官方信件，近几周来由于路况不佳，本人仅收到一封信件。为此，本人已请滨江关税务司向哈尔滨邮政局查询是否留有海关通过"海澄"号轮船邮寄信件的记录。

至于俄籍关员撤离一事，艾华诺先生和蓝金先生两家人已于今日乘坐运货马车离开瑷珲，并将卡车留在瑷珲口岸海关办公楼大院以待孔士洋行取回。瑷珲口岸主事关员卜乐喀郭夫先生待收到本人通过军方信使发送的汇款后亦将前往梁家屯。此前留在村落等待消息的帕维各夫先生业于今日乘坐运货马车启程。四组家庭将于今晚在梁家屯分卡汇合，停留期间，运货马车亦将留于其身边。待他们可以继续前往齐齐哈尔时，如有危险，瑷珲口岸的信差将会前去报信。此外，他们不仅佩有左轮手枪防身，还带有道尹和镇守使签发的文件，可保途中安全。

俄籍关员撤离后，本人批准华籍关员以每日5银圆的价格租赁运货马车，停放于海关办公楼大院以备不时之需，因为到最后关头再去租用，恐怕无法租到。此外，瑷珲关华籍外班杂项职员均为大黑河当地人士，应该能够照顾好自己，因此本人并未制定他们的撤离计划。

本人与施密先生和思诺先生会尽量留在大黑河，但若苏联军队跨江而来，吾等可能须于袭击期间撤离，因为苏联军队纪律如何，能否分辨洋人和白俄人，着实无法确定。待苏联军队第一次袭击过后，本人便可与军队指挥官取得联系，请其保护海关免受伤害，当然这只是在苏联军队试图跨越黑龙江的情况下之安排。

如今所有贸易均已停滞，瑷珲关已无业务可办。更糟糕的是近两日来电报线路中断，本人无从得知外界局势如何。而且大黑河地区天气状况不佳，黑龙江水位再次上涨，大黑河与齐齐哈尔之间的道路上也满是积水。与撤离的关员相比，留在大黑河的人目前更为舒适，而且此地亦很有可能会平安无事。

很抱歉此函篇幅过长，当然内容亦可精简，但兹认为，将事件全部记录下来更为有宜，以便日后出现类似危机时可作参考之用。

您真挚的

铎博赉

9. 铎博赉致梅乐和函

（第 113 号半官函）

S/O No. 113.

CUSTOM HOUSE.

........Aigun...,7th August, 1929

~~INDEXED~~

Dear Mr. Maze,

SINO-SOVIET CRISIS: In my last S/O written on the 27th July, when excitement was at its height, I reported that the Russian Staff with families had been evacuated and were expected to arrive at the Liangchiat'un Barrier that night and that carts had been engaged here to stand by in case the Chinese Staff had to leave. Messrs. Ivanoff and Lankin with families did not reach the Barrier, however, until the 29th and the Pravikoffs and Bulgakoffs not until the 1st August. The roads, owing to the continuous rains of the past month, were well nigh impassable while a fair sized stream, which the first party crossed without great difficulty, rose directly afterward and held up the second party for three days. They are all remaining at the Barrier until the crisis is passed. The carts engaged for the Chinese Staff were kept for five days and then paid off as the situation seemed easier and as the Taoyin had taken similar action with the carts he had retained for the evacuation of his family and staff.

My last visit to Blagovestchensk, as reported in my

F.W.Maze, Esquire

preceding

Shanghai.

preceding S/O, was on the 22nd July. Since that time the frontier has been closed and communication has been difficult. The representations that had been made for the release of the Chinese passengers on the three Chinese steamers seized, some 600 in all, met with only a partial response 183 being brought over by Chinese junk that had been sent to fetch them. These were mostly the very old, the young and the decrepit. they reported that, of those detained, the better class had been confined on one steamer and the coolies to another and that it was the intention to send the latter to the gold mines, whether with or without their consent I did not learn. They said they had been fairly well looked after being fed from flour, millet, etc., forming part of the steamers' cargo. I also learned that the S/S "Aigun", which was captured up-river in the neighbourhood of Moho, was fired on by field guns before being boarded. Two guards were wounded and two missing passengers were supposed to have been blown overboard by shells. It was further reported that all valuables were taken from the luggage of the travellers on the three steamers possibly on the plea that gold, foreign money, etc., are contraband that cannot be taken out of the country. On the 30th July the Habarovsk Chinese Consul, staff and effects were evacuated to Tsheiho via Blagovestchensk. The Consul reported that there was

very

347

very little bread in that region while meat was hardly to be
had. 100 more refugees, of the same class as those sent over
on the 29th, arrived on the 31st July. They were from the
Chinese vessels seized on the Ussuri (I hear 6 steamers were
seized there) and taken to Habarovsk from where they were
transported by a Soviet steamer to Blagovestchensk. It is not
known why they were sent to this distant place, which they
cannot leave at present, unless it is to cause as much
inconvenience as possible. On the same day the Blagovestchensk
Consul and Vice Consul who had been detained were sent across
and a Blago paper was received showing photographs of the
contraband seized in the Consular luggage. There were shown
some 40 rifles, much ammunition, loose gold, American and
Chinese bank notes, roubles, etc., all contraband in the eyes
of the Soviet authorities. On the next day another paper was
received dated the 31st containing the names of 16 "Whites"
who had been executed as contra-revolutionists. It was not
mentioned, in connection with the announcement, that these men
were seized on the 3 Chinese steamers. Many of the victims
were known here and amongst them were several of the steamers'
officers. While they may have been "White" in sympathy it was
not known that they were active in the cause. On the 5th August
I sent a representative from his office across in the Customs
motor boat at the Taoyin's request. He was told that no further

crossing

crossing was to be made unless signals were first exchanged
between the two sides by raising and lowering of the flags of
the Chinese Customs and the Soviet Frontier Office.

Largely through my efforts the local military advanced
money to the Telegraph Office for repair of lines and of late
messages have been coming through regularly though a heavy storm
last night crippled the service again. Communication by post
is especially aggravating. For the past month continuous heavy
rains have made the overland route from Tsitsihar to Taheiho
very difficult to travel for the post carts. A large mail was
received by steamer on the 16th July since when no mail has
arrived. It is said that there was a heavy mail for Taheiho
from Harbin on the "Hai Cheng" seized by the Soviet on the
19th July. In my S/O I reported to you that I had addressed the
Soviet Authorities asking them to send over any Customs mail
taken. Up to now they have taken no action. On the 29th ultimo
I wired you that mail had been seized and suggested that any
instructions posted by the Inspectorate to this office between
the dates 20th June and 10th July be repeated. I also took
the liberty of intruding my private affairs into this telegram
and inquired as to whether the cheque for my R/A, if sent to
me between those dates, could not be cancelled and a new
cheque paid into my account in the Hongkong & Shanghai Bank.
I further inquired about a reply to my private letter of the

7th

7th June which may also have gone astray. Ordinarily the mail
from Harbin overland via Tsitsihar takes 6 days in the summer.
The mail seized by the Soviet was despatched from Harbin on
the 12th June giving an interval of 26 days for another mail
to arrive by cart. I have wired to the Harbin Commissioner to
represent to the Chinese Post Office there that after making
all due allowance (for bad weather) I could not believe that
a determined effort was being made in this crisis to get mail
through from Tsitsihar.

Repairs are being taken in hand by the local authorities
to the road to Tsitsihar and, as Aids affairs are now very slack
the Taoyin has asked Mr. Ignatieff to take charge of the work.
This he is doing with his characteristic energy. The future of
Aids is now very problematical and it remains to be seen if
Chinese steamers can continue to navigate the Amur and under
what conditions. All collection of River Dues (and duty) also
ceased but payments to the other side having been stopped for
the time being we have a balance large enough to carry us on
for some time.

With the confusion that has existed since the crisis
began and with the shortage in Staff since the departure of
Mr. Lee Peng Sheo for his oral examination in Shanghai for
a Travelling Scholarship, only the bare routine has been carried
on.

on. During the present lull, however, I have got things
practically back to normal. Despatches prepared on the Aids
budget and the bunding of the foreshore early in July were
held up by the uncertainties of the occasion but are going
forward now. I trust that Mr. Lee is already on his way back
or that a successor has been appointed. It would seem that
whoever is coming will have to proceed overland entailing great
hardship and long delay.

You are probably much better acquainted with the
political situation as it now stands than myself. Cut off from
all postal communication as I have been since the beginning
of the crisis (my last Tientsin paper was dated the 4th July)
I am entirely dependant on the Harbin Commissioner for news
by wire. His last telegram, despatched on the 3rd August, said
that though the position was unchanged he was hopeful of a
peaceful outcome. Foodstuffs such as Flour, Rice, Compradores'
supplies, etc., normally derived from Harbin, are now rapidly
mounting in price owing to a prospect that no more will be
received until the Tsitsihar road freezes in November.

Yours truly,

第113号半官函　　　　　　　　　　　　　**1929年8月7日于瑷珲关**

尊敬的梅乐和先生：

为中苏危机事：

本人于7月27日（局势最为紧张之时）半官函中汇报称，瑷珲关俄籍关员及其家人均已撤离大黑河，预计将于当晚抵达梁家屯分卡，另已于大黑河雇用运货马车以备华籍关员需要撤离时使用。

但实际上，艾华诺（T. Ivanoff）先生和蓝金（V. Z. Lankin）先生两家人至7月29日方抵达梁家屯分卡，帕维各夫（V. V. Pravikoff）先生和卜乐喀郭夫（S. M. Bulgakoff）先生两家人至8月1日才抵达。上个月降雨连绵不断，前往梁家屯的道路泥泞难行，途中还有一条小溪，艾华诺先生和蓝金先生两家人通过后，溪水迅速上涨，拦住了帕维各夫先生和卜乐喀郭夫先生两家人的去路，因此他们延误三日方至梁家屯。四组家庭在梁家屯分卡汇合后便一直停留在此地，直至危机结束。

为华籍关员雇用的运货马车仅留用了五日，之后见局势有所缓和，而且道尹也将此前为撤离家人及道尹公署职员提前雇用的运货马车退回，本人便结清运货马车的费用，不再租用。

如7月27日半官函中所述，本人最近一次前往布拉戈维申斯克（Blagovestchensk）是在7月22日。自那日以来，中苏边境一直关闭，双方往来通信十分困难。中方要求苏方释放三艘被扣押轮船上的600余名中国乘客，但苏方仅释放了183名，由中国此前派出的民船带回大黑河。而这些中国乘客大多为老人、幼童和体弱多病之人。据返回的乘客报告，乘坐较好舱位的乘客被抓到一艘轮船上，苦力被抓到另一艘轮船上。据称苏方打算将苦力运去开采金矿，但是否已经苦力同意，并不知晓。返回大黑河的乘客表示苏方并未苛待他们，每日三餐均是来自中国轮船上的货物，如面粉、小米等。据悉，苏方从黑龙江上游漠河附近截获的"瑷珲（Aigun）"号轮船，因苏联军队在登船前发射了野战炮而失火，船上有两名卫兵受伤，两名乘客可能被炮弹炸入江中失踪不见。据报告称，三艘轮船上乘客行李中的所有贵重物品均被苏方掠走，其理由可能是因为黄金、外国货币等物品为不可带出国境之违禁物品。

7月30日，驻哈巴罗夫斯克（Habarovsk）中国领事及官员携带物品经布拉戈维申斯克返回大黑河。中国领事称哈巴罗夫斯克地区的粮食和肉类都十分紧缺。

7月31日，100多名难民抵达大黑河，与7月29日到达的难民一样皆为老弱妇孺。

他们在乌苏里江上乘坐中国轮船时被苏方截获（据悉苏方于乌苏里江上共截获了六艘轮船），之后被带至哈巴罗夫斯克，随后又被一艘苏联轮船运送至布拉戈维申斯克。但不知他们为何会被送至如此偏远之地，现下又不能离开，除非日后不便之处过多，或许会有被转移的可能。同日，此前被苏方扣留的驻布拉戈维申斯克中国领事和副领事也被遣返回大黑河。当日布拉戈维申斯克报纸上刊登了从领事行李中搜查出的违禁品照片，包括 40 多把步枪、大量弹药、零散黄金、美钞及中国钞票、卢布等物品，这些物品均被苏方视为违禁品。

8 月 1 日又收到另一份日期为 7 月 31 日的布拉戈维申斯克报纸，上面刊登了 16 名"白"俄人以反革命的罪名被处决的新闻，但报纸上仅有这 16 人的姓名，并未说明他们是否为苏联军队在三艘被扣押的中国轮船上抓捕。他们当中有很多人都为大黑河当地人所熟知，有几人还是轮船的驾驶员。他们或许曾支持过白军，但从未听闻积极参与其中。

8 月 5 日，本人按照道尹要求使用海关摩托艇将道尹公署的一名代表送往布拉戈维申斯克。但该名代表被告知，凡过江者，均须于中国海关和苏联边境检查处（Soviet Frontier Office）通过升降旗帜交换信号后，方可通过。

经过本人的不懈努力，当地军方终于向电报局预支了维修电报线路的费用，近日信息方得以如常传递，但昨夜骤降暴雨，电报线路再次中断。邮政通信方面的情况更是糟糕。上个月大黑河地区连续降雨，齐齐哈尔至大黑河的道路太过泥泞，邮递马车难以通行。7 月 16 日，大批邮件由轮船载运而来，但之后再无邮件运抵本地。据称 7 月 19 日被苏方截获的"海澄（Hai Cheng）"号轮船上载有大量自哈尔滨发来的信件。本人于此前半官函中曾汇报已向苏联当局致函请其返还轮船上与海关有关的信件，但至今未果。7 月 29 日，本人向阁下发送电报汇报信件已遭苏方扣押，建议再次发送 6 月 20 日至 7 月 10 日期间海关总税务司公署致瑷珲关的令文，冒昧询问如果在此期间已向本人发送房租津贴支票，能否将之取消，重新以本人在汇丰银行的账户为收款方开立支票，同时希望可对本人 6 月 7 日私人信函做出回复。估计阁下之回函亦已不知所踪。

通常夏季期间，信件自哈尔滨通过陆路经由齐齐哈尔运来需要六日。被苏方扣押的信件乃于 6 月 12 日自哈尔滨发出，而时隔 26 日，由邮递马车运送的另一批信件方送达。本人已向滨江关税务司发送电报，请其转告哈尔滨中国邮政局，即使将天气状况等因素全部考虑在内，本人亦难以相信邮政局对于在此危机期间通过齐齐哈尔运送信件一事已竭尽全力。

大黑河政府已开始修缮通往齐齐哈尔的道路，因航路标志事务目前需要处理者甚少，道尹已命易保罗（P. I. Ignatieff）先生负责修路之事。易保罗先生如今干劲十足。依目前情况来看，航路标志工作日后能否如常开展仍难以确定，主要取决于中国轮船能否继续于黑龙江上航行，取决于届时的具体情况。瑷珲关现已停止征收江捐（和关税），亦暂停向苏方支付联合维护航路标志的摊款，因此目前账户余额还可以支撑一段时日。

由于自中苏危机开始以来，一切都陷入了混乱，黎彭寿先生前往上海参加海关行政考察员口试后，瑷珲关人手又一度紧缺，所以在此期间，本关只开展了一些日常事务。但现今局势又暂时恢复平稳，本关工作也逐步回归正轨。此前航路标志预算及7月初筑堤工程的相关报告因局势不稳而暂时搁置，如今皆已开始重新编制。相信黎彭寿先生现已在返回大黑河的途中，或者接任者已获任命，不过无论何人，都将须经由陆路而来，旅途必定十分艰难，延误之期亦会很长。

目前，阁下对当前政治局势的了解或许比本人更多。自中苏危机爆发以来，大黑河地区的邮政通信便被阻断，本人收到的最近一份《天津日报》还是7月4日的。消息方面，只能依靠滨江关税务司通过电报传来。滨江关税务司上一封电报发于8月3日，内称当前局势虽未有所缓和，但相信会恢复和平。此前，大黑河地区的面粉、大米等粮食物资均自哈尔滨运来，但如今在11月份齐齐哈尔通往大黑河的道路结冰之前都不会再有货物运抵大黑河，各类粮食价格因此迅速上涨。

您真挚的

铎博赉

10. 铎博赉致梅乐和函

（第114号半官函）

CUSTOM HOUSE,

Aigun   15th August, 29.

Dear Mr. Maze,

SINO-SOVIET CRISIS: I have very little to
add to the news given in my last S/O dated the 7th August.
There has been no communication with the Soviet side since
the 3rd August.   Various requests made by the local
Chinese Authorities for the release of those still detained
on the seized steamers, and regarding other questions of
a pressing nature, have been studiously ignored by the
Soviet Authorities who maintain a consistent attitude of
hostile aloofness.   Rifle, machine gun and big gun
practice goes on daily in Blagovestchensk causing continued
uneasiness here and reminding one of the "daily hate"
indulged in on the Western front during the Great War.
Rumours have it that two regiments of Chinese soldiers,
supported by field pieces, are coming overland from
Tsitsihar.   Judging by the almost impassable condition
of the roads they will have great difficulty in getting

through

F. W. Maze, Esquire.
SHANGHAI.

through.   An elaborate system of trenches has been
constructed along the bund and one trench just in front
of my office windows invites firing on the Custom House
should hostilities eventuate.   Taheiho has a semi-deserted
appearance, most of the shops are closed and martial law
prevails.

More troops seem to be arriving in Blagovestchensk
pointing to mobilization.   There are, of course many
rumours of trouble in the interior of Siberia, that there
is not enough food for the army, that the farmers are
opposing mobilization, that the Soviet dare not arm the
older men of fighting age, etc.,etc., but these cannot be
verified.   Many Russian escape across the river every
night and it is dangerous to walk along the bund after
dark as the Soviet soldiers fire at everything suspicious
seen in the water.   All who escape to this side are
rounded up by the Chinese military for fear "Red" spies
may be amongst them.   Strict search in this district is
now being made by the Chinese police of all Russian
residents for firearms of any description.

Mail is filtering through at last being 19
days enroute from Harbin.   Judging by the dates of the

Shanghai

Shanghai papers I now estimate that all mail from there,
posted between the dates of the end of June and 12th of
July, was confiscated by the Soviet on the Chinese steamers
seized.   I.G. despatches Nos.470 to 473 inclusive and
many Circulars are missing.   I trust copies of these
despatches have already been sent as suggested in my telegram
of 29th July, 1929 reporting the loss of mail by Soviet
seizure.   I am addressing the Statistical Secretary asking
for the missing Circulars and any other printed instructions
sent at the same time.

I hear regularly from the evacuated Russian
Staff now living in the Barrier building at Liangchiat'un.
The last letter from there said that they were short of
food and spent most of the time exploring for it in the
neighbouring villages.   However considering that they
left with the bare necessities they appear to be making
the best of the situation.   I have asked Barentzen to
wire me as soon as he considers it safe for them to return
as I am out of touch with the situation having to rely on
the meagre information received by the local authorities,
who seem badly informed, on an occasional telegram from
Barentzen and on papers 19 days enroute from Harbin.   As
work is very slack here they are not greatly missed and

it

it would be unwise to bring them back until the situation
takes a turn for the better.

RENEWAL OF CONTRACT OF TECHNICAL ADVISER: in
Aigun despatch No.441 going forward today I report that
Mr. Ignatieff's contract expires on the 15th September. He
was originally taken on in 1922 for three years and since
1925 his agreement has been annually extended for a period
of one year from the 15th of each September.   Under the
present conditions it is difficult to foretell the future
of Aids and whether the present system of joint maintenance
will be continued.   The Chinese Commission has not discussed
the question of the continued employment of Mr. Ignatieff
and as there is a balance of some $15,000 in Aids funds it
is presumed that he will be kept on regularly for the time
being.   At present, as reported in my last S/O, he has
been detailed by the Taoyin (President of the Chinese Aids
Commission) to superintend the repairing of bridges between
here and Tsitsihar.   This work has been attempted before
in the past with the result that considerable money was
squandered and little accomplished.   Under Mr. Ignatieff's
supervision, however, order has been brought out of chaos.
It is probable that he will get no special remuneration

(other

(other than his Aids pay) for this work he is doing; **but**
as it is for the improvement of communications in this
crisis I have made no protest of this diversion of Mr.
Ignatieff from his regular duties.　It is probable that
any conference arising out of the present situation will
take up the question of the joint navigation of the frontier
rivers where it was dropped by the Sino-Soviet Conference
of Moukden.　For the time being, it seems to me, the
question of the renewal of Mr. Ignatieff's contract might
be left open, as long as the Chinese Aids Commission do not
raise the question and pending developments in the present
crisis.

　　　　AIGUN STAFF: I received today your telegram of
the 14th August to the effect that under present circumstances
it did not seem desirable to appoint new Clerks to Aigun
and that leave was granted to Messrs. Li P'eng-tse, 2nd
Clerk B, and Chang Yuan Yang, 3rd Clerk B, from any convenient
date they could be spared.　I am replying that I desire to
retain Messrs. Li and Chang for the present pending news of
the appointment of a successor to Mr. Lee Peng Sheo, 4th
Assistant A, who proceeded to Shanghai in July for an oral
examination in connection with a Travelling Scholarship.　At
　　　　　　　　　　　　　　　　　　　　　　　　　　　the

the time of the latter's departure I wired, on the 5th July,
asking that he be temporarily replaced as I was left without
an accountant.　You replied on the 19th July that in view
of developments the replacement of Mr. Lee did not seem
necessary: however if necessary the Harbin Commissioner
could be asked to supply a Clerk for a few weeks.　I replied
on the 25th July that I could carry on under the circumstances.
I have no news yet as to whether Mr. Lee is to be replaced
and the instructions in that connection may have gone astray.
Since the latter left here Messrs. Li and Chang (now selected
to be removed from the strength of the port) have been
picking up the work of the Secretary's and Accounts Office,
with my assistance, and will qualify in time.　Neither of
the other two Clerks here, Mr. Wang Te-mao, 2nd Clerk A, nor
Mr. Li Fong-lin, 2nd Clerk B, now in charge of the General
Office and Returns Office, respectively, have had any
experience in secretarial or accounts work while the latter
cannot typewrite.　I have now instructed Mr. Wang Te-mao
to look after the Returns work in connection with his duties
in the General Office, and Mr. Li Fong-lin to learn the
Accountant's duties.　I don't know how quick and reliable
he will prove to be but if he picks up accounts quickly I
　　　　　　　　　　　　　　　　　　　　　　　　　　　can

can let Mr. Li P'eng-tse proceed on leave at an early date.
I trust, however, that an Assistant or experienced Clerk
with a good knowledge of accounts and secretarial duties
will be sent in place of Mr. Lee Peng Sheo's place in which
case I can let Messrs. Li and Chang go at once providing
the present political deadlock continues and roads permit.
A certain amount of duty is still being collected on postal
parcels and a small amount of River Dues are being paid by
junks and rafts.   I had considered the advisability of
wiring you, before the arrival of your wire, regarding a
rearrangement of the Staff with a view to its possible
reduction until trade resumes but I was so out of touch with
the situation that I thought it best to leave the question
to be decided by yourself when it was raised by that of
whether Messrs. Li and Chang should be granted their leave.
Another important factor I had to reckon with in considering
the reduction of the Staff, and which influenced my reply
when I said that I desired to retain Messrs. Chang and Li
for the present, was that of the condition of the overland
route to Tsitsihar.   For the two Clerks in question to
proceed on leave at this time with their families and personal
effects would mean great hardship for them and expense to the
                                                        Service

Service as prices of carts to Tsitsihar are almost prohibitive
now.   While on the subject of the reduction of Staff I would
recommend that, of the two Examiners stationed here at present,
only one be retained.   As conditions have been the past year,
even before the present crisis, one Examiner could carry on
with a 1st Class Tidewaiter doing the examining work at the
Post Office.   Mr. H. W. Snow, Assistant Examiner A. would
seem to be the logical man to shift, if my suggestion is
adopted, as he has been here since the spring of 1928 while
Mr. Ivanoff, Examiner A. arrived here from Harbin this spring.
However, it happens that Mr. Snow desires to proceed on leave
next autumn and if he were to be transferred from here now
it would cut into his savings and he would be forced to sell
his furniture and effects at a time when there are no buyers due
to the unsettled conditions.   Mr. Ivanoff, on the other hand,
would, I believe, welcome a transfer.   The health of neither
he nor his wife seems robust enough for the rigorous winters
we have here while their two sons ought to be in a place where
they can continue their schooling.   There are now three
foreign and two Chinese Tidewaiters in the port.   If there
is no prospect of Chinese trade on the Amur next spring one
of the foreign Tidewaiters could also be spared now.   As in
                                                        the

the case of the Chinese Clerks, transfers would have to wait
on improved road conditions.

I was very pleased to receive Mr. Walsham's
inquiries in his S/O of the 25th July, as to the welfare of
my family and to learn that he had reported the matter of
their seizure to the American Consul in Shanghai. The family
remained in Blagovestchensk where my daughter could be under
medical care, which she could not have if she came here. I
have had no news from them for two weeks, as communications
have stopped, and though I can see people walking on the bund
at Blagovestchensk through binoculars I cannot see them and
am worried. In view of the uncertainty of the future, and
on the advice of the doctor that my daughter should not travel
through the tropics, I have cancelled the passage I had booked
via Suez this autumn. If steamers do not run between here
and Harbin my successor will have to come overland and it
may be that this cannot be done until the road freezes early
in November. As I cannot go until he arrives the time when
I can embark by steamer on leave is very uncertain as conditions
are at present.

Yours truly,

第 114 号半官函　　　　　　　　　　　　　　　**1929 年 8 月 15 日于瑷珲关**

尊敬的梅乐和先生：

　　为中苏危机事：

　　续本人 8 月 7 日半官函。中苏双方自 8 月 3 日以来便再无通信往来。对于当地中国政府提出的释放被扣押轮船上剩余中国乘客等各项要求，苏联当局表现出了一贯的敌视态度，故意不予回复。布拉戈维申斯克（Blagovestchensk）每日都在进行步枪、机关枪及大型枪械演习，大黑河地区因此人心惶惶，不禁让人想到第一次世界大战西线战场的情形。现有谣言称齐齐哈尔有两个团的中国士兵正在经由陆路来至大黑河，但如今道路难行，想要抵达大黑河，恐怕十分艰难。目前，堤岸沿线均已修筑战壕，其中一条战壕就在本人办公室窗前，如果双方开战，海关办公楼必然会成为射击目标。大黑河现处于半荒废的状态，商铺多已歇业关门，政府也已实施了戒严令。

　　据悉，现已有越来越多的部队抵达布拉戈维申斯克，开始进行战时动员。不过，西伯利亚境内也是流言四起，如军队粮食不足，农民反对动员，苏联政府不敢征募年龄较大的士兵作战，等等。但这些流言均无法证实。每晚都有俄籍人过江逃难至华岸各地，中国军方因担心其中会有"红军"间谍，已将他们围捕关押起来。大黑河地区的中国警察业已开始对俄籍居民进行严密搜查，以防有私藏枪支者。夜幕降临后，在堤岸附近行走十分危险，因为苏联士兵会对江中任何可疑目标进行射击。

　　信件终于陆续送达，不过自哈尔滨运来需耗时 19 日。根据上海方面文件上标注的日期判断，上海自 6 月末至 7 月 12 日期间邮寄的信件均在苏方扣押的中国轮船上。海关总税务司公署致瑷珲关第 470 号至 473 号令及多封通令均已丢失。相信相关令文已照本人于 1929 年 7 月 29 日发送电报汇报信件丢失一事时之建议再次发出。本人已致函造册处税务司申请重新提供丢失的通令及其他印谕。

　　撤离至梁家屯分卡的俄籍关员会定期来函汇报情况。他们于上一封信函中汇报称现在缺少食物，大部分时间都在附近的村庄寻找粮食。他们离开时只携带了最基本的必需品，可以看出，现下已是在尽力维持生活。本人如今已无法直接获悉外界的局势变化，只能从地方政府处获取少量信息，实际上他们的信息似乎亦不太灵通，偶尔亦会收到巴闻森（P. G. S. Barentzen）先生的电报，或是通过自哈尔滨经过 19 日邮递而来的报纸了解外界情况。因此本人已请巴闻森先生在其认为局势已经安全，俄籍关员可以召回之时电告本人。瑷珲关现今公务甚少，俄籍关员暂不返回亦无太大影响，因此还是待局势转好，再将他们召回,更为妥当。

为与航务专门顾问续约事:

本人于今日发出的瑷珲关第 441 号呈中汇报,易保罗(P. I. Ignatieff)先生的合同将于 9 月 15 日到期。其最初于 1922 年被任命为黑龙江航务专门顾问,任期 3 年,自 1925 年起,每年 9 月 15 日续约一年。

现今局势不稳,很难确定未来航路标志工作会如何开展,中俄双方是否还会继续联合维护边界河道的航路标志。中国水道委员会尚未讨论易保罗先生的续约问题,但航路标志经费余额还有 15000 银圆,据此推测,其或许还可暂时留任一段时日。

如本人上一封半官函所述,道尹(兼任中国水道委员会委员长)现已命易保罗先生监管大黑河与齐齐哈尔之间的路桥修缮工程。在此之前,当地政府亦进行过此类工事,但最终都是花费巨大,收效甚微。不过,此次在易保罗先生的监督下,情况已明显好转,只是其最终可能不会获得额外酬金(除航路标志薪俸)。虽然此项工事不在其正常职责范围之内,但考虑此亦是为改善中苏危机期间的通信渠道,因此本人并未提出异议。在当前形势下,只要中苏双方举行会议,便有可能重提奉天中苏会议搁置的边界河道联合航运问题。就目前情况而言,兹认为,易保罗先生的续约问题可以暂且搁置,待中国水道委员会提及此事,中苏危机有新进展后再做定夺。

为瑷珲关人事事:

阁下 8 月 14 日电报收悉,内称鉴于当前之局势,似乎暂无为瑷珲关任命新税务员之必要,批准二等二级税务员李鹏泽先生和三等二级税务员张远扬先生于公务允许时开始休假。特此回复,鉴于四等一级帮办黎彭寿先生于 7 月前往上海参加海关行政考察员口试后,尚未有关员接任其职位,因此计划在收到其接任者的任命消息之前,暂时留任张远扬先生和李鹏泽先生。

黎彭寿先生离开瑷珲关时,本人曾于 7 月 5 日向阁下发送电报说明瑷珲关已无能够处理会计事务之人,申请暂时委派他人接任其职位。阁下于 7 月 19 日回复称,鉴于局势发展,暂时应无须任命关员接替黎彭寿先生之职位,如有必要,可请滨江关税务司派遣一名税务员暂至瑷珲关任职数周。本人于 7 月 25 日回复称,目前尚可应对。但迄今为止,本人仍未收到关于黎彭寿先生接任者任命的指示,或许阁下已有指示,只是因中苏危机爆发而不知所踪。

黎彭寿先生离开以后,李鹏泽先生和张远扬先生便在本人的协助下负责文案房和会计课的公务,应该很快可以胜任。但另外两名税务员,即现今负责总务课和统计课的二等一级税务员王德懋先生和二等二级税务员李芳林先生，对文案和会计公务均毫无经验，李芳林先生甚至不会打字。本人现已指令王德懋先生负责处理与总务课相关的统计工作，让李芳林先生学习会计课相关事务，但不知其何时能够接手，若其能够尽快担起此职，李鹏泽先生便可尽早开始休假。但相信阁下定会派遣一名帮办或是熟悉会计和文案知识的税务员前往瑷珲关接替黎彭寿先生的职位。若如此，则只要当前政治局面继续僵持，且道路畅通，李鹏泽先生和张远扬先生便可即刻开始休假。

目前，瑷珲关对邮政包裹仍可征收一定关税，对民船和木筏亦能够征收少量江捐。在收悉阁下电报之前，本人已考虑发送电报申请在贸易恢复之前精简人员，重新调整瑷珲关的人事安排，但因不了解局势发展，觉得还是由阁下在处理李鹏泽先生和张远扬先生的休假问题时对瑷珲关的人事调整下达指示为宜。另外，大黑河至齐齐哈尔的道路状况亦是本人在精简人员问题上的顾虑所在，同时也是暂时留任张远扬先生和李鹏泽先生这一决定的影响因素。若该两名税务员此时携家眷及个人财物离开大黑河，于他们自身而言，路途必定十分艰难，于海关而言，费用亦太过高昂，运货马车至齐齐哈尔的价格现已涨至难以承受的程度。

对于精简人员一事，建议在大黑河现有的两名验货员中择一名留用，因为去年中苏危机爆发之前，一名验货员和一名负责邮政局包裹税征收处工作的一等稽查员便可完成相关公务。若此建议得以采用，按理应调离一等副验货员思诺（H. W. Snow）先生，因其自1928年春季便开始在瑷珲关任职，而一等验货员艾华诺（T. Ivanoff）先生今年春季才自滨江关调任至此。但思诺先生希望可于明年秋季休假，若此时被调离，积蓄便会受到影响，还须变卖家具和个人物品，而且如今局势不稳，根本无法寻得买家。不过，艾华诺先生应该愿意被调离此地，因为他与妻子的身体状况均难以抵抗大黑河的严冬，两个儿子也需迁至适合继续上学之地。大黑河口岸目前有三名洋籍稽查员和两名华籍稽查员。如果明年春季黑龙江华岸无贸易往来，洋籍稽查员中亦可调离一名。至于华籍税务员，调离之事需待道路状况改善后再议。

华善（Walsham）先生7月25日半官函收悉，内称已将本人家人被苏联当局扣留一事呈报驻上海美国领事，对此深表感激。因女儿生病须于布拉戈维申斯克接受治疗，他们仍留在当地。但近两周来由于中苏双方停止通信往来，本人一直没有收到他们的消息，虽然可以通过望远镜看到有人在布拉戈维申斯克堤岸上走动，但见不到家人，甚是担忧。鉴于局势发展无法确定，医生又不建议女儿前往热带地区，本人已取消了原本预定今年秋季通过苏伊士运河返回美国的船票。如果哈尔滨与大黑河之间的轮船无法通行，本人的继任

者则只能经陆路而来,也就是要待 11 月初道路结冰后才能动身出发。 在其到来之前,本人只得继续留在大黑河,依目前情况来看,本人休假登船日期暂无法确定。

您真挚的

铎博赉

11. 铎博赍致梅乐和函

（第 115 号半官函）

S/O No.115.

CUSTOM HOUSE.

A i g u n 24th August, 1929.

Dear Mr. Maze,

SINO-SOVIET CRISIS: during the past week there
have been more "excursions and alarums" than at any time
since the present trouble began. On the 19th instant I
telegraphed you that the local military authorities, on
the instructions of their higher authorities, had issued
orders for the evacuation of all civilians, that they were
themselves removing all military supplies and provisions,
that I was evacuating the Chinese Staff and that the
apparent reason for the order given was frequent forays of
Soviet troops across the Amur. Shortly afterwards I had a
wire from Barentzen that the Chinese delegates had returned
to Harbin from Manchouli and the situation was critical.
I received advance information of the intended evacuation
from the Taoyin late on the evening of the 18th and at
midnight Mr. Acting Tidesurveyor Smith, Mr. Assistant
Examiner Snow and a Chinese Tidewaiter went outside Taheiho
to nearby villages and managed to round up 16 two-wheeled

carts

F. W. Maze, Esquire,
SHANGHAI.

carts before dawn. They were not able to get more because
of the activity of the military and police in the same
direction. These carts were for the evacuation of our two
foreign families, the Native Indoor and Outdoor Staffs,
with families and effects, amounting to some 55 people in
all. Five dollars per day was the least I could get the
carts for as they could get as much or more from others,
9/10ths of the population being unable to get any means
of transportation. Though the prices were exorbitant I
saw no alternative but to incur the expense involved to
secure the safety of the Staff, in accordance with your
instructions. All the yamens and banks were similarly
providing for their staffs. As it was, the number of
carts I was able to get was about half of what was required.

The morning of the 19th was one of confusion
what with again packing up, paying the staff and securing
funds before the bank left, etc., but at noon a heavy
downfall of rain came, after a week of good weather, and
again made the roads impassable. By night the excitement
had died down somewhat and I wired you accordingly and that
the evacuation of the Chinese Staff had been postponed. The
military duly issued the order of evacuation offering
protection to those who went. A large number took

advantage

advantage of the offer to leave. Those who did not go
were given to understand that the Sau Ling Pu no longer
undertook the responsibility of their safety when they were
to leave.

I have had no wire from Barentzen since that
of the 18th, spoken of above, but the Japanese community
received a telegram from their Tsitsihar Consul on the 21st
instant that rather deprecated the necessity for immediate
evacuation. After keeping the carts for three days I
paid them off to avoid the mounting expense and trusting
to the reputation of the Customs for fairplay to obtain
them again should another crisis arise.

The raids across the Amur seem to have ceased for
the time being. Early in the present crisis a boat load of
armed Soviet soldiers crossed in the dark just below Taheiho.
It is not known that their purpose was for they ran into a
Chinese armed patrol as they landed and recrossed at once with
several casualties. At a village called Hsin-Tung (興東)
some distance down the river they crossed and raided the town
killing several Chinese soldiers and civilians. It is
thought they came after supplies as they went back with all
they could carry. A more serious affair occurred at
Chao-Hsing-Chen (肇興鎮), near Lahasusu, where they

crossed

crossed in force and occupied the place for several days
threatening the rear of Lahasusu. I presume this affair
was reported to you by the Harbin Commissioner. Not long
ago some eight or ten Soviet soldiers crossed secretly to
the populous town of Chikote (奇克特), about 100 miles
below Taheiho, hid in the outskirts and at a signal began
to fire at random. In the great panic which ensued they
seized what they could carry and escaped back to their own
side. In addition many raids have been made across to the
Chinese side above Taheiho. It would appear that in some
instances bad characters, who had been armed, conducted the
attack; in all instances considerable looting seems to have
occurred. It is well known that food is daily becoming
more scarce in Siberia. From reports from those escaping
to this side Soviet troops no longer guard the frontier and
anyone is allowed to cross to the Chinese side in search
of food. It was this series of events, aggravated by the
rupture of negotiations at Manchouli, that decided the
military to consider Taheiho as indefensible and that
preparations should be made against its complete evacuation.
It was intended that the military should remain after the
others left but when it would become known by the other side

that

that evacuation was beginning they would probably take it
as an invitation to try and occupy the place.

We have rigged up a radio but as all we hear is
propaganda from both sides in Russian, Chinese, Japanese and
Korean the information we receive cannot be depended on. The
roads remain in a bad condition and mail is very irregular
still requiring from 18 to 24 days between here and Harbin.
Because of the difficulties of communication and the stoppage
of steamer traffic food is daily becoming more scarce and
dear. To make matters worse the local banks destroyed all
their surplus notes when the scare began and money is now
exceedingly difficult to obtain. So far the Bank of China
has accommodated the Customs with funds to carry on with
but they will not cash cheques on Shanghai to transfer money
here. Steps are being taken by the Taoyin to relieve the
money stringency.

In rereading my S/O No.112, in which I state that
I might have to leave Taheiho in case of an attack and that
if I did I should await my chance to get into communication
with whoever was in control, after hostilities had died down,
to secure protection for the Customs, the thought suggests
itself that you may have received the impression that I am

preparing

preparing to leave on the first alarm. Such is not my
idea; my intention is to remain throughout any trouble that
may occur if at all possible.

The June quarter's accounts are being forwarded
today. They have been prepared under considerable difficulty
owing to the nervous tension that has prevailed the past
five weeks and the lack of any experienced accountant. I
trust that due allowance will be made for the delay and for
any errors that may have crept in.

Yours truly,

第 115 号半官函   1929 年 8 月 24 日于瑷珲关

尊敬的梅乐和先生：

为中苏危机事：

自中苏危机爆发以来，上周局势最为"紧张混乱"。本人于 8 月 19 日向阁下发送电报汇报称，大黑河军方已奉上级指示命令所有居民撤离大黑河，同时开始搬离军用设备和物资，瑷珲关华籍关员已开始撤离，军方有此命令皆因苏联军队已多次过江突袭。随后不久，本人便收到巴闯森（P. G. S. Barentzen）先生发来的电报，内称与苏联谈判的中国代表已从满洲里返回哈尔滨，如今局势更加恶化。

8 月 18 日深夜道尹提前告知本人撤离大黑河的消息。当日午夜代理监察长施密（Smith）先生、副验货员思诺（Snow）先生及一名华籍稽查员离开大黑河前往附近的村庄，在天亮前成功租到 16 辆两轮运货马车，当时军方和警察亦在四处搜寻车辆，因此他们只能弄到这么多。瑷珲关需要撤离的人员包括两名洋籍关员及家人、华籍内外班关员及家人，共约 55 人，此外还有个人物品，这些都将由租用的运货马车运送撤离。每辆车每日租金为 5 银圆，虽然过高，但为按照阁下指示确保关员安全，已别无选择，而且大黑河撤离居民中十之八九都无法租到交通工具，他们当中愿意出此价格甚至更高者比比皆是。本地区所有公署和银行也为其职员做出了相应安排。但本人租用的运货马车数量亦只是实际所需的半数。

8 月 19 日早情况十分混乱，本人忙于打点行装，支付职员薪俸，在银行撤离之前办理钱款等事，不料中午突降大雨，道路再次无法通行，但此前一周皆是晴好天气。至当日夜晚，躁动逐渐平息，本人便向阁下发送电报汇报情况，说明华籍关员撤离之事已遭延误。军方随即下令保护民众撤离，并说明凡未随此次队伍撤离者，司令部日后不再为其离开提供保护，大批民众已借此机会离开大黑河。

自上述 8 月 18 日电报后，巴闯森先生再无电报发来。但本地日本人于 8 月 21 日收到驻齐齐哈尔日本领事电报，内称不必立即撤离。运货马车在瑷珲关停放了三日后，本人便将租金付清，停止租用，以免租金累计过多。日后如再遇危急情况，相信以海关的良好声誉必定可以租回所需车辆。

目前，苏联军队似已暂时停止过江突袭。当前危机爆发之初，有一支苏联武装队伍于夜间乘船过江来至大黑河下游，登岸后与中国武装巡逻队相遇，造成部分士兵死亡，随后立即乘船返回俄岸，因此不知其目的究竟为何。嗣后，苏联军队又过江突袭黑龙江下游的兴东村,导致数名中国士兵和当地居民死亡,返回时还将在村中搜刮之物全部带走,据此推断,他们突袭的目的应是获取物资。此外,拉哈苏苏附近的肇兴镇亦遭到苏联军队突袭,而且情况更为严重。当时苏联军队强行渡河并占领了该镇数日,对拉哈苏苏后方造成极大威胁。滨江关税务司应已将此事汇报给阁下。不久之前,约有八到十名苏联士兵秘密过江袭击了人口众多的奇克特镇,该镇位于大黑河下游约100英里处。当时苏联士兵躲藏在郊外,收到信号后立即开始扫射,随后又趁民众慌乱之时掠夺物资,逃回俄岸。除此之外,苏联军队还多次偷袭大黑河上游华岸各地。据悉,其中有些应是武装匪徒所为,但所有袭击事件中,均有大量物资遭到抢掠。

如今西伯利亚地区的粮食危机日益严重。据从苏联逃至华岸的难民所述,苏联军队现已不再对边境设防,允许所有人跨越边境到华岸地区搜寻粮食。正是由于苏方的不断侵扰,满洲里举行的中苏双方谈判破裂,中国军方才认为大黑河已无法防守,才会下令要求全部撤离。按照计划,待百姓撤离后,军方将继续驻守大黑河,但苏联军方若得知撤离之事,很有可能会借机攻占大黑河。

本关已草草搭建一台无线电设备,但只能收到黑龙江华俄两岸使用俄语、汉语、日语和朝鲜语发出的宣传信息,并无任何参考价值。前往齐齐哈尔的道路状况依然不佳,信件亦无法如常送达,大黑河与哈尔滨之间的邮递时间仍需18到24日。由于陆路交通受阻,轮船运输又已停止,大黑河地区的粮食日益减少,价格却节节攀升。更糟糕的是,大黑河陷入恐慌之后,当地银行便将剩余纸币全部销毁,如今想要弄到货币,已是万难之事。迄今为止,中国银行一直为瑷珲关提供运营资金,但拒绝兑现上海支票。道尹已开始采取措施缓解货币紧缩状况。

本人曾于第112号半官函中提出,如遇苏军来袭,本人或将撤离大黑河,待战火平息再与军队指挥官取得联系,请其保护海关免受伤害。如今再次翻阅此函,发现上述提议可能会让阁下认为本人会在警报拉响时立即撤离。但并非如此,无论局势如何发展,本人都将竭力坚守岗位。

瑷珲关第二季度账簿已于今日发出。由于近五周来局势紧张,瑷珲关又无熟悉会计事务之人,账簿编制工作完成得颇为艰难。虽然呈交时间有所延迟,账簿中或许亦会有错误疏漏之处,但相信会得到阁下谅解。

您真挚的

铎博赉

12. 铎博赉致梅乐和函

（第 116 号半官函）

S/O No.116.

CUSTOM HOUSE.

Aigun 8th September, 1929.

Dear Mr. Maze,

    SINO-SOVIET CRISIS; my last S/O was dated the 24th August. In it I reported a tense situation created by an order by the Military Authorities to evacuate and its gradual easing. I also reported that many raids had been made across the Amur by Soviet armed troops. On the 25th a Soviet gunboat with guns trained on the town crossed to this side of the river and steamed slowly the entire length of the bund in a very provocative manner. On the 26th this action was repeated when the gunboat had on board several hundred Chinese soldiers in Soviet military uniform. To my mind such demonstrations are similar to those of May and June, 1925, in Shanghai and Canton respectively (inspired by Communists), and were calculated to create an international incident. Fortunately the Chinese troops on shore did not fall into the trap. On the 28th instant at midnight, as reported in my wire to you of the 29th, a large explosion occurred on the bund.

The

F. W. Maze, Esquire,
SHANGHAI.

The Officer on duty sent to my house reporting that the Custom House had been struck by a shell. On proceeding there I found the Staff very excited and learned that not the Custom House but the S/L "Yung Ping", lying along the foreshore a short distance above the Custom House, had been damaged by an explosion. I made a short examination of the launch and concluded that an attempt had been made to blow up the vessel by a bomb. The force of the explosion was very great. Mr. Assistant Examiner H. W. Snow, who lives over the Custom House, was thrown to the floor from his bed. He with his family took refuge in my house for the remainder of the night and others of the Staff who lived along the bund removed temporarily to places of greater safety. In the morning I inspected the damaged launch and found that a bomb had been exploded on her forward deck blowing out the port side of the vessel, destroying the roofing, wheel, etc., badly denting the boiler and destroying the iron floor-plating for some distance. Luckily the bomb had fallen on a pile of firewood which took up a great deal of the force of the explosion. A fast motorboat on the Soviet side was heard proceeding up river before the explosion and down river afterwards. The military conjecture

that

that a man had been placed in the river above Taheiho by
the motorboat with something buoyant to keep him afloat,
that he had approached close to the launch in the darkness
and had either placed or thrown a bomb aboard her after which
he floated on down and was again picked up.

The "Yung Ping" has been put out of commission for
the time being but the damage to the hull was not great and
she did not sink. Neither the Custom House nor adjacent
buildings were damaged structurally but they were badly
shaken and the Custom House had many windows broken. As
the "Yung Ping" was the only steam propelled vessel left
to Taheiho it would appear that the Soviet wished to remove
the last means by which a crossing of the river might be
effected. I have not removed the Customs launch from the
water as I do not feel that any attempt will be made on her.
At my request, however, she is specially guarded at night by
the military. Since the bombing incident the Chinese troops
have been on the <u>qui vive</u> along the bund at night and it is
kept in darkness. At the same time the bund is now kept
clear of all civilians day and night.

Two days ago a Soviet motor launch came close to the
bund along the upper part of Taheiho and when Chinese soldiers
ran

ran to their positions fire was opened on them from her by
rifles. This fire was returned and the motorboat quickly
turned back. There appear to have been no casualties on
either side. At Aigun, and doubtless in other places,
all Chinese who approach the river are fired at from the
other side. It is reported that a few days ago a Soviet
steamer stopped at the Chinese village of Ma Chang (馬 厰)
some 30 miles above Taheiho, and looted the place of flour
and provisions. The Military report that at midnight on
the 6th they discovered two bombs and 6 large pieces of
dynamite which were placed on a large government gold dredge
moored just above the Tungpei Steamship Company's wharf last
night. The fuse had burned out without firing the charge!
Method can be seen in the destruction of a launch but not
in an attempt to destroy a dredge unless a systematic
campaign is now on foot to inspire terror on this side of
the river. A continuous trench is now being dug along our
new bund the soldiers working on it in the daytime. It is
calculated to draw fire from the other side and places the
Custom House and the Tidesurveyor's House in a dangerous
position. Such acts, coupled with the Soviet demonstrations
reported above, creates a situation that a tiny spark will
set

set off. Locally the Chinese soldiers have acted with great
self restraint so far but I have no confidence that it will
continue.

Despite the well nigh impassable conditions of
the road a caravan of 28 carts set out 5 days ago in an
attempt to reach Tsitsihar. It included the Harbarovsk
Chinese Consul and party, the wife and daughter of Mr.
Assistant Examiner Snow and many of the families of the
principal Russians remaining in Taheiho. After the explosion
on the bund Mrs. Snow's nerves gave away and it became
necessary to send her away.

I hear frequently from the Russian Staff at
Liangchiat'un. They report that they are alright for the
present but that it is getting cold and warm clothes are
needed. They also state that the Military have commandeered
all carts in the vicinity for the evacuation of Taheiho and
they fear that it will be impossible to retire further if it
becomes necessary. I am endeavouring to remedy the situation-
it is only one phase of many problems I am facing here. The
Taoyin/Superintendent has asked permission to quarter his
immediate family in the Liangchiat'un building too. I am
giving him three rooms, the use of two of which has already
                                                        been

been sanctioned in I.G. despatch No.466/122,131 for Cattle
Inspection Bureau. It will make the building very crowded.

The last few days the weather has improved
somewhat and the mail is a little more regular. I received
covers dated the 5th August from Shanghai on the 6th September.
I had a wire yesterday from the American Consul, Harbin, who
is keeping in touch with my family in Blagovestchensk through
the Japanese Consul there. He reports that they are under
no restrictions and that my daughter's health is better;
further that should hostilities break out he will arrange for
the family to proceed at once to Japan. The Consul further
states that the general situation seems to be improving from
which I conclude that negotiations must be proceeding in
some manner.

It has now been 7 weeks since we were placed
"under the guns", so to speak, and a change for the better
is devoutly to be hoped for. All personal effects of the
Staff that could not be taken in case of evacuation have been
stored in the Custom House. We are living out of bags ready
packed while such archives as should be taken are now kept in
iron despatches boxes that they may be removed to a place of
safety if a bombardment began. Such an atmosphere, with
                                                        troops

troops lining the trenches under the office windows, is not
conducive to constructive work but the routine is being kept
up-to-date and the morale of the Staff is good.   The occasion
is being taken to repaint and colour-wash all the quarters
where necessary.   The money and food situation continues
acute.

Because of the poor communications I have not
heard from you since the present crisis became acute but I
trust that the action I have taken so far, as reported, will
meet with your approval.

Since writing the above two seaplanes appeared
over Taheiho and flew above the Chinese frontier defences.
This is the first time planes have appeared here.   I wired
you today (9th September) to this effect and that it is
reported that Soviet troops have crossed the Amur some 30
miles above Taheiho.   I have no confirmation of the latter
report yet.   It would appear that the Soviet is intent
on ending the present suspense one way or another.

Yours truly,

第 116 号半官函   1929 年 9 月 8 日于瑷珲关

尊敬的梅乐和先生：

为中苏危机事：

本人于 8 月 24 日半官函中汇报称，当地军方下令撤离后，大黑河地区局势更加紧张，但随后已有所缓解，苏联武装队伍屡次过江突袭黑龙江华岸各地。

8 月 25 日，一艘苏联武装炮艇过江来至华岸演练，以极其挑衅的方式缓慢驶过大黑河前滩。8 月 26 日，该炮艇故技重施，只是这一次船上载有数百名身着苏联军装的中国士兵。本人认为，此事与 1925 年 5 月和 6 月上海广东两地（由共产主义者发起）的示威事件如出一辙，意欲让事态发展成为国际纠纷。所幸驻守在黑龙江沿岸的中国军队并未落入苏联军队设下的陷阱。

8 月 28 日午夜，大黑河堤岸发生大规模爆炸（参见本人 8 月 29 日电报）。爆炸发生后，当值关员到本人住所汇报称海关办公楼被炮弹击中。本人立即前往堤岸查看，发现被炮弹击中的并不是海关办公楼，而是停在海关办公楼上游不远处的"永平（Yung Ping）"号汽艇，快速查看汽艇后，发现是有人试图用炸弹将之炸毁。此次爆炸威力巨大，在海关办公楼居住的副验货员思诺（H. W. Snow）先生甚至从床上被震到地板上，不过爆炸过后已携家人暂至本人住所避难，其他住在堤岸附近的关员也都暂时移居到其他更加安全之处。次日上午，本人又对被炸毁的汽艇进行仔细检查，发现炸弹在前甲板上爆炸后朝左舷方向喷发，船舱室顶板、轮子等处皆被炸毁，锅炉因爆炸已严重变形，船底板亦有受损。所幸炸弹掉落在一堆薪柴之上，爆炸威力得以减轻。据悉，俄岸有一艘摩托艇在爆炸前曾驶向黑龙江上游，爆炸后又驶向下游。军方据此推断，该摩托艇应是先行至大黑河上游，将一人放入水中，让其利用可以漂浮之物，趁着夜色游向汽艇，将炸弹扔到或放在汽艇上，之后顺流而下，再由摩托艇接回。

"永平"号汽艇船体的损毁程度并不严重，船只本身亦未有下沉迹象，只是出于安全考虑已暂停使用。海关办公楼和附近的建筑，结构都未有损坏，但在爆炸过程中都有震颤，而且海关办公楼的许多窗户玻璃也都被震碎。"永平"号汽艇是大黑河仅剩的一艘由蒸汽驱动的船只，苏联方面定是希望将中方唯一的过江工具破坏掉。但考虑苏方不会再对该汽艇有所图谋，本人并未将之拖拽上岸，不过已请军方在夜间严加看护。自爆炸事件发生以来，中方军队便加强了堤岸夜间的守卫，时刻保持警惕。如今，无论日夜，堤岸附近均无民众往来。

两日前，一艘苏联摩托艇向大黑河上游堤岸靠近，发现有中国士兵接近后立即开火，随后遭到反击便迅速掉头返回俄岸。此次交火并未造成人员伤亡。

在瑷珲，乃至华岸其他地区，凡有中国人靠近江岸者，均会遭到苏方的枪击警告。据报，数日前一艘苏联轮船行至大黑河上游约 30 英里处的中国村庄马厂，停靠后将村中面粉等粮食物资洗劫一空。据军方报道，他们于 9 月 6 日午夜在东北航务局码头上游停泊的一艘政府采金船上发现了两枚炸弹和六大包炸药，炸弹引线已经燃尽，但所幸炸药未被引爆！此次炸弹投放的办法应与炸毁汽艇时一样，炸毁采金船，定是为了在华岸制造恐慌。如今中国士兵已开始于日间沿着大黑河的新堤岸挖掘战壕，此举很有可能会引来苏军火力，海关办公楼和监察长宿舍亦会被战火波及。中苏双方现正处于紧张对峙的状态，稍有不慎，局势便会迅速恶化，引发战争。中方军队已保持了相当程度的克制，但恐怕不会保持太久。

虽然道路依旧难以通行，但已有 28 辆运货马车于 5 日前出发前往齐齐哈尔。随行人员包括驻哈巴罗夫斯克（Habarovsk）中国领事及其随扈、副验货员思诺先生的妻女及许多在大黑河居住的苏联人。自爆炸事件发生以来，思诺先生妻子的精神便一直处于失常状态，须转移至安全之地好生调养。

撤离至梁家屯分卡的俄籍关员常有书信送来，最近汇报称目前一切安好，唯天气渐冷需要御寒衣物，并告知中国军方已征用了附近所有运货马车，以供大黑河撤离之用，因此担心日后撤离时无马车可用。本人已在竭力解决此事，不过除此之外，眼下需要解决之事还有很多。道尹兼海关监督希望可允许其家人搬至梁家屯分卡避难。本人已为其安排三间房间，其中两间已由海关总税务司公署第 446/122131 号令批准供兽疫检验所使用。如此一来，分卡房屋将会十分拥挤。

近几日来，天气已有所转好，信件送达时间亦日趋正常。上海方面 8 月 5 日寄出之函已于 9 月 6 日收悉。昨日，本人收到驻哈尔滨美国领事的电报，其一直通过驻布拉戈维申斯克（Blagovestchensk）日本领事与本人家人保持联系。其于电报中告知，本人家人的行动并未受到限制，女儿的病情也有所好转，如果战争爆发，将立即安排他们前往日本避难，最后还表示，如今总体局势似有改善的趋势。本人据此推断，谈判之事应该已有新进展。

大黑河地区的紧张局势已持续七周，真心希望可以转好。为准备撤离，关员无法携带的个人物品均已存放于海关办公楼。目前留守在大黑河的关员都已打点好行装，需要带走的档案业已装入铁箱之中，以便发生炮击时可立即转移至安全之地。如今海关办公楼窗外皆是成排的战壕和部队驻军，在此氛围下，本关难以开展有建设性的工作，但日常事务仍在有序进行,关员士气亦未受到影响。此外,借此机会已按需重新粉刷关员宿舍。但货币和粮食问题依然十分严峻。

由于通信状况不佳,自危机严重以来,本人便再未收到阁下来信,但相信上述举措定会得到阁下批准。

在撰写此函时,有两架飞机出现在大黑河上空,并在中国边防上空盘旋。这是第一次有飞机出现在本地区。本人已于今日(9月8日)向阁下发送电报汇报此事,并说明据称苏联军队已在大黑河上游约30英里处过江。但该消息是否属实,尚不确定。显然苏联方面打算以某种方式结束目前僵持的局面。

您真挚的

铎博赉

13. 铎博赉致梅乐和函

（第 119 号半官函）

S/O No.119

CUSTOM HOUSE.

Aigun 3rd October, 19 29

Dear Mr. Maze,

SINO-SOVIET CRISIS: Since my last S/O, the lull spoken of then as prevailing along the frontier has continued and nothing of importance has occurred. Mails from Harbin still require some 18 days enroute so that I continue to be quite out of date in knowing the trend of the situation. From what I gather, however, it seems to me safe to bring back those evacuated to Liangchiat'un but as there is little to do here at present and the Service is at no expense in keeping them at the Barrier, now they have arrived there, it is probably wiser to defer this move until the future is more certain and until I hear from you in reply to my proposals to transfer one Examiner and to replace a foreign Tidewaiter with one of Chinese nationality (my S/Os Nos. 114 and 117).

Yesterday a Russian Second Mate from a Chinese steamer escaped from Blagoveschensk to Taheiho and is being held by the local military until he obtains a guarantor. He was

F. W. Maze, Esquire,
SHANGHAI.

was employed on the S/S "Hung-tai" at the time she was seized by the Soviet and taken to Habarovsk. I have talked with her owner and he says that the Second Mate was confined until recently in a Habarovsk prison where he received a half a pound of bread per day for his rations. Recently he was transferred to the Blagoveschensk prison for some reason where he received only a quarter of a pound of black bread per day but was allowed out of the prison every day from 8 a.m. to 5 p.m. to obtain more food if possible by begging. However, the streets there were nearly deserted, little food was to be had at any cost (black bread is Roubles 1.50 per lb.) and he resolved to try and escape to the Chinese side. For some time he explored the bund there and ascertained that only two guards were stationed along it, one at the upper and one at the lower end of the city. While proceeding along the bund day before yesterday at 2 p.m. he noticed a small boy playing with a row boat and approached him asking for the loan of it. On the boy refusing he gave him some money and told him to go to the shops and buy some sweets and return. The boy departed at once on the errand when the Second Mate jumped into the boat and started rowing for this side. When half-way across a Soviet guard saw him and started firing. By good fortune he was

not

not hit and arrived safely just below Taheiho. As stated,
he reports the food situation to be very acute in Siberia.
The passengers seized near Blagovestchensk on the three
Chinese steamers have been sent to Habarovsk, according to
his statement, where they receive little food and are made
to work.

I am in close touch with Civil and Military
officials here and from I have been told and have observed
I am satisfied in my mind that there are no White Russian
bands operating along the Amur despite Soviet claims to
the contrary. Nor do I believe that there has been any
instances of Chinese troops crossing over to the Siberian
side of the Amur. Undisciplined Chinese troops at remote
places may have fired an occasional shot at passing Soviet
steamers but their provocation has been great as nearly all
outlying Chinese villages on the Amur seem to have been
attacked and looted in organised raids at different times
generally supported by Soviet gunboats and employing field
pieces. It is freely reported by those who have crossed over
from the other side that the young bloods of Blagovestchensk
have long wanted to attack this place and are only held
back by the older heads. Our protection here is the fact
that Blagovestchensk is within range of the Chinese guns and
she

she stands to lose much more in a bombardment than the
Chinese do. At Suifenho and Manchouli the Soviet soldiers
are not deterred by the close presence of a Soviet town
to the Chinese frontier.

A military supply train of some 150 carts arrived
yesterday from Tsitsihar. I am told that they brought a
great deal of much needed ammunition, hand grenades, Stokes
mortars, etc., and, what is also very important, a considerable
amount of money. You may remember I reported that during
the first panic all the banks destroyed their supplies of
bank notes leaving the community in a very difficult
financial position. The carts were 45 days in making the
journey from Tsitsihar, an eloquent testimonial of the
condition of the road, the average distance travelled per
day being some 7 miles!

APPOINTMENT OF MR. DAWSON-GROVE AS AIGUN COMMISSIONER: I duly
received your telegram of the 25th ultimo notifying me of
the appointment of Mr. Dawson-Grove from S.U.L. as my
successor. As he probably will not arrive in Shanghai much
before the 15th of October I do not expect him to put in
an appearance here before the 1st November by when, I trust,
the roads will be frozen and he can travel by motor car
in some comfort.

METEOROLOGICAL:

METEOROLOGICAL: I find that the total rainfall for the months of June, July, August and September for the last four years has been as follows:

1926	1927	1928	1929
10.50 in.	12.20 in.	27.18 in.	24.35 in.

As the normal figures for these months is some 10" it can be seen that the last two years have been exceptionally wet accounting for the floods and bad roads. The maximum temperature for this summer was only 89° F., the minimum in July and August being 55° F. As heavy frosts have now set in and a slight fall of snow occurred on the 26th September, we feel that we have been cheated out of our summer which we had looked forward to after being shut in by 7 months of winter weather. Yesterday small particles of ice appeared in the Amur some two weeks earlier than usual.

LOCAL: owing to the uncertain conditions and the prospects that they will be much worse when the river freezes and it can be easily crossed by looters from the Soviet side large numbers of people continue to leave the place for Harbin. As a consequence the streets are presenting a deserted appearance. In discussing the future of Taheiho with the Taoyin/Superintendent he deplored this as well as any reduction of the Customs Staff saying that just before the

the trouble began he had obtained a free hand from the Heilungchiang authorities to throw the frontier open to trade with the other side (my S/O No.110) through semi-official Chinese trade agencies which would have meant a big trade in grain, flour and certain other commodities and he still had high hopes of carrying out his plans if a turn came for the better in the present situation. As regards the Staff I told him that it could be easily strengthened on short notice if occasion arose and that there was always some reduction during the winter season.

Yours truly,

P.S. I received to-night an urgent telegram from Barentzen dated 3rd October to the effect that Manchouli had been fiercely bombarded and part of the Staff had been evacuated to Hailar. This news would indicate that the situation is far from being settled. Locally all still remains quiet.

第 119 号半官函   1929 年 10 月 3 日于瑷珲关

尊敬的梅乐和先生：

为中苏危机事：

自本人发出上一封半官函以来，边境地区一直较为平静，并未有何重要事情发生。信件自哈尔滨发出后仍需约 18 日方可送达，因此对于外界局势的发展趋势，本人依然无法及时收悉。不过，据目前所收到的信息判断，撤离至梁家屯分卡的关员似乎已可以返回大黑河，只是大黑河口岸目前并无太多公务需要办理，而且关员于梁家屯分卡停留期间的支出亦无须海关承担，因此兹认为，关员们既已留于梁家屯分卡，建议待局势更加稳定，待阁下下达关于调离一名验货员，委派一名华籍稽查员替代洋籍稽查员（参阅本人第 114 号及 117 号半官函）之指示后，再令关员们返回大黑河。

昨日，一名中国轮船的俄籍二副从布拉戈维申斯克（Blagovestchensk）逃至大黑河，现已被当地中国军方收押，待寻得担保人后方可获释。该名二副此前受雇于"鸿泰（Hung-tai）"号轮船，并在该轮船被苏联军队截获后被一并押往哈巴罗夫斯克（Habarovsk）。本人与"鸿泰"号轮船船主交谈后得知，该名二副此前一直被苏联当局关押在哈巴罗夫斯克的一座监狱之中，每日仅能获得半磅面包作为口粮。近日苏联当局出于某种原因将其转移至布拉戈维申斯克的监狱，在这里二副每日只能得到四分之一磅黑面包，但获准于每日早 8 时至晚 5 时去街上乞讨获取食物。然而现今布拉戈维申斯克的街道门可罗雀，无论花费多少卢布都无法换来食物（每磅黑面包需 1.50 卢布），因此二副决定想办法逃至黑龙江华岸地区。经过一段时日的探查后，二副确定布拉戈维申斯克堤岸上仅有两名警卫驻守，一名于上游驻守，一名于下游驻守。前日下午 2 时许，二副在堤岸附近乞讨时，发现一个小男孩正在划艇上玩耍，于是靠近向其借用划艇，遭到小男孩拒绝后，又拿出一些钱让他去店铺买些糖果回来。小男孩拿了钱后立即离开去买糖果，二副趁机跳上小船，向黑龙江华岸方向划去，不料划至江心时被苏联警卫发现，遭到扫射，所幸并未受伤且安全抵达大黑河下游地区。据悉，二副称，西伯利亚地区的粮食危机已十分严重，苏联当局已将在布拉戈维申斯克附近截获的三艘中国轮船上的乘客押送至哈巴罗夫斯克，乘客们只能获得很少的食物，还要被迫劳作。

本人一直与大黑河地区的文武各官保持密切联系，根据他们提供的消息和本人的切身观察，兹确信，黑龙江沿岸已无俄国"白军"，尽管苏联方面一直持反对观点。另外对于中国军队过江袭击西伯利亚地区的传闻，本人亦无法相信。当然，驻扎在边远地区的中国军队或因纪律性不强偶尔会对往来的苏联轮船开枪射击,但是黑龙江华岸几乎所有边远乡村都曾遭受过苏联炮艇的袭击和劫掠,与之相比中国军队的行为并不算是挑衅。据从黑龙江俄岸逃至大黑河的民众报告,布拉戈维申斯克的年轻人一直渴望进攻大黑河,但是当地的长者们纷纷劝阻不要鲁莽行事。苏联军队之所以一直未对大黑河发起进攻,是因为布拉戈维申斯克恰位于中国军队的射击范围之内,而且一旦发生轰炸事件,苏联方面的损失将远高于中方。而绥芬河和满洲里两地,因附近的中苏边境上并无苏联城镇,苏联军队方敢于对之进行轰炸。

昨日,一列由齐齐哈尔发出的载有军用物资的火车抵达大黑河。据称火车上载有军方急需的弹药、手榴弹、斯托克斯迫击炮等物资,更重要的是也带来了数量可观的经费。本人曾经汇报过,在大黑河地区第一次陷入恐慌时,本地区内的所有银行都将纸币尽数销毁,以致经济异常紧张。该列火车从齐齐哈尔出发后历经 45 日才抵达大黑河,火车平均每日的行进里程仅有约 7 英里! 由此证明自齐齐哈尔至大黑河的道路的确难行。

为克勒纳(H. Dawson-Grove)先生被任命为瑷珲关税务司事:

阁下 9 月 25 日电报收悉,内称已任命在江海关任上休假的克勒纳先生为瑷珲关新任税务司。鉴于其可能不会于 10 月 15 日之前抵达上海,因此推断其应不会于 11 月 1 日之前抵达大黑河。若如此,届时道路应已结冰,克勒纳先生可乘坐更为舒适的汽车来至大黑河。

为气象变化事:

经查,近四年来 6 月至 9 月的总降雨量如下所示:

1926 年	1927 年	1928 年	1929 年
10.60 英寸	12.20 英寸	27.18 英寸	24.35 英寸

正常而言,每年这四个月的总降雨量应在 10 英寸左右,但从数据可知,近两年的同期降雨量远超平均数额,因此导致洪水泛滥,道路难行。今年夏季的最高气温仅有 89 华氏度,7 月和 8 月的最低气温已降至 55 华氏度。如今已开始出现霜冻,9 月 26 日还迎来少量降雪,经历七个月严冬苦苦期盼的夏季就这样悄然离去。昨日黑龙江上已有浮冰出现,较往年提前了约两周时间。

为地方局势事:

由于地方局势发展一直不稳,待江面结冰后甚至会有恶化的可能,届时黑龙江俄岸的匪徒过江来袭亦会更加便利,因此大黑河地区的民众仍在大批量地向哈尔滨撤离,街道更是呈现一片荒芜的景象。与道尹兼海关监督讨论大黑河未来发展时,他认为形势不会一直如此,而且亦不赞成瑷珲关裁减关员。道尹表示,就在中苏危机爆发之前,其关于通过设立半官方中国贸易机构与苏方开展边境贸易之建议已获得黑龙江省政府的批准(参见本人第110号半官函),若可实行,中苏双方便可就粮食、面粉及其他特定货物开展大量贸易,而且其依然相信待局势稍有缓和后即可实现此项建议。至于瑷珲关裁减关员一事,本人已向其说明,如有贸易和征税需要,瑷珲关可随时增加人手,但冬季公务减少,的确经常会有裁减关员的情况。

您真挚的

铎博赉

注:本人今晚收到巴闰森(P. G. S. Barentzen)先生10月3日紧急电报,内称满洲里遭到猛烈炮击,部分关员已撤离至海拉尔避难。此则消息表明如今中苏局势并不安稳。不过,大黑河地区目前暂无任何异常。

14. 铎博赉致梅乐和函

（第120号半官函）

S/O No.120.

CUSTOM HOUSE.

Aigun   15th October, 1929.

Dear Mr. Maze,

SINO-SOVIET CRISIS: in my last S/O of the 3rd October I reported a continuation of the lull on this front and the receipt of an urgent wire from Barentsen that Manchouli had been bombarded on the 2nd instant and part of the Customs Staff had evacuated to Hailar. The situation here has continued quiet though tense and the last two days much excitement has prevailed over the news of a serious engagement at Lahasusu the reports being that 3 Chinese and 3 Soviet gunboats were sunk. The authorities at Chikote, a village some 100 miles below here, report the arrival of a Soviet gunboat with a small transport in tow loaded with infantry. The gunboat has anchored opposite Chikote and it remains to be seen what her object is in stopping there. As I write sounds of heavy guns can be heard down river.

STAFF: as time passes and the condition appears to grow more serious my concern about the safety of the

staff

F. W. Maze, Esquire,
SHANGHAI.

Staff increases. The situation of the Aigun Staff is different from that of the other ports in that it now requires not less than two weeks to reach Tsitsihar by cart and if evacuation is not carried out before hostilities begin their chances of reaching Harbin and safety are very small. Not to reach there would mean a severe winter in the mountains with only rude huts to live in and no foreign food. In I.G. S/O of the 18th September Mr. Walsham says that my recommendations about the strength of the Outdoor Staff will be acted on. I trust that this means the early transfer of Messrs. Ivanoff, Examiner A, and Pravikoff, 1st Class Tidewaiter (both with families). The Acting Tidesurveyor, Mr. H. A. Smith, has approached me with the query as to whether or not the Service would assist him toward the expenses of sending his wife and three children to Harbin for the winter (they are now at Liangchiat'un) as present prospects point to a condition here the next few months that will make life for foreign women and children extremely difficult. The place is being evacuated as rapidly as possible, all foreign women having left some time ago. I have told Mr. Smith that I would refer the question to you for your sympathetic consideration. The cost would

not

not be less than $350, equals Hk.Tls.150 at the present
rate of exchange.   The price of the necessities of life
such as flour, sugar, etc. are going up by leaps and bounds.
The financial situation, too, continues to be extremely
acute.   Funds were recently sent to the military but
local banks have only a limited supply and banks in other
places will not accept remittances on Taheiho so money
cannot be sent here.   The Bank of China has met the
demands of the Customs so far but it is not known how
long they can continue to do so.

Yours truly,

第 120 号半官函   1929 年 10 月 15 日于瑷珲关

尊敬的梅乐和先生：

为中苏危机事：

本人于上一封 10 月 3 日半官函中汇报称，大黑河地区局势持续平稳，巴闰森（P. G. S. Barentzen）先生发来紧急电报，告知满洲里于 10 月 2 日遭到苏联军队炮击，部分满洲里分关关员已撤离至海拉尔避难。目前，大黑河地区虽然并无任何异常，但形势依然紧张。两日前，中苏双方于拉哈苏苏激烈交战的消息传来后，当地又掀起一阵波澜。据报告称，在此次交战中，有两艘中国炮艇和三艘苏联炮艇沉船。位于大黑河下游约 100 英里处的奇克特村政府汇报称，发现一艘苏联炮艇拖拽一艘装载步兵的小型运输船向村庄靠近。该炮艇现已停靠于奇克特村对岸，目的为何还有待进一步查证。就在本人撰写此函之时，黑龙江下游地区传来巨大的枪炮声。

为人事事：

随着时间的推移，局势愈发严峻，本人也愈发担忧关员的人身安全。瑷珲关关区的关员情况与其他口岸不同，现今乘坐运货马车前往齐齐哈尔至少需要两周时间，如果不能在战争爆发前撤离大黑河，关员安全抵达哈尔滨的几率将会十分渺茫。如果未能撤离至哈尔滨，关员们将只能前往深山中度过严冬，居住简陋的棚屋，难觅日常所需的食物。在总税务司 9 月 18 日半官函中，华善（P. R. Walsham）先生曾表示日后可照本人建议调整瑷珲外班关员的人员配置。据此判断，相信一等验货员艾华诺（T. Ivanoff）先生和一等稽查员帕维各夫（V. V. Pravikoff）先生（均有家人相随）应可尽早调离。

日前，代理监察长施密（H. A. Smith）先生前来询问，鉴于未来数月的局势变化将不利于洋籍妇女和儿童继续在此地生活，不知海关是否可以出资协助其妻子和三个孩子前往哈尔滨过冬（如今他们都住在梁家屯分卡）。现今愈来愈多的民众开始迅速离开大黑河，所有洋籍妇女均已于此前离开此地。本人已告知施密先生会将此事提请总税务司裁定。预计其家人此次旅费不会少于 350 银圆，按照现行汇率计算，应为 150 海关两。

目前，大黑河地区的面粉和白糖等生活必需品的价格飞速上涨，经济形势也依旧十分严峻。虽然军队已经收到拨款，但是大黑河地区的银行所获数额却十分有限，其他地区的银行又不可能向大黑河汇款，因此本地根本无法获得钱款。不过到目前为止，中国银行一直按照海关要求提供资金，只是不知道还可以持续多久。

您真挚的

铎博赉

15. 铎博赉致梅乐和函

（第 121 号半官函）

S/O No. 121.

CUSTOM HOUSE.

Aigun 30th October, 1929.

Dear Mr. Maze.

SINO-SOVIET CRISIS: I have not addressed you semi-officially for some time as there has been nothing definite to report until the last few days. I duly received your two semi-official letters of the 2nd October and was greatly encouraged to learn that the action I had taken to secure the safety of the Staff and to keep the office going has your approval and that the conditions under which the Staff are carrying on meets with your sympathetic consideration. While it is true that this place has not been attacked openly, as have the other frontier places, still we have lived under the constant threat that it would be aggravated by the foreknowledge that our retreat will be cut off if it is. There is no hiding the fact that our nerves have suffered from the ordeal during the past 3½ months and that it would be well if all had a change.

In my last S/O I reported that the news of the bombardment of Lahasusu had just been received (15th October) and

F. W. Maze. Esquire,
SHANGHAI.

and that much excitement prevailed. Following the battle at that place the Soviet gunboats moved up in this direction and the local populace were in a panic for fear that our turn had come the evacuation of the place, which had been going on steadily since the trouble began, being greatly accelerated. The threat of the gunboats did not materialize, however, (though they came as far as Tahsiho) and we were left in peace until midnight of the 26th instant when sounds of rifle firing were heard in the western part of the town followed by a heavy explosion and more firing. Simultaneously with the explosion the lights went out. It occurred to me at once that the electric light station had been bombed but could not go out into the street to see what was happening as all was in darkness and firing was promiscuous. As it died down the sky was lighted up from a large fire and I soon learned that my surmise as to the destruction of the electric light station was correct. Next day full details were available. Five men, presumably Russians, disguised in the uniforms of Chinese soldiers, had calmly approached the station, shot the soldier and policeman on duty at the gate and had placed a bomb in the station near the boilers. The bomb was so large that it had to be carried by two men on a pole! The resulting

explosion

explosion was tremendous wrecking the whole plant and
starting a fire that practically completed the work of
destruction. Many windows were broken in the Custom
House a quarter of a mile away. The plant was a large
one valued at some $250,000 local money. In the confusion
none of the conspirators were caught. That such a thing
could happen, after all the other attempts with bombs that
have been made in the town, reveals a lamentable and
characteristic lack of preparedness and alertness on the
part of the military. Since the incident, reported to
you in my telegram of the 28th instant, the town is in
complete darkness at night and it is extremely dangerous
now to move on the streets after 6 p.m. for fear those on
guard will mistake one for the enemy. The stock of kerosene
lamps in the town was very limited and of an inferior quality
but the Customs has secured a supply of sorts to carry on
with.

The ice began to drift heavily on the 28th
instant, the same date as last year, and the thermometer has
dropped to +11° F. In ten days the river should be frozen
over solidly enough to be crossed anywhere. When this
occurs it is expected, with every reason, that Soviet raids
will begin in earnest and that life along the frontier here
will

will be increasingly dangerous. The soldiers in Taheiho
cannot number more than 1,500 with (say) another thousand
within a few miles on either side. This force is not
large enough to make any resistance if a determined attack
is made by the Soviet troops.

I had a long interview with the Taoyin/
Superintendent yesterday and he deplores the situation
Taheiho is in as regards means of defense. I asked him if
he had any plan for evacuation in case of attack pointing out
that should one come in the night it would be impossible
for civilians to leave the place without some prearranged
scheme as the Chinese soldiers would probably fire at
everyone they saw on the streets as they did on the night
of the raid on the electric light station. He agreed that
some plan should be worked out with the military and said
he would call a meeting shortly to discuss the subject.
He also said that if the situation became very serious the
military would remove their Headquarters back a few miles
from the frontier and that his and the Customs Staffs
could go with them. Such a dropping back of the Headquarters
would presuppose the evacuation of Taheiho by all but the
military and in such a case the Customs would have to
leave. However, in the case of raids, such as are now
occurring

occurring on the Sungari and at Moho upriver, we would have
no warning and the chances are that the place would be
surrounded at night and our retreat would be cut off. If
such a situation arises it remains to be seen if the name
of the Customs would be any protection.

If war is not declared any fighting that may
occur here will only be along the frontier and if there is
warning the Customs Staff can be evacuated back into the
hills a few miles (possibly with the military) to await
developments. To live under such conditions for long,
however, would be extremely difficult owing to poor
accommodation, extreme cold, scarcity of food and bad
characters.

If war is declared, as now seems very possible,
the nearest place of safety for the Staff is Harbin.
Tsitsihar will not be safe as it will be the first objective
of the Soviet from Manchouli while the region between
Taheiho and Tsitsihar will be a theatre of war as the winter
road connecting the two places will be a route of great
strategic importance in these days of rapid motor
transportation. To fail to reach Harbin would mean a life
of indescribable hardship in the mountains, as just described.
If motor cars could be engaged the trip to Harbin could

be

be made in three days. But, as the supply is very limited,
it is highly probable that they will all be seized by the
military in a crisis and the only means of transportation
would be carts requiring a minimum of ten days for the trip.
And carts are now very scarce and difficult to hire.

As the post still requires some 14 days enroute
from Harbin, I continue to be that much behind the trend
of events. Under such circumstances I cannot plan ahead
for the safety of Staff. Mr. Barentsen is very good in
keeping me advised telegraphically of events as they happen
but he cannot be expected, under present circumstances, to
venture information as to the general situation and probable
developements as it is so difficult to know what is going
on behind the scenes. However, he is probably in the best
position to study the situation (especially if the Mukden
Government has declared its independence as is rumoured)
and as he has been stationed at Taheiho and understands
conditions here it would be well, in my opinion, if he could
be instructed by yourself to consider Aigun in the same
category as his out-stations during the present crisis and
to keep me informed of the trend of events, in addition to
actual happenings, and that he should recommend to you the
evacuation of Aigun if, and when, the general situation

warranted

warranted it, bearing in mind the time required to reach Harbin after the warning is received. This arrangement would relieve me of a great deal of worry and I could confine my anxieties to coping with local emergencies as they arose. I.G. despatch No. 1/85,630 to Aigun instructs that, though Aigun is to be independent of Harbin in the future, the Harbin Commissioner may be said to stand *in loco parentis* to his colleague at Aigun.

I need hardly assure you that the evacuation of Aigun is the last thing I wish to do but if the place becomes untenable I consider that Service interests would best be served by closing the Custom House temporarily and moving the Staff to a place of safety where they can continue to be of use to the Service instead of wintering in the mountains. I wrote you early in the crisis that I may be able to get into touch with the attackers after the first rush is over. Since then experience has shown that the Soviet raiding parties are largely composed of Cossacks, Chinese and Koreans of the renegade type, out for looting and killing, and the chances of their distinguishing between foreigners and White Russians is very small. The Chinese Staff, of course, would be treated by them like the rest of the population.

I

I have thought the last two days to lay the situation before you telegraphically and may do so yet with the request that you instruct Mr. Barentsen as recommended above. There is the question, of course, as to how the Superintendent may view the matter of the evacuation of the Customs Staff but he may be counted on to do the reasonable thing. I think that if the Customs decided to leave he would be the first to go if, indeed, he had not already left. I hope I do not sound panicky in what I write (I am freely criticized for not appearing to take conditions more seriously) but the situation seems daily to become more acute. The military has news of continued serious fighting down river along the Sungari as far as Fukochin and that a large force of some 800 has crossed up river at Moho and is trying to occupy that place. With the river about to close there is no reason why similar activities should not be started here. To read the newspapers an outsider would get the impression that conditions were not very serious on the frontier, battles like that at Lahasusu being dismissed in an obscure paragraph.

A continuous stream of carts is now leaving Taheiho for Tsitsihar due to firmer roads and the fear of
what

what may happen after the Amur freezes. By the time the
river is frozen there will be few civilians left. Following
the bombing of the electric plant all Russians with Soviet
passports, most of whom are Whites at heart, were arrested.
Many have since been released and the balance will be on
the production of acceptable guarantees, but all Russians,
whether White or Red, are now being compelled to leave
Taheiho for Harbin within three days. Messrs. Smith,
Snow and myself will soon be the only non-Chinese here.

I had heard many rumours that the Bank of
China was about to close and interviewed the Manager
yesterday. He told me that his instructions were to
continue here as long as the other banks remained open and
that his plans were uncertain. As all business has come
to a standstill, however, the other banks may decide to
move to Tsitsihar, where their Head Offices are, at any
time. If the banks go it will be very difficult to
finance the Customs. I could only do it by keeping cash
in hand and this would be extremely dangerous under present
conditions.

The food situation, which I have remarked on
before, grows increasingly acute. Shops have practically
all evacuated so that very little is obtainable and the

one

one butcher's stall remaining open may close at any time.
Naturally the price of things mount as they grow more
scarce; Chinese feeling the pinch as well as foreigners.

STAFF: owing to the gloomy outlook and the
close of navigation I wired you on the 20th instant
recommending the transfer of Messrs. Pravikoff and Bulgakoff,
1st Class Tidewaiters, and was very glad to get your
instructions the next day appointing them to Shanghai. At
the time I received your despatch transferring Mr. T. Ivanoff,
Examiner A, to Ningpo. All these employees had been evacuated
to Liangchiat'un early in the crisis as already reported.
They left on the 28th instant overland on a two weeks
journey with a cavalcade of 8 carts, one of which was loaded
with my personal effects. I regret to report that Mr. Ivanoff
was unreasonable in his demands for transportation before
he left and that I had to reprimand him for his manner of
addressing the Tidesurveyor. I would not mention the matter
were it not for the fact that his attitude has been anything
but helpful to his colleagues while they were occupying the
cramped quarters at Liangchiat'un.

While on the subject of the reduction in staff,
I should report that I came to the conclusion, even before

the

the present crisis set in, that it was not necessary to have
both a Writer and a Ho Shui-yüan to take care of the small
amount of Chinese secretarial work now required. The Ho Shui-
yüan, Mr. Li Yung-p'o, is a hard working and capable employee
and might well be transferred to another port at any time,
if convenient to the Service, leaving the Writer, Yang Ts'un-
hou to carry on by himself.

On the 22nd instant I received a wire from Mr.
Fletcher at Ichang inquiring as to the route beyond Tsitsihar
from which I concluded that the appointment of Mr. Dawson-
Grove had been cancelled. As this will mean a further delay,
owing to the remoteness of Ichang, I am concerned about my
family whom I had thought to join before this. They have
been waiting in Blagovestchensk for me since they were taken
from the Chinese steamer on the 16th July it having been
arranged that I should go from here to Japan and thence via
Vladivostock to a junction near Blagovestchensk where they
could join me and we could continue via Siberia to Europe.
I should have sent them to Japan to await me there but I
had to consider the expense. As the Japanese Consul was
looking after them in Blagovestchensk, and I have been in
touch with him through the Consular Authorities at Harbin,
and

and as my wife preferred staying there in preference to
Japan, I have let them remain though I have not been at all
easy regarding her situation . I have had no time nor occasion
as yet to arrange anything in advance for my passages, etc.,
and may have to do some telegraphing to the Inspectorate
at the last minute.

I was very gratified to learn that I had received
a promotion through the creation of new ranks for the Foreign
Indoor Staff. This addition to my pay will be a great help
to me when I am on home leave as will your generous act in
fixing home pay at the rate of $10.00 to the Pound Stirling.

I duly informed Mr. Acting Tidesurveyor Smith
of your sanction of his request that he might evacuate his
family to Harbin at Service expense. He has not sent them
away yet, though I have strongly advised him to do so, as he
is doubtful if he can meet the expensive living conditions
in Harbin. They are at Liangchiat'un at present.

A copy of this S/O is being sent to Mr. Barentsen
for his possible comments.

Yours truly,

Tientsin

Tientsin papers just received report the bombardment of Taheiho on the 14th instant. Needless to say there is no truth in the report or I would have informed you. It may develop, however, to have been "an intelligent anticipation of events".

第 121 号半官函   1929 年 10 月 30 日于瑷珲关

尊敬的梅乐和先生：

为中苏危机事：

因近半个月以来，大黑河并无值得汇报之事，故未向阁下发送半官函。阁下两封 10 月 2 日半官函已收悉，内称对本人为保护关员安全，确保瑷珲关正常运营所采取的各项举措表示支持，对瑷珲关关员的处境深表同情。本人因此备受鼓舞。虽然大黑河未如其他边境城镇一样遭到苏联军队的攻击，但本地区的民众依然生活在被苏联进攻的威胁之中，皆知一旦受到攻击，撤离路线就会被阻断。在过去的三个半月中，关员们一直生活在担惊受怕之中，如果局势有所好转，相信紧张情绪应会得到缓解。

本人于上一封 10 月 15 日半官函中汇报称，拉哈苏苏遭到轰炸的消息传来后，当地又掀起一阵波澜。中苏双方于拉哈苏苏交战结束后，苏联炮艇便向黑龙江上游进发，大黑河民众再次陷入恐慌，担心炮艇会攻击大黑河，于是此前一直稳步进行的撤离活动因此而变得更加迅速。不过之后，当地民众对苏联炮艇的担忧并未成为现实（虽然苏联炮艇已来至大黑河附近），形势依然较为平稳。然而就在本月 26 日午夜，大黑河西部突然传来巨大的爆炸声，随即又传来交火和步枪射击的声音。在爆炸声传来的同时，电灯也突然熄灭。本人当时预感到应是供电站遭到炸弹攻击，但因当时情况十分危急，外面一片漆黑，枪击声此起彼伏，无法到街道上探查究竟。爆炸声和枪击声消失后，天空又被一场大火照得通亮。随后很快传来消息，的确如本人猜测一样，是供电站遭到了袭击。

次日，本人了解到了爆炸事件的详细情况。当时有五名匪徒，据称可能是苏联人，身着中国士兵的军装，从容地走近供电站，击毙了门口值班的士兵和警察后，进入供电站在锅炉附近安置了一枚炸弹。此枚炸弹十分沉重，需由两个人使用木棍才能抬动，而且威力巨大，炸毁了整个供电站，爆炸发生后引起的火灾又将整个供电站烧成废墟。海关办公楼距离供电站有 0.25 英里，但许多窗户都已被震碎。供电站总价值约达哈大洋 250000 元。据悉，事发后匪徒趁乱逃离了现场。

此次爆炸事件的发生表明中国军方对突发事件毫无警觉，未能事先做好应对预案。自爆炸事件发生以来（已于 10 月 28 日通过电报呈报），夜幕降临后，大黑河便完全陷入黑暗之中。每晚 6 时天黑以后再到街上行走便会十分危险，随时可能被警卫误认为是敌人而遭到射击。大黑河镇内煤油灯的存货量十分有限，质量也很差。所幸瑷珲关还有一定存量，暂时无忧。

10月28日，黑龙江上出现大量浮冰（与去年时间相同），本地区的气温也降至零下11华氏度。十日之后，江面应会全部结冰，足供行人安全行走。一旦江面结冰，苏联方面很有可能会开始突袭，黑龙江华岸各地居民的生命将受到严重威胁。大黑河现有兵力不足1500人，据称上游或下游地区还有1000余名士兵。但如果苏联军队发动进攻，此等兵力根本不足以抵抗。

昨日与道尹兼海关监督进行了长谈，道尹对大黑河的防御办法亦有谴责之意。本人询问其是否已有应对苏联军队攻击的撤离方案，指出如果夜间遭到苏军突袭，没有应对预案，民众恐怕难以安全撤离，因为中国士兵很有可能会向出现在街道上的任何一个人开枪射击，就像供电站发生爆炸当晚的情形一样。道尹表示的确应与军方商讨制订一套撤离方案，并称会尽快召开会议讨论此事，还指出如果局势发展到十分严重的地步，军方会将司令部撤离至距离边境数英里以外之地，届时政府官员和海关关员可与之一同撤离。若如此，则意味着除军方，其他一干人等均须撤离大黑河，也就是说届时海关必须撤离。不过如果大黑河与松花江和漠河上游地区一样遭遇苏联军队突袭，事先根本不会收到任何警报，而且很有可能会于夜间被苏军包围，退路亦会被阻断。如果发生上述情况，海关之名能否为关员提供保护，实难确定。

如果中苏双方不宣战，所有对战都将仅限于边境沿线。如能提前收到警报，海关关员便可暂时撤退至数英里以外的群山之中避难（可能与军方一同撤离），等待局势转好。然而山中住宿环境极差，天气又极其寒冷，再加上食物紧缺，匪徒横行，长期居住，必是艰难无比。

如果中苏双方宣战（依照当前形势判断极有可能发生），于瑷珲关关员而言，最近的安全避难之地便是哈尔滨。至于齐齐哈尔，届时必会成为苏联军队自满洲里进攻内陆地区的首要目标，绝对不会安全。大黑河与齐齐哈尔之间的区域必会成为主战区，因为冬季期间两地之间的道路可供汽车快速通行，是极其重要的战略路线。如果无法及时到达哈尔滨，瑷珲关关员们就只能如上所述撤离至深山之中艰难度日。若可雇用到汽车，三日便可到达哈尔滨，只是目前当地汽车数量十分有限，而且危机一旦爆发，很有可能会被当地军方征用，届时海关唯一的交通工具就是运货马车，如此一来至哈尔滨的行程便将延长至十日。但是目前，本地区所余运货马车业已为数不多，很难租到。

如今邮政信件自哈尔滨发出后仍需十四日方可送达大黑河，本人依然无法及时知悉时局的发展趋势，因此亦无法为保障关员的安全提前制定方案。凡有事件发生后，巴闰森（P. G. S. Barentzen）先生都会通过电报告知本人，但对于局势的总体情况和日后发展趋势，因目前形势如此，难以知晓暗中是否有何秘密进行之事，他亦无法提供相关信息。不过，巴闰森先生可能更便于调查局势发展趋势（尤其如果奉天当局如传闻所述已宣布独立），而且还曾驻于大黑河，十分了解本地区的情况，故此认为，阁下若可指令其在中苏危机期间暂时将瑷珲关视为滨江关分关，除实事，还可随时发来局势发展趋势的相关信息，待因形势变化瑷珲关需要撤离之时，再于考虑瑷珲关自收到警报到抵达哈尔滨所需时间后，向阁下呈请批准，必将更为有益。若可如此安排，本人便可将精力从撤离一事上转移出来，集中应对当地需要处理的紧急事件。海关总税务司公署第 1/85630 号令曾指示，瑷珲关虽将自哈尔滨关独立出来，但哈尔滨关税务司对瑷珲关税务司仍有顾问资格。

诚然，本人亦不愿撤离瑷珲关，但是如果大黑河地区失守，为维护海关利益起见，最好还是暂时关闭瑷珲关，将瑷珲关关员撤离到较为安全的地方避难，以便继续为海关工作，而不是前往深山中过冬。本人曾于危机爆发之初向阁下致函表示或许可于苏联军队第一次进攻结束后，与其指挥官取得联系，请其保护海关安全。然嗣后才发现，苏联的突袭部队中有哥萨克人、叛变的中国人和朝鲜人。他们抵达黑龙江华岸地区后便开始抢掠财物，屠杀百姓，根本不会区分外国人和俄国"白军"，对待华籍关员的态度与对待百姓的态度也并无不同。

本想于前两日通过电报呈报近期的局势发展，现今借此机会详细汇报，特此申请按照上述建议对巴闰森先生下达指令。虽不知海关监督将会如何看待瑷珲关关员撤离大黑河之事，但相信其应会予以支持。兹认为，如果海关决定撤离大黑河，海关监督届时若仍在本地，应会加入第一批撤离队伍当中。

希望阁下不会通过此函认为本人已开始恐慌，（若通过此函批评本人对现今的局势未能给予足够的重视，本人欣然接受），不过本地区的局势确实已经日益严峻。军方收到消息，松花江下游至富克锦一段区域的战况依然十分激烈，另外已有 800 余名苏联士兵在黑龙江上游过江抵达漠河，现下正在试图攻占该镇。江面即将结冰，苏联军队很有可能会以同样的办法进攻大黑河。外界通过报纸可能会认为边境地区的局势并不危急，毕竟像拉哈苏苏那样的战事在报纸上的报道都十分模糊，根本无法引人注意。

如今通往齐齐哈尔的道路更加便于通行，当地民众因担心黑龙江结冰后苏联军队会趁机采取行动，纷纷租用运货马车撤离大黑河。待黑龙江完全结冰之时，大黑河的居民应已所剩无几。供电站发生爆炸后，凡持苏联护照的俄人均被逮捕，其中多数为俄国"白军"的支持者，不过嗣后已有很多人被释放，其余人等在出具合理担保后亦将获释。如今，大黑河当局已下令，命所有俄人，无论为"白军"支持者或为"红军"支持者，均须于三日之内离开大黑河前往哈尔滨。不日之后，施密（H. A. Smith）先生、思诺（H. W. Snow）先生和本人将成为大黑河地区仅存的洋籍居民。

因有谣言盛传中国银行即将关闭，本人遂于昨日与中国银行大黑河支行经理会面，得知其收到的指示为只要大黑河其他银行继续营业，中国银行便不得关门，但具体如何安排，现下还不确定。目前本地区贸易均处于停滞状态，其他银行随时都有可能决定撤离至其总行所在地齐齐哈尔。银行搬离后，瑷珲关将难以寻得资金来源维持日常所需。本人能够想到的应对之策唯有预留足够现金，不过在当前情况下，亦是极其危险之举。

本人此前曾汇报过大黑河的粮食危机，而近期该危机更是愈演愈烈。所有粮店都已经撤离大黑河，居民们可以获得的粮食少之又少，唯一营业的肉铺也有随时关闭的可能。粮食、肉类的价格自然也因为稀缺而猛增；如今中国人和洋人的生活都十分拮据。

为人事事：

鉴于当前形势不甚明朗，航运亦已关闭，本人遂于10月20日向阁下发送电报，建议将一等稽查员帕维各夫（V. V. Pravikoff）先生和卜乐喀郭夫（S. M. Bulgakoff）先生调离瑷珲关。次日收到阁下将两名关员调至江海关的指令后，甚为欢喜。与此同时，阁下关于将一等验货员艾华诺（T. Ivanoff）先生调往浙海关的令文业已收悉。

如此前汇报所述，以上三名关员均早于中苏危机爆发之初撤离至梁家屯分卡。10月28日，帕维各夫先生、卜乐喀郭夫先生和艾华诺先生雇用8辆运货马车携家人经由陆路出发，开始了为期两周的行程，其中1辆运货马车装有本人的私人物品。特此遗憾汇报，艾华诺先生在离开前对撤离的交通方式提出了无理要求，又对监察长出言不逊，为此，本人已将其斥责。若不是因艾华诺先生的态度对在梁家屯分卡避难的关员百害而无一利，本人亦不会呈报此事。

至于裁减瑷珲关关员一事，兹认为，即使是在中苏危机爆发之前，瑷珲关少量的汉文文案工作亦无须由汉文文牍员和核税员两人共同处理。核税员李永坡先生十分勤勉，亦很有能力，可根据公务需要随时调往其他口岸任职，汉文文牍员杨存厚先生可留在瑷珲关独自处理文案工作。

本月22日收到富乐嘉（H. G. Fletcher）先生从宜昌关发来询问自齐齐哈尔至大黑河路线的电报后，本人猜测，阁下已经取消了对克勒纳（H. Dawson-Grove）先生的任命。然因宜昌关与大黑河距离遥远，富乐嘉先生抵达此地的时间还将延后，本人着实担心不能按照约定时间与家人会合。

自7月16日本人家人乘坐的中国轮船被苏联当局截获以来，他们一直滞留在布拉戈维申斯克（Blagovestchensk），等待与本人会合。而本人亦已计划好先自大黑河前往日本，经符拉迪沃斯托克（Vladivostock）到达布拉戈维申斯克附近，待与他们会合后再经西伯利亚前往欧洲。此前本应先将家人送往日本，但在费用方面还是有所顾虑，之后他们又得到驻布拉戈维申斯克日本领事的照顾，本人亦可通过驻哈尔滨领事与之保持联络，而妻子也更愿意留在布拉戈维申斯克而非日本，本人便暂且同意如此安排，不过还是很难知悉他们的处境。鉴于目前已无时间预先安排离开大黑河之后的行程等事，恐怕只得于最后关头再向海关总税务司公署发送电报请示批准。

得知本人因洋籍内班关员改制已获擢升，甚为欢喜。而阁下又慷慨地将休假期间的薪俸发放汇率调整为 10.00 银圆兑换 1 英镑，这将为本人休假返家期间带来极大的帮助。

本人已告知代理监察长施密先生，阁下已批准由海关支付其家人撤离至哈尔滨的旅费，业已强烈建议其家人尽快动身，但是施密先生担心无法承担家人在哈尔滨高昂的生活费用，因此迟迟未能出发，现仍居住在梁家屯分卡。

此函抄件已发送给巴闰森先生，以征询意见。

您真挚的

铎博赉

据刚刚收到的天津报纸报道，本月 14 日大黑河发生爆炸事件。显然该报道毫无事实依据，如有此等事件发生，本人此前便会向阁下汇报。不过该报道或已演变成为"对实事的明智预判"。

16. 富乐嘉致梅乐和函

（第 124 号半官函）

S/O No.124.

CUSTOM HOUSE,

Aigun(Harbin) 16th January, 30.

Dear Mr. Maze,

GENERAL CONDITIONS IN AND WITH REGARD TO THE AIGUN OFFICE: I have now had time to have a good look at things in the office and to make myself acquainted with the conditions governing our return to Aigun (Taheiho). It is my present intention to return to Aigun when the river opens again in the spring. There is not much object in going earlier since there will be no collection before then; the hardships of the overland journey are very real; that route is reported unsafe for person or property owing to bandits; and a Staff has yet to be appointed and collected. As regards the office, there is at present only one Linguist, Chang Yuan Yang, 3rd Clerk B, and he is here with me in Harbin. I have written to you about him officially in my despatch No.464 and I hope that you will be able to do something for this deserving and intelligent employee who has borne so disproportionately large a share both of the hardships and of the actual

work

F. W. Maze, Esquire,
etc. etc. etc.
SHANGHAI.

work of the last half-year. He works willingly, energetically and for long hours but, owing, I suppose, to the successive withdrawals from Aigun since last July of member after member of the Indoor Staff, the condition of affairs inside the office is nothing less than tragic. The I.G. Official, semi-official and circular indices and the non-urgent correspondence register have not been written up since last May. The capture by the Soviets of the original copy of I.G. Circular No.3919 caused the September Quarter Accounts to be made up on the old lines; they have not yet been despatched and must be revised as soon as the necessary time can be found; such cognate matters as the necessary revision (July 1928 - June 1929) of the June Quarter's cumulative account on the Abstract Sheets and the compilation on the same lines of the Annual Summary and Statement and of the Annual River Dues (local moneys) Account have been attended to during the past fortnight, some by Chang, some by myself. Till those were done, the Annual Budget could not be framed; it will now be done as soon as possible. We are doing our best to clean things up but Chang is finding it next to impossible to tackle the back work and at the same time carry on the current work including all quarterly and Annual Reports and including the

Annual

Annual Trade Returns - for him the last straw - of which
he has absolutely no experience.   I have therefore wired
you requesting the immediate reappointment of Wang Te-mao,
2nd Clerk A, who is a Returns expert, knows the Aigun
General Office work, and possesses that knowledge of
Russian which is very necessary for the General Office
and which was specially solicited in Aigun despatch No.54,
§ 12, when the Staff required for the River Dues Collection
was stated.

    May the Audit Secretary be shown this letter, please.

    Your truly,

第 124 号半官函　　　　　　　　　　　　　　1930 年 1 月 16 日于瑷珲关（哈尔滨）

尊敬的梅乐和先生：

为瑷珲关办事处现状及相关事务事：

本人现下终于有时间仔细查看瑷珲关（哈尔滨）办事处的情况，以便熟悉各项事务，为日后返回大黑河做好准备。依照目前情况来看，兹计划，待今年春季航运开通后再行返回大黑河，一则因在此之前大黑河口岸无税可征，二则若通过陆路返回，路途着实艰难，且据报沿途常有匪徒出没，人财往来皆十分危险，再则瑷珲关人员配置尚不齐全，有待重新任命安排。

至于办公方面，目前仅有一名通事与本人留于哈尔滨办理瑷珲关各项事务，即三等二级税务员张远扬先生。本人已于瑷珲关第 464 号呈中正式汇报过张远扬先生的情况，近半年来，其承担了瑷珲关实际工作的大半，历尽艰辛，还望阁下可予以嘉奖。张远扬先生才智过人，对待工作能够做到全心全意的投入，而且自去年 7 月起，瑷珲关内班关员相继离开，相信各项事务已是乱无头绪。自去年 5 月起，海关总税务司公署令文、半官函及通令的索引和非紧急中文往来函摘由簿便再未更新。由于海关总税务司公署第 3919 号通令抄件被苏方截获，瑷珲关第三季度账簿只得按照此前规定编制，不过账簿目前尚未呈交，待时间允许时将立即修改。过去两周间，张远扬先生和本人已分别完成了一些必要的修订（因 1928 年 7 月至 1929 年 6 月间的账目需要调整）和编撰工作，包括收支总簿中第二季度累计账目的修订和年度财务报表及年度江捐（地方公款）账簿的编制。上述工作完成后，年度预算的编制工作方可开始，如今已尽快赶制。

吾等已竭力厘清各项事务，但张远扬先生发现难以同时处理旧时积压与当前需要完成之工作，这其中包括所有的季度、年度报告，以及其从未接触过的年度贸易统计表，压力着实不小。有鉴于此，本人已向阁下发送电报请求立即将二等一级税务员王德懋先生调回，因其不仅善于编制报表，熟悉瑷珲关总务课的各项事务，而且还精通俄文，这一点于总务课工作而言十分重要。瑷珲关第 54 号呈（第 12 项）在汇报瑷珲关江捐征收工作人员需求时，特别提出大黑河口岸需要一名精通俄文的税务员。

烦请将此函亦交与会计科税务司查阅。

您真挚的

富乐嘉

17. 富乐嘉致梅乐和函

（第 127 号半官函）

S/O No. 127.

CUSTOM HOUSE.

Aigun(Harbin) 14th March, 19 30.

Dear Mr. Maze,

Opening of through traffic to Aigun and return of In-door Department thither: I sent you a long telegram on the 6th March 1930 but have so far had no reply. The situation therein outlined arose suddenly. I have little to add to what I said therein, succinctly but, I hope, clearly enough. I could not promise when navigation would open, there were many reasons why an immediate return was inadvisable, yet I did not want you to think that I was gallivanting in this centre and delaying our return to my post. This has, in fact, been a most unfortunate position in which I have found myself: I would much sooner be settled down in my own home in Aigun than be a vagrant in Harbin, but I am only just now approaching the end of my labours clearing up the accounts etc. mess that was left in the wake of the evacuation - and I do not want it all over again in in a hurry!

Quite

F. W. Maze, Esquire,
　　etc. etc. etc.,
　　S H A N G H A I.

Quite possibly things will turn out all right after all. Who can predict either way? Some say the Russians will allow Amur navigation by Chinese in return for Sungari navigation by themselves. Some say the Chinese steamers will not enter the Amur till either the Soviet—captured ships are returned or immunity from further capture is guaranteed. And when will all this be decided? Before, or at, the Moscow Conference? And when will that be held? How big a pawn in the game is Chinese navigation of the Amur anyway? Will it be considered as a special and urgent question, or will it be allowed to lapse for the time being? Who can say? Meanwhile, I would say that we will go there as soon as ever we can with some degree of comfort and safety.

Later: I have just sent you a telegram that the Superintendent, who is still at Moukden, has got out of going to Moscow after all but will remain here in Harbin endeavouring to arrange with Russian authorities (Consul here and Consul-General at Moukden) for Chinese vessels to ply on the Amur

Yours truly,

[signature]

第 127 号半官函   1930 年 3 月 14 日于瑷珲关（哈尔滨）

尊敬的梅乐和先生：

为至瑷珲关区的直通路线开通及瑷珲关内班关员返回大黑河事：

兹已于 1930 年 3 月 6 日向阁下发送电报一封，但是迄今仍未收到回复。电报中所述之情况事发突然，本人的叙述已经尽量简明扼要，几无需要补充之内容。

航运何时能够开通，根本无法确定，不宜立即返回瑷珲关区的原因亦有很多，但希望阁下不要认为本人是在哈尔滨闲游，是在故意拖延返回大黑河任职的时间。实际上，本人目前的状况最为可悲，在哈尔滨就像一个流浪者，真心希望能够早日返回大黑河安稳下来，只是现下刚刚整理完瑷珲关撤离期间混乱不堪的账目等工作，已是精疲力竭，实不希望再次陷入仓促混乱的局面！

当然或许形势终会好转，但谁又能够预料呢？有人称，苏方会同意中国船只在黑龙江上航行，以换取自己在松花江上航行的权利，有人称，在苏方将此前截获的中国轮船释放之前，或是承诺不会再有此等截获行为之前，中国轮船不会再进入黑龙江航行。而这一切究竟何时会有定论？在莫斯科会议之前还是期间？莫斯科会议何时会召开？中国轮船在黑龙江上的航行问题在会议上能有多重要？属于特别紧急议题？还是可以暂且搁置？谁能确定？不过，吾等定会在情况允许之时，在确保旅途较为安全且不必遭受太多艰难之时，尽快返回。

附记：业已向阁下发送电报汇报，现今仍在奉天停留的海关监督已不必前往莫斯科谈判，将留在本地与苏联当局（驻哈尔滨苏联领事及驻奉天苏联总领事）商议中国船只在黑龙江上航行之事。

您真挚的

富乐嘉

18. 富乐嘉致梅乐和函

（第 132 号半官函）

CUSTOM HOUSE,

S/O No.132   A I G U N 15th July 1930.

Dear Mr. Maze,

TRADE: RESTRICTED IMPORTS ALLOWED. On 7th July I received a letter from the Mayor allowing a specified amount of imports (Soda, 100 boxes; Soap, 20 boxes; Kerosene, 1,000 cases; Benzine, 36,000 lbs; Sugar, 36,000 lbs; Medicine, 5 bundles) under his Huchao and on payment, of course, of duties and River Dues. This, at any rate, is a beginning but I have little hope that the frontier will be opened as far as this side is concerned unless the other side proves itself more amenable to the renewal of the Aids Agreement on which the Mayor has set his heart. Russia is now quite ready for a certain amount of trade -- to be conducted, of course, through the Government Trade Bureau -- but it is China who holds back.

DUTY FREE PRIVILEGES: The Superintendent asked for the duty free privilege on some benzine sold him by the Blago authorities and privately brought over from the other side of the river for him, practically smuggled, in fact. There is no general official trade at present, so that no vessels can officially enter from or clear

for the other side. Any such amenities between the officials of the two nations must, therefore, be arranged more or less surreptitiously. After a friendly personal argument, I agreed on the understanding that such an attitude on my part only holds good so long as the frontier is officially closed and the opportunities for such transactions are rare. He also asked for the same privilege for some benzine similarly brought over for the Soviet Consul, basing his request on the plea that the Blago Authorities allow free importation to the Chinese Consul-General and Japanese Consul. Again I agreed. Such small concessions oil the wheels enormously and cause the revenue but little loss, especially under present conditions when trade is officially prohibited.

CHINESE CONSUL-GENERAL AT BLAGOVESTCHENSK: The newly appointed Chinese Consul-General to Blagovestchensk, Mr. Ch'üan Shih-en (權世恩), together with the Vice-Consul Chang Ta-tien (張大田) and suite, arrived here on 9th July and crossed to the other side on 11th. We exchanged calls here and they came over and dined with me on the 12th, proving to be very pleasant companions.

CUSTOMS MOTOR-LAUNCH: The Ferry boat that used to run between Taheiho and Blagovestchensk last year and that was then captured by the Russians was the only means of communication except the Customs and the Soviet

F. W. Maze, Esquire,
    Inspector General of Customs,
        S H A N G H A I

Consul's

Consul's motor-launches. The fare was $2.00 per crossing
for non-officials and $1.00 per crossing for officials.
Even then the loan of our motor-launch was quite
frequently asked for by officials, and my predecessor
suggested the propriety of a charge which was agreed to
but never enforced. This year, however, owing to there
being no ferry boat, such loan requests(principally from
the Superintendent) are becoming more frequent, and will
become still more so now that the Chinese Consulate-
General on the other side is reopened. I therefore
verbally informed the Superintendent(=Mayor) that our
finances could not stand the racket and that I should
be obliged to make a charge of $1.00 per crossing to
cover cost of running (that is just about what it does
cost); that I would willingly lend the launch to himself
and other officials (including Blago Consul-General) under
those conditions provided that she was not wanted by us
and that it was understood that she is not a ferry boat
and that the loan of her is a favour to be asked for
of me personally each time; but that as a courtesy to
him as Superintendent I would not charge him when he
went personally (he goes rarely), though I would charge
members of his staff (who go frequently). He fully
agreed that my proposals were only fair. The proposed
charge of last year failed owing to being collectable in
the

the future; this year it will be a cash one (though I
did not say so). Moreover, steps have been taken to
prevent the launch being detained on the other side.
So shall we help local officials out of the present
dearth of transport without inflicting financial injury on
ourselves.

AIDS TO NAVIGATION: AMUR RIVER DUES ACCOUNT: Aigun
S/O No.122 reported that on evacuation the Mayor (=President
of Chinese Aids Commission) had insisted on the Commissioner
handing over $4,500.00 of the balance. Aigun S/O No.125
referred pessimistically to this subject and your S/O of
18th March 1930 stated that the Taoyin will doubtless
account in due course for the advance of $4,500.00. He
has done so! On 7th June I wrote to him politely
asking how this $4,500.00 handed over to him for safe-
guarding was to be accounted for, and on 20th he replied
that it was expended in providing passages, etc. for
people from neighbouring districts, who, coming to Taheiho
to seek refuge during the Sino-Soviet trouble, could not
return home without government aid. He stated that he
had duly reported this expenditure (to Moukden ?). This
correspondence appears in my Summary of Non-urgent Chinese
Correspondence for June 1930. To me it appears totally
wrong that River Dues collected for Aids to Navigation
should be expended in this manner, especially considering
that

that the River Dues Account is in debt to the Sungari
Aids for $25,000.00, at least. I have, however, taken
no further steps since my attitude depends largely on
your attitude towards the Mayor's request that the River
Dues be handed over to him monthly (reported in my
despatch No.492 requesting instructions).

    Yours truly,

第 <u>132</u> 号半官函　　　　　　　　　　　1930 年 7 月 15 日于瑷珲关

尊敬的梅乐和先生：

为允许限量货物进口事：

7 月 7 日黑河市政筹备处处长来函请海关允许定量货物（100 箱苏打、20 箱肥皂、1000 箱煤油、36000 磅轻质汽油、36000 磅白糖及 5 捆药物）持其签发之护照在完纳税捐后进口。无论如何，这都是中苏跨境贸易的开始。不过兹认为，如果苏方不能在黑河市政筹备处处长最为关心的中苏黑龙江航路标志协议续约一事上做出让步，中方边境应不会有重新开放的希望。现今苏联方面迫切希望通过苏联政府贸易公司开展一定量的与华贸易，但中国方面迟迟未予允准。

为免税特权事：

日前海关监督告知，布拉戈维申斯克（Blagovestchensk）当局出售给他一批轻质汽油，将自俄岸私运过来，希望海关可免税放行。这批轻质汽油实际上就是走私而来。现今中苏双方并无正式贸易往来，苏联船只不得进入华岸，中国船只亦不得办理结关前往俄岸，因此两国官员之间的此等往来只得秘密进行。经过一番私下友好协商，本人表示同意，但说明此决定仅适用于两国边境正式关闭期间且此等交易少有发生的情况。此外，海关监督还提出，苏联领事亦有类似情况，希望海关同样免征税款，并表示有此请求乃因布拉戈维申斯克当局已允许中国总领事和日本领事免税进口。对此本人业已答允。此等让步微不足道，于税收亦不会有太大影响，尤其是在贸易皆遭禁止的情况之下，但可以极大地拉近与海关监督的关系。

为驻布拉戈维申斯克中国总领事事：

新任驻布拉戈维申斯克中国总领事权世恩先生和副领事张大田先生及随扈于 7 月 9 日抵达大黑河，并于 7 月 11 日过江至俄岸，随后又于 7 月 12 日又返回大黑河与本人共进晚餐，本人亦已回访，双方关系非常融洽。

为海关摩托艇事：

去年往来大黑河与布拉戈维申斯克的渡船是当地唯一的水上交通工具，但已遭苏联当局扣押。除此之外便只有海关和苏联领事的摩托艇可做此用。渡船当时的收费标准为，非政府官员每次过江 2.00 银圆，政府官员每次 1.00 银圆。然而，在渡船未被苏方扣押之前，中国官员便已开始频频借用海关摩托艇。为此瑷珲关前任税务司建议收取费用，然虽已获得同意，但一直未能实行。由于今年已无渡船可用，中国官员借用海关摩托艇越发频繁（主要为海关监督借用），而且如今布拉戈维申斯克中国总领事馆又重新开放，借用之事只怕会愈来愈多。有鉴于此，本人已口头告知海关监督（黑河市政筹备处处长），瑷珲关的财务状况难以承担中国官员对摩托艇的免费借用，因此计划每次收取 1.00 银圆以抵消使用成本，同时表示在海关不需要摩托艇时，愿意将之借给其本人及其他官员（包括驻布拉戈维申斯克中国总领事），但说明海关摩托艇并非渡船，每次借用时均须向本人提出，不过出于对其海关监督身份的尊重，当他个人需要借用时（海关监督很少单独出行），不会收取费用，但其下属官员（频繁往来于两岸）均须照常收费。海关监督认为此提议十分合理，表示同意。去年收取费用之计划未能成功实行，主要因采用了远期收费办法，今年将直接收取现金（不过本人并未向海关监督说明此事）。另外，中国当局已经开始采取措施，防止苏联方面再次扣留中国船艇。故此请示，瑷珲关是否可以在不损害海关经济利益的前提下帮助地方官员缓解交通工具紧缺这一问题。

为航路标志：黑龙江江捐账户事：

瑷珲关第 122 号半官函汇报称，瑷珲关撤离大黑河之时，黑河市政筹备处处长（即中国黑龙江水道委员会委员长）坚持让瑷珲关税务司向其移交黑龙江江捐账户余额中的 4500.00 银圆。瑷珲关第 125 号半官函认为此事不甚乐观。总税务司 1930 年 3 月 18 日半官函回复称，道尹（黑河市政筹备处处长）定会在适当之时为此 4500.00 银圆报账。如今其已完成报账之事！本人于 6 月 7 日致函黑河市政筹备处处长，礼貌地询问前税务司移交给他保管的 4500.00 银圆应如何入账？黑河市政筹备处处长于 6 月 20 日回函称，因中苏危机期间，附近地区来至大黑河避难的民众若无政府援助，将无法返回家乡，他已使用该笔款项为难民发放旅费等，并表示该项支出已经及时上报（也许是上报至奉天）。该两封信函已收录于 1930 年 6 月非紧急中文往来函摘由簿。

兹认为，专为黑龙江航路标志工事所征收的江捐税款不应用于援助难民，尤其如今黑龙江航路标志账户还亏欠松花江航路标志账户 25000.00 银圆。但是，本人对此事并未进一步表态，待阁下对黑河市政筹备处处长要求海关按月移交江捐税款一事下达指示后（已通过瑷珲关第 492 号呈申请指示），再遵照办理。

您真挚的

富乐嘉

19. 富乐嘉致梅乐和函

（第 133 号半官函）

CUSTOM HOUSE,

S/O No.133   A I G U N 30th July   19 30.

Dear Mr. Maze,

AMUR AIDS TO NAVIGATION ETC.: pourparlers re renewal of
Agreement, Amur trans-frontier trade and Russian navigation
of Sungari River: discussions in re: On 24th the
Chief Director of the Amur River Water Transport
Bureau in Harbarovsk, accompanied by the Interpreter
of the Soviet Consulate here, called on me with a
view to obtaining my opinion, as a member of the
Amur Aids Commission, on the general principle of
the reopening of frontier trade. He meandered
discursively from subject to subject, starting with
the non-repair of Aids on the Chinese side of the
river, branching to the reopening of frontier trade
along the Amur, and ending up with an expression
of the Russian desire to navigate the Sungari River
in return for the Chinese right to navigate the
Amur between Harbarovsk and the sea (Nikolaevsk).
To all his requests for opinion I turned a more

or

or less deaf ear. I stated that the question of
trade communications was in this instance a
political one: that trade relations had not been
broken off by the Amur Aids Commission and that
they could not be reopened by that Commission.
My opinion as a member of the Amur Aids Commission
was therefore uncalled for. As Commissioner of
Customs I shall of course be glad to see the
Amur frontier trade resumed, for financial reasons;
but I deprecated the idea of opening additional
offices which could hardly justify their existence.
Trade that did not report either at Aigun or at
Lahasusu would have to be considered as smuggled,
as was the case before it ceased. I refused to
say a word about the Sungari question except that
that district was outside my province. But I
assured him that I welcomed any cooperation between
the two countries, such, for instance, as the
activities proper to the Amur Aids Commission.
Whilst recording his regret that I could not
express myself more definitely, he stated his
satisfaction at the courtesy of his reception.
What he was out for, I imagine, was to drive a
wedge between the Mayor and myself by getting me

to

F. W. Maze, Esquire,
    etc., etc., etc.,
        S H A N G H A I.

to express opinions contrary to the former's, but
on that score he obtained no satisfaction whatsoever
for I soon divined his objective, cleverly
camouflaged with much politeness and flattery though
it was.

On 26th I returned the call. Noon was
nominated as a convenient hour and, the Russian
talent for discussion being much in evidence, we
conversed animatedly from that hour till 3.30, all
of us missing tiffin on a very hot day when, as
a matter of fact, its loss was not a matter of
great moment. The Soviet Consul was present and
my "Tidesurveyor", N. S. Ivanoff, a faithful
interpreter, fulfilled that rôle. So what was
intended to be a formal visit developed into a
most interesting conversation. I must presage a
brief account of it by saying that I had already
fully informed the Mayor of what had occurred at
the original interview and that he had endorsed my
attitude as eminently correct. Boiled down, in
order not to be wearisomely verbose, the fact
appears that the Russians this year do not want
(will, in fact, refuse) to renew the Annual Amur
Aids Agreement, on which the Mayor has set his
heart.

heart, unless they are offered some very
considerable outside advantage. They claim that
at the time of the conflict last year China
deliberately destroyed some of the Aids on its
side of the river, and moved others in order to
lure Russian vessels to destruction. They say
that they have therefore spent huge sums (Roubles
350,000) to light and guide the river from the
Russian side alone and that they are now totally
independent of China; in any case, they say,
China's miserable contribution ($22,000p.a.) was only
a fleabite as regards the total expenditure and
that, therefore, China has everything to gain and
Russia everything to lose by a renewal of the
Agreement on the old lines. They cannot, therefore,
recommend such renewal to their Authorities, though
they would undertake the work of repairing Chinese
Aids, acting as contractors only, should China so
desire, at estimated cost of Rs.200,000. They
would like to have trans-Amur trade between the
two countries, though they claim that such trade,
whilst advantageous to themselves, would be just as
advantageous to China. But they complain that the
strictly restricted trade that has at times been
allowed

allowed during past years proves that China's main
idea is to get rich quickly -- that she leans
towards only allowing official and not open trade,
that is, towards only allowing trade with some ~~our~~ one
official institution, and that she will tax it to
the uttermost limit in Customs Duties, River Dues
increased to 5% this year for direct imports and
exports (my despatch No.492, §1), and all kinds of
other taxes after passing the Customs.   It must,
however, be remembered that all Russian foreign
trade is also transacted by one official institution,
the Government Trade Office.   Then they came to
what they really want: Russian navigation of the
Sungari in exchange for Chinese navigation of the
Amur between Harbarovsk and the sea (Nikolaevsk).
Whilst not denying advantages for themselves (otherwise they would not be wanting it !) they claim
that it would do much good to the Manchurian bean
trade which now reaches the London market _via_
Harbin and is often held up for nine months by
the Sansing shallows in its passage from the Lower
Sungari to Harbin, whereas it could then proceed by
steamer direct to Nikolaevsk for transhipment, rail
transport not being used and much loss of time
avoided.   To my quotation, from the newspapers, of
the

the recent Sino-Hongkong negotiations showing the
difficulties nowadays of obtaining Chinese inland
navigation in exchange for any other advantage,
they countered that, though the parallel was well-
drawn, yet there was indeed an immense difference,
that is, the fact that British subjects and their
vessels are extraterritorialised whereas the Russians
want navigation of inland waters on a non-extra-
territorial basis.   Such a move on the part of
China would, they contend, inevitably support the
Chinese claim that abolition of extrality would in
the end actually benefit foreigners.   These are the
conditions, to be embodied in the "Aids to
Navigation" Agreement, on which they would consent
to sign that document.   On my stating that inland
navigation was a thorn that would require protracted
reference to the Central Government, they replied
that Manchuria in 1923/4 had shown her ability to
deal with such questions herself by including the
very terms now proposed by Russia in a draft
agreement which it was not then convenient for
Russia to sign.   That, however, was before Chinese
national consciousness became so resentful of
allowing anything that can be construed as loss of
sovereign rights.   Moreover, whatever may have been
the

the case then, Sungari trade is at present a practical monopoly of the Moukden authorities and any encroachment by Russia means a loss to the authorities themselves.

The interview then concluded with mutual expressions of esteem and the expressed desire of the Russians that the gist be communicated by me to the Mayor, for, when national susceptibilities may so easily be aroused, it is, I take it, far easier and less fraught with peril for frank views and direct criticisms to be expressed through the medium of a third party than face to face.

On the 28th I reported the above conversation to the Mayor who expressed his pleasure at the trouble I had taken and his appreciation of my attitude.

The whole question is extraordinarily difficult. It is obvious that the Russians are trying to obtain locally what they begin to fear it will be impossible to get at Moscow. Yet some concession may well have to be granted before it will suit them to sign a purely Aids Agreement.

STATIONERY: SERVICE ECONOMY IN. Your Circular No.4044 enjoins strict economy in stationery and as a step in in this direction I have refused any longer to provide Service stationery for the use of the office of the Technical Adviser on Amur Aids to Navigation. It is true that we take one-tenth of Collection of River Dues as "Cost of Collection", but the Technical Adviser's Office is purely administrative and has nothing whatever to do with the cost of collection.

Yours truly,

第 133 号半官函　　　　　　　　　　　　　　　1930 年 7 月 30 日于瑷珲关

尊敬的梅乐和先生：

为黑龙江航务等事（关于续签黑龙江航路标志协议、黑龙江跨境贸易及苏联船只于松花江上航行等问题的非正式会谈）：

7 月 24 日，哈巴罗夫斯克（Habarovsk）阿穆尔水运局局长在苏联领事馆翻译的陪同下来至大黑河与本人会面，以期获得本人作为黑龙江水道委员会委员对于重新开放边境贸易的意见。只是在会谈过程中，阿穆尔水运局局长不断更换话题，东拉西扯，不着边际，从黑龙江华岸一侧航路标志未经修理之问题，谈到黑龙江沿岸边境贸易重新开放一事，最后又提出苏联方面希望获得在松花江上的航行权利，并表示作为交换，中国轮船可自哈巴罗夫斯克航行至黑龙江入海口处尼古拉耶夫斯克（Nikolaevsk）。

对于阿穆尔水运局局长寻求的意见，本人一直避而不答，并表示如今两国开展贸易之事乃为政治事件，而且中断两国贸易关系的并非黑龙江水道委员会，重新开放跨境贸易亦非委员会职权范围以内之事，因此无法以黑龙江航路标志委员会委员的身份提供意见。不过作为瑷珲关税务司，从经济角度考虑，本人自然乐见黑龙江边境贸易重新开放，但不建议增设税卡，因为贸易有限，不值得如此操作，凡往来贸易未至瑷珲关或是拉哈苏苏分关报明者，均应如贸易停滞之前一样被视为走私行为。至于松花江的问题，本人仅对阿穆尔水运局局长说明松花江不在黑龙江省辖区以内，但表示支持两国的任何合作，正如黑龙江水道委员会的合作活动一样。阿穆尔水运局局长对于本人未提出任何明确观点表示遗憾，但对其受到的礼待仍然十分满意。兹认为，阿穆尔水运局局长此行之目的在于让本人提出与黑河市政筹备处处长相左的观点，以此挑拨我们之间的关系，但终究未能如愿，因为本人早已识破其恭维背后的意图。

本人于 7 月 26 日中午回访了阿穆尔水运局局长。苏联代表十分健谈，我们从中午一直激烈讨论到下午 3 时 30 分，在这样炎热的夏日，所有人居然都忘记了吃午餐，不过与会谈相比，午餐着实不甚重要。出席此次会谈的还有苏联领事和作为本人翻译的瑷珲关"监察长"亿万纳福（N. S. Ivanoff）先生，此人很可靠并且恪尽职守。此次正式访问最终变成了一次颇为有趣的会谈。需要声明的是，本人在拜访阿穆尔水运局局长之前便已将此行程告知黑河市政筹备处处长，并汇报了该局长与本人第一次会面的情形，黑河市政筹备处处长对本人的表现表示赞赏。

关于此次会谈内容，为避免赘述，特此归纳说明。实际上，苏联方面今年并不希望（将会拒绝）续签黑河市政筹备处处长正在极力促成的年度黑龙江航路标志协议,除非中方可在其他方面让利。苏联代表宣称,去年两国冲突期间,中国方面故意破坏黑龙江华岸一侧的部分航路标志,还将一些航路标志移位以误导苏联船只发生事故,为此他们已经斥巨资（350000 卢布）单独于俄岸一侧增设灯桩导标引导船只航行,现在已完全不需要与中国方面联合修建航路标志。苏联代表表示,与他们每年航路标志的总支出相比,中国对航路标志所投入的经费（每年 22000 银圆）完全不值一提,所以如果仍照此前航路标志协议所定条款续签新协议,于中国而言自然有百利而无一害,但于苏联则是有百害而无一利,因此他们无法向苏联政府提议续签黑龙江航路标志协议,但提出如果中国方面愿意,他们可以以承包商的身份承接黑龙江华岸一侧的航路标志工程,预算为 200000 卢布。

苏联代表希望两国可以开展跨江（黑龙江）贸易,认为如此于双方皆为有利之举,还抱怨称,过去几年间中国对跨境贸易一直施行限制性政策,偏向官方性、非开放性贸易,只允许苏联与特定的官方机构开展贸易,还最大限度地征收海关关税,今年甚至将直接进出口货物的江捐税率提高 5%（参阅瑷珲关第 492 号呈第 1 项）,而且货物于海关完纳关税后还须缴纳其他税项,并据此认为中国之意图显然为迅速致富。但是值得注意的是,苏联所有出口贸易亦只通过政府贸易公司这一家官方机构办理。

苏联代表最后提出了他们真正的意图? 希望得到苏联船只在松花江上的航行权利,作为交换,将允许中国船只自哈巴罗夫斯克航行至黑龙江入海口处尼古拉耶夫斯克。苏联代表并不否认他们在这一交换中能够获得利益（若无利益苏联方面亦不会提出此建议!）,但也表示此举亦会促进满洲地区的大豆贸易。如今满洲地区的大豆已开始通过哈尔滨运至伦敦市场,但是由于自松花江下游至哈尔滨需经过三姓浅滩,此处航道不利于轮船航行,因此往往需要 9 个月的时间才能抵达目的地,但如果由轮船直接运至尼古拉耶夫斯克再进行转运,便无须通过火车运输,也可节省大量时间。

对此本人引用报纸上的报道回复,指出近来中国与香港之间的谈判表明,中国不愿以任何利益交换内河航道的航行权利。苏联代表反驳称,虽然两件事情确有相似之处,但归根结底有本质上的不同,因为英国国民和船只在中国享有治外法权,但苏联方面要求的内河航行权利并不是以索要治外法权为基础的,并指出如果中国方面不能答允苏联轮船在松花江上航行的这一要求,便证明中国人认为废除治外法权最终将使洋人受益。苏联代表还说明,只要中国方面同意将其要求列入"航路标志"协议,便同意签署。本人表示内河航行权利的要求需提请中央政府裁定,但如此一来必将耗费过多时日。苏联代表则称,满洲政府早于 1923/1924 年便可独立决定此类事务,当时草拟的协议中已列入他们现在所提的条款,只是当时苏联方面不便于签署而已。

但是当时中国人的民族意识并未觉醒,因此才会草拟如此丧失主权的协议。而且,无论当时情形如何,松花江贸易如今已被奉天当局垄断,苏联当局的介入则意味着奉天当局将遭受损失。

会谈结束时,双方都表示尊重对方的立场。苏联代表希望本人可将会议要点转述给黑河市政筹备处处长,因为考虑到值此国家矛盾极易被激化之时,中苏两国代表最好不要直接会面交谈,而是通过第三方转达,以避免双方在袒露观点,直接提出意见时会引发冲突,让事情更加难办。

本人于 7 月 28 日将上述会谈内容呈报黑河市政筹备处处长张寿增,其对本人所做努力和所持立场表示感谢与赞赏。

整件事情非常棘手,苏联代表显然开始担心无法再如从前一般从莫斯科方面获得拨款等利益,于是试图通过地方协议从中方获得一些。不过,如欲让苏联代表签署纯粹的航路标志协议,可能还需给予一些让步。

为用于办公用具的海关经费事:

鉴于海关总税务司公署第 4044 号通令已指示要严格限制海关办公用具方面的支出,兹已据此指示停止为黑龙江航务专门顾问办事处提供海关办公用具。虽然海关于江捐税收中扣留 10% 作为"征税佣金",但是航务专门顾问办事处仅负责行政管理事务,并不涉及江捐征收工作,因此与海关所得征税佣金亦无干系。

您真挚的

富乐嘉

20. 周骊致梅乐和函

（第 139 号半官函）

CUSTOM HOUSE,

S/O No. 139.　　　　　Aigun　11th Nov., 30
　　　　　　　　　　　　　　　　　　　　19

Dear Mr Maze,

　　　　　I must thank you for my
promotion to the rank of Deputy Commissioner, and
I take this opportunity to express my thanks for
my appointment as Acting Commissioner.

Staff: Miscellaneous Outdoor Staff:

　　　　　The Miscellaneous Outdoor Staff of
this Office have handed me a petition asking that
they be given some reward for services rendered
during the period of evacuation of the port. They
base their request on the last paragraph of Aigun
Order No. 1300, copy of which was forwarded to
the Inspectorate in Aigun Despatch No. 450,
wherein Mr Talbot promised that they would be
specially recommended to you for reward after the
re-opening of the port. Mr Fletcher, in his
Despatch No. 488, duly reported the re-opening of
the Aigun Customs and stated that Service property
　　　　　　　　　　　　　　　　　appeared

F. W. Maze, Esquire,

　　SHANGHAI.

appeared to have been well looked after. In your
Despatch No. 128,774, you conveyed your thanks to
the staff and instructed that they be given an
extra allowance of Hk. Tls.10.00 a month as
authorised in your Despatch No.125,397, i.e., a
charge allowance of Hk. Tls.10.00 to the two
Watchers Yü Fu Shou and Ko Chin-chiu who had been
placed in charge of Customs property at Taheiho
and Aigun, respectively. In view of Mr Talbot's
promise, made in the last paragraph of his Order
No. 1300, the Miscellaneous Staff, including the
two Watchers who consider the Hk. Tls.10.00 a month
already issued as a charge allowance for extra
responsibilities shouldered and not in the nature of
a reward, feel that they have not been fairly
treated. From what I have been told, it would
appear that my predecessor refused to consider the
question of reward to the Miscellaneous Staff and
pointed out that the two senior men had already
been compensated for the extra responsibilities
thrown on them. In my opinion, the whole staff
deserves a reward as they could have disposed of
furniture and of the entire stock of firewood with
little fear of detection. Besides, the staff need
not have stayed here at the time of evacuation.

　　　　　　　　　　　　　　　　　I

I regret having to raise this question as it was one for my predecessor's decision, but I feel that the staff has not received its just due and that it would be unwise, apart from being ungenerous, to economise by failing to fulfil a promise made at a time of crisis. Failure to give due recognition for services satisfactorily rendered would react against the best interests of the Service by undermining the spirit of loyalty displayed by the Miscellaneous Staff at and during the time of evacuation. I would beg to recommend that all members of the Miscellaneous Staff be granted a reward of either Hk. Tls.15.00 or Hk.Tls. 20.00 each, and I now write to enquire whether I may apply officially for authority to make such payments. An English translation of the petition from the staff is appended hereto.

Trade:

In July last the Heiho Mayor gave permission for the Soviet Trading Bureau, the Gostorg, to import the following articles into Taheiho:-

Soda:	100	cases.
Soap:	20	"
Kerosene Oil:	1,000	"
Benzine:	1,000	poods.
Sugar, white:	1,000	"
Medicinal Substances, Vegetable:	5 Bundles.	

So

So far nothing has arrived, but the Gostorg has been authorised to open an agency here. There are rumours that the Gostorg is to be permitted to buy beans at Chikote, a place some 350 li below Taheiho and not controlled by the Customs, for export to Russia. Should such permission be granted during the winter it would mean that the beans would be transported across the ice and I should have to request the Mayor/Superintendent to ensure that I be informed in time to enable me to send an Officer to control the cargo, after receipt of a deposit sufficient to cover all duties. In 1929 the Russians wanted to convey beans by Russian vessels from Chikote - please see Aigun S/O letter No. 91 - but the transaction fell through as crops on the Chinese side were destroyed by flood. Although it is not specifically stated in any of the local regulations or instructions, I presume that the Aigun Customs' district extends from Mohoting (漠河處), if not further, to the mouth of the Sungari.

There is no likelihood of the frontier on either side being opened in the near future and the Gostorg will only be allowed to import and export certain articles for which special permission

permission will have to be obtained on each
occasion, but there is no prospect of any
substantial movement of cargo. Local timber dealers
are troubled by the reported dumping of Soviet
timber on the Harbin market at prices with which
Taheiho merchants are unable to compete. If there
is any truth in the report, I fear that our
receipts, both revenue and River Dues, will be
seriously affected next navigation season. There was
a tendency amongst certain local officials to try
to form an official trading organisation to deal
with the Gostorg, but the latest report is that
Moukden has definitely squashed any such attempt on
the grounds that in China individual trading is
permitted.

Officials: Mr Chang Shou-tseng (張壽增), Mayor/
Superintendent:

In my last S/O letter I remarked
that Mr Chang had left for Harbin on being
appointed one of China's delegates to the Moscow
Conference. I am now informed that he is returning
to Taheiho in the course of the next few days,
viâ Suifenho, Habarovsk and Blagoveschensk, as the
Moscow Conference has been indefinitely postponed.

Thirteenth

Thirteenth Anniversary of the Russian Revolution:

In company with all the local
Chinese officials, I attended an official reception
at the Soviet Consulate on the 7th. It was a
dismal affair and the Consul made a short,
non-committal speech explaining what the occasion was
and expressing the hope that the Moscow Conference
would be successful. The representatives of the
Mayor and the General confined themselves to wishing
good luck to the Soviet Government.

Travelling Expenses: incurred in connection with the
evacuation of the Aigun staff to Harbin: Mr
Chipourin's claim for additional payment of
H.$1,133.80:

Mr Chipourin has handed me copy
of a letter that he has addressed to the Mayor/
Superintendent in connection with the non-payment by
the Customs of his claim for an additional amount
of Harbin $1,133.80 for evacuating the Aigun staff
to Harbin in November 1929. The letter, which is
in Russian, is now being translated and will be
submitted officially to you later. Mr Chipourin
intimated that he had written to the Mayor/
Superintendent at the latter's request and that he
would place the matter in the hands of a lawyer

if

if the Customs again refused to meet his claim.
He tried to give me the impression that the Mayor
thinks his claim just. As soon as Mr Chang returns
to Taheiho I shall discuss the question with him
and obtain his real views on the subject. Before
his departure, Mr Fletcher informed me that Mr
Chipourin was not satisfied with the ruling of your
Despatch No. 127,549 and that he intended presenting
his claim again. The references are: Aigun Despatches
Nos. 460 and 483; I. G. Despatches Nos. 125,732 and
127,549.

Yours truly,

第 139 号半官函　　　　　　　　　　1930 年 11 月 11 日于瑷珲关

尊敬的梅乐和先生：

　　首先感谢阁下将本人晋升为副税务司，同时借此机会感谢阁下任命本人担任瑷珲关署理税务司。

　　为杂项外班职员事：

　　瑷珲关杂项外班职员近日递交请愿书一份，希望可因在瑷珲关撤离期间看管海关关产而得到一些奖励。杂项职员有此请求，是因为铎博赉（R. M. Talbot）先生此前曾于瑷珲关第 1300 号谕令（抄件已随瑷珲关第 450 号呈呈交至海关总税务司公署）中承诺会于大黑河口岸重新开放之后向总税务司申请对他们予以特殊奖赏。

　　富乐嘉（H. G. Fletcher）先生于瑷珲关第 488 号呈中汇报了瑷珲关重新开放一事，并称海关关产得到了妥善看管。海关总税务司公署第 128774 号令对看管关产的关员表示感谢，并指示按照海关总税务司公署第 125397 号令批准之额度，为看管关产的关员每月发放额外津贴 10.00 海关两，即为在大黑河和瑷珲看管海关关产的巡役于福寿和郭敬九每人发放 10.00 海关两的职务津贴。

　　鉴于铎博赉先生此前于瑷珲关第 1300 号谕令末段有所承诺，因此杂项职员，包括于福寿和郭敬九两名巡役（他们认为海关发放额外津贴是因其承担了额外的工作，并非奖金），均认为自己未得到海关的公正待遇。

　　据本人所知，瑷珲关前任税务司拒绝为杂项职员申请奖金，并指出海关已为两名巡役所做的额外工作给予了补偿。然兹认为，瑷珲关所有杂项职员都有权得享奖金，因为他们本可在无人知晓的情况下将关产内的家具和储藏的所有薪柴低价售出，但是他们并没有这样做，而且在瑷珲关撤离大黑河之时，他们本不必留守，但最终却同意留下看护关产。

　　虽然瑷珲关前任税务司已对此事做出决定，但本人依然认为杂项职员并未得到他们应有的奖励。而且海关如果为了节约资金，未能履行危机期间所做的承诺，不仅会略显吝啬，而且极不明智，拒绝承认杂项职员在瑷珲关撤离期间所表现出的忠诚，为保护海关关产所做出的努力，也就是在损害海关的最大利益。兹建议，为瑷珲关所有杂项职员发放奖金，每人 15.00 海关两或 20.00 海关两。另请告知，奖金一事是否需要本人提出正式申请。杂项职员的请愿书英文译文已随函附上。

　　为贸易事：

　　黑河市政筹备处处长于今年 7 月批准苏联贸易公司向大黑河进口如下货物：

货物名称	数量	单位
苏打	100	箱
肥皂	20	箱
煤油	1000	箱
轻质汽油	1000	普特
白糖	1000	普特
药物和蔬菜	5	捆

截至目前,尚未有何货物运抵大黑河,不过苏联贸易公司已获准于本地设立办事处。而且有传闻称,苏联贸易公司将获准于位于大黑河下游约350里处的奇克特收购大豆并出口至苏联,且不受海关管控。如果收购之事最终于冬季获得批准,也就意味着大豆将通过结冰的黑龙江运输出口。若如此,本人则应提前请黑河市政筹备处处长兼海关监督及时通知海关,以便关员前去管理货物,收取足够的关税押款。1928年,苏联方面就曾计划由其轮船自奇克特运输大豆(参见瑷珲关第91号半官函),但由于当年黑龙江华岸的庄稼皆被洪水淹没,最终未能实现。虽然地方规章或指令中并无明确规定,但兹认为,瑷珲关的管辖范围应自漠河厅至松花江与黑龙江交汇处。

中苏双方在近期内均无开放边境之可能,苏联贸易公司亦仅被允许进出口特定货物,而且每次均须事先获得中方的特批,不过应该不会有大宗货物运输。据报道称,苏联木料已大批进入哈尔滨市场,而且价格十分低廉,大黑河木料经销商根本无法与之竞争,现下十分困扰。若此报道属实,恐怕瑷珲关下一航运季期间的税捐收入将受到严重影响。大黑河地方官员试图成立官方贸易组织,以便与苏联贸易公司进行交易,但有最新消息称,奉天当局已明确表态,中国既允许进行私人贸易,成立官方贸易组织则无甚必要。

为黑河市政筹备处处长兼海关监督张寿增先生事:

本人于上一封半官函中提及,张寿增先生因被任命为出席莫斯科会议的中国代表之一,已动身前往哈尔滨。但刚刚收到消息,莫斯科会议已无限延期,黑河市政筹备处处长近日将经由绥芬河、哈巴罗夫斯克(Habarovsk)和布拉戈维申斯克(Blagovestchensk)返回大黑河。

为苏联革命十三周年事:

11月7日,驻黑河苏联领事馆举办了一场官方招待会,本人与大黑河中国官员均列席参加。此次招待会氛围沉重,苏联领事仅简短地介绍了此次宴会的主旨,还表示希望莫斯科会议可以顺利召开。黑河市政筹备处处长代表和大黑河司令代表均表达了对苏联政府的祝福。

　　为瑷珲关关员撤离大黑河的旅费事（查普林（Chipourin）先生索要额外费用哈大洋1133.80元）：

　　查普林先生近日向本人呈交了一封其致黑河市政筹备处处长兼海关监督的信函抄件，主要为1929年11月将瑷珲关关员撤离至哈尔滨一事索要额外费用哈大洋1133.80元。此封信函以俄语书写，现已在翻译当中，嗣后将正式呈交给阁下。查普林先生透露，他是按照黑河市政筹备处处长兼海关监督的要求撰写此函，表示如果海关再次拒绝付款，此事将交由律师处理。从其言辞中可以判断，他意在表明黑河市政筹备处处长认为他索要费用是合理之举。待张寿增先生返回大黑河后，本人将立即与之商议此事，以明晰其本意。富乐嘉先生离开大黑河前曾告知本人，查普林先生对海关总税务司公署第127549号令的规定不甚满意，打算再次索要费用。此事详情可参阅瑷珲关第460号和483号呈，海关总税务司公署第125732号和127549号令。

您真挚的

周骊

21. 周骊致梅乐和函

（第 141 号半官函）

CUSTOM HOUSE.

S/O No. 141   A I G U N . 24th December 30.

Dear Mr. Maze,

RIVER DUES: The Mayor wrote to me on the 4th instant requesting that River Dues on cart-borne goods from and to Russia be levied at ordinary rates instead of at the increased rate of 5% reported in Aigun despatch No. 492. The Soviet Trading Bureau has since paid these dues without protest. The Mayor is now considering a general increase in the River Dues Tariff, to be effective from the opening of the navigation season, and he intended drawing up two different rates, one for trade with Russia and another for trade from Chinese places. At a meeting with him on the 3rd instant, I pointed out that the Soviet would undoubtedly protest strongly if its imports into China were discriminated against as compared with other foreign goods arriving here $\underline{via}$ Harbin, and he finally saw the point of this argument and decided to have two different rates,

one

F. W. Maze, Esquire,
  Etc., etc., etc.,
    S H A N G H A I.

one for foreign, and another for native, goods. His reason for an increase in the tariff is that, by the last agreement, China's contributions for the upkeep of Aids have been enhanced to the tune of about 70% and that trade and shipping must supply the additional money by subscribing to a larger extent to river dues funds. I heard to-day, through the Technical Adviser, that the Tsitsihar Government has now vetoed the levy of river dues on cart traffic. If this is the case, the Mayor will no doubt write asking that such levy be discontinued.

WHEAT FLOUR. As I am in some doubt concerning the applicability here of the instructions of your Circular No. 4140, notifying the temporary withdrawal of the prohibition on the exportation abroad of flour, I am telegraphing to-day to ask whether these instructions partially supersede those of your telegram of the 19th June, 1930, which read as follows :

"Export to Russia of cereals and flour prohibited". The Superintendent has received the same instructions from the Ministry, but I have not discussed the matter with him as it is said that he has large stocks of flour for disposal to the Russians. The

report

report may be unfounded, but it has decided me not to raise the question locally until I hear from you.

CHANGE OF OFFICIALS: The former Heiho Ssüling, General Pa Ying-o (巴英額) has been appointed Superintendent of the Harbin Customs and his successor is General Ma Chan-shan (馬占山) from Hailun (海倫).

ABOLITION OF LIKIN STATIONS, ETC.: Your telegram of the 20th instant arrived on the 21st. The season precludes all possibility of a really thorough investigation into each tax office along the Amur as there are no regular means of conveyance and the cost of hiring sledges, arranging for guards, etc., would be so exorbitant that it would be out of all proportion to the value of the information to be obtained. The Mayor/Superintendent, who formerly as Taoyin controlled the district from the mouth of the Argun to the mouth of the Sungari, no doubt has information concerning the various tax offices along the Amur and I am applying to him for assistance in gathering the particulars called for in your telegram. As regards the establishment of Customs stations along the frontier, under present conditions it would appear necessary to have such only at the larger places to enable us to say that we control the frontier. With the Russian frontier closed

closed and all trade prohibited, the Soviet is actually doing our preventive work for us and, from all accounts, doing it very successfully. There are reported to be two battalions of Frontier Guards, assisted by about 2,000 G.P.U. agents, engaged directly or indirectly in preventive work on the Russian side between Moho and Lahasusu. Furthermore, would-be smugglers must not overlook the innumerable spies of the G.P.U. We know from observation and information that very little smuggling is done now as the risks are too great. The principal duties of Customs stations at the larger places on the frontier would be to supply information concerning each district and to see that no illegal tax offices spring up, and their only real value would be as evidences of Customs control of the frontier and of trans-frontier trade. If, later, the Russian frontier is opened and individual trade permitted, we should have to build up a proper preventive service with an increased number of stations and with both land and water patrols, but such a possibility appears unlikely for a long time and, even if a change did occur in the Soviet's fiscal policy, recuperation on both sides of the Amur would be slow and tedious. The Russian side has been denuded

denuded of all resources and money and, on the
Chinese side, the Amur along its whole length is
sparsely populated. In addition, the configuration
of this region, and the difficulties and expense
of transportation, would restrict its development as
a "feeder" for inland places until railways had been
extended to various points along the Amur. All
these contingencies are, however, far too remote and
uncertain to warrant serious consideration and a
nucleus for future expansion is all that seems
necessary at present.

As instructed by you, I am consulting with
the Harbin Commissioner and have already written to
him semi-officially on the subject.

There is only one experienced man on my
Chinese Staff, Mr. Wang Tê - mao, 1st Clerk B, and
he cannot be detached until the Annual Returns have
been completed as he is the only Clerk with a
sound knowledge of this work. I shall do my best
to despatch the necessary report as early as possible
but communication with Harbin is slow and irregular
at this time of the year and I fear it will be
some time before I can hope to have all the
necessary material.

Yours truly,

第 141 号半官函　　　　　　　　　　　　　　　1930 年 12 月 24 日于瑷珲关

尊敬的梅乐和先生：

为江捐事：

黑河市政筹备处处长于 12 月 4 日来函请海关仍按照原税率对中苏两岸往来车载货物征收江捐，而非瑷珲关第 492 号呈中所汇报之 5% 的新税率。苏联贸易公司已开始按照原税率缴纳江捐，且未提出任何抗议。

不过，黑河市政筹备处处长现下正在考虑于明年航运季开始时全面提高江捐税率，并计划为与苏联往来贸易和与中国其他地区往来贸易各定一套税率标准。12 月 3 日与黑河市政筹备处处长会面时，本人指出，苏联方面如果发现其进口至中国的货物与其他经由哈尔滨运抵大黑河的洋货所享待遇不同，遭到区别对待，定会提出强烈抗议。黑河市政筹备处处长终于看出此举的争议所在，决定仅为洋货和土货分别制订税率。其提高江捐税率的原因为，按照中苏双方最新签订的黑龙江航路标志协议，中方为联合维护航路标志工事所摊款项总额已上涨约 70%，多出的款项只能通过对贸易货运征收更多的江捐税款来筹得。今日据航务专门顾问透露，齐齐哈尔当局已经否决了对车辆运输征收江捐的提议。若此消息属实，黑河市政筹备处处长定会来函要求停止征收江捐。

为面粉事：

海关总税务司公署第 4140 号通令指令各关临时取消对面粉出口外国的禁令。关于该项指示，本人对瑷珲关是否应遵照执行一直心存疑惑，因此已于今日向阁下发送电报，询问该项指示是否取代总税务司 1930 年 6 月 19 日电令：

"禁止向苏联出口谷物和面粉。"

海关监督业已收到相同指令，但听闻其手上存有大量面粉要出售给苏联方面，因此本人并未与之商议此事。当然，此消息或许并不属实，但兹已决定在收到阁下指令之前，暂不与地方官员讨论此事。

为地方官员调动事：

前任黑河司令巴英额将军现已被任命为滨江关海关监督，其继任者为来自海伦的马占山将军。

为裁撤厘金税卡等事：

阁下 12 月 20 日电报已于 12 月 21 日收悉。现下正值冬季，常规交通工具已停止通行，租赁雪橇，安排卫兵等费用势必会过于高昂，甚至远高于最终获取信息的价值，有鉴于此，此次只怕无法对黑龙江沿岸所有税卡进行一一调查。黑河市政筹备处处长兼海关监督，曾任黑河道尹时，管理自上游额尔古纳河口至下游松花江口所有各卡，必然了解黑龙江沿岸各税卡之情况，本人已请其帮助提供阁下电报所要求之各项信息。至于增设海关分关一事，依目前情况来看，似乎唯有于规模较大之城镇设立，方可证明边境乃于海关管辖范围之内。

苏联方面自施行封锁边境政策，禁止私人贸易以来，一直严守边防，实际上亦是在为华岸国防代劳，而且卓有成效。据报告所称，现在苏联界防军约有两营人，另有秘密警探两千人相辅而行，均以直接或间接之方式参与俄岸自漠河至拉哈苏苏一段的边防事务。私贩之徒既见密探如此之多，必会有所忌惮。经查，因风险过高，走私之事已不多见。

在边境地区规模较大城镇设立的海关分关应主要负责搜集各地区的信息，确保无非法税卡设立，而其价值之体现便是证明边境及跨境贸易为海关所辖。如果日后苏联方面开放边境，准许进行私人贸易，海关应于边境地区增设分关并设立水陆巡防往来稽查，然此项时期为日尚远。即使今苏联经济政策骤变，而俄岸资源资金紧缺，华岸人口稀疏，若求其恢复旧观，当需时日。此外，大黑河地区的城镇布局和交通弊端（不甚便利且费用高昂）均是其发展成为内地"供给站"的阻碍，除非黑龙江沿岸各地均有铁路通达。然此项事实发生渺茫，似不必急之深虑，目前仅为日后发展考虑关键之事即可。

按照阁下指示，本人已开始与滨江关税务司商议调查黑龙江沿岸税卡之事，并已就此事向他发送半官函。

瑷珲关华籍关员中，只有一等二级税务员王德懋先生有相关经验，但他亦为本关唯一熟悉年度统计表编撰工作的税务员，因此唯有在他完成此项工作后，方可接受派遣。本人会竭尽全力尽早呈交报告，但每年此时大黑河与哈尔滨之间的通信往来总是较慢，而且极不规律，因此要备齐所有必需材料，只怕还需一段时日。

您真挚的

周骊

22. 周骊致梅乐和函

（第 143 号半官函）

CUSTOM HOUSE.

S/O No.143　　　　　A I G U N 22nd January 19 51.

Dear Mr. Maze,

<u>River Dues</u>: The Mayor wrote on the 29th December, 1930, requesting that the collection of River Dues on cart-borne goods from and to Russia be discontinued. The question of increasing the River Dues Tariff is being referred by him to the Provincial Government and I asked him to mention that any change in the Tariff should be referred to the Ministry of Finance for approval and for the issue of instructions to the Aigun Customs through the Inspector General. He said he would do so.

<u>Change of Officials</u>:　Mr. Chang Shou-tseng (張壽增), Mayor/Superintendent, handed over office on the 6th instant to Mr. Ch'i Chao-yu (齊肇豫) from Manchouli. The latter is a much younger man and was very helpful to me when I was in Manchouli in 1923. I am sorry that Mr. Chang has been replaced as he has always
　　　　　　　　　　　　　　　　　　　　upheld

F. W. Maze, Esquire,

　　Etc., etc., etc.,

　　　S H A N G H A I.

upheld Customs rights and requirements. He is not certain what appointment he is to receive in the future, but thinks that he will ultimately proceed to Moscow as one of China's delegates to the Conference. Mr. Ch'i has so far not been notified of his appointment as Superintendent of the Aigun Customs and has asked me to withhold the issue of the monthly allowance until he writes to me officially. He has requested the Tsitsihar Government to take up the matter with the Ministry of Finance.

<u>Abolition of Likin</u>: The local Tax Office continues to function. The only levy that has been suspended is the Parcel Tax. All goods, including those despatched by Parcel Post, leaving the port still have to pay a Consolidated Tax of varying amounts, a Military Surtax of 8% <u>ad valorem</u>, and a Local Tax (for Education and Volunteer equipment) of 5% <u>ad valorem</u>. Skins and furs, for instance, pay a Consolidated Tax of 11% <u>ad valorem</u> so that the total amount payable to the Tax Office is 24% <u>ad valorem</u>, but this figure is, I think, only nominal as the values accepted are so low that the actual amount levied is between 5% and 10% <u>ad valorem</u>. The director of the Tax Office claims that these taxes are not "Likin". The Consolidated Tax is leviable once; thereafter a fee of 10 cents is charged by each Tax
　　　　　　　　　　　　　　　　　　　　Office

Office for verification of documents. The Military Surtax and the local Tax are levied by each Tax Office passed. The Tobacco and Wine Bureau is still operating and levying the special duties entrusted to it. In addition to the taxes already mentioned there are: Business Tax; Consumption Tax; Opium Tax; Gambling Tax; Cattle Inspection Tax; and Municipal rates and taxes. The local taxes on skins and furs sent by Parcel Post, however low they may be, have led to the transportation of these articles by car and by cart to Harbin, where, it is said, such charges are not demanded.

Amur Aids Commission: indebtedness of to, and proposal of Heilungkiang Government that further financial help of $30,000.00 be extended to by, Sungari Aids Commission: Copy of the Harbin Commissioner's Comments on your despatch No. 132,077 reached me some days ago, but, before preparing the report called for by you, I shall await a reply to my despatch of the 13th instant to Harbin on these subjects. It appears to me that the Heilungkiang Government intends trying to throw on the Sungari Aids Commission the full responsibility for financial assistance to the Amur Commission and, with this in view, I have suggested to the Harbin Commissioner that it would be far more economical in the long run if the Sungari Commission could

could offer to assume such responsibility in exchange for control of the finances of the Amur Commission.

Yours truly,

第 143 号半官函　　　　　　　　　　　　　1931 年 1 月 22 日于瑷珲关

尊敬的梅乐和先生：

为江捐事：

黑河市政筹备处处长于 1930 年 12 月 29 日来函要求瑷珲关停止对中苏两岸往来车载货物征收江捐。关于提高江捐税率一事，黑河市政筹备处处长已向黑龙江省政府呈交报告，本人业已提前请他在报告中指出，须请财政部批准税率调整办法，并通过海关总税务司向瑷珲关下达指令。他表示会照此办理。

为地方官员调动事：

黑河市政筹备处处长兼海关监督张寿增先生已于 1 月 6 日将职位移交给自满洲里调来的齐肇豫先生。齐肇豫先生年纪较轻，1923 年本人于满洲里分关任职期间便受到过其襄助。张寿增先生任职期间一直维护海关权利，满足海关需求，如今调离此地，令人备感惋惜。不过其目前还不知日后将前往何地任职，估计会作为中国代表团的成员之一出席莫斯科会议。迄今为止，齐肇豫先生还未收到担任瑷珲关监督的指令，不过已请齐齐哈尔当局向财政部提请指示，并告知本人待收到其正式函文后再为之发放海关监督津贴。

为取消厘金制度事：

地方税捐局仍照常运作，唯一暂停征收之税项为包裹税。所有货物，包括通过邮政包裹运输者，离开口岸后还须缴纳不同税率的统税、货价 8% 的军费附加捐及货价 5% 的地方捐（系作本地教育金及其他地方自治之经费）。以皮货为例，离开口岸后须缴纳货价 11% 的统税，再加上军费附加捐和地方捐，最终向税捐局纳税总额高达货价的 24%。然兹认为，皮货估值较低，此数值并不属实，实际征收金额应在货价的 5% 至 10% 之间。税捐局局长宣称此等税项并非"厘金"。统税仅征收一次，嗣后经各征收局卡查验税票后，每张收取 10 分的税票验讫费，但军费附加捐和地方捐均照常征收。烟酒事务稽征局亦正常运作，继续征收由其代收之专项税。除以上各税，本地区还征收营业税、消费税、洋药税、赌博税、牲畜检疫税及市政税。另外，虽然由邮政包裹运输之皮货需缴纳的地方捐捐率或许已经很低，但皮货商人已纷纷选择使用汽车或是运货马车将皮货运至哈尔滨。据称哈尔滨并不征收此税。

为黑龙江水道委员会仍未向松花江航路标志委员会偿还欠款及黑龙江省政府再次提出借款 30000.00 银圆事：

滨江关税务司关于海关总税务司公署致瑷珲关第 132077 号令的意见已于数日前收

悉，兹计划在收到滨江关税务司对本人就此事于 1 月 13 日向其发送之信函的回复后，再开始撰写阁下要求的报告。依吾之见，黑龙江省政府是在试图令松花江水道委员会全权承担为黑龙江水道委员会提供财务援助之责任。兹已据此向滨江关税务司提议，如果松花江水道委员会能够以承担财务援助之责换取黑龙江水道委员会财务管理之权，从长远经济角度来看，尚属有益之举。

您真挚的

周骊

23. 周骊致梅乐和函

（第 145 号半官函）

CUSTOM HOUSE.

S/O No. 145   A I G U N   19th February, 31.

Dear Mr. Maze,

    I have duly received your S/O letter of the 28th January, 1931.

    <u>Trade: district of Aigun Customs: assumption that it extends from Moho (漠河), if not farther, to the mouth of the Sungari River</u>:

    My assumption is based on the following correspondence:

1.- Harbin despatch No. 164/I.G., §4;
2.-   "   "   "   1055/I.G.;
3.-   "   "   "   1294/I.G., §5;
4.-   "   "   "   2273/I.G., Appendix - "Customs Control";
5.- Aigun despatch No. 32/I.G., §4, 5, C, and 10;
6.-   "   "   "   37/I.G., §6, Heading and §1 of Enclosure No. 1, and section headed "General" and §2 of Enclosure No. 3;
7.-   "   "   "   41/I.G., §8;

See also No 17 from §§. cml.

F. W. Maze, Esquire,
    Etc., etc., etc.,
      S H A N G H A I

8.- Aigun despatch No. 123/I.G., paragraphs 1 and 2 of Enclosure; and
9.-   "   "   "   240/I.G., §10 of Enclosure No. 2: *See also S/O No. 110 to §§.* and on the procedure followed in 1928 (<u>vide</u> Aigun S/O letter No. 91) to control grain exported from Chik'ot'e (奇克特). I stated, in my S/O letter No. 139, that no beans were exported in 1928, but found later that 22,248 piculs of wheat were shipped by Soviet steamer from Chik'ot'e on the 25th September 1928 for Blagovestchensk, under special permission from the Chinese authorities. The steamer was made to enter at Taheiho; to take Customs Officers on board for whose services special examination fees were charged (<u>vide</u> Account <u>A</u> for the September Quarter 1928, Schedule Z/1, Voucher No. 4); to pay export duty on the wheat; and to return to, and clear at, Taheiho. The correspondence enumerated above shows that, although vague at first, the view that the Aigun Customs' district extends from Moho, if not farther, to the Sungari River, gradually developed until definitely expressed in §1 of the Enclosure to Aigun despatch No. 123, wherein Mr. Boezi went so far as to claim that it includes the Argun frontier as well as that along the Amur River. The former Mayor/Superintendent, Mr. Chang Shou-tsêng (张寿增), who was thoroughly acquainted

428

acquainted with this district, was of the opinion that anything exported or imported across the frontier, irrespective of locality, is liable to Customs duties. When discussing with me the possibility of the Gostorg being permitted to export beans across the ice from places on the Lower Amur, he told me that he would supply me with the necessary particulars to enable me to collect duty without having to send Officers overland in the middle of winter to supervise the beans. As I felt some doubt regarding our right to collect duties on goods exported from places which we do not control, I mentioned in my S/O letter No. 139 the procedure I proposed following in the hope that you would enlighten me on the subject. The Gostorg has now been given permission to export 100,000 poods, about 27,000 piculs, of beans from Taheiho, Aigun, Chik'ot'e, Wuyün (乌云), and other places on the Lower Amur and, as duty was levied in 1928 on the wheat from Chik'ot'e, I have, with the concurrence of the Superintendent, demanded the payment of export duties. The question of control of these beans does not raise any great difficulty as the Gostorg has been supplied by the Mayor/Superintendent with a huchao, which has to be presented for endorsement to the Magistrate of each district from which the beans are sent

sent across the frontier. The Gostorg will keep me informed of the quantities exported, and this information will be checked with particulars to be supplied by the Mayor/Superintendent to whom the huchao must ultimately be returned. The procedure appears irregular, but, in view of what has gone before, I have thought it advisable to maintain our right to collect. I shall be glad to receive your instructions on the subject

Yours truly,

第 145 号半官函　　　　　　　　　　　1931 年 2 月 19 日于瑷珲关

尊敬的梅乐和先生：

1931 年 1 月 28 日半官函收悉。

为瑷珲关区贸易事（推断瑷珲关管辖范围应自漠河至松花江与黑龙江交汇处）：

本人对瑷珲关管辖范围之推断依据如下：

1. 滨江关致海关总税务司公署第 164 号呈（第 4 项）；

2. 滨江关致海关总税务司公署第 1055 号呈；

3. 滨江关致海关总税务司公署第 1294 号呈（第 5 项）；

4. 滨江关致海关总税务司公署第 2273 号呈附录"海关管控"；

5. 瑷珲关致海关总税务司公署第 32 号呈（第 4、5、6、10 项）；

6. 瑷珲关致海关总税务司公署第 37 号呈（第 6 项，附件 1 标题及第 1 项，附件 3 通则及第 2 项）；

7. 瑷珲关致海关总税务司公署第 41 号呈（第 8 项）及总税务司第 17 号半官函；

8. 瑷珲关致海关总税务司公署第 123 号呈（附件第 1 和第 2 段）；

9. 瑷珲关致海关总税务司公署第 240 号呈（附件 2 第 10 项）、瑷珲关致总税务司第 110 号半官函及瑷珲关至总税务司第 91 号半官函（1928 年奇克特谷物出口管理办法）。

本人此前于瑷珲关第 139 号半官函中汇报称 1928 年并无大豆出口，但嗣后经查发现，1928 年 9 月 25 日有 22248 担小麦经中国政府特别批准由苏联轮船自奇克特运往布拉戈维申斯克（Blagovestchensk）。该艘轮船当时按照要求至大黑河口岸报关，为小麦缴纳出口税并于此办理结关，瑷珲关关员还登船检查并收取特别查验费（参阅瑷珲关第三季度 /A 账户 / 费用项目 2：1/ 传票字号 4）。

从以上所列各函可知，瑷珲关管辖范围最初的确有些模糊不清，但嗣后皆已逐步认为应自漠河至松黑两江合流处，而且包安济（G. Boezi）先生于瑷珲关第 123 号呈附件第 1 项中明确指出黑龙江及额尔古纳河两条边界河道的运输皆由瑷珲关管辖。前任黑河市政筹备处处长兼海关监督张寿增先生对大黑河地区之情形极为熟悉，也认为凡跨境进出口之货物，无论地点为何，均须缴纳海关关税。张寿增先生此前与本人商议批准苏联贸易公司在黑龙江下游地区收购大豆并通过结冰的江面运输出口至苏联一事时，表示会为瑷珲关提供必要信息以便于征收关税，免去冬季派遣关员经由陆路前往奇克特监管大豆出口之麻烦。不过当时对于海关是否有权对在关区以外地区出口之货物征收关税，本人的确存有疑虑,因此方于瑷珲关第 139 号半官函中提出建议办法,希望可得阁下指示。

苏联贸易公司已获准自大黑河、瑷珲、奇克特、乌云及黑龙江下游其他地区出口 100000 普特(约合 27000 担)大豆。鉴于瑷珲关已于 1928 年对自奇克特出口的小麦征收关税,经海关监督同意,本人已要求此批大豆缴纳出口税。于瑷珲关而言,监管此批大豆并非难事,因为苏联贸易公司已获得黑河市政筹备处处长兼海关监督签发的护照,出口大豆时,此护照须呈交给过江运输地区的行政长官签字,最后再交还给黑河市政筹备处处长兼海关监督。而本人则将根据此护照上的信息核对苏联贸易公司随时汇报的出口数据。此办法或许有违常规,但鉴于此前之情况,兹认为还是保留瑷珲关对此等货物征收关税之权力为宜。如蒙指示,不胜感激。

您真挚的

周骊

24. 周骊致梅乐和函

（第 149 号半官函）

CUSTOM HOUSE.

S/O No.149   A I G U N, 22nd April 1931.

Dear Mr. Maze,

Amur Aids Commission: balance of collection, after deduction of Customs one-tenth and salary and allowances of Technical Adviser, to be handed over to Mayor at the close of each month (I. G. despatch No. 569/132,077):

     I think it necessary to point out well in advance that, although there should be no difficulty in applying these instructions during the summer months, complications similar to those reported in Aigun despatch No. 532 will arise when the river freezes and there is no River Dues collection from which to pay the Technical Adviser's salary and allowances for the winter months of 1931-1932. The difficulty has been solved this year by the Sungari Aids' advance of $15,000.00 (Aigun despatch No. 539), which I retained, but the last instalment of $11,300.00, due to the Russians for 1930, still remains unpaid and the Mayor will, no doubt, apply for all available funds when this and the first payment for 1931 have to be met. The

F. W. Maze, Esquire.

Etc., etc., etc.,

S H A N G H A I.

     The more I study local Aids matters the more puzzled am I by the following:-

(1). Why the Technical Adviser was ever engaged as a Customs employee. The only possible explanation I can think of is that the Inspectorate was under the impression at the time of his first appointment that the Amur Commission would develop along the same lines as that of the Sungari.

(2) Why, after it was definitely expressed in I. G. despatch No. 93/92,051 that it was the Aids Commission and not the Customs which controlled Aids' funds, the Inspectorate later issued instructions regarding payments from River Dues Account.

(3) Why, when it was realised that the Customs did not control the Amur Commission, the re-employment of the Technical Adviser was not left to the decision of the Aids Commission after the expiry of his first contract.

(4) Why financial assistance was given from Sungari funds when such should have emanated from the provincial authorities.

(5) Why, if financial assistance were absolutely essential to ensure the smooth working of the Aids Agreement, such assistance was not made subject to absolute control of Aids' funds by the Customs as a quid pro quo.

It

It appears to me that too much importance was attached
in the past to Customs control of Aids' funds for
which there was no legal justification and that, as a
result of a general misconception regarding the relative
status of the Aids Commission and the Customs, the
interests of the latter received scant consideration and
were left unprotected.

Two alternatives in regard to Aids' matters are
now open to the Customs, 1.- to assume complete
financial control, and 2.- to act merely as a
collecting agency. The first is impractical for the
reasons set forth by the Harbin Commissioner in his
despatch No. 103/Aigun, copy of which was appended to
Aigun despatch No. 536/I.G., The second has been
achieved in part by the instructions of your despatch
No 569/132,077, but by inference it would seem that the
Customs are still responsible for the continued
employment of the Technical Adviser by the Amur
Commission and for the issue of his salary and allowances, and as far as I can see the question now is
what to do with the Technical Adviser in order to
achieve the second alternative in full. He is
certainly entitled to special consideration for his very
valuable services to China, but is such consideration
due from the Customs or from the Amur Aids Commission
and the Kirin and Heilungkiang authorities ? The
Customs have already paid heavily for their failure to
realise

realise that the Aids Commission and the Customs are
two entirely separate institutions. In my Confidential
S/O letter of the 7th February to the Staff Secretary,
I recommended that Mr. Ignatieff be appointed River
Inspector for the Sungari and Amur, but this recommendation was made from a purely local point of view and
assumed that the Sungari Aids would continue to be
controlled by the Harbin Customs. If the Sungari Aids
are likely to be taken over by the provincial
authorities, there would certainly be no object in
giving Mr. Ignatieff the above appointment, especially
as there is no scope for a Customs River Inspector on
the Amur where we have no control whatsoever over aids
matters.

As you will see from the foregoing, Amur Aids
have puzzled me a good deal since my arrival here and
the views now expressed are written with the object of
getting a clearer insight into a question which appears
~~unquestionably~~ beset with anomalies. I shall much
appreciate correction where my conclusions are wrong.
Personal effects of Baron von Grot:

In Aigun S/O letter No. 108, Mr. Talbot asked
for instructions regarding the disposal of these personal
effects. In your S/O letter of the 2nd July 1929,
you stated that the matter was being attended to, but
no instructions on the subject have been received and
the articles are still stored in the strong room.
Refugees

<u>Refugees from Siberia</u>:

   Large numbers of refugees escaped from Siberia this winter and were allowed to proceed to Harbin. The local authorities have now received orders to return all such refugees to the Soviet authorities and a batch of 80 was sent back from Aigun at the end of last month and another batch of 18 - men, women, and children all trussed together like cattle - was escorted across the river from Taheiho last night. I am afraid this means death for the men and work in the penal settlements (timber camps and mines) for the women.

    Yours truly,

第 149 号半官函　　　　　　　　　　　　　　**1931 年 4 月 22 日于瑷珲关**

尊敬的梅乐和先生：

黑龙江水道委员会：为每月月末扣除 10% 海关征税佣金及航务专门顾问薪俸津贴后将江捐税收余额移交给黑河市政筹备处处长事（海关总税务司公署第 569/132077 号令）：

兹认为有必要提前说明的是，夏季执行上述指令应无困难，但冬季江面结冰后因无江捐收入，只怕会再次出现瑷珲关第 532 号呈所汇报之情形，即与 1930—1931 年冬季一样，1931—1932 年冬季仍无江捐税收可供为航务专门顾问发放薪俸及津贴。今年已通过从松花江航路标志账户预支 15000.00 银圆为航务专门顾问发放薪俸及津贴（参阅瑷珲关第 539 号呈），但 1930 年中中方摊款尾款 11300.00 银圆仍未向苏方支付，黑河市政筹备处处长定会于需要支付此笔尾款及 1931 年第一笔分期款项时，想尽一切办法申请使用江捐账户中的全部可用余额。

深入研究地方航路标志相关事宜后，兹对以下问题颇为不解：

（1）为何航务专门顾问最初由海关雇用？本人能想到的唯一原因便是海关总税务司公署认为黑龙江水道委员会的发展将会和松花江水道委员会如出一辙，因此方有此决定。

（2）海关总税务司公署第 93/92051 号令既已明确表示，黑龙江航路标志经费应由黑龙江水道委员会管理，而非海关，为何嗣后又对江捐账户支出之事下达指令？

（3）海关既无权管理黑龙江水道委员会，为何未于航务专门顾问合同首次期满时，将续约事宜交由黑龙江航路标志委员会决定？

（4）黑龙江航路标志账户资金紧缺时，本应由黑龙江省政府负责解决，为何由松花江航路标志账户提供财务援助？

（5）如果由松花江航路标志账户提供财务援助是为确保顺利履行黑龙江航路标志协议，那么为何不借提供援助之机会换取海关对航路标志资金的绝对管理权？

兹认为，海关此前过于重视对航路标志经费的管控，但此行为实际并无合理依据。另外各方对黑龙江水道委员会与海关之间的关系普遍存在误解，海关的利益一直未得到充分的考虑，也未得到保护。

对于航路标志问题，海关现有两套方案可选：（1）全权管理航路标志经费；（2）仅负责征收江捐。

其中，第一套方案并不切实际，滨江关税务司已于致瑷珲关第 103 号函中做出了解释，此函抄件已随瑷珲关第 536 号呈发送至海关总税务司公署。第二套方案已按照海关总税务司公署第 569/132077 号令指示实施了一部分,但海关仍在负责为黑龙江水道委员会雇用航务专门顾问,并为之发放薪俸和津贴。兹认为,当务之急是如何处理航务专门顾问之事以便彻底实施第二套方案。

航务专门顾问所做之工作于中国而言颇有价值,的确值得予以特殊考虑。但是此等特殊考虑应由何方做出? 是海关还是黑龙江水道委员会和黑吉两省政府? 海关已因黑龙江水道委员会和省政府未能意识到海关与委员会是完全独立的两个机构而付出了沉重的代价。

瑷珲关 2 月 7 日致铨叙科税务司机密半官函中曾提议任命易保罗(P. I. Ignatieff)先生为海关巡江事务长,负责松花江和黑龙江上的事务。有此提议完全是出于地方上的考虑,而且是以松花江航路标志事务仍由滨江关管理为前提的。如果松花江航路标志事务将由省政府接管,那么对易保罗先生的任命便无意义,因为黑龙江上的航路标志事务不在海关管辖之列,海关巡江事务长亦无用武之地。

如上所述,黑龙江航路标志问题是本人自调任至瑷珲关以来一直颇为困惑之事,如今所陈种种,皆为厘清这一看似有些反常的问题。如推断有误,还望予以指正。

为男爵柯乐德(Von Grot)私人物品事:

铎博赉(R. M. Talbot)先生曾于瑷珲关第 108 号半官函中请示男爵格鲁特私人物品的处理办法。总税务司 1929 年 7 月 2 日半官函回复称此事正在处理中,但并未下达具体指令。如今相关物品依旧保存在瑷珲关保险库中。

为西伯利亚地区难民事:

今年冬季,大批难民自西伯利亚地区逃至大黑河。当时,地方政府已允许难民前往哈尔滨避难,而今又收到指令要将这些难民遣返回苏联。上月末,有 80 名难民从瑷珲被遣返;昨晚,又有 18 名难民,男女老幼皆像牲畜一样全部被绑在一起,从大黑河遣返回苏联。只怕其中的男性难民将全部被杀,女性难民将被判服劳役刑(即在木料厂和矿井内劳作)。

您真挚的

周骊

25. 周骊致梅乐和函

（第 150 号半官函）

CUSTOM HOUSE.

S/O No 150   A I G U N, 7th May, 19 31.

Dear Mr. Maze,

<u>Staff: Mr. P.I.Ignatieff, Technical Adviser on Amur Aids to Navigation, to be appointed Customs River Inspector:</u>

Your S/O letter of the 11th April and your despatch No. 595/134.203, finally dispose of the difficulties mentioned in my S/O letter No. 149. I am very glad you have found it possible to place Mr. Ignatieff's employment on a regular basis. The Mayor at first was rather inclined to oppose the new arrangement on the ground that, however satisfactory and **attractive** it might be now, it would probably result in the course of time in the Aids Commission being deprived of Mr. Ignatieff's services.

<u>Wharfage Dues:</u>

No more has been heard of the proposed levy of wharfage dues by the police. I explained to the Superintendent that the collection would be most irregular and I think he took the necessary action to have the suggestion dropped. I shall report by despatch

W. Maze, Esquire,

Etc., etc., etc.,

S H A N G H A I.

despatch if anything further develops.

<u>I. G. Circular No. 4166: Steam and Motor Vessels of less than 100 register tons prohibited from engaging in direct trade between China and abroad:</u>

In your S/O letter of the 20th April, 1931, you direct my attention to Kuan-wu Shu telegram No. 735 of the 20th March, 1931. May I point out that the instructions of this telegram have not been received by this Office.

<u>Mr. Chang Shou-tsêng (張壽增) former Mayor/Superintendent</u>

Mr. Chang, who is now attached to China's delegation to the Moscow Conference, arrived from Moscow viâ Blagovestchensk on the 24th April to take his family to Moukden by the first steamer, after which he will return to Moscow. I called on him on the day after his arrival. He informed me that the Conference is progressing satisfactorily; that it is at present busy with Chinese Eastern Railway questions; and that he has hopes of being able to recover the merchant vessels seized by the Soviet in 1929. He said that he had heard from the present Mayor that Mr. Ignatieff was to be appointed as a Customs River Inspector and he asked me to convey to you his thanks for this settlement of a troublesome question. He is especially appreciative of your action as he considers that the Heilungkiang authorities have failed in this matter.

Repairs

Repairs to Service Property:

My original intention was to commence repairs about the middle of June, but owing to the peculiarities of the local labour market, I had to change my decision and allow work to commence on the 3rd May. The contractor came to me about ten days ago and explained that there would soon be a general exodus of labourers from Tahsiho to the opium fields and that, if he did not engage his men at once, he would be left stranded later on. It appears that there is an annual pilgrimage of labourers, policemen, and soldiers to the opium producing districts where work is plentiful and pay satisfactory.

Navigation Season:

The ice began to move on the 2nd instant, but the river is not yet clear. We have had it very cold during the past few days. The water has not risen much and it is feared that the river will remain at a low level throughout the summer.

Yours truly,

第 150 号半官函   1931 年 5 月 7 日于瑷珲关

尊敬的梅乐和先生：

为任命黑龙江航务专门顾问易保罗（P. I. Ignatieff）先生担任海关巡江事务长事：

随着总税务司 4 月 11 日半官函及海关总税务司公署第 595/134203 号令指示的下达，瑷珲关第 149 号半官函所汇报之难题终于得以解决。易保罗先生能够正式成为海关雇员，令人颇为欢喜。黑河市政筹备处处长最初听闻此安排时仍有反对之意，认为虽然目前看来如此安排甚好，但久而久之，黑龙江水道委员会很有可能会失去易保罗先生这一得力干将。

为码头捐事：

当地警方所提议的征收码头捐一事暂无任何进展。兹已向海关监督说明此类征税完全有违常规，相信其已采取必要措施阻止此事。如有进展，将通过呈文正式汇报。

海关总税务司公署第 4166 号通令：为禁止注册一百吨以下之轮船及电船于中国与外国各埠间进行直接贸易事：

总税务司 1931 年 4 月 20 日半官函中指示参阅 1931 年 3 月 20 日关务署第 735 号电令，但瑷珲关并未收到过此电令。

为前任黑河市政筹备处处长兼海关监督张寿增先生事：

张寿增先生现被任命为参加莫斯科会议的中国代表，已于 4 月 24 日经布拉戈维申斯克（Blagovestchensk）抵达大黑河，计划携其家人乘坐今年航运开通后的第一艘轮船前往奉天，之后再独自返回莫斯科。在其抵达的第二日，本人便前去拜访，得知此次会议进展较为顺利，如今中苏双方正在商议中东铁路之事，1929 年被苏联方面截获的中国商船亦有希望收回。张寿增先生表示，已从现任黑河市政筹备处处长处听闻易保罗先生被正式任命为海关巡江事务长，特请本人代为转达他对总税务司帮助解决这一难题的感激之情。张寿增先生对这一安排给予高度赞赏，主要还因他认为黑龙江省政府未能解决此事。

为修缮海关关产事：

修缮工事原计划于 6 月中旬开始，但是由于当地劳务市场情况特殊，只得改于 5 月 3 日开工。十日前，工程承包商前来告知，不日之后，大黑河将有大批劳动力前往罂粟田劳作，如果不尽快预订人手，最终恐将无人可雇。似乎每年都会有大批劳工、警察和士兵前往罂粟产区，产区不仅有大量工作，而且报酬丰厚。

为航运季事：

5月2日,黑龙江江面上的冰层开始移动,但浮冰至今仍未完全消融。近几日来天气十分寒冷。黑龙江的水位上涨幅度不大,恐怕今年夏季黑龙江的水位会维持在一个较低的水平。

您真挚的

周骊

26. 周骊致梅乐和函

（第 158 号半官函）

S/O No. 158.　　　　Aigun　　5th Sept., 31

Dear Mr Maze,

Entered in Card Index.

Floods:

　　Owing to heavy rains in the Hingan Mountains (興安嶺) near Humaho (呼瑪河) and in the upper reaches of the Zeya River, Taheiho was for a day or two in danger of inundation when the waters of the Amur rose to within two feet of the flood level of 1929. Luckily, the Upper Amur was not affected and the rise here had almost stopped before the rise in the Zeya made itself felt. Humaho was flooded and has appealed for financial assistance, and several low-lying villages were partially under water and had to be abandoned for a few days. The river at Taheiho rose ten feet in seven days, but the fall was equally rapid.

Russian gunboats at the mouth of the Sungari River:

　　Several Russian gunboats and seaplanes lay off the mouth of the Sungari for some days and were the cause of much nervousness and many rumours. The

F. W. Maze, Esquire,
　SHANGHAI.

The Soviet land, air and river forces carry out manoeuvres along this frontier each summer, but since the 1929 conflict the population along the Chinese bank of the Amur is very nervous and ascribes sinister motives to all Soviet actions. Four gunboats and three seaplanes arrived at Blagovestchensk on the 22nd August and have since been carrying out manoeuvres above and below Taheiho. My impression is that the Soviet authorities are aware of the prevailing nervousness and think that by playing up to it they add to their prestige. Their patrol boats circle round Chinese vessels under way, but this may be done more with a view to frightening White Russian passengers and members of the crew. I see from the Tientsin paper that a Soviet gunboat was reported to have stopped and searched a Chinese steamer on the Ussuri River. The local agent of the Shipping Syndicate informed me that the gunboat circled round the vessel several times but did not actually interfere with her. I hope there was no truth in the report as Mr Ignatieff is on his way to the Ussuri and the Soviet authorities would never release him if they once got hold of him. He will be able to obtain more reliable information at Lahasusu.

Collision:

Collision: Chinese s.s. "Hsiching (西京)" and
Soviet raft:

The s.s. "Hsiching" left for Harbin in the
early afternoon of the 7th August. On reaching a
point about ten miles below Taheiho, she ran into
a heavy storm and was driven on to the Soviet
bank where she collided with, and broke up, a
Soviet raft. The local G. P. U. agents fired
across her bows when she tried to steam into
mid-stream and detained her until the Captain had
paid compensation for the damage to the raft. The
Captain suggested that a joint statement be prepared
and sent to the authorities of both countries at
Taheiho for negotiation, but the G. P. U. agents
informed him that such a course would necessitate
the detention of the vessel until settlement of
the case. The Captain decided to pay the sum
demanded and proceeded on his journey without further
incident. I do not know whether the Chinese
authorities have protested against this high-handed
action.

Staff: Entered in Card-Index.

I telegraphed to you yesterday recommending
that one Clerk be transferred from this port. Having
been here during one navigation season, it is now
                                        possible

possible for me to see that one Assistant, helped
by me, can perform the work of the Secretary and
Accounts offices and that two Clerks, one senior and
one junior, can do the work of the General and
Returns Offices.

Title Deeds: Entered in Card-Index.

The question of registration of our Title
Deeds still remains unsettled. The Magistrate has
repeatedly promised to complete the necessary
formalities as soon as possible, but the delay is
due to the Tsitsihar authorities to whom he had to
refer regarding the waiving of registration fees.

Property: Liangchiat'un Barrier: Entered in Card-Index.

I have been informed verbally that the
Aigun Magistrate has agreed to use the building for
the local police, on our terms, but I must await
an official communication before I can proceed further
in this matter.

                                        Yours truly,

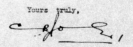

第 158 号半官函   1931 年 9 月 5 日于瑷珲关

尊敬的梅乐和先生：

为洪水事：

由于呼玛河附近的兴安岭地区及结雅河上游一带连降暴雨,黑龙江水位一度上涨,最高时仅与 1929 年洪水水位相差两英尺,大黑河有一两日都面临着被洪水淹没之危险。幸而黑龙江上游地区并未受到影响,而且在结雅河水位上涨之前,黑龙江大黑河一段的水位已停止上涨。呼玛河地区遭遇洪水侵袭后,已申请财务援助,但地势低洼处的村庄已被洪水淹没大半,只得暂时放弃救援。大黑河处的水位在七日内上涨了 10 英尺,不过之后水位下降得也十分迅速。

为苏联炮艇停靠于松黑两江交汇处事：

近日来,苏联几艘炮艇和水上飞机一直停靠于松花江与黑龙江交汇处,一时间流言四起,气氛十分紧张。每年夏季,苏联陆军、空军和海军都会在中苏边境地区集结演习。但自 1929 年中苏军队在此地爆发冲突以来,黑龙江华岸各地民众便一直生活于紧张之中,认为苏联当局所采取的一切行动均是出于战争目的。8 月 22 日,苏联四艘炮艇和一架飞机抵达布拉戈维申斯克(Blagovestchensk),随即开始于大黑河上游和下游地区开展军事演习。兹认为,苏联当局是在故意制造紧张局势,希望借此提高威望。在此期间,其巡逻艇一直绕着中国船只巡弋,不过此举或许是为了恐吓白俄乘客及船员。据《天津日报》所载,苏联炮艇曾在乌苏里江上拦截一艘中国轮船,并登船搜查。哈尔滨官商航业总联合局大黑河代理人亦告知,其轮船在航行过程中曾遇炮艇围绕巡弋,幸而未受到实质干扰。希望上述消息皆为子虚乌有之事,因为易保罗(P. I. Ignatieff)先生现正在乌苏里江上巡查,一旦被苏联当局抓获,便不会再被释放返回大黑河。不过其将于拉哈苏苏分关获取更为准确之情报。

为中国 "西京(Hsiching)" 号轮船与苏联木筏碰撞事：

"西京" 号轮船于 8 月 7 日下午启程前往哈尔滨。在行至大黑河下游约 10 英里处时遭遇风暴浪潮,一时失控驶向俄岸,造成一艘苏联木筏倾覆。事件发生后,该轮船试图返回华岸一侧,但船头遭到当地政治部士兵的射击,随后被扣留,直到船主赔偿了木筏损失后,才获释放。当时船主建议双方起草联合声明,并交由大黑河的中俄两方政府审议,但政治部长官表示,若如此则须于事情得以解决之前暂时扣留轮船。为防止事态继续扩大延误航期,船主决定支付苏方要求的赔款,随后继续起航前往哈尔滨。不知中国政府是否会抗议苏方的粗暴行径。

为人事变动事：

本人已于昨日向阁下发送电报，建议调离一名税务员。经历一个航运季后，可以确定，一名帮办在本人的帮助下可以完成文案房和会计课的工作，两名税务员（初级、高级各一名）可以完成总务股和统计课的工作。

为地契事：

瑷珲关关产地契登记一事至今仍未解决。瑷珲县县长一再表示会尽快完成必要的登记手续，但因其向齐齐哈尔当局提出免除登记费用，故有所延误。

为梁家屯分卡关产事：

据悉，瑷珲县县长已同意按照海关要求将此关产移交当地警察使用，但本人须待双方正式沟通后，方可采取进一步行动。

您真挚的

周骊

27. 周骊致梅乐和函

（第 159 号半官函）

S/O No. 159.　　　　　　Aigun　　1st Oct.,　　31

Dear Mr Maze,

Political Situation:

Very little news regarding the situation in South Manchuria has been received here. For a few days there were many wild rumours, but these appear to have ceased and the place remains quiet. I believe the Military authorities have been instructed to give Japanese residents special protection. The Telegraph Administration refused to accept telegrams up to the 24th ultimo for places beyond Harbin, but has since transmitted them at Sender's Risk. The Wireless Station has all along transmitted telegrams without restriction. The latter are sent to Tsitsihar and from there to Peiping. Your WIGE telegrams have come through by land line and by wireless after some delay. The last, of the 28th September

F. W. Maze, Esquire,
　　etc., etc., etc.,
　　　　SHANGHAI.

September, arrived yesterday morning. The Post Office informs me that mails are getting through from Shanghai and Tientsin. From the Blagovestchensk newspaper it would appear that the Soviet's sympathies are with China, but the local Military have been instructed to enforce martial law along this frontier to ensure that no incident arises to disturb friendly relations.

Russian Consul:

A new Russian Consul, a Mr Mihailoff, arrived on the 26th September from Moscow where he was attached to the Chinese Department of the People's Commissary for Foreign Affairs. He is a man of about 34 years of age and has a fair knowledge of English. He was formerly stationed in Peiping and Kalgan.

Amur Aids Agreement:

The Amur Aids Agreement, signed here on the 16th August 1930 (Aigun Despatch No. 504), expires on the 31st December next. Both the River Inspector and I have recommended to the Mayor the advisability of commencing negotiations as early as possible for a new agreement, but he thinks it better to wait until later. As the Commissioner's
position

position is now that of collector of Navigation
Fees (I. G. Despatches Nos. 569/132,077 and
612/135,648), I do not like to take too active
a part in Aids matters. From private sources I
hear that the Russian Consul wants if possible
to have the new Aids Agreement negotiated in
Moscow.

Rainfall: Entered in Desk Index.

It rained almost continuously throughout
September and the river is very high for this
time of the year. Considering the amount of rain
that has fallen this year Taheiho was lucky not
to have been flooded. A short spell of fine
weather at the end of August saved us from a
repetition of 1928 conditions.

Property: Liangchiat'un Barrier Entered in Desk Index.

The Aigun Magistrate has agreed in writing
to use the house, on our terms, for the local
Police and I am now waiting for the roads to
dry sufficiently to permit of my proceeding
thither, in company with the Superintendent and
the Magistrate, to hand over the building.

Yours truly,

第 159 号半官函   **1931 年 10 月 1 日于瑷珲关**

尊敬的梅乐和先生：

为政治局势事：

关于南满洲地区局势的消息，本地鲜少听闻，日前曾有许多流言，但如今似已平息，大黑河又恢复平静。相信军方已收到指示要为本地日本居民提供特殊保护。自上月 24 日起，大黑河电报局便拒绝接收哈尔滨以外各地发来之电报，但可以发送电报，只是须由发送人自担风险。无线电台一直可以发送电报，且不受限制，但须先发报至齐齐哈尔再转发至北平。关于阁下发送之"收税率"电报，有线和无线两种方式均已传递成功，只是无线电报有些延迟，上一封 9 月 28 日的无线电报，昨日上午方收悉。邮政局方面告知上海和天津发来的邮件依然可以顺利接收。据布拉戈维申斯克（Blagovestchensk）报纸所载，似乎苏联当局更支持中国，并已指令地方军队于中苏边境实行军事管制，以确保不会有事故发生影响两国友好关系。

为苏联领事事：

新任驻黑河苏联领事米海依罗夫（Mihailoff）先生已于 9 月 26 日自莫斯科抵达大黑河，在莫斯科期间曾任职于人民外事委员会中国部（Chinese Department of the People's Commissary for Foreign Affairs），年约 34 岁，精通英文，此前曾在北平和张家口担任领事。

为黑龙江航路标志协议事：

中苏双方于 1930 年 8 月 16 日在大黑河签署的黑龙江航路标志协议（参阅瑷珲关致海关总税务司公署第 504 号呈）将于 1931 年 12 月 31 日期满。巡江事务长与本人已建议黑河市政筹备处处长尽早与苏方协商新协议，但其认为此事最好稍后再议。鉴于税务司如今仅为航务费的征收者（参见海关总税务司公署致瑷珲关第 569/132077 号和 612/135648 号令），本人不愿在航路标志一事上表现得过于积极。据悉，新任苏联领事希望可于莫斯科协商新航路标志协议。

为降雨事：

9 月几乎日日都有降雨，以致黑龙江水位暴涨，比往年此时水位高很多。所幸的是今年雨量虽大，但大黑河地区并未爆发洪水。8 月末出现的短暂晴朗天气使得大黑河免于重蹈 1928 年之覆辙。

为梁家屯分卡关产事：

瑷珲县县长已同意以书面形式说明将按照海关要求将此关产暂供当地警署使用，待前往梁家屯之道路可以通行后，本人将与海关监督和瑷珲县县长一同前去办理房屋交接手续。

您真挚的

周骊

28. 周骊致梅乐和函

（第 160 号半官函）

S/O No. 160.　　　　　　　　Aigun　　16th Oct., 31

Dear Mr Maze,

Political Situation: Entered in Conf.Index.

　　　Conditions continue quiet here, but very little is known of developments in the rest of the country. The Heiho Ssu-ling (司 令), General Ma Chan-shan (马占山), left for Tsitsihar via Harbin on the 12th instant. I believe he has been ordered by Nanking to take control of the Heilungkiang Government during General Wan Fu-lin's absence in Peiping. It is reported that the Japanese are trying to induce a certain General Chang at Taonan (洮 南) to usurp General Wan's office and that Nanking has taken this step to counteract these activities. Whether there is any truth in these reports I am unable to say, but there seems to be no doubt that conditions at Tsitsihar are not altogether normal. We have had a perfect epidemic of dinners since the arrival of the

F. W. Maze, Esquire,
　　etc.,　etc.,　etc.,
　　　　SHANGHAI.

new Soviet Consul - with the usual accompaniment of speeches - but on each occasion there has either been no mention whatsoever of the political situation or it has been referred to in a vague and indirect manner.

Accident to Shipping: Entered in Conf.Index.

　　　The Tung Pei Shipping Syndicate's tow-steamer "Hangchow" ran aground on the 7th instant at a point about ten miles below Aigun and it is probable that she will not be re-floated this year. Being a tow-steamer she could not be lightened beyond the dismantling of her engines. The captain telegraphed to Taheiho on the 8th for assistance, but there were no vessels in port at the time and nothing could be done until the 9th when the s.ss. "Tungshan" and "Tahsing" reached the stranded vessel on their way up river. The Syndicate's local agent did not apply to the River Inspector for advice and did not seem to welcome it when it was volunteered so that it has not been possible for this office to render much assistance. With the river falling fast, every twenty-four hours' delay added seriously to the difficulties of salvage

salvage, but the agent preferred to wait, before
taking any action, for a report from the s.s.
"Tahsing" and for instructions from his head
office. Salvage work undertaken by the "Tungshan",
"Tahsing" and a Soviet steamer, chartered for the
purpose, has failed and the "Hangchow" is now
nearly high and dry. The captain of the latter
vessel is a young, inexperienced man and he seems
to have done very little to re-float his ship
immediately after she grounded.

    Yours truly,

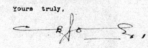

第 160 号半官函　　　　　　　　　　　　　　1931 年 10 月 16 日于瑷珲关

尊敬的梅乐和先生：

政治局势：

大黑河地区目前平静如常，但不知其他地区之情形如何。黑河总司令马占山先生已于本月 12 日经由哈尔滨前往齐齐哈尔。兹认为，其必是接到南京方面之指示，将于万福麟总司令滞留北平期间接管黑龙江省政府。据报告，日军现正设法引诱洮南某位张总司令篡夺万福麟之职，南京政府亦正因如此方有此命令，以期对此加以阻挠。虽不知此消息是否准确，但齐齐哈尔之形势的确有反常之态。虽然新任驻黑河苏联领事到来后，经常与海关摆宴相谈，但往往不会涉及政治局势之相关话题，即使有涉及，亦十分含混婉转。

船运事故：

东北联合航务局之拖船杭州（Hang chow）号于 10 月 7 日在瑷珲下游 10 英里处搁浅，今年或将无法再次漂浮起来，只有拆除引擎才能使其重量变轻。该船船主于 10 月 8 日向大黑河发送电报求救，但当时大黑河港口内并无可用之船只，10 月 9 日东山（Tung shan）号轮船和大兴（Tah sing）号轮船在向上游行驶之途中遇到该搁浅之轮船。东北联合航务局大黑河之代理并未向巡江工司征询意见，亦不愿听取巡江工司提出之建议，因此，瑷珲关无法提供过多之帮助。目前水位急速下降，每昼夜之延迟皆会增加营救之难度，然该代理表示在收到大兴号轮船之汇报以及其船运协会之指示前，不愿采取任何行动。但东山号轮船、大兴号轮船以及一艘获得特许之苏联轮船所采取之营救行动均已失败告终。而杭州号拖船目前之处境十分艰难，该拖船之船主非常年轻，毫无经验，似乎并未于船只搁浅后有何作为。

您真挚的

周骊

29. 周骊致梅乐和函

（第 169 号半官函）

S/O No. 169.   Aigun   1st March, 32

Dear Sir Frederick,

Political Situation:

        It is reported here that General Ma Chan-
shan is definitely co-operating with the Japanese
and the Moukden faction and some of the local
officials are preparing to leave for China, via
Siberia, Germany, France and the Suez route. Wan
Kuo-p'in, Wan Fu-lin's son, has been told by
General Ma that he is persona non grata with the
new administration. He is therefore leaving by
the above route, and the Mayor/Superintendent and
General Ma's son, who is opposed to his father's
policy, are planning to accompany him. Beyond press
reports, nothing is known here regarding the
proposed "Manchurian-Mongolian Republic". Your
telegram of the 20th February reached me on the
23rd ultimo.

Long Leave:

        I have duly received your S/O letter of
the

Sir Frederick Maze, K. B. E.,
        etc.,   etc.,   etc.,
        S H A N G H A I.

the 10th February 1932, in reply to mine numbered
165, and have noted your remarks regarding the
probable shortage of senior Indoor employees
throughout the years 1932 and 1933. The two
principal reasons which prompted my request are :-

    1.- My two eldest boys will both be in the
        Senior School at Clifton next year and,
        as their present guardian desires to
        relinquish his responsibilities, plans for
        their future must be re-arranged; and

    2.- My third son, who is here, is aged
        eleven and must be sent to school this
        year. If I cannot get leave, my wife
        will have to take him to England, which
        will mean maintaining two households and
        will add greatly to expenses.

I fully understand that private affairs must always
be subordinated to Service interests and do not
wish in any way to inconvenience you by applying
for special consideration. Perhaps my S/O letter
No. 165 was not clear on the point, but my
intention was to inform you that, in the event of
a sufficiency of staff, I should be amongst those
who would be glad to be granted leave from a
date earlier than that on which it is actually
due.

        Yours truly,

452

第 169 号半官函   1932 年 3 月 1 日于瑷珲关

尊敬的梅乐和先生：

政治局势：

据报,马占山总司令现已确定与日军合作,奉天方面以及一些当地官员正准备经由西伯利亚、德国、法国及苏伊士之路线返回中国内地。万福麟之子万国宾于马占山总司令处获悉新政府对其之敌意后,亦计划通过上述路线逃离,而黑河市政筹备处处长兼海关监督 [①] 以及马占山总司令之子(反对其父之政策)计划与他共同离开。但关于提议之 "满洲蒙古共和" 一事,大黑河方面仅能通过报纸获得消息。本人已于 2 月 23 日收悉阁下 2 月 20 日之电报。

长期休假：

1932 年 2 月 10 日半官函(回复本人第 165 号半官函)收悉,关于阁下提及 1932 年和 1933 年超等内班关员之人手或将不足一事,兹说明本人提出休假申请之理由：

1. 两名长子将于明年进入克里弗顿(Clifton)学院高中部,而其现监护人已打算放弃监护权,因此本人需要为二人之将来重新安排；

2. 三儿子现居于此地,但已满 11 岁,到了入学之年龄,若本人无法休假,则将由妻子带其回英国,如此一来,一家人两地分居,费用亦会大大增加。

当然,本人知道,海关之利益远高于个人之事,亦不希望因提出特殊要求而为阁下带来任何不便。或许本人第 165 号半官函未能清楚表意,但本人之初衷乃为谨向阁下说明在人手充足之情况下,若可提前蒙阁下批准休假,将不胜感激。

您真挚的

周骊

---

① 即齐肇豫。

30. 周骊致梅乐和函

（第 170 号半官函）

S/O No. 170   Aigun   16th March, 32

Dear Sir Frederick,

Mutiny of Local Troops:

As reported in my telegram of the 12th, the local troops mutinied at 2.30 in the morning of the 10th March. The flag question was merely a pretext for concerted action after various other grievances had been ignored by the senior military officer at Taheiho. For one thing, their pay had not been issued for three or four months and it now transpires that, with a minimum of care and forethought on the part of General Tsui, the officer left in command here by General Ma, the mutiny could have been averted. He was, however, too busily occupied with his opium-smoking, brothel-frequenting, and gambling cronies to keep in touch with his officers and men and averred to the last moment that there was no danger. The President of the Chamber of Commerce, a man of marked ineptitude, is also reported to have miscalculated the gravity of the

Sir Frederick Maze, K. B. E.,
     etc.,   etc.,   etc.,
          S H A N G H A I.

the situation, and to have purposely hidden the facts at his disposal from the merchants. Whatever the reasons, the outbreak took the town by complete surprise and cash, goods, opium, jewelry, and gold, to the tune of about $1,000,000, a first rough estimate, were looted. The mutiny must have been planned for weeks as it was carried out to schedule and the mutineers knew exactly what was to be found in each house, office or shop.

The signal for the outbreak was three rifle shots fired at four points in the town, after which looting, accompanied by indiscriminate shooting, continued throughout the day. One centre of activities was General Ma's house, right opposite the front gate of the Commissioner's house and till 4.30 p.m. there was a constant stream of soldiers up and down the street. To make my position more difficult, there was another post in the street behind my house so that it was impossible to move without passing through a large number of mutineers. For some unknown reason, the Commissioner's and Tidesurveyor's houses were not entered. The Custom House was entered by a group of four at 4 a.m. in the morning of the 10th March

March, but they interfered with nothing except the desk of the Bank of China shroff. For this immunity, Mr Chên Pei Yin, 4th Assistant A, deserves special credit. He was in the General Office with his wife and Mr Fan Chin Tsao, 1st Class Tidewaiter, and he explained that they were in the Customs' office, requested that no official documents be touched as there was no money anywhere, and offered to take them up to his quarters to enable them to help themselves from his personal belongings. They took all available money and all Mrs Chên's jewelry. He also had the unpleasant experience of having a Mauser and a rifle placed against his body. At 11 o'clock of the same morning, another party of soldiers entered the Custom House compound, but they confined their attention to one half of the quarters of the Miscellaneous Staff.

The house occupied by Mr Ignatieff was entered by eight different parties and he lost money, clothes, and household goods, but one brute in the eighth party, for no accountable reason, led him into the backyard to be shot. On arrival there he told Mr Ignatieff to return to the house, and proceeded to brand him and his wife on the body with a red hot poker. Mrs Ignatieff also received three heavy kicks in the lower part of the

the abdomen. They were both badly wounded, but, apart from the pain, no serious injury was inflicted. They are recovering slowly but satisfactorily. After the eighth attack they left their house and sought refuge in the Custom House. This was about 4.30 p.m., when the main body of the mutineers had moved off to gather their loot and to prepare for flight.

The Old Custom House Building, occupied by Mr Ch'ang Fu Yüan, 3rd Clerk A, was broken into two or three times, but he and his family hid themselves in the stable as soon as they heard the first shots and were not molested. They lost clothes and household goods.

The houses of all other members of the staff, with the exception of that of Mr Yang Ts'un-hou, Writer, were visited by several parties and clothes, money, jewelry and household goods were removed. Mr Yang is indebted to his neighbour, a junior military officer in league with the mutineers, for his good fortune.

At 9 a.m. of the 10th March, Mr Crossland, whose house is conveniently situated on the bund, sent his family to Blagovestchensk and then managed to make his way to the Custom House

House. At 2 p.m. of the same day, Mrs Chên and Mrs Ch'ang, the latter with two children, succeeded in getting to Blagovestchensk.

From the outbreak of the mutiny to 5 p.m. of the 10th March, my family and I were unable to leave our house owing to the large numbers of mutineers congregated both in front and at the back of the compound. From 3 to 7 a.m., I was waiting at the front gate to admit any mutineers that might seek entrance as I felt that it would be better to throw the house and its contents open to them at once so as to avoid damage and to lessen the shock to my wife and two small boys. At 10 a.m. I made an attempt to leave for the office, but decided that such a course would be unwise with so many troops about, especially as He had so far not been molested and my presence might draw attention to this fact. At 5 p.m., the main body of the mutineers having left our vicinity, I accompanied my family to the Custom House and instructed Mr Crossland to take them to Blagovestchensk. The relief at getting them away was immense. Having at last gained the Custom House, I took control of the staff and arranged for a general withdrawal to the river and, if conditions became too bad, to Blagovestchensk. We could not resist entry by armed troops and the best policy was

/ to be prepared to get every one away before they arrived. To enable us to get sufficient warning, the back gate was heavily barred and barricaded and a watch was set. Luckily, the bund was deserted as, apart from the Custom House, there is hardly another building with its main entrance facing the river. Looting proceeded throughout the night, and the situation was no less dangerous as a part of the troops, which had abstained from looting earlier, started in the evening and was joined by the riff-raff of the town, the poorer elements, escaped prisoners from the Magistrate's compound, peasants from the neighbouring villages, the police - in fact every one including the owners of small shops. The return of some of the looters of the morning of Kietkhand aggravated the situation on the 11th March, but on the 12th March some attempt was made to gain control of the situation. Most of the responsible officials had, however, disappeared and there was no one to take the lead. On the 13th, some of the officials reappeared and the troops were reported as willing to resume their duties on the understanding that they would not be punished. The merchants also organised a force to search for looted articles. The situation throughout the 14th and 15th continued uncertain with no one to coordinate co-ordinate the efforts of each department. There was also the danger of attack by mutineers from the up river districts, and, when news of the despatch of troops from Tsitsihar became known, it was feared that the old troops might again loot and make off before the new forces came within striking distance. In the evening of the 14th, an advance guard of 100 of the Tsitsihar troops arrived under a junior officer and entered without opposition, but they were too few to ease the situation and conditions at the time of writing are still doubtful, although outwardly better. I therefore continued the precautions taken on the first night and any of the staff and their families so wishing were allowed to sleep at the Custom House. I remained with them until last night as my presence gave them a rallying point and seemed to re-assure them - not that I could do more than organise a general dash for the river if a body of troops attempted to enter the Custom House. The atmosphere is less tense today, but the authorities are still unable to give more than a vague reply when asked whether they consider the town safe. Conditions will not return to normal until the main body of the new troops arrives to take up garrison duty. General Hsü and his men are at present in pursuit of the mutineers below

below Aigun.

The wholesale looting of Taheiho has impoverished the business community and it will probably be years before it regains its former prosperity. Local inhabitants, although hard hit by the business depression of the past eight years, have had much capital at their disposal since the boom years 1918-1923, but another boom on a similar scale is not likely to occur again.

Staff losses have, fortunately, on further investigation been found to be much less than was anticipated. Many articles thought lost were later found. Service property, apart from two panes of glass in the River Inspector's house, was undamaged.

All important archives were packed in cases and stored in the basement of the Custom House. Some, which I had removed to my house owing to the political situation, were concealed in the kitchen cellar amongst the potatoes.

The Custom House was open throughout the trouble, but it will probably be a long time before any cargo is declared for import or export.

Aigun was looted in the morning of the 11th March and the Custom House was broken into. No Service loss has been reported, but Mr Sun Hung Tsao

Tsao, 3rd Class Tidewaiter, lost many of his clothes and other personal effects. His cook was wounded in the foot by a rifle shot fired at him when he was running away.

In conclusion, I beg to report that the staff on the whole deserve commendation for their steadiness, loyalty, willingness to carry out orders, and cheerfulness. That all were at times very nervous, there is no harm in admitting as, in my humble opinion, a mob of heavily armed mutineers, interspersed with the worst elements of the town and surrounding districts, supplies just cause for apprehension.

Before closing, I should like to record my appreciation of the assistance and courtesy shown by the Soviet officials at Taheiho and Blagovestchensk in facilitating the evacuation of families of the Customs' staff.

Yours truly,

P.S. 17th March: The situation is improved but will continue uncertain until the arrival of the new General from Tsitsihar. He is at present fighting the mutineers and is reported to have met with success. General Tsui, who was taken away by the mutineers, returned last night, but I do not know how he escaped.

第 170 号半官函　　　　　　　　　　　　　1932 年 3 月 16 日于瑷珲关

尊敬的梅乐和先生：

地方军队发生暴动：

如本人于 3 月 12 日电报中所述,大黑河地方军队于 3 月 10 日凌晨二时三十分发起暴动。国旗之事仅为联合行动之借口,此前士兵们已有诸多不满,如军饷之事,据说已有三四个月未予发放,但一概未得大黑河高级军官之理会。马占山总司令当时将崔司令①留于大黑河指挥,若该崔司令对士兵有所顾虑,或可避免此次暴动之发生,然为与其他官员等拉拢关系,他整日忙于吸食鸦片、招妓、赌博等事,甚至于暴动前夕,依然认为不会有何危险。黑河商会主席亦属无能之辈,据报告称,他当时对事态之发展判断失误,并擅自做主,故意向商人隐瞒真相。然无论暴乱之原因为何,大黑河已遭突袭,现金、商品、鸦片、珠宝和黄金无一不遭掠夺,初步估计,此次损失高达 1000000 银圆。此番暴动定已筹谋良久,且按计划行事,而暴动之人必对各处房屋、办公室以及商铺之内所有之物了如指掌。

暴动开始前,暴动者于城内四个地点连放三声枪响以作行动之信号,随后大批暴动者便涌入街头开始掠夺,肆意射杀,整整一日皆是如此。马占山总司令之住所为暴动者的主要突袭地点,而税务司住所之前门恰与之相对,下午四时三十分,士兵不断涌入街道,税务司住所后门所对街道亦被暴动者包围,如此一来,本人之处境愈发艰难,无法离开。然不知为何,税务司和监察长之住所并未有暴动者闯入,凌晨四时许,有四人闯入海关办公楼,但除中国银行管账员之办公桌,并未损坏其他任何物品。关于此次暴动,应特别嘉奖四等一级帮办陈培因先生。陈培因先生当时与妻子和一等稽查员樊金藻先生皆在总务课办公室,见有暴动者闯入便向其说明,此乃海关办公室,并无钱财,不可擅动海关文件,随后又指引暴动者至其宿舍,让他们自行拿走其私人之物以及妻子所有珠宝。陈培因先生还于此次暴动中中枪。当日上午十一时,另外一批士兵闯入海关办公楼大院,但仅闯入部分杂项职员之宿舍。易保罗(P. I. Ignatieff)先生之住所遭到八批不同士兵闯入,不仅钱财、衣服、家居用品皆遭掠夺,就连其自己亦被一残暴士兵无故拖拽至后院射伤。该士兵闯入易保罗先生住所之时,命其返回屋中,并用烧红之烙铁在其与妻子二人身上烙印,其妻子小腹之处更是被重重踢了三脚,二人受伤严重,但除此之外未受其

---

① 即崔柏山。

他严重伤害，现正于缓慢恢复之中，状况已有所好转。遭受八次袭击后，易保罗先生与妻子二人逃至海关办公楼避难。下午四时三十分，暴动者主要部队开始收敛战利品，为后续战争做准备。

三等一级税务员常福元先生一直居于旧海关办公楼，此处亦遭遇三四次袭击，但其与家人在听到第一声枪响之后，便藏于马厩之中，因此并未遭到攻击，仅丢失衣物等。

除汉文文牍员杨存厚先生以外，海关其他关员之房屋均遭到数次袭击，衣物、钱财、珠宝以及家居用品皆被掠走。杨存厚先生幸得其邻居庇护，方躲过此劫，该邻居是一名初级军官，亦参与了此次暴动。

克思澜（J. A. Crossland）先生之住所靠近码头，暴动当日，于上午九时将其家人送至布拉戈维申斯克（Blagovestchensk），随后返回海关办公楼。当日下午二时，陈培因妻子以及常福元的妻子和两个孩子均被成功转移至布拉戈维申斯克。

3月10日自暴动开始至下午五时，本人及家人因房屋周围皆有暴动者而一直无法逃离。本人自上午三时至七时一直于前门等待暴动者闯入，当时考虑若将房屋及屋内各物拱手让与暴动者，便可减少妻子及两个幼子遭到袭击之险。上午十时，本人曾试图前往海关办公楼，但之后考虑到既有重兵包围，若有此举，实不明智，尤其当时本人尚未遭遇袭击，若贸然出现定会引起暴动者之注意。下午五时，本人见住所周围之暴动者已基本撤离，便携家人前往海关办公楼，委托克思澜先生带其前往布拉戈维申斯克。待家人逃离后，本人方略有放松之感，并于海关关员皆聚集于海关办公楼后，开始布控安排向江边撤离一事，以便于事态严重之时，向布拉戈维申斯克撤离。然考虑到若有暴动者持械闯入，海关关员根本无力抵抗，因此最为妥善之办法便是在其闯入之前，做好撤离之准备。幸运的是，除海关办公楼，再无其他建筑之入口面江而开，因此码头尚无暴动者出没，本人遂命众人将海关办公楼后门插严，用重物挡住，并派人把守，以期随时可发现暴动者之举动。然掠夺之事一直未有停歇，当日夜里依然如此，情势十分危急。白天未参与掠夺之军队于夜间开始行动，不仅如此，其他所有人，包括镇上的下等人、穷人、逃犯、邻村村民、警察甚至小商铺店主均加入掠夺行动之中。3月11日，前日上午参与掠夺行动之军队再次返回，以致形势更加严峻。3月12日，有人试图控制局势，然而当地官员大多已消失了踪迹，无人出面主事。3月13日，部分官员露面，据报，军队方面愿意重新担起责任，但前提条件是不得受到惩罚。商人方面，亦成立队伍开始搜寻被掠夺之物。3月14日和15日，形势依然不甚明朗，无人出面统领大局。此外，上游地区之暴动者亦有可能袭击大黑河。而齐齐哈尔方面派遣军队之消息传开后，暴动者亦有可能在军队进入之前再次行掠夺之事，而后逃跑。3月14日晚,齐齐哈尔100人的先行部队在一名初级军官的带领下进入大黑河,未遭抵抗,但人数太少,无法缓解局势。本人写此函之时,从表面看来,局面虽已有所好转,但依然未明,故于当晚继续布防,但允准关员及其家人如有需要可于海关办公楼睡觉。作为众关员之精神支柱,本人至3月15日晚一直与大家在一处,以安定人心。当然,对于此事,本人亦只能于军队试图闯入海关办公楼之时,率领众人冲向江边。3月16日,情况有所缓和,但政府方面对于大黑河是否已安全之问题依然无法给出明确答复。只有待新主力军队抵达大黑河接管守备任务之后,此地之情况方有回归正常之可能。目前徐司令①已带领其人马于瑷珲口岸下游搜寻暴动者。

大黑河遭遇此番掠夺后,商业方面已然受到重创,恐怕需数年之后,方能重获此前之繁荣。过去八年间,大黑河当地居民虽因贸易萧条而备受打击,但早已于1918年至1923年经济繁荣期间赚得大量钱财,不过,如今恐难再有如此繁荣之势。

幸运的是,进一步调查后发现,海关关员之损失比预计要小很多,此前以为丢失之物品已于后期寻回。海关关产方面,除巡江事务长住所之两片玻璃窗被损坏,再无受损之物。

凡重要之文档皆已封箱保存于海关办公楼地下室,此外,本人此前考虑到政治局势动荡,已将一些文档转移至税务司住所处,藏于厨房地窖中,以马铃薯掩盖。

动乱期间,海关办公楼并未关闭,但恐怕要许久之后方会有货物进出口报关之业务。

3月11日清晨,瑷珲遇袭,海关办公楼亦有暴动者闯入,但目前尚未收到损失汇报,唯三等稽查员孙鸿藻先生丢失大量衣物。其厨子在逃离过程中,脚部中枪。

兹申请,嘉奖瑷珲关全体关员,他们在此次暴动中沉着冷静、忠诚乐观、甘于服从命令,虽偶有慌乱焦虑之表现,但在被大批持械暴动者包围,镇上和周边情况又不断恶化之环境中亦属情有可原。

最后,望于此对苏联驻大黑河和布拉戈维申斯克之官员帮助撤离海关关员家人一事聊表感激之情。

您真挚的

周骊

---

① 即徐景德。

另：3月17日，情况有所好转，但直到齐齐哈尔方面派遣之新总司令到达大黑河后，局势方得以稳定。目前该总司令正与暴动者交锋，据报，已获胜。此前被暴动者劫走之崔司令昨晚已返回，但不知其如何得以逃脱。

周骊

31. 周骊致梅乐和函

（第 171 号半官函）

S/O No. 171.   Taheiho   22nd March, 32

Dear Sir Frederick,

Local Situation:

The situation here was easier from the 16th to the 19th instants, but it has again become tense and uncertain as no more than 100 of the new troops have arrived and the garrison still consists mainly of returned mutineers, who are becoming restive as they fear that General Hsü will give them short shrift when he comes with his forces. He and his men are somewhere near Chik'ot'ê and they are reported to have accounted for over two hundred of the looters. Cavalry is proceeding from Hailun to Chik'ot'ê via Lungmên to cut off the retreat of the survivors, who are not likely to try to proceed down river as the Hingan Mountains run down to the Amur below Chik'ot'ê and the country is wild and thinly populated. In the meantime, the

returned

Sir Frederick Maze, K. B. E.,
        etc.,   etc.,   etc.,
        S H A N G H A I.

returned mutineers are a very disturbing factor here. They all profess to be innocent, but it is definitely known that they all participated in the shooting and looting of the 10th, 11th and 12th instants. We are all passing through a very anxious time as the families that were evacuated to Blagoveatchensk had to return when things looked a bit brighter as the food and accommodation at the Chinese Consulate were insufficient for a prolonged stay. The Acting Mayor/Superintendent advises a continuation of precautions and any member of the staff and his family so wishing is allowed to sleep at the Custom House. My family and I are sleeping in one room in the quarters above the Custom House as there are still posts of ex-mutineers both in front and behind the Commissioner's House. Work at the office is being performed normally, but all important archives are still hidden. I see that I omitted to mention in my S/O letter No. 171 that the report that the mutineers and other looters were taking people as hostages was the reason for my deciding that the best policy was to get the staff out of the way in case of an attempted entry into the Custom House. In

the

the event of further trouble, this danger must not
be overlooked, also the possible kidnapping of
people for ransom. There is not one official with
the ability, energy or authority to take the lead
and developments are in the hands of a group of
juniors with no definite policy. There are also
reports of bandits congregating in the Humaho district
for a descent on Taheiho. This information was
received from Blagovestchensk and the Soviet is
supposed to be behind the move.

Losses in money, gold, etc., are now
estimated at over $2,000,000. Personally, I am
inclined to believe that many of the officials and
some of the bankers and merchants knew of the
impending mutiny and did nothing to prevent it as
they saw a chance of enriching themselves by
reporting that they "had been looted of everything.
The real cause for the trouble will probably never
be ascertainable.

Soviet Troop Concentration:

Large numbers of Soviet troops have arrived
in Blagovestchensk, where there are said to be
between 15,000 and 20,000 men.

Yours truly,

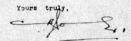

第 171 号半官函   1932 年 3 月 22 日于大黑河

尊敬的梅乐和先生：

地方局势：

3 月 16 日至 19 日期间，大黑河之局势已有所缓和，但因新军队驻于大黑河之人数不足百人，且守备队中那些此前参与暴动之人因担心徐司令带其部下返回后会不再受到重用，而显得焦躁不安，以致局面再次紧张起来，将来之事亦难以预料。目前徐司令正带领其部下于奇克特附近搜寻此前之掠夺者，据报，现已抓获两百余名。骑兵部队已从海伦经由龙门前往奇克特以阻挡掠夺者之退路，但应该不会向奇克特下游行进，毕竟奇克特下游之黑龙江已与兴安（Hingan）岭相依，当地荒无人烟。大黑河方面，重返军队之暴动者着实令人不安，虽其自称为无辜之辈，但实际的确参与了 3 月 10 日、11 日和 12 日的射杀掠夺行动。目前，海关关员再次陷入不安之中，此前撤离至布拉戈维申斯克（Blagovestchensk）之家人因当地中国领事馆无法长期提供膳宿已于局势缓和之时返回大黑河。暂代黑河市政筹备处处长兼海关监督建议继续布防，且凡海关关员及其家人如有需要均允许于海关办公楼休息。本人及家人因税务司住所前后仍有此前暴动者在把守，故于海关办公楼楼上一间宿舍内休息。海关各项事务均如常进行，但重要文档皆已收藏妥当。本人于第 171 号半官函中未提及，当时有报告称，暴动者和其他掠夺者有挟持人质之举，故为防后患，避免关员有被绑架要挟之险，本人当时决定如遇暴动者试图闯入海关办公楼，立即带领海关关员撤离。当地官员中竟无一人有能力、精力或是权力来统领大黑河，事态之发展皆由一群初级军官所掌控，且毫无章法可言。同时有报告称，呼玛河一带亦有土匪聚集正欲赶来大黑河。该消息由布拉戈维申斯克方面传来，此举应为苏联之谋划。

目前各项损失包括钱财、金子等预计已达 2000000 余银圆。兹认为，关于此次暴动，多数官员，甚至一些银行和商人，均早已知晓，只是未予阻拦，以期借汇报被洗劫一空之名，谋取个人丰厚之利。无论怎样，此次暴动之真实原因，恐怕永远无法水落石出。

苏联军队集结：

布拉戈维申斯克现已集结苏联大批军队，据悉，约有 15000 至 20000 人。

您真挚的

周骊

32. 周骊致梅乐和函

（第172号半官函）

S/O No.172　　　　A I G U N 30th March 32.

Dear Sir Frederick,

　　Local Situation: Although the situation is much easier since the arrival of the 200 cavalry on the 23rd instant, the new General and Mayor have so far not arrived and there is a general feeling of nervousness and uncertainty. Nearly all business remains suspended, and everyone continues cautious.

　　Political Situation: The general situation seems most confused and General Ma Chan-shan is suspected of waiting for an opportunity to change his present policy. His family has been told to stay at Taheiho and this is regarded as an indication of his future plans. No attempt has been made by anyone to interfere in any way with the Customs here. I shall adhere closely to your instructions should any interference develop. There is always the possibility that all archives may be detained by force, but I shall do my best to circumvent this by

moving

Sir Frederick Maze, K.B.E.,
　　Etc., etc., etc.,
　　S H A N G H A I.

moving those concerned to my house at the least sign of action on the part of the new government.

　　Shipping: It is feared that shipping will not ply normally on the Amur this year as complications are expected with the Soviet regarding the flag question. It is, however, too early to predict anything in this connection and we can only wait and see. I hope ships do arrive fairly regularly as we shall be almost cut off from the rest of the world after the overland route is impassable.

　　Aigun S/O letters of 16th and 22nd March: Will you please be so good as to have the numbers of the above letters altered from 171 and 172 to 170 and 171. I regret the error, but all my archives were hidden at the time of writing and I had to number from memory.

Yours truly,

第 172 号半官函   1932 年 3 月 30 日于瑷珲关

尊敬的梅乐和先生：

地方局势：

3 月 23 日，200 名骑兵进驻大黑河后，局势已有所缓和，但新任总司令和黑河市政筹备处处长尚未抵达，因此紧张之势并未消散，将来之事仍难以预料。商业活动几近中止，人人自危。

政治局势：

整体局势尚不明朗，据悉，马占山总司令或正等待时机改变策略，其家人现仍留于大黑河，或可作为其下一步计划之暗示。目前尚未有人试图对海关加以阻扰，如有此类行为，本人将谨遵阁下之指示行事。然而，目前随时皆有文档全部被迫扣留之可能，但一旦发现新政府有何举动，本人将不遗余力将文档转移至税务司住所以避免发生扣留之事。

船运：

今年，苏联方面因其国旗一事将陷入混乱之中，因此黑龙江上本年之船运工作恐怕难以如常进行。不过，现在对船运之事做出推测为时尚早，只能静观其变。希望届时船只可如期而至，毕竟自陆路无法通行后，与外界之沟通已几近断绝。

瑷珲关 3 月 16 日及 22 日半官函：

望阁下将本人 171 号和 172 号半官函之编号分别改为 170 号和 171 号，对此疏漏，深感抱歉，然因写信之时，所有文档皆已收藏起来，故本人当时只能凭借记忆编号，望阁下体谅。

您真挚的

周骊

33. 周骊致梅乐和函

（第 173 号半官函）

S/O No. 173.　　　　Aigun　　15th April, 32

Dear Sir Frederick,

OFFICIALS: APPOINTMENT OF NEW MAYOR/

SUPERINTENDENT:

Mr Ch'i Chao-yü (齊摩豫), the former Mayor/Superintendent, left for Shanghai, <u>via</u> Siberia, Europe and Suez, on the 4th March. He notified me officially that he was proceeding on sick - leave, but informed me privately that he wanted to get away whilst it was still possible as he was opposed to General Ma Chan-shan's policy. His Chief Secretary acted for him until the 3rd instant, when Mr Lang Kuan-p'u (郎官普), appointed by General Ma, arrived from Tsitsihar to take over the office of the Mayor/Superintendent. It looked at first as though it would be necessary to treat the new man as the appointee of a <u>de facto</u> government, but, with General Ma's arrival here and his co-operation, through Marshal Chang Hsüeh-liang, with the Central Government, I shall regard

Sir Frederick Maze, K. B. E.,
　　etc., etc., etc.,

　　SHANGHAI.

regard him as holding his commission from the Central Government. He seems a pleasant, capable and energetic man.

POLITICAL SITUATION:

General Ma Chan-shan escaped from Tsitsihar on the 2nd or 3rd April and arrived here in the afternoon of the 7th, accompanied by General Hsü Ching-tê (徐景德), who was recently engaged in rounding up the Taheiho mutineers. General Ma is very busy organising a provincial government in opposition to the new state and his troops hold Hailun (海倫), Kêshan (克山), Noho (訥河), Nênchiang (嫩江), Lungmên (龍門), and all the district to the north of the Hingan Mountains. The general at Tsitsihar is also his man, and he is said to be supported by the forces at Hailar, Manchouli and Sansing. General Ma called on me on the 12th instant and stayed two hours telling me his experiences and explaining how he escaped. My confidential telegram of the same date was sent at his request. This turn in the situation disposes for the time-being of the question of interference with the Customs at this port. The prospective members of the new government at Taheiho are planning to open a local bank with its own note issue, based on opium and gold as security, and I fear the project is surrounded by many, and insufficiently considered

considered, dangers.

LOCAL SITUATION:

Another mutiny was only just averted during the night of the 6th instant by the energy and initiative of the new Mayor. The situation was very critical until midnight. We fortunately were warned in good time and were able to take precautions. General Ma's arrival has done much to restore confidence and shops are slowly opening for business. General Ma has taken very strong action against the officials responsible for the mutiny of the 10th March: General Tsui Po-shan (崔 柏 山) is in prison under threat of execution; the Regimental Commander is under supervision; the Chief of Police has been dismissed and has been ordered to make good a sum of $10,000.00 reported to have been lost by his office; and the Chairman of the Chamber of Commerce has been severely warned.

AIDS AGREEMENT:

The new Mayor/Superintendent has asked the Soviet Consul to agree to an extension of the 1930-1931 Agreement for another year. It is still doubtful whether shipping will ply on the Amur, and I have not been informed yet whether the Lahasusu Sub-Office will be able to collect Navigation Fees and to remit them to Taheiho.

Yours truly,

第 173 号半官函　　　　　　　　　　　　　**1932 年 4 月 15 日于瑷珲关**

尊敬的梅乐和先生：

官员：新黑河市政筹备处处长兼海关监督之任命：

前任黑河市政筹备处处长兼海关监督齐肇豫先生已于 3 月 4 日离开大黑河,欲经由西伯利亚、欧洲、苏伊士路线前往上海,其官方通知为因病休假,但已于私下告知本人其反对马占山总司令之政策,须于尚可逃离之际离开此地。4 月 3 日,郎官普先生奉马占山总司令之命自齐齐哈尔抵达大黑河,以接任黑河市政筹备处处长兼海关监督之职,此前一直由齐肇豫先生之秘书代理。依最初之情势来看,本人应将郎官普先生作为政府任命之官员相待,然随后马占山总司令亦抵达大黑河,且通过张学良少帅之关系已与中央政府达成合作,因此实应将其作为中央政府任命之官员相待。郎官普先生看似为人和善,精力充沛,应属有能力之辈。

政治局势：

马占山总司令于 4 月 2 日或 3 日自齐齐哈尔逃离出来,并于 4 月 7 日下午抵达大黑河,随行之人为徐景德司令,徐司令即为此前参与围捕大黑河暴动者之军官。马占山总司令现忙于重组黑龙江省政府以抵抗新政府,目前海伦、克山、讷河、内江、龙门以及兴安(Hingan)岭以北所有地区皆被其军队占领,齐齐哈尔方面主事之人亦为其部下,据说海拉尔、满洲里及三姓等地之军队亦开始响应其号召。3 月 12 日,马占山总司令前来海关拜访,于逗留之两小时间向本人讲述了其种种遭遇及逃离之事。本人于 3 月 12 日发送之机密电报亦是按其要求所为。局势扭转后,瑷珲关暂时将不会受到阻扰。大黑河新政府各候选官员目前正筹划于当地开办一家银行,发行自己的纸币,以鸦片和金子作为担保;但恐怕此事并非深思熟虑之结果,而且会面临诸多艰险。

地方局势：

4 月 6 日晚大黑河再次发生暴动,情势一度十分危急,至午夜方有所缓和,此次暴动之发起者为新任黑河市政筹备处处长。幸而海关方面及时收到消息,得以提前采取防范措施。马占山总司令至此后采取了一番行动,使得当地人们重拾信心,店铺亦逐步开张营业,另对 3 月 10 日暴动一事之负责官员进行了严肃处理,崔柏山司令已被收监,将被处决,团指挥官已被监管起来,警察长已被革职,并须奉命报告因其失职造成了 10000.00 银圆之损失,商会主席已受到严重警告。

航路标志协议：

新任黑河市政筹备处处长兼海关监督已向苏联领事提出要求,望 1930/1931 年航路标志协议可再次续约一年。但目前仍无法确定黑龙江上是否会有船只往来通行,至于拉哈苏苏分关是否能够完成航运费之征收,并将税收汇至大黑河一事,本人尚未收到消息。

您真挚的

周骊

34. 周骊致梅乐和函

（第 174 号半官函）

S/O No. 174.　　　　　　Aigun　　6th May, 32

Dear Sir Frederick,

HEILUNGKIANG PROVINCIAL GOVERNMENT:

General Ma Chan-shan's provincial government was inaugurated here on the 21st April, when a public welcome and a procession through the town were organised to celebrate the occasion. The Mayor/Superintendent is now also acting as Finance Commissioner, Bandit Suppression Commissioner, Chief of Police Affairs, Special Representative of the Ministry of Foreign Affairs, and Director of the Provincial Bank. At General Ma's request, all Japanese residents, including women married to Chinese, left Taheiho _via_ Blagovestchensk.

LOCAL:

Although the inauguration of the provincial government has removed the scares and alarums of March and the first week of April, the future is most uncertain. There is a general lack of confidence and every one feels nervous. The troops have

Sir Frederick Maze, K.B.E.,
　　etc.,　etc.,　etc.,
　　　SHANGHAI.

have not been paid since January and it is considered that the situation would become critical if Generals Ma and Hsü left the place.

SHIPPING:

From present indications, it appears fairly certain that there will be no shipping between Sungari and Amur ports.

OFFICE:

There is very little for me to do in the office. All important archives are packed in cases and I can only exercise patience and watch developments. The lack of work and the general uncertainty are trying, and the confidential archives worry me greatly as, in case of necessity, there is no safe place to which they could be moved.

STAFF:

If no steamers come this year, I could recommend the transfer of one clerk and one tidewaiter, but the only route by which they could travel would be _via_ Blagovestchensk and the Soviet authorities are at present not willing to grant a transit visa to Chinese.

NAVIGATION FEES:

The Mayor/Superintendent has written requesting that Navigation Fees be collected on the Harbin Dollar basis (please see my S/O letter No.

No. 164).

<u>HEILUNGKIANG BANKNOTE:</u>

The Heilungkiang banknote has depreciated heavily on the Harbin market during the past month and the rate today is Harbin $100.00 = Heilungkiang $145.00. The price of everything is soaring, and, if steamers do not come, there will be a general shortage of foodstuffs and a further increase in the cost of living.

<u>CHINESE CONSUL GENERAL AT BLAGOVESTCHENSK:</u>

The Blagovestchensk authorities have withdrawn the Consul General's telegraphic facilities as he used the Soviet lines for the transmission of some of General Ma's circular telegrams. The Japanese are reported to have protested that this was a breach of Soviet neutrality - hence the excitement. The Soviet has now requested the Manchukuo to recall the Consul General, an appointee of the Chinese Government! I think the personal element has had much to do with the case as the Consul General is not popular in Blagovestchensk.

<u>TITLE DEEDS:</u>

I am taking advantage of the presence of the provincial government officials to try to have the rest of the Aigun Customs' Title Deeds registered. As reported in my S/O letter No. 163, certain irregularities require reference to the provincial government.

Yours truly,

473

第 174 号半官函　　　　　　　　　　　　　1932 年 5 月 6 日于瑷珲关

尊敬的梅乐和先生：

黑龙江省政府：

马占山总司令之省政府已于 4 月 21 日正式成立，当日政府组织全镇举行公开欢迎和宣言仪式，以示庆祝。黑河市政筹备处处长兼海关监督现亦兼任财政特派员、剿匪特派员、警务处处长、外交部特派员及省银行经理等职。按照马占山总司令之指示，当地日本居民，包括嫁与中国人之妇女均已经由布拉戈维申斯克（Blagovestchensk）离开大黑河。

地方：

省政府成立之后，3 月乃至 4 月初之恐慌虽已消逝，但将来之势仍难以预料，依然是人人自危之局面。自 1 月以来，军队一直未发放军饷，一旦马占山总司令及徐司令离开此地，大黑河恐怕又将陷入危难之中。

船运：

依目前之情势来看，似乎可以确定松花江与黑龙江沿线各口岸之间将不会有船只往来。

办公：

目前，鉴于重要文档均已封箱保存，本人可做之事甚少，只能静观其变，然于本人而言，无事可做，加之局势不稳已十分难熬，而今考虑到如有万不得已之时，机密文档竟无安全之地可存放，心头又添重担。

人事：

若大黑河口岸今年无轮船往来，兹提议调离一名税务员和一名稽查员，由布拉戈维申斯克离开大黑河是目前唯一之途径，但苏联政府现不愿向中国人发放通行签证。

航运费：

黑河市政筹备处处长兼海关监督已呈交书面请求，望以哈大洋征收航运费（参阅本人第 164 号半官函）。

黑龙江纸币：

上个月，黑龙江纸币在哈尔滨市场上严重贬值，5 月 6 日汇率为哈大洋 100 元兑换黑龙江银圆 145.00 元。大黑河物价急剧上涨，若再无轮船至此，食物将严重不足，物价亦将继续上涨。

中国驻布拉戈维申斯克总领事：

布拉戈维申斯克当地政府因中国总领事使用苏联线路传递马占山总司令之通令电报已撤掉其电报设备。据报,此前日方辩称中国总领事此举破坏了苏联中立之状态,导致苏联方面方有此过激之行为。目前,苏联方面要求伪满洲国(Manchukuo)召回该总领事,但该总领事乃为中国政府任命之官员! 兹认为,此事亦有个人因素,毕竟该总领事在布拉戈维申斯克并不受欢迎。

地契:

本人打算借省政府官员在任之际完成瑷珲关剩余地契登记之事。如本人第 163 号半官函中所报告,有一些不合乎规矩之处须提交省政府裁定。

您真挚的

周骊

35. 周骊致梅乐和函

（第 176 号半官函）

S/O No. 176.　　　　　Aigun　　7th June, 32

Dear Sir Frederick,

SITUATION: Entered in Card-Index.

There is nothing special to report. We have just emerged from another mutiny scare, but I have been unable to find out what did actually occur. The officials are non-committal on the subject.

ECONOMIC CONDITIONS: Entered in Card-Index.

Although the Heilungkiang dollar has appreciated and is now quoted at Harbin $100.00 = Heilungkiang $131.30, the price of everything has risen substantially as, with no ships running, merchants are unable to replenish their stocks. Firewood will be much more expensive than last year. The Upper Amur district was badly hit by the depredations of mutineers during January, and the raftsmen will be unable to return to their villages in time to float down a second lot of timber. No shipping will be a serious enough matter for Taheiho, but

but it will probably mean that the Upper Amur region will have to be abandoned as the settlers will find great difficulty in laying in their winter stocks of flour and other daily necessities.

Yours truly,

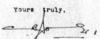

Sir Frederick Maze, K. B. E.,
　　etc.,　　etc.,　　etc.,
　　　S H A N G H A I.

第 176 号半官函   1932 年 6 月 7 日于瑷珲关

尊敬的梅乐和先生：

局势：

无特殊之情况，只是海关关员刚刚从一次暴动中幸免于难，但尚无法查明具体情况，而政府官员对于此次暴动亦未表态。

经济状况：

黑龙江银圆已贬值，兑换汇率为哈大洋 100.00 元兑换黑龙江银圆 131.30 元，因无轮船往来，大黑河物价飞涨，商人已无法补充储备。木桦价格与去年相比涨幅较大。黑龙江上游地区于 1 月间遭到暴动者之掠夺，已受重创，筏夫将无法及时返回其村庄将第二批木桦运至黑龙江下游地区。于大黑河而言，无船只往来已然成为十分严重之事，但如此一来，黑龙江上游地区之居民亦将难以储备冬季所需之面粉及其他日常必需品。

您真挚的

周骊

36. 周骊致梅乐和函

（第 177 号半官函）

S/O No. 177.   Aigun   21st June, 32

Dear Sir Frederick,

SITUATION: Enclosed in Card-Index.

It looks very much as though this place were slowly but surely being isolated. The food question here is already serious, and the shortage is acute at places both above and below Taheiho. Ships from Harbin are running as far as Fuchin on the Sungari only, and the overland route is almost impassable after heavy rain and is also bandit-infested. The telegraph line has either been down for three weeks or the Nenchiang Office is not receiving or transmitting messages from and to Taheiho. Wireless communication with Harbin is now suspended, the Harbin station having notified the local station that it would not work with it any longer. We have had no mails for a week, but it is not known whether this is due to bandits, to the commandeering of the mail-carts by the military,

to

SIR FREDERICK MAZE, K.B.E.,
    etc.,   etc.,   etc.,
        SHANGHAI.

to the suspension of the mail service by the Manchukuo authorities, or to the bad roads. Disorders are reported from Wuyün, Lungmen, Nenchiang, and Sanchan, and conditions at Aigun are said to be none too good. The authorities are taking precautions to maintain good order here, but there is a general feeling of nervousness and uncertainty. If no ships run to Amur ports before August, something should be done by the Central Government for humanitarian reasons to arrange for the despatch of foodstuffs to this district. After all, it is claimed that a state of war does not exist, and I feel sure the authorities concerned would not detain food ships if they received assurance that these would not be used for military purposes. At present the peasants and labourers are the greatest sufferers.

HEILUNGKIANG BANKNOTE: Enclosed in Card-Index.

The Heilungkiang banknote has risen in value on the Harbin market, but this has done nothing to lower prices here as merchants are unable to remit funds to Harbin. The price of everything has gone up by 40% to 50%.

RIVER: Enclosed in Card-Index.

The river is very high and it is still raining. A further rise of four feet will flood

all

第 177 号半官函   1932 年 6 月 21 日于瑷珲关

尊敬的梅乐和先生：

为地方局势事：

根据当前形势判断,大黑河地区已被日渐孤立。本地区的粮食问题已十分严峻,大黑河上游和下游地区均出现了严重的食物短缺现象。交通方面,哈尔滨的轮船仅于松花江上航行至富锦,而陆路交通则因暴雨和土匪之故几乎无法通行。电报方面,有线电报已有三周无收发往来,或因电报线路出现故障,或因嫩江方面未向大黑河收发电报,大黑河与哈尔滨的无线通信现已停止,哈尔滨无线电报站此前已通知大黑河无线电报站日后不再相互收发电报。邮件方面,已有一周无邮件到来,或因土匪之故,或因邮递车辆被军方征用,或因满洲政府已暂停邮政服务,或因道路交通不畅,究竟为何,实难知晓。据报,乌云、龙门、嫩江、三站等地已发生动乱,瑷珲地区之情形亦不乐观。大黑河地方政府虽已竭力维持秩序,但整体氛围依然十分紧张,形势不甚明朗。若 8 月之前仍无轮船行至黑龙江沿岸各口,中央政府应会出于人道主义为本地区提供粮食等物资,毕竟目前并未进入战争状态。兹认为,相关当局若可确定运来的粮食并非军用物资,便不会扣留运输轮船。目前老百姓才是最大的受害者。

为黑龙江纸币事：

黑龙江纸币在哈尔滨市场的价格已有所上涨,但在本地的价格依然较低,主要因商人无法将资金汇至哈尔滨。大黑河地区所有商品的价格均上涨了 40% 到 50%。

为黑龙江水位事：

黑龙江水位现已非常高,且降雨仍在继续。

> 您真挚的
>
> 周骊

注：后文未存档。

海关总税务司署名录

安格联	总税务司　1912—1927 年
梅乐和	总税务司　1929—1942 年
包　罗	总理文案税务司　1910—1911 年 总务科税务司　1913—1918 年 /1921—1922 年 代理总税务司　1920 年 /1923 年
李家森	总务科税务司　1919—1920 年
威厚澜	总务科税务司　1923 年
泽　礼	代理总务科税务司　1924—1925 年 代理总税务司　1925 年
易纨士	总务科税务司　1926 年 代理总税务司　1927—1928 年

瑷珲关历任税务司名录

包安济	署理税务司 1921.01.01—1923.06.01
贺智兰	税务司 1923.06.01—1925.10.16
裴德生	暂行代理税务司 1925.10.16—1926.05.15
瑚斯敦	税务司 1926.05.15—1926.10.12
铎博费	署理税务司 1926.10.12—1929.12.01
巴闰森	滨江关税务司（代理瑷珲关关务） 1929.12.01—1930.05.16
富乐嘉	署理税务司 1930.05.16—1930.10.14
周　骊	署理税务司 1930.10.14—1932.10.13

后　记

　　《瑷珲海关历史档案辑要》是 2020 年国家重点档案保护与开发项目成果，在国家档案局专项资金的支持下，历时两年，终于付梓出版。

　　本套书是在对瑷珲海关档案进行数字化、翻译整理、开放鉴定的基础上汇编而成，由满文和外文档案开发处负责项目申报、统筹海关档案翻译及书稿编辑等各项工作，由信息处、整理处、保管处等相关处室承担档案的数字化以及开放鉴定等工作。编辑人员本着对档案及历史负责的精神，反复推敲编排体例、筛选档案资料、审核档案内容，力争客观、真实、全面反映瑷珲海关从初设到闭关的历史活动轨迹。

　　本套书内的海关机关、职衔名称及关员姓名、海关关船、灯标等海关术语主要参考陈诗启、孙修福主编《中国近代海关常用词语英汉对照宝典》（2002 年版），孙修福编译《中国近代海关高级职员年表》（2004 年版），对历史资料无着者，或加"注"，或从汉文附件，或由编译者研究酌定。编译过程中主要参考了陈诗启著《中国近代海关史》（1993 年版），《旧中国海关总税务司署通令选遍》（第二、三卷）（中国海关出版社，2003 年）等资料。书中的"地方见闻卷"编选自 1921 年至 1932 年历任瑷珲关税务司写给总税务司的半官函（s/o），所有信件均按照时间排序，原信件有编号者，均按原编号标出。汉译内容全部由原档客观翻译而来，不代表编者立场。

　　本套书的编译出版也得到史学专家、翻译人员以及出版社的大力支持和帮助。感谢厦门大学中国海关史研究中心各位专家的权威指导和专业审读。感谢常唤等翻译人员对海关档案汉译工作的深入研究和精雕细琢。同时也感谢社会科学文献出版社的积极配合。

　　由于编译内容庞杂、年代久远且数量巨大，缺点和错误之处，敬请读者指正。

编　者

2021 年 12 月